Slavery in the Twentieth Century

The Evolution of a Global Problem

SUZANNE MIERS

ALTAMIRA
PRESS

A Division
ROWMAN & LITTLEFIELD
Walnut Creek • *Lanham*

D1424027

18 056202

ALTAMIRA PRESS
A Division of Rowman & Littlefield Publishers, Inc.
1630 North Main Street, #367
Walnut Creek, CA 94596
www.altamirapress.com

Rowman & Littlefield Publishers, Inc.
A Member of the Rowman & Littlefield Publishing Group
4720 Boston Way
Lanham, MD 20706

PO Box 317
Oxford
OX2 9RU, UK

British Library Cataloguing in Publication Information Available

Library of Congress Cataloging-in-Publication Data

Miers, Suzanne.
  Slavery in the twentieth century : the evolution of a global problem / Suzanne Miers.
    p. cm.
  Includes bibliographical references and index.
  ISBN 0-7591-0339-9 (hardcover : alk. paper)—ISBN 0-7591-0340-2 (pbk. : alk. paper)
    1. Slavery—History—20th century. 2. Antislavery movements—History—20th
century. I. Title.

HT867 .M54 2003   2002010560
306.3'62'097304—dc21

Printed in the United States of America

♾™ The paper used in this publication meets the minimum requirements of American
National Standard for Information Sciences—Permanence of Paper for Printed Library
Materials, ANSI/NISO Z39.48-1992.

"The suppression of the slave trade arouses much sympathy but little actual support."

—C. D. Prior, Political Resident, Bushire, 31 July 1940.

"We are a small company in a small room, but I am persuaded we represent a great moral movement in this country, for the anti-slavery sentiment which some years ago was so strong, powerful, and enthusiastic cannot be dead, but only needs to be reawakened."

—C. Wright Brooks, Anti-Slavery Reporter, March–May 1907, p. 40.

"Freedom is a good thing but it means a dearth of slaves."

—Lucien Hubert at the 13th Assembly of the League of Nations, 12 October 1932, quoting a former slave a year after he had been freed and appointed headman of a French village de liberté in West Africa in the 1890s.

"It is only the younger generation of today that has not known the sweetness of slavery. . . . A Slave is your property, just like the money in your pocket . . . you could send him anywhere, sell him at any price, or even give him away. . . . This was not a secret business but a sacred one."

—The District Governor of Asosa (Ethiopia) 1972. Quoted in A. Triulzi, Salt, Gold and Legitimacy, p. 136.

"People may at any moment find the security of slavery preferable to the starvation of freedom and sell themselves or their children."

—C. D. Prior, Political Resident, Bushire, 31 July 1940.

"The unweary, unostentatious, and inglorious crusade of England against slavery may probably be regarded as among the three or four perfectly virtuous pages comprised in the history of nations."

—W. E. H. Lecky, quoted in R. Coupland, The British Anti-Slavery Movement, p. 2.

Plus ça change plus c'est la même chose.

To Roland Oliver

Contents

Preface

In 1980 I attended for the first time a meeting in Geneva of the United Nations Working Group of Experts on Slavery "in all its forms" including the "slavery-like practices of apartheid and colonialism." It was a disheartening experience. Of the five experts, only the chairman seemed interested in the proceedings, and he wasted time on long-winded speeches presumably aimed at a nonexistent public, since their content was well-known to the few nongovernmental organizations (NGOs) which, at considerable expense to themselves, came to Geneva to present evidence to the group. The experts wandered in and out in an apparently endless need to be somewhere else. They appeared bored with the proceedings. Although billed as "experts," some of them looked astonished when presented with harrowing evidence of abuses that had been raised many times before. There was little or no dialogue between the committee and the NGOs. Committee members were often defensive and quick to deny allegations of abuses in the area of the world they represented. The meeting was bedeviled by Cold War politics and "North/South" animosity. Scoring political points appeared to take precedence over the search for truth and justice, let alone formulating plans for action. As I saw it then, the Group, which had been ardently desired by NGOs to combat important social ills, seemed determined to paralyze and decry their efforts to create a better world.

Most of the time I was alone in the public gallery, and the press gave little coverage to either the Working Group or the "forms of slavery" it was designed to combat. In fact, few members of the public even knew there was such a group, although this was its sixth meeting. I had only just heard about it myself. Even my colleagues working on slavery were surprised to hear of its existence, and most people believed that slavery had long disappeared.

Why, I wondered, did this group exist? What purpose did it serve? Who were these "experts"? How had they been chosen? Did they really have any expertise? Why did the

United Nations fund the Group? Were its aims really humanitarian or had it been set up as a smokescreen to deflect public criticism and avoid action? This had in the past been one manifestation of what may be called the "antislavery game." Another was the use of a humanitarian issue to cover action wanted for other reasons. Both devices are all too often used in international relations.

This led to another set of questions: How, when, and why had the definition of slavery been stretched to include practices as disparate as apartheid and female genital mutilation? Finally, and most importantly: To what extent could these widely different practices, labeled "contemporary forms of slavery," be eradicated with the existing international machinery? Was the Working Group an effective weapon against slavery in any form?

I came back from Geneva determined to write a book entitled "The Antislavery Game," showing how the antislavery campaign had been used since its outset by various powers to further their political and economic interests—a theme I had begun to develop in my first book. However, the research took me so long that the international climate changed for the better. The end of the Cold War and of the apartheid regime in South Africa, together with the increase in the numbers of NGOs and their successful publicity campaigns, changed the picture dramatically. The group was rechristened the Working Group on Contemporary Forms of Slavery. These forms, which include forced labor, sweated labor, forced prostitution, forced marriage, the exploitation of child labor and of migrant and contract labor, as well as other abuses, were well publicized by the late 1990s. Most people in the Western world, and many in other areas, were now aware of them, although they might not know the dimensions of the problem, or consider all the practices under attack as slavery. Nongovernmental organizations had proliferated to an extraordinary extent and secured funding on an unprecedented scale. UN specialized agencies such as the ILO, UNESCO, UNICEF, UNCTAD and others attended the Group's meetings, although not always regularly. As small wars proliferated, as poverty and runaway population growth became more and more widespread, the media ran frequent stories of women tricked into prostitution far from home, of illegal aliens dying in the sealed trucks in which they were hidden, or drowning in attempts to reach the promised land, of children abused in back-street workshops or forcibly enrolled as soldiers and made to commit atrocities, of workers exploited in sweat shops supplying brand-name goods to consumers in rich countries, of contract laborers tricked into debt-bondage, and an increasing number of other forms of bondage.

As I began to know more about the subject, my initial harsh judgment on the Group began to mellow. The problem, of course, was not merely with the Group itself. It was due to the lack of the political will on the part of the members of the United Nations to give it powers of enforcement. As the Group collected more and more information and the public became better informed about "contemporary slavery," the problems of eradication were greater and more intractable than they had ever been. In this book, I set out to trace the history of the international antislavery movement in the twentieth century, showing how and why the definition of slavery was continually expanded to include more and more practices, many of which are even crueler than the chattel slavery so familiar to the public mind. To keep the book within manageable proportions, I centered the story on British policy. The rationale for this was that for some two hundred years, from the late eighteenth century to the late twentieth, the British led the antislavery movement. Successive governments, responding to parliamentary and public pressure, had prided themselves on leading the campaign. Their efforts waxed and waned according to political dictates, but that Britain was leading an antislavery "crusade," usually with scant support from other nations, became firmly embedded in the national consciousness. From 1839, the campaign was spurred on by a society, now called Anti-Slavery International, which was still the foremost NGO in the field at the outset of the twenty-first century.

A full diplomatic history of the antislavery movement has still to be written, but its early history and British efforts to suppress the slave trade are well-known. Much less research has focused on the years from 1919 to 2000, which form the heart of this book. It was during this period, for reasons that will be made clear, that the definition of slavery came to be stretched to cover so many practices, as to become almost meaningless. It was also during this period that many of these practices came to be generally condemned in international conventions, and some abuses were carefully defined in these instruments. During this period, too, so-called contemporary forms of slavery became more widespread and pernicious, affecting more people than at any time in human history. At the outset of the twenty-first century, it is fair to say that while more is known of these evils, and much effort has been spent in describing and analyzing them, the goal of eradication seems as distant as ever.

This book highlights on the one hand the campaign by dedicated members of NGOs, particularly the British Anti-Slavery Society, to persuade first the League of Nations, and then the United Nations, to establish international machinery to end these abuses, and, on the other, the efforts of governments, including sometimes the British government, to avoid action and evade criticism. The introduction, based mainly on secondary sources, sets the scene. The main part, based primarily on British archival documents, traces the campaign from 1919 to 1969. The epilogue discusses the events of the last thirty years of the century. Since the British official archives were closed at the time of writing, from 1970, the epilogue is necessarily based on published sources, including United Nations documents. However, I have had the benefit of the archives of Anti-Slavery International and of interviews with some of the participants.

This work is not definitive. Time and space forced me to limit the research to British sources, with only short forays into other archives. Hence, all but the last chapters of this book are heavily weighted towards the British role in promoting and sustaining the antislavery campaign. This means that the voices of other nations have not been given due weight. The earlier chapters also draw heavily upon African examples because this is the region with which I am most familiar, and which attracted the greatest humanitarian and international attention. Almost entirely missing from this book is the slave voice, a subject that invites further research. In some parts of the world, notably Arabia, slavery is still considered too sensitive to attract serious research. In parts of Africa, it has been deliberately covered up by the descendants of both slaves and owners. The former are reluctant to reveal servile origins and the latter are unwilling to admit that their forebears were involved in an institution now generally considered abhorrent. Information, however, exists and I trust that scholars will step up the research on these areas before it disappears from the oral record. Further research on the documents will also yield valuable information.

The epilogue is primarily based on the reports of the Working Group. It is merely an introduction to a very wide set of questions both on the various forms of servitude they describe and on the efficacy of the existing machinery of the United Nations and the International Labor Organization. I have sought to place both modern slavery and the efforts of the United Nations into their historical context. Ideally, such research should be undertaken by a team consisting, for instance, of a political scientist, a sociologist, a lawyer, and a human rights worker, as well as a historian. Unfortunately, the arbitrary division of academic disciplines under which we labor usually precludes such cooperative work. As a result, few scholars, and even fewer activists, have any idea of the history that led to the present situation.

I am all too sadly aware that I have barely scratched the surface of a broad subject. Much more research remains to be done, both on the ground and in the archives, particularly on the period after the Second World War. I trust, however, that this book will stimulate research into one of the most harrowing and pressing problems of our time. I also hope that in its small way it may stimulate some public pressure for more effective action by the United Nations.

Acknowledgments

It is not possible in the short space at my disposal to thank the many people who inspired and helped me during the twenty-odd years I worked on this book. I must pay particular tribute to the staff of Anti-Slavery International. I interviewed at length the former secretary, Patrick Montgomery, and his successor, Peter Davies, the first director. More recently, Mike Dottridge gave me invaluable help. David Ould and Jeff Howarth have also assisted me in many ways. I was privileged to serve for a few years, in the 1990s, on the Society's General Committee and to accompany the delegations to the meetings of the Working Group on Contemporary Forms of Slavery.

From the coeditors of my earlier books, Igor Kopytoff, Richard Roberts, Maria Jaschok, and Martin Klein, and from our contributors, I learned much of relevance to the present volume. I owe a particular debt to those people who read and commented on various parts of my manuscript. They include Maureen Alexander Sinclair, Indrani Chatterjee, Gifford Doxsee, Dr. Taj Hargey, Sir Donald Hawley, Leila Ingrams, Roger Sawyer, and Claude Welch. David Weissbrodt and Kevin Bales provided valuable information for the epilogue. Walter Clark sent me information on Henri de Monfried. Joseph C. Miller has helped me in many ways over the years.

Eleanor Casbon and Christian Curtis kindly sent me relevant extracts from their father's papers, and Michael and Anne de Halpert talked to me at length about the life of his uncle, Frank de Halpert. The Rev. Professor Anthony Orbell gave me his papers on slavery in Sudan. Peter Calvocoressi discussed with me his experiences on the UN Sub-Commission on the Prevention of Discrimination and the Protection of Minorities.

The Rockefeller Foundation gave me a Humanities Fellowship in 1980, and Ohio University provided me with several grants over the years. The staff of the many libraries and archives in which I worked rendered me invaluable service, particularly those in Rhodes House, Oxford. The book would never have been finished without the help of Helen Allen and John Fogle, who helped me prepare the manuscript and control my often-wayward computer. Rosalie Robertson at AltaMira Press encouraged me to bring the book to a conclusion and submit the manuscript. John Calderone and Diana Edwards worked patiently on the manuscript in its final stages.

Finally, I owe the greatest debt to my husband, Roland Oliver, who introduced me to African history, and who nobly read and commented on every page more than once as successive drafts came off my printer. It is to him that this book is affectionately dedicated.

Abbreviations and Acronyms

AASG	American Anti-Slavery Group
ACD	Association for Community Development
ACE	Advisory Committee of Experts on Slavery
AFL	American Federation of Labor
AIDS/HIV	Acquired Immunodeficiency Syndrome/ HIV virus
AS Annual Report	Annual Report of the Anti-Slavery Society
Anti-Slavery Society	(AS in notes) Note: To avoid confusion this name is used throughout the text to denote the British Anti-Slavery Society. The Society's actual name changed as follows: British And Foreign Anti-Slavery Society 1839–1909, Anti-Slavery and Aborigines Protection Society 1909–1947, Anti-Slavery Society 1947–56, Anti-Slavery Society for the Protection of Human Rights 1956–1990, Anti-Slavery International 1990–present.
Anti-Slavery Reporter	Note: This name is used throughout the text, but the title of the periodical changed as follows: *Anti-Slavery Monthly Reporter* 1823–1830, *Anti-Slavery Reporter* 1830–1909, *Anti-Slavery Reporter and Aborigines Friend* 1909–1980, *Anti-Slavery Reporter* 1981–to present.
AOF	Afrique Occidental Française (French West Africa)
AS	Anti-Slavery Society, British (used in endnotes)
ASAPS	Anti-Slavery and Aborigines Protection Society (see note above)
ASI	Anti-Slavery International—name of the British Anti-Slavery Society from 1990
BBC	British Broadcasting Corporation

BFASS	British and Foreign Anti-Slavery Society (see note above)
BFSP	*British and Foreign State Papers*
BIDI	Ligue Suisse pour la Défense des Indigènes (Bureau for the Protection of Indigenous Peoples)
BMAE	Ministère des Affaires Étrangères (Belgian Ministry of Foreign Affairs)
BNA	Botswana National Archives, Gaborone
CAB	Cabinet Papers (British)
CATW	Coalition Against Trafficking in Women
CEAWC	Committee for the Eradication of Abduction of Women and Children
CES	Committee of Experts on Slavery
CJAHS	*Canadian Journal of African Historical Studies*
CHR	Commission on Human Rights
CO	Colonial Office
COCP	Colonial Office Confidential Print
CRO	Commonwealth Relations Office, London
CSDHA	Center for Social Development and Humanitarian Affairs (United Nations)
CSI	Christian Solidarity International
DO	Dominions Office, London
Documents	*Documents relatifs à la Répression de la Traite des Esclaves 1893–1913*
ECOSOC	United Nations Economic and Social Council
ECPAT	End Child Prostitution in Asian Tourism
FAO	Food and Agriculture Organization
FCO	Foreign and Commonwealth Office, London
FMAE	Ministère des Affaires Étrangères (French Ministry of Foreign Affairs)
FO	Foreign Office, London
FOCP	Foreign Office Confidential Print
GAATW	Global Alliance Against Trafficking in Women
Hansard	British Parliamentary Debates
HC	High Commissioner
HRI	*Human Rights: a Compilation of International Instruments,* United Nations 1978
HPR	de Halpert Papers, Rhodes House, Oxford
HRW	Human Rights Watch
HSO	His/Her Majesty's Stationery Office, London

ICC	International Criminal Court
ICFTU	International Confederation of Free Trade Unions
IGO	Inter-Governmental Organizations
IJAH	*International Journal of African Historical Studies*
ILO	International Labor Organization
IMADR	International Movement Against all forms of Discrimination and Racism
INGO	International Non-Governmental Organizations
Instructions	*Instructions for the Guidance of H.M. Officers Engaged in the Suppression of the Slave Trade*
IO	India Office, London
IPEC	International Program for the Elimination of Child Labor
JAH	*Journal of African History*
JICS	*Journal of Imperial and Commonwealth History*
LON	League of Nations Archives
MOD	Ministry of Defence, London
NANI	National Archives of Nigerian Ibadan
NGO	Non-Governmental Organizations
NLF	National Liberation Front, Aden
OAS	Organization of American States
OAU	Organization of African Unity
PP	*British Parliamentary Papers*
RC	Resident Commissioner
S & A	*Slavery and Abolition*
SACCS	South Asia Coalition on Children in Servitude
SDN	Société des Nations (League of Nations), Geneva
SIR	Sudan Intelligence Reports
SM notes	Notes taken by author at meetings of the WGCFS
SOAS	School of African and Oriental Studies, University of London
SPDPM	Sub-Commission on the Prevention of Discrimination and the Protection of Minorities
TSC	Temporary Slavery Commission
UDI	Unilateral Declaration of Independence (Rhodesia)
UN	United Nations Organisation
UNA	United Nations Association
UNCTAD	United Nations Conference on Trade and Development
UNDP	United Nations Development Programs
UNESCO	United Nations Educational, Scientific, and Cultural Organization

UNHCHR	United Nations High Commission on Human Rights
UNHCR	United Nations High Commission for Refugees
UNICEF	United Nations Children's Fund
USNA	United States National Archives, College Park, Maryland
WGCFS	Working Group on Contemporary Forms of Slavery
WGS	Working Group on Slavery (later WGCFS)
WGIP	Working Group on Indigenous Populations
WHO	World Health Organization

1

The Rise of the British Antislavery Movement

THE BEGINNINGS OF THE BRITISH ANTISLAVERY MOVEMENT

In the eighteenth century, Britons prided themselves on being a "free" people. By this they meant that they were free to live where they wished, work for whom and on what terms they wanted, marry whom they chose, raise their own children, and own, inherit, and pass on property. They enjoyed hard-won political rights to freedom of religion, of speech, of the press, of association, and of election, and could not be arbitrarily imprisoned. In practice, few people had freedom of choice in all aspects of their lives. Men without landed property, all women, and the inhabitants of many newer towns were excluded from political participation. Property rights were oppressive. Common lands could be enclosed and tenants evicted at will, and vestiges of bondage still existed in sections of the labor force.[1] Nevertheless, the British considered themselves to be free and they certainly enjoyed more rights than most contemporary Europeans. Yet this free people sanctioned chattel slavery in its most oppressive form in their overseas possessions, where slaves were commodities owned and fully controlled by individuals, without the right to choose their occupation, to enjoy the fruits of their labor, to marry, to control their own children, or to own property. They were forced to work, were subject to arbitrary punishment, sometimes to the point of death, and were bought, sold, inherited, and transferred at will.

In the second half of the eighteenth century, however, slavery came increasingly under attack. Philosophers denounced it as incompatible with the inalienable rights of man. Economists claimed it was less profitable than wage labor. Religious activists considered it a sin. The dichotomy of free labor at home and slave labor in the colonies posed problems when owners brought their slaves to Britain. No laws recognized slavery, but such slaves were bought and sold, and forced to work without pay. Some who absconded were even kidnapped and returned to the colonies. Law courts were inconsistent in their handling of cases involving claims over slaves.[2] A small group of

1

humanitarians, spurred by moral indignation, took up their cause, and, in 1772, achieved a significant legal victory, when the Lord Chief Justice ruled that James Somerset, a runaway slave, whose master had had him kidnapped to sell in Jamaica, could not be forcibly taken out of the country. This decision did not outlaw slavery, or end its vestiges in Britain, but it made it possible for slaves to desert their masters with impunity.[3]

Publicized as a moral struggle between the right to property and the basic human right to freedom, this case was the first victory in what quickly became a full-scale campaign against slavery. It raised two questions, which were to plague the government as long as slavery existed in the British Empire. The first concerned the sanctity of property. Owners now stood to lose valuable assets, albeit human, which they had acquired legally and brought to England in the belief that their rights would be respected. The second concerned the rights of slaves in Britain, who could now, in theory, sue their masters for back wages. At issue was whether masters should be compensated for the loss of their slaves, or whether slaves should be compensated for being forced to work without pay in a country where slavery had no legal standing. At the time compensation was not given to either slaves or owners. The question remained unanswered. Equally unresolved was whether slaves automatically became free by setting foot on British soil, and, if so, what constituted British soil?

The handful of activists, who had taken up the Somerset case, banded with others to mount a campaign against slavery. The Society of Friends (Quakers), who had long denounced it, began active propaganda in 1783, and was joined by a small group of leading Anglican Evangelical philanthropists known as the Clapham Sect, of whom the best known was William Wilberforce, who led the campaign in Parliament. Together with other evangelicals, particularly Methodists, and more traditional Anglicans, they formed the Society for the Abolition of the Slave Trade in 1787.[4] Building on Quaker methods, they devised successful tactics to put pressure on Parliament and the government, and opened a new era in politics by launching the first mass agitation for a humanitarian cause.

Their methods became models for the future.[5] Public meetings, sermons, and lectures rallied even illiterate audiences. Local auxiliary abolitionist societies raised support and money. Since accurate information was vital, they collected and disseminated material on slavery and the slave trade through tracts, books, booklets, periodicals, advertisements, and articles. The publication of a schematic plan of a loaded slave ship was an effective forerunner of modern pictorial propaganda. A medallion, designed by Josiah Wedgwood, depicting an African in chains, kneeling with arms raised in a gesture of supplication, surrounded by the inscription "Am I not a man and a brother?" became the enduring emblem of the movement.

A number of factors contributed to their success. Churches served as meeting places. Burgeoning local newspapers allowed the wide dissemination of propaganda. The disenfranchised could participate, and the iniquities of slavery became a popular topic in debating societies, where women, voteless and officially unable to sign petitions, played an active role, particularly in the 1820s.[6] Consumers of both sexes and all ages could boycott slave-grown sugar, demonstrating their potential economic power, while shopkeepers could make money selling free (non-slave grown) sugar.[7]

The ultimate goal of the abolitionists was to end slavery everywhere, but for strategic reasons their first target was the outlawing of the British Atlantic slave trade. Its inhumanity was easily demonstrated, especially after the captain of the slaver, *Zong*, had 132 sick slaves thrown overboard to collect insurance, and was tried for fraud and not murder.[8] The movement soon attracted followers from all walks of life, including landed gentry, businessmen, missionaries, and thousands of ordinary people, particularly artisans in the new manufacturing towns.[9] Petitions were presented to Parliament. Politicians were lobbied. The message was clear. The slave trade was a sin against humanity and must be ended. Moreover, it was argued, slavery itself was inconsistent with economic progress in the possessions of a nation whose prosperity was more and more based on capitalist enterprise, a growing wage labor force, and an increasingly free market economy.

THE OUTLAWING OF THE BRITISH SLAVE TRADE

It, nevertheless, took many years before even the slave trade was banned. It was an important branch of British commerce, believed to be vital for the prosperity of the slaving ports and the slave-holding colonies. If Britain alone outlawed it, it would simply pass into the hands of foreign rivals to the benefit of their shipping and colonies. Since the trade could not be ended without international agreement, British abolitionists opened private talks with their counterparts in France and the United States, while the French and British governments explored the issues in 1787.[10] The French, however, were not willing to risk the prosperity of their colonies, particularly since their colony of Saint Domingue was the fastest developing sugar producer of the day.

The British government tried to appease the abolitionists by measures to ameliorate rather than end the traffic. Rules against overcrowding on slave ships made British carriers less competitive,[11] so British merchants financed foreign slave ships, and sold them the goods and equipment needed for the trade.

The French revolution of 1789, followed by wars with France, caused a reaction in Britain against reforms, and a successful slave uprising in Saint Domingue raised fears that antislavery agitation would lead to insurrections in British colonies.[12] However, in 1805 the British had won command of the seas and had conquered many of the slave colonies of rival powers. They could have developed these colonies in their own interest with slave labor. Instead they limited the trade to the conquered colonies and the next year prohibited British participation in the slave trade to any foreign territory. These measures, presented as being in the national interest since they were blows against foreign possessions, eliminated much of the British slave trade, and paved the way for the coup de grace—the Abolition Act of 1807. This outlawed the slave traffic to British subjects from 1808 and forbade the import of slaves into any British colony.[13] In 1811, slave trading was made a felony punishable by transportation to a penal settlement.

The actual reasons for this volte-face by the leading slave-trading nation at the height of its power, when it controlled the largest number of slave-using colonies, have been the subject of academic debate. It has been portrayed on the one hand as the triumph of humanitarianism over vested interests, and on the other as the result of changing economic interests unleashed by the industrial revolution.[14] Clearly ideology, economics, and politics were intertwined, but scholars have reached no consensus as to how they interacted or why the movement gained such popular support. It seems true that most members of the British public had no direct interest in the traffic and could afford to be humanitarian, yet the trade found fewer and fewer defenders in Liverpool, the leading British slaving port, which profited from it right up to 1807.[15] Changes in economic theory and the growing importance of commercial and industrial sectors unrelated to the traffic played their part, but so did the evangelical revival with its humanitarian attack on slavery and its emphasis on personal Christian conduct. The debate need not detain us here, but the struggle between national interests and philanthropy was to be an ongoing one, still unresolved at the outset of the twenty-first century.

Important for our story is the fact that, after twenty years of effort, the antislavery movement had mustered deep and enduring popular support. The public had been mobilized to secure "a great political object" and in the process had been educated on all aspects of slavery. Its defenders stressed the economic importance to Britain of the trade, and of the colonies using slave labor, and even argued that the traffic benefited its African victims by introducing them to Christianity and "civilization" in the New World. The abolitionists countered with political and economic arguments, but the one with the greatest appeal was humanitarian. It was this that gave the campaign its high moral tone. It came to be accepted that the slave trade violated British ideological norms by turning human beings into chattels, brutally uprooting them from their homes, destroying their family life, and condemning them to lifelong often brutal servitude.

This wide acceptance by the British public that both the slave trade and slavery were morally wrong—a complete reversal of the eighteenth-century views that it was either acceptable or simply an unpleasant fact of life—was an important step towards a new conception of universal human rights. For most of the vocal public as well as politicians, the debate henceforth was to turn on the methods of eradication and not on the necessity for abolition. The question became a matter of calculating how far the country could afford to put its humanitarian ideology into practice and what methods would best attain the goal.

THE ABOLITION OF SLAVERY IN BRITISH COLONIES

In the 1820s, the British abolitionists turned their attack to slavery in British possessions. The same core of Quakers, dissenters, and evangelicals formed the Society for the Miti-

gation and Gradual Abolition of Slavery, in 1823. They advocated a policy of "amelioration" or "gradualism"—improving the condition of slaves by regulation, preventing the
smuggling in of more victims, and ensuring that all children born after a certain date
were free.[16] As in the past, they mobilized public opinion by mass propaganda. Antislavery societies again sprang up all over the country with support from all classes, although
there was strong opposition from traditional Anglicans, conservatives, and vested interests, and from some radical working-class leaders, who believed that the campaign diverted attention from the deplorable condition of free British workers.[17]

When slave owners blocked amelioration, the movement became more radical. The
Agency Committee, formed in 1831, was dedicated to the immediate abolition of slavery in British colonies.[18] It paid lecturers to persuade audiences to sign petitions and
launched over a thousand auxiliary societies. It secured parliamentary support by urging voters for the first reformed Parliament to vote only for candidates supporting
immediate abolition.[19]

It worked in favorable times. The opposition was crumbling. Some planters, fearing
slave revolts and faced with falling profits, opted for emancipation, provided they were
paid compensation. The declining importance of the slave colonies to the expanding
British economy, combined with the spectre of the cost of suppressing slave uprisings,
made it easier for the establishment to contemplate universal emancipation.[20]

Thus a combination of factors led to the passing of the Emancipation Act in August
1833.[21] This outlawed slavery in the British Caribbean colonies, Bermuda, Canada,
Mauritius, and Cape Colony, but not in India or other eastern possessions or the trading posts on the west coast of Africa, which were not Crown colonies. Slaveholding by
British subjects also became illegal everywhere except in the eastern possessions. For
convenience, I have called this form of abolition the "Caribbean model."[22]

Under this model, the possession of slaves became illegal and owners were compensated on the principle that legally acquired property should not be arbitrarily confiscated. No one contemplated compensating the slaves for their suffering. Moreover,
complete freedom was not to be immediate. In those colonies that wanted it, an apprenticeship system bound all ex-slaves over the age of six to remain with their former
owners for a period of years. Their pay and hours of work were regulated and they
could buy their freedom if they could earn the means to do so. This was intended to
ease the transition to wage labor by giving the colonies time to learn new techniques of
production and labor management, to replace the slave codes with new laws, to develop
banking institutions, and to build up sufficient supplies of currency to pay wages.[23] In
1834 over 800,000 slaves were freed, and £20,000,000 was offered in compensation.

Neither the government, nor the slave owners, nor even most of the abolitionists
had wanted the freed slaves to leave the labor force. Some abolitionists saw virtue in
former slaves becoming small-holders producing for market, but this was to comple-
ment not replace the plantation system.[24] Few people thought ex-slaves should have

complete freedom of choice. The idea that they might opt for subsistence farming was viewed with horror as a return to African "barbarism." It was believed that, once free to choose their employers and profit from their own efforts, former slaves would work harder and more efficiently as wage labor, proving, as Adam Smith had asserted, that this was more productive than slave labor. Production was expected to rise and costs to decline. Abolitionists hoped that the British Caribbean colonies would become the "shining example" and induce foreign slave owners, particularly in the United States, to abolish slavery in their own interests.[25]

Neither the ex-owners nor the government wanted to dismantle the plantation economy or the political hierarchy. To maintain production, therefore, the planter-dominated assemblies in the Caribbean passed laws affirming the former owners' rights to their land, denying ex-slaves access to political power, and preventing them from organizing to express grievances. Penalties were introduced for vagrancy and non-fulfilment of contracts. Eviction laws and regressive tax policies were designed to discourage ex-slaves from leaving their former owners.[26] Thus slaves were given "freedom" but a freedom modified by laws carefully crafted to keep them in place and at work.

The apprenticeship system did not satisfy owners, slaves, or humanitarians.[27] Masters found it hard to renounce old habits of labor control by intimidation, and government supervision was inadequate. Apprentices agitated for the complete freedom they had been led to expect and ardently desired. The more radical elements in the Agency Committee, led by Joseph Sturge, the Quaker secretary of the Birmingham Anti-Slavery Society,[28] organized mass protests against the system.[29] Finally the Caribbean assemblies ended it rather than risk having further reforms forced upon them. Apprenticeship was abandoned in 1838 before most of the preparations for an orderly transition to free labor had been completed.[30]

The ex-slaves took matters into their own hands. Wherever possible they became small-holders, artisans, and subsistence farmers, avoiding wage labor.[31] Like the British working classes they regarded real freedom as self-employment.[32] In many areas there was a labor crisis and a fall in production.[33]

A NEW FORM OF SERVITUDE: INDENTURED OR CONTRACT LABOR

To meet this crisis, planters turned to new sources of labor. Attempts to replace slaves with European immigrants failed miserably.[34] The enlistment of Africans freed by the Royal Navy from slave ships led to charges that this was a disguised slave trade.[35] Attempts to recruit laborers in West Africa promoted war to capture recruits.[36] Finally a solution was found in the expanding British Empire in India, where thousands of indentured workers were recruited for Mauritius, the British Caribbean, and other colonies.[37] In theory, they came voluntarily and signed contracts for a limited period, after which they were to be repatriated. In practice, many were kidnapped or bought, or coerced, or given an idealized impression of conditions in the colonies. The transport ships were overcrowded. Discipline was harsh. Mortality rates were high. Many recruits were forced to sign on after their contracts expired and some never returned home. Few workers were accompanied by their families. They thus became a new form of coerced labor, tied to the plantations. Abolitionists denounced the system as a disguised form of slavery, and over time the government introduced measures to safeguard the recruits, resorting again to amelioration rather than abolition.[38]

Under the new rules, recruitment was to be by government agents only. The number of immigrants carried on each ship was to be restricted. Immigrants could bring their wives and children without charge and could choose their employers upon arrival. Contracts were to be for one year only. Repatriation was to be free after five years of service. Anyone who wanted to leave earlier could do so but at his own expense. A deaf ear was turned to the abolitionist demand that medical care, housing, and welfare should also be supervised.[39] The extent to which these safeguards were implemented is a matter of debate. That there were abuses at times is certain, but as time went on, recruiting and repatriation were regulated and scholars now believe that the worst features of the Indian system tended to disappear.[40] However, in 1915 the viceroy of India, for political reasons, charged that it was a form of forced labor little different from slavery, and recruiting in India was ended a year later.

From the humanitarian viewpoint, the system, even when reformed, was invidious. It kept down the price of labor, thereby hampering the attempts of freed slaves to get higher pay and better working conditions. It also introduced a new set of workers—contract laborers. Uprooted from their homes, implanted in an alien environment, they were bound by penal contracts to work long hours for low wages. When their contracts expired they were often subject to laws which rest̃ ̃ed their mobility and access to land in an attempt to turn them into a pๆl ๐ ๐ ge labor.[41] Their need for legal protec̃ ̃

THE BRITISH Al
SOCIETY AND l

Once slavery hac   rned their attention
to ending it wor   ıti-Slavery Society[42]
(henceforward tl   ; inaugural meeting
in Exeter Hall on   ınants of earlier societies, and most   It became and remained, under va   ̃ and international
conscience. Know   ̤ end of the twentieth century, the   rganization.

The Society established its headquarters in London, employed a paid full-time executive known as the "Secretary," and published a journal, *The Anti-Slavery Reporter*. It kept up a far-flung correspondence with its branches all over the country, and with individuals and organizations at home and abroad. It sent articles and letters to the press, produced books and pamphlets, and organized meetings and lectures. It also carried on a direct correspondence with government offices offering gratuitous criticism and advice.

Its membership was, and remained largely middle class, as well as Quaker and nonconformist. Until the late twentieth century, it was financed almost entirely by the modest annual dues of its members and the generous contributions of a few rich business or professional men. Its secretaries were high-minded men prepared to accept little more than nominal salaries. The General Committee consisted of philanthropists ready to give their time freely in a good cause. In the early days they were accused of caring more for the welfare of Africans than for the very real sufferings of the British working classes.[44] Probably none of them were radical enough to want reform of the class structure, but many of them contributed time and money to a wide range of philanthropic causes in Britain. They were men of conscience with strong religious beliefs, and doubtless hoped for reward in the next world.[45] Many were closely connected by marriage and business ties, and they often passed the torch to their descendants. Peases, Sturges, Buxtons, and Gurneys served on the committee in the 1880s just as they had done in the 1840s and Barclays, Buxtons, Gurneys, and Wilberforces were members of Anti-Slavery International at the beginning of the twenty-first century.

The Society's aim—to end slavery throughout the world—was daunting. It required winning the support of foreign governments and foreign public opinion. In the 1840s it was believed that there were some six and a quarter million slaves in the New World alone—the greatest number in the United States and Brazil, and the rest spread through the colonies of Spain, France, Holland, Denmark, and Sweden.[46] In Africa and Asia, unknown numbers were to be found in diverse and often barely understood forms of bondage, in societies ranging from small social formations to large empires.

As an unofficial body, the Society had only a limited range of weapons. The most effective up to the late twentieth century was its ability to pressure the British government, and this depended on rallying public opinion. This raises the vexed question of what constituted public opinion, or more important for our story, what constituted the public opinion to which governments were sensitive and which the Society could mobilize. In nineteenth and early twentieth-century Britain, this was essentially the informed reading public, which expressed its views directly through the press and at the polls. Originally this consisted mainly of the middle and upper classes, but both the literate public and the middle classes expanded steadily; and the electorate was widened through a series of franchise reforms beginning in 1832, until by the late twentieth century it included all adults of both sexes over eighteen.

The Society could put pressure on the government through press and Parliament. It will be seen over and over again in the pages that follow that ministers and civil servants, picking up their morning edition of *The Times* or other newspapers, were spurred into action, or at least suffered fits of anxiety, when an article or a letter criticized their policies. Criticism in the press meant sooner or later criticism in Parliament and vice versa. The Society had no difficulty in inspiring such criticism.

In fact one of its greatest and enduring strengths was its ability to co-opt members of Parliament to serve on its committee and to press them into asking questions in both Houses. There were always members ready to attack government policies, either because they believed in the abolitionist cause, or because they wanted to please their constituents, or simply in order to embarrass the administration. Support for the Society also came from the churchgoers in all walks of life. The missionary movement was closely identified with the antislavery cause and the Society co-opted leading churchmen and missionaries to sit on its committee.[47]

In the mid-nineteenth century, to generate discussion on how best to achieve its aims, it organized international antislavery conventions.[48] The first of these was attended by all the leading British abolitionists, by delegates from the British colonies, the United States, France, Spain, Switzerland, and Haiti, as well as from the provincial antislavery societies, church groups and other benevolent societies, and by five thousand spectators. To prepare for it, the Society launched investigations into slavery around the world. One of its methods—the use of questionnaires—set precedents for enquiries by both the League of Nations and the United Nations. They were sent to sister organizations, to missionary societies, and to British consuls. Information was elicited on questions such as slavery in the Muslim world, the total world slave population, and the attitudes of different governments to slavery. At the convention, papers were presented on a range of subjects, including slavery among Native Americans, slaving by Egyptians in Sudan, and a host of other issues. The Society thus became the recipient of a vast body of information, and henceforth was the acknowledged spokesman of the world antislavery movement.

It soon built up a network of correspondents, including explorers, missionaries, consuls, and colonial officials.[49] It became the organization to which anyone wishing to publicize facts about slavery, whether from humanitarian motives or in pursuit of a private grudge, could write and be sure of sympathetic attention. The great dilemma was the difficulty of separating fact from fiction. When funds permitted or the occasion arose, the committee sent out fact-finding missions, but until the late twentieth century most of its information came from interested individuals.

With its limited resources, the Society was, and remained, primarily a pressure group. It did not finance philanthropic schemes, although it sometimes contributed money for particular projects, or established subsidiary organizations for the purpose. Its main brief was to collect and disseminate information, and to promote official action by appeals to the national and international conscience, and by suggesting remedies for abuses. It constantly spurred on the British government to urge other powers to end the slave trade and slavery. It wrote, or even sent delegates, to discuss abolition with foreign heads of state or ministers. It asked British consuls abroad to persuade the countries to which they were accredited to take action. It maintained and still maintains close relations with antislavery societies and other humanitarian organizations abroad. As will be seen, in the twentieth century it was to become an important pressure group and source of information at the United Nations. Its international activities could be a two-edged sword for, particularly in the days of empire, they reinforced the suspicion that the British were trying, under humanitarian guise, to interfere in the internal affairs of other nations in their own interests.

The Society embarked on its great crusade under a self-imposed handicap. Reflecting the principles of its Quaker members, it insisted that universal abolition was to be achieved by "moral, religious and pacific" means only. This split the antislavery movement and won the Society some strange bedfellows. Its pacifism, for instance, put it in the ludicrous position of being unable to support the North during the American civil war of the 1860s, although the Northern victory led to the outlawing of slavery in the United States. Basically the Society remained pacifist, although by the 1880s, as the European imperial powers began to conquer large areas of the world, it sometimes applauded attacks on slave traders, and even advocated the extension of British rule in Africa. Imperialism, of which it was always highly critical, could be accepted if it promoted the antislavery cause.

Thanks to the long antislavery campaign, by the time of the great expansion of the British Empire in the last quarter of the nineteenth century, all classes shared the image of an empire in which slavery had no place. This was an integral part of the belief in what came to be seen as Britain's civilizing mission—an ideological package, which included the spreading of British democratic ideas, British views of freedom, British commerce, and the Christian religion to the "backward races" of the world. This enduring ideal was embedded in the national conscience. Thus, although popular enthusiasm for the antislavery cause never again reached the heights attained in the late eighteenth and early nineteenth centuries, the Society could still attract wide support and wield an influence out of proportion to its minute numbers and minuscule budget. It did not always get the government to do what it wanted, but ministers of the Crown and colonial governors appreciated its nuisance value and were anxious to gain its approbation.

Moreover, just as the Society learned to manipulate the government, so the government learned to use the Society. It could be called upon, for instance, to drum up support for policies and get money from Parliament for actions presented as antislavery measures, but desired for other reasons. It could be used to put pressure on reluctant foreign governments by publicizing their shortcomings. The Society became the joker—the wild card—in colonial policy and international relations. It could be used or resisted according to circumstances, but could rarely be ignored. Thus the British government, like foreign powers, learned to play what may be called the antislavery game.

NOTES

1. Eltis 1993.

2. Drescher 1987, 25–49; Drescher 1989.

3. Historians disagree on the interpretation of the famous Mansfield judgment of 1772, but it seems clear that it enabled slaves brought to Britain to leave their masters. For a discussion of the case, see Davis 1975, 469 ff.; Drescher 1987, 35–43, Drescher 1989.

4. I am following here the usage by Davis 1975, 21, in which Evangelical means the "movement for personal devotion" in the Church of England, while evangelical refers to revivalist movements such as Methodism. Historians disagree on the role of religion in the antislavery movement, see inter alia Anstey 1975, 91 ff., and Drescher 1987, 111–34.

5. See inter alia Drescher 1987, 50 ff.; Temperley 1972, 3–4; Turley 1991, 47–81; Walvin 1982.

6. Walvin 1982, 61–63; Midgley 1992; Halbersleben 1993.

7. Drescher 1987, 79.

8. Temperley 1972, 6–7.

9. Drescher 1987, 67 ff.

10. Temperley 1972, 4–5.

11. Drescher 1987, 71–73.

12. This revolution led to the establishment of the independent state of Haiti. For the repression of other reformist movements, particularly to reform Parliament, see Thompson 1966.

13. For a detailed discussion, see Anstey 1975, 343 ff.

14. Reginald Coupland saw it as a humanitarian triumph, Coupland 1933; whereas Eric Williams, 1944, in a seminal work, argued that abolition was the result of economic changes linked to the industrial revolution. This sparked an academic debate, which has yielded much new evidence and demonstrated the complexity of the question.

15. Drescher 1988.

16. Temperley 1972, 10–11.

17. See Drescher 1986, 89 ff.; Hollis 1980. However, the movements for reform at home and for the end of colonial slavery were closely related.

18. Temperley 1972, 12–15.

19. Parliamentary leadership passed from Wilberforce to Thomas Fowell Buxton in 1824.

20. The reasons for the success of the movement for the abolition of slavery in the British colonies have been the subject of the same intense scrutiny and disagreement as the movement for the abolition of the slave trade. For the Caribbean factors, see Craton 1992; Green 1976; Higman 1976, 1984.

21. See inter alia Blackburn 1988 (a), 419–71.

22. Miers and Roberts, eds., 1988, 10. It is perhaps more correctly called the British colonial model since it applied also to Bermuda, to Mauritius, which ranked third among British colonies in slave numbers, and to Cape Colony. For slavery in Mauritius, see Allen 1999; Barker 1996; Burroughs 1976; Nwulia 1981. For the Cape, India, and the West African outposts, see below, chapter 3.

23. Green 1976, 129 ff.

24. Eltis 1987, 21.

25. Green 1976, 126-27; Temperley 1977, 113–15. For a recent discussion of the hopes of the abolitionists and their failure, see Drescher 2002, 121 ff.

26. See, for example, Craton 1974, 293 ff., 1988; Bolland 1986; Eric Foner 1983, 39–73; Packwood 1975, 185.

27. Green 1985, 129–61.

28. See particularly Temperley 1991, 33–36.

29. Temperley 1977, 19–41.

30. Green 1976, 164–228.

31. See inter alia Green 1976, 64 ff.; Sheridan 1993.

32. Eltis 1987, 19.

33. Engerman 1982, 1985; Green 1985; Eltis 1982.

34. Temperley 1972, 128–29.

35. Asiegbu 1969. However, see also Green 1976, 409–10 for a critique of some of Asiegbu's assertions about African emigration to the Caribbean.

36. Temperley 1972, 133–34.

37. I use the terms indentured and contract labor interchangeably. Strictly speaking, an indenture is a particular kind of contract usually binding the worker to work for a set period to repay the cost of his or her fare.

38. Temperley 1972, 124–33; Green 1976, 276–93; Tinker 1993; Rodney 1981, 32–35. Cumpston 1953, 78–83; Benedict 1980; Carter 1993; Northrup 1995; Allen 1999; Musleem Jumeer 2000. Indentured labor was not limited to the former slave-using colonies but was widely used elsewhere, nor was it limited to Indian labor as will be seen.

39. Temperley 1972, 124–33.

40. See in particular Northrup 1995.

41. For examples of the restrictions to which they were subjected, see Allen 1999 and Dasgupta 2000.

42. For the Society's changes of name, see Abbreviations and Acronyms.

43. Temperley 1972, 65 ff. For the Society's constitution, see *Slavery in British Protectorates*, BFASS London 1897.

44. For the antislavery movement and the working classes, see Temperley 1972, particularly 70–77, 137–67; Walvin 1977, 1980; Hollis 1980; McCalman 1986.

45. For a detailed discussion and for the range of the social causes they supported, and the deep-seated sense of guilt that drove some of them, see Temperley 1972, 70–77.

46. Temperley 1972, xii–xiii, citing *Proceedings of the General Anti-Slavery Convention of 1840*, 3.

47. For a list in the 1880s, see Miers 1975, 32.

48. These were held in London in 1840, 1843, and 1854, and in 1867 in Paris, sponsored together with French and Spanish sister societies; see Temperley 1972, 52 ff.

49. Miers 1975, 31–32.

Forging a Treaty Network against the Slave Trade

THE DECLARATION OF VIENNA 1815

From the day the British outlawed their slave trade, they tried to persuade other nations to follow suit in order to stop this lucrative traffic from falling into foreign hands, and to prevent rival colonies from undercutting British producers faced with higher labor costs. The Danes had already outlawed the slave trade largely for economic reasons in 1802, while the United States did so in 1808 for political reasons.[1] Both gave slave owners plenty of time to stock up with supplies and neither ended slavery. While the Napoleonic wars lasted, the British used their command of the seas to attack the foreign trade and extort treaties from their allies. They sent naval squadrons to patrol the African coasts, paid sailors bounties for every slave they freed, and established a vice-admiralty court to try captured slavers. Since these were often seized with questionable legality, their actions provoked diplomatic protests and claims for compensation for wrongful arrest. This built up a legacy of ill will, convincing foreign powers that the real aim was to disrupt their trade. By the end of the war, the Swedes and the Dutch had outlawed the traffic outright, but Portugal, Spain, and France, anxious to rebuild their colonial and commercial prosperity, would only agree to treaties which left them free, or gave them time, to stock their colonies with slaves.[2]

The British foreign secretary, Lord Castlereagh, would have agreed to this, but the abolitionists collected nearly a million signatures on petitions against the foreign slave trade.[3] At the peace Congress of Vienna, therefore, he tried to get a treaty outlawing the traffic within three years, and giving powers mutual rights to search each other's ships. All he could get, however, was a declaration appended to the Act of Vienna stating that the slave trade was "repugnant to the principles of humanity and universal morality." It was not declared illegal. No time limit for abolition was set. No policing system was established. Even the arrest of slavers was not sanctioned.

This declaration, although useless in practical terms, was the first hesitant step in the direction of the present international human rights movement—the first declaration by the great powers that the slave trade was a violation of the rights of man. For the colonial powers, it was also the beginning of the process by which what was to be called "native welfare," and later "trusteeship," became a matter of international concern.

In 1816, Castlereagh convoked a conference of the ambassadors of France, Austria, Russia, and Prussia, hoping that it would lead to the establishment of a permanent bureau to collect information about the slave trade, to negotiate with recalcitrant powers, and to form a "Christian league" against the traffic. This foundered in the face of French opposition and lack of support from other powers. Taken together, his proposals contained the three ingredients vital for success in all humanitarian projects—effective laws, effective policing (in this case of the seas), and a body to monitor results and ensure that all signatories carried out their obligations. Had Castlereagh succeeded, the future of the antislavery campaign would have been very different.

As it was, the British, convinced of the righteousness of their cause, and willing and able to police the seas, continued to demand the cooperation of all maritime nations and the moral support of others. They were opposed by France, Portugal, Spain, the United States, and Brazil, who believed that British humanitarianism cloaked political and economic ambitions. Measures to end the traffic were inextricably bound up with vested interests, national pride, maritime rights, and colonial and commercial rivalry. The British soon came to think of themselves as the "traditional leaders" of the antislavery movement—lone crusaders fighting for a righteous cause in an immoral world.

BUILDING THE BRITISH TREATY NETWORK

Since a general treaty against the slave trade could not be obtained, Britain, by bribery and cajolery, gradually negotiated bilateral agreements with the maritime powers. These gave signatories mutual rights to visit suspected slavers, to verify their right to the flag they were flying, search them for slaves, and take them for trial in the courts of mixed commission which were set up in Africa and the New World.[4] These rights were mutual in theory, but only Britain had the will and the means to exercise them consistently. British efforts to obtain treaties waxed and waned according to circumstances, and other nations signed them if they wanted British support or had to bow to British pressure. At times all participants found ways to use the humanitarian movement to their own advantage—to play the antislavery game.

Since the capture of slavers at sea, unsupported by an intelligence service on land, was a haphazard affair, naval officers blockaded the African coast and attacked the barracoons housing slaves awaiting shipment. They negotiated treaties with Africans giving them the right to seize slaves destined for export both on land and in territorial waters. These efforts reduced the traffic and increased the risks and price of slave trading, but did not end it. The lesson learned was that as long as there was a market for slaves, they would continue to be smuggled out of Africa, and the markets could not be closed without the cooperation of the authorities in the importing areas.

By 1870, all New World markets had been closed,[5] but slaves were still exported to the Middle East from Africa, from the Caucasus, and the eastern shores of the Persian Gulf. The British had tried to end this traffic by agreements with the authorities in both the exporting and importing regions, including the small polities along the Red Sea and Indian Ocean coasts, the shaykhdoms of the Persian Gulf and the Hadhramaut, and the rulers of important states, such as the sultan of the vast Ottoman Empire, the khedive of Egypt, and the sultan of Zanzibar.

These areas were predominantly Muslim. Whereas most of the Western world had come to accept that slave trading was morally wrong, most Islamic peoples had no such qualms. Slavery was recognized by the Qur'an.[6] By Islamic law, only infidels captured in war could be enslaved. This was believed to be morally justified, and to benefit the victims by giving them the opportunity to convert to Islam.[7] However, this restriction was rarely observed. Slaves, Muslims and others, were captured in wars and raids, kidnapped or sold, from a catchment area which included the Balkans, the Caucasus, Baluchistan, India, Southeast Asia, and the Philippines. Those most central to our story in the nineteenth century came from Africa along trade routes stretching into the heart of the continent. Those from the eastern Sudan, Ethiopia, Somalia, and the country west of the great lakes were marched, shackled, to the coast, crammed into dhows and taken across the Red Sea or the Gulf of Aden to markets in Arabia, the Persian Gulf, and even India. Those from the western and central Sudanic belt, and the Southern Sudan made the dangerous journey across the Sahara by caravan or sailed down the Nile and were exported from North African ports, sometimes in European steamships, and sold throughout the Ottoman Empire. While the sea journey was less horrendous than the Atlantic crossing, the march to the coast left a trail of desolation and death. Slaves trudging across the Sahara, without shoes or clothes, died of exposure, or were left to a lingering death when their feet were so swollen that incessant beating could spur them no further. On the journey from the interior to the east coast of Africa the weak were abandoned, children were torn from distraught mothers, and the recalcitrant were killed to terrorize the remainder. Slaves were thrown overboard from dhows or abandoned on inhospitable shores by cornered slavers trying to hide evidence of their misdeeds.

The British gradually obtained treaties against the export or import of slaves with the more important Muslim rulers. The sultan of Zanzibar, through whose ports thousands of slaves had been exported, signed a comprehensive treaty with Britain in 1873, under threat of bombardment.[8] Egypt, whose predatory rule in Sudan had led to the capture of untold numbers of victims, followed suit in 1877, when the ruler,

Khedive Ismail, wanted British support for the extension of his rule along the Red Sea coast and up the Nile into central Africa.[9] The Ottoman Empire, which stretched from the Balkans to the Gulf of Aden and along the North African coast to Tripoli, was of major strategic importance to Britain, particularly after the opening of the Suez Canal in 1869, since it straddled the short route to India. Its demise would have unleashed a power struggle between Britain and its main rivals, Russia and France, each anxious for a share of the pickings. Hence, the British were cautious in pressing for a treaty, for fear of dealing the empire a coup de grace.[10] However, when they needed British support, the Turks yielded to pressure. The result was piecemeal legislation against the traffic. This was rarely enforced, particularly in the Hijaz.[11] This province contained the holy cities of Mecca and Medina, which the sultan had to control to support his claim to be caliph of the Islamic world and leader of Sunni Muslims. Thus, when a law to prohibit the import of African slaves in 1857 provoked a rebellion, the province was exempted from the law. However, after the Turks lost a war with Russia in 1877, they were anxious enough to retain British support to agree to the Anglo-Ottoman Convention against the traffic in 1880.[12] But, predictably, they did little to carry out its provisions in Arabia.[13]

The sultan of Morocco, on the other hand, refused to agree to a treaty, claiming he could not enforce it.[14] In view of his country's strategic position and the threat of French intervention, the British, wary of doing anything to weaken him, merely asked him to keep slave dealing out of sight of foreigners by stopping public sales in his ports. Politics predictably prevailed over humanitarianism.

By the 1880s, Britain stood at the center of a great network of treaties against the export and import of slaves by sea. No other power had acquired such rights or shouldered such responsibilities. It was not lost on other nations that these treaties had played a part in the building of British paramountcy on much of the African coastline. In western Africa, for instance, officers of the Royal Navy had become the virtual policemen of the coasts and navigable rivers, with orders to use "every endeavour to encourage" legitimate commerce, collect information about the country, and protect British subjects, as well as combat the slave trade.[15] The treaties had political ramifications. Those with small polities, considered "barbarous chiefs," were regarded as sufficient to prevent other European powers from taking them under their protection. They also opened the way to interference in local affairs. From mid-century, consuls were appointed to strategic areas. Together with the antislavery squadron, they became the spearhead of a creeping British informal domination along the east and west coasts. The slave trade was also sometimes used to justify territorial expansion wanted for other reasons. Parliament was more willing to sanction high-handed action and provide money for measures against the slave trade than for other ventures.[16]

THE PARTITION OF AFRICA AND LOOPHOLES
IN THE MARITIME TREATY NETWORK

By the 1880s, the export of slaves from Africa to the Muslim world had been reduced but not ended. The great territorial expansion of the European imperial powers, known as the "scramble for Africa," was under way. Britain could no longer hope to contain the export traffic by patrolling the coasts, exerting informal domination over indigenous societies, and obtaining the cooperation of rulers by force or bribery. Powerful rival colonial powers were replacing pliant native authorities. Moreover, the treaties were a hodgepodge of agreements, negotiated at different times, with different provisions, and there was no treaty with France.

Although French philosophers had been in the vanguard of the antislavery movement, and France had outlawed slavery in its colonies in 1848, there was little grassroots support for abolition.[17] The French had outlawed the slave trade in 1818, but had refused to give the British the power to search their shipping, or even to visit their vessels to confirm their right to fly the French flag. They regarded such rights as an infringement of national sovereignty, and did not try to acquire them themselves. As long as even one maritime power remained outside the treaty network, slaves could be carried with impunity under the protection of its flag. In 1839, Britain, by act of Parliament, assumed the right to arrest vessels not flying a flag. But if there was a flag at the masthead, without a treaty, British naval officers could not even visit a suspect to verify its right to fly the flag, and slavers evaded arrest by shifting from flag to flag.

After a series of unsatisfactory treaties, Britain and France agreed, in 1855, on measures to prevent fraudulent use of their flags. Henceforth a vessel had to show her flag if challenged by a man-of-war. If there were grounds for suspecting she had no right to it, the warship's officers might visit her. Detailed instructions for these visits were laid down. Their whole tenor, even after they were revised in 1867, was to discourage visits in order to minimize friction. The visiting officer had to have strong grounds for suspicion and could only inspect the vessel's papers. If she had the right to fly the French flag, he could take no action, even if the dhow was full of slaves clamoring for help.[18]

By the late 1880s, the British feared that the eastern African slave trade was growing. The French, anxious to build up their carrying trade, were allowing residents of their footholds in the Comoro Islands and Nosi Bé, off the west coast of Madagascar, and their base on the Red Sea at Obock, to sail under the French flag. They did not inquire too closely into the character of the captains, but made sure they knew that the British had no power over them.[19]

Another loophole was that the treaties with the European colonial powers did not allow the patrolling of territorial waters. As these powers annexed the African coastline, the Royal Navy could only cruise offshore in the hope of falling in with a slaver—

a remote chance in the absence of cooperation from authorities ashore and a good intelligence service. This was a particular problem in Mozambique where underpaid Portuguese officials connived at the slave trade and claimed areas they did not control. Potentially even more serious was the fact that the treaties did not cover the traffic in contract labor, which had escalated as the European powers freed their slaves. In the 1880s, the French were buying slaves in Mozambique and sending them to their possessions in Madagascar and the Comoros as *libres engagés*.[20] They were captured upcountry, brought to the coast, sold to recruiting agents, ostensibly freed, sometimes furnished with a contract, which they rarely understood, and shipped off to French colonies. Alternatively, slaves were bought from their masters in a transaction passed off as an advance of wages.[21] The Portuguese were also sending a thousand workers a year to produce cocoa on their islands of São Tomé and Principe in the Gulf of Guinea. Most came from Angola and none returned.[22]

This kind of disguised slaving seemed likely to get worse as the European powers took over large areas of Africa and needed workers and soldiers. Since it was theoretically a migration of free people, armed with contracts and under government supervision, existing treaties did not cover it. Naval officers could not interfere with the European or local craft in which the victims traveled, since technically they were passengers traveling legally to regions under European rule in which slavery had been outlawed.

Another problem was that each European power, as it established itself in Africa, dealt with slavers in its own way. The British had clear rules of procedure, and slavers convicted in the vice-admiralty court in Zanzibar usually served a light sentence in the sultan's prison, but the Germans, just then establishing themselves on the East African coast and new to the problem, sometimes hanged them.[23] In the interests of justice, the powers needed a concerted policy for the arrest and punishment of slavers.

THE BERLIN DECLARATION 1885

In 1884, as the European colonial powers began occupying and claiming large parts of Africa, the German chancellor, Otto von Bismarck, called a conference in Berlin of the leading colonial and maritime powers. The purpose was to find a formula for coastal annexations, and to ensure that the two great navigable rivers—the Congo and the Niger—remained open to the trade of all nations. The British, "anxious to carry off all the honors of the meeting," and please the humanitarian lobby, proposed that the conference should also condemn the slave trade as a crime against the law of nations (or human rights), liable to prosecution by the tribunals of all "civilized countries," whatever the nationality of the offender. However, the other powers would only agree to a declaration in the Berlin Act that the export slave trade was forbidden by international law and that the operations, which supplied it on land and water "ought to be regarded as forbidden." The powers with territories in the conventional basin of the Congo, however, agreed to

watch over the preservation of the native tribes, and to care for the improvement of the conditions of their moral and material well-being, and to help in suppressing slavery, and especially the slave trade.[24]

The slave trade on land was thus condemned for the first time in a multinational treaty, and the principle that "native welfare" was a matter of international concern was accepted. Once more, however, no practical measures were suggested. No machinery was established for monitoring results and no common action was envisaged.

THE BRUSSELS ACT OF 1890

By the 1880s, a number of Christian missions had established themselves in the interior of East Africa, initially in response to the revelation of the British missionary, David Livingstone, that slave raiding and trading were devastating large areas, and his appeal to bring "Christianity, commerce, and civilization" to the heart of the continent.[25] As the threat of European conquest became explicit, the Swahili/Arab perpetrators of these raids and their African allies tried to preempt the European advance by conquering large areas for themselves. The Christian missions were threatened. They reported these wars not as a reaction to European encroachment but as the desperate onslaught of slavers, hunting down victims with "fiendish passion." The Scottish missionaries around Lake Nyasa appealed to the British government for help and the Anti-Slavery Society pressed for action, but the most spectacular call came from the French Cardinal Lavigerie, founder of the Roman Catholic Society of Our Lady of Africa, commonly known as the "White Fathers." In 1888, he launched a "crusade" to protect his missions.[26] With papal blessing, he toured Western Europe, preaching fiery sermons calling for volunteers to go to Central Africa to combat the slave traffic. Christians of all denominations flocked to hear him, astonished that the slave trade still existed. Before his appearance, the finances of the Anti-Slavery Society had been at such low ebb that it was considering amalgamating with a sister organization, the Aborigines Protection Society. This plan was jettisoned as the cardinal breathed new life into the antislavery movement.

Since the Society, with its pacifist policy, could not support the cardinal's warlike plans, it urged the government to cooperate with other powers, reminding it that the public expected Britain to play its "traditional" role as leader of the antislavery movement. The government, alarmed at the prospect of armed crusaders loose in Africa, and anxious to retain leadership of the movement, decided that the safest response was to call a conference of the African coastal powers to consider measures against the export of slaves. They asked King Leopold to hold it in Brussels to disarm foreign suspicions that they might have ulterior motives.[27]

The cardinal's hopes of founding an international order of military knights financed by Christians of all denominations bore little fruit,[28] but the Brussels Conference resulted in the signing of the Brussels Act of 1890.[29] This treaty went far beyond the British proposal for an agreement against the export traffic. King Leopold II of the Belgians, who was carving out a personal empire in the Congo, ably assisted by the other colonial powers, seized the opportunity to craft a treaty to serve their purposes, and carried the antislavery game to an apogee unequalled before or since.

THE BRUSSELS ACT AND THE JUSTIFICATION OF COLONIAL RULE

All the colonial and maritime nations, together with the other signatories and adherents to the Berlin Act, were invited to the conference, to avoid offending them and to secure their support.[30] The treaty they hammered out was the first comprehensive multilateral treaty against the African slave trade. All existing treaty rights, mostly British, to visit, search, arrest, and try suspected slavers on the high seas and in territorial waters were retained, but, in an attempt to win over the French, they were to be limited to vessels under 500 tons and to a "slave trade zone." This zone included the eastern African coast north of Quilimane in Mozambique, Madagascar, the Red Sea, the Persian Gulf, and the Indian Ocean north of a line drawn from the northern tip of Madagascar to the border of British Baluchistan. Vessels suspected of slaving or of flying a flag to which they were not entitled were to be arrested and turned over for trial to the authorities of the country whose flag they were using. Compensation was to be paid for wrongful arrest.

The signatory powers were to issue flags and ships' papers only to respectable nationals. African passengers were only to board at ports where they could be given identity papers, and only to land where these could be verified. African crewmen were to be interviewed to ensure they were serving voluntarily. Procedures for stopping, visiting, searching, arresting, and trying suspects were carefully laid down.

At the instigation of King Leopold, the treaty declared that the best means of attacking the slave trade on land was by establishing colonial administrations, controlling the trade routes, constructing road, rail and water communications, and telegraph systems, and protecting trading companies and missionaries of all denominations. Africans were also to be "civilized" and—most ominously—their welfare was to be promoted by initiating them into agricultural labor and the "industrial" arts. Because the other powers were wary of these open-ended commitments, these changes could be introduced gradually.

Having thus established that the occupation and exploitation of Africa was an antislavery measure, the signatories bound themselves to pass and enforce laws against the capture, transport, and sale of slaves on land, and the castration of males. Freed slaves, and fugitives, if they had been illegally acquired or ill-treated, were, if possible, to be repatriated to their place of origin. Otherwise, they were to be protected and enabled to earn a living. Refuges were to be established for women and children, and the latter were to be educated. The signatories in whose territories slavery was legal—Zanzibar, Persia, and the Ottoman Empire—agreed to prohibit the import and export of African slaves, and to free those illegally acquired.

Measures to control the arms traffic, to limit the liquor trade, and to allow King Leopold to levy import duties in the Congo were slipped into the act as either antislavery measures or measures to promote African welfare. Their effect was to give governments a monopoly of the lucrative arms and liquor traffic, and hence an edge over commercial rivals.

THE BRUSSELS AND ZANZIBAR BUREAUS

To supervise the working of the Act, a special bureau was to be established in Brussels to which signatories were to send annual reports on the numbers of slaves they had freed, the dealers they had arrested, the laws they had passed, and the penalties they had imposed. These were to be published, together with the reports of a bureau in Zanzibar, to which each local power was to send any information that would assist in the suppression of the maritime trade. The British failed to get a similar bureau established in the Red Sea.

Since these offices in Brussels and Zanzibar were, in a sense, forerunners of the twentieth-century League of Nations and United Nations slavery committees, their composition and powers merit examination. The British had wanted to bind all signatories to supply the Brussels bureau with information, and proposed that it should monitor the working of the Act and suggest measures to make it more effective. The French, Russians, Portuguese, Italians, and the Turks all objected to giving it such powers, fearing that it would infringe national sovereignty if it were allowed to criticize, comment on, or even draw conclusions from the information it gathered. These objections, as will be seen, were to be raised again and again in the twentieth century, and prevent any effective monitoring of antislavery treaties.

The Brussels bureau was therefore so emasculated that it was merely an office attached to the Belgian Foreign Ministry. It collected, exchanged, and published whatever information signatories cared to send it about the measures they were taking to carry out the Brussels Act, together with statistical information on the slave, arms, and liquor traffics, and on the numbers of slaves liberated. The International Maritime Bureau in Zanzibar consisted of representatives of the five colonial powers in the region: Britain, Germany, France, Italy, and Portugal. They met monthly from November 1892. Their mandate was vague. However, they drew up their own rules of procedure, agreed on a budget, and decided to ask for the information they needed. They struggled to find common formulas so that naval officers could identify a vessel, check its papers, and ensure that it had been legally cleared for embarkation. They drew up lists of registered vessels and prototypes of the identification papers issued to dhows, and passengers and crews. They also kept records of naval patrols, and of the trials of suspects.[31]

Although too emasculated to form an effective monitoring system, these bureaus gathered useful statistics and kept the slave trade question alive.

THE IMPACT OF THE BRUSSELS ACT

The Brussels Act came into force on 2 April 1892. The Anti-Slavery Society was to look back to it with nostalgia half a century later as a model treaty. It was certainly a land-mark in the development of the doctrine of trusteeship. It reaffirmed the process begun at Berlin by which the suppression of the slave trade, and by implication eventually slavery, was part and parcel of the European civilizing mission—part of an ideological package which justified not only colonial conquest but also the reshaping of African social, political, and economic systems, and religious beliefs. Its importance went far beyond Africa since the slave trade could not be condemned as inhuman in Africa while being tolerated elsewhere. It also reaffirmed the principle that "native welfare" was an international responsibility. Finally, it was a step towards the establishment of standards of international morality by which governments might be judged.

As a practical measure against the slave trade, however, it had many shortcomings. It lacked effective supervisory machinery. It applied only to the trade in Africans. The slave trade zone did not include the Mediterranean, although slaves were still exported from North Africa to the Ottoman Empire and the Middle East, often on European steamers.[32] It did not explicitly attack slavery or cover colonial labor practices such as the hiring of slaves from their masters, or the acquisition of freed slaves for contract labor or for service in the colonial armed forces. The colonial powers had no desire to hamper development by risking the mass departure of slaves or by restrictions on their labor or military recruitment. Finally much of its force was lost by the insertion of such phrases as "as far as possible," or "in so far as circumstances shall permit," so that signatories would not need to carry out its provisions before it suited them—a device copied in later antislavery treaties. The act was to prove a two-edged sword for the colonial powers. For some two decades after it came into force, they were fully occupied with establishing administrations in their vast territories in Africa. Their goal was to make them economically self-sufficient by turning their people into producers of primary products for export, and consumers of European manufactured goods. Hundreds of small wars of conquest were fought and the suppression of the slave trade was a heaven-sent excuse for campaigns which otherwise might have raised a storm of criticism at home. Not all opponents could be written off as slavers, but, conveniently, the fiercest resistance often came from Africans heavily involved in slave raiding and trading.

Most colonial conquerors were genuinely convinced that they were bringing civilization to "darkest Africa." Hence, the killing of innocent people, the burning of their homes, the looting of their villages, the seizure of their lands, the desecration of their shrines, and the killing of their leaders were justified as the necessary means to a laudable end. Although the suppression of the slave trade was only one facet of this "civilizing" mission, it produced visible results faster then Christianity or commerce. Once a region had been "pacified," slave raids ended and slave caravans and public slave markets vanished.

The Brussels Act, however, could also be used by interested parties to force a reluctant government into action. In the 1890s, when the Imperial British East Africa Company announced its withdrawal from Uganda, imperialists, missionaries, and humanitarians successfully pressured the government into assuming control. Prominent among the reasons advanced was that Britain had a moral duty to suppress the slave trade in accordance with the Act.

Although it was clearly in the interests of the imperial powers to suppress raiding, and prevent their subjects—potential producers, consumers, and taxpayers—from being exported as slaves, they only slowly mustered the strength to do so. For at least two decades, and much longer in some areas, European officials were thin on the ground and the military forces at their disposal were minimal. Wars of conquest were undertaken piecemeal and usually with African cooperation. Africans served in colonial armies, or were enlisted as allies or irregular troops. In the early days, these campaigns increased slaving, as Africans on both sides freely enslaved their prisoners, and European commanders were in no position to deny their allies the spoils of war.[33]

Once an area was "pacified," colonial ventures produced an insatiable demand for labor. Administrators, planters, farmers, merchants, and army officers, desperate to satisfy this need, and even missionaries trying to build up their congregations, often began by buying slaves.[34] Thus, the Congo Independent State and the Portuguese bought slaves from the Ovimbundu, who first sold them their own captives and then replaced them with fresh supplies from ever more distant regions.[35] The French in Ubangi-Shari not only bought slaves outright but even attacked slave caravans in order to get labor.[36] Both the French and Belgians settled freed slaves along lines of communication and used them as forced labor. Slaves were also hired from their masters, who all too often managed to appropriate the lion's share of their earnings. Theoretically, slaves employed by the colonial rulers were voluntary paid labor but they were rarely given any option about their employment or their terms of service and, if ransom was paid for them, the cost was deducted from their minimal wages. Small wonder, then, that Africans, both slaves and masters, usually concluded that the colonial rulers were freeing slaves to use them themselves.

Eventually, as European control was extended over the whole continent, except for Liberia and Ethiopia, the wars and raids that had been such a fertile source of slaves came to an end and the supply declined. Nonetheless, raiding continued for many years on the borders between colonial territories, on the frontiers of Ethiopia, along the Saharan fringe, and in the desert oases.[37] On the borders of French Mauritania and

Spanish Rio del Oro, raiding by the *grands nomades* was endemic, even after they submitted to the French in the 1930s.[38] However, by the end of the second decade of the twentieth century, large-scale raids and the great caravans of slaves, which had characterized earlier decades, had disappeared from the regions under colonial rule, although petty raiding continued in remote areas.

Small-scale slave dealing was harder to eradicate. Victims, mostly children, were kidnapped or acquired by trickery, and taken surreptitiously to secret markets in private homes. This traffic was hard to detect and the ingenuity of the traders often baffled the authorities. For instance, girls from Adamawa would be bought by a merchant, kept for a year in Cameroon learning Hausa, and then be smuggled into Nigeria for sale in, say, Kano, for concubinage, domestic service, or even genuine adoption.[39] Similar undercover operations continued in many areas throughout the twentieth century.

Operations of this sort could only be ended with African cooperation and this often took years to win. Moreover, there were different interpretations as to what constituted slave trading. In Mauritania in 1918, a French official "closed his eyes" to sales if both the buyer and the seller belonged to his subdivision and the sale took place in front of a Muslim *qadi* (judge). The governor maintained that the transfer of a slave as part of bride price arrangements was not slave dealing, whereas sale to a stranger would be.[40] Endless questions arose over transfers of women.[41] For instance, if a French soldier redeemed a slave woman in order to marry her, was he buying her freedom or on his return to his village would she simply be viewed as his slave?[42] Control over women and children, and transactions in women went to the heart of domestic relations and are relevant to the ongoing problem of what was denounced in the twentieth century as "servile marriage."

The eradication of the maritime traffic posed fewer problems, and it declined as the colonial powers established control over the coast. The records of the Zanzibar bureau in the early 1890s show that the British freed nearly two hundred slaves destined for Arabia in 1893. Other powers also reported captures.[43] As in the past, French policy impeded British efforts for a while. The French Parliament refused to accept some of the provisions of the Brussels Act, claiming that they amounted to the right to search and would be used to the detriment of French commerce. Since no one wanted the treaty to founder, France was allowed to exclude these clauses when it ratified the Act. In return, the French government agreed to abide by the regulations of 1867 and to impose more rigorous rules for the issue of their colors. Nevertheless, old habits die hard, and slaving continued on French dhows, particularly those registered at Muscat, where France was anxious to maintain influence. Omani vessels under French colors brought slaves to Arabia and the Persian Gulf from as far away as Mozambique. This loophole was only closed in 1905, when the Hague International Tribunal decided that France should curtail the issue of French flags to Omani dhows. Thereafter, the traffic died down, but as will be seen, small-scale smuggling of slaves to Arabia continued far into the twentieth century, and only ended with closure of the markets in the 1960s.

NOTES

1. The Danes wanted to keep labor in West Africa to build up their possessions on the coast, and they believed that the slave population of their West Indian Islands would be self-sustaining. Norregard 1966, 172–85; Johansen 1981; Kea 1995. The United States wanted to limit the representation in Congress of the southern states, in which slaves counted as two-thirds of a person in the population count.

2. For a brief discussion with further references, see Miers 1975, 9–10.

3. This was out of a total population of some twelve million. For British policy, see Drescher 1977, 142–61; Bethell 1970, 12; Walvin 1981, 67–68; Temperley 1972, 8.

4. For the building of the network and the terms of the treaties, see inter alia Miers, 1975, 9 ff.

5. Slavery was still legal in Brazil (until 1888) and in Cuba (until 1878) but the traffic had been reduced to a minute smuggling trade.

6. Many sources could be cited, but see inter alia for Muslim attitudes, Lewis 1990; for Muslim law, see Brunschvig 1960. See also Toledano 1993, 1998. For a discussion of the prevalent European belief that Islam sanctions rather than recognizes slavery, see Ali 1972.

7. See below, chapter 7, for further discussion of Muslim slavery.

8. For the events leading to this, see Gavin 1962, Cooper 1977, and Sheriff 1987.

9. Many sources could be cited, but see particularly Gray 1961; Ali 1972; Ewald 1990; Hargey 1981, chapter 1.

10. For a detailed study of the Ottoman slave trade and its suppression, based on Ottoman as well as British sources, see Toledano 1982.

11. For this subject, see Toledano 1982, 91 ff. For the gradual decline of slavery in the Ottoman Empire, see Toledano 1993.

12. See for further references, Miers 1975, 84; and Toledano 1982, 235.

13. Memos by Marinitch, 23 July 1889, enc. in White to Salisbury, no.14 Africa, 9 September 1889, FO 84/1971, and 13 January 1890, enc. in White to Salisbury, no. 2 Africa, 15 January 1890, FO 84/2056; Wylde 1888, II, ch. 9; Renault 1971, II, 65–69.

14. Miers 1975, 62–68; the *Anti-Slavery Reporter* published many articles on the subject particularly from May 1883, and sent out investigators in 1884 and 1885. See also Miège 1961, III and IV.

15. See *Instructions* 1844, para. 1.

16. A well-known example was the annexation of Lagos in 1860.

17. It was briefly also abolished during the revolution in 1794, and again in 1814. For French policy, see inter alia Daget, 1980, 1981; Drescher 1980; particularly for West Africa see Klein 1998 and Getz 2000.

18. Memo by Euan Smith, 31 July 1889, FOCP 5977.

19. Ibid.

20. For French policies on *libres engagés*, see Renault 1976. For a recent study of the contract labor question, see Northrup 1995.

21. O'Neill to Granville, no. 55, 31 December 1880, FO 84/1565; Renault 1971, I, 133–34; Renault 1976, 124 ff.

22. For this traffic, see Duffy 1967. For the later history of this question, see below, chapter 4.

23. Miers 1975, 220–21.

24. Article VI, Berlin Act, E. Hertslet, *The Map of Africa by Treaty*, II, 474. For British efforts and aims, see Miers 1975, 169–89, 1988; Gann 1988.

25. Livingstone 1857; Oliver 1965; Hanna 1956.

26. For Lavigerie's crusade, see Renault 1971, vol. 2, 73 ff.

27. Miers 1975, 190 ff.

28. Renault 1971, vol. 2.

29. General Act for the Repression of the African Slave Trade, Hertslet, *Map* II, 488 ff.

30. The participants were France, Britain, Portugal, Germany, Italy, Spain, the Netherlands, Belgium, Russia, Austria, Sweden and Norway, Denmark, the United States, the Congo Independent State, the Ottoman Empire and Zanzibar. Persia was included as a cooperative Muslim power. For the conference, see Miers 1975, 229–91.

31. The reports of the bureau are to be found in *Documents*.

32. Boahen 1964, 157. The Mediterranean had never been covered by British treaties. Because of its strategic and commercial importance, no power would grant the British the right to search its ships there. By the 1880s, there was the added complication that slaves carried on steamers were hard to distinguish from legitimate passengers, many of whom were from parts of North Africa under French protection.

33. For specific examples from areas far apart, and further references, see inter alia Miers and Roberts, eds., 19; Klein 1993a, 175–76.

34. Oliver 1965, 22–23; Renault, I, 142, 188 ff., 203; Miers 1975, 154–55; Cordell 1988, 156–57.

35. Heywood 1988. See below for further discussion of the Angolan slave trade.

36. Cordell 1988, 156.

37. For examples, see chapters in Miers and Roberts, particularly Cordell, McDougall, Lovejoy and Hogendorn 1993, 274–77; Vaughan and Kirk-Greene 1995; Miers 1997.

38. McDougall 1988, 366–67.

39. Harris to resident, Kano 24 January 1922, NANI/ 50127 vol. 1; Lovejoy and Hogendorn 1993, 267–70; Miers 1975, 296–98.

40. McDougall 1988, 368.

41. For some examples, see McDougall 1988, 369–73.

42. For an interesting discussion of this point, see McDougall 1988, 369–73.

43. *Documents* for 1892–1893.

3

Emancipation in Theory and Practice

LIMITING THE IMPACT OF EMANCIPATION:
THE BRITISH PROTECTORATE MODEL

The British were soon disillusioned with the results of the Caribbean model of emancipation. A quickening racism and pseudoscientific theories of human evolution fueled the belief that Africans were lazy, childlike, and unresponsive to market incentives; and that only white tutelage could lead them from barbarism to "civilization."[1] Even the abolitionists, upset by the decline in production in the West Indies, by the contract labor system, and by the continuing poverty of the freed slaves, had second thoughts about this model. Moreover, in the Cape Colony it was one of the reasons that a number of Afrikaner owners, already disaffected and finding the compensation inadequate, left the colony in the great trek of the 1830s[2]—leaving the British wary of alienating slave owners.[3]

The tiny British footholds in West Africa were not included in the Emancipation Act until, largely due to abolitionist pressure, they became colonies in 1843.[4] These were trading stations existing by courtesy of their African neighbors. The local administrators soon convinced their superiors in London that any interference with African slave ownership would lead to widespread resistance within the colonies and that traders from surrounding regions, fearing their slave porters might claim freedom under the British flag, would take their goods to the posts of rival European powers. The first solution was to free the slaves of the Europeans without compensation, but to allow African residents to keep theirs. The law officers of the Crown, however, ruled that the colonies were actual British soil and, on British soil, all slaves had to be freed. Thereafter, colonies were kept as small as possible. As new areas were annexed, they were designated "protectorates," in which Britain exercised influence, established customs posts, warded off encroachments by rival powers, discouraged slave trading, and even mounted the occasional military expedition to keep the inhabitants in line, but in which Africans ruled themselves. This solution enabled the British to avoid the expense of establishing full colonial administrations, and avoid the dangers of attacking slavery.

For the next three decades, British policy in West Africa remained one of minimal interference with African affairs outside the actual colonies. In 1842, a select committee of Parliament confirmed that Britain had no legal right to interfere with African slavery in the protectorates around the colonies, except "by persuasion, negotiation and other means"—whatever that might mean.[5] Even in the colonies, little changed, as owners found ways to control their freed slaves, and runaways from the surrounding areas were routinely returned to their owners.[6] In the 1840s, however, a better solution was worked out in India.[7]

THE BRITISH INDIAN MODEL OF EMANCIPATION

The Emancipation Act of 1833 did not cover India, Ceylon, or St. Helena, and was not applied in the far eastern dependencies of Singapore, Malacca, Penang, or Province Wellesley. British India was at the time ruled by the East India Company. Slavery was an ancient institution and took many forms according to Muslim, Buddhist, and Hindu law, and local customs.[8] Most slaves were women and children and few were used for commercial enterprises. Although some Africans were imported, the majority of slaves and owners were Indian. Slaves might be domestic servants, concubines, dancing girls, soldiers, and agricultural, agrestic, or predial slaves, who like serfs were sometimes traded with the land. Some were well-off. Others were worked hard and were subject to arbitrary punishment, including mutilation or death. In 1841, it was estimated that one million people were in various forms of servitude. Modern estimates suggest there may have been nine million. Either figure makes this the biggest body of slaves in the British Empire at the time. The great majority had sunk into bondage either because they had sold themselves or because their parents had sold them as children, to save their lives in times of famine, or because they had fallen into debt. The giving of food or hospitality was tantamount to purchase and, in this land of recurrent famine, many people became debtors and hence slaves of their creditors.[9] The East India Company's tax and land tenure policies, its misgovernment, and its inability to provide famine relief compounded the problem.

The Company had few officials and vast territories. It only slowly suppressed the slave trade and was reluctant to interfere with slavery, about which it knew little. Officials tended to have their own definitions of slavery and slave trading. Some regarded sales of children for domestic service as a form of adoption, but considered sales for prostitution as enslavement.[10] Under humanitarian and parliamentary attack, the Company found an ingenious solution—one that was to become the model of the future.[11] It did not outlaw slavery, but simply declared that it had no legal standing in British India.[12] Henceforth, if slaves left their owners, they could not be recovered by legal action or force, nor could they be made to work. No case could be brought against them, nor could property be taken from them on the grounds that they were slaves. However, it was not illegal to own slaves, and slaves did not have to change their status. Theoretically, therefore, those who remained as slaves did so voluntarily. Thus, the idea of "voluntary" or "permissive" slavery was born. The exact meaning of this was to be the subject of argument in the future.

Owners in India were not compensated since their slaves were not actually taken away from them. Moreover, there were too many owners and they had no clout in Parliament. Hence, they had no incentive to change the status quo. The administration, equally anxious to maintain it, assumed no obligation to tell slaves that they were free to leave, or to help them secure a livelihood if they did so. Much more research is needed before the overall results of these measures can be assessed, but many persons were said to be still in slavery a decade later.[13] Slaves were often the last to hear of their liberation. Masters, on the other hand, were quickly aware of it, and found ways to protect their interests. Thus, for many slaves freedom meant eviction, or a demand for rent for houses and land that they had hitherto used for nothing. Unable to meet these exactions, some, forced to borrow from their former owners, fell into hereditary debt bondage, swelling the numbers of unfortunates already suffering from this form of oppression.[14] Not until 1860, after the British government took over the administration from the East India Company, did it become an offense to own slaves.[15]

If the Indian model of abolition did little for the slaves, it was ideal for the government. It was cheap. It caused no discernible social or economic disruption, produced no political backlash, and required no special measures of enforcement. Its advantages for the administration were so clear that it came to be accepted as the ideal method of ending slavery among non-European peoples. It was applied in Ceylon where some thirty to forty thousand slaves were "freed" and in Singapore, Malacca, Penang, and Province Wellesley.[16]

However, it was not applied in the Indian Princely States under British "protection." Britain had treaties with them precluding interference in their domestic affairs, including labor questions. Since they covered two-fifths of the subcontinent, this was a serious omission. It was also not applied in Assam or other border areas.[17]

THE CONCEPT OF "BENIGN" SLAVERY AND THE BRITISH DEFINITION OF SLAVERY

This model of abolition was acceptable to the humanitarians in Britain, because they believed that Indian slavery, unlike its Western counterpart, was "benign," meaning that it could benefit the slaves as well as their owners.[18] The fact that people enslaved themselves or their children to avoid starvation was a powerful argument. Slavery, it was said, provided the poor with a protector, and access to land or other forms of livelihood. As long as it could be argued that no one could now be legally bought, sold, or captured, and that those slaves who remained in slavery did so voluntarily, it was believed that there was no need to force them to change their status. The fact that no steps were taken to provide them with an alternative livelihood was simply overlooked by governments unwilling to take responsibility for their fate, or to bear the cost of re-settling the "freed." Modern scholars no longer accept the argument that all forms of Indian slavery were benign,[19] nor did all humanitarians believe it at the time. Never-theless, the British decided that Indian slavery was free of the worst cruelties of West-ern slavery and, in theory at least, after 1843 discontented slaves could leave.

The concept of benign slavery raises the complex question of what we understand by the term "slavery." The humanitarians, the British public, and the government in the nineteenth century all had in mind the Western model of chattel slavery practiced in the New World. In this model the contrast between slave and free was clear-cut in theory, even though in practice freedom was never absolute and slaves often found ways to resist domination. Faced with a whole range of non-free statuses in India and other non-Western regions, administrators made their own decisions as to who was and was not a slave. The application of the English term "slave," and its French coun-terpart "esclave," with their connotations of Western chattel slavery, to a wide range of non-Western forms of servitude has created confusion. Scholars, faced with this prob-lem in colonial literature, have engaged in long debates about the definition of slav-ery.[20] The academic debate need not concern us here, but it is important to note that "slave" was a term used by British officials and abolitionists very loosely to cover many different statuses. Important, too, is the fact that by the middle of the nineteenth cen-tury, the idea had been born that non-Western slavery might be benign and could be tolerated and even defended.

BRITISH ANTISLAVERY POLICY IN AFRICA[21]

In the great imperial expansion of the late nineteenth century, once an area was con-quered the main concern of the colonial rulers was to keep the economy going or to reorient it to suit their own needs. Their policies differed widely even between differ-ent regions of the same territory, and they changed over time. These new empires put great strain on the resources of manpower and money in the metropoles, forcing them to introduce measures to increase colonial revenues and to use local leaders in their administrations. Hence, the British, who controlled the biggest empire, relied largely on indirect rule—government through local rulers or institutions.[22] This system, al-ready operating elsewhere in the empire, was widely applied in Africa. Originally a matter of expediency, it came to be based on the concept that different people pro-gressed towards civilization—meaning Western civilization—in their own time and by their own route. Therefore, subject peoples, dubbed "child races," were best ruled through their own institutions, but under the guidance of the colonial administration. The worst cruelties, such as human sacrifice and slave trading were immediately out-lawed, but slavery, polygyny, and other "benign" practices could be modified gradually or allowed to wither away as circumstances changed. These theories were commonly voiced in the 1890s, and effectively propagated by Frederick Lugard, who was to play a prominent part on the League of Nations antislavery committees.[23] Indirect rule was not applied everywhere and it also took many different forms. Whether rule was direct or indirect, Africans were used in the lowest echelons of local government. Where there were no existing rulers, "chiefs" were appointed.

These rulers, chiefs and other notables, including traders, used slaves as soldiers, administrators, servants, porters, trading agents, canoe men, and agricultural labor.[24] Women served as domestics, as concubines, and farm labor, and were valued both for their production and their role in reproduction. African slavery, like Indian slavery, was considered benign, and, as in India, the term covered many different forms of servitude, some clearly more oppressive than others. There were slaves owned by subsistence farmers, who lived much like junior kinsmen. There were the slaves of coastal merchants, often quite harshly treated and not integrated into the merchants' households. There were trusted slaves used as trading agents, who had considerable freedom. There were slaves settled in separate hamlets to grow cash crops and food for their owners. There were royal slaves valued not for their labor, but as loyal supporters who swelled the retinues and enhanced the power and prestige of rulers. Some became army commanders or high officials with power over free people. There were slave women who, in matrilineal societies might be preferred to free wives because their progeny would be under the control of their husbands, who otherwise only had control over their sisters' children. There were also various forms of cult slavery in which children were dedicated to a temple by their parents and served the priests. Treatment varied with the type of servitude, the degree of acculturation of the slave, and the character of his or her owner. The most harshly treated were the newly enslaved, called trade slaves in colonial literature. Some societies used slaves for human sacrifices performed in times of trouble or on the death of a "big man." Second and later generation slaves, born into the society, fully acculturated, known in colonial literature as domestic slaves or *captifs de case*, were not usually sold and were normally treated better than trade slaves. However, even the latter might be well treated once they found a permanent home, and the former might suffer ill-treatment. Although slaves lost their kin affiliations and were thus marginalized outsiders, with no social standing of their own, not all were foreigners. Some societies enslaved their own people, usually as punishment for crime.

Slaves were acquired by capture in wars or raids, and by purchase. Some were reduced to slavery as a punishment, and some sold themselves or their children to escape famine. They could be transferred by purchase, by inheritance, or as gifts and tribute. Apart from their labor, they were valuable capital assets in the absence of a universal currency and banking system. A man's power and prestige depended on having many dependents—wives, children, kinsmen, and slaves. Slaves thus increased the standing of leaders, and gave added status to the heads of households. Where slavery existed—and it was not universal in Africa—it was more than a means of mobilizing labor; it served political, social, and religious functions, and in the late nineteenth century, it was a thriving and widely practiced institution.

INDIAN MODEL OF EMANCIPATION IN BRITISH AFRICAN TERRITORIES

The colonial rulers all feared that sudden liberation would lead to economic collapse, famine, disorders, and revolts by former masters. In the early days, when European administrators were few and their resources scanty and wars of conquest were still being fought, the political and economic cooperation of the masters was needed to keep public order and maintain discipline in the workforce. This cooperation could only be won if their authority and prosperity were not threatened. Slaves had, therefore, to be kept in place and at work for as long as possible. The Indian model of abolition seemed the ideal solution and it was hoped that it would force owners to treat their slaves well in order to induce them to stay.

Most colonial officials opposed slavery. They were products of societies that had outlawed it in the metropoles and in their older colonies, and, in the British case, they had been brought up to believe in Britain's antislavery crusade. Many administrators in the first flush of conquest actually began by freeing slaves, but the realities of the African situation soon cooled their ardor.[25] However, even when they switched to upholding slavery, they expected it to be a temporary solution. It was believed that European rule by ending wars and raids, and opening new commercial opportunities, would lead to the development of a free mobile wage labor force, and a free tax-paying peasantry producing for the market. Meanwhile the Indian model of abolition seemed the least disruptive and most humane way of easing the transition.

If the theory seems simple, it was by no means clear how it was to be applied. It was introduced to Africa in 1874, when the British annexed the Gold Coast Protectorate and were forced to reconsider policies in protectorates, hitherto ill-defined, pragmatic, and constrained by the unwillingness of the home government to shoulder costly responsibilities. The coastal settlements, together with Lagos, now became the Gold Coast Colony, where British law applied and slave holding was already illegal. The adjacent areas became the Gold Coast Protectorate. The colonial secretary had no desire to do more about slavery than was needed to disarm criticism from the humanitarian lobby.[26] A variation on the Indian model was thus introduced. British and native courts were forbidden to enforce any claims arising out of slavery. A new feature was that all children born in, and all persons entering, the Protectorate after 1 January 1875 were to be considered free. Although this seems illogical if the legal status of slavery no longer existed, it reflected the fact that existing slaves, if they did not exercise their right to leave, were still slaves. It also, of course, set a time limit—the lifetime of existing slaves—with whose death slavery would be extinguished.

Another departure from the Indian model was that debt bondage or pawning was also declared illegal.[27] Pawning was the temporary transfer of a person as collateral for a loan. In the absence of banking institutions, this might be the only method to enable a kin group to pay bride wealth, or acquire food in time of famine, or for an individual to raise credit for trade goods. People sometimes pawned themselves, but more often, they pawned a dependant. The practice was widespread in Africa. The kinship structure, together with local custom, determined who might be pawned and their terms of service. Sometimes the work of the pawn counted as interest. It rarely reduced the debt. Pawns were distinct from slaves. They remained members of their kin group. Their status was not a disgrace. Their fate could befall anyone in hard times. In theory at least, their kinsmen were on hand to see that they were not ill-treated and their position was temporary. Most were children, usually girls. Many ended up marrying the creditor and the bride wealth was adjusted to cancel the debt. Not all were well treated and those who were not redeemed often ended up as slaves. Slaves were also frequently given as pawns, and pawns could be used to raise credit to buy slaves.

As in India, the failure to introduce compulsory emancipation of slaves on the Gold Coast was justified on the grounds that it would cause hardship to the slave, as well as the master. However, there was a more cogent reason. It was argued that, in all fairness, if slaves were completely emancipated, masters should be compensated, particularly as slaves were often the only capital Africans possessed. But compensation was not only expensive, it was impractical. Since the government had no way of knowing who was a slave and who was not, opportunities for fraud and collusion were limitless. Schemes to buy slaves and use them on public works until they had earned their redemption were dismissed. The governor argued that they would probably desert their jobs.[28]

Had these ordinances been fully enforced, they would have struck at the heart of African systems of credit, capital accumulation, and labor, and enabled slaves to leave their owners or renegotiate their terms of service relatively quickly. However, the governor was careful to minimize their impact. He explained to African rulers and chiefs that slaves would not be encouraged to leave, and that the emancipation of a pawn would not cancel the debt. In deference to African feelings, the penalties for breaking these laws were moderate—seven years in prison.[29] The administration hoped that, as in India, most slaves would stay with their owners and the immediate effects of the ordinances would be almost imperceptible, particularly as, here too, officials were under no obligation to inform slaves of their rights.[30]

The onus of demanding their freedom lay with the slaves, who had to make a formal complaint to a British official. There were very few officials in the interior and chiefs were usually able to stop slaves from reaching them. If they did succeed, officials were often reluctant to free them. Slaves were also under strong societal pressure not to bring complaints against their owners[31] and it was virtually impossible to get evidence against

chiefs, or to secure a conviction in an African court. Finally, there was not much wage labor to attract slaves away from their owners. As for the chiefs, they continued to hold
slaves, but used the ordinances as an excuse not to provide labor for public works, saying they could no longer control their slaves.[32] So lax was the enforcement of the laws
that slave dealing continued in the protectorate and even in the colony, where, although
cases were brought to court, there was no concerted effort to end it until after 1911.

Likewise, little was done to enforce the law against pawning, which did not become a
criminal offense until 1892. Humanitarians suggested various methods to end it but they
were not pursued. These included capping interest rates, which were 50 percent or higher,
and counting the pawn's work towards paying off the debt and not just as interest.[33]

As more areas of Africa were conquered and became protectorates, variations on
the Indian model were introduced. Although there was much discussion between the
British government and the governors of colonies, particularly in the crucial years between 1895 and 1907, there was little agreement on the details of policy, even in the
Colonial Office. British administrators struggling, often alone, to control whole regions in which slavery was entrenched, worked out their own solutions to stop slaves
downing tools or departing. Colonial administrations were forced to do a balancing
act—supporting slavery to maintain the viability of their conquests, while seeming to
attack it in order to ward off criticism at home. The result, as a few examples will show,
was a hodgepodge of pragmatic solutions.

In theory, there were three different types of British administrations. There were
colonies, in which slavery was definitely outlawed and it was an offense to own a slave.
There were protectorates, where slavery might continue, but its legal status was usually
abolished, and there were "spheres of influence," areas which the British claimed but did
not administer, and in which they had no wish to incur any responsibilities other than
for external defense. It took many years to work out the meaning of the terms protectorate and sphere of influence, and no clear policy towards slavery was universally
applied in them or even in colonies, where the legal position should have been unam-
biguous. For instance, in the Gold Coast Colony, slave owning was outlawed. In the
surrounding Protectorate, it merely lost its legal status. So far so good, but when the
powerful kingdom of Asante was conquered in 1896, its chiefs were assured that they
would be allowed to keep their slaves. In 1901, both the Protectorate and Asante became
colonies and slave holding should have been outlawed. But, as the British explained to
the League of Nations many years later, a clear statement to this effect would have led
to "internal disorganization." So ordinances in 1902 merely made it a punishable offense
to "compel or attempt to compel the services" of any person.[34] Only after complaints
from missionaries did the governor issue instructions in 1908 to end the legal status of
slavery—treating the colony of Asante as if it were a protectorate.[35] Moreover, the ordinances freeing slaves born or entering both these territories after a certain date were not
applied—a fact that was only realized in the colonial office in the 1920s.

In the Sierra Leone Protectorate, the legal status of slavery was not abolished.[36] For the first few years, the British encouraged slaves to leave their owners and freely resettled fugitives, but this policy was abandoned in the face of opposition from chiefs. Ordinances made it illegal to leave a chiefdom without permission. Fugitive slaves who fled to Freetown could be forcibly repatriated unless they found work within three weeks. In theory, district commissioners' courts protected slaves. Owners were forbidden to sell them and they could ransom themselves. In practice, slaves found it difficult to get a hearing. Moreover, in their administrative capacity officials often upheld the rights of masters in disputes about ownership, redemption, and inheritance, and even returned fugitives to their owners. Children were still born into slavery. Slaves were still transferred between owners, and were inherited by their legal heirs. Yet, in some areas of Sierra Leone, slavery was far from benign. First generation (trade) slaves had no rights to property or access to land. Slave marriages were not recognized. Husbands and wives could be separated. Their children could be taken from them and pawned, married, or put to work without their consent. Slavery thus continued in Sierra Leone with administrative support until changed economic circumstances and international scrutiny led, as will be seen, to a change of policy in the 1920s.

In Zanzibar, the government feared that if slaves were freed the plantation economy controlled by Muslim Swahili and Arab landlords would decline.[37] A humanitarian outcry, however, forced it to end the legal status of slavery in 1897. In this rare case, compensation was paid to owners, for fear of alienating the sultan and perhaps stimulating repercussions among Muslims in India. The compensation was merely the equivalent of five months' wages, and did not do as much to soften the blow as it had in the Caribbean. However, slaves were discouraged from leaving in various ways. They had to go to courts controlled by their owners to get their freedom. The freed were subject to vagrancy laws and had to pay rent for their homes and land. Out of an estimated one hundred forty thousand slaves in the 1890s, only some eleven thousand had been freed by 1907. Moreover, an important category of slaves—concubines—was not freed until 1909, for fear that interference in domestic arrangements would arouse resentment.

On the sultan's strip of the Kenya coast, British power was so tenuous that the legal status of slavery was not abolished until 1907. But a blow was dealt to the institution in 1897, when humanitarian pressure forced the British to stop returning fugitives to their owners and many slaves left. In 1907, Muslim owners were compensated, but at a low level, and only if their slaves left or refused to work. In the area behind the coastal strip, where social formations were small and owners were not Muslim, slavery was simply not recognized. Neither slaves nor masters were informed of this, however, and owners only found out slowly when the authorities refused to return runaways. It took a decade for the news to permeate fully down to the grassroots level.[38]

The Protectorate of Northern Nigeria had one to two and a half million slaves—one of the largest slave populations in the world. Raiding and trading were rife and thousands of slaves were paid in tribute to the powerful sultan of Sokoto, his emirs, and other rulers. The first British high commissioner, Lugard, abolished the legal status of slavery without compensation, and declared all children born after 31 March 1901 free.[39] To prevent the wholesale departure of slaves, he made them pay for their redemption. In blatant contravention of the Brussels Act, he ordered his subordinates not to help those who left without permission, unless they had been ill-treated, in which case they could connive at their "escape" to avoid antagonizing owners.[40] Otherwise, fugitives were not to be found jobs or given land. Many were handed over to Muslim courts, which unlike British courts could hear slavery claims and restore them to their owners.

Lugard covered his tracks by ordering that male fugitives be treated as vagrants, while women were brought before Islamic courts, which could award compensation to their owners under guise of damages for matrimonial disputes. These and other devices discouraged slaves from seeking freedom. Lugard was fortunate that the humanitarian lobby did not understand his policy and soon regarded him as an ally and an authority on slavery.

As these examples show, the "abolition of the legal status of slavery," considered "blessed words" in the Colonial Office because they satisfied British public opinion, could mean much or little depending on administrative policy. As long as slavery cases could be tried in Islamic or native courts or settled by official action, as long as fugitives could be returned to their owners and slaves could be forced to buy their redemption, the impact of the loss of legal status was more theoretic than real.

EMANCIPATION IN THE AFRICAN TERRITORIES OF OTHER COLONIAL POWERS

Space precludes a detailed examination of the policies of the other colonial powers, but a few examples will show that they were as pragmatic as the British. The French, theoretically, outlawed slavery in all their colonies in 1848, including their tiny footholds in Africa, but in practice the law was only applied to French citizens and areas under actual sovereignty.[41] Even in these cases, owners managed to keep control over former slaves since they controlled both land and housing. As the empire expanded, the people of newly conquered regions were considered subjects not citizens, and the law did not apply to them. In effect, the French created a system much like the British one. During the period of conquest, they captured large numbers of slaves or accepted them in payment of taxes, and distributed them to their African allies, and even their own officers. Like the other powers, they generally interfered as little as possible with slavery, except to use it as a weapon—freeing the slaves of their enemies, and returning those of their allies, unless they had been ill-treated. Ill-treatment, however, could be defined differently depending on whether the master was a friend or foe.

Between 1903 and 1905, their policy changed in West Africa. Antislavery sentiment in France, although less popular than in Britain, had some support among politicians. The laws against slave trading were tightened. The return of runaways was forbidden and slaves were allowed to leave if they wished. An exodus followed, notably in Banamba, and administrators, faced with the prospect of famine when cultivators downed tools just before the planting season, ordered those who left without permission to be returned as vagabonds. But by 1906, as more slaves left, they tried to pressure them into share-cropping arrangements or offered them freedom if they continued to farm. The realization grew that productivity increased with freedom, as owners had to till their own fields and freed slaves worked more vigorously for themselves. Moreover, some provided much needed labor in the burgeoning towns.

From 1905 to 1908, several hundred thousand slaves ceased to work for their owners out of a servile population of several million. The institution was dealt another blow by the large-scale conscription of both slaves and owners for labor and for the army during the First World War. Slaves who had served in the trenches refused to return to bondage. In spite of these events, however, most former slaves in French West Africa are believed to have remained with or near their former owners, and some retained vestiges of servile relations through the twentieth century.

In Equatorial Africa, the French reported to the League of Nations that they had never recognized slavery and had employed slaves as village chiefs and protected those who asserted their freedom.[42] In fact, policy varied with the area. In remote Dar Kuti, until 1908, they countenanced even slave trading and raiding by the sultan and supplied him with arms and ammunition—not because they approved of his operations but because the economy would have been ruined if he and his followers had decamped into British territory.[43] Only in 1911 did they attack him and proclaim the slaves free. Elsewhere in the colony, slavery continued in some areas into the 1920s. In Mauritania and parts of the Sahara, slavery and slave trading continued to the end of French rule.[44]

The Portuguese passed laws in 1854 designed to end slavery in their colonies in twenty years—allowing time for the emergence of a free labor force.[45] However, even after 1878, when all slaves became *libertos*, theoretically free to contract their services for wages, little actually changed. A vagrancy law made them liable to forced labor for the government or private employers. There was also little difference in treatment between *libertos* and free contract laborers. Both could be bought and forced to work. After an outcry in Britain, the Portuguese outlawed slavery in their colonies in 1910, but it was many years before this took effect. Portuguese officials were even thinner on the ground than the British and their resources were more limited. In many areas, they had no power to implement their laws.

In Somaliland, Italian policy was much the same as that of other colonial powers, but the options open to slaves seeking their freedom were somewhat more diverse than in some other areas.[46] An Italian chartered company established its rule on the Somali Benadir coast from 1893. For a decade, it returned fugitives to owners if they belonged to friendly clans. Only a humanitarian outcry in Italy led to the issuing in

1903–1904 of ordinances prohibiting the slave trade, and providing for the emancipation of all slaves born after 1890. The government took over the colony in 1906, but it
was in no hurry to implement these ordinances. When officials freed some slaves in
the coastal towns, they compensated the owners and made the ex-slaves pay them a
stipend for board and lodging. This satisfied urban masters, but as news that slaves
were being freed spread inland ahead of the Italian forces, fugitives came in increasing
numbers from the interior, fueling the hostility of their owners. Officials tried to stop
the exodus, but under pressure from the home government, many were freed. The fact
that they had a number of options speeded up their departure. Many joined villages
of runaway slaves or religious settlements founded by Muslim shaykhs. Others were
able to find a niche among client-cultivators working the lands of Somali clans.

In the Congo Independent State, slavery was not recognized as having any legal status.[47] However, King Leopold's agents redeemed thousands of men, women, and
youths from their Swahili Arab masters in the eastern Congo between 1886 and 1892,
and conscripted many into the militia (*Force Publique*)—in accordance with a protocol, which the king had been careful to insert into the records of the Brussels Conference. Captives taken in the wars of conquest in the early 1890s were used as laborers
or soldiers, or given to militiamen or to local chiefs who put them to work on their
own plantations. Many freed slaves were also settled along the main roads to grow
food and furnish porters for the administration. Once its control was established, the
Congo Independent State freely called on chiefs for laborers and soldiers. At first they
sent their own slaves, and then raided their neighbors.

In 1908, the State was taken over by Belgium and renamed the Belgian Congo. Slavery was still rife in the eastern region. In 1910, the Belgians declared it illegal, but were
slow to enforce the law for fear of reducing the control of chiefs over labor, hence curtailing their ability to meet government demands. Over time, however, the distinction
between slave and free in the Belgian Congo became less and less important as more
and more people were conscripted for forced labor for private and public projects.[48]

The Germans in Tanganyika were fearful of ruining the economy of the coast, and
anxious to conciliate slave owners who formed the lower echelons of the administration.
They did not forbid new enslavements until 1901, and then they only forbade commercial slave trading. Unlike the other colonial powers, they allowed, but supervised, private
sales, recording over a thousand transactions, mostly of women, between 1911 and 1914.
All children born after 1905 were declared free and none under twelve could be parted
from their parents. Slaves could also ransom themselves and those who had been ill-
treated were freed.[49] Over fifty-two thousand purchased their freedom between 1891
and 1912, and many more decamped, finding the Germans unable to prevent their departure.[50] Thus, although slavery was a legal status, the worst features of the institution
were suppressed, and overall, numbers of slaves declined. By 1914, the Germans were

considering total abolition, but announced that there were an estimated one hundred forty-five thousand slaves, and they could not afford to compensate their owners—a decision the British were to turn to their advantage in the 1920s, as will be seen.

In Cameroon, the Germans took little action even against the slave trade until 1902. In that year they declared that all slaves were to be what they called half free—they were not to be treated as property, but they still suffered the social stigma of servile origins. Moreover, all children born to slaves from the date of this ordinance were to be free.[51] In Northern Cameroon, however, local rulers continued to acquire slaves by raids and trade, right through the German period and beyond it.[52]

The Spanish actually outlawed slavery in Fernando Po and Rio Muni (Spanish Guinea), but not in their other colonies. Their motives were not philanthropic. They merely wanted to avoid having to return slaves who fled to their territories from the Portuguese islands of São Tomé and Principe. They also did not want to give the British an excuse to intervene in Fernando Po. Instead of slavery, they resorted, as will be seen, to an abusive form of contract labor.[53]

THE SLOW DECLINE OF SLAVERY IN AFRICA

Given the fact that the colonial powers initially wanted to keep slaves in place and working, it is not surprising that slavery lingered on in Africa. Slaves seeking freedom had to assess their prospects, and these varied with their age and gender, and with prevailing economic and political conditions. The newly enslaved, who remembered their homes and could count on a welcome, were the most likely to run away or claim their freedom. Slaves living in separate slave settlements could sometimes safely leave en masse. Slaves who had been integrated into lineages and were relatively well treated, and those born into servitude, who knew no other home than that of their owners, were less likely to want to leave.

The good faith of the colonial rulers could be gauged by their treatment of fugitive and freed slaves. The Brussels Act bound them to repatriate them but this was rarely observed. It was impossible if their natal communities had been destroyed, or if they might be re-enslaved, or if they did not remember their origins. However, administrators, underfunded as they were, feared having to support numbers of former slaves until they could provide the men with land or work, the women with a male protector or a safe haven,[54] and the children with shelter and education. Worried administrators, like discontented slaves, had to assess their options in the light of what was practicable. Small numbers posed little problem, particularly if there were Christian missions or an established labor market for them to join. The children were often shared among the missions, and were thus the first Africans to receive a Western education leading to jobs in the administration or in business.[55] Women were placed in "respectable" (usually Christian) families,[56] or given as wives to African soldiers or officials,[57] and the men were sometimes recruited as soldiers or policemen.[58]

Large numbers, however, posed a serious problem particularly where slaves num-bered perhaps half the population. Many fugitives and freed slaves were settled around the posts of the various colonial powers, or were accepted into neighboring African communities, or simply given to friendly chiefs as followers. The French hit on the in-genious idea of creating *villages de liberté*, to which they pointed with pride in the 1920s. Supposedly these were places where the freed were helped to find a new niche as independent producers or wage labor. Runaways belonging to owners friendly to the French were either not accepted in these villages or were handed back. All too of-ten, those settled in them were used as forced labor for the administration, and the de-mands were sometimes so excessive that they fled.[59]

Whether slaves left or stayed with their owners was usually determined by their prospects of finding a better life, rather than by government policy, although this could help or hinder them.[60] Where there was a wage labor pool, their chances of mak-ing it as free people were good and many drifted into the growing urban centers. If there was unused land, those who left might be welcomed by a chief anxious to build up his following and hence his prestige and power base, or by a colonial official eager to see his region developed. Many thousands, for instance, settled along the line of the railway in Nigeria and grew cash crops. Where this was not an option, unless they were suffering severe ill-treatment, slaves tended to remain with their owners, renegotiating their terms of service, and often arriving at sharecropping arrangements.

It was not always easy to free a slave even when colonial officials wished to do so. In many African societies, there was no mechanism for manumission. In some societies, intermarriage with the free was taboo, and in some, slaves were not even considered to be human.[61] In others, such as Benin, and in Muslim areas, they could be manumitted or could redeem themselves. However, those freed under Muslim law remained in a state of clientage to their former owners and their progeny, needing, for instance, their permission to marry. Colonial officials soon found that though they could free slaves under colonial laws, they could not raise their status in the eyes of the community. Slaves freed by the administration sometimes insisted on paying ransom to their own-ers so that they would be free in their masters' estimation as well as their own. In some societies, even this was not acceptable. Both the British and the French sometimes is-sued freedom certificates at the request of slaves, but, since slavery had no legal status, the wisdom of this was debated.[62] The British were still issuing them in 1925 in South-ern Nigeria.[63] In the Anglo-Egyptian Sudan, on the other hand, by the 1930s slaves were insulted when offered them because it emphasized their servile origins.[64]

This whole question raises the issue of what freedom actually meant to Africans—a question upon which scholars have not reached a consensus. The meaning varied with the society and with the sex of the slave, and changed over time. Where slaves were held by lineages or clans and lived in or around their masters' households or compounds, it doubtless meant closer integration into the kin group on a par with the free, but complete equality was often not possible, particularly when it came to questions of marriage, ritual, and inheritance. Where slaves lived in their own settlements or were held in large numbers, they wanted to be free of obligations to their owners, to be able to profit from their own labor, to choose their own wives, to control their own children, and start their own kin groups. Whether this correlated with the Western concept of the autonomous free individual is debatable since African kin groups had considerable control over individual members and the freed doubtless formed their own households along lines with which they were familiar. However, as time went on, social and cultural attitudes changed with economic development, the spread of Western education and ideas, and, in many cases, the acceptance of Christianity.

As the colonial powers established settled administrations, so their fears of interfering with slavery declined. Government policies were important in that they determined the legal framework within which slavery operated, and above all, they cut off the supply of fresh slaves. Slavery was progressively undermined by the economic and political changes set in motion by colonial conquest, and sometimes by natural disasters such as drought or disease. By the outbreak of war in 1914, in most of colonial Africa, the slave trade had ended or been much reduced, and slavery itself was on the wane, but the colonial powers were introducing their own forms of labor exploitation.

NOTES

1. See inter alia Philip D. Curtin 1964, 363 ff.

2. For slavery and its abolition in South Africa, see Crais 1990; Watson 1990; N. Worden 1986, forthcoming; Peires 1988; Eldredge and Morton, eds. 1994; J. R. H. Davenport 1977, 33 ff.; Robert Ross 1993; Monica Wilson and L. Thompson, eds. 1983, vol.1, 297 ff. For the problems with compensation, see Meltzer 1993, 187–99. Once established beyond British control, they found new ways to exploit Africans; see Morton 1994.

3. Uzoigwe 1974, 157–58, citing Salisbury memorandum, 16 December 1895, FOCP 6709.

4. Getz forthcoming; C. W. Newbury 1965, 294–98; Dumett and Johnson 1988, 73–78; G. McSheffrey 1983, 352–53. These consisted of a small colony of freed slaves in Sierra Leone, a fort on the Gambia River, and forts on the Gold Coast.

5. Raymond E. Dumett 1980, 196.

6. Getz forthcoming.

7. I have called this the Indian model of emancipation for convenience, although strictly speaking it applied only to the area under direct East India Company rule and is sometimes called the Bengal model.

8. Very little research has been done on slavery in India; see Chatterjee, forthcoming. For a recent study, see Chatterjee 1999.

9. Chatterjee forthcoming.

10. Ibid.

11. For the parliamentary struggle, see Chattopadhyay 1977, 204–51; Temperley 1972, 93–108.

12. The India Act (V. of 1843) Abolishing the Legal Status of Slavery.

13. Temperley 1972, 107–108; Hjejle.

14. Hjele, 93. For modern debt bondage, see below, chapter 24.

15. Chattopadhyay, 253. Slave dealing was also prohibited. The Government of India was transferred from the company to the Crown in 1858.

16. Temperley 1972, 108–109.

17. For Assam, see below, chapters 11 and 17. For the border states, see Chatterjee forthcoming. For the treatment of the Indian states in the twentieth century, see below, chapter 17.

18. Chattopadhyay, 215, 221–32, 254; Temperley 1972, 93–110; Hjejle, 93–96.

19. Hjejle, 93–96.

20. See for instance: Kopytoff and Miers 1977; Finley 1980, 67–77; Watson 1980; Lovejoy 1981, 1983, 1–8; Patterson 1982; Meillassoux 1975, 1991; Martin A. Klein 1993.

21. I am using African examples here because it was African slavery that was principally under attack in the late nineteenth and early twentieth centuries and African slavery upon which there has been the most scholarly research.

22. For a recent discussion of the meaning of this, see C. W. Newbury 2000.

23. Later Sir Frederick and then Lord Lugard.

24. For a discussion of slavery in Africa with examples from various areas, see Meillassoux 1975; Miers and Kopytoff 1977; Lovejoy 1983; Miers and Roberts 1988; Miers and Klein 1999. For a discussion of women in slavery, see Robertson and Klein 1983.

25. Many examples can be cited, but see inter alia chapters in Miers and Klein.

26. Frere to Carnarvon, 25 June 1874, Carnarvon Papers, P.R.O. 30/6/43, quoted in Dumett 1980, 209.

27. For pawning in Africa, see Falola and Lovejoy, eds. 1994.

28. G. E. Metcalfe 1964, 373, 377.

29. Carnarvon to Stahan, secret, 29 October 1874, CO 879/7 3198.

30. Griffiths to Knutsford, confidential, 26 January 1891, CO 96/215; Dumett and Johnson, 85; McSheffrey 1983, 349–68.

31. Dumett and Johnson, 85.

32. Metcalfe, 400.

33. Dumett and Johnson, 94–95.

34. LON A.25 (a) 1924, VI British reply to the League of Nations for the Gold Coast.

35. Dumett and Johnson, 96–99. The same laws were introduced in the Northern Territories Protectorate as in Asante.

36. Grace 1975, 84. For slavery in Sierra Leone, see Grace 1975; Rashid 1998.

37. See Cooper 1980, chs. 2, 3, appendix. For a detailed discussion of the various arguments put forward as to the model of abolition to be adopted, see Uzoigwe, 155–71.

38. See Miers interview with Kiponda wa Mavuo, 1974.

39. For a comprehensive discussion of his antislavery policy in Nigeria, see Lovejoy and Hogendorn 1993.

40. Lugard 1906; Hogendorn and Lovejoy 1988; Lovejoy and Hogendorn 1993, 31ff.

41. For French policy, see inter alia Klein 1993 (a), 1993 (b), 1988, 1998; Roberts and Klein 1980; Roberts 1987, 1988; Clark 1994, 1998, 1999.

42. Compare note communicated by the French government, LON. A.18.1923 VI with A.25. 1924 VI. Reply from the government of France.

43. Cordell 1988, 158–61.

44. McDougall 1988; see below, chapter 24.

45. See Duffy 1967; Heywood 1988; Clarence-Smith 1985.

46. See Cassanelli 1988; Eno forthcoming.

47. Northrup 1988.

48. For a discussion of forced labor, see below, chapters 4 and 10.

49. See, for example the German report for 1901 in *Documents* 1901–1913, 30–31; Deutsch 1998, 2001.

50. Deutsch 1998, 2001; Byatt to CO no.13, 12 February 1917, CO 691/4 139586.

51. Austen 1977, 308, 325; Eckert 1998.

52. Vaughan and Kirk-Greene, 1995; note communicated by the French government to the League, LON A. 18 1923. VI.

53. Sundiata 1996. For contract labor in Fernando Po, see below, chapter 10.

54. For an interesting discussion of the difficulties of assuring the safety of freed women, illustrated with graphic case histories, see Wright 1993.

55. See inter alia examples in Herlehy and Morton 1988; Dumett and Johnson 1988.

56. See inter alia examples in the reports of the Zanzibar bureau, *Documents*.

57. See inter alia examples in Wright 1993.

58. See examples cited in Miers and Roberts, 36; Echenberg 1991; Grace 1975, particularly 201; Hargey 1981, 248–62; Lovejoy and Hogendorn.

59. Bouche 1968; Klein 1988 and 1993, 178–79; Roberts 1988; Clark 1995, 1999.

60. For examples with fuller discussion, see Lovejoy and Hogendorn 1993; Klein 1993.

61. See, for instance, Ohadike 1988, 443.

62. Miers 1975, 304; Igbafe 1975, 422–23.

63. Secretary, Southern Provinces, to chief secretary, Lagos, 28 January 1925, resident, Cameroons Province to secretary, Southern Provinces, 31 January 1925; minute by governor, Southern Provinces enclosed in secretary, Southern Provinces, to chief secretary, Lagos 14 January 1925 ibid. NANI CSO 26/2 1 11799 vol. 1.

64. Hargey 1981, 308.

4

From Slavery to New Forms of Exploitation

EARLY COLONIAL LABOR PROBLEMS

Although at the time of the partition some Africans were integrated into the world economy and producing cash crops or hunting products for export, most were subsistence farmers or herders meeting their own needs and requiring only a small surplus to barter in local markets for the things they could not produce themselves. There was a division of labor between sexes and age groups, and there were specialized groups of craftsmen, hunters, miners, and the like, but basically each household met its own needs, and in much of the continent, the main means of extracting and mobilizing labor in the past had been through the slave trade and slavery. A flourishing trade in legitimate goods, before the conquest, had shown that Africans would respond to market incentives if offered an adequate return for their efforts. But the wage labor force was small and largely consisted of target workers who returned to their own lands once they had earned enough to invest in, say, a gun, cattle, or bride wealth.

The goal of the colonial rulers was to turn Africans into a pliant, disciplined, tax-paying workforce producing for the market. This required divorcing numbers of them from the means of production—land and labor—and turning them into wage laborers or peasant producers. Colonial governments were short of capital and not able to extract sufficient money in taxes to fund their administrations and pay market rates for the labor needed to build the infrastructure—the roads, railways, docks, and other projects—to develop their new possessions. European companies and individual employers did not offer wages or working conditions that would attract free labor. Africans had little incentive to leave their fields or herds to work for low wages, often far from home and in bad conditions. Moreover, for many households the loss of an able-bodied man for a long period, or at crucial times in the farming cycle, interfered with their ability to produce adequate food for themselves.

To meet their demands for public works and private enterprises, colonial rulers resorted to a wide variety of devices to produce cheap labor. These differed from slavery in the ways in which recruits were obtained, in the length of time served, and in their ideological basis. However, since the laborer was no longer a saleable capital asset and the powers of coercion of the colonial state were greater than those which had been available to most African owners, the emerging labor systems were often more oppressive than slavery. The worst scandals after the conquest, before and during the First World War, were not over slavery but over the abuses of the colonial rulers, most of whom believed that development along Western lines was morally as well as economically sound. They saw themselves as bringing "civilization" to the "backward" areas of the world, uplifting the "child" races, raising their standard of living, bringing them the "blessings" of Christianity and eventually Western education. Their technological expertise, administrative know-how, and Christian morals enabled them to lead this onward march of humanity. It took no mental gymnastics to decide that if the black man did not willingly take up his designated role—the provision of unskilled labor for development—then in his own interests he must be forced to do so.

The colonial rulers need to extract labor led to ad hoc experiments, some of which resulted in atrocities causing scandals on an unprecedented scale. Much has been written about them and many examples could be given. Some will be considered later in conjunction with the Forced Labor Convention of 1930, but three are discussed here because they brought Britain into conflict with other powers over forced and contract labor. They were thus the background against which the antislavery campaign was waged after the First World War. Furthermore, they illustrate the diplomatic dilemmas that face governments when breaches of human rights occur in other countries. They thus raise one of the most intractable issues of the twentieth century—how to protect labor from the depredations of its own government.

CONTRACT LABOR: BRITAIN'S DILEMMA OVER SÃO TOMÉ AND PRINCIPE

The scandal which erupted over Portuguese recruitment and use of contract labor for the cocoa plantations on the islands of São Tomé and Principe in the Gulf of Guinea posed serious dilemmas for British businesses as well as the government, and left a legacy of distrust which was to hinder the international antislavery movement for decades.

Although slaves in the Portuguese empire were free from 1878, all Africans were obliged by law to work.[1] Work was defined as cultivating their own land, following a recognized trade, working on public works or for European plantations and other projects, or serving in the police or militia. The cocoa islands suffered from chronic labor shortages, and some ninety-seven thousand people were shipped to them from Angola between 1876 and 1915. Theoretically, these were "free" contract laborers. In practice, many were seized in the interior, marched to the coast in shackles, and forced to accept contracts. In the late nineteenth and early twentieth centuries, the British, alerted by reports from their consuls, and pressured by humanitarians, complained to the Portuguese, who simply denied that there was any slaving.

The government, however, did not want to alienate Portugal by pressing the point, for two main reasons. First railway routes, vital for the economies of Southern Rhodesia, Nyasaland, and the Transvaal, ran through Portuguese Mozambique, and secondly migrant labor from Mozambique was needed for the mines and sugar plantations of South Africa.[2] In 1903, the main buyers of the islands' cocoa crop, the British chocolate manufacturers Cadbury, Rowntree, and Fry, owned by Quakers with strong humanitarian ties, were accused of buying slave-grown goods. William Cadbury, anxious not to have to pay more elsewhere for his cocoa, urged the British government to appoint an agent to watch over the interests of the laborers. This raised an ongoing question—whether or not Britain had any right to interfere in a matter in which British nationals were not directly involved. The Foreign Office decided it could not do so, and suggested that the companies stage a cocoa boycott.[3]

The Portuguese suspected that the humanitarian outcry concealed political and economic designs on their colonies. Theirs was a small poor country without the resources to develop the vast regions it claimed. These islands were the "pearls of the empire." Their cocoa trade was vital to the economy of the metropole, and produced budget surpluses used to reduce the chronic deficit in Angola.[4] They were aware of a secret treaty in 1898 in which Britain and Germany agreed to divide the Portuguese colonies if Portugal had to give them up. Both powers had pressured Portugal to mortgage its colonies in return for loans.[5] Moreover, Mozambique was being developed with British and South African capital. It would clearly be to Britain's advantage to get possession of it. Cocoa was also now being produced in increasing quantities in the British West African territories, raising the suspicion that Britain was threatening the labor supply to the Portuguese islands in order to protect exports from its own colonies.[6] Finally, the Portuguese thought Britain applied a double standard, complaining about the few thousand workers a year who went to their islands, while themselves recruiting tens of thousands in Mozambique by doubtful methods.[7]

In 1903, the Portuguese, faced with the threat of a cocoa boycott, a humanitarian agitation in Britain, and protests in Angola and at home, issued new rules to regulate contracts, improve living conditions, and ensure repatriation at the end of five years of service. By 1906, the British consul reported that the contracts and living standards were satisfactory, but workers were still recruited by force. Missionaries, African traders, and an investigator sent out by the British cocoa companies reported that in the far interior villages were raided by their neighbors and that a man or woman kidnapped and sold to coastal traders fetched enough gunpowder to buy three slaves. Elsewhere, ill-paid Portuguese officials organized raids themselves, or levied fines that

had to be paid in slaves, or simply arrested innocent people and sent them to the islands. Officers who tried to suppress these iniquities risked being removed in response
to complaints from influential traders.[8]

The humanitarian lobby kept up the pressure on the British government,[9] and was
supported by a new player on the scene. Revelations that some forty-seven thousand
Chinese indentured laborers recruited for the gold mines in South Africa were being
made to work long hours in bad conditions, and were kept as virtual prisoners in their
compounds for fear of miscegenation, outraged British labor, which was increasingly
aware of its potential political power and demanding more protection and security for
itself. The power of organized labor, as will be seen, was to become more important in
the course of the twentieth century. The scandal helped give the Liberal Party a sweeping majority in the elections of 1906. Chinese recruitment was stopped in 1907.[10] This
squared the British conscience but made it even more imperative for South Africa to
continue to recruit labor in Mozambique.

In 1907, the Liverpool Chamber of Commerce called on the British firms to boycott cocoa from the Portuguese islands. Cadbury objected, using arguments which
were to become all too familiar: It would end any influence English firms had over the
Portuguese; the government would lose its grounds for protest if no British trade was
involved; and foreign buyers would replace the British.[11] By the beginning of 1909,
however, British patience, official and unofficial, was wearing thin. Cadbury yielded to
pressure from fellow Quakers and humanitarians,[12] and the four British companies
stopped buying their cocoa from the islands.

The Portuguese government, under attack in its own press as well as in Britain, reduced contracts to three years, limited recruiting to areas under a semblance of control,
and finally suspended it in Angola. In 1910, the Portuguese monarchy was overthrown
and replaced by a republican government. The British hoped it would introduce last-
ing reforms. But the new labor law promulgated in 1911 had the same fatal flaw as its
predecessors—Africans who did not work in some approved fashion could still be
forced to do so. Moreover, recruiting for the islands, now forbidden in Angola, switched
to Mozambique. Press gangs rounded people up and charged them with vagrancy.
Those unable to pay the fine were handed over to recruiters and kept, corralled and
drunk, until the boat for São Tomé arrived. The curator of natives received a bonus for
each recruit. Only a few returned, ill, poor, and exhausted.[13] Thus, the slave trade as a
means of obtaining labor had now been replaced by official recruiters using intimidation and trickery.

Schemes to repatriate workers to Angola as their contracts expired were instituted
in 1908, but of the 2,864 laborers whose five-year contracts ended that year, only 793
were offered repatriation, and of these only 19 accepted.[14] In subsequent years, numbers increased, but they were the old and sick. Plantation owners forced the fit to re-
new their contracts. Dumped without wages, some of the repatriated died destitute in

the streets of Benguela. Others clamored to return to the islands where they had spent the greater part of their lives.[15] These abuses led the Anti-Slavery Society to recommend that all contract workers should be compulsorily repatriated at the end of their term—a question with implications for the future.[16]

In 1912, the British foreign secretary, under unremitting humanitarian attack, described the Portuguese colonies as "sinks of iniquity," which should be sold at once.[17] The Colonial Office agreed on a division of the spoils with Germany. The outbreak of war in August 1914 ended the negotiations, but not before the Portuguese had heard of them.[18] In 1916, Portugal came into the war on the allied side. By this time, conditions on the islands were reported to be improving. Genuine short-term contract workers were employed, and recruiting in Angola had resumed.[19]

What of the cocoa boycott? In December 1914, an Anglo-Portuguese commercial deputation asked that it be rescinded. Cadbury asked for Foreign Office approval. This posed a dilemma as the boycott benefited British West African cocoa producers. However, officials decided that, in view of the supportive attitude of the Portuguese towards the war, it would be "unfair" not to end it. Nevertheless, Cadbury never again bought his cocoa from the islands. The Portuguese accused him of buying it indirectly through another firm.[20]

At the level of international diplomacy, the controversy reinforced the distrust between Portugal and Britain that had existed from the outset of the international antislavery campaign. British suspicions that the Portuguese were abusing labor, and Portuguese suspicions that British humanitarianism had ulterior motives were further entrenched. Color was lent to this by the fact that the secretary of the Anti-Slavery Society, John Harris, advocated giving parts of the Portuguese empire to Germany, and many humanitarians were pacifist and pro-German before 1914.[21] As will be seen, Portuguese ill-treatment of African labor continued almost to the end of colonial rule, and Portugal consistently opposed attempts to establish effective supervisory mechanisms for the antislavery treaties of the twentieth century.

The whole episode highlighted the dangers inherent in the contract labor system. This case is only one example of the widespread abuse of such labor. It was particularly devastating as it dovetailed with a preexisting slave trade. Illiterate recruits were marched to the coast and forced to accept contracts the terms of which they could not enforce even if they understood them. Even after the reforms, the standards for the recruitment and treatment of "native" contract labor fell short of those acceptable for free labor in the Western world, raising questions that would be passed to the International Labor Organization when it was formed after the First World War.

THE POWER OF HUMANITARIAN AGITATION: BRITAIN AND THE CONGO SCANDAL

The case of the Congo Independent State raised a different set of questions.[22] King Leopold II of Belgium was the personal ruler of this territory many times the size of his tiny kingdom, which had no desire to acquire colonies. He soon found himself unable to pay the inevitable start-up costs of colonial rule, including the building of railways. He, therefore, parceled out large areas to be directly exploited by the state or by concessionaire companies, which were given monopoly rights to all natural resources in their areas. The state was a shareholder in these companies. Africans outside the concession areas could only sell their products to the state. Control over labor was established by taxes in kind. In 1903, Africans were also required to perform up to forty hours a month of productive work for the state for which, in theory, they were to be paid a fair wage. This forced labor system was defended as a humanitarian measure to give Africans the incentive to work in their own interests. The result was a highly exploitative and oppressive system in which the state had a direct stake in commercial enterprises.

The agents of the king and of the companies forced Africans to produce goods for export, as well as to provide the administration with food, wood, and labor for porterage and road building. They were rarely paid for their goods or their services. The worst cruelties took place in the rubber bearing areas. With the expansion of the automobile and bicycle industries, the demand for rubber increased rapidly and profits were high. The wild landolphia rubber vines in the Congo forests required a recuperation period after tapping and were easily damaged.[23] Officials, whose bonuses depended on results, arbitrarily set excessive quotas. Failure to produce led to military reprisals, beatings, and mutilation. Hostages were held until quotas were met. As the vines wore out, starving people, unable to till their own fields and forced to go farther and farther into the forests in search of rubber, fled into the bush or across the borders, or rebelled. Resistance was brutally crushed.[24] Far from opening the Congo to the trade of all nations and promoting "native welfare," King Leopold's state was actually a highly monopolistic trading enterprise extracting its products as tribute from its embattled people, and spending the proceeds on public works in Belgium and pensions for the royal family.

As early as 1896, the British were aware of these abuses,[25] but the government was anxious not to alienate the king. They feared he might help a French expedition coming up the Congo trying to reach the upper Nile before the British, who were fighting their way south in Sudan. Moreover, they were afraid that if the king had to relinquish the Congo, it would revert to France in accordance with an agreement made by the wily monarch. In 1898, however, the French, confronted by the British on the upper Nile in the famous incident at Fashoda, backed away. The British, now free of this threat, began to keep a record of Congo atrocities against the day when it might prove useful.[26]

The next year, the French granted concessions similar to the king's to French companies in the French Congo. This brought them into conflict with English traders. John Holt, the head of a company whose goods had been seized, claimed that these concessions created monopolies, which infringed the Berlin Act. He lost his case in a French court, but was at once recruited by E. D. Morel—a passionate humanitarian—to join the struggle to end a system which both oppressed Africans and excluded foreign trading companies. The two joined forces in a happy combination of economic and philanthropic motives. Holt had influence and money. Morel prided himself as a strategist.[27] The government was bombarded with memorials from chambers of commerce and appeals from humanitarians and missionary societies. The Aborigines Protection Society held a great meeting in 1902 to drum up public support. It called on all signatories of the Berlin and Brussels Acts to cooperate in securing reforms in the Congo, and demanded that the British government call a conference inviting the powers to abide by their treaties. A press campaign aroused wide support. Britain's role as leader of the antislavery movement was invoked as a reason to take the initiative, and a resolution in Parliament requested the government to confer with other signatories of the Berlin Act.

In 1902, the Foreign Office appointed Roger Casement as British consul to the Congo Independent State to investigate the question. His report confirmed the case against the Congo. In 1904, Casement and Morel formed the Congo Reform Association,[28] which orchestrated debates and resolutions in Parliament, called public meetings, and enlisted support in the United States.

In Belgium, the agitation was seen as a plot to get the Congo for Britain or to divide it with Germany.[29] King Leopold denied all accusations. Other powers did not rally to the cause. Congo reform was thus primarily a British issue, led by British businessmen and humanitarians. In Belgium, a reform movement developed in close touch with the British reformers and the upshot was that Leopold II appointed a commission of inquiry. This concluded that the charges were substantially true, and the scandal forced him to hand over the government to Belgium in 1908. The episode brought colonial forms of labor exploitation forcibly to public attention. It showed that nongovernmental organizations run by determined reformers could bring about an international demand for reform, which given the right circumstances could shame governments into action. The association was disbanded in 1913, but the problems that had given rise to the abuses remained. Belgians were still reluctant to invest in their vast colony and took little interest in its affairs. As a result, the new government built largely on Leopold's framework. Although it ended the atrocities and violence that had characterized the Independent State, it maintained and expanded the system of concessionaire companies, alienating more African land. It coerced labor by regressive taxation, and a new device—compulsory growing of cash crops for export, which had to be sold at minimal prices set by the concessionary companies.[30] The reformers had hoped a democratic Belgian government would foster a workforce free to sell its labor in the best market and reap the rewards of its own efforts, but as will be seen, this did not happen.

EXTRATERRITORIAL JURISDICTION: BRITAIN AND THE PUTUMAYO SCANDAL

Scandals like those in the Congo occurred elsewhere in Africa, as well as in other regions of the world. Only one example can be included here, the Putumayo scandal. This concerned the operations of a British rubber company—the Peruvian Amazon Company—in a remote region disputed between Peru and Colombia.[31] It began with rumors in the local press claiming that the rubber collectors were virtual slaves of the company and that some had been tortured and mutilated. An American traveler, on the advice of the Anti-Slavery Society, sent an article to *Truth* entitled "A British Owned Congo." Questions in Parliament prompted the government to send Roger Casement to investigate the charges, together with a commission set up by the company itself.

This inquiry raised the already vexed question of extraterritorial crime. Did the government have the power to try Britons for crimes committed abroad; and did it have the right to investigate abuses in foreign territory not committed by, or against, British subjects? This question was not new, and it was to be an ongoing one.

In the case of slavery, slave trading, and crimes such as piracy, Britons who broke British law in other countries were prosecuted under British law. However, the law was not clear and there was doubt as to whether those convicted should be punished in Britain or in the state in which the crime was committed. Moreover, it was difficult to collect sufficient evidence abroad to satisfy a British court. In this case, Casement was instructed only to investigate the actions and treatment of the British Barbadian employees. The indigenous people collected the rubber and suffered the worst abuse. The Barbadians were better treated but were in debt to the company and hence were not free to leave. Their grievances had been reported to the Foreign Office in 1905 and an official protest had resulted in the dismissal of one of the company's agents.

Casement exceeded his instructions by investigating the treatment of the indigenous people. He found evidence of atrocities and his published report aroused considerable interest.[32] A select committee was established to decide if the company's directors could be held responsible for the actions of their agents, and whether changes were needed to prevent similar abuses by British companies abroad in the future. The Anti-Slavery Society wanted the government to negotiate treaties to enable British consuls to care for indigenous peoples in foreign territory. Casement suggested that British companies employing labor abroad should be required to notify the government of their terms of service. But if consuls were to extend their duties beyond the protection of British subjects, they would have to be paid more. Moreover, the unpaid honorary or "trading consuls," who had ties to local business, would have to be replaced by professionals who could report abuses without conflicts of interest. An idea melding the two recommendations was that treaties should be made with other nations providing for an international consular service to serve as a watchdog against the abuse of indigenous peoples. This was, and remained, unrealistic.

The select committee recommended appointing career consuls to districts where "colored labor" was employed with orders to visit British companies and report all labor abuses in their districts, just as they were already bound to report slave trafficking under the Slave Trade Act of 1843. It also recommended the consolidation of the laws against the slave trade and slavery and their extension to allow prosecution of other abuses of labor. Finally, it proposed that suspected companies should be forced to carry out inquiries and furnish information on labor conditions.

The directors of the Putumayo company, although judged guilty of "culpable negligence," could not be prosecuted under the Slave Trade Act, and most of their underlings—the perpetrators of the atrocities—were never arrested, let alone punished. The Foreign Office continued to make representations to the Peruvian government urging their arrest, but Casement's trial and execution for high treason in 1916 discredited his evidence,[33] and Peruvians thought his fate vindicated the company.[34]

The results, though unsatisfactory, were not wholly negative. The question of consular powers and of extraterritoriality had been thoroughly discussed and in 1913 the Foreign Office sent a circular dispatch to consuls ordering them to report the existence of any conditions amounting to "virtual slavery or entailing the ill-treatment of colored laborers." They were to note how British companies in their districts treated their labor, and to report on mortality rates, and local labor laws. They were not required to investigate conditions on the spot, but were to report cases of ill-treatment perpetrated by British subjects. The Anti-Slavery Society urged the government to consolidate and extend the Slave Trade Acts to cover peonage and forced labor.[35] In the summer of 1914, two such bills, one drafted by the Society,[36] were under consideration but they were halted by the outbreak of war and never revived.

The Putumayo scandal increased sensitivity in Britain to labor practices in other parts of the world. It highlighted, but did not resolve the difficulties in the way of prosecuting persons for crimes committed abroad, and it called attention to another ongoing problem—debt-bondage. Both of these questions were, as will be seen, to become important issues in the last decades of the twentieth century.

NOTES

1. For the stages by which they were liberated, see Duffy 1967, 7 ff. For the discussion that follows, see particularly Duffy 1967, 168 ff; but also Heywood 1988; Hodges and Newitt 1988; Newitt 1981, Clarence-Smith 1985, 1993 (a), 1993 (b).

2. In 1905 for instance, they delayed making representations to Portugal until negotiations on the labor and railway agreements had been resolved. See minutes, 28 August 1906, on Nightingale Report on the *Serviçal* System, 28 August 1906, FO 367/18. These negotiations were over changing the *Modus Vivendi* of 1901, which made the railway and labor recruitment arrangements contingent upon each other.

3. Memorandum respecting contract labor (*Serviçaes*) for São Tomé and Principe by Gye, 30 December 1905, FO 367/18 23071.

4. Clarence-Smith 1985, 87; Hodges and Newitt, 34–36.

5. Vail and White 1980, 129–31, and see Grey, I, 45, in which the author states that the Portuguese knew about this agreement at the time.

6. Clarence-Smith 1985, 86–87; Hodges and Newitt, 35–36.

7. Newitt 1981, 38–40. The Anti-Slavery Society claimed that recruiters for South Africa traveled with Portuguese tax collectors and offered to pay the taxes of defaulters if they signed up for the mines, falsely promising that they would not have to work underground. Duffy 1967, 159–60, notes 31, 32.

8. Some raiders were deserters from King Leopold's army. Others were neighboring peoples who needed slaves to ransom relatives who had been captured in order to meet demands for compensation for murder or witchcraft, or to exchange for weapons. This description of conditions in the interior is based on accounts in the following: Extract from Schindler to FO, 29 April 1904, FO2/876; Teixeira-de-Mattos to Beak, 2 January 1909, enclosed in Beak to Thesiger, 11 January 1909, FO 367/156; Report on the Condition of Coloured Labour employed on the Cocoa Plantations of S. Tomé and Principe and the Methods of Procuring it in Angola by Joseph Burtt, 24 December 1906, with a confidential supplement, FO 367/46 28725; Mackie to Grey, confidential, no. 5, 15 March 1908, FO 367/87; Report by Mr. C. Swan on his Recent Journey to Africa, enclosed in Swan to FO, 2 June 1909, FOCP 9547 [FO 403/407].

9. For a detailed discussion, see Duffy 1967, 168 ff.

10. For a brief discussion of this question, see Ensor 1966, 376–78, 390.

11. Statement made by Mr. William A. Cadbury to the Council of the Liverpool Chamber of Commerce, 21 October 1907, FO 367/46.

12. See article by Morel in *The African Mail*, 9 October 1908, vol. 2, no. 53, and E. W. Brooks to Morel, 11 October 1908, and Morel's reply, 13 October 1908, FO 367/87 37273. Cadbury won a libel case against the *Standard* over the boycott issue.

13. Vail and White 1980, 184–85, citing Maugham to Grey, 28 August 1911, FO 367/234.

14. The rest presumably had died. Duffy 1967, 210.

15. Duffy 1967, 216–18.

16. Duffy, 222–23.

17. Vail and White 1980, 187.

18. Ibid.

19. Duffy, 226–27.

20. Cadbury to Grey, 3 December 1914 and minutes, FO 371/1960 78790; Duffy, 205–206.

21. See Harris, *Dawn in Darkest Africa.* For more on Harris, see chapter 5 below. Even the Foreign Office wondered how far Germany was behind the humanitarian antislavery agitation, minute by Eyre Crowe, 21 December 1912, on Hardinge to Grey no. 106, confidential, FO 367/287 53971.

22. Much has been written on King Leopold's regime, but a very useful recent work is Nelson 1994, 79–112. See also, Louis and Stengers 1968; Northrup 1988 (a), 37 ff. and 1988 (b), 29 ff; Samarin 1989. For a recent popularized version, see Hochschild 1999.

23. Nelson 1994, 80–84.

24. Nelson 1994 provides an interesting study of African strategies of resistance, see 104–111.

25. Cookey 1968, 42–43.

26. Cookey 1968, 51–54.

27. See for instance Morel to Brooks, 13 October 1908, in which he came to the defense of Cadbury when he was attacked for not instituting a cocoa boycott, FO 367/87.

28. Cookey 1968, 108–112.

29. I can personally confirm that this view was still held in the 1960s even by my own mother, an American who was in the Kasai from 1919–23.

30. See below, chapter 10.

31. The discussion that follows is based on Sawyer 1984, 77 ff.

32. *Report by H.M. Consul at Iquitos on his Tour in the Putumayo District,* Miscellaneous no. 6 1913 (Cd.6678) LI, *PP.*

33. An Irish nationalist, he was arrested after being landed in Ireland by a German submarine.

34. Sawyer 1984, 106–107.

35. Resolution passed by the ASAPS at the AGM, 23 April 1914.

36. Slavery, Peonage and Forced Labour Bill, Bill 134, 4 Geo.V., FO 371/2222 and minutes on parliamentary questions, 7 May, 8 July 1914, ibid.

5

New International Machinery

THE LEAGUE OF NATIONS

When the First World War ended in November 1918, the victorious allies had conquered all Germany's colonies and occupied much of the Ottoman Empire. Germany was in ruins, the Austro-Hungarian empire had dissolved, the Turks controlled only the heartland of their empire, and Russia was in the throws of the Bolshevik revolution. Out of the carnage of war, the League of Nations was born at the Paris Peace Conference. Its most powerful promoter was the idealistic president of the United States, Woodrow Wilson. One of the statesmen who drafted its Covenant was Lord Robert Cecil (later Viscount Cecil of Chelmwood) who was to play an important part in the antislavery movement. The hope was that by bringing together the statesmen of the world to diffuse quarrels and stop aggression at its outset, war could be prevented. "Collective security" was to replace the "balance of power" as the mechanism for keeping the peace. Members agreed to take joint action against aggression, to refer international disputes to arbitration, to reduce their armaments, and end secret diplomacy.

The League's headquarters were established in Geneva—on neutral Swiss territory. Its directing organs consisted of an assembly of representatives of all member states, and a council of permanent delegates from the leading allied powers together with those of lesser powers chosen on a rotating basis. The Secretariat presided over by a secretary-general, the first of whom was an Englishman, Sir John Drummond, formed its staff of permanent officials, and was divided into different sections. Committees of the Assembly dealt with specific problems. The Sixth Committee was concerned with social questions, including slavery.

The Covenant did not include a formal declaration on human rights or slavery, but article 23 bound members to "secure fair and humane conditions of labor" for men, women, and children, not only in their own countries but in all countries with which they had commercial and industrial relations, as well as to secure the "just treatment" of the natives under their rule. These were large but vague commitments. Taken literally, the first would have infringed national sovereignty. Neither "fair and humane conditions" nor "just treatment" were defined, nor was there any way to enforce these obligations. However, they propelled the whole question of native labor, not just slavery, into the international arena, and laid the groundwork for further agreements.

THE MANDATES SYSTEM

The peace settlement also established the mandates system.[1] This was a compromise born of the need to reconcile the conflicting policies of the powers that had won the war. Britain and its self-governing dominions, Australia, New Zealand, and South Africa, and its allies, France, Belgium, Italy, Portugal, and Japan, all expected to get parts of the defunct German and Ottoman empires. Woodrow Wilson, on the other hand, opposed territorial annexations; and sections of the British public believed that imperialism and the rivalries it generated among the colonial powers had been a cause of the war—a view supported by Bolshevik propaganda. Since much had been made during the war of the brutality of German rule, even Wilson did not want the German colonies restored. The mandates system was designed to satisfy the conflicting aims of the architects of the peace treaties. It was the price that the European colonial powers had to pay to get the support of President Wilson, and to a lesser extent to quiet domestic opposition and counter Bolshevik propaganda.

The German colonies and Turkish provinces were shared out among the victors to be administered under the supervision of the League as mandates—"a sacred trust of civilization." This meant that they were to be ruled in the interests of their inhabitants and to be prepared for eventual self-government in accordance with the Wilsonian ideal of self-determination for all peoples. Theoretically the system was based on some of the same principles as the Berlin and Brussels Acts with their twin aims of ensuring "native" welfare and keeping these territories open to the trade of all nations—or in this case all members of the League, which it was anticipated all "civilized" states would join. The League was to be no more successful in ensuring native welfare than the Berlin and Brussels Acts.

Those territories considered close to being able to govern themselves became Class A mandates. These were the predominantly Arab states of Iraq and Palestine, which became British mandates, and Syria, which became a French mandate. Their inhabitants bitterly resented this tutelage. Class B mandates were those considered to require European rule for the foreseeable future. These were the former German African colonies of Cameroon and Togo, which were divided between France and Britain, Tanganyika which became British, and Ruanda-Urundi which was given to the Belgians. Finally, C mandates, classed as the most backward, were given to British dominions, which were now virtually independent, and sent their own representatives to the

League. South West Africa was allotted to South Africa, and the German Pacific islands passed to New Zealand and Australia. At the insistence of these dominions, the C mandates were more closely integrated into the territories of the mandatory power than the others. They were not open to the trade of all League members and were less closely supervised by the Permanent Mandates Commission, which was formed to see that the colonial powers ruling the mandates carried out the terms of their trust.[2]

These terms included the suppression of slavery and were most stringent for class B mandates. In these territories the mandatory powers were bound to suppress the slave trade, to "provide for the eventual emancipation of all slaves and for as speedy an elimination of domestic and other slavery as social conditions will allow," and to prohibit forced labor, except for "essential public works and services" and then only if it was paid. They were also to protect natives by supervising labor contracts and recruitment. These were far-reaching provisions, clearly binding the colonial powers to protect labor from all abuses. That they would be taken to task if they failed to do so became apparent almost as soon as the Permanent Mandates Commission began its work.

This was a permanent body of independent experts all of whom had been senior colonial officials. Hence, they were well acquainted with the problems of colonial rule and with the devices used by administrators to avoid action. Moreover, when it came to discussions of labor questions, a representative of the International Labor Organization had the right to attend their discussion "in an advisory capacity," thanks to the initiative of its director, Albert Thomas, the French socialist and former minister of war, who had been responsible for the stringent provisions of the B mandates.[3]

Influenced by the head of the Mandates Section of the League Secretariat, the Swiss William Rappard, the Commission alarmed the colonial powers as early as 1921. Unimpressed by their official annual reports, it sent them exhaustive questionnaires covering all aspects of administration. Colonial officials had to come to its meetings to explain their policies, and the minutes of these meetings were published, effectively publicizing the failings of colonial policies. Publicity was the Commission's main weapon, since it was an advisory body, without the power to conduct investigations or enforce its recommendations. However, publicity was, as always, a powerful weapon and the Commission used it to full advantage.

The Permanent Mandates Commission had a twofold influence when it came to League action against slavery. It made the colonial powers wary of appointing committees, particularly permanent ones, which could in any way oversee their policies. Secondly, the Commission, in spite of the opposition of the colonial rulers, set standards for the treatment of all colonial labor. Although these standards were not realized even in the mandates, the colonial powers had at least to pay them lip service. Moreover, the ideal that colonies were to be governed for the benefit of their inhabitants and that colonial labor should be protected from abuse took root in the public mind and was to be passed to the United Nations after the Second World War.

THE ABROGATION OF THE BERLIN AND BRUSSELS ACTS IN 1919

At the end of the war, Britain, France, and Belgium were determined to sweep away both the Berlin and Brussels Acts. Discussions began in 1916 and continued for three years.[4] They claimed the Acts were out of date. Neither had fully served its purpose. They had not ensured free access to trade on the Congo or the Niger. The commercial clauses designed to provide such access had prevented the riverine powers from setting their own tariffs and they wanted to be free of them. The restrictions on the arms and spirits trades had not proved satisfactory.

As for the slave trade, in 1912 the Foreign Office complained that the Brussels Act was not "working properly."[5] There was evidence that the traffic was often carried on in big ships, which no one could search even in the maritime zone. A stronger treaty was required, extending and updating the Brussels Act, and including slavery and colonial labor abuses. Instead, the negotiators when discussing renewal of the Act simply claimed that the slave trade was so reduced in scale that it was no longer needed. No investigations were launched, and the colonial powers took advantage of the general peace settlements to abrogate both treaties.

At St. Germain-en-Laye in 1919, they negotiated three new conventions covering the spirits and arms trades, and the tariffs on trade. One dealt with the spirits traffic and need not concern us here. One dealt with the arms trade. The restrictions on this traffic in the Brussels Act had not stopped smuggling, and the end of the war unleashed the prospect of a massive unloading of surplus arms on the world market, which alarmed the colonial rulers. Thus, the Arms Convention signed at St. Germain was a far-reaching treaty designed by the colonial powers to prevent modern arms from reaching their colonies. It was no longer disguised as a measure against the slave trade. In any event, it never came into full force as neither it, nor the subsequent arms agreements negotiated by the League, were ratified by all powers. The arms question continued to worry the British, particularly, as will be seen, in connection with Ethiopia. The third convention revised the commercial clauses of the Berlin and Brussels Acts. Free navigation and trade on the Niger and the Congo were retained for all powers who joined the League of Nations or who adhered to the convention, but each riparian power was now given the right to set its own tariff and navigation dues.

The slave trade was dismissed in a single article in this convention. It read:

> The Signatory Powers exercising sovereign rights or authority in African territories will continue to watch over the preservation of the native population and to supervise the improvement of their moral and material well-being. They will in particular endeavor to secure the complete suppression of slavery in all its forms, and of the slave trade by land and sea.[6]

This was the first commitment to end slavery in an international instrument, and it was to cover "all its forms." But these were not specified.

However, all the practical measures of the Brussels Act were swept away, including the bureaus in Brussels and Zanzibar, which had ceased to function during the war. As will be seen, the British were later to regret this thoughtless abrogation of a treaty, which, for all its faults, had given them rights to search foreign shipping, which were never again granted. The Royal Navy soon deplored its demise, while the Anti-Slavery Society hankered after it as late as the 1950s. At the time, however, the British were as keen as their allies to be rid of it. They created confusion for the future, however, because the allies could only abrogate the Brussels Act for themselves and for those other signatories who chose to ratify the St. Germain treaties. For those who did not do so, the British claimed that the Act was still in force, but for all practical purposes, it was now dead.

THE INTERNATIONAL LABOR ORGANIZATION (ILO)

Article 421 of the Peace Treaty of Versailles bound signatories to apply all the labor conventions, which they ratified to their non-self-governing possessions. A significant step towards the general protection of labor was taken in 1919, when the International Labor Organization was established. This was a specialized agency affiliated to the League, funded from the same budget, and inspired by the same desire to iron out conflicts between nations before they led to war. It grew out of the movement for international social legislation. A congress in Berlin in 1890 and subsequent meetings in Berne in 1905 and 1906 had concluded the first conventions for the protection of labor. Now the ILO was formed to find ways to improve living and working standards for labor throughout the world.

This body—still in existence at the beginning of the twenty-first century—was composed of representatives of governments, employers, and workers nominated by each member state. They met annually at the International Labor Conference. It had an elected governing body of twenty-four, of which twelve represented governments, and the rest were drawn from persons nominated by business and labor interests. Its office and permanent secretariat were in Geneva. Founded on the premise that labor standards could only be raised by international agreements, and that labor could not be protected in one area unless it was protected everywhere, the ILO defined minimum labor standards and negotiated conventions embodying them. Although it provided a forum for the public discussion of labor questions and gave organized labor a voice in these discussions, it could not force governments to sign its conventions or carry them out. Moreover, although article 421 bound the colonial powers to apply any conventions they signed to their overseas possessions, they could, and did, delay doing so by claiming that conditions in these territories were not yet "suitable."

JOHN HARRIS AND THE ANTI-SLAVERY AND
ABORIGINES PROTECTION SOCIETY

That slavery would be a decreasing problem and colonial labor practices an increasing one was reflected in the amalgamation of the British and Foreign Anti-Slavery Society with its sister organization—the Aborigines Protection Society (APS)—in 1909. The combined society was called the Anti-Slavery and Aborigines Protection Society (ASAPS). Colonial labor policies had always been within the brief of the APS and it had never been possible to draw a rigid line between the spheres of the two organizations. From time to time in the past, they had considered amalgamating and in 1909, the death of the Secretary of the APS provided the occasion. Members were told that:

> Now that slavery is so commonly found under a disguise, and the great evil which has to be fought is the exploitation and coercion of natives in order to secure their labor for the white man, it has appeared to those interested that nothing but good could result from uniting the two similar bodies, and that one strong Society, representing the cause of the native races of mankind, could more effectively serve their interests than two separate organizations working independently and often hampered by want of adequate resources.[7]

The combined society, like its predecessors, was predominantly middle class, mostly Protestant and largely Quaker, and had only a few hundred members. Its dual role, however, gave it a broader mandate and enhanced its influence. In 1910, it appointed a new secretary—the dynamic and dedicated Reverend John (later Sir John) Harris. He was born in 1874, and as a young man worked for seven years in a London commercial firm before joining a group called the Young Evangelicals in Business. With their support, he became a missionary in the Congo Balolo Mission. There he witnessed the atrocities perpetrated by the agents of the Independent State and was a star witness at King Leopold's commission of inquiry. He played a prominent part in the Congo Reform Association. He was described as "truly lovable," vital, genial, "boyish" in his eager conversation, and endowed with "engaging simplicity." He was to lead the society with telling effect for over thirty years until he died in 1941.[8]

However, there was a downside to his leadership. His boundless enthusiasm and single-mindedness led him at times to fudge the facts to prove his point, while his unrestrained optimism often caused him to make unrealistic suggestions. Relations between the antislavery society and the British government had only occasionally been close. In the immediate prewar years, Harris's unremitting criticism of Portuguese recruiting methods and of Britain's treatment of contract labor in South Africa irritated the Foreign Office and laid the seeds for future distrust. Foreign Office officials believed he distorted evidence and lacked candor.[9] They thought him "mischievous" and often unsympathetic to what they regarded as vital imperial interests. He was not a radical reformer and was as paternalistic as most of his contemporaries, but he differed from many members of the colonial establishment because he was skeptical about the benefits of imperial rule for indigenous peoples. He wanted them to be a free and prosperous peasantry rather than low paid wage laborers working on European projects, divorced from the means of production. He was dedicated to improving conditions of labor and ending all forms of abuse. Officials tried to keep him at bay, but they had a healthy respect for his ability to embarrass them in press and Parliament.

He used all the well-tried methods of putting pressure on reluctant governments, and developed new tactics suitable for the postwar world.[10] The Society still operated on the proverbial shoestring, but Harris, like his predecessors, gave it an importance out of all proportion to its minute membership and slender budget. His particular strength lay in his close links with members of both Houses of Parliament. He himself served briefly as a Liberal M. P. His ability to mobilize parliamentary support enabled him to expose government shortcomings. He carefully courted members, noting their particular interests and the subjects on which they were prepared to speak. He promoted debates, preparing for them weeks in advance, doing all the necessary research in his office, writing speeches for his supporters and feeding them information and questions. He sat in the lobby during debates and at question time, ready to produce additional information and point out weaknesses in government answers.

He was indefatigable in his efforts to inform and rally public opinion. He orchestrated press campaigns. He flattered editors, telling them, for instance, that there were "no truer friends of the unfortunate backward races than editors of the British press."[11] He published books and pamphlets, wrote letters to newspapers, offered articles to magazines, solicited reviews of his books, and proposed talks on the radio—a new medium. He sought support from missionary societies and businessmen. He traveled incessantly, speaking to humble church gatherings and prestigious civic groups. He carried on a worldwide correspondence that included missionaries in Papua, civic-minded English women in Hong Kong, Methodists in America, and a man he described as an "influential Roman Catholic" who might have the ear of the Pope, as well as newspaper and magazine editors, politicians and humanitarians at home and abroad. As time went on Africans also wrote to him. His correspondents also included the well-known former colonial officials Lugard and Sir Harry Johnston, as well as the Mayoress of Birmingham, the socialist Wedgewood-Benn, the future fascist leader Oswald Mosley, the conservatives Sir Arthur Steel-Maitland and Lord Robert Cecil, and Lord Islington and the Duke of Atholl. The list was endless. Harris was wise enough, however, to forge links not just with members of the British government and the Opposition, but also with officials in the Foreign and Colonial Offices. He had his supporters among civil servants, colonial administrators, diplomats, and even government ministers. Their role is hard to estimate, as it was necessarily covert.

In the period immediately after the First World War, when the colonial powers were recovering from the conflict and extending their control over new regions, slavery was a minor issue, and not a priority of the nascent League of Nations, beset as it was by urgent political questions. The commitment to attack it "in all its forms" would probably have been forgotten had not events soon shown that the slave trade was still very much alive, and had the Anti-Slavery Society not been under the determined leadership of Harris. He watched events like a hawk, ready to take advantage of every opening to force the powers to take action.

Nor was slavery his only concern. During the war, he had been very much concerned with the abuse of African labor, particularly in the British East African Carrier Corps, into which Africans had been impressed. Tens of thousands had died from overwork, poor food, exposure, and disease. As early as 1918 he had hoped that the League would enforce international agreements on the treatment of "native" labor. Article 23 of its Covenant was an international commitment covering all forms of labor virtually everywhere, but it had been carefully crafted by the colonial powers to have little practical value. To make it effective the League needed to negotiate a treaty defining the terms "fair and humane conditions" and "just treatment," as well as to set a time limit for action, and establish supervisory machinery. It was Harris who, as will be seen, was to set the League in motion with this in mind.

NOTES

1. Much has been written on the League of Nations and the Mandates system and I have drawn on many sources, but see particularly Louis 1967 and van Ginneken 1996.

2. For a discussion of the work of the Permanent Mandates Commission, see van Ginneken 1996.

3. See van Ginneken 1996, citing note by Rappard, 20 May 1921, LON S 300.

4. For a discussion with further references, see Miers 1975, 309–14.

5. Minutes on Hardinge to Grey confidential no. 106, 12 December 1912, FO 367/287 53971.

6. Article 11, convention of St. Germain-en-Laye, 10 September 1919. For the three conventions see CMD 414, 477, 478 LIII 1919, *PP*.

7. *Anti-Slavery Reporter*, XXIX, no. 2, series 4, March–May 1909.

8. This information comes from a fragmentary autobiography by Harris and Mrs. Harris, and obituaries filed with it in AS MSS Brit.Emp.s 353, and from *Who Was Who 1929–40* and Hochschild 1999.

9. Duffy 1967, 219, is strongly critical of Harris.

10. The discussion which follows is based on Harris's voluminous correspondence and papers in the AS archives in Rhodes House, Oxford.

11. Harris to St. Loe Strachey, 18 October 1926, AS MSS. Brit.Em. s.19, D3/40.

6

Ethiopia, the League of Nations, and Slavery

THE NEWS FROM ETHIOPIA

Late in October 1919, Foreign Office officials were stunned to hear that slaving was far from dead in west and southwest Ethiopia. Britain and Ethiopia had sent a joint commission to pinpoint the frontiers between the Anglo-Egyptian Sudan and the British territories of Kenya (then called East Africa) and Uganda. They were also to apportion blame for Ethiopian incursions into British territory.[1] The reports of the two British commissioners, Majors Darley and Athill, were to cause the British government extreme embarrassment.[2]

They reported that the country from Addis Ababa to Jimma was peaceful, prosperous, and well populated, but when they crossed the Gojeb into Kafa they met utter devastation from slave raiding. Darley had traveled there before the war when an industrious people were producing food in abundance. Now food was unprocurable, and "for days and days," he wrote, "one can travel through country in which the date of each raid can be clearly marked by the height of the bush growing in what was formerly cultivated fields." In what had been a fertile agricultural district, blessed with water, timber, and beautiful scenery, the few remaining inhabitants were hiding in caves. "Nothing remained but overgrown fields, burnt houses and ruined shrines." Charred corpses lay in smoldering ruins. Cultivation was abandoned. A few starving old women in native houses were kept alive by their menfolk, who crept back from the bush at night with roots. One of them had had all of her six children carried off. Standing on Maji Mountain, the commissioners had looked over a vast expanse of terraced hillside dotted with stone circles on which houses had once stood, but where there was now no trace of people, huts, or crops.[3]

Evidence of slave trading was everywhere. Caravans marched openly along the roads, occasionally deviating to avoid government posts, not for fear of arrest but to escape taxes. One convoy walked through the middle of the commissioners' camp with seventy captives, the men chained, the toddlers strapped to mules. The chief of Shawa Ghimira was selling off local people fast—little boys for MT$5 and big ones for MT$10. When Darley and Athill picked up a starving small slave boy eating roots by the roadside, the Ethiopian commissioners told them they were wasting their efforts as he was a cripple and "would never be any good."[4]

The devastation was spreading into British territory. The Ethiopians had been outraged when shown the border. They claimed the whole country east of the Nile and south for sixty miles beyond Lake Turkana, far into Sudan and British East Africa, and had been operating there freely for many years. Darley and Athill subsequently walked for eighteen days in British territory. Once flourishing Toposa villages were abandoned. Three survivors, living on roots and berries, told them that a raiding party a hundred strong was at that moment devastating Didinga. They found the marauders' camp. It was well entrenched with over thirty houses and room for four hundred head of cattle. The nearest British post was miles away in the Boya Hills.

Darley laid the blame squarely on the Ethiopian system of government.[5] Officials were virtually unpaid. They and their hundreds of retainers and soldiers—*neftenya*—lived off the land, supported and served by local peasants—*gabbar*—who were virtual serfs. Each soldier was allotted a number of gabbar, from whom he collected money, food, firewood, and other necessities. They did his housework and produced women for his sexual needs. A good governor might keep some control over his inferiors and have a prosperous province, but when he left, having no security of office, he and his followers plundered the local people, seizing livestock and possessions, and carrying off men, women, and children as slaves, to insure against their own uncertain future. Their successors, finding a province denuded of food and people, had to raid ever farther a field. At one time ivory had provided the major source of income for these officials, but it had been replaced by slaves by 1912, as elephants were hunted out in Ethiopia. Now the hunters had to go farther and farther into British territories in search of tusks and livestock. There were constant incursions over the frontier. Darley and Athill had met a party of poachers in Sudan and confiscated their ivory, and had seen evidence of cattle rustling in British territory.

Darley had been in Maji in 1910 when a relatively good governor, Walda Giyorgis Aboye, left the province after a long term in office. Before leaving, his followers had plundered and seized the local people. Those who could, fled into the bush and then attacked the departing caravan trying to free their relatives and retrieve their animals. Darley had watched from the top of the mountain as the soldiers, with their captives roped together carrying their loot, accompanied by shopkeepers and even robbers—some ten thousand people—literally fought their way out of the area. He had bought babies for MT$1 (two shillings) each to restore them to their parents hiding in the bush.[6] A series of short-term governors had followed, and as

each departed, the cycle of violence had been repeated and the situation had become more and more desperate.

These reports should not have come as a surprise. In 1912, the British minister in
Addis Ababa, Wilfred Thesiger, among others, had reported a great increase in slaving
and raiding in west and southwest Ethiopia since 1910, and continuous incursions
over the borders into British territory. Thesiger, like Darley, who was one of his informants, blamed it on the system of government, and described the havoc created by
a rapid change of governors, whose pillaging provoked rebellion, which in turn was
brutally crushed by further raiding and enslavement of the luckless inhabitants. The
Emperor Menelik II, who had fostered relatively good government, had been incapacitated by a stroke, and his heir, Lej Yyasu, was campaigning in the west and southwest,
amassing great numbers of slaves himself. Several Europeans had met large caravans
on the roads going north.[7]

When raiders killed a British officer in 1913, the British reviewed their options.
They believed that only joint pressure from the three rival powers interested in the
Horn of Africa—Britain, France, and Italy—could force a change in the administrative system, but any such attempt might bring chaos and precipitate the partition of
the country between the three powers.[8] Under the tripartite agreement of 1906, the
three powers had guaranteed the independence and integrity of Ethiopia, but had demarcated "spheres of influence" for themselves if the government collapsed. In 1913,
with the emperor incapacitated and the heir to the throne himself out raiding, the
British were afraid to do anything that might precipitate partition. This would give the
Italians control of part of the Blue Nile and enable them to impede the flow of water
to Sudan and Egypt, both under British control. France and Italy were in any case reluctant to cooperate. The British alone had no leverage. They considered a military expedition to be "out of the question." There was no money market they could close, and
if they withheld duties at Galabat or Gambela, they would hamper the very trade they
wished to develop between Sudan and the highlands.[9]

They recognized the need to police their own frontier. The raids were causing depopulation, preventing the development of legitimate trade, and robbing the southern
Sudan of its ivory. The Ethiopians were also offering the people on the British side of
the border arms and ammunition in return for ivory and cattle. In the absence of any
British forces, these unfortunates were faced with the unenviable choice of joining the
pillagers or being plundered. But neither the Anglo-Egyptian Sudan nor the British
East African Protectorate were ready to assume the cost of policing, let alone administering, these remote areas.

Slave raiding and trading were the main sources of revenue for all the chiefs in
western Ethiopia, and the heir to the throne, the principal *rasses* (provincial governors
and other high officials) and ministers were all implicated. At Dangela, where caravans
arrived twice weekly, men sold for MT$80 and children for MT$30. A small propor-

tion of the captives was eventually shipped across the Red Sea to Arabia, but most were absorbed in Ethiopia. Thesiger had warned the Foreign Office that the Ethiopian slave and arms trades would soon become known in Europe, and the humanitarian outcry might force the tripartite powers to partition the country. Otherwise, the only solution was for the British to police their borders and protect the people under their rule.[10] There the matter stood when Britain was engulfed in the First World War, during which reports of slaving continued to come in from Gore and Gambela.[11] By the time the war ended, the situation had changed.

Menelik II had died in 1913 and his successor, Lej Yyasu, had been deposed in 1916. He was succeeded by a weak triumvirate, headed by the conservative Empress Zauditu, dependent on the support of the very officials involved in slave trading and raiding. The only progressive figure in the triumvirate was the regent, Ras Tafari, the future Emperor Haile Selassie I. He was regarded as a reformer, but was faced with entrenched opposition.

Ethiopia had not adhered to the Brussels Act, but had enacted various laws against the slave trade.[12] The country felt threatened by the European powers and the latest proclamation had been issued in 1918 in order to forestall any attempt to turn Ethiopia into a League of Nations mandate.[13] Like its predecessors, this remained a dead letter. When, late in 1919, Foreign Office officials considered their options in the light of the Maji reports, these seemed as limited as they had been in 1913. Neither the Anglo-Egyptian Sudan nor British East Africa, their resources depleted by the war, had occupied the frontier regions. The prospect of provoking a partition of Ethiopia seemed more dangerous than ever. The British feared that France and Italy might close their spheres to British enterprise. France was already obstructing British trade on the railway from Jibuti, in spite of free trade agreements. Italy was believed to be angling for exclusive commercial privileges, and the threat to the waters of the Blue Nile remained.[14] Partition might also encourage France and Italy to flood British territories with modern arms and ammunition, which were already being imported, mostly through French Somaliland, in spite of agreements with both countries.

With partition to be avoided at all costs, Britain had to protect its interests in an atmosphere of intense rivalry with France and Italy, as all three powers struggled for concessions and influence at court and the Ethiopians played them off against each other. The central government was too weak to attack the slave trade. The British suspected the French would support Ethiopia in order to obtain economic concessions, and that the Italians would be glad to see the country drift into chaos ending in partition.[15] They feared that if Britain alone put pressure on the Ethiopians to end slaving, it would jeopardize their other interests, the most important of which was the building of a dam on Lake Tana to regulate the flow of the Blue Nile to the Sudan. They wanted this in order to expand cotton production in the Gezira to supply the mills of Lancashire, but the Ethiopians had steadfastly opposed the plan.[16]

Foreign Office officials were in a dilemma. They did not want the Ethiopians to think they could continue slaving with impunity, but they did not want to publish the Maji reports for fear that the resulting outcry would force Britain to take action.[17] They decided simply to send a consul to Maji, and to urge the Anglo-Egyptian Sudan and their East African territories to police their borders. They also protested to Addis Ababa at the border incursions, with a view to having the governor of Maji, Desta Birru, removed.

Birru claimed that he was not slaving but collecting tribute or suppressing rebellions within his own borders. The frontier had been agreed between Britain and Ethiopia in 1902, but it was generally believed that the officials in Maji had never been told where it was. Since the British had not occupied the border area, they admitted they could not blame the Ethiopians for treating it as their territory.[18] To make matters worse, the ivory poachers included British subjects—a motley collection of Baluchis, Swahili, and others who had left British territory to install themselves in Maji, where they had fallen into debt to Ethiopian creditors.[19] The British minister feared that insisting on Birru's removal would simply trigger another slaving orgy by his departing retainers. It was decided to limit action to trying to get a good working relationship between the governor and the newly appointed British vice-consul in Maji, Brian Hawkins.[20]

Foreign Office officials salved their consciences by maintaining that it was not their duty to suppress slaving in independent countries, particularly "semi-barbarous" ones in which slavery was entrenched in the social system.[21] They well knew that the Anti-Slavery Society would challenge this view, and they were relieved later to hear that Darley was unreliable.[22] However, everything in his reports had been corroborated by Athill, and was quickly confirmed by Hawkins when he reached Maji, where his reception was so "chilly" that he felt like a policeman in a robber's house.[23] Not only had nothing changed, but between Maji and Kafa, he found the local people, their villages hidden in inaccessible places, attacking their oppressors and selling slaves themselves in exchange for arms.[24]

Nevertheless, no further action might have been taken by the Foreign Office had the humanitarian outcry officials had long dreaded not been provoked by a series of sensational anonymous articles in the *Westminster Gazette* in January 1922, exposing the misgovernment and slaving in Ethiopia.[25] Robert Sperling, the architect of Britain's Ethiopian policy in the Foreign Office, typically decided that the authors were not motivated by humanitarianism. The principal author, Dr. Sharp, former physician to the British legation, was said to have left with a grievance. His coauthor, Darley, needed money and was reported to have a grudge against the Ethiopian government.[26] This was not the last time that such theories were advanced by officials to cast doubts on inconvenient revelations. There is no reason to believe that Darley, although generally conceded to be an adventurer and an ivory poacher, was not genuinely outraged by the devastation in an area where he had friends among the victims, particularly since he had reported the raiding to the legation in Addis Ababa before the war, and had warned both the British minister there and the governor of Uganda of Ethiopian intentions to launch raids into British territory.[27] Harris, at the Anti-Slavery Society, had reservations about Darley, but believed Sharp to be an unimpeachable witness.[28] Sharp's correspondence with the Society shows a sincere sympathy for slaves, some of whom had been his patients.[29] He also maintained that he had told the British minister in Addis Ababa that he intended to publish the facts.[30] The articles suffered from some inaccuracy and exaggeration, but they pointed correctly to a flourishing slave trade in Ethiopia, and rightly accused the Foreign Office of "hushing up" the whole question. Moreover, they accused the British legation of employing slave owners as servants and stated that some of their slaves were British subjects.

These revelations attracted considerable attention in Britain and abroad.[31] The Foreign Office was censured for failing to take action and not publishing the facts.[32] Officials were unrepentant. Russell in Addis Ababa was told to show the articles to the regent, Ras Tafari, before either the French or Italians did so, and make it clear that the British government was neither responsible for, nor approved of, them.[33] Nevertheless, he was to suggest to Tafari that Ethiopia might be well advised to take action. Tafari replied that slavery was an old institution, that slaves were well treated, and that if the Ethiopian people saw the articles there "would be a revolution." But he issued an order stating that all slaving was illegal and hanged two men as an example. These were small fry rounded up in the slums of Addis Ababa. None of the high officials involved were punished. Since the royal family was believed to accept slaves as gifts and tribute, this injustice upset the British minister and made him wary of further protests.[34]

To absolve Britain from any charge of condoning slavery, the Foreign Office ordered the legation to free the slaves of its employees and compensate their owners. Two servants refused to comply and were dismissed with two months' pay. Three signed papers testifying that their slaves were free adopted children. The wives of two other employees claimed that the slaves were theirs and refused to allow their husbands to liberate them. The men divorced their wives. This "domestic catastrophe" dismayed the British minister, but the husbands assured him they would soon find other wives ready to abide by the new British rules! Eighteen slaves received manumission certificates from Ras Tafari. Three, who had been purchased, were given the money to buy their freedom from their owners in the presence of the minister. The total came to MT$223. Three owners of bought slaves refused compensation, as did three owners who had inherited or been given their slaves.

The striking thing was that most of the freed were under eighteen and some had been acquired as babies. Although Dodds did not altogether believe all the owners who claimed to have adopted them, many had clearly been acquired when too young to work. They had known no other home and freedom was probably meaningless for them. Some had been designated as their masters' heirs. Some of the older ones also chose to remain with their owners.[35] The picture that emerges is of an active market in children, with whom strong bonds of attachment were often formed, and who often had considerable social mobility. Most slaves were used by women as domestic servants. Of the twenty-two slaves listed by the legation, fifteen were female. Since these were household slaves, there is no reason to believe that they were not well treated. The fact that so many were so young, however, clearly meant that they had recently been snatched from their parents to supply the buoyant market in Addis Ababa.

Meanwhile the agitation continued in Britain and abroad. Questions were asked in Parliament.[36] In May, a deputation from the Anti-Slavery Society was received at the Foreign Office. Harris had been watching developments carefully and he now put forward a novel plan—the League of Nations should be asked to take up the question.

HARRIS GOES TO THE LEAGUE OF NATIONS

Harris had led a delegation from the Anti-Slavery Society to Geneva in 1920 to lobby delegates on a wide range of questions. These included slavery in the Portuguese colonies, the alienation of African land in Rhodesia, the form of the League mandates, the Armenian question, and the trade in women and girls, particularly little Chinese girls. His tactics were to feed information to every member of the Assembly and follow this up with personal interviews. He spent five of the "most strenuous weeks" of his life in Geneva and came home jubilant, convinced that the League opened up "an entirely new method" of dealing with such issues.[37] He had found sympathetic ears among delegates and League officials, and hoped that "the personnel behind the scenes" would get the League to establish machinery to promote reforms.[38] Colonial governments could ignore requests for information, let alone action, from the Society, but he believed they would have to respond to the demands of the League. Moreover, article 23 of the Covenant, provided a vehicle for an attack on all the various forms of abuse under which slavery, as he said, now "masqueraded" including forced labor, contract labor, and debt bondage.

Ethiopia was the catalyst that spurred him into action. Sharp had called on him the day before the first articles came out in the *Westminster Gazette* to see if the Society would take up the matter and had put him in touch with Darley.[39] Both wanted questions asked in Parliament about the attitude of the British government. The Society reprinted the articles in a pamphlet and Sharp distributed a hundred copies to Members of Parliament. They were also sent to American editors, as Sharp believed the United States was planning to send arms to Ethiopia which would be used for raiding. Harris encouraged Darley to write a book about his experiences and helped him find a publisher.[40]

In February, Harris engineered a question in Parliament asking whether the government had information on slave trading in Ethiopia and if so would it publish it in a Blue Book. The reply was that it had the reports but would not publish them.[41] Harris wanted "one or two suitable administrators" appointed as League commissioners to help the Ethiopians end slave raiding and trading. He inspired articles on the League's possible role in the *Westminster Gazette* in May, as well as letters from Lugard, and other luminaries, and followed them up with a deputation to the Foreign

Office.[42] He sounded out League officials as to how to proceed, and collected information for a memorial to the Assembly.[43]

His plan had to overcome a major obstacle—Ethiopia was not a member of the League. He searched for persons with influence to induce it to apply.[44] He wrote to Dr. Martin (Warqenah Eshete),[45] an Ethiopian educated in Bombay, who now lived in Addis Ababa, had the ear of the government and had written to the *Westminster Gazette*. Martin reiterated what Harris knew—the government was too weak to take action that might provoke rebellion. He suggested that combined pressure from "all the civilized powers" might force them to do something, provided the integrity and independence of the country were guaranteed. Martin advised the empress that joining the League would ensure the country's status and security.[46] Harris had no desire to see Ethiopian independence threatened. He preferred "native states" to evolve "naturally," but he also believed that "civilized powers" could not allow slavery to "drift on." He sought international support. For instance, he sent the *Westminster Gazette* articles to the sub-editor of *L'Europe Nouvelle* to publish, and asked him to "sound out" the views of French officials, but it was August and the French were "*en vacances*." He denied French suspicions that he supported unilateral action by Britain.[47]

In June 1922, HMS *Cornflower* captured the *Al Mosahil*—a dhow carrying thirty Ethiopian slaves in the Red Sea—dramatic proof that slaves were still being exported to Arabia. Reports of a lively trade had already reached the Foreign Office the previous year, but here again strong action had been precluded by imperial considerations, as will be seen. In August 1922, twenty-six of the slaves liberated from the dhow arrived in Addis Ababa with a British escort. This proof that slaves were being illegally exported caused a sensation in the capital and put the government on its mettle. The regent freed them and offered money and an escort to those who wanted to return to their homes and proposed to educate the children in monasteries and convents. He also asked for information so that he could trace and punish their captors.[48]

For the Anti-Slavery Society this capture was grist to the mill. In September, Harris gained what he called a "first class victory" when the New Zealand delegate to the League of Nations, Sir Arthur Steel-Maitland, submitted two resolutions to the League Assembly.[49] The first requested the Council to inquire into slave trading in Ethiopia and report to the next Assembly. The second requested that they inquire "with the help of competent African administrators" into the whole question of slavery. Steel-Maitland was supported by the representative from Haiti. The Assembly duly resolved on 22 September that the recrudescence of slavery should be included on its agenda for 1923—and set in motion an inquiry into slavery all over the world. This all-embracing resolution was intended to disarm suspicions that it was an attack on one country.[50] Moreover, it had been so designed that the League could now inquire into what Harris called "all forms of labor which encroach on slavery," including forced labor and contract labor, as well as "crude" (chattel or classic) slavery, slave trading, and what was commonly called by the British in Africa "domestic slavery." Domestic slaves were those born in their owners' households.[51]

Thus the Anti-Slavery Society had finally projected the whole question of labor abuse onto the official international stage in pursuit of the objective for which it been founded over eighty years before—the ending of slavery everywhere. The hope was that this would be the first step in the creation of international machinery to protect the weakest members of society and improve the quality of life for millions of people all over the world. It was a great achievement for a minute organization. But it did not come cheaply. The Society was left with a deficit of several hundred pounds in its annual budget for 1922–1923. It pared its expenses to the bone. Harris reduced his own salary for the second year running. Only £1,000 was needed to wipe out the deficit and pay for upcoming expenses, but Harris had to beg for donations from individuals and businesses.[52]

Now that the League had been induced to take up the question, the hard work of translating its request for information into effective action began.

BRITAIN AND ETHIOPIAN ADMISSION TO THE LEAGUE OF NATIONS

The British Foreign Office was outraged by Steel-Maitland's "entirely unauthorized" introduction of the resolution on slavery, particularly as he was a Member of Parliament. They were even more irritated when he asked them to publish their reports on Ethiopia in a White Book. When the League itself asked for information on slavery everywhere, they worried about the effects that divulging it would have in Ethiopia, particularly the likelihood of endangering the Lake Tana dam negotiations.[53] "I see no reason," wrote Sperling, "why we should give the League any information about Abyssinia. It is not a British colony or protectorate and we are not responsible for its manners or customs." Moreover, since slavery could only be ended by force and none of the tripartite powers would spend money on its suppression, there was not "the least use in the League's discussing it."[54]

Dissenting voices pointed out that the League would discuss it whether the British liked it or not; that they would be expected to provide information they were known to have; that they already bore the cost of naval patrols and were under an "obligation to put down slavery in general" and that a treaty with Ethiopia of 1884 provided grounds for interference.[55] The Foreign Office, however, merely informed the League that nothing had occurred in British territory to justify fears of a recrudescence of slavery.[56]

Since the League could only circulate documents received from governments, Harris sent the government a memorandum incorporating his evidence, hoping they would publish it in a White Book together with official reports, and send it to the League.[57] He needed reliable accounts and asked consuls and colonial officials to produce sworn affidavits, but the Foreign Office refused its consent for fear of prejudicing relations with Ethiopia and endangering the life of the consul in Maji.[58] Darley jeopardized his credibility by demanding £25 for his affidavit—a request turned down by the Society because it could not compromise its integrity by buying information.[59] However, the Swiss Bureau pour la défense des indigènes (BIDI) prepared a report for the League based on the accounts of Athill and Darley, and other witnesses.[60]

Harris continued his relentless feeding of questions and comments to members of both Houses of Parliament hoping to force the government to either publish its information or send it to the League.[61] Ministers claimed that slave trading was declining and Darley's reports were out of date, and with more truth, that the raids into British territory were for cattle and not slaves. Under duress, however, they finally published the long sought White Book. To Harris's great disappointment, it was designed to support their position.[62]

His persistence finally paid off late in July 1923, when his supporters took the foreign secretary, Lord Curzon, to task in the House of Lords for not showing as much zeal in furnishing information to the League as other powers, and not publishing the reports from Ethiopia. Relying on information furnished by his officials, Curzon maintained that the Foreign Office had no up-to-date information. When an incredulous Archbishop of Canterbury inquired why consuls had kept a "severe rule of silence" on a matter of such great interest to the country, Curzon, taken by surprise, answered that those in the remote areas of Ethiopia were not ordinary consuls, but persons engaged "very likely in business or hunting" who were appointed to "foster trade and promote British interests." "I do not imagine," he added, "that it ever occurs to them that it is any part of their duty to send a report upon Slavery to us, because they do not send any report at all."

This was too much for the peers, well briefed by Harris. Curzon was forced to promise to send for up-to-date information and pass it on to the League.[63] During the debate the peers and, on the following day, the press, reminded him of Britain's "traditional role" as leader of the antislavery movement. Clearly, slavery still commanded sufficient public interest for the government to ignore it at its peril. Deeply mortified, Curzon accused his subordinates of misrepresenting the facts and demanded a memorandum on the whole question. After perusing the evidence, he rebuked them for not realizing that the matter could not be "trifled" within Parliament. He ordered the consuls in Ethiopia to send him all the information they could glean on slavery in a form suitable for publication.[64] He minuted:

> I hope that when the replies come from the elephant hunting consuls, the Department will treat the case with greater seriousness. Nobody suggests the invasion of Abyssinia. But that slave raiding has existed on an atrocious scale is indisputable. That it exists still is more than likely.[65]

He was right. The new consul in Maji, Arnold Hodson, confirmed that Kafa and Gimira had been denuded of people. The main road to Maji was closed by "Tishana" rebels.[66] However, he had been well received by officials in Maji, who had actually intercepted a caravan of fourteen slaves, and nineteen others had been freed in Gore.[67]

But neither he, nor Russell, the minister in Addis Ababa, thought the improvement would last.[68] Provincial officials were still not paid, and most people still saw nothing wrong with slavery. Fitwrari Hapte Giyorgis, the third member of the ruling triumvirate, minister of war, and a slave by origin, told Russell that "pagan savages who live like dogs get food and clothing and are made into Christians when they become slaves."[69] The incentive for acquiring slaves was as strong as ever, both as a form of conspicuous consumption, and as valuable and useful assets. Ras Tafari, upon whom the British pinned their hopes for reform, owned many.

The question, however, now entered a new phase with the maneuvers that were to bring Ethiopia into the League of Nations.

THE SECRET TRADE OF THE RED SEA

These maneuvers were instigated by the French. They feared that the agitation in Britain presaged an attack on Ethiopian independence, and believed that determined action against slavery by the ruling triumvirate would provoke rebellion.[70] The French representative in Addis Ababa corroborated the British reports and, with shame, informed his government that some three hundred slaves a month reached Tajura, in French Somaliland, where the sultan taxed them at MT$1 a head before they were exported across the Red Sea.[71] Tajura, under its own sultan, was only some twenty miles from the colony's main port of Jibuti, the railhead for Addis Ababa. The French had not occupied it for lack of troops.[72] Until they did so, their minister warned, slaves would continue to be exported.

The problem was not new. During the years that the Brussels Act had been in force, long stretches of the Somali and Eritrean coast had been barely policed. In 1907, for instance, the French at Obock and the Italians at Assab each had only one European official. Both had been many years in the country and had considerable influence over the Danakil, but the British believed that they either connived at, or were powerless to stop, the smuggling of slaves and arms. The French agent had Ethiopian wives reputedly given to him by slavers in return for permission to pass through French territory. Although he had six armed dhows at his disposal, he seemed unable to stop the traffic. As late as 1915, the British had captured a French dhow carrying nine slaves. The Italian had not prevented the chief of Raheita from supplying two dhows, which had carried over a hundred slaves to Arabia, including eunuchs, in 1905.[73]

Suppressing this traffic was not easy. A French adventurer, businessman, and prolific author, Henry de Monfreid, described how the traders evaded capture. Like them, he was smuggling arms and drugs to Arabia in the early decades of the twentieth century.[74] He was also suspected of slaving by the French, and in 1930, the Ethiopians accused him of making a fortune from the traffic, but both had other reasons to dislike him. His description of the Red Sea trade tallies with the evidence of freed slaves, the crew of the *Al Mosahil*,[75] and of British naval officers.

Since the French refused to allow Europeans to visit Tajura, de Monfreid sailed there in his own boat, disguised as a local, to do business with a fellow arms smuggler—Shaykh Maki, "a very holy man" credited with supernatural powers—who kept wives in Tajura and in Yemen, and thus had a firm foothold on both sides of the Red Sea. De Monfreid was taken secretly by night to his camp in the mountains above Tajura, guarded by some fifty armed men. A thorn *zeriba* enclosed goats, camels, and five or six round huts covered with palm frond matting. In the morning twenty-four "mules," as the slaves were called—well-built young women and little boys—emerged singing and laughing from the huts and began milking the animals. All were negroid in feature and were described as "Chancallas" (Shankalla), the derogatory Amharic term for the Nilo-Saharan speaking peoples of the west and southwest fringes of Ethiopia, and "Wallemos" from Christian Walamo, also in the southwest. They moved freely about the camp, were given the best food—goat's milk, rice, and dates—and slept in the huts, while their escort ate "parched durra" and slept in the open. The scene resembled a typical Bedouin camp.

The dealer told de Monfreid that Ethiopian chiefs obtained the slaves as tax or tribute, and that they came willingly, expecting a better life in Arabia, while their parents were happy to get money for them. Although de Monfreid probably had reasons for presenting a picture of happy victims, his is not the only such description.[76] It is likely that, once torn from their homelands, the slaves were pacified with promises of a comfortable future. That they were well enough treated on the way is also credible since they were valuable property. Moreover, slavers would not have wanted to draw attention to themselves by having obviously reluctant victims in their midst.

Once obtained, the slaves were sold to traders, who kept them in underground storage rooms until they had enough for a caravan. They then escorted them to the Danakil frontier, paying a tax to every chief along the way. Dankali merchants then took them to villages visited by Arabian traders, who bought them in exchange for cotton goods and copper leaf. These traders took them for shipment to the neighborhood of Tajura, or Raheita and Eid in Italian Eritrea, or Zeila in British Somaliland.

Occasionally Danakils themselves took them across the Red Sea, but more often, they met up with sailors from Arabia, who smuggled arms and tobacco as well as slaves, and turned pirate when given the opportunity. They would put into inlets hidden from the sea by brush and mangrove, and often only accessible over the coral reefs at high tide. They beached their boats, buried the stores of food and water needed for slaves, stretched sails over spars as shelter, and settled down as apparently peaceful fishermen, drying their catch. A slave caravan would halt in the mountains some hours' march away and send a messenger to warn of their arrival. A lookout posted on the hills would put up a smoke spiral if there were no naval patrols about and at nightfall the fishermen would light a fire to show that the coast was clear for embarkation. The caravaners would respond with an equally short-lived fire and escort the slaves down to the boats.

Under cover of dark, they were packed twenty to thirty into the well of the dhow and, if a ship approached, they were covered with a tarpaulin over which the crew would walk to disarm the suspicion that they carried live cargo. The slavers would then dash for the Arabian coast at night. From north of Tajura, the fifteen-mile or so crossing might only take two hours running before a strong south wind. The favored boat was a fast, light *zaroug*, with no ballast, manned by six or seven men, who under full sail balanced the boat by leaning outwards clinging to the shrouds. These craft could outrun any patrol boats and, moving fast in the dark, were unlikely to be challenged. Tactics and the type of vessel used by the smugglers varied with time and place, but de Monfreid's account probably gives an accurate picture of the mechanics of the Red Sea slave trade.

Once across the sea, slavers, landing by day and sailing at night, made their way up the coast, keeping close to shore, under cover of islands and reefs and the frequent Red Sea mist. Naval officers complained that their warships could not enter these waters and their ship's boats, which did the patrolling, were no match in speed or seaworthiness for the smugglers' vessels. The navy sometimes hired dhows for its patrols.[77] Once the slavers put to sea, it was almost impossible to intercept them. If a dhow was stopped, the slaves could not be counted on to make their presence known, having probably been told that the Europeans would kill them.

The trip along the Arabian coast to Jiddah, or its neighborhood, might take a considerable time. The slaves liberated on the *Al Mosahil* had been twenty-three days out of Maidi, crowded amidships on filthy matting. Of the twenty-nine who had been newly enslaved, eight were women, seven were little girls, and fourteen were small boys, including a ten-day-old baby. Six of them came from Walamo. They had all changed hands several times and had traveled by night.

In 1922, the French were embarrassed at the revelation that slave caravans were still crossing their territory. Even more shaming was the Ethiopian belief that France had not occupied Tajura because French colonial officials were making money trading in arms through the sultanate in contravention of the agreement with Britain.[78] Thus, the Ethiopians considered the French partners in crime. In the face of these revelations, the French, as will be seen, began to cooperate with the British and Italians and took steps to improve the policing of their coast and caravan routes.

ETHIOPIA JOINS THE LEAGUE OF NATIONS

At the League, the French recognized that the slave trade laid Ethiopia open to attack.[79] Like the British, they freed the slaves of their legation servants and warned their citizens against employing slaves.[80] They found that the British agitation cemented their relations with the Ethiopians who believed that they alone of the tripartite powers had no territorial ambitions over the country.[81] Moreover, they were anxious to supply the government with arms to boost their munitions exports, and increase traffic on the Jibuti-Addis Ababa railway, which badly needed more freight to make it pay.[82] Unlike the Sudan, their small colony of Somaliland did not suffer from Ethiopian raids, so the arms traffic could do them no harm.

When Steel-Maitland first brought the question of slaving in Ethiopia before the subcommittee of the Sixth Commission of the League Assembly, the French tried to brush it off as rumor, earning Ras Tafari's gratitude.[83] In response to the League request for information on slavery, they produced a long memorandum showing that Ethiopian slavery was "benign," a description with which the British minister in Addis Ababa agreed.[84] This was to prepare the way for Ethiopian admission. It was so well received that the French advised Ras Tafari to apply for membership at once so that the application could be rushed through the Assembly in 1923 before the British could muster opposition.[85] The Ethiopians doubtless hoped that membership would protect them from British or Italian aggression, and help them resist British pressure for the Lake Tana dam and end the slavery agitation.[86] They applied immediately.

The British were outraged. They thought Ethiopia was "unfit" for membership,[87] and that its admission would mean that in the future there would be no "ground for excluding anybody."[88] They believed the application was part of a French plot to flood the country with arms, and feared that Ethiopia would now be less likely to take action against the slave traffic or to agree to a dam on Lake Tana. Moreover, the League might appoint European advisors, who would either be ignored or start costly and contentious operations.[89] However, unable to rally support, and not wanting to be the lone dissenter, they accepted the inevitable,[90] on condition that Ethiopia furnish the League with information on slavery, accept its recommendations on the subject, and agree not to import arms without the agreement of the signatories of the Arms Traffic Convention of St. Germain-on-Laye. They also realized that the rejection of Ethiopia would be regarded in India as an example of racism, and that it would also make it more difficult to get Iraq (a British mandate) admitted to the League.[91]

As the British had foreseen, Ethiopia, with French support, soon began to press for the unrestricted import of arms, claiming they needed them to enforce the orders of the central government. The various local arms agreements between the tripartite powers need not detain us here, except to note that the French argued that arms were needed against slavers. The British dismissed this as a cynical attempt to further French commercial and political interests. The Foreign Office was convinced that if the Ethiopian government imported arms freely, the unpaid levies, which made up the bulk of the army, would use them to raid British or Italian territory.[92]

To allay criticism, the Ethiopian government issued a proclamation reaffirming that slave trading was illegal and imposing the death penalty for offenders. The British did not believe it would be effective.[93] The admission of Ethiopia to the League, at the end of September 1923, was a triumph for the Ethiopians, the French, and the Anti-Slavery Society, and a defeat for Britain. However, every cloud has a silver lining. Henceforth, the Foreign Office could tell Harris and his cohorts that the Ethiopians were now responsible for sending the League reports on slavery.[94] Britain, absolved from the responsibility of denouncing a fellow member, could simply say that it would support any action the League decided to take.

However, in 1924 the first Labor government took office. Harris, who had been elected to Parliament as a Liberal the year before, served in it. This short-lived administration was sympathetic to the antislavery cause and privately sent the secretary-general its latest reports, omitting only names and places in order not to jeopardize its sources.[95]

The result of these machinations was that the suppression of slavery in Ethiopia was now an international question. It had been merged into a general attack on the institution mounted by the League of Nations, thus ensuring that it would be the subject of much talk but no effective action.

NOTES

1. For these raids, see Barber 1968.

2. These reports are scattered. A summary is in Campbell to Curzon, no. 100, 21 September 1919. Separate reports by each commissioner are enclosed in Campbell to Curzon, no. 102, 22 September 1919. Darley also wrote in greater detail to Dodds on 1 November 1919; this is enclosed in Dodds to Curzon, no. 121, 7 November 1919. The original reports and minutes are in FO 371/3498. They are printed in FOCP 11640. For a survey of the whole question of British policy towards slavery in Ethiopia from c.1910 to c.1942, see Miers 1997.

3. Memorandum by Athill, 11 September 1919, enclosed in Campbell to Curzon, no. 102, 22 September 1919, FO 371/3498, FOCP 11640 (FO 403/450).

4. They nursed him back to health and he became Athill's stable boy in Addis Ababa, Darley 1972, 201.

5. For the system of government, see Perham 1969, Marcus 1995, Tibebu 1995, 21–101.

6. Darley 1972, chapter 9.

7. Thesiger to Grey, confidential no. 76, 29 August 1912, Doughty Wylie to Grey, 31 December 1912, FO 371/1294; Sudan Intelligence Report (SIR) no. 216, July 1912, no. 218, September 1912, FO 357/311. Report on the situation in Abyssinia for 1912, enclosed in Thesiger to Grey no. 6, 20 January 1913, FO 371/1571. A number of secondary works deal with frontier raiding and the position in western and southwestern Ethiopia. For detailed studies of the Maji area and further references, see Hickey 1984, chapter 2; Garretson 1986. For the western frontier, see Zewde 1976.

8. Minute on Thesiger to Grey, no. 76, 29 August 1912, FO 371/1294. See also Miers 1997.

9. See minutes on Thesiger to Grey no. 41, 19 June 1913, FO 371/1572.

10. Annual Report 1912, enclosed in Thesiger to Grey, no. 6, 20 January 1913, FO 371/1571.

11. Report from Gambela, no. 12, 4 June 1916, and from Gore no. 9, 10 April 1916, and no. 6, 14 February 1917 and Walker to Thesiger no. 3, 24 April 1919, FO 371/9985.

12. This is a vexed question. Italy had tried to adhere for Ethiopia at the Brussels conference but this was regarded as an attempt to get other powers to recognize that Ethiopia was an Italian protectorate. It was arranged that Italy should announce after the conference that Ethiopia had agreed to the Act. The procedure was followed but the Foreign Office did not believe in 1912 that Ethiopia had actually adhered to the Act. For the conflict at the conference, see Miers 1975, 270–72.

13. Campbell to Curzon, no. 102, 22 September 1919 FO 403/451, and minute by Lidderdale, 12 December 1919, FO 371/3498.

14. Sperling minute 12 January 1920, on Thesiger to Tilley 1 January 1920 and Campbell to Sperling, 31 December 1919, FO 371/3498; Memorandum by Sperling, 27 September 1920, FOCP 11692 (FO 403/451) A6812/5369/1.

15. Memorandum by Sperling, 27 September 1920, FOCP 11692 (FO 403/9453) A6812/5369/1.

16. See inter alia minutes 15 December 1922 on Steel-Maitland to MacNeill, 5 December 1922, FO 371/7148 A 7382/486/1.

17. For discussion of the whole question, see minute by Sperling, 27 February 1923, on parliamentary question, FO 371/8404; minutes on Campbell to Sperling, 31 December 1919, minutes on Thesiger to Tilley, 1 January 1920 and enclosed memorandum, FO 371/3498; Campbell to Sperling, 31 December 1919, Thesiger to Tilley, 1 January 1920 and enclosed memorandum, FOCP 11692 (FO 403/451) 167212; Dodds to Curzon, no. 139 secret, 10 December 1919, ibid. 167815; Dodds to Curzon, no. 101 very confidential, 14 September 1920, ibid. A 7355/5369/1.

18. Dodds to Curzon, no. 125, 2 November 1920, A8236, FO 371/4390.

19. See below, chapter 12.

20. Dodds to Curzon, no. 125, 2 November 1920, FO 371/4390 A 8236.

21. Minute by Sperling, 12 January 1920, on Thesiger to Tilley, 1 January 1920, and Campbell to Sperling, 31 December 1919, FO 371/3498 167212; memorandum by Sperling, 27 September 1920, FOCP 11692 (FO 403/451) A 6812/5369/1. This was in line with a decision not to press for better labor conditions on the Portuguese islands of São Tomé and Principe on the grounds that it would be interfering in the internal conditions of another country. Also the expense of appointing consuls to the Portuguese islands was considered "unjustified."

22. Minute 13 June 1923, FO 371/8404 A 3512. Darley had been an elephant hunter operating in British territory. He maintained that he had had a permit to shoot in 1907, but had moved into Ethiopia. He claimed he did not know his permit had been revoked until 1919, when Athill arrived in Addis Ababa with a warrant for his arrest but also with orders to go to Maji under his care. Darley 1972, 1–2. The Ethiopian government accused Darley of leading armed bands and murdering Ethiopians. He was also described as "a fearless adventurer without too many scruples as to the niceties of international law and a wonderful command over natives," minute on Dodds to Curzon, no. 4, 8 January 1920, FO 371/3498 178186. However, Athill and C. W. Hobley, the Kenya administrator, and other reputable people were to come to his defense. The latter described him as "a gallant Yorkshireman . . . of the blonde Nordic Viking Type to whom adventure is the salt of life" but with a tendency to "fall foul of colonial governments through disregard of local regulations and possibly the inability to assess the difficulties of the situation when international questions are involved." All doubtless true. Darley 1972, xii–xiii.

23. Hawkins to Lockhart, 20 March 1921, FO 371/5501.

24. Hawkins report, 1 February 1923, FOCP 12114 (FO 403/453) A 2187/2187/1.

25. *Westminster Gazette* 18, 19, 20, 25 January 1922.

26. Memorandum by Sperling, 20 July 1923, FO 371/8404.

27. Darley 1926. For his communication to the governor of Uganda, 10 August 1910, see Barber, 112, citing East African Archives 145/09.

28. For further discussion of Darley, see Miers 1998.

29. Sharp to Harris, 8 November 1922, AS MSS Brit.Emp. s.22 G.444/1.

30. ASAPS to Johnston, 20 January 1922, Buxton to Bentinck, 20 January 1922, AS MSS Brit.Emp. s.22 G444/1.

31. See references in memorandum by Sperling, 23 May 1923, FO 371/7148 A 3326/486/1.

32. See for instance *New Statesman*, 21 January 1922.

33. Minute by Dodds, 24 January 1922, FO 371/7147 A 486.486/1.

34. Dodds to Curzon, no. 89, 7 July 1922, FO 371/7148 A 4990/486/1.

35. Dodds to Curzon, no. 114, 5 September 1922, FOCP 12114, (FO 403/453) A 6010/486/1.

36. Question by Lord H. Cavendish Bentinck, 1 March 1922, Hansard.

37. Buxton to Mrs. Haslewood and Harris to Mrs. Haslewood, 23 December 1920, no. 126, AS MSS Brit.Emp. s.22, G 361.

38. Harris to Mrs. Cadbury, 20 December 1920, AS MSS. Brit. Emp. s.19, D3/26.

39. Harris to Darley, 17 January 1922, ASAPS to Johnston, 20 January 1922, Buxton to Bentinck, 20 January 1922, Harris note of conversation with Sharp, 17 January 1922, AS MSS Brit.Emp. s.22 G444.

40. Harris to Moore, 4 April 1922, and Harris to Darley, 25 April 1922, AS MSS Brit.Emp. s.22 G444. The book was eventually published; see Darley 1972, first published in 1926.

41. Hansard, 1 March 1922.

42. Harris to Lugard, 4 and 24 April 1922, Harris to Gilbert Murray 26 April 1922, Johnston to Harris 29 April 1922, AS MSS s. 22, G444; memorandum by Sperling, 23 May 1922, FO 371/7148 A3326/486/1; Balfour to Russell no.79, 6 June 1922, A3428/486/1, ibid.

43. Harris to Nitobe, 9 March 1922, and to Rappard 24 April 1922, and other correspondence and papers in the same volume AS MSS Brit.Emp. s.22 G444.

44. Harris to Lugard 4 April 1922, AS MSS Brit.Emp. s.22 G444.

45. Martin's Ethiopian name was Werqneh Eshete; for further information, see below, chapter 12.

46. ASAPS to Martin, 16 August 1922, and Martin to Buxton, 25 September 1922, AS MSS Brit.Emp. s.22 G444.

47. Harris to Roger Levy, 20 July 1922, Levy to Harris, 4 August 1922, AS MSS Brit.Emp. s.22 G 444/1; Harris to Alcindor, 8 November 1922, AS MSS Brit. Emp. s.22 G444.

48. The report of the capture is in Campbell to Commander-in-Chief Mediterranean Station, 4 July 1922, no. A125/4 in FO 371/7148. The report of their arrival in Addis Ababa and Ras Tafari's letter of 12 August 1922 are enclosed in Dodds to Curzon, no. 104, 26 August 1922, FOCP 12114, FO (403/453). Sadly, I have not been able to follow them further.

49. Harris to Cadbury, 22 November 1922, AS MSS Brit.Emp. s.22 G444/1.

50. Harris to Roberts, 18 and 29 December 1922, AS MSS Brit.Emp. s.22 G444/1. He reported conversations with Rappard, Director of the Mandates Section of the League and with Grimshaw of the International Labor Office (ILO).

51. Harris to Withers Gill, 16 October 1922, and Harris to Cadbury, 22 November 1922, and draft letter undated headed "Slavery in Abyssinia. A Possible Solution," AS MSS Brit.Emp. s.22 G444/1.

52. Harris to Cadbury, 22 November 1922, AS MSS Brit.Emp. s.22 G444/1.

53. Minutes on Steel-Maitland to MacNeil, 5 December 1922, FO 371/7148 A 7382/486/1.

54. Minute by Sperling, 4 December 1922, FO 371/7148 A 7575/486/1.

55. This treaty was signed with Menelik's predecessor, the Emperor Yohannes, in return for a treaty assuring Ethiopia free trade through Massawa, Miers 1975, 114.

56. Minutes by Tufton, Sperling and E. A. C., 30 November 1922, 4 and 6 December 1922, FO 371/7148 A 7575/486/1 (see also W 8530/8041/98 and verbatim minutes of the Assembly, 6 September 1922 W91/91/98); Harris to Lugard, 25 January 1923, AS MSS Brit.Emp. s.22 G444/1.

57. Harris to Roberts, 29 December 1922, AS MSS Brit.Emp. s.22 G 444; Harris to Lugard, 25 January 1923, ASS MSS Brit.Emp. s 22 G444/1.

58. Harris to Sharp, 19 March 1923, AS MSS Brit.Emp. s.22 G 444/1. Thus Hawkins was refused permission to send a letter to *The Times*, minute by Dodds, 27 April 1923, on War Office to FO, 26 April 1923, FO 371/8404 A 2464 and Sperling draft reply to parliamentary question, 10 July 1923, FO 371/8405 A 4215/142/1.

59. Harris to Lugard, 29 January 1923, and to Sharp, 30 January 1923, and 19 March 1923, AS MSS Brit.Emp. s.22 G 444/1.

60. These included its vice-president, the explorer Dr. Georges Montandon, who had travelled in Ethiopia a decade earlier and Dr. Schrenk who had been there in 1921–1922, ASAPS to Simonetti, 26 January 1923, and to Roberts, 9 February 1923, AS MSS Brit.Emp. s.22 G 444/1. A copy of the Swiss publication, *L'eslavage en Ethiopie*, is in FO 371/8406 A 4953/142/1. For further information on the BIDI, see chapter 8, note 5.

61. Harris to Lugard, 2 February 1923, to Cavendish-Bentinck, 19 February 1923, to Sharp, 19 March, to Chapple, 4 April, and various draft questions filed in AS MSS Brit. Emp. s. G 444/1. For the questions actually asked, see Hansard, 4 July, 9 July, 11 July, 19 July, 23 July 1923.

62. *Abyssinia*, no. 1 1923 Cmd 1858, *PP*.

63. Hansard, 31 July 1923.

64. Tyrrell to consuls at Harar, Gardula, Maji, Gore, and Dangela, 1 August 1923, FO 371/8405 A 4567/142/1.

65. Minutes by Curzon, 7 August 1923 on memoranda by Sperling, 20 and 25 July 1923, in FO 371/8404 A 3972/142/1 and on article by Darley in *Outward Bound*, 2 September 1923, FO 371/8406. See also minute by Curzon, 13 September 1923, on Russell to Curzon no. 77, 13 August 1923, ibid. A 5379/142/1.

66. Tishana was the name given by the Amhara rulers of Ethiopia to a conglomeration of local peoples living around Maji.

67. Hodson to Russell, private, 6 June and 26 June 1923, enclosed in Russell to Curzon no. 76, 14 August 1923, FOCP 12390 (FO 403/454) A 5378/2781/1. Walker to Russell no. 12, 11 July 1923, enclosed in Russell to Curzon no.77, 13 August 1923, ibid. A 5379/142/1.

68. Hodson to Russell, private, 6 June and 26 June 1923, enclosed in Russell to Curzon no. 76, 14 August 1923, ibid.; Hodson to Russell, confidential, 26 October 1923, enclosed in Russell to

Curzon no. 120, 23 November 1923, FO 371/8047 A7392; Russell to Curzon no. 91, 29 September 1923, FO 371/8406 A6281/142/1.

69. Russell to Tyrell, 23 May 1923, 4 FO 371/8404 A 3562/142/1.

70. Note on *Westminster Gazette* articles undated, filed in FMAE SDN 939.

71. See FMAE SDN 939, note by Famin on slavery in Ethiopia, 25 March 1922.

72. Sarraut (Ministry of Colonies) to MAE, 25 July 1923, FMAE SDN 939.

73. Eustace, HMS *Fox* at Perim to Poe C. in C. East Indies, 16 December 1906, Admiralty reference S. N. Q. 9/2, FO 371/191.

74. De Monfried recounted his adventures in the Red Sea in many books written between 1931 and 1940; while not strictly accurate, they are based on fact. I am indebted to Mr. Walter Clarke for much information on de Monfreid, who was born in 1879. For a biography, see Grandclément 1990. References to the slave trade are on pp. 236, 253, 267, 278, 284, 287–89, and 302. See also, de Monfreid 1930, Treat 1934.

75. This discussion is based on de Monfried 1930, chapter 8. References to slavers are scattered through this book and another that he published with Ida Treat in 1934; and on the evidence given by the *Al Mosahil* crew and captives in Captain HMS *Cornflower* to C. in C. Mediterranean, no. A125/4, 4 and 5 July 1922, FO 371/7148.

76. See Abir 1968, 53–70; although he is discussing the nineteenth century, there is no reason to think that this was different in the second decade of the twentieth century.

77. Minutes on the Red Sea Slave Trade enclosed in Cromer to Lansdowne no. 2 Africa, 17 May 1902, FO 78/5327; Eustace, commander HMS *Fox*, to Scallon, resident Aden, 31 August 1905, FO 2/948, and Eustace to Poe, C. in C. East Indies, 1 March 1907, FO 371/901.

78. De Coppet to FMAE, 1 October 1922, FMAE SDN 939.

79. FMAE to LaGarde, 7 September 1922, FMAE Papiers d'Agents, LaGarde; aide memoire, 2 November 1922, ibid., 219.

80. De Coppet to FMAE, 1 October 1922, FMAE SDN 939.

81. Undated note on *Westminster Gazette* campaign in FMAE SDN 939.

82. For British fears about the arms trade, see Miers 1997.

83. FMAE to De Coppet, 9 October 1922, and De Coppet to FMAE, 24 November 1922, FMAE SDN 939.

84. Russell to Curzon no. 77, 13 August 1923, FO 403/454 A 5379/142/1.

85. Gout to De Coppet, 5 May 1923, and to Poincaré, 20 July 1923, Poincaré to secretary-general League, 12 June 1923, note for Gout, 14 June 1923, Poincaré to French legation, Addis Ababa, telegram 14 July 1923, FMAE SDN 939.

86. Memorandum by Sperling, 29 August 1932, FO 371/8409 A 5205/5097/1.

87. Russell to Curzon no. 76, 14 August 1923 enclosing Hodson to Russell, 6 June 1923, and minutes of 12, 13, 14 September 1923, FO 371/8409 A 5378/2781/1.

88. Curzon to London for Cecil no. 81 telegram, 17 September 1923, FOCP 12390, (FO 403/454) A 5527/142/1.

89. See inter alia memorandum by Sperling, 29 August 1923, FO 371/ 8409 A 5205/5097/1; memorandum by Sperling on Abyssinia's admission to the League of Nations, 31 December 1923, FOCP 12390 (FO 403/454) A 7678/5097/1; Draft Sperling reply to parliamentary question, 20 July 1923, FO 371/8405 A 4543/142/1.

90. Tufton to Sperling, 11 September 1923, FO 371/8409 A 5485/5097/1. A detailed discussion of the proceedings of the League and the British attempts to prevent Ethiopian admission against the advice of their own delegate, Lord Robert Cecil, is given in a memorandum by Sperling, 31 December 1923, FOCP 12390 (FO 403/454) A7678/5097/1.

91. Tufton to Sperling, 11 September 1923, FO 381/8409.

92. Foreign Office Memorandum on the Arms Traffic in Abyssinia, 20 April 1925, FOCP 12910 (FO 401/18) J 1151/130/1. For the Arms Trade Convention, 10 September 1919, see *PP* Cmd 414 LIII 705 1919.

93. Abyssinian Ministry of Foreign Affairs to Russell, 21 September 1923, enclosed in Russell to Curzon no. 91, 29 September 1923, FOCP 12390 (FO 403/454) A6281/142/1.

94. Minute by Sperling 16 October 1923 on Russell to Curzon no. 89, 22 September 1923, FO 371/8406 A 6047/142/1.

95. This was against the wishes of Foreign Office officials. Minutes on Russell to Curzon, no. 120, 23 November 1923, FO 371/8407 A7392/142/1. Cadogan to Drummond, private and confidential, 3 March 1924, ibid., A 7392/142/1/1423, also in LON MSF S 1669 no. 5. For the discussions on this question in the Foreign Office, see minutes on Russell to Curzon no. 89, 22 September 1923, and on Russell to Parmoor no. 120, 23 November 1923, FO371/2407 A 7392.

7

Slavery in Hijaz

ARABIA AFTER THE FIRST WORLD WAR

The First World War brought dramatic changes to the Middle East.[1] In 1914, the Ottoman Empire came into the conflict on the German side. In 1916, the Arabs of the Hijaz under the Hashemite Sharif of Mecca, Husayn ibn Ali, rose in rebellion. His sons, Faysal and Abdallah joined the British in driving the Turks out of Arabia. At the end of the war, Husayn expected to become the overlord of the whole Arab "nation." Instead, when the victorious allies divided the spoils, he was recognized only as king of the new little kingdom of Hijaz on the Red Sea coast. In 1921, one of his sons, Faysal, was installed by the British as king of Iraq, and another, Abdallah, became emir of Transjordan. Instead of being independent states, these became League of Nations mandates under British control, while the rich provinces of Syria and Lebanon became French mandates. The Arabs, and many British, saw this as a betrayal of wartime promises made to them as allies. To add to Husayn's bitterness, Palestine west of the Jordan was declared a Jewish homeland and opened by the British to large-scale Jewish immigration in the face of intense Arab opposition.

Thus, in Hijaz, the relatively pliant and weak Turks were now replaced by an embittered ruler, whose position depended on the veneration he could command as a descendant of the Prophet, and guardian of the Holy Places. Any attack on a Muslim institution, even if he could be induced to mount one, would have undermined his standing, particularly as, in 1924, he assumed the title of caliph, or head of the Islamic world, in succession to the sultan of the defunct Ottoman Empire.

To the south of Hijaz, Husayn also claimed Asir. The British had helped the Idrisi Sayyids of Asir to drive out the Turks, and acquire the port of al-Hudaydah, which was claimed by Yemen, also now independent under its Zaydi imam, Yahya. Thus, the whole eastern shore of the Red Sea was now under Arab rulers, most of whom had grievances against the British.

In east and central Arabia, the dynamic Abd al Aziz ibn Saud had been building up his power since 1902. His success was due to his fighting force of militant Islamic fundamentalists, the Wahhabi *Ikhwan*. Like Husayn, he could not afford to interfere with institutions recognized by Islam. However, he had good reason to seek British support. He had expelled the Turks from al-Hasa in 1913, giving him a footing on the western shores of the Persian Gulf, where the small shayhkdoms of Bahrain, Kuwait, Qatar, and the Trucial States of Dubai, Abu Dhabi, Sharjah, Ajman, Fujairah, Ras al Khaimah, and Umm al-Qaiwan were theoretically independent, but Britain controlled their foreign relations.[2] During the war, the British had recognized Ibn Saud as independent and paid him a subsidy. When hostilities ended, his need for their support prevented him from attacking Hijaz in 1919. The following year, however, he eliminated a rival dynasty and was proclaimed sultan of Nagd. Thereafter he waited his chance to attack Husayn, his remaining rival for control of most of Arabia.

The British did not anticipate any recrudescence of the Red Sea slave trade when they abrogated the Brussels Act, although the trade was reported to be "rife" in Hijaz in 1917.[3] It soon became clear, however, that the successor states of the Ottoman Empire did not consider themselves bound by Turkish treaties. This threw to the winds Britain's treaty network with its rights to search on the high seas and in territorial waters, and to arrest and try slavers, which had been confirmed by the Brussels Act. It also opened to question its long-established practice of asking the Turks to free slaves illegally imported, or who took refuge at British consulates or on British warships—a practice known as consular manumission. These problems came to the fore from December 1921, as reports arrived of a brisk traffic in slaves to the new kingdom of Hijaz.[4]

SLAVERY IN HIJAZ IN THE EARLY 1920s

Hijaz was a poor and barren land, much of it desert, without permanent rivers or good harbors.[5] Its population of less than three quarters of a million consisted mainly of Bedouin pastoralists. In the mountain valleys and desert oases farmers produced dates, fruit, and other crops. The townsmen were sophisticated and cosmopolitan, but they numbered less than one hundred thousand. There was almost no industry. King Husayn jealously guarded the right to import cars, motor launches, airplanes, and steamers and discouraged technological development. The railway between Medina and Damascus, sabotaged during the war, lay in ruins. Transport was mainly by camel or donkey. Imports far exceeded the value of exports. The country's prosperity depended on its unique asset—the Hajj—the pilgrimage to Mecca, which it was the duty of every Muslim to make at least once in a lifetime, and the optional pilgrimage to Medina. The ceremonies took only a few days, but the faithful often came months before and stayed on afterwards, sometimes for years. This influx of people from all over the Muslim world was the main source of income—an annual "rain of gold" benefiting all sections of the urban population. Landlords, food producers, traders, water carriers, and the pastoralists, who supplied camels, donkeys, and guides, all at inflated prices, while the government levied taxes on the possessions—even the clothes—of the pilgrims.[6]

Wage labor was rare and slaves provided much of the labor force. Most were domestic servants, but some were craftsmen, seamen, pearl divers, fishermen, agricultural laborers, herdsmen, camel drivers, water carriers, porters, washerwomen, cooks, and shop assistants.[7] The most fortunate men were the armed retainers and officials of emirs, and the business managers of merchants. The most attractive women became concubines of the elite. The most expensive and privileged, because of their rarity, were eunuchs.[8] Since they could not have families of their own, they were valued for their loyalty and many held responsible positions, looking after their owners' property or businesses, or serving as officials with authority over free people. Some owned their own slaves. Privileged ones served in the harems around the Kaba in Mecca, and the tomb of the Prophet in Medina.

The numbers of slaves in Hijaz can only be guessed. In 1930, they were said to make up 10 percent of the population of Mecca, the largest town. They were also widely used in the countryside. Owners ranged from the rulers to poor shepherds and fishermen. Some hired their slaves out to work and lived on their earnings. Poor men found it cheaper to buy a slave woman than to pay the dowry for a free wife. A rich man, limited to four wives at one time by Muslim law, could build up his household by buying concubines, who bore him free children. In the desert, where a man's power, security, and prestige depended on the number of his followers and dependents, slave retainers were particularly valuable since they had no outside loyalties.

The Hijazi regarded slaves as the most profitable and desirable investment. They were self-supporting and completely under their owner's control. They could be sold, bequeathed, used as gifts, or to pay tribute or dowry. Other than eunuchs, who were rare in the 1920s, the most prized, because they were so few, were Chinese or "Javanese" girls, who might fetch £500 if they were Christian and educated, while "red" (non-Negroid) Ethiopian girls cost at most £100 if they were trained in household duties.[9] Prices varied over time.

The British believed that there was no social stigma attached to slavery and that slaves in Hijaz were often better off than the free poor. Islam bade owners treat them well and, although the lot of the slave of a desert Bedouin "working all hours as herdsman, camel driver or porter, inadequately fed, and clothed in rags," might be unenviable, it was no different from that of his owner—all shared the bare necessities of life. The slaves of the poor were often treated as members of the family, while those of the rich might live comfortable lives and have considerable social mobility. One must avoid, however, painting too rosy a picture, for, as will be seen, there was always a small minority anxious to gain their freedom, usually because, in contravention of Muslim law, they had been illtreated, or feared they were about to be sold, or because they wanted to return to their homeland. The British belief that Muslim slavery was "benign" and that most slaves were content was based on the fact that few sought manumission through the consulate even when they had the chance. Further research, however, is needed to recover the voice of the slaves themselves, and new research elsewhere is tending to modify the belief that there was no social stigma attached to slaves in Muslim societies.[10]

Manumission reinforced slavery by providing the slave with an incentive for loyal service. Freeing slaves was a meritorious act and dying owners often freed them. Sometimes heirs refused to recognize such manumissions, or an owner might free a slave but not provide the necessary certificate, or he might free one too old to work, saving his pocket as well as his soul. Devout pilgrims sometimes ransomed a slave as an act of charity, but when they left, the same slave was sometimes offered to others. Many slaves, however, were genuinely freed, while many gained their freedom through the normal working of Muslim law, under which, for instance, the children of concubines were usually free, and a man had to free a woman if he married her.[11] This produced a steady attrition in the numbers of slaves and kept up the demand.

The Hajj was the high point in the demand for slaves—the time when prices peaked, for the Hijaz was the market for the Muslim world. Pilgrims came from places as far apart as China and Morocco, South Africa and Senegal. In 1923 more than twenty-four thousand Indians and thirty thousand Malays came, as well as Persians, Iraqis, Egyptians, Syrians, and Africans from all over the continent—over one hundred thousand in all. They might pay for their journey by selling off a woman or child on the way or in the Hijaz itself, or they might buy a slave to take home. Although the European powers tried to police the pilgrimage, it remained a fertile source of supply. Whole families traveled overland, sometimes taking years on the way, crossing the Red Sea in small craft embarking from out-of-the-way places. It was almost impossible to prevent them from acquiring or selling slaves on their travels. Dealers coming to or leaving Mecca could pass the children off as their own offspring and claim that the adults were their wives or servants.

Some slaves were victims of trickery.[12] Indonesian children, for instance, might be entrusted to a guardian to take them to Mecca for religious instruction but be sold on arrival. A stranger might settle for a while in Africa and marry four wives, and then announce, to the delight of their families, that he was taking them on the pilgrimage.[13] When some did not return, he could claim they had died, or, more likely, he would settle elsewhere and start again. Some unfortunates sold themselves or their relatives when they were widowed, or rendered destitute by the depredations of the Hijazi. Whole parties of pilgrims were sometimes seized by Bedouin marauders. The Turks had tried to prevent this by paying a subsidy to the Bedouin but King Husayn discontinued this, and poverty often drove them to banditry.[14] Thus, the Hajj offered endless opportunities to enslave the helpless or the unwary, and an incomparable market for their disposal.

Apart from the pilgrimage, dealers also imported slaves, mostly Africans from nearby Ethiopia or the Sudan, but some came from as far away as West Africa. Some were captured in raids. Children were kidnapped, or were sold by their parents in hard times. Small numbers came from Baluchistan, India, Indonesia, Malaya, and even China. Arabs were imported overland from Yemen and doubtless from other parts of Arabia, but little is known of this traffic.

BRITAIN AND THE HIJAZI SLAVE TRADE

The whole question came forcibly to British attention in December 1921, when the captain of HMS *Cornflower* heard from his interpreter that slaves had landed in Jiddah, while his ship was actually in the harbor. In January 1922, just as the storm broke in the press over slaving in Ethiopia, the vice-consul in Jiddah confirmed that Ethiopian slaves were being shipped from Obock and Assab to Maidi in Asir, where it was later reported that the Idrisi government levied a tax of MT$15 a head. The victims were then transported by small *sambuks* to Jiddah, disguised as free passengers. At Jiddah, the local authorities had confiscated some of them but only to sell them themselves for £35 a head, giving the dealers 25 percent. In April, the consul reported that two to three hundred had arrived from Tajura during the previous three weeks and more were expected. Most were aged between seven and fifteen. Police sometimes shepherded them from the city gates to the houses of the brokers, watched by curious spectators. Demand was keen and prices high. There was no public market but private dealing was brisk. The government, far from stopping the traffic, was taking 15 percent of the slaves and charging a heavy sales tax on the remainder. There had been no patrol in the Red Sea for some time and this had apparently encouraged the slavers, who had accumulated large stocks at Maidi.[15]

The British governor of the Red Sea Province of the Anglo-Egyptian Sudan complained that Sudanese slaves on pilgrimage with their owners were also being sold in Hijaz. He could not take action as the dealers did not reside in Sudan and the crime was not committed there. Both he and the commander in chief of the Royal Navy's Mediterranean squadron pressed the Foreign Office to protest to King Husayn.[16] But the king saw nothing wrong in slavery. The British did not want to alienate him, as they hoped he would agree to a treaty recognizing their mandates over Iraq and Transjordan. Tactful protests, however, merely elicited the reply that slavery was recognized by the Qur'an, the trade was legal and, since the British had command of the sea, it was up to them to prevent slaves leaving Africa.[17]

Now that Hijaz was an independent state, the British had no legal rights to search its ships on the high seas or any shipping in its territorial waters, but the navy insisted that searches were essential if the traffic was to be stopped. As a compromise, the Red Sea patrol was ordered to search suspicious dhows everywhere, but not to arrest them in Hijazi territorial waters unless the officer was sure that a conviction could be obtained. This exceeded British legal rights and placed naval officers in a dilemma, since it was difficult to detect slaves hidden among legitimate passengers, particularly during the busy pilgrimage season.[18] The capture, in Hijazi waters, by HMS *Cornflower*, of the *Al Mosahil* with its cargo of Ethiopian slaves drew attention to the dimensions of the traffic and the loopholes in the treaties. The commander of the *Cornflower* on hearing that over two hundred slaves were awaiting shipment at Maidi, had "swept" the coast, but had caught only this dhow. He had interviewed the authorities at Al Qunfudhah, Birk, Jizan, and Maidi—all of whom had denied any knowledge of the trade, although he had heard it was in full swing. Treaties to search in territorial waters were needed not just with Hijaz, but also with Asir and Yemen. Moreover, the navy required six light craft to do the actual patrolling, and cooperation with France and Italy was essential.[19] As it was, the one or even two British ships in the Red Sea, whose movements were clearly visible for many miles, could do little. The Admiralty decided the increase in the traffic did not warrant sending another ship.[20] However, after the capture of the *Al Mosahil*, slavers temporarily brought their slaves from Maidi overland rather than by sea.

The trial of the *Al Mosahil* slavers in the Prize Court in Aden raised the old problem of extraterritoriality. They could not be punished in British courts because neither the dhow and crew, nor the traders, were British subjects, and the offense had not been committed in British waters. Fortunately, the traders were French subjects. They were sent to Jibuti, where the main offender was sentenced to ten years in prison and a fine of 3,000 francs. His twelve-year-old nephew was released and his slave assistant was imprisoned for a month and fined 200 francs.[21] The dhow's crew, however, were from Asir. They were sent there, and the Idrisi ruler was asked to punish them. Since he had been making money on the traffic, it was a surprise when he complied. He also prohibited slave landings, refused to allow slave dhows to take on provisions, and threatened to confiscate the property of his subjects who imported slaves. This drove slavers to land their cargoes at small ports in Hijazi territory just north of his frontier, where King Husayn's officials could warn them by radio of the approach of a British patrol.[22] Slavers also began using dugout canoes with sails, or smaller dhows, which hugged the coast and sailed at night.[23]

So the traffic continued, with hundreds of victims reported shipped to Arabia. Good intelligence work, for which the British paid informers, led to the arrest of a few slavers when they attempted to return home to Jibuti via the British colony of Aden. The French imprisoned them. International cooperation was essential, as the following case will demonstrate. A French Somali embarked from the Italian port of Assab, but sent his twelve-year-old son with a cargo of thirty slaves from Tajura in French Somaliland to Hijaz, on a dhow owned by a Yemeni but captained by an Italian subject from Eritrea. The matter only came to light because the captain quarreled with the trader and reported the case to the Italian consul in Jiddah. He informed the British, who arrested the slavers in Aden. Such a breakthrough was rare even when the three powers cooperated.

The governor of French Somaliland estimated that it would take two companies of *tirailleurs* to suppress the traffic through the colony, and this was too much for his budget, but he set up a "*poste de garde indigène*" at Khor Anghar. To patrol French territorial waters, he had to make do with a launch (*vedette automobile*) armed with a machine gun, which was no match for an armed dhow. In 1923, however, because of the outcry over the traffic, the French increased the colony's budget by 50,000 francs, and sent the *Diana* to patrol the Red Sea in cooperation with British and Italian ships, and ordered the governor to police the caravan routes.[24] In 1925, however, the colony still had no troops and too few police to do the job, and communications were so erratic that even if a local ruler informed the governor that slaves were awaiting shipment, the news usually arrived in Jibuti too late to intercept them.[25]

Early in 1924, the British consul in Jiddah, R. W. Bullard, reported that a "sudden boom" in imports had reduced the price of young women from £65–70 a head to £30–35. Slavers were growing bolder. Most now shipped their cargoes from the Italian coast near Massawa, touched at the Farasan Islands, and then sailed straight into Jiddah, where the Hijazi government was still openly taxing the traffic.[26] The French and Italian navies were cooperating with the British, patrolling their coasts and coordinating their efforts by radio, and holding conferences, but neither France nor Italy had sent vessels fast enough to overhaul dhows. What was needed was constant patrolling by small fast craft supported by a good intelligence service on land. As it was, the British blamed the Italians and French, and they blamed each other for not stopping the traffic from their African coasts.[27] Naval cooperation, although achieved for a while, was hampered by mutual suspicion. The Italians tried to make their cooperation conditional on the British agreeing that they might participate in patrols along the Arabian coast. The British refused, fearing the Italians wanted to build up their navy in the Red Sea and establish a submarine base in the area.[28] As in the past, the suppression of the slave trade was secondary to national interests.

As for the British, they came up with what was primarily a publicity stunt. They sent four destroyers to reinforce the Red Sea patrol for a few weeks in the summer of 1924, not because they believed it would end the slave trade, but for its "moral and political effect." This cost some £10,000 for extra fuel and £1,320 in Suez Canal dues, but the government believed it would put them in a stronger position to press France and Italy to act on land. Moreover, it would show the League of Nations that Britain was "in earnest" about suppressing the traffic and might disarm criticism from "inquisitive M.P.s like Mr. Harris" of the Anti-Slavery Society.[29] The ships sailed in secret but their arrival was announced in a press release designed to catch public attention.

The Foreign Office also invited the three other powers with consuls in Jiddah—the French, Italian, and Dutch—to join them in a protest to the king,[30] but got little cooperation.[31] Husayn denied that he was taxing slave imports.[32] Bullard also made the embarrassing discovery that British Indians were freely buying, selling, and keeping slaves, apparently unaware that it was illegal under British law. He advised them to free them and warned them they could be prosecuted if they returned to India. He could do no more as they had not broken Hijazi law, but he dismissed the consulate dispenser for buying and selling a girl.[33]

CONSULAR MANUMISSION

The increase in the slave trade brought to the fore the problem of consular manumission. Slaves manumitted at the request of British consuls were of two kinds: persons from British or other colonial possessions who had been imported by dealers or sold once they arrived in the country; and slaves who took refuge at a British consulate or on a British ship and asked to be freed, often claiming ill-treatment. The numbers were small, but consular manumission ultimately threatened the institution of slavery by presenting an avenue of escape. The Hijazi had bitterly opposed it almost from the day the British had appointed a consul in Jiddah in the 1870s, but the British public and the Anti-Slavery Society were adamantly opposed to the return of fugitives.[34] In the 1880s, when numbers were small, the Turks had manumitted slaves at the request of the consuls,[35] and consuls had behaved with restraint, trying to reconcile the fugitives with their owners, or arranging for them to change masters.[36]

Once the Brussels Act came into force in 1892, the Turks, in common with other signatories, were bound to free and repatriate any slaves illegally brought into the Ottoman Empire. This gave the consuls of all the signatory powers the right to claim and send home, or require the manumission of their nationals imported since 1889, when the slave trade had been outlawed. The grounds for interference were even stronger after 1908, when the status of slavery ceased to exist under a new Ottoman constitution. Although the laws against the slave trade were never seriously enforced in Hijaz, numbers of slaves were freed at the instance of the British and French consuls before the First World War. At one point when thirty or forty a month were being manumitted, feeling ran so high that the Turks warned the British consul they could not be responsible for his safety.[37]

During the war, consular manumission fell into disuse and now King Husayn vehemently opposed it. During his reign, slaves were rarely able to get their complaints heard by the authorities or catch the attention of the consuls, let alone reach a consulate. Occasionally he freed a slave, but usually this was if the traders were nationals of European possessions, thus proving his contention that the colonial powers were to blame for the increase in the traffic by allowing slavers to cross the Red Sea. Occasionally he also freed slaves who could prove that they were Muslims, and had therefore been enslaved illegally according to Islamic law. Such proof was rare. In August 1924, the Dutch consul, with great difficulty, secured the release of some Javanese children, whose parents had entrusted them to supposedly reputable people to take them to Mecca for "religious instruction" or to visit relatives elsewhere in the Dutch East Indies. These cases had only come to light by chance. In one instance, the buyer boasted that he had Christian girls as concubines. In another, the girl's brother came on the pilgrimage and found her. They had to be carefully handled to prevent the children from "disappearing" before they could be freed. The king, professing to be horrified, released some of them, but allowed them to be re-enslaved when the Netherlands vice-consul went on leave. Small wonder that Bullard decided that as long as Husayn reigned, consular manumission in the Hijaz was worthless.[38]

When a woman and her child, newly arrived from the Anglo-Egyptian Sudan, took refuge in the British consulate after being sold in Jiddah by a man from the French Soudan, the *kaimakam* (governor) maintained that the sale was legal as they were slaves of the seller. The consuls protested that all persons under British and French protection were free. Bullard himself escorted the woman on board a ship bound for the Sudan, after an acrimonious correspondence with the authorities.[39] The representatives of Britain, France, Holland, and Italy were on the point of making joint representations to the Hijaz about the freeing of their nationals when Ibn Saud invaded the Hijaz. Husayn abdicated in September 1924 in favor of his son Ali, who was soon beseiged in Jiddah—the beleaguered ruler of the bankrupt rump of the kingdom.

Because of the war, only one ship was available for the Red Sea patrol. The others had to remain in Jiddah to protect British subjects. By early 1925, the ruler of Asir had stopped preventing slave landings at Maidi and was again taxing imports.[40] Thus six months after the flight of King Husayn, the slave trade was as active as ever and the British consulate was faced with a flood of fugitives demanding manumission. A few Ethiopians went to the Italian consul, but he and the French consul distanced themselves from the proceedings.[41] Bullard decided to harbor only two or three of these refugees in the consulate at a time, and then only when he could put them aboard steamers bound for the Sudan. He warned them on arrival that, if freed, they would have to stay in Jiddah and risk re-enslavement until he could embark them.[42] He then told those unwilling to take the risk to sneak back home and return only in time for the next boat. Having sent their names privately to the Hijazi foreign secretary to ensure they were not criminals evading justice, he shipped them out when he could. Some were mere children. There were five Ethiopian boys between nine and eighteen, for instance, and one little eleven-year-old who came by himself.[43] But most were Sudanese and Takruri (West and Central African) men. To his regret, Bullard had nowhere to house women while he investigated their stories—a necessity as wives sometimes tried to escape by posing as slaves. Occasionally, however, he managed to slip a woman onto a boat at the last minute.[44]

Another reason he rationed the number of slaves repatriated was that he had to pay their fares and quarantine fees. The Anglo-Egyptian Sudan paid for its nationals, but for West Africans Bullard was reduced to milking the Nigerian Repatriation Fund, founded to help destitute pilgrims.[45] As for Ethiopians, he had not the money to pay their fares to Massawa, but some were given free passage by the Italians.[46] By these means, Bullard had shipped out forty slaves by June 1925.

In August, when twenty slaves had been repatriated in a month, and nine more were in the consulate, the foreign minister of Hijaz begged Bullard to stop harboring fugitives. Resentment was rising in Jiddah, the town was besieged, and owners were in-creasingly fearful of losing the capital they had invested in slaves. The king pleaded that his subjects were at breaking point.[47] Desperate owners took to charging fugitives with theft and demanding that they be tried in the Shari'a Court. They were searched on arrival at the consulate and evidence of theft was rare. The consul believed the court was corrupt and worried that the fugitives, if convicted, would suffer amputa-tion. He, therefore, claimed the right to try them under the capitulations, which the British maintained had not lapsed with the end of Ottoman rule. King Ali promised that if the consul would stop receiving fugitives, he would end slavery when the war was over. However, Foreign Secretary Austen Chamberlain, fearing a public outcry in Britain, refused to sanction any such deal and the exodus of fugitives continued.[48]

Thus in 1926, when King Ali fled and Ibn Saud's forces marched into Jiddah, the prac-tice of consular manumission was in full swing. Ibn Saud, now ruler of the combined kingdom of Hijaz and Nagd, proceeded to establish a protectorate over Asir, uniting much of the Arabian peninsular under his rule. The British were now faced with an able, strong, and determined ruler in place of the weak Hashemites. By this time, however, the slavery question had been well and truly placed on the agenda of the League of Nations.

NOTES

1. See inter alia Baker 1979, Busch 1971, Gavin 1975, Muhammad Al-Amr 1978, Goldberg 1986, Holden and Johns 1981, Fromkin 1989.

2. See below chapters 11, 13, 16, and 20 for their relations with Britain.

3. Consul Jiddah to governor Red Sea Province (Sudan) no. 64 M (206), 14 January 1922 quoting letter of December 1917 to inspector at Suakin, FO 686/103, 388.

4. Commander HMS *Cornflower* to governor Red Sea Province and British consul, Jiddah, 5 December 1921, FO 686/103.

5. See report by Graffity-Smith on the Economic and Financial Condition of the Hijaz, secret, enclosed in Bullard to Curzon no. 12, 31 October 1923, FOCP 12518 (FO 406/52); Baker 1979.

6. Graffity-Smith to Curzon no. 14, secret, 28 February 1922, enclosed in Jeddah Report 11–28 February 1922, FOCP 12068 (FO 406/49) E2959/656/91.

7. The description of slavery in Hijaz is based on the following documents: Note on Slavery in the Hedjaz [sic] with Suggestions for Checking it, enclosed in Bullard to Chamberlain no. 54, 9 June 1925, FO 371/10617 E3679/1780/91 (henceforth Note on Slavery); Memorandum on Slavery and the Slave Traffic in the Kingdom of the Hejaz [sic] and Nejd [Nagd] and its

Dependencies, enclosed in Bond to Henderson no. 60, 6 March 1930, FOCP 13886 E1541/1054/91; Memorandum on Slavery in Saudi Arabia, enclosed in Ryan to Simon no. 149, 15 March 1934, FOCP 14573 E3764/722/25. For more detailed references, see Miers 1989.

8. Since mutilation was against the tenets of Islam, most were imported from the fringes of the Muslim world, many from Ethiopia, where de Monfreid was told they were castrated at their parents' request in their own villages by "sorcerers" skilled in producing anesthetics and poultices from local plants. The crude operation varied from removal of the testicles to complete severance of all genital organs, de Monfreid 1930, 115–16. De Monfreid's informants estimated that 60 percent died, either from hemorrhage or bladder infections. Prices fluctuated with supply and demand. Prices in the Hijaz in 1906 were around MT$400 for eunuchs, whereas girls fetched only MT$300, and uncastrated boys some MT$250, senior naval officer, Aden to C. in C. East Indies, 16 December 1906, FO 371/191. The traffic was active in the first decade of the twentieth century, commander HMS *Fox* to political resident Aden, confidential, 31 August 1905, FO 2/948. I have not found information on this trade for the 1920s in British archives, but journalists reported it as late as the 1950s.

9. Marshall to Commander HMS *Cornflower* no. 1520 M (206), 399, 13 December 1921, FO 686/103; A Note on Slavery in the Hijaz; sub-enclosure to memorandum by Onraet, 20 October 1924, FO 686/104; Bullard to MacDonald no. 78, 7 August 1924, FO 371/10011 E7495/1841/91.

10. See Chouki El Hamel 2001, for a discussion of this in Morocco. For pioneer studies on the "slave voice" in Arabia, see Hutson 2002; Miers forthcoming (b).

11. Muslim law varied with the different sects of Islam.

12. For concrete examples of such trickery, see Note on Slavery.

13. I was told of this sort of deceit in Burundi in 1961.

14. Report by Graffity-Smith on the Economic and Financial Condition of the Hijaz, enclosed in Bullard to Curzon, no. 12, 31 October 1923, FOCP 12518 (FO 406/52).

15. Commander HMS *Cornflower* to governor Red Sea Province and consul Jiddah, A.59.6, 5 December 1921; vice-consul Jiddah to commander HMS *Cornflower* no. 1520 M (206), 13 December 1921, and no. 48 M 92060, confidential, 10 January 1922, and to senior naval officer Red Sea Patrol, confidential, no. 395 M (206), 5 April 1922, FO 686/103, pp. 381–400; Graffity-Smith to Curzon, no. 7 secret, 20 January 1922, E 1378/656/91, and no. 23 secret, 31 March 1922, E4085/656/91 FOCP 12068 (FO 406/49). Barrett to colonial secretary no. 115, confidential, 27 July 1922, FO 371/7723.

16. Governor Red Sea Province to consul Jiddah 133, 28 December 1921, FO 686/103; C. in C. Mediterranean to Admiralty no. 358/250/152, 9 February 1922, enclosed in Admiralty to Foreign Office, confidential, M 0220/22, 28 April 1922, FO 371/7723 E 4453/4453/91.

17. Marshall to King Husayn, 29 June 1922, and Fuad-el-Khatib to Marshall, 1 July 1922, enclosures 1 and 2 in Bullard to MacDonald no. 27, 19 March 1924, FOCP 12604 (FO 406/53).

18. SNO RS patrol to C. in C. Mediterranean, no. M/15, 29 April 1922, C. in C. to SNO RS patrol no. 250/152, 12 June 1922, SNO RS patrol report, 21 April 1922, enclosed in Admiralty to FO M 0808/22, 14 July 1922, FO minutes 18, 19, 25 July 1922, FO to Admiralty, 1 August 1922, FO 371/7723 E 7045/4453/91.

19. Report of commander HMS *Cornflower* 31 July to 5 August 1922, enclosed in Admiralty to FO M42516/22, 18 September 1922, FO 371/7148 A 5897/486/1.

20. Admiralty to FO M 42516/22, 18 September 1922, and minute by Snow, 28 September 1922, FO 371/7148 A 5897/486/1.

21. Governor Aden to CO, no. 159, 18 October 1922, enclosed in CO to FO no. 54157/22, 6 November 1922, FO 371/7723 E 12174/4453/91.

22. Barrett to CO no. 115, confidential, 27 July 1922, enclosed in CO to FO no. 38807/22, 18 August 1922, E 8227/4453/91, and CO to FO no. 51720/22, 21 October 1922, E 11454/4453/91, FO 371/7723, Marshall to Curzon no. 92, secret, 31 December 1922, FOCP 12283 (406/51) E 653/653/91; Fazluddin to first resident Aden, 6 and 14 December 1922, FO 686/103, 297–301.

23. Fazluddin to first resident Aden, 6 December 1922, FO 686/103, 297 ff.

24. Minister of colonies to MAE no. 148, 19 November 1923, FMAE SDN 939 folder esclavage.

25. Report of commander of *Diana* no. 6, enclosed in MAE to SF SDN no. 110, 6 March 1924, FMAE SDN 939 folder esclavage 1924; extract from the report of proceedings of HMS *Clematis* for the period ending 7 June 1925, FO371/10812. Thus, the British gave the French the names of dealers in vain.

26. Bullard to MacDonald no. 9, secret, 29 January 1924, FOCP 12604 (FO406/53).

27. Graham to MacDonald no. 231, 11 March 1924, and minutes, A 1803/1023/52; reports from HMS *Clematis* no. 124/58 A 18 March 1924 and no. 114/28 28 March 1924 enclosed in Admiralty to FO no. M.1788/24, 9 May 1924, A 2896/1023/52, FO 371/9533.

28. Bullard to MacDonald no. 91, 20 August 1924, and minute by Spring-Rice, 13 September 1924, FO 371/10012 E 7532/1841/91.

29. Admiralty to FO, no. M.0395, urgent, 9 April 1924 enclosing C. in C. Mediterranean to Admiralty, telegram 6 April 1924, with FO minutes, A 2253/1023/52; minutes on Admiralty to FO M.0675, 1 May 1924, A2703/1023/52, minutes and draft press release FO 371/9533.

30. FO to Bullard no. 112, 11 June 1924, FO 371/10011 E 4324/1841/91.

31. The French decided to hold their protest until their consul returned from leave. The Italian consul received no instructions. Only the Dutch consul was ordered to support the general British protest, but the issue became merged with the delicate one of consular manumission.

32. Bullard to MacDonald no. 69, 30 June 1924, with enclosure and minutes, FO 371/10011 E 6471/1841/91.

33. Bullard to MacDonald no. 50, 21 May 1924, and no. 51, 21 May 1924, FO 371/10011 FOCP 12604 (FO 406/53) E 5067/1841/91 and E 5068/1841/91.

34. For the history of this question outside the Hijaz, see Miers 1975, 163–64, and for a study of it in the Hijaz and Saudi Arabia, see Miers 1989.

35. Only thirty-five were freed between 1881 and 1883, the only years for which numbers are available.

36. Ochsenwald 1980, 121–22.

37. Note on Slavery.

38. Bullard to MacDonald no. 78, 7 August 1924, E 7495/1841/91, and no. 88, 18 August 1924, E 7716/1841/91, FO 371/10012; Note on Slavery.

39. Bullard to MacDonald no. 78, 7 August 1924, E 7495/1841/91, and no. 87, 18 August 1924, E 7715/1841/91, FO 371/10012.

40. Political resident Aden to CO, secret no. 24, 4 March 1925, and no. 40, 1 April 1925, and no. 147, 28 October 1925, FO 371/10812; commander HMS Clematis to C. in C. Mediterranean, no. 114/45, 25 March 1925, enclosed in Admiralty to FO, confidential, M.1721/25, 6 May 1925, E 2865/13/91, ibid.

41. Jordan to Chamberlain, no. 81 (206), 26 August 1925, FO 686/104, FOCP 13028, (FO 406/56), E 5534/1780/91.

42. Those who were freed and remained in Jiddah were employed as servants in private families under government supervision.

43. Bullard to Fuad El-Khatib, private, 30 May and 16 July 1925, FO 686/104.

44. Note by Bullard, 16 July 1925, FO 686/104.

45. This fund was created from donations from rich pilgrims and from the property of British subjects who died intestate in the Hijaz.

46. Howard to Bullard, 7 January 1925, 225, and note by Bullard, 16 July 1925, FO 686/104.

47. Jordan to Fuad El-Khatib, 15 August 1925, and Fuad El-Khatib to Jordan, very urgent and private, 16 August 1925, FO 686/104; Jordan to Chamberlain no. 81 (206), 26 August 1925, FO 686/104, FOCP 13028 (FO 406/56) E 5534/1780/91.

48. Jordan to Chamberlain no. 81 (206), 26 August 1925, FO 686/104, FOCP 13028 (FO 406/56) E 5534/1780/91; Jordan to Fuad, 15 August 1925, FO 686/104, Jordan to FO telegram no. 127, 20 August 1925, FO to Jordan telegram no. 56, 25 August 1925, FOCP 13038 (FO 406/56), FO 686/104.

The Temporary Slavery Commission and the Expanding Definition of Slavery

THE LEAGUE OF NATIONS CALLS FOR INFORMATION ON SLAVERY

In 1922 and 1923, when the League asked all governments for information on slavery, officials expected there would also be a flood of petitions from nongovernmental organizations. The prospect raised two crucial questions. First, should the League accept information from unofficial sources? Secondly, what information should it circulate to members, or publish? The colonial powers could not prevent NGOs from sending in information, but they insisted that only evidence from governments could be circulated.[1] The Anti-Slavery Society tried to circumvent this by asking the Foreign Office to forward a petition to the League, with a disclaimer stating that it was not an official document— a solution suggested privately to Harris by the head of the League Mandates Section.[2] The Foreign Office refused, saying that it contained misleading information, which they would seem to be endorsing.[3] This highlighted the problem constantly facing NGOs— the difficulty of getting reliable information without official help.

In this case, the petition was a scrappy document based on scanty publications and official replies to parliamentary questions. What it lacked in substance, however, was compensated for by the illustriousness of its signatories. They included ten peers, fifty-five politicians from all parties,[4] four bishops, six mayors and lord mayors, the editors of the *Manchester Guardian* and *Spectator*, and such well-known figures as Sir Harry Johnston, E. D. Morel, and George Bernard Shaw. The antislavery cause clearly still had wide appeal across the social and political spectrum.

The only other petition to reach the League in 1923 came from the Geneva-based Bureau International pour la Défense des Indigènes (International Bureau for the Defense of Native Races) known as the BIDI.[5] It denounced slave trading in Arabia, slavery in Ethiopia, Sudan, Tanganyika, and the French colonies, and condemned South African labor laws, forced labor in Mozambique, and peonage in Latin America. Unlike the British government, the Swiss forwarded this document to the League.[6]

Both these NGOs wanted a permanent office established in Geneva to deal with slavery, like one recently formed to combat trafficking in women and children. The colonial powers were afraid that it might monitor their policies. However, governments were slow to send information and when, in September 1923, there was still not enough to form the basis of a report, the Assembly decided to appoint a "competent body" to pursue the inquiry. The cheapest solution would have been to turn the question over to the Permanent Mandates Commission, but it had already alarmed the colonial powers by criticizing their policies. If they had to have a committee, France, Belgium, and Britain wanted to control it.

The Council circulated a questionnaire in December 1923 to all countries in which slavery had existed, asking them what measures they had taken to eradicate it, what the effects had been, and whether they contemplated further action. They were also asked to name individuals or organizations who might provide reliable additional information. Governments now had either to launch an investigation into slavery, to admit ignorance, or to send in partial answers. Some thirty-five states, mostly European and American, replied that there had never been any slavery in their territories or that it no longer existed.[7] Some states did not reply. Some sent detailed answers. Others were curt, or untruthful. Some colonial officials misled their governments. Thus, the Anglo-Egyptian Sudan replied that it had disbanded its Slavery Repression Department because the slave trade was so minimal that it was no longer needed. The British high commissioner reported that there was no slavery in Bechuanaland, and the government of Hong Kong sent no reply for the same reason. In both cases, as will be shown, this turned on the definition of slavery. The resident in Aden admitted that slavery existed in the Protectorate but claimed that slaves were better off than the free poor and would resent liberation. The British Government of India acknowledged that slavery continued in remote areas, but said it was dying out.[8]

The Spanish reported a mild domestic servitude in Spanish Sahara (Rio de Oro), too deeply rooted to tackle without causing grave disruption. In fact, slave raiding continued even among nomadic pastoralists.[9] The Dutch said that slavery existed in the remoter parts of the East Indies, but they were unsure of its form. The Belgians, in a long and detailed report, stated that slaves in the Congo were well treated, lived like their owners, and willingly accepted their situation but, since they were the cultivators, sudden liberation would threaten the African food supply. They apparently saw no contradiction in these statements. The Portuguese claimed that they had suppressed the slave trade and that their labor laws were "perfect." Their natives enjoyed complete liberty, and allegations to the contrary were inspired by "sinister," even criminal, motives.[10] Liberia, the only independent African state other than Ethiopia, replied that slavery was illegal but that, to avoid social and political upheaval, no steps had been taken to forcibly disrupt the institution, which was slowly dying out.

The French sent no report on Morocco, where they had not yet outlawed slavery. However, they produced a long report on their West African colonies stating that all slaves were legally free and those who remained did so voluntarily. Many had tried leaving, but had returned to their owners, finding that freedom required harder work than slavery and did not provide the same security. This idealized and widely held view of a benign form of slavery, blaming the "lazy slave" for his inability to profit from freedom, begged the question as to what freedom meant and what opportunities existed for those who had left their owners. It also justified inaction.[11]

The French and British both sent in information on Ethiopia, and the Ethiopian government described its new measures against slavery. The slave trade, it claimed, was almost suppressed, and sales, gifts, and inheritance of slaves had been forbidden. All children born after 1924 were to be free. All bought slaves were to be freed within seven years of their masters' deaths. All captured slaves were to be freed on the owner's death. Ill-treated slaves were to be freed at once, together with any who had been baptized, educated, had fought as soldiers, or saved their masters from death or injury. Judges were to be appointed around the country to try offenders, hear disputes between slaves and owners, free slaves, collect fines, and send in reports on the numbers manumitted. Fugitives could only be reclaimed within eight days and their cases had to be heard in court. Freed slaves were to be sent back to their homelands, and exempted from taxes for seven years until they became self-supporting. Those who did not want to return home could take wage labor wherever they wanted. The young were to be sent to a special school to learn to read and write. Others were to go to trade, language, or military schools or to seminaries.[12] On paper, therefore, a considerable advance had been made towards bringing slavery to an orderly end.

THE TEMPORARY SLAVERY COMMISSION (TSC): CHOOSING THE EXPERTS

By the spring of 1924, the League had agreed to appoint a "competent body" to inquire into slavery. This was known as the Temporary Slavery Commission. The colonial powers wanted it to be pliant, short-lived, and without the power to conduct investigations. Lord Parmoor, handling the matter for the newly installed Labor government,[13] proposed a small group of "impartial" delegates including one from the International Labor Organization (ILO). They were not to include members of NGOs, and, most important, they were to be appointed by their governments and take instructions from them.[14] He was thwarted by the secretary-general of the League, whose prerogative it was to appoint members of League committees. The Secretariat was determined to see that the committee was not "packed" with colonial officials bent on "paralyzing" it.[15] They decided on a body of seven "independent experts." "For expediency," they included nationals of the three great powers permanently represented on the Council of the League—France, Britain, and Italy—and either a Belgian or a Portuguese. One of them was to represent the ILO, to please its director, Albert Thomas.

These "independent experts" were chosen in consultation with their governments, except for Lugard. The secretary-general, Drummond, thought him such an obvious British choice that he nearly appointed him without reference to the Foreign Office.[16] Lugard was considered the leading expert on the subject, was a member of the Permanent Mandates Commission and had promoted himself tirelessly behind the scenes, letting it be known months ahead that he would be willing to serve, and advising Drummond to read his newly published book, *The Dual Mandate in British Tropical Africa*, with its two chapters on slavery.[17] From 1920, he had kept himself in the public eye, taking an active part in the controversy over Ethiopian slavery, and carrying on a voluminous correspondence with Harris and other influential persons, as well as with informants on the ground. He wrote articles and letters to the press, and made it plain he would consider some role in the suppression of slavery in Ethiopia if it were offered.[18] The Anti-Slavery Society thought him an admirable choice. Although he was not a member of the Society, and did not always approve of their methods, they consulted him and always sought his support.

Parmoor insisted that the experts could not commit their governments to any course of action.[19] Drummond, presumably at the British request, hinted to Lugard that he should consult his government on their policy,[20] but Lugard regarded himself as genuinely independent, believing that if the members of the committee saw themselves as defenders of national interests, its value would be destroyed.[21] However, although he considered the suppression of slave raiding and trading to be "the essential work" of his life,[22] he was well aware of the political and economic consequences of hasty action against slavery itself, and it would have been difficult to find anyone with more practical experience or more "know-how" on how to discourage slaves from seeking freedom.

The other colonial powers kept their representatives more closely in line. The French delegate, Maurice Delafosse, had an equally appropriate background.[23] He had given up medical studies in 1890 to join Cardinal Lavigerie's Armed Brothers to fight the slave trade in the Sahara. In 1913, he had joined the Commission Anti-Esclavage de France. As a colonial administrator in French West Africa, he had initiated many reforms and became the leading French expert on African languages and civilization. A distinguished scholar, he was a member of the Académie Coloniale. The last years of his career were spent as a professor at the École Coloniale, which trained colonial administrators, and the École des Langues Orientales Vivantes. He wrote a major work on the upper Niger-Senegal, and many articles, and translated works from Arabic manuscripts. He respected African institutions, whereas Lugard tended to dismiss non-Muslim peoples as savages. However, he agreed with Lugard's policies of indirect rule and believed that colonial governments should interfere as little as possible in indigenous affairs and should rule in the interests of the governed. He opposed all forced labor and, like Lugard, was convinced that Africans were not lazy and would work in their own interests. Lugard called him "the best Frenchman" he had ever known and they worked "cordially" together.[24]

Delafosse was carefully briefed by his government. He was warned, for instance, to be sure that the Commission's report showed the progress made in suppressing slavery in French colonies, and paid tribute to Ethiopia's antislavery efforts. He was cautioned to avoid any discussion of slavery in Morocco,[25] and to ensure that the BIDI was not allowed to give evidence.[26]

The Portuguese member, Alfredo Freire d'Andrade, had been governor-general of Mozambique from 1906–1910 and foreign minister of Portugal. Like Lugard, he was on the Permanent Mandates Commission. In Mozambique, he had promoted African agriculture, and initiated reforms to improve the lot of Africans and keep them from fleeing to neighboring territories. He was considered an enlightened governor even by critics of Portuguese colonial rule, although he believed firmly that Africans would not work unless forced to do so.[27] As a staunch patriot, he had been much upset by the Anti-Slavery Society's attacks on Portuguese colonial policies before the First World War,[28] and had opposed the League's taking up the antislavery cause for fear that it would lead to a condemnation of Portuguese policies. Portugal was the most vulnerable of the colonial powers and was as concerned as ever about losing its colonies. Chronically verging on bankruptcy, it could not develop them without foreign capital and enterprise, and South Africa was clearly trying to gain control of the Mozambican port of Lorenzo Marques.[29] Freire d'Andrade admitted to his colleagues on the TSC that when he spoke in the Assembly as a representative of his government his tune was different from when he voiced his own opinions in the TSC.[30]

The Belgians, when they heard that a committee was to be appointed, proposed Albrecht Gohr. He was a lawyer, who had been a judge in the Congo Independent State, and then director of justice in King Leopold's scandalous administration. After eleven years in Africa, he had been appointed to the Congo State's Justice Department in Brussels. In the last years of the king's rule and the early years of Belgian rule, he had been employed drafting reforms in the judicial and administrative system of the Congo. In 1915, he became director general in the Ministry of the Colonies. His experience covered "native" administration, including employment contracts.[31] He published widely on legal questions and taught colonial courses at the University of Brussels. On the TSC, as a serving colonial official, he was nervous of offending governments, and careful to defend Belgian interests.

Italy was represented by Commandant Roncagli, secretary-general of the Italian Geographical Society. He played a minor role on the commission, but used it to further his government's colonial policies. The Dutch member was van Rees, formerly vice-president of the Council of the Netherlands' East Indies, who had long service in the colonies and was vice-president of the Permanent Mandates Commission. He was a conscientious member of the TSC but was hampered by the fact that he was not an expert on slavery, and his country had no African colonies. Moreover, he spoke no English.[32] In his zeal to defend Dutch policies, he was ever ready to dissent from the majority opinion. Of the African colonial powers, only the Spanish were missing. The two independent states of Liberia and Ethiopia were also not represented.

A particularly important member, eagerly supported by the Anti-Slavery Society, was the chief of section of the Diplomatic Division of the International Labor Organization, Harold Grimshaw. He was also on the Permanent Mandates Commission, and had drawn up its report on slavery and labor in 1922–1923. He was well versed on the subject and worked closely with Harris, who thought him a kindred spirit, prepared to go "quite far" in "busting up the world in general."[33] By 1924, Grimshaw had decided that slavery should be dealt with by the ILO, which could put pressure on governments through its publications and its conference, and could negotiate conventions.[34]

The last member of the TSC was a delegate from Haiti to the League, Louis Dante Bellegarde. He had been minister of agriculture and had represented his country in Paris. He had tried and failed to get on the Mandates Commission, and asked to be appointed to the TSC. Rappard thought his appointment would be welcomed by "the black race" and by Latin Americans and hence was "sound League policy." Since he had shown considerable knowledge of slavery in the Assembly discussions, and was a moderate "although a Negro," he was considered safe as well as useful.[35] Although his appointment was mere window dressing, he was to prove valuable in reminding his more nervous colleagues that the purpose of the commission was to serve the interests of the slaves, rather than their governments. He warned against too ready an acceptance of the official view that slavery was benign, and provided the nearest thing to the "slave voice" on this commission.

Two nominations to the TSC were rejected. The Secretariat had proposed Henri Junod, the dominant force in the BIDI, thinking he would be impartial. He had been a missionary in the Swiss Evangelical Mission in Mozambique and was well-known for his respect for African religions and civilization. However, the French objected strongly to the BIDI, because its petition to the League in August 1923 denounced the export of slaves through French Somaliland and complained of slavery in the French protectorate of Morocco, of forced labor in the French Congo, and of the kidnapping of workers from the Anglo-French condominium in the New Hebrides. The French believed it was anti-French and had connections with the communist and pan-Islamic organizations then attacking French colonialism. The nomination was rejected on the tactful grounds that the bureau would be more useful as a source of information, and that if one NGO was represented others would demand to be included.[36]

Drummond had wanted to appoint an American. Although the United States had withdrawn from the League in 1920, it still took part in some of its committees. He suggested a sociology professor, Edward A. Ross, from the University of Wisconsin, but dropped the idea when he found that Ross wanted to extend the committee's functions beyond acceptable bounds.[37] Ross conducted research in Angola and his report on conditions there and in Mozambique was published on the eve of the second session of the TSC,[38] frightening the already jittery Portuguese. Both Ross and Junod would have provided a channel for the "slave voice" so lacking at the TSC.

The British feminist Women's Freedom League protested that there were no women on the commission, eliciting the acid reaction in the Foreign Office that any further enlargement of the commission "was undesirable even if these indignant ladies could produce a candidate who had any genuine practical experience" with slavery.[39]

THE COMMISSION DEFINES ITS MANDATE
AND EVALUATES ITS EVIDENCE

Its composition established, the members of the Commission held seven meetings in Geneva in the summer of 1924. They had not accepted the job for money or pleasure. Only their travel expenses and living costs were reimbursed.[40] Where the Brussels conference had been enlivened by a glittering succession of dinners, receptions, and balls, the TSC settled down to hard work.

Before the commission was even constituted, Lugard asked Drummond for its terms of reference. But the League's guidelines were vague and the Secretariat looked to him to pull the slavery question out of the "morass" in which the League had left it.[41] This enabled the TSC to take the initiative.

The eight experts began their work with marked cordiality.[42] Lugard declined the chairmanship because of his poor French. Delafosse refused because too many League honors fell on British and French representatives, and tactfully proposed the Belgian, Gohr, who was duly elected, with Freire d'Andrade as vice-chairman.[43] A distinguished and conscientious group of practical men, they were uncertain of what they were to discuss and wary of overstepping their mandate. They decided to draw up a program of work to submit to the Council. If it were accepted, they would meet the following year to draw up a final report.

The first session was spent trying to agree on the scope of their investigation and the type of evidence they could use. Initially, the more cautious members, knowing that colonial governments were unwilling to open the door to outside scrutiny of their policies, argued that they should only investigate slave raiding and trading. These were legitimate international issues because they operated across borders, caused disorder, and diverted trade towards countries that tolerated the traffic. Slavery, on the other hand, they argued, was a domestic question, concerning only the relations between indigenous people. Colonial governments were reluctant to interfere with it and would regard international discussion as an infringement of their sovereign rights.

However, article 23 of the Covenant of the League binding members to secure "fair and humane conditions of labor" in all countries with which they had commercial relations implied that slavery and, indeed all labor conditions, were now matters for international action. Grimshaw reminded the Commission that the ILO's dedication to raising the living and working standards of workers everywhere was based on the premise that this could not be done in one country or colony without having an economic and social impact elsewhere. Goods produced by slaves might undercut those produced by free labor, and a power that eradicated slavery might find itself at an economic disadvantage. The argument was decisive and the Commission decided that slavery was indeed within its brief.

The vital question was to define slavery. This proved so difficult that the Commission decided not to attempt a watertight definition but to list in their report all practices restricting personal liberty, including slave raiding, trading, and dealing, as well as slavery, serfdom, and all forms of debt bondage. The discussion over the meaning of the terms slavery, domestic slavery, predial slavery, and serfdom illuminated the prevailing confusion. The problem was a familiar one. What Europeans had called slavery covered a wide range of practices, and the colonial powers used different terms to describe them. Thus in many African societies, first generation or trade slaves were distinct from their descendants, who had more rights and were rarely sold. The French called the latter *captifs de case* and the British called them "domestic slaves." Some people called them serfs; others thought they were not slaves at all. To the British and Belgians, slave "dealing" was the transfer of persons already enslaved and included all exchanges, sales, gifts, and inheritance, whereas slave trading was the selling of someone who was previously free—a more serious offense. Since the French maintained that all their subjects were free, they could not make such a distinction. To overcome these difficulties, the TSC included all these terms and all forms of transfer in their report.[44]

Another vital question was whether freed slaves would be given "nothing but freedom" or whether they would be assured access to homes and land, or wage labor. An even broader question was how far free labor, including contract labor, was to be protected. Wage labor could be more oppressive than slave labor, depending on how what the British called "master and servant" laws were framed. Highly controversial was the inclusion of forced labor. Lugard and Grimshaw insisted that this could degenerate into slavery if not rigorously restricted, and their colleagues were keenly aware that the compulsory labor exacted by the colonial powers could be more oppressive than the slavery still practiced by indigenous peoples. They also realized that the colonial powers would resent any attack on their labor policies. They had not been asked to set labor standards, but they slipped it in cautiously by suggesting that they should discuss measures to smooth the transition from servile to free labor. To disarm any attempt by the Council to keep it from discussing these sensitive questions, the TSC stressed that they were merely fulfilling their mandate to investigate slavery in all its forms. To sweeten the pill, however, they made it clear that they envisaged only a very gradual transition from slave to free labor and that their recommendations would be designed to help governments make the transition.

They realized that to do an effective job, they had to take account of information from unofficial sources. Although the League had not circulated them, these petitions were kept by the Secretariat for the TSC to consult. To enable them to be used for its report, the Secretariat had asked the powers to name individuals or NGOs whose evidence would be acceptable. France, Belgium, Poland, Switzerland, and Portugal had done so and the Secretariat had contacted the various institutions, but they had produced little information. The TSC was only too aware that all the colonial powers were uneasy about admitting evidence from unofficial sources for fear the Commission might be turned into a tribunal bringing accusations against particular states.[45] To calm these fears, they stated that they would only take account of information from sources "whose competence and reliability" were recognized by their own governments. This was the forerunner of the system of "accrediting" certain NGOs to the United Nations. However, although it enabled a government to rule out information from individuals or organizations based in its own territories, it did not protect them from evidence from foreign NGOs or individuals whose governments certified them as reliable. To meet this difficulty, the TSC proposed that unofficial information would be sent to the government concerned, and would only be used in the report after its comments had been received. This enabled governments to refute charges or to avoid reference to them in the report by delaying their answers until after the TSC finished its work.

On the question of unofficial evidence, the British were in a particular dilemma. Their long experience with the Anti-Slavery Society had convinced the Foreign Office that NGOs lacked discrimination and that Harris, especially, was certain to present his material "with the object of creating prejudice instead of assisting in the production of a judicial and impartial report."[46] They tried to sidestep the issue by refusing to name "reliable" organizations, offering instead to comment on the reliability and reports of any NGOs referred to them by the League. Eventually, and not until the TSC had almost finished its meetings, seeing no alternative, they reluctantly designated the Society as reliable. In view of its high-level support in Parliament and the country, they could hardly do otherwise.[47] But they wanted all unofficial reports channeled through the Foreign Office on the excuse that they could then refer them to colonial administrations for comment.[48] In the end, since no power wanted to be seen as preventing the use of unofficial sources, the League accepted the TSC's plan.

As public opinion had played so important a part in promoting the antislavery cause, a vital question was whether the report of the TSC should be published. Caution prevailed and it was decided that the Council should decide this point. The even more important question of whether or not League members would be committed to act on the recommendations of the TSC had already been decided when the British made it plain that they certainly would not be bound by any of its proposals.[49] Thus, Britain took the lead in ensuring that the TSC would be merely a "paper tiger."

With the main hurdles as to its scope, its powers, and its sources of evidence overcome, the members of the Commission went home to study their material. All but Delafosse, who was elected rapporteur, and Freire d'Andrade, whose views had been incorporated in the Portuguese reply to the League questionnaire, prepared memoranda for the draft report. The second session of the TSC was devoted to hammering this draft into final form for presentation to the League.

This took place in the summer of 1925. The TSC held twenty-one meetings in thirteen days.[50] "We sit," wrote Lugard, "from 10 A.M. to 7 P.M. with an interval for lunch—and waste 3/4 [sic] of the time in the most futile and exasperating speeches. I am usually up till 1:30 dealing with papers."[51]

Nevertheless as documents continued to arrive throughout the session, members could not read all their material before it ended, much less refer it to governments for comment.

In the year since their last meeting, they had themselves collected voluminous information from official and unofficial sources—documents, books, journals, and newspapers.[52] They now faced the problem of how to evaluate it and use it in their report—problems which were to beset all future committees. Disagreements on these points almost brought work to a standstill and deliberations were suspended while compromises were worked out. Basically, all their material was suspect. That furnished by governments was incomplete, or untruthful. That from NGOs and individuals was often biased, out of date, or rested on dubious evidence. Even the information that members produced themselves was challenged. Lugard was in a quandary because he had been shown British consular reports but was not allowed to divulge his sources. He persuaded his colleagues that his information was reliable—that children were sold in Liberia for domestic work, and women were being pawned, or bought as wives.[53] But when he asked them to believe that girls were sold in China on the basis of a statement made in the House of Lords by the Archbishop of Canterbury, they were skeptical.[54] When Grimshaw, quoting from a book published in 1921, claimed that children in Haiti were sold by their parents for domestic service, Bellegarde protested that peasants often placed their children with families in towns so that they might go to school in return for light housework. He intimated that the author, the son-in-law of the American high commissioner, had distorted the picture to support U.S. occupation of Haiti.

To avoid arguing over every piece of evidence, the TSC decided that, if a government did not comment on allegations, their report should make it clear that they were citing evidence they could not verify. Moreover, they avoided directly contradicting a government. Thus, they merely stated in their report that they had received evidence of slave dealing in Liberia and China, but could not send it to either power for comment because both had denied that there was any slave trade in their territories.

THE REPORT OF THE TEMPORARY SLAVERY COMMISSION: PLAYING THE ANTISLAVERY GAME

The members of the TSC used their report to play the antislavery game for the benefit of their own countries. They began by stating that slavery was no longer recognized
by law in any Christian state or its colonies, or in China, Japan, and Thailand, and that
the maharaja of Nepal had announced measures to end it. It was still legal, however,
in some Muslim states, including Hijaz. They recommended that these states should
not be allowed to join the League unless they gave clear evidence that they intended to
end slavery. They could not insist that it should actually be ended, as this would have
called Ethiopia's membership into question. Lugard stated that the Tafari had neither
the power nor resources to end slave raiding and trading, and suggested sending a
League commission to ascertain the facts. His reasons are a mystery.[55] The Foreign Office had warned him not to give "mischief makers" a chance to accuse Britain of "acting in an unfriendly or underhand way" towards Ethiopia,[56] yet this is exactly what he
did. Delafosse, however, defeated the proposal, paying tribute to Tafari's efforts in the
report. In Ethiopia, the French told Tafari that the British had wanted the inquiry in
order to get Ethiopia expelled from the League.[57] Thus France's position as the defender of Ethiopia was strengthened.[58]

The TSC report stated that slave raiding had disappeared in all the areas controlled
by European powers, except in and around the Sahara. This enabled France and Italy to
justify their military operations in northern Africa. Delafosse claimed that raids in the
northern and western Sahara were encouraged, perhaps even organized, by Muslim
sects, and Roncagli claimed that the main activity of the Sanusi, a Muslim brotherhood
resisting conquest in the Libyan desert, was slave trading. Certainly, slave raiding and
trading continued in the desert and on its fringes.[59] However, the report described
French and Italian "penetration" of the Sahara, and their plans to establish petrol depots
and workshops to support aerial patrols, as antislavery measures. It also urged the Saharan powers to grant mutual rights to pursue slavers over their frontiers. This would enable the French to pursue opponents into the unoccupied "backcountry" of the Spanish
colony of Rio de Oro.[60] The Italian delegate, anxious to prevent Egypt from helping the
Sanusi, proposed that the League also call on Egypt, newly independent of British rule,
to cooperate against slave raiding and trading across both the desert and the Red Sea.

The report stated that the slave trade, already outlawed by all members of the
League, continued in Ethiopia, in the British protectorate of Aden, and some Muslim
states, particularly Hijaz, but only possibly in China and Liberia. It praised the efforts
of Britain, France, and Italy to prevent the export of slaves from their territories and
commended them on the naval patrols in the Red Sea. At the instigation of Roncagli,
it urged them to reach agreement between themselves to allow mutual rights of pursuit in territorial waters in the Red Sea.[61] Egged on by Lugard, the TSC also suggested
that all transport of slaves by sea should be declared piracy—a proposal made and re-

jected many times in the past, as it would automatically have allowed all maritime powers the right to search suspect shipping on the high seas worldwide. The British, hoping to get other powers to share the unpopularity and financial burden of consular manumission, saw that the report urged that the successor states of the Ottoman Empire be pressed to grant foreign consuls the "right of asylum" for fugitives. It also recommended the repatriation of freed slaves, the establishment of a depot to receive them on the west coast of the Red Sea, and a bureau to gather information about their capture and the routes along which they had traveled. To police the pilgrimage, the TSC recommended that all travelers to the Hijaz should carry passports, all servants of pilgrims should be registered and given freedom papers, and that travel with children and young people should be controlled.

SLAVERY IN ALL ITS FORMS: THE PROTECTION OF WOMEN AND CHILDREN

The TSC suggested clear laws against all methods of transferring or acquiring slaves, including sale, gift, inheritance, exchange, adoption, and pledging. This was dangerous ground. Lines between acceptable transfers and servile ones were not always easy to draw. Certain African marriage customs, for instance, were quite distinct from slavery in the African, but not the Western, mind. Payment of bride wealth could disguise slave dealing, but did not normally do so. Yet bride wealth itself, child betrothal, the inheritance of widows by their husband's kinsmen, even polygyny because it might lower the status of less-favored wives, seemed analogous to slavery to some Western women's organizations. The TSC made it clear it was not advocating interference in normal marriage practices. The lot of women, Lugard argued, could only be ameliorated slowly by "civilization and education."[62] Nevertheless, it had opened the door to consideration of what was to be called "servile marriage" as a form of slavery in the future.[63]

Concubines posed another problem. Under Muslim law, they had to be slaves. The British, reluctant to interfere with domestic arrangements, had not always included concubines when they abolished the legal status of slavery. They considered them as wives. The TSC, however, recommended that, like other slaves, they should be allowed to leave their owners if they wished. Lugard pointed out that freedom might not be to their advantage. Normally they were not sold if they had borne a child and could not be divorced like wives. Their children were usually free. If they were freed, their children might become bastards, and the mothers might lose their privileged position in the household. Interference in such questions could have unforeseen results.

The TSC branded the transfer of children for domestic service under guise of adoption as slave dealing. They were careful to say that this was only alleged to be practiced in Liberia and China and they credited the British wrongly with having recently outlawed it in the Straits Settlements and Hong Kong.[64] The buying of children by missionaries "or other charitable bodies" in order to free them was also condemned. By providing a market, this encouraged the capture of more slaves. Missionaries, particularly Catholic ones, had habitually bought young slaves to educate them or settle them as the nucleus of their Christian communities. Other well-meaning people purchased slaves to free them. The British had long deplored the practice, believing that it encouraged further slaving. This question was to become a bone of contention in Sudan in the 1990s.[65]

SLAVERY IN ALL ITS FORMS: DEBT-BONDAGE

The report dealt with various forms of debt-bondage. Pawning had been outlawed by most colonial and Eastern powers. The commission recommended that pawning of a third party should be outlawed everywhere, but self-pledging for a limited period might be allowed. Pawning in Africa, which was believed to be the result of a debt between persons of equal standing and contracted only by individuals, was distinguished from the more vicious forms of debt-bondage known as peonage in the southern United States, Latin America, and the Philippines, where the peon and his creditor were persons of unequal standing. The agricultural peon was usually given seeds and tools, or land, and then charged interest in the form of a proportion of the crop, or other proceeds of his work. The rate was so fixed that the debt could never be repaid. Alternatively, an employer advanced money for food, housing, and other necessities and then charged his employees rent and interest, or forced them to buy necessities in a company shop thus keeping the debt mounting. The debtor could not leave until the debt was paid. He and his family and even his descendants, trapped in this cycle of escalating debt, fell into lifelong bondage, living at subsistence level, and working for a privileged class of landowners, officials, or even clergy. Although theoretically not saleable, debtors could be transferred with the land or the business, or their debts could be purchased, so that in practice they could be virtually bought and sold. No government had sent the TSC any information on peonage, but the BIDI had called attention to it.[66] Grimshaw, quoting American sources, described various forms of it in his memorandum.[67]

The TSC recommended that all peonage be outlawed. An individual might be allowed to work off a debt under controlled conditions and within a limited time. They did not discuss the various forms of debt-bondage widespread in the Indian subcontinent. They were entering uncharted waters. Branding peonage as analogous to slavery was to cause serious trouble in discussions in the 1950s, while debt-bondage in many forms and many areas of the world was to be a perennial problem into the twenty-first century.[68]

The TSC recognized that indigenous forms of servitude, which they called domestic or predial slavery or serfdom, existed, de facto if not de jure, in a number of colonial territories in Africa, as well as in Burma, New Guinea, Borneo, and Assam. None of the colonial powers wanted to interfere with it, and Delafosse went so far as to describe the institution in tropical Africa as totally benign, painting a rosy picture of the domestic slave as a serf with few obligations, who benefited from the institution.

Bellegarde, supported by Grimshaw, protested that this description in the report might encourage governments not to take action. The commission felt they knew too little to accept Delafosse's description and stated that indigenous slavery varied from abject servitude to an approximation of "medieval European serfdom." This question was to become the subject of acrimonious discussion in the next League committee.[69]

Since, like most colonial governments, the TSC believed that the sudden abolition of indigenous slavery would cause economic and social upheaval, they recommended ending its legal status rather than outlawing it, thus endorsing the Indian model of abolition the British had found so satisfactory. However, its attraction, at least in India, had been that its impact had been gradual, partly because slaves had not been told that they could leave their owners. The TSC, urged by Bellegarde, recommended that in the future they should be told of their rights.[70]

SLAVERY IN ALL ITS FORMS: FORCED LABOR

The most controversial and potentially explosive subject in the TSC report was forced labor, including the forced growing of certain crops.[71] From the start of its deliberations, the TSC had recognized that these practices were now far more oppressive than the remaining vestiges of slavery, particularly since they usually benefited the mother country or white settlers rather than the native population. The committee had received a considerable amount of information on the iniquities of forced labor, particularly in the Portuguese colonies. In 1923, the BIDI had accused Portugal of forcing men and women to work for a pittance for six months at a time for private enterprises. Late the following year, the Anti-Slavery Society had sent in a report by G. A. Morton, accusing Portuguese officials of impressing Africans to work for private companies or on their own plantations, and of taking women and children as hostages if the men fled. Then in 1925, E. A. Ross published a report on the deplorable conditions in Angola and parts of Mozambique.[72] The Portuguese denied these accusations, claiming that the authors were hostile, and their information out of date or unreliable.[73] They were not the only offenders. Grimshaw and Lugard, both, covered the question in their memoranda showing the various devices by which indigenous people were being forced to work. These varied from outright conscription to land alienation and vagrancy laws, of which the British were particularly guilty in settler colonies, and regressive forms of taxation widely imposed in the British Empire.

Lugard, who had already discussed the question in the *Dual Mandate*, advocated eliminating all such forms of coercion. Although he believed like his colleagues that indigenous people should work, and that the colonial powers owed it to the world to "develop the tropics," he did not believe that Africans were lazy and argued that if wage labor or the return on crops was attractive enough there would be no need for compulsion. The example of a few European-run plantations and a "proper system of education" might be used, he wrote, to convince the "natives" that it was in their interests to work, but they should be free to sell their labor in the best market or to cultivate their own land or to simply "gather sylvan produce." If labor was short, then labor-saving machinery should be introduced. Taxation should only be used to raise revenue. Vagrancy laws should aim only at keeping order. Wages should always be paid in cash. He suggested drawing up a "labor charter" to regulate colonial labor conditions and contracts. Grimshaw, anxious that the ILO be the body deputed to deal with these questions, also made comprehensive suggestions, endorsing many of Lugard's proposals.[74] Bellegarde supported them.[75] Harris had long advocated such a charter and the idea had been bandied about in the League Assembly in 1924, supported by Freire d'Andrade and the British and French delegates.[76]

However, while there was general agreement in the TSC that forced labor came within its province, members recognized that their governments would not agree to their setting labor standards. The French Ministry of the Colonies had warned Delafosse that labor regulation was an internal question, and any discussion of it would infringe national sovereignty.[77] Lugard dropped his proposal at the request of the British Ministry of Labor.[78] Grimshaw insisted that the ILO considered labor regulation an international and not a domestic matter, but for him the important question was not whether the TSC dealt with it, but simply to have it record that it was a matter to be taken up by the ILO.

After much discussion, the TSC stated in their report that forced labor was often a disguised form of slavery, but refrained from accusations against any power. They recommended, that, as in the Mandates, it should be used only for essential public works, and never for private employers; and that it should always be adequately paid, unless—a loophole insisted on by the Dutch and Portuguese—this was "completely impossible." They urged that forced labor for chiefs be prohibited, especially for personal services, a practice widespread in colonial Africa. Some of the force of their recommendations was lost because they suggested that governments should be allowed to define "essential" public works, and issue their own regulations for the recruitment and treatment of the workers.

They maintained that forced crop cultivation was only justified if there was a danger of famine or it was an "educative measure," as the Belgians insisted. They condemned all forms of direct or indirect pressure to force people into private wage labor. Grimshaw also succeeded in getting them to recommend that the ILO should take up labor legislation to protect "backward peoples,"[79] although the Dutch, Italian, and Belgian delegates, all concerned at even the mention of forced labor, objected that this was not part of their mandate. They were careful, though, to record that they personally favored a labor charter.

Lugard, mindful of the Putumayo scandal, and supported by Grimshaw, wanted to include a recommendation that consuls should visit private enterprises abroad run by their nationals to ensure there was no abuse of native labor, but this was not included in the report, which did not mention extraterritorial loopholes.

The final chapter of the report consisted of recommendations to facilitate the change from servile or forced labor to free wage labor or independent production. Since labor was often not forthcoming in sufficient quantity to increase or even maintain production, the TSC recommended that instead of resorting to forced labor, or tolerating slave labor, governments should foster peasant production, and gradually replace communal land tenure systems with private landownership.

A major problem in promoting economic development along Western lines was that indigenous people had few wants and hence little incentive to work for wages. As prosperity increased, the TSC anticipated that their perceived needs would rise, fueling a desire to work for money. To speed this up, they urged that payment should always be in cash rather than kind, and that wages and working conditions should be attractive enough to lure slaves away from their owners.

Finally, efforts should be made to end the "servile attitude of mind" of "backward peoples" by providing "suitable" education, permitting them to conduct their own affairs and "allowing them to participate in the working of enterprises conducted by the more advanced races," and even giving them a share in the profits—ideas that were nothing short of visionary.

THE RESULTS OF THE TEMPORARY SLAVERY COMMISSION

Their report finished, the life of the Temporary Slavery Commission came to an end. Gohr presented their findings to the Council on 25 July 1925, with a covering letter containing its most fruitful proposal—that the League should negotiate a new treaty, binding signatories to abolish the legal status of predial slavery and serfdom; to declare the slave trade by sea to be piracy; to grant rights to pursue slavers over land frontiers and in territorial waters; to impose severe penalties for raiding and trading; to prohibit peonage; and to ban forced labor except for essential works.

The TSC had debated at length whether or not to recommend the negotiation of this convention.[80] Lugard, who had already drawn up a draft, and Delafosse both found that their governments would support it, providing it was only against slavery and did not cover forced labor, or include a labor charter. Gohr supported it in order to ensure a practical outcome from the work of the TSC. Grimshaw naturally favored it. Finally, it was put to the vote and carried over the opposition of the Dutch, Portuguese, and Italian members.

Clearly, the attitude of the TSC to indigenous peoples left much to be desired. They were regarded as children to be protected and brought up to become consumers working for wages or producing crops like the workers of the Western world. The voice of indigenous people and of slaves was completely lacking. The report was watered down and direct accusations were avoided to make it palatable to the colonial powers. Nevertheless, the Commission—the first of its kind to consider slavery—had collected much information and given much thought not just to slavery but to all related institutions—including forced labor—and general conditions of labor.

With its mandate to discuss "slavery in all its forms," it had propelled into the international arena questions not previously identified as slavery, including servile child labor, servile marriage, debt-bondage, and forced labor—all questions which would be taken up as forms of slavery by the United Nations later in the century. It thus set important precedents for the future. Similarly, its composition—a small group of independent experts—set the pattern for future slavery committees.

By no means all its recommendations bore fruit at the time, but in the development of the modern concept of human rights, it was a milestone on the hard-fought road from Vienna in 1815 to Helsinki in 1945. At Vienna, the great powers of Europe took the first halting steps towards the protection of Africans by proclaiming the slave trade "repugnant to the principles of humanity and universal morality." Further steps were taken at Berlin in 1885 and Brussels in 1890. Now in 1925, the TSC recommended the protection of all peoples from all forms of restriction on personal liberty in the economic and social spheres. This was a significant step towards the acceptance of the idea that there should be a general standard of human rights in the workplace. The TSC was the product of the ideal of trusteeship, enshrined in the Mandates agreements, but it was a step towards a wider ideal accepted at least in the Western world—that infringements by a government of the rights of its own citizens are matters of international concern. This ideal was to be significantly extended in the years to come.

NOTES

1. Tufton minute, 28 August 1923 on ASAPS to Curzon, 28 August 1923, FO 371/8406 A5163/142/1.

2. Rappard to Harris, private and confidential, 18 August 1923, LON MSF S1669, file 3. The petition is enclosed in ASAPS to FO, 28 August 1923, FO 371/8406 A 5163/142/1.

3. FO to ASAPS, 4 September 1923 and minutes, FO 371/8406 A 5163/142/1.

4. Among them were the Fabian, Sidney Webb; the Labor politicians, Ramsay MacDonald, Arthur Henderson, Philip Snowdon; the Liberals, Noel Buxton, W. Wedgewood Benn, Charles Trevelyan, and Sir John Simon, who was to play an important role in the future.

5. This had sprung from a Swiss organization founded in 1908 to educate the public on the Congo atrocities. In 1913, after Mrs. Harris toured the country lecturing on the iniquities of Portuguese recruiting in Angola for the cocoa islands, a central bureau had been formed to coordinate several small national societies. After the war, this was revived, renamed the BIDI, and expanded to combat the new "disguised" forms of slavery. Claparède to Crane 5 November 1924, Claparède Papers, LON. Its president was a well-known philanthropist, René Claparède. Like the ASAPS, it depended on donations from NGOs and individuals.

6. *L'esclavage sous toutes ses formes*, 2 August 1923, LON s.1670 file 9; For background, see Claparède to Crane, 5 November 1924, Claparède Papers LON.

7. These replies are all in LON A.18.1923.VI, and LON A.25.1924. VI.

8. The situation in Sudan, Bechuanaland, Aden, Hong Kong, and India will be discussed in later chapters.

9. McDougall 1988, 367; Klein 1998.

10. LON A.18.1923.VI, p. 15.

11. LON A.25.1924.VI. For further discussion of this question, see chapters 3, 11.

12. The report and the provisions of the edict are in LON C.209.M.66.1924.VI.

13. Lord Parmoor was lord president of the Council, and seems to have dealt with this question for the foreign secretary and prime minister, Ramsey MacDonald, in the Labor government formed in January 1924, which resigned in November the same year.

14. Drummond to Cadogan, 22 February 1924, and minutes A 1186/366/52, Record of proceedings of Deputation Received by Lord Parmoor, 22 February 1924, and minutes A 1292/366/52, memorandum 7 March 1924, A1503/366/52, League of Nations to FO, 17 March 1924 and minutes, A 1709/366/52, FO 371/9531.

15. For the League memoranda and correspondence over the composition of the committee and the selection of delegates, see LON S.1670 file 9 and notes by Rappard and Drummond on Melot to secretary-general, 14 March 1924, LON R.70 dossier 34440 file 34661.

16. Rappard to Drummond, 17 March 1923; Drummond minute, 19 March 1923, LON s.1670 file 9.

17. Cecil to Lugard, 22 November 1922, and further correspondence in Lugard Papers.

18. See, for example, his correspondence with Drummond in 1922 in Lugard Papers.

19. Parmoor minute on League of Nations to FO, 17 March 1922, FO 371/9531 A 1709/366/52.

20. Drummond to Lugard, 31 March 1924, and Drummond to Crowe, personal, 18 April 1924, FO 371/9531 A 2607.

21. Lugard to Catastani, 6 February 1925, LON R 34440/35843 VIII.

22. Lugard to Milner, 23 May 1920, Lugard Papers.

23. See Deschamps 1971, 556–58; Manchuelle 1987; Klein 1998, 213.

24. Lugard to Lady Simon, 22 January 1930, Lugard Papers.

25. Slavery was only outlawed in Morocco in 1925.

26. Aide mémoire enclosed in Clauzel to Delafosse, 8 July 1924, FMAE SDN 939 Esclavage 1924. If such evidence were allowed, the Académie des Sciences and the missionary Holy Ghost Fathers would have to be heard.

27. G. A. Morton to ASAPS October [sic] 1924, enclosed in Buxton to Grimshaw, 13 November 1924, and forwarded by Grimshaw to Rappard, 27 January 1925, LON 1/41255/23252 C.T.E. 24. For a summary of his reforms, see Vail and White, 188–92. See also Duffy 1967, 224.

28. Duffy 1967, 224–25.

29. Vail and White 1980, 221–22.

30. See, for instance, the minutes of the 15th meeting of the TSC, LON C.428.M.157.1925.VI.

31. For further information and a list of Gohr's publications, see *Bulletin des Sciences, Institut Royale Coloniale Belge*, 1937, no. 1, 32–6, *Biographie Coloniale Belge* 3, Brussels 1952, 301–6. I am indebted to Professor Jean Stengers for these sources.

32. Lugard to Harris, 11 December 1931, Lugard Papers.

33. Harris to Grimshaw, 5 January 1926, ASAPS MSS Brit.Emp, s.19, D3/39.

34. Gertrude E. and C. W. Newbury 1976, 314–35. For a further discussion of ILO methods, see below, chapter 10.

35. Rappard memoranda for Drummond, 12 May 1924 and 7 June 1924, and note by Drummond 8.4.1924, LON S.1670 file 9, minute 1/36398/34440; Parmoor's record of conversation with Drummond 23 May 1924, FO 371/9531 A 3297.

36. For this correspondence, see note by Clauzel, 15 June 1924, FMAE SDN 939 Esclavage 1924. League to BIDI, 18 June 1924, LON S.1670, file 9. The French objections are in Minister of Colonies to FMAE, 27 December 1923, FMAE SDN 939 Esclavage 1924.

37. Drummond notes of 8 April and 10 June 1924 in LON MSF S.1670 no. 9.

38. E. A. Ross 1925. For a discussion of the report, see Duffy 1967, 166–68, Vail and White 1980, 222.

39. Women's Freedom League to Baldwin, 28 January 1925 and minute, 3 February 1925, FO 371/10617 A 531/531/52.

40. The total budget was a meager 15,000 Swiss francs, LON R 34440/34440.

41. Rappard to Drummond, 26 April 1924, LON R 34440/35843 III. For a summary of the League's resolutions and debates and the many unanswered questions as to the terms of reference of the TSC, see Lugard's note in the minutes of the first session, LON A 18.1924.VI, 5–6.

42. The discussion that follows, unless otherwise indicated, is based on the minutes of the first session of the TSC and its reports to the Council 12 July 1924, published as LON A.17. and A.18. 1924.VI.

43. Note by Delafosse, 20 July 1924, FMAE SDN 939 Esclavage 4.

44. Minutes of the First Session of the TSC, LON A. 18. 1924.VI.

45. For the discussions on this point, see documents in LON S.1670 file 9, particularly the notes on the discussion in the subcommission of the Sixth Commission on 13 September, and note by Friis, 4 October 1924, LON R.71 34440/38860.

46. Minute by Mallet, 7 August 1924, on LON A 17.1924.VI, FO 371/9531 A4703/366/52.

47. Minutes on LON A.17.1924.VI, FO 371/9531 A 4703/366/52; Minute by Snow, 28 June 1925, on Drummond to Chamberlain, 20 June 1925, LON 1/28029x/23252, FO 371/10617 A3181/531/52.

48. Minutes on League of Nations to FO, 19 July 1924, A 4703/366/52 and *League of Nations Journal* Extract no. 20, 23 September 1924, A. 5631/366/52, FO 371/9531; minutes on League of Nations to FO, 20 June 1925, A 3181/531/52, FO 371/10617.

49. Parmoor minute on League to FO, 17 March 1924, FO 371/9531 A 1709/366/52; Rappard to Drummond, 17 March 1924, and note on meeting of subcommission of the Sixth Commission, 13 September 1924, LON s.1670 file 9.

50. The discussion that follows unless otherwise indicated is based on the memoranda of the members of the TSC, CTE 30, 31, 32, 39, 41, minutes of the Second Session of the TSC, 13–25 July 1925 C.426 M.157. 1925. VI, Report of the TSC Adopted at its Second Session, LON A.19 1925 VI.

51. Lugard to Cecil, 20 July 1925, FO 371/10617 A 3757/531/52.

52. These sources included *The African World* and *L'Afrique Francaise*.

53. Murray to Lugard, 26 June 1924, and Lugard to Lady Simon, 22 January 1930, Lugard Papers.

54. See Hansard for 13 May 1925.

55. He had offered to be Tafari's "mouthpiece" at the TSC, and may have believed that this would strengthen his hand against his opponents. Lugard's notes to Rey for Tafari, 24 May 1924, Lugard Papers.

56. Murray to Lugard, personal and confidential, 26 June 1924, Lugard Papers.

57. To ensure they got the credit for this, the French sent a copy of Lugard's memorandum to Leonce Lagarde, a former governor of French Somaliland and French minister in Ethiopia, who was on intimate terms with Tafari, to whom he showed it. Clauzel to Delafosse, 8 July 1924, enclosing aide mémoire, FMAE SDN 939 Esclavage 1924, Delafosse note, 29 July 1925, FMAE Afrique 1918–1940, Question Generales, Series K, carton 1, dossier 2.

58. Delafosse note, 29 July 1925, and Briand to Gaussen, no. 58, 21 August 1925, FMAE Afrique 1918–1940, Question Generales 2. series K. carton 1, dossier 2, 4–6.

59. There were reports of a slave market in the Sanusi center of Kufra in 1929, Holmboe 1936, 187–88. Mauritanian pastoralists raided in southern Morocco and Rio del Oro, McDougall 1988, 367. Slaves could be bought in Timbuktu at least as late as 1958; see below, chapter 21.

60. McDougall 1988, 307.

61. See pp. 35–36 of the minutes of the 2nd session of the TSC, LON CTE.426.M.157.1925.VI. For further discussion of this question, see chapter 12 below.

62. Minutes of the TSC, pp. 54–55, LON C.428.M.157.1925.VI.

63. See below, chapter 24.

64. See below, chapter 11.

65. See below, chapter 24.

66. BIDI memorandum, 2 August 1923, LON s.1670 file 9, and BIDI to STC, 11 July 1925, LON CTE.46. For the BIDI, see chapter 8 above, note 5.

67. Grimshaw memo, 15 April 1925, LON CTE.31.

68. See below, chapter 24.

69. See below, chapter 13.

70. Minutes of the TSC, p.62, LON C.426.M.157.1925.VI.

71. For examples of the abuses to which this gave rise, see below, chapter 10.

72. E. A. Ross 1925.

73. See Grimshaw to Rappard, 27 January 1925, enclosing Morton to ASAPS October 1924, LON CTE 24 and the Portuguese replies of 22 June 1925, LON CTE 43, and 20 June 1925, LON CTE 44; Ross Report and the Portuguese reply to secretary-general, 26 September 1925, in documents presented to the 6th Committee of the League Assembly.

74. Gertrude E. and C. W. Newbury 1976, 314–15. For Grimshaw's statement, see minutes of the 14th meeting, LON C.426.M.157.1925.VI, pp. 69–70.

75. Bellegarde memorandum, 14 March 1925, LON CTE 32.

76. Fifth Assembly, 22 September 1924.

77. Note for French representative, 25 August 1924, no. 11, and Minister of Colonies to FMAE 26 August 1924, and no. 713, 4 September 1924, SDN 939, Esclavage 1924. FMAE.

78. See minutes and his Note on Forced Labor annexed I to the minutes, LON C.426.M.157.1925.VI, Cecil to Lugard, 8 July 1925, Lugard Papers.

79. See minutes, pp. 85–86, LON C.426.M.157.1925.VI.

80. TSC Minutes pp. 90–93, LON C.426.M.157.1925.VI.

The Slavery Convention
of 1926

THE BRITISH DRAFT PROTOCOL AGAINST
SLAVERY AND THE SLAVE TRADE 1925

The colonial governments did not welcome the Temporary Slavery Commission's recommendation that the League should negotiate an international treaty against slavery. Unlike the experts, they had no desire to disturb the status quo and the proposal would probably have been ignored had Lugard not forced the issue. He sent Cecil[1] a draft convention, and asked if the government would support him if he presented it at the forthcoming second session of the Commission.[2] The Anti-Slavery Society advocated it,[3] and Cecil, having assured the House of Lords that the government was still committed to leading the antislavery campaign, felt bound to support it. However, he asked Lugard not to make any commitment to the TSC until he had convened an interdepartmental committee of representatives of the Foreign, Colonial, India, and Sudan Offices, the Admiralty, the Board of Trade, and the Ministry of Labor to prepare a draft that Britain would accept.[4]

The Foreign Office wanted a treaty to clear up the confusion created because only Britain, France, Portugal, Belgium, and Japan had ratified the St. Germain Convention. In theory, therefore, the Brussels Act was still in force for the other signatories.[5] In practice, it was ignored and the legal position was not generally understood. However, the other departments did not want a new treaty, and downgraded the proposal to a protocol. This would still enhance their antislavery image but would not have the same force as a convention. Moreover, they drafted it to ensure that it would not force the various components of the British Empire to take unwanted action.[6]

They were ready to take a firm stand against the slave trade and agreed that slavers on the high seas should be treated as pirates, liable to search and seizure anywhere, irrespective of their nationality, the flag they flew, or the size of their vessel.[7] Lugard's other proposals, however, were whittled down. These included expelling from the League states which allowed slave trading, imposing a mandatory death penalty for slaving, allowing signatories to prosecute their nationals for possessing, or dealing in slaves, no matter where the offense was committed, and the immediate abolition of slavery—not simply its legal status. These were rejected as impractical, or because new laws would have to be passed assuming extraterritorial jurisdiction, or for fear of precipitating social upheaval. Instead, the committee proposed that enslavement should be a penal offense, but that each power should impose its own penalties, and that signatories should merely be bound to end slavery as speedily "as social conditions will allow." The protocol was thus robbed of all force and meant that even Ethiopia, where slavery was legal, could sign it.

The committee was nervous about the definition of slavery. Where would the line be drawn, members asked, between slavery and other forms of forced labor, or even some forms of marriage? They decided to define it as "the exercise of the right of property by one person over another" without listing the various forms of servile status laid out in the TSC report.

Lugard's proposal to end forced labor, particularly for private purposes, and to draw up a general labor charter to prevent such abuses as debt bondage, the forced extension of contracts, and failure to repatriate migrant workers at the end of their term of service, caused considerable alarm. The India Office protested that banning forced labor for private purposes would "cut at the root" of Indian land tenure systems in both British India and the Indian States. The Sudan and Colonial Offices objected to having to pay forced labor for "essential public works." The Ministry of Labor raised the red herring that it would rule out work in asylums, prisons, and workhouses,[8] although Lugard had expressly exempted work in such institutions. They were also afraid that a labor charter might propel the ILO into "injudicious" action.[9] The protocol, therefore, merely stated that "great evils" might arise if forced labor was used for other than "essential public services" and signatories should "take all necessary precautions," particularly in the case of "less advanced races" to prevent its becoming "analogous" to slavery. Against this wishy-washy article, Lugard protested in vain that the Mandates agreements already banned forced labor except for essential public works and services.[10]

To water down the protocol still further, signatories could reject some articles altogether, and exclude some of their territories from any of its provisions. This was to protect the Government of India, which claimed large areas it did not administer, and was afraid of having to conquer still unexplored areas "inhabited by primitive aborigines amongst whom slavery or practices akin to slavery are believed still to exist."

THE LEAGUE OF NATIONS DRAFT CONVENTION 1925

Cecil thought this emasculated draft had the merit of being weak enough to be accepted by the League.[11] He presented it to the Sixth Commission of the Assembly, hastening to get it in before any other power stole his thunder, or made "objectionable" proposals.[12] The Assembly appointed a drafting committee consisting of Cecil, Gohr, and delegates from France, Italy, Portugal, and the Netherlands to revise the text. To the dismay of the British, who had hoped to "gain kudos in the press," it met privately. This committee raised the protocol to a convention. It was to replace all existing international agreements on slavery and the slave trade. The French predictably refused to consider the slave trade at sea as piracy or allow the right to search.[13] However, since the arms agreements allowed vessels under 500 tonnes flying the French flag in the Red Sea to be searched for arms, they suggested that suspects might be stopped and if slaves were spotted on board, the vessel could be arrested and handed to the nearest authorities of the flag it was flying.[14] The Royal Navy, aware of the difficulty of distinguishing slaves from legitimate passengers, insisted that they needed powers to search and arrest vessels of all sizes and nationalities in the Red Sea and Persian Gulf.[15] This impasse was solved by an article stating that, in areas in which the slave trade was active, the local powers would negotiate agreements giving each other "special rights" of search. France and Italy could agree to this, where they would not grant such rights as a principle in a general convention.[16]

The British secured the addition of an article binding signatories to give each other "every assistance" in abolishing slavery and the slave trade.[17] They hoped that this would open the way for agreements on the pursuit of slavers over land frontiers, for the extradition of offenders, and even for foreign consuls to collaborate with them in consular manumission.

The definition of slavery in the draft convention was altered for legal reasons to the following: "The status or condition of a person over whom any or all of the powers attaching to the right of ownership are exercised." Although somewhat stronger than the British draft, this was still vague and the various forms of ownership identified by the TSC were not listed. To weaken the convention still further, signatories were only bound to secure the "progressive" disappearance of slavery. Cecil defended this on the usual grounds that sudden freedom would cause "hardships" for the freed slaves and precipitate "grave social upheavals."[18]

The Portuguese objected to the forced labor clauses. Cecil tried intimidating them by brandishing a copy of the Ross report on Angola and Mozambique[19]—a strategy that later backfired, as will be seen. All that could be agreed was that forced labor should only be used for "public purposes"—but neither these nor the terms of service were defined, leaving each government free to identify them.[20] Nevertheless, there was one advance. Where the Mandates agreements allowed forced labor for "essential public works and services," services were dropped from the convention. These included the "customary work" exacted by "native chiefs" and conscription by governments under guise of a "fiscal tax." The French and others maintained that if forced labor could be commuted to a cash payment, and if it applied to all classes, it was not forced labor but a tax, which people could commute by work and for which they might be conscripted.[21]

The new text stipulated that signatories were to "endeavor progressively and as soon as possible" to end it. Meanwhile it was always to be "exceptional," to be paid, to be performed near home, and to be controlled by the central authorities. Cecil argued that it was better policy to accept this minimum standard, rather than demand an immediate end to all private forced labor, which some colonies would insist was impossible. Although unsatisfactory, it was the first definite attempt to deal with forced labor in an international agreement.[22]

As the Government of India had wanted, a signatory could exclude part of its territories from some of the new obligations and could reject certain articles altogether. Otherwise, the treaty bound all parties to introduce laws to carry it out, and to exchange information about them.

The convention was delayed a year to give governments time to study it, ending Cecil's hope of pushing it through the League in 1925. Aware that it would not satisfy the humanitarians, he emphasized, when introducing it in the Assembly, that Britain had proposed a stronger treaty and this convention was merely a first step.[23] To minimize the impact of the delay, the Assembly ordered the draft circulated to all members as well as to Afghanistan, Germany, Ecuador, the United States, Egypt, Mexico, Russia, Sudan, and Turkey. They were asked to put it into immediate operation and to send the League information on their antislavery and forced labor legislation. The powers concerned were also requested to conclude their special agreements for policing the maritime slave trade.

The Norwegian delegate, Dr. Nansen, made three further proposals, which were also postponed. The first mandated that disputes arising from the convention be referred to the Permanent Court of International Justice, or some other tribunal. The French and Portuguese objected, fearing the Court would interfere with their colonial administrations.[24] The Portuguese also thought it might open the way for an attack on their colonies.[25] The second proposal bound signatories to send the League annual progress reports. The French, Portuguese, Italians, and Belgians all objected that this would infringe national sovereignty, and reduce their colonies to the status of mandates.[26] Finally, Nansen wanted the ILO to study conditions of native labor and take action if they were not fair and humane, in accordance with article 23 of the League Covenant. Prompted by the Ministry of Labor, Cecil did not support this.

HUMANITARIAN CRITICISM OF THE DRAFT CONVENTION

The British press, the Anti-Slavery Society, and Lugard were dissatisfied with the draft convention, and Cecil had urged his government to propose a stronger treaty at the 1926 meeting of the League Assembly.[27] He suggested that the Anti-Slavery Society try to get the French public to pressure the Ministry of the Colonies,[28] but the French antislavery society was a small exclusive Roman Catholic monarchist organization, taking its cue from the pope and the pretender to the throne. Since it would not cooperate, Harris contacted a French Quaker organization,[29] but he was not to be diverted into action abroad, and welcomed the year's delay, which enabled him to continue lobbying for stronger forced labor provisions. He marshaled his supporters in the House of Lords for a debate on 16 December 1925, alerted the British Broadcasting Corporation (BBC) to ensure coverage, and occupied his usual position under the gallery to provide material to the speakers. He was well pleased with the result.[30] Liberal and Labor Peers, and the Archbishop of Canterbury—one of the vice-presidents of the Society—pointed out the weaknesses in the forced labor clauses, citing abuses that the provisions would not have prevented, and complaining that even Portugal could sign the draft in its existing form.

Cecil maintained that forced labor for public purposes was necessary where an "ignorant and half educated" population could not see the need for development. It was allowed with safeguards in British territories, and even in Britain! When challenged, he said that householders were forced to clear snow from their doorsteps. The peers pointed out that they could hire someone else to do the job. Lord Raglan came to his rescue by suggesting jury service might be considered forced labor. Cecil gratefully agreed that the principle was the same, but the House clearly thought this ridiculous. Cecil took refuge in the argument that a more stringent convention would be rejected by other powers, and that the ILO had virtually been invited to take up the whole question of "native labor."

The peers also complained that the government should give them the same information it gave the League, claiming in a flight of fancy that, had they been furnished with the facts on, for instance, Ethiopia, Nepal, and Burma, steps against slavery in these areas would have been taken sooner. They demanded information on slavery in Sudan, Sierra Leone, Hijaz, and Ethiopia, on labor in Liberia, and on the treatment of British workers in Cuba—all questions being publicized in the *Anti-Slavery Reporter*.

Cecil managed to get this motion withdrawn by promising to look into the matter, and he subsequently made several appeals to the Foreign Office to supply Parliament with the information. It was in vain. The Foreign Office took the view that, since slavery was a League question, it was not their business to publish information on foreign powers, which might have serious diplomatic repercussions and compromise their sources.

PROTECTING BRITISH INTERESTS: THE MARITIME ARTICLES OF THE DRAFT CONVENTION

However, the government itself now reviewed the draft convention to see if humanitarian demands could be met without compromising British interests. They feared that the special agreement between the coastal powers against the maritime trade would simply drive slavers to avoid the flags of the signatories. The navy still insisted that a general treaty was needed giving rights not just to verify the flag, which was all that France would concede, but a clear mandate to search for slaves. As hopes of reaching an agreement with the French faded, the British decided to revert to trying to get the slave trade on the high seas treated as piracy, on the grounds that it was a crime so heinous that it merited special treatment. Privately, however, the foreign secretary, now Austen

Chamberlain, agreed with the French that slavers could be arrested under cover of the search for arms. If they failed to get a new general maritime treaty, the British decided to try to maintain the Brussels Act in force for powers not parties to the St. Germain Convention, such as Spain and the Netherlands, and to retain their other treaties, particularly those with Muscat and the rulers on the coasts of the Red Sea and Persian Gulf.

Alarm bells had also been raised by the TSC's recommendation that slave dhows could be pursued in territorial waters. As has been seen, the Italians had tried to get Britain to grant them the same rights to patrol and search on the Arabian coast as the Royal Navy exercised, raising the specter of increased Italian naval forces in the Red Sea and greater Italian influence in Arabia. The Admiralty was unwilling to offset this by increasing its ships in the area. The navy regarded patrolling for slavers as a disagreeable duty, which did nothing to increase its efficiency. The most it would promise was to send an occasional flotilla to the Red Sea "to conduct an intensive campaign" but only in the cooler months! What the British really wanted was an extension of their own rights to search, without any increase in the Red Sea forces of their European rivals or any challenge from local powers in Arabia and the Persian Gulf.

PROTECTING BRITISH INTERESTS: THE SLAVERY AND FORCED LABOR ARTICLES

All ideas of strengthening either the slavery or the forced labor clauses to meet the demands of the humanitarian lobby were dropped from the British program after inquiries made it clear that it would be difficult even to apply the weak clauses of the draft convention to all parts of the British Empire, let alone more stringent ones.

The major problem concerned India and Burma.[31] Slavery, newly defined as "the status and condition of a person over whom any or all of the powers attaching to the right of ownership are exercised," could with some stretch of the imagination be said to have virtually died out in most of British India. But it had not died in the Naga and Lushai Hills, the Abor Tracts, and other areas not under direct administration in Assam. Slavery also existed in the Hill States of the Northwest Frontier Province, in the Baluchi tribal territory, in the Chin Hills and Myityina in Burma, and perhaps in the Wa states, which had not even been explored. Slaves were still captured in unexplored areas. In Chitral, slavery not only existed, but women were reported to be sold into marriage. Slave girls from Baluchistan were exported to Sind. In Bihar and Orissa, the Kamiauti system of agricultural bondage bordered on slavery.

Forced labor, widely used for public works in British India and Burma, was considered essential. In the petty states under British rule, the rulers exacted it for private and public service. In some areas it was described as "feudal service" based on custom. Little was known about this type of forced labor, except that it would be difficult to end by legislation. Chiefs and landlords could legally command labor in return for charging reduced rent from tenants, or they could accept remuneration in kind rather than cash. Since steps were being taken to end all practices "savoring of slavery" in British India, and some were simply dying out, the convention as it stood, merely demanding progressive elimination, could be accepted for most areas. However, if it were strengthened, many regions would have to be excluded.

Similarly, the Indian Princely States, comprising one third of India, would have to be excluded.[32] The imperial government conducted their foreign affairs, but treaties with the rulers precluded interference with their internal administration and the princes were becoming sensitive to such interference. They did not consider the British entitled to commit them to international treaties that impinged on domestic policy. Only some of the princes were under a clear obligation to suppress both the slave trade and slavery. In the Rajput and frontier states, conditions analogous to slavery persisted, although they were reported to be dying out.

In the Princely States, forced labor was part of the "administrative machine," usually because there was no free labor market or public transport. This labor took various forms and was performed for "feudal lords," for temples, for moneylenders, and for such essential services as putting out fires and irrigation. Normally this labor was not paid, although rents might be remitted and rations provided. Some states were not prepared to accept the draft convention and the British felt they would be infringing treaty rights if they agreed to it on their behalf.

The Dominions and Colonial Offices also raised problems. The high commissioner in South Africa wanted to exclude the three high commission territories of Basutoland, Swaziland, and Bechuanaland from the forced labor provisions, or change the wording to commit signatories merely to taking all "practicable" instead of all "necessary" precautions to prevent such labor from deteriorating into slavery. This was because customary services for chiefs included working on their land and other labor. The resident commissioners who administered all three territories claimed that these services were not forced labor, but tribute willingly performed. The Colonial and Dominions secretary, Leopold Amery, was disturbed by accusations reported in the press that the Tswana and other dominant groups in Bechuanaland had enslaved the Sarwa (Bushmen), and he ordered a full inquiry into the matter.[33]

Amery was faced with a problem that was to last as long as Britain continued to rule its far-flung empire. All components had different laws and customs, and the power of the metropole to impose policy differed in different territories. Treaties could only be signed if they did not conflict with local legislation. Every administration had to be consulted and even if no conflict existed, this was a long and arduous task taking up much official time.[34] In 1926, when the empire was at its greatest geographical extent, Amery did not want to weaken the convention to accommodate the different conditions in each territory. He could only accept it as long as the commitment was merely to end slavery and forced labor gradually, and as long as chiefs could continue to call out labor for public works.

The British, therefore, returned to the League in 1926, determined to try to strengthen the naval provisions of the convention and to ensure that the slavery and forced labor clauses were only as strong as their interests allowed.

FINAL NEGOTIATIONS AT THE LEAGUE OVER THE SLAVERY CONVENTION OF 1926

In 1926, the League Assembly appointed a subcommittee to revise the convention. Neither France nor Italy would agree to the slave trade being declared piracy, as this would give Britain, the only country with a fleet "scattered over the whole globe," the right to search any ships they pleased on the pretext of looking for slaves. They were sure it was a ruse to enhance British prestige.[35] Defeated, the British proposed a general treaty against the maritime slave trade. This, too, was impossible, but a compromise was reached by which signatories were committed to take all appropriate measures to end the slave trade in their territorial waters and under their flags and to negotiate "as soon as possible" a general convention giving them the same rights against suspected slavers as those against arms smugglers.

The British got agreement that the Brussels Act and all their other treaties remained in force for powers that had not acceded to the Convention of St. Germain.[36] In the maritime discussions, Persia and the Government of India objected to "native vessels" being treated differently to others under the Brussels Act and it was agreed that when the projected general maritime convention was concluded, the vessels of all signatories would be treated in the same way. This sent a clear signal that the rising powers of the non-Western world would henceforth challenge the differential treatment to which they had been subjected in the days of gunboat diplomacy.[37]

Predictably, the slavery and forced labor provisions of the convention were not strengthened. The struggle over them was long and drawn out. The Portuguese quibbled about the definition of forced labor, and proposed dropping the forced labor articles pending an investigation by the ILO.[38] They claimed that their colonial labor policies were aimed at development and were color-blind—a dig at South Africa where many skilled jobs were reserved for whites only—a matter which the ILO was eventually to take up.

Late in the day, the Belgians tried to slip in an amendment allowing forced labor not just for public works but also for the "education and social welfare of the natives" on their own land and for their own profit. This was an attempt to legitimize an ordinance imposed in their mandated territory of Ruanda-Urundi in 1924, permitting forced labor for plantations and other undertakings. They maintained that this would only be enforced through African chiefs in the interests of African-owned plantations. However, it was under attack in the Mandates Commission as an infringement of the terms of trusteeship, and it opened the door to the kind of abuses already practiced in

the Belgian Congo ostensibly for local "social purposes," such as forced crop production. The amendment was defeated because of Harris's vigilance.[39]

Only the Germans, newly admitted to the League, tried to strengthen the treaty.
Stripped of their colonies at the end of the war, they had no vested interests to defend.
Like Lugard, they suggested that slavery itself should be immediately banned, together
with forced labor for private purposes. These and their other suggestions would have
benefited the slaves but were not acceptable to the colonial powers. In the end, the
German delegate withdrew his proposals, but to please him, a resolution was passed
stating that "as a general rule" forced labor should only be used when voluntary labor
was not to be had, and that it should always be adequately paid.[40]

Nansen's proposal to refer disputes to the International Court at The Hague was accepted. His proposal that signatories should send progress reports to the League was
reduced to a commitment to send the League and each other information on legislation to implement the convention. His proposal that the ILO be invited to investigate
the question of native labor was whittled down to a resolution of the League Assembly urging the ILO to study the best means of preventing forced labor from becoming
analogous to slavery. The ILO had already begun to collect information and consult
experts. Significantly, it had decided to limit its inquiries to forced and indentured labor rather than to try to get agreement on a labor charter to protect native labor.[41]

The Slavery Convention was opened for signature at Geneva on 25 September 1926
and was signed by thirty-six members of the League, including Belgium, Holland,
Italy, Portugal, and Spain. Britain signed for the empire except the dominions and the
Anglo-Egyptian Sudan, which signed for themselves. Ethiopia, Liberia, Persia, and
China also signed, as well as Colombia, Cuba, Panama, and Uruguay. Over the next
decade, most of them ratified the convention. The British, with an eye to publicity,
were among the first, but to their embarrassment, the Government of India excluded
all the territories of the Indian princes and the chiefs under its suzerainty, as well as
the un-administered tracts in Burma and Assam from the slavery and forced labor
provisions. Portugal and Italy also soon ratified the Convention, as did the Spanish,
but they excluded their protectorate in Morocco. The French, on the other hand, did
not ratify it until 1931, in spite of persistent efforts by their Foreign Ministry to get it
past the Senate. The Ministry was anxious to be seen as solidly *abolitioniste*, in order
to be in a stronger moral position to defend French interests at the ILO when it took
up the forced labor question—as well as to combat British efforts to get a permanent
slavery committee established by the League—a question which, as will be seen, became the next item on the British agenda.[42] When the French finally did ratify, they excluded their protectorates of Morocco and Tunisia.

A number of states that were not members of the League acceded to the Convention.
The most important of these was the United States, where missionaries had aroused
public interest, and the government had expressed sympathy for the antislavery cause

from the start.[43] However, when it acceded in 1929, it made a reservation over the out-lawing of forced labor for private purposes, because convicts were used in private enter-prises in certain southern states. The Americans had originally hoped that the treaty would be negotiated by an international conference including all signatories of the Brus-sels Act, in which they would have participated. However, the British had opposed this for fear other powers might steal their thunder. The Soviet Union, also not a member of the League, refused to have anything to do with the Slavery Convention.

On the whole, British diplomats were well pleased. They had saved their existing naval treaties from abrogation, and other powers had agreed to negotiate a general maritime treaty. They had a convention they could sign without worrying about its impact in India and elsewhere in the empire. They could show that other powers had prevented the negotiation of a stronger agreement and they hoped their "leading role" would be "appreciated in the world at large."[44]

THE IMPORTANCE OF THE SLAVERY CONVENTION OF 1926

This Convention was still in force at the beginning of the twenty-first century. It was important primarily as a legal document establishing a moral position. It was the first international treaty against slavery as well as the slave trade. By widening the definition of slavery to include "all its forms," it marked the beginning of the attack on a wide range of exploitative practices, and was the first step in an ever-expanding definition, as more and more practices came to be described as "analogous" to slavery. Although the Convention did not specifically name all such practices—an obvious weakness—they were on record in the Report on the Convention presented to the Assembly,[45] as well as in the report of the Temporary Slavery Commission. The Convention thus sent a clear signal to all governments that henceforth these types of oppression were under attack. It was the foundation upon which later agreements would be built.

As a practical instrument for ending even the slave trade, it left much to be desired. The commitment to negotiate a maritime agreement was never honored. Since no time limit was set for the eradication of slavery or forced labor, signatories could allow them to continue. Worst of all, no mechanisms were established for enforcement or even for monitoring its results. These were rejected as infringements of national sovereignty. Thus, for all the hoopla surrounding its signature, the Convention was and remained a paper tiger—dependent upon the good faith of governments to give it teeth.

NOTES

1. Lord Robert Cecil became Viscount Cecil of Chelwood in 1923. In 1925, he was Chancellor of the Duchy of Lancaster. A dedicated supporter of the League, he took an active part in its affairs.

2. Lugard to Cecil, enclosed in Cecil to Chamberlain, confidential, 19 June 1925, FO 371/10617 A 3180/531/52.

3. ASAPS to Drummond, 20 May 1925, LON C.T.E. 37, 28 May 1925, 1/28029/23252, enc. in Drummond to Chamberlain, 20 June 1925, 1/28029x/23252, FO 371/10617 A3181/531/52.

4. Cecil to Lugard, confidential, 22 June 1925 and 8 July 1925, Lugard Papers.

5. Minute by Snow, 29 June 1925, on Lugard to Cecil, 23 June 1925, FO 371/10617 A3225/531/52. See also Cecil to Chamberlain no. 30, 28 September 1925, ibid. This question was to remain confused into the 1950s.

6. Unless otherwise indicated the discussion which follows is based on the minutes of the meetings of the interdepartmental committee on 7 and 13 July 1925, together with the appended minutes and the draft conventions in FO 371/10617 A 3541/531/52, A 3557/531/52, A3673/531/52.

7. This went much further than the Brussels Act, which France had never completely accepted; see above, chapter 2. For the implications of treating slavers as pirates, see FO to League of Nations, 29 May 1926, FO 371/11134 A 2858/110/52.

8. These objections are listed in the minutes on Henty to Snow, 21 July 1925, FO 371/10617/ A3728/531/52.

9. Cecil to Lugard, confidential, 8 July 1925, filed with minutes of the interdepartmental committee, FO 371/10617 A 3541/531/52.

10. Lugard to Cecil, 18 July 1925, and enclosed memorandum, FO 371/10167 A 3728/531/52.

11. Cecil to Lugard, confidential, 16 July 1925, FO 371/10617 A 3728/531/52.

12. Cecil to Chamberlain, no. 30, 28 September 1925, FO 371/10617 A 5177/531/52. He was especially concerned that Germany, now robbed of its colonies and soon to enter the League, might make such proposals.

13. Bentinck to Vansittart, 15 September 1925, FO 371/10617 A 4688/531/52.

14. For discussion of these points, see Berthelot to Phipps, 21 May 1926, and minutes and FO to Admiralty, 4 June 1926, all filed as Crewe to Chamberlain no. 958, 26 May 1926, FO 371/11134 A 2837/110/52. The treaty referred to was the Convention of 1925 for the Supervision of the International Trade in Arms and Ammunition and in Implements of War of 1925, which never came into force.

15. Admiralty to FO, very urgent, 22 September 1925, FO 371/10617 A 4778/531/52. For the difficulties of distinguishing slaves from legitimate passengers, see below, chapter 12.

16. Cecil to Chamberlain, no. 30, 28 September 1925 and minute by Bentinck, 10 November 1925, FO 371/10617 A 5177/531/52. For further discussion of both the British and French viewpoints, see Crewe to Chamberlain no. 958, 26 May 1926, FO 371/11134 A 2837/110/52.

17. Report Presented to the Sixth Assembly by the Sixth Committee, 26 September 1925, annex C in Cecil to Chamberlain, no. 30, 28 September 1925, FO 371/10617 A 5177/531/52.

18. Ibid.

19. Minute by Cavendish Bentinck, 13 November 1925, on Incomati Estates to FO, 10 November 1925, FO 371/10617 A 5624/2190/52. For the report by E. A. Ross, see above, chapter 8.

20. For Cecil's defense of this, see House of Lords debate, 16 December 1925, Hansard.

21. See Lugard memorandum, 15 July 1925, to TSC enclosed in Cecil to Lugard, 18 July 1925, FO 371/10617 A 3728/531/52.

22. Report Presented to the Sixth Assembly by the Sixth Committee, 26 September 1925, annex c in Cecil to Chamberlain, no. 30, 28 September 1925, FO 371/10617 A 5177/531/52.

23. Cecil to Chamberlain, no. 30, 28 September 1925, ibid.

24. Cecil to Chamberlain, 25 September 1925, FO 800/258.

25. Reply of the Government of Portugal to the League of Nations, 27 August 1926, LON A.10 (b) 1926.VI.

26. See replies in ibid., and Bentinck minute, 2 September 1926, FO 371/11134, pp. 21–27.

27. Cecil to Chamberlain, no. 30, 28 September 1925, FO 371/10617 A 5177/531/52.

28. Bentinck minute, 10 November 1925, on Cecil to Chamberlain no. 30, 28 September 1925, FO 371/10617 A 5177/531/52.

29. Harris to Behrens, 18 March and 7 April 1926, AS MSS. Brit.Emp. s.19, D3/39.

30. For the debate that follows, see House of Lords Debate, 16 December 1925, Hansard cols.1503 ff.

31. For the discussion that follows, see Patrick to Snow, 19 April 1926, and enclosed tels. from the Government of India and memo by Patrick, FO 371/1113 A 2150/110/52. See also, Chatterjee forthcoming.

32. For further discussion of slavery and forced labor and the Indian Princely States, see below, chapter 17, and Chatterjee forthcoming.

33. High Commissioner (HC), South Africa to DO tel. 27 April 1926, DO to HC, confidential, 28 July 1926, Resident Commissioner (RC), Swaziland to HC, confidential, no. 147, 21 April 1926, RC Bechuanaland to HC, confidential, 21 April 1926, acting RC Basutoland to HC, no. 39, 21 April 1926, FO 371/11134, pp. 139–45. For further discussion on Bechuanaland, see below, chapter 11. For a brief period at this time, the Dominions and Colonial Offices were under one minister.

34. Personal communication from M. Baker-Bates.

35. Memorandum by Bentinck for Cecil, 2 September 1926, FO 371/1114, pp. 22–27; for the French view, see Ministry of Marine to FMAE no. 987, 30 July 1926, FMAE SDN IM4.

36. The British found unexpected support over retaining the Brussels Act from the Catholic powers, Italy, Portugal, and Belgium, and the Vatican. This was because the Act included clauses for the protection of missionaries of all denominations, which had been slipped in as an antislavery measure on the excuse that it promoted "civilization." British missions also supported it for the same reason. Conference of Missionary Societies in Great Britain and Ireland to FO, 24 June 1926, FO 371/11134 A 3394/110/52. For this clause, see Article II, 3, Brussels Act, Hertslet, *Map*, II.

37. British delegation to Tyrell, no. 35, 18 September 1926, and Cecil to Tyrell, no. 44, 25 September 1926, FO 371/1135 A5104/110/52. For further discussion of the Persian question, see below, chapter 16.

38. For the Portuguese views, see Reply of the Portuguese Government to League, 27 August 1926, LON A.10. (b) 1926. VI; Slavery Convention (report on discussions of 17 September) FO 371/11135, pp. 114–15.

39. Harris to Travers Buxton, 10 and 22 September 1926 and enclosure after p. 2, AS MSS. Brit.Emp. s.19, D3/40; British Report from Geneva, 20 September 1926, FO 371/11135, p. 122. The ordinance referred to is no. 52, of 5 November 1924. For Belgian practice and the powers of chiefs in the Belgian Congo, see inter alia Buell, II, ch. 85, section 4, and Northrup 1988 (b), ch. 5.

40. For the German proposals, see Reply from the German Government 1926, LON A.10. (a). 1926.VI and LN A. VI/2/1926 (copy in FO 371/11134). For the discussions which ensued, see British Delegation to FO, 11 September 1926, FO 371/1135 and British Delegation to FO, 13 September 1926, ibid., and Bentinck to Tyrrell, very urgent, no. 39, 22 September 1926, ibid. A 5051/110/52. For the British concern over wording, see Tyrrell to Bentinck, 7 December 1926, ibid. A 6396/110/52. For the resolution, see Cecil to Tyrrell no. 44, 25 September 1926, ibid. A 5104/110/52. For the description of the German delegate, see Harris to Buxton, 11 September 1926, AS MSS Brit.Emp. s.19 D3/40.

41. Enquiry by the ILO into Native Labor, ILO 163/1925 FO 371/11134.

42. Documents on this subject are to be found in FMAE SDN Esclavage—convention de 1926— Rafications, Carton 941 and SDN IM 4. They include letters to French senators complaining of the embarrassing position created by the delay.

43. See correspondence between the ASAPS and the International Missionary Council and the Federal Council of Churches of Christ in America in AS MSS Brit.Emp. s.22 G 448/5. The American Federation of Labor promised support to the International Missionary Council, Warnshuis to Harris, 24 May 1926, ibid.

44. Minute by Snow, 27 September 1926, on British Delegation, Geneva, no. 44 (L.N.A.), FO 371/11135 A 5104/110/52.

45. See LON A.104. 1926.VI.

10

The International Labor Organization and the Forced Labor Convention

HARRIS, THE ILO, AND FORCED LABOR

Once the Slavery Convention was under negotiation, humanitarian efforts centered on the protection of labor from practices "analogous to slavery." Harris set the ball rolling by asking Grimshaw whether the ILO would call a conference to discuss a labor charter for colonial peoples. The director, Albert Thomas, needed a formal proposal to put to the governing body. Harris got the League of Nations Union to send the ILO the necessary telegram. It was drafted by Grimshaw, who watered down Harris's proposal to the more realistic goal of a convention against forced labor—the abuse which had most concerned the Temporary Slavery Commission and which was to be closely tied to the antislavery campaign in the future. The convention was seen as the thin end of the wedge, which would open the way to further treaties.[1] Hitherto, the ILO had been primarily concerned with the protection of labor in the industrialized countries, negotiating agreements on rights of association, unemployment benefits, minimum age for employment, and so forth. The colonial powers had applied few of these to their overseas territories, claiming the conditions were not suitable.

Now, at Grimshaw's suggestion, the governing body appointed a committee of experts to examine forced and indentured labor. It included Lugard, Gohr, Freire d'Andrade, Van Rees, and members from India, France, Japan, South Africa, Germany, and Spain.[2] They held three sessions between 1927 and 1930 to examine the various forms of compulsion exercised by colonial governments. In 1929, the ILO circulated a draft report on colonial legislation with proposals for limiting forced labor, and asked the powers concerned if they would accept them as the basis for a convention.[3]

Forced labor was broadly defined as "all work or service that is exacted under menace of any penalty for its non-performance and for which the worker concerned does not offer himself voluntarily." It differed from slavery as defined by the 1926 convention since no rights of ownership were exercised and it often lasted for a limited time. However, as the following examples will show, it might last a lifetime and be even crueler than slavery since the forced laborer, unlike a slave, had no capital value. These examples drawn from Africa in the late 1920s are designed to show why the Temporary Slavery Commission attacked the practice as liable to deteriorate into slavery.

FORCED LABOR FOR PUBLIC WORKS

Forced labor for public works took many forms. Administrators in most African colonies habitually called on chiefs and headmen to supply labor for public works. Restrictions on the numbers of men who could be recruited in each area, limits on the length of service, regulations on minimum wages, rations, housing and health care, and prohibitions on the use of force and intimidation often went unheeded. Men, and sometimes women, were paid a pittance, if at all, and forced to serve for long periods away from home, without regard to the impact on their own agricultural cycle. In the British colonies, however, as the result of earlier scandals, from 1921 forced labor for public works had to be authorized by the secretary of state and used only for approved projects for a limited time and for the benefit of the community performing it. The use of private contractors was forbidden, experience having shown that they perpetrated some of the worst abuses.

The British, therefore, wanted a convention that would force other powers to abide by the same rules.

At the very time when the ILO was sitting, the need for such a treaty was amply demonstrated by events in French Equatorial Africa. In 1921, to speed up the development of this stepchild of their empire, the French began building a railway from Brazzaville to the sea. Theoretically, a quota of workers was conscripted from each region for one year. The burden on the sparse population, already suffering from other exactions, was immense. High mortality rates caused an outcry in the French parliament and there was an inquiry in 1926. Nevertheless, three years later the British district commissioner at Tambura reported that French subjects were fleeing into Sudan to avoid being sent to the railway, hundreds of miles away. Far from observing a quota, the French official in Obo and Djemah, deeply ashamed, confided that he had had to send all the able-bodied men in his district and was being asked for more. He was also ordered to send food, although his people were starving. Only one woman was sent to the railway for every four men—apparently consigned to forced prostitution. Other witnesses testified that recruits traveled under escort, many dying of starvation on the way.[4] Before the line was completed in 1934, over one hundred twenty-seven thousand people had been conscripted and the official death toll was more than fourteen thousand. Later estimates put it at over twenty thousand—one for every seven recruits.[5]

This was a tragedy born of ignorance—the unforeseen consequences of moving people into a new disease and climatic environment, and feeding them unfamiliar foods, rendering them liable to disease and malnutrition. But it was also due to callous mis-management. Unrealistic demands were made on a sparse population. Quotas and time limits were ignored. It was not the first such disaster. The British East Africa Carrier Corps, for instance, had suffered thousands of deaths from illness and poor conditions during the First World War, and many other instances could be cited, but this human tragedy at this time amply demonstrated the need for the protection of native labor.

By the 1920s, the French had institutionalized another method of recruiting labor for public works—forced labor disguised as military service.[6] As early as 1912, they had introduced partial conscription into their African colonies. Over two million Frenchmen died in the First World War and the postwar birthrate was lower than Germany's. To reinforce their manpower permanently, they introduced universal conscription in West and Equatorial Africa in 1919. Africans were recruited for three years. Only a small proportion of them actually served in the army. The rest were placed in what was called the Second Portion. By the late 1920s, this was formed into labor brigades. The conscripts were given minimal pay, and used to build docks, railways, canals, dams, and other public works constructed by private contractors. Bad working conditions and brutal treatment caused high mortality. The French defended this conscription as a national security measure, denying it was forced labor.

FORCED LABOR FOR PRIVATE ENTERPRISES

Whereas forced labor for public works might last months or even years, it was usually limited in time. Forced labor for private enterprises, however, could last a lifetime and, although it was not hereditary, children might find themselves in the same position as their parents. Moreover, the borderline between public and private works was not always clear, particularly in the case of concessionary companies. In French Equatorial Africa and the Portuguese colonies, these companies actually administered large areas and in return were given the right to exploit all or some of their products. By the late 1920s, they were being phased out and their rights were, at least in theory, more limited, but abuses were still rampant. Thus in French Equatorial Africa the Compagnie Forestière Sangha-Oubangui, had the right to all wild rubber collected in its area. The company demanded an arbitrary quota from the sparse population, already ravaged by tripanosomiasis.[7] The writer André Gide described conditions at the grassroots level in 1925.[8] Defaulters were fined the equivalent of a month's pay. Those who could not pay were imprisoned, flogged, or subjected to other physical abuse. Company agents underpaid villagers for their rubber. When the men fled, they took women and children as hostages. Women were made to work on roads all night. French administrators were too few to exercise control, and the badly paid lower ranks often colluded with the company's agents. In this case, children were born and brought up in conditions of virtual slavery.

Similar conditions existed in Portuguese Mozambique. Here large areas were leased to plantations and chartered companies with a monopoly of their produce in return for collecting taxes, keeping order, and producing crops.[9] Chiefs were ordered to conscript men, women, and children. If a man was sick, his wife was forced to work without wages in his place. One company employed twenty thousand children, some only six years old, for one hundred and twenty days a year. Too young to be useful, they were conscripted so that their parents, out of pity, would take their places at the children's lower rate of pay. A woman might receive a yard of inferior calico for a month's work, or scrip that could only be redeemed for shoddy goods in the company shops. A particularly vicious form of punishment—beating with the palmatoria—was inflicted for offenses as minor as selling a chicken without permission. "Zambesia," wrote a Portuguese official, "looks more like an open slave trading camp" than Portuguese territory.[10]

Some of the worst cases of forced labor for private enterprises took place in settler colonies. In Kenya, white farmers, undercapitalized and unwilling or unable to pay attractive wages, expected the administration to provide cheap labor for their farms and transport for their crops.[11] After the First World War, in response to settler demands, officials, chiefs, and elders were told to step up their efforts to provide male recruits for private use, and to press women and children into paid labor. Workers were registered and forced to carry passes, making evasion more difficult. Finally, an ordinance was proposed which would have obliged all African men who had not performed three months of wage labor in the preceding year to work for sixty days a year on public works for pay below the market rate, as well as to give six days a quarter to unpaid communal labor. This raised such a storm of protest from Parliament, the Anglican Church, the Anti-Slavery Society, Lugard, and others that Churchill cut the Gordian knot in 1921. Henceforth, the only labor obligation was six days a quarter of paid communal service performed in the Native Reserves.

However, large numbers of Africans became squatters or resident labor, living with their families on European farms. In a modern form of serfdom, they were forced to work for 180 days a year for the landlord in return for minimal pay, a plot of land, and grazing rights, and had no security of tenure.[12] In theory, they were free to leave, but, as time went on, many found it increasingly difficult to return to their homelands in the Reserves. To cement this system, Africans were not allowed to live outside the Reserves except as squatters or wage laborers. Master and Servant Ordinances made all breaches of contract penal offenses. Fines and prison sentences were imposed for offenses such as failure to pay taxes or to carry a pass.

In sum, forced labor in its crudest form had been much reduced in Kenya by the late 1920s, but less obviously oppressive forms of labor extraction had been devised which were so successful that the governor worried that the siphoning off of adult males from their communities would impair the African population's ability to sustain and reproduce itself.[13]

The same worry beset the Belgians. In contrast to the poverty of both French Equatorial Africa and the Portuguese colonies, the 1920s were years of rapid economic

growth in the Belgian Congo. Railways and roads were built, capital poured in, and copper, diamonds, gold, cobalt, uranium, and other minerals flowed out. Local secondary
industries were established and food and cash crop production was stimulated. The result was an acute labor shortage. The Belgian public, in reaction to the scandal of King
Leopold's administration, was determined not to allow any compulsory labor for private enterprises. However, in their eagerness to "develop" the Congo, the administration
made it clear that Africans had an obligation to work, and officials an obligation to see
that they did so. The results were impressive. Where there had been some one hundred
thousand wage earners in 1918, seven years later, the number had more than quadru-
pled, with about half working for European enterprises, often hundreds of miles from
home.[14] This was only achieved because illegal recruiting by the administration was
pervasive. Officials threw their weight behind recruiting agents. Chiefs were pressured
to cooperate on pain of removal or lowered salaries. One appalled official complained
that villagers fled at his approach as though he were a slave trader.[15]

By 1924, the government feared that the excessive demand for labor was depleting the
manpower of rural communities to the point that they would not be able to reproduce
themselves. Two commissions recommended curbing recruitment and economic development, and in 1928, administrators were ordered to stop direct recruiting for private enterprises. However, wages were still too low to attract voluntary labor and administrative
pressure continued. Thousands of men, women, and children were still conscripted to
build roads and perform other services. The demands of business kept up the pressure.
Forced labor continued, deplored by the Belgian public and agonized over by ministers.

FORCED CROP GROWING

Another form of forced labor in the French, Portuguese, and Belgian colonies at this time
was the compulsory growing of cash or food crops, defended as educational measures.
Forced growing of food was justified as a measure against famine, and was supposed to
be solely in the interests of the African farmer. But, in the Belgian case the crops were often requisitioned by the administration to feed workers in the mines or towns. They paid
low prices, and the porterage, performed mainly by women and children, was unpaid.
Moreover, to pay their taxes, farmers had to produce more than their quota.[16] This cheap
source of food for their workers contributed to company profits and enriched the coffers
of the colony as a whole. If prices went down the loss was passed on to the African farmer.

Forced growing of export crops was tried by the Portuguese, French, and Belgians.
Thus, in 1920–1921 the Belgians, to lessen their dependence on American and Indian
cotton, gave a number of concessionary companies the right to buy the whole crop
produced in their areas.[17] Government agronomists assigned each productive male a
plot of land on which to grow cotton. Mechanization was ruled out as too expensive.
Peasants with rudimentary tools had to clear the land, plant and weed the cotton,
harvest it, sort it, and carry it to trading stations in homemade baskets. Women and

children, not officially recognized as producers in order to avoid criticism in Belgium, played an important part in the work, including the porterage. In 1925, for instance, hundreds of women, carrying head loads of over sixty pounds, were forced to walk for seven days to distant buying stations, for no pay and with only the food they could forage. The men worked all year for such a small return that some one hundred thousand people were impoverished.[18] Failure to plant or tend the crop was punished by imprisonment, flogging, or fines. Desperate peasants, trying to convince officials that cotton would not grow on their land, cooked the seeds before planting them. In some areas, men no longer had the time to supplement their protein intake by hunting or fishing, and women had to grow less nutritious and less labor intensive crops, such as cassava, in place of millet, causing malnutrition. The peasants carried the risks and costs of floods, droughts, crop disease, and price fluctuations.[19]

COMMUNAL LABOR

Communal labor was defined as "a common effort to carry out rapidly a public work for the common benefit." This was work people supposedly performed free "traditionally" for the good of the community, or as tribute for their chief. Once slaves were freed, this labor became an important perquisite for chiefs and village heads. Colonial authorities, knowing little about African traditions except what the chiefs and elders chose to tell them, believed it was hallowed by custom and willingly performed. They valued it because it enabled them to avoid paying chiefs adequate salaries, and provided them with labor for minor local projects. The chiefs valued it as a status symbol and because they could use it to their economic advantage. The British were the great defenders of communal labor. This was particularly important in the 1920s when they were extending indirect rule to areas where there were no traditional rulers, by appointing chiefs and establishing native administrations.

In some areas, there was little problem. In the tiny territory of the Gambia, where there was only one all-weather road, no settlers, and one main cash crop grown by Africans, the only compulsory service was communal labor. It was performed by adult males around their own villages. Payment was distributed by chiefs, who were handed the money in public, ensuring that everyone knew the work was to be paid. No one, not even porters, worked any distance from home. In such a situation, the proposed ILO convention could be accepted without problems.[20] In Sierra Leone, equally without settlers, the only unpaid compulsory labor was on the roads. Chiefs supplied the labor and men were normally only away from home for fourteen days. The governor insisted that the people wanted roads and if he had to pay market wages, taxes would have to be raised, and this would be unpopular. Moreover, when chiefs called out villagers for local communal work, certain tasks, such as weeding, reaping, rubbing the walls of houses, and cooking for the workers, were traditionally performed by women. Interference with such customs would be resented.[21] Difficulties of this sort could be resolved by careful wording of the ILO proposed convention, and by excluding minor community services from its provisions.

In Uganda, however, there were more serious problems. Here, African rulers had considerable power and independence, and many were growing cash crops in response to market incentives. Ganda rulers and chiefs exacted various forms of labor as tribute. This could be used to increase their output of cash crops, particularly cotton, or it could be commuted to a cash payment, or payment might be in food and beer. The governor maintained that these obligations were "thoroughly understood and willingly accepted." Only men were conscripted and they worked in gangs under their chiefs. All young males were called out, but the unfit were given only tasks they could perform. The governor believed that a convention requiring medical examinations and the conscription of only a percentage of men at one time would be resented. Moreover, in some cases the rights of chiefs and rulers had been guaranteed by treaties made during the period of conquest.[22] In the little kingdom of Swaziland, chiefs protested that communal labor was "an absolutely essential support to the chiefs." It was the contribution of the people to the "dignity" of their chosen leaders and was purely voluntary.[23] Like the chiefs, the governors of all colonies tended to paint a rosy picture of communal labor—happy Africans willingly giving their time to their chiefs for the benefit of their communities. There is ample evidence, however, that this labor was often resented. Chiefs and headmen were agents of the colonial state. Many abused their powers, demanding labor for their own fields, keeping a cut of the taxes they collected, sending the recalcitrant as forced labor for the administration and exacting a share of their pay, extending the number of days of work, and conscripting women and children. This was an inevitable result of the colonial situation. Those chiefs who genuinely tried to shield their people from exactions risked removal or other punishment. Those who pandered to the administrations were rewarded.

THE FORCED RECRUITMENT OF CONTRACT LABOR

Contract labor was also open to abuse. Workers for the Portuguese islands of São Tomé and Principe, for instance, were still forcibly recruited. Officials sentenced tax defaulters, together with troublemakers, and "vagrants" to work on the islands. Angola was paid for the recruits and they were only repatriated in return for further consignments. All a discontented worker could really expect at the end of his contract was to be allowed to change employers.[24] Spanish recruiting methods for the cocoa plantations of Fernando Po were equally suspect.[25] Under various agreements, the Spanish paid the impecunious government of Liberia for each recruit. In 1928, a private syndicate run by Liberian officials was using the Liberian Frontier Force to recruit workers by force. Between 1922 and 1929, over nine thousand were sent to the island on one- to two-year contracts. By this time, the American Firestone Company was oper-

ating in Liberia with unrealistic plans to hire three hundred and fifty thousand workers from a total able-bodied population of perhaps four hundred thousand.[26] It was
accused of using forced labor. The American government tried to ward off this brew-
ing scandal by accusing Liberia of slave trading in 1929 under guise of labor recruitment. The Liberians, believing, with some reason, that the United States had designs
on their independence, asked the League to mount an investigation. As will be seen the
question was soon mired in politics.

BRITAIN AND THE ILO PROPOSAL FOR
A FORCED LABOR CONVENTION

Unlike the other colonial powers, Britain wanted a forced labor convention. This was
the result of the rise of the Labor Party, which in 1920 had passed a resolution against
the import of goods made with sweated labor. The party was taking an increasing interest in colonial labor policies. William Ormsby Gore, the parliamentary undersecretary at the Colonial Office, had been embarrassed when Grimshaw pointed out that
there was no legislation in African colonies requiring even safety devices on equipment. In 1925, he warned the Office that the old excuse for not applying ILO conventions to the colonies on the grounds that "conditions were not suitable" was becoming
untenable as more and more people were employed on public works and in light industries. If the government wanted to gain the support of the Labor Party for the economic development of the empire, it would have to show that native labor was safe-
guarded, or make a good case in Parliament for not safeguarding it.[27] This, and the ILO
circulars, forced the Colonial Office into action.

Early in 1929, colonial governors were sent the ILO report and asked if they could
accept its recommendations. Their replies showed that the principles were acceptable,
but modifications would be needed if the convention were to be applied to all components of the "dependent" empire without changing existing practices. The Colonial
Office appointed a committee to ensure that the provisions of the proposed convention would not conflict with "some unhappy custom" in the middle of the Pacific.[28]
They were concerned only with the territories under British control, and not with self-
governing colonies, notably Southern Rhodesia, or with the dominions or India.

The biggest problem was to reconcile the proposed convention with indirect rule.
Some treaties, such as those with the Malay sultans, the emirs of Northern Nigeria, and
the kings in Uganda, precluded interference in internal administration, except for
gross abuse.[29] Even where there were no such treaties, some provisions conflicted with
"traditional" practices and chiefs' rights. Thus the principle that forced labor should
only be used for essential public works was acceptable. However, the ILO proposed
that only the government of the colony or the metropolitan government should have
the power to authorize such works. This was only compatible with indirect rule if the

authority could be delegated to rulers, chiefs, or native authorities. In cases where chiefs normally called out all adults, or where women performed "traditional" tasks without pay, requirements that forced labor should be paid, that only able-bodied men should be recruited, and that workers should be ensured good working conditions and health care might conflict with "native law and custom." The ILO proposed to solve this by excluding communal labor for minor projects benefiting only the local community. However, the Colonial Office wanted road building classified as a minor project in order to avoid having to pay wages for it. These exclusions would enable chiefs and native authorities to continue to exact free services.

The British were in full agreement with the ILO principle that forced labor should never be used for private enterprise. However, it was not always possible to distinguish between work the chiefs exacted as personal services, such as tilling their personal land or repairing their houses, and that to which they were entitled in their official capacity, such as the maintenance of roads and guest houses. The Colonial Office, unwilling to pay chiefs enough for them to hire labor, decided to insist that chiefs should not be classified as private employers. Officials agreed, however, that colonial administrations should ensure that they only used forced labor for public services, and that they abide by the proposed regulations.

Since there were no concessionary companies in Colonial Office territories, and no forced cultivation except to avoid famine, the British could support the ILO proposals to eliminate them.[30] However, the ILO's proposed sixty-day limit for all compulsory work, or six months in exceptional cases, was only acceptable if it could be waived in cases where it was impractical. The regulations to protect porters—limiting their loads and days spent away from home, and requiring medical examinations—would raise difficulties for officials on tour in remote areas. The committee accepted the other provisions to protect the health of workers and limit workloads. They also agreed with the ILO proposal that workers' compensation should be paid for illness, accident, and death, but went further suggesting it should be paid to all workers, not just those conscripted for forced labor.

They agreed that indirect methods of forcing people into wage labor—such as taxation, vagrancy and pass laws, land alienation, and restrictions on the growing of the more lucrative cash crops—the very things of which the British were most guilty, should all be forbidden. They believed the assurance of the governor of Kenya that there was sufficient land for the African population in the colony, and that taxes and vagrancy laws were not imposed in order to promote a supply of labor for private purposes. Apparently, they thought they had set their house in order in Kenya and elsewhere. At the level of general policy, they also agreed with the suggestion that further development in a colony should only be permitted if it would not put such pressure on the local population as to require forced labor, even if this meant curtailing industrial, agricultural, and mining enterprises, and limiting "non-native" settlement. They knew, of course, that there were problems in Rhodesia and South Africa, but since these territories ran their own affairs, they could be left to "look after themselves." The Colonial Office committee recommended that under the convention, governments should have the power to prevent labor from going to places where conditions were not satisfactory. This would give international sanction to efforts to stop voluntary labor from going, for instance, from Nyasaland to Mozambique, or from Northern Rhodesia to the Belgian Congo, or from Nigeria and Sierra Leone to Fernando Po. It was thus a potential threat to foreign powers allowing labor abuse.

The election of a Labor government in June 1929, dependent on Trades Union support and sympathetic with the aims of the ILO, made it inevitable that Britain would not just support a convention, but would attempt to make it as strong as possible. The whole question was being closely followed in labor circles.[31] The new colonial secretary, Lord Passfield, reminded colonial governments that Britain was under a moral obligation to apply all ILO conventions "with the smallest possible modifications" in all its territories. He also asked for annual reports, which could in the future be the basis of the reports to the ILO required under article 408 of the Treaty of Versailles.[32]

While the Colonial Office pondered the forced labor questions from the viewpoint of the "dependent empire," Foreign Office officials wrestled with the diplomatic problems. As in the past, there were difficult choices, raising questions as to how far humanitarian sentiments should override the protection of British commercial and diplomatic interests.

THE COLONIAL POWERS WATER DOWN THE CONVENTION

France, Portugal, Belgium, and Italy viewed the ILO proposals with undisguised alarm. They would have liked the negotiations to fizzle out. They could sabotage or delay the resolutions of the League of Nations, but it was more difficult to deflect the ILO with its large unofficial membership and strong labor representation. They tried to organize a united front to water down the convention. In 1930, after abortive overtures to enlist their support,[33] they invited the British to meet representatives of the French, Belgian, Portuguese, Italian, Spanish, and Dutch governments in Paris. They each had specific practices to defend, and they had more general fears about opening a Pandora's box if the ILO were given powers to interfere in colonial policy.

The Portuguese were the most concerned. In May 1926, the corrupt and inefficient Republican government had been overthrown by a Fascist military dictatorship. One of the reasons for the coup was fear that Portugal might lose its empire in view of South African designs on Mozambique and a deteriorating political situation in Portugal. The new government reorganized the colonial administration with the aim of turning the colonies into producers for the metropole. New laws were promulgated in 1928 and 1930. Henceforth, forced labor was to be used only for public purposes or penal correction. It was to be paid and could only be called upon when urgently needed in the public interest. Contracts were to be supervised. The old concession system was phased out. This looked good on paper and the Portuguese boasted that indigenous peoples had complete freedom to choose the work that suited them best. But—and it was a big but—for his own development the "native" had to be "rescued" from his "traditional idleness." He had a "moral duty" to work and, of course, work meant wage labor or some other approved means of earning money. In practice, in order to pay their taxes, men had to work as contract labor for private or public employers for at least six months a year and were often recruited by the administration by force. More efficient government and a pass system made evasion more difficult. The old abuses continued.[34]

Although they maintained that their labor legislation was now perfect, the Portuguese were mortally afraid of investigation, and used threats and bribery to silence critics. The missionaries who had helped Ross with his investigations were persecuted, and their congregations targeted for forced labor and harassed.[35] In 1925, Incomati Estates, a British company operating in Mozambique, was told by Freire d'Andrade's son that because Cecil had "backed" the Ross report at the League, they could expect "distinct opposition" to their business proposals.[36] Using attack as the best means of defense, the Portuguese also accused foreign companies of labor abuses, including—with reason—the British owned Sena Sugar Estates in Mozambique.[37]

They feared the ILO would appoint a permanent committee of experts to oversee colonial labor policies, or that the ILO might demand the imposition of economic sanctions if they did not comply with the convention—a fear shared by France and Italy. They tried to enlist British support by bribery, intimating that they could further the interests of British companies. Foreign Office officials toyed with this idea only to be sharply reminded that the Labor government

> desire[s] the abolition of forced labor as soon as possible. The Portuguese see no need for this and deny the necessity of a Convention . . . we must oppose the Portuguese attitude and associate ourselves with progressive Colonial powers.[38]

This was a dream—there were no such powers. The British persuaded the French to invite the ILO to send an observer to their Paris meeting. They hoped he would support them, and that his presence would deflect attacks from "labor groups," who realized that the colonial powers were plotting to undermine the convention. The ILO director, Thomas, came himself.[39] He tried to resolve the differences between the diehard views of Portugal and those of the British, which other powers thought "unduly progressive" if not "quixotically impractical."

The British wanted complete abolition of forced labor in five years. The others wanted no time limit or at least ten years' delay. The British wanted forced labor limited to sixty days. The others opposed this. The French and others wanted to exclude military conscription from the definition of forced labor. The British had a large volunteer army in India and elsewhere and did not conscript young men for military service. They were prepared to allow conscription, but only for a year and if recruits were paid market wages and used strictly for military purposes. This would have spelled the end of the French military labor battalions.

To please workers' groups, and particularly the Trades Union Congress,[40] the British did not want the convention to mention that administrators should encourage people to "engage in some form of labor." The other powers objected. Thomas supported them. He believed that the ILO had a duty to promote "habits of free labor." The British wanted to ban the use of forced labor by contractors engaged on public works. The Belgians protested that they could lay down more stringent requirements for contractors than for administrators. The Portuguese objected to all restrictions on forced labor, but took particular exception to the proposal that it should only be resorted to if voluntary labor was not forthcoming at market wages. The prestation—unpaid labor as a tax—was considered forced labor by the British but defended as a fiscal measure by the other powers. The British lost this argument, and agreed that it could be exacted if protected by the same regulations as other forms of forced labor.

The Belgians were upset when the British objected to forced crop growing. They complained the British were trying to protect Ugandan cotton producers from competition. When the British suggested that forced cultivation be limited to five years, the Belgians would only agree to consider ending it in ten years, as it would take at least that long to overcome the "backwardness and indolence" of the farmers.

To meet British concerns about the impact of the convention on indirect rule, the powers agreed that colonial governments might delegate their authority to recruit forced labor to subordinate authorities, provided these were subject to the same regulations. The British announced that they intended gradually to curtail chiefs' powers to conscript labor, and to phase in payment at market rates. In "exceptional cases," it was agreed that local authorities might keep porters away from home for long periods.[41]

After the Paris meeting, Thomas and his staff, in consultation with the committee of experts, redrafted the convention to make it more palatable to the colonial powers, and presented it to the Fourteenth International Labor Conference in June 1930. A drafting committee of representatives of governments, labor, and employers drew up the final convention.[42] The British were supported by Workers' Groups, while the other colonial powers were backed by Employers' Groups.

The Portuguese were "hand in glove" with the French and Belgians. The French regarded the convention as unwarranted interference in their colonial affairs. At the time, their plans for the economic development, *mise en valeur*, of their colonies were being much criticized. The British thought their intransigence was dictated by financial and industrial interests anxious to develop French Indo-China and the Pacific

Islands.[43] The continental powers were well served by an African, Blaise Diagne, a deputy to the French parliament from the Four Communes of Senegal—who, to the dismay of the British, not only supported military labor as necessary for national defense, but declared:

> I speak as an African . . . on behalf of my race and of my people and my country, and I say that we are by nature indolent and so incapable that we really require force and compulsion; that even under stress and famine we are not capable of finding food in the forest unless someone compels us to do it.[44]

These views coming from such a source made a great impression on the delegates, although they were contrary to all evidence that Africans responded to market forces.

THE FORCED LABOR CONVENTION OF 1930

The Forced Labor Convention was necessarily a compromise.[45] It bound all signatories to end forced labor "in all its forms within the shortest possible period," a weak provision that all could accept. However, in five years, the ILO was to "consider the possibility" of immediate abolition. Meanwhile, it could be used only for public purposes for which there was a clear need and for which voluntary labor could not be procured. It was to be an exceptional measure, subject to strict regulation and not to put too severe a burden on the population concerned. A 25 percent limit was put on the male labor to be conscripted in any community. Forced labor of all kinds was to be restricted to sixty days in twelve months—a provision strongly resisted by the French. Forced cultivation as an educational measure was ruled out, to the disgust of the Belgians. If it had to be used to avoid famine, the food was to remain the possession of the producer. The prestation or labor tax, on which the French and others insisted, was allowed.

All forced labor was to be the responsibility of the "competent authority"—defined as the highest central authority of a territory or the metropolitan country—but it could delegate its powers as long as workers did not have to leave home, or if it was necessary for the transport of government officials or supplies—thus British wishes were met. As a further concession to indirect rule, forced labor for chiefs was allowed if they had administrative functions, but it was subject to the same conditions as other forced labor and was to be phased out. Chiefs who were not adequately paid in other ways were also to be allowed to enjoy "personal services" subject to regulation to prevent abuse.

Only males, "who had the appearance of being between 18 and 45," were to be conscripted and certain categories, such as teachers, pupils, and officials were to be exempted. Where possible, conscripts were to be medically examined to ensure they were fit. Working hours and pay were to be the same as for voluntary labor. Wages were to be paid to individuals and not to chiefs, and were to cover traveling time. No deductions from wages were to be made for taxes, food, clothing, tools, or accommodation. Workers' compensation was to be the same for conscripts as for voluntary workers. Laborers were not to be sent to a different climate, given strange foods, or forced to perform unaccustomed work without being acclimatized and given adequate health care. If they were away from home for long periods, provision was to be made for their sustenance, and for the remittance of wages to their families. Regulations were laid down for the employment of carriers and boatmen but they were to be replaced by other forms of transport as soon as possible. Forced labor was never to be used for work underground in mines, and, to the chagrin of British governors, was never to be imposed as a collective punishment.

Forced labor for private purposes was completely ruled out. Concessions to companies were to be rescinded as soon as possible. The British objection to allowing official "encouragement" of recruiting for private purposes was met by careful phrasing: "Officials of the administration, even when they have the duty of encouraging the populations under their charge to engage in some form of labor, shall not put any constraint upon them to work for private enterprises."

As the French wanted, military service was excluded from the definition of forced labor but—here came the sting in the tail—the British carried the day by insisting that it had to be "purely military in character," thus banning the French labor battalions. Penal labor was also excluded from the definition and was thus allowed—but again there was a sting in the tail—it was not to be hired out for private use, as it was, for instance, in India, South Africa, and certain states in the United States.

Minor communal services were also excluded, in deference to the British, so that chiefs and native authorities administering "small native communities" could continue to call on "traditional" services. At the suggestion of the Workers' Group, however, these services were only to be allowed if the members of the community agreed to them. This meant that the "traditional rights" of chiefs as the theoretical basis for conscription was to be replaced by the democratic principle of the "will of the people." When this was later discussed at a conference of governors and officials in the Colonial Office,[46] the governors of the larger British territories feared that any interference with the rights of chiefs and rulers would diminish their standing. They also argued that "the will of the community" would be hard to establish. The young men called out to build roads, for instance, might well object, while the women, who would be relieved of the heavy work of porterage, might welcome the advent of motor transport. In contrast, the governors of Sierra Leone and the Gold Coast thought the "communal will" could be easily ascertained.

For political reasons, British negotiators accepted this provision, with its democratic implications. It reflected the debate that was just beginning about the merits of indirect rule as a method of preparing indigenous people for eventual self-government, as against more democratic forms of local administration. At this stage, the controversy was still in its infancy and more emphasis was laid on the "rights" of the chiefs and rulers, whose legitimacy was derived from the colonial government for whom they provided a cheap form of administration, than on their obligations to their people. How far they had the support of their followers in accordance with an understood "moral economy" was not under serious discussion.

Finally, the convention stipulated that signatories must provide facilities for complaints about forced labor, must inform workers of their rights, and take measures to ensure that the regulations were enforced. They were also to send annual reports to the ILO.

RESULTS OF THE FORCED LABOR CONVENTION

This convention was the first of its kind. It opened the way to further agreements to protect indigenous labor; and it protected the workers of the industrial world from the competition of the still unorganized colonial workforces. It laid down principles for the treatment of native labor, which, if observed, would ensure that they did not fall into virtual slavery.

The other colonial powers and Employers' Groups abstained from voting for the convention, so the British were proud of having secured a two-thirds majority at the ILO for a treaty which contained almost all the provisions they thought essential, and none that would embarrass them by requiring modification or exclusion. They recognized that some articles might be difficult to carry out, but as a public relations exercise they had achieved their goals. The British Empire had been shown to be generally "on the right side."[47]

The British had no illusions that the convention would really benefit "native races." They believed it would only be applied in territories where its principles were already accepted and not in those where the need was greatest. In this they were right. It had, anyway, built in delaying mechanisms. No time limit was set for the end of forced labor, for the rescinding of concessions, or for the phasing out of unpaid labor for chiefs. Signatories could exclude part of their possessions from its provisions, and did not need to apply the convention for twelve months after they ratified it. They could renounce it after ten years. If they did not do so, they would be bound for further periods of five years. At the end of each five-year period the Governing Body was to present the General Conference of the ILO with a report on the working of the convention and its revision was to be considered.

Britain and the Netherlands both ratified the convention in 1931. Spain ratified it in 1932—the year it came into force. The other colonial powers simply delayed ratification, Italy only until 1934, France until 1937, Belgium until 1944, and Portugal until 1956. Ratification merely meant that the principles of the treaty were accepted. Henceforth, forced labor was theoretically distinguished from slavery and clear standards had been set for its use. Enforcement was another matter. As will be seen, the question entered a new and more explosive phase when an important new player, the Soviet Union, came into the fray after the Second World War. Then, as in 1930, it was closely tied to the antislavery campaign.

NOTES

1. For Harris's maneuvers, see Harris to Grimshaw, 20 December 1925, 11 and 14 January, and 5 February 1926, to Hills, 11 January 1926, to Murray, 14 January 1926, to Goldring, confidential, 15 January 1926, AS MSS. Brit.Emp. s.19 D3/39; Grimshaw to Harris, private, 9 January and 1 February 1926, AS MSS. Brit.Emp. s. 22, G 466, G. and C. W. Newbury, 315.

2. For a useful article on this committee, see Gertrude E. and C. W. Newbury.

3. The questionnaire with the British replies and discussion are in CO to FO, important, 23 May 1929, FO 371/13481 A 3473/594/52.

4. Burges Watson to governor, Bahr el Ghazal, confidential, 28 July 1929, and Nesib Bas to D. C. Tambura, 25 July 1929, Huddleston to Hoare, no. 163, 10 August 1929, extract from letter from Rushby at Bangui, 15 June 1929, FO 371/13880.

5. Bouche 1991, 193.

6. Echenberg 1991, 47–64.

7. For a history of these companies, see Coquery-Vidrovitch 1972.

8. Gide 1962, 64–73, 183–87, 257–60.

9. This section is based on Vail and White 1980, 221–25, and Allen and Barbara Isaacman 1983, 29–59.

10. Vail and White 1980, 224.

11. For this section, see Clayton and Savage 1974, 20ff; Wrigley 1971, Buell 1928, 351–59, Okia 2000.

12. Wrigley 1971, 248–49.

13. Acting governor, Kenya, to Amery, 9 April 1929, CO 323/1027.

14. Buell II, 534; Jewsiewicki 1986, 476.

15. Buell II, 542.

16. Northrup 1988(a), 144–48; Buell II, 500.

17. For this section, see Likaka 1997, and Northrup 1998(a).

18. Northrup 1988(a), 142–44.

19. Likaka 1997, 12–56.

20. Governor, Gambia, to Amery, no. 60, 5 April 1929, CO 323/1027.

21. Governor, Sierra Leone, to Amery, no. 173, 6 April 1929, CO 323/1027.

22. Governor, Uganda, to Amery, no. 113, 2 April 1929, CO 323/1027.

23. Acting resident commissioner to acting government secretary, no. 81, 10 February 1933, SNA, RCS 133/33 file forced labor 1932–1948.

24. Smallbones to Carnegie, confidential, 11 September 1927, enclosed in Carnegie to Chamberlain no. 336, 13 October 1927, FO 371/11990, and Smallbones to Chamberlain, confidential, no. 17, 23 February 1928, FO 371/12758 A 2001/230/52.

25. This section is based on Sundiata 1980, 28–32, and 1996, as well as reports from the British consul in Monrovia in FO 371. The full complexities cannot be considered here.

26. Buell 1928 I, 833–36.

27. Memorandum by Ormsby-Gore for Sir S. Wilson, "Labor Conditions in Crown Colonies and Protectorates," 28 August 1925, CO 323/941. At this time, the Convention on Unemployment had not been applied in any dependent territories. The Convention on the Right of Association of Agricultural Workers had been applied only in British Guiana, Ceylon, the Straits Settlements, and some Caribbean islands. The conventions on Workmen's Compensation had not been applied anywhere in Africa. The only African colony covered by an ILO convention was the Gold Coast, and this merely laid down the minimum wage for employing children at sea.

28. Eighth meeting of the Colonial Office Conference, 8 July 1930, COCP 885/32, miscellaneous, no. 416, confidential, copy in FO 371/15036.

29. There were similar problems with the Indian Princely States, which will be considered separately, and were handled by the India Office and not the Colonial Office.

30. The only forced cultivation was in the Western Pacific and was to ensure an adequate food supply.

31. Third Report of the Forced Labor Committee of the Colonial Office, 21 November 1929, FO 371/15034.

32. Colonial Office memorandum: International Labor Conventions, 1930, and Circular Letter 29 April 1930, CO 885/32.

33. See for instance, Paskin to Howard Smith, no. 70188/2/30, 31 January 1930, FO 371,15034 W1141/34/52; Report by the Colonial Office Delegates to the Preliminary Conference held in Paris, 12–23 May 1930, in CO to FO, 27 May 1930, FO 371/15035 W 5544/34/52; Lindley to Henderson, no. 27, 10 January 1930, and minutes, FO 371/15034 W 801/34/52.

34. Allen and Barbara Isaacman, 41–42.

35. Bell to Harris, 12 February and 18 November 1926; Warhuis to Harris, 26 August 1926, ASS MSS Brit.Emp. s.22 G 448/5.

36. ASAPS to FO, 25 January and 16 March 1927, and minutes, FO 371/11989 A 581/230/52. Incomati Estates had not given Ross any information or been mentioned in his report but presumably this was d'Andrade's response to Cecil's attempt to intimidate Portugal into accepting the Slavery Convention by displaying the Ross report in Geneva.

37. A British consul investigated Sena Sugar Estates and reported that there had been abuses, but they had ended, Pyke to Chamberlain, no. 210, confidential, 8 November 1927, and minutes, FO 371/11990 A 6511/230/52. For a history of the company, see Vail and White 1980.

38. Lindley to Henderson, telegram no. 65, 2 May 1930, and FO to CO and Ministry of Labor, 5 May 1930, FO 371/15035 W 4422/34/52, and Drummond Shiels to Henderson, 6 May 1930 and minutes, ibid., W4534/34/52.

39. He was accompanied by C. H. Weaver, who had drafted the ILO reports and had replaced Grimshaw, who had died.

40. Third Report of the Forced Labor Committee of the Colonial Office, 21 November 1929, FO 371/15034.

41. Minutes of the meeting are in FO 371/15036. The report by the Colonial Office delegates is in CO to FO, 27 May 1930, FO 371, 15035 W 5544/34/52. The comments on amendments to the draft convention which resulted are in ibid., 293–96.

42. It consisted of representatives of all the colonial powers except Spain, and all the British dominions except Canada, and of representatives of Liberia, China, Japan, and Germany.

43. Speech by Vernon to the 8th Colonial Office Conference, 8 July 1930, COCP 885/32 Miscellaneous no. 416 confidential and FO 371/15036 W 8250/34/52, pp. 128–44.

44. Ibid., 131.

45. Only the main provisions are listed here. For the text, see *Human Rights: Instruments (HRI)*, E.78.XIV, 2, 1978.

46. Eighth Colonial Office Conference, 8 July 1930, COCP 885/32, Miscellaneous no. 416, confidential, copy in FO 371/15036 W 8250/34/82.

47. Report of the Colonial Office Members of the Delegation of H. M.'s Government in the United Kingdom on the 14th International Labour Conference, Geneva, 10–28 June 1930, COCP 885/32 Miscellaneous no. 14 and FO 371/15035.

11

The League of Nations and Slavery in the British Empire

THE BRITISH EMPIRE IN THE 1920s

The 1920s and early 1930s were the heyday of the British Empire. It had reached its geographical limits. The wars of conquest were over. Although colonial rivalry still bedeviled relations, there were no great internal or external threats. However, resources were limited and governors, still fearful of precipitating rebellion or flight, gave the slavery question low priority. In the metropole, four different departments—the Colonial Office, the Dominions Office (separated in 1930 from the Colonial Office), the Sudan Office, and the India Office—struggled to keep the policies of the territories under their control in line with the new demands of the treaties negotiated by the League of Nations and the ILO. Their task was not made easier by the resistance and subterfuges of the men on the spot.

In some cases, notable advances were made, particularly on the frontiers and in remote areas, where the British now felt strong enough to act. They reported in 1924 that, as the result of their efforts and of the spread of Christianity, the Bawi in the Lushai Hills in Assam could now ransom themselves for forty rupees and were no longer called by a term denoting slavery. This was a reversal of their prewar policy when they had insisted that the Bawi were not slaves and that owners were merely providing poor relief.[1] In other parts of Assam and in certain frontier tracts, however, slavery continued.[2] In 1925, the India Office informed the League that it had negotiated a system of self-redemption with the rulers of the still unadministered Hukawng Valley in Upper Burma.[3] The government had advanced slaves the money to ransom themselves and proposed to recover it in easy installments, from those able to pay. The selling of slaves, their use for paying dowries and blood money, and the splitting up of families was immediately forbidden. Emancipation was to be completed by 1926 and an official was to visit annually to monitor results. The total cost of freeing two thousand people was estimated at Rs1,250,000 (rupees). It was cheaper than establishing an administration, kept critics at bay, and gave slaves less incentive to flee into the adjacent administered areas.[4]

Elsewhere, as the examples below, drawn from very different parts of the empire, will show, the local administrators were only forced into action by the revelations of the antislavery lobby—a lobby now reinforced by the backing of the League of Nations.

SLAVERY AND THE SLAVE TRADE IN SUDAN

The case of the Sudan is of particular interest in view of the apparent revival of slavery there in the 1990s. Slavery was widespread when the British conquered Sudan in the late nineteenth century and established joint rule with Egypt, known as the Anglo-Egyptian Condominium. Most owners were the Muslim Arabic speaking peoples who predominated in the north, and most slaves came from the Nilotic and other non-Muslim ethnic groups of the south and west. However, both sedentary and pastoral peoples in the south and west also had slaves. Originally fearing that action against slavery would provoke rebellion and disrupt the economy, the British concentrated on suppressing the slave trade. Owners were assured that they could keep their slaves, and administrators returned those who left "without due cause," or made them pay ransom. Vagrancy laws stipulated that everyone had to be in "acceptable employment" on pain of imprisonment.[5] The administration tried to keep these policies from attracting the attention of the Anti-Slavery Society and even the Foreign Office—the department in charge of Sudan.

Thus in 1923, agriculture in northern Sudan was still based on slave labor. Children, theoretically free, were still born into slavery. Although a circular in 1919 stated that slaves did not have to pay ransom, officials still illegally imprisoned runaways until they could be "persuaded" to return to their owners. Slavery cases were dealt with in Shari'a courts controlled by the slave-owning class, and masters manipulated Muslim law to their advantage, particularly when it came to control over women and children. There were still slave raids from Ethiopia and French Equatorial Africa. Individuals were still kidnapped and some were exported to Arabia.

In that year, an agricultural officer, P. W. Diggle, began to manumit numbers of slaves. He was outraged at seeing slaves neglected or beaten, children taken from their parents, and girls hired out as prostitutes.[6] His superior supported him and asked for a clear statement of government policy. The administration denied that slaves were badly treated and claimed that if they were freed, agricultural production in the north would collapse. Diggle resigned and embarked on a personal crusade, alerting press and Parliament, and the Anti-Slavery Society forwarded his evidence to the League just as the Temporary Slavery Commission was preparing for its second session.

The fact that the British were attacking slavery in Ethiopia while allowing it to continue in Sudan was bound to fuel suspicion that they were playing a devious game to promote their interests in Ethiopia.[7] Moreover, they were engaged in a struggle with Egypt for control of the Sudan and slavery became a pawn in this game. The Egyptians assured Diggle that if the northern Sudan reverted to their control, slavery would "automatically" cease.[8] The British feared that they might at the same time tell the Sudanese they would support slavery in accordance with Muslim law.[9] To prevent Egypt indirectly asserting its claim to joint sovereignty over Sudan, the British arranged for League questionnaires and correspondence to be sent directly to Khartoum and for Sudan to sign the 1926 Convention in its own right.[10] Against this background, pressed by the Foreign Office to answer Diggle's charges, the administration denied that slaves were ill-treated and claimed that abolition would involve "political risk."

This reply, together with a manifesto from Muslim leaders saying that they desperately needed labor, and that freed slaves would not work, was sent to Lugard at the TSC with an appeal for his forbearance, since he, of all people, would understand the risk of taking unpopular action in "so lightly held and explosive a country as the Sudan."[11] In the nick of time, he was also sent a circular issued on 6 May 1925, stressing that all persons born since 1898 were free, that slaves had a right to leave and would not be returned to their owners. He duly informed the TSC that action was promised. What he was not told was that the circular was only sent to British officials.[12] However, Harris now instigated a debate in the House of Lords in which peers demanded that its provisions be enforced and slaves be informed of their rights.[13] This finally drove the administration into action.

Slaves were registered and freed on demand without ransom. Those born since 1898 were considered free.[14] Fugitives were no longer returned. The freed were given access to land, loans, implements, and cattle. Some were placed in supervised settlements. Claims over the children of concubines and proxy marriages to secure control over women were forbidden.[15] The laws were publicized and enforced. Efforts were made to control the pilgrimage and a clearinghouse was established in Port Sudan to receive slaves repatriated from Arabia—over eight hundred of whom were resettled between 1925 and 1935.[16]

While these reforms were under way, a flourishing two-way slave trade over the Ethiopian border was uncovered. Ethiopians were launching raids into Funj and White Nile provinces and returning with Berta, Gumuz, and Burun captives. Southern Sudanese Arabs were crossing into Ethiopia to buy slaves and arms, or were buying them in Sudan from Ethiopian dealers, the most prominent of whom were Khojali al-Hassan, the "Watawit" shaykh of Bela Shangul in Wallaga and his principal wife, Sitt Amna.[17] She had established herself and her followers in Sudan in 1905 and the unsuspecting British had recognized her as head of an administrative unit. Khojali and his supporters collected slaves in Ethiopia, many of them his own subjects, and sent them to Sitt Amna to sell. The victims, mainly adolescent girls or young boys, were either born in servitude, captured in raids, kidnapped, or acquired through debt or as tribute. To disguise their origins, they were given Watawit scarification and sometimes kept for a while and trained as domestics in the homes of Sitt Amna's and Khojali's wives and concubines in Ethiopia. Most buyers bought only one or two slaves, but profits could be high. A slave bought from Sitt Amna for eight to ten pounds, Egyptian, could fetch thirty-five to forty pounds in Kurdufan. The traffic was hard to detect and to prove, as even children with still unhealed wounds from recent scarification or circumcision were so terrorized by tales of what the white men would do to them that they claimed they were slaves of long standing, traveling legitimately with their owners.

The Sudan report to the League in 1927 did not mention slave trading,[18] so the accidental discovery of this traffic in 1928 was embarrassing, particularly when the scale of the operations was uncovered. Over a thousand slaves were freed. Some two hundred traders and buyers were arrested, and about three hundred firearms were confiscated. Anthony Arkell, who headed the investigations, believed that only a fraction of recently imported slaves had been discovered and that there was a substantial complementary arms traffic. The administration blamed its failure to detect the trade earlier on the fact that the migrant pastoral people on the frontiers, as well as native government officials and local notables, were heavily implicated. There was still only a token British presence in the area.[19]

New border posts were now created and secret agents were employed to infiltrate trading networks. Heavy fines and prison sentences were imposed[20] and warnings were issued against slave trading. The freed slaves, who called themselves "sons of Arkell," were resettled, some near their masters, others in colonies of former soldiers, and some as wage labor in Gezira or elsewhere. The girls were married off as quickly as possible.[21]

As well as this traffic, there was a constant flood of fugitives from Ethiopia, including runaway slaves, subjects of Khojali fleeing to avoid being sent to Addis Ababa as tribute, men trying to avoid conscription, and girls fearing they would be forced into prostitution for the army.[22] Masters petitioned the British to return fugitives. Those who could not be persuaded to go home were settled away from the frontier for fear raiders would recapture them or local notables would return them. Their presence inflamed relations with Ethiopia, upset slave owners in Sudan, who feared their own slaves might join them, and saddled the British with the expense of resettling them. From 1924, largely as the result of pressure from the Anti-Slavery Society, no fugitives were returned[23] and the problem festered on.

As the result of the change in government policy from 1925, most men who wished to leave their owners had been able to do so before the outbreak of the Second World War in 1939. Progress was slower for women. As elsewhere, they had fewer opportunities for wage labor, and freedom could mean abandoning their children. Laws were passed to give them the same rights as other women, but as late as the 1950s in rural areas, masters often found ways to retain control.[24]

As in so many cases, legal emancipation did not give ex-slaves or their descendants of either sex social and economic equality with the free born. Half a century later, although their condition varied greatly,[25] many had no land, lived in separate settlements, were socially despised, and did not intermarry with the descendants of the freeborn. Since social attitudes and structures had not changed, it should have been no surprise when in the 1990s, as a by-product of the war between the northern and southern Sudan, many southern peoples found themselves captured by government-sanctioned Arabized militias and sold north into bondage.

THE FINAL ATTACK ON SLAVERY IN SIERRA LEONE

Revelations of slavery in Sierra Leone surfaced in the mid-1920s. As in Sudan, the administration had done little to change the lot of slaves in the Protectorate.[26] After more than three decades of British rule, there were still over two hundred thousand of them, 15–20 percent of the population, comprising half the inhabitants of some areas. They still suffered serious disabilities. They still changed hands and officials still returned fugitives. The hardships of the First World War, and the food shortage and economic stagnation which followed, had led to many of them decamping to the towns and either taking wage labor or turning to crime. They were becoming increasingly restive, and the administration and the business community now saw slavery as a disincentive to growth. The freeborn regarded manual labor as "slaves' work" and slaves risked having their earnings taken by their owners. Officials were few and they resented time spent settling claims over slaves. Prodded by the Colonial Office from 1919, the administration finally passed an ordinance forbidding officials from recognizing slavery in either their judicial or administrative capacities.[27] It was still legal to own slaves and chiefs were assured they would not be forced to free them, but any who applied for redemption were to be manumitted without charge.

Difficulties about interpreting the law soon surfaced. Masters recovered runaways by force or chastised them in accordance with customary law. Some slaves refused to work for their owners. Such cases were taken to court and in 1927 it was decided that it was still legal for masters to use "reasonable force" to regain their slaves.[28] This caused an uproar in England and questions were asked in the Sixth Commission of the League. The ordinance was repealed and slavery lost its legal status in 1928. The government promised Parliament that slaves would be told they were free, would have access to land, and be otherwise supported, and none would be sold across the Liberian border.[29]

In practice little changed. Although slaves were told of their rights, few left their owners.[30] Most continued to work without pay in return for access to land, lodging, food, or some other consideration. Instead of being called slaves, however, they were now known as "cousins" or by some other euphemism. Nearly thirty years later, in 1956, a commission of inquiry reported that many complained they were still working just as when they were slaves, and in the 1970s their servile origins were remembered.[31] As usual, legal equality did not bring much change in social or economic status. However, the British reported in 1929 to the League that they had fulfilled their obligations.[32]

What they had not suppressed, however, was a new form of captive labor, known as "wardship." This was the acquisition of children disguised as adoption, which grew in scale as the supply of slaves declined. In Sierra Leone in the 1920s, it usually involved a rural family in the Protectorate sending a child to a "Creole" family in the Colony. Theoretically, they were to go to school and learn the customs of "civilized" urban life, in return for performing light household duties. In practice, all too often they became household drudges or overworked "apprentices." This disguised trade in children, akin to the infamous traffic in little Chinese girls known as mui tsai, which will now be discussed, was to grow into a trade of unknown proportions in West Africa at the end of the twentieth century, and included a regular cross-border trade in children.[33]

"LITTLE YELLOW SLAVES UNDER THE UNION JACK": THE SALE OF MUI TSAI

Mui tsai[34] were Chinese girls sold by poor parents to richer families usually for a paltry sum. In theory, they were adopted, and suitable husbands were to be found for them when they grew up. The transaction was recorded in a deed of "presentation." Boys were rarely sold and when they were it was usually a genuine case of adoption. At best, a mui tsai was saved from infanticide, starvation, or a life of toil with her natal family. The Chinese elite saw their adoption, and their descendants in Hong Kong still see it, as an act of charity. If the parents lived nearby, adopters would probably treat the child well so as not to lose face, and parents could redeem her by repaying the purchase price. Many girls doubtless bettered themselves, but unknown numbers became overworked, abused domestics. Dealers exported them to overseas Chinese communities, including the United States. The least fortunate were sold into prostitution, although this was not the normal fate of a mui tsai.

When the British occupied Hong Kong in 1841, they proclaimed that the Chinese would be governed according to their own laws and customs, although they outlawed both slavery and the slave trade. The British regarded all sales of persons as slave dealing, whereas in a Chinese patriarchal family, the male head could sell, pledge, or betroth all its members, including wives, children, younger siblings, and servants. It was only slave trading if they were sold by someone other than their legal guardian.[35] It was not until 1879 that a British judge pronounced the sale of mui tsai to be slave trading. The governor, fearing this would drive away the Chinese merchants upon whom the prosperity of the colony depended, persuaded the colonial secretary not to press the point. An ordinance in 1887 strengthened laws against sales for prostitution but did nothing to stop the acquisition of mui tsai. The British simply did not recognize such transactions. Theoretically, the girls could leave. In practice, they did not know their legal rights and usually believed it was their filial duty to remain with and obey their purchasers.

In 1880, the Chinese founded Po Leung Kuk, a society formed to care for persons who were destitute, or had been kidnapped, forced into prostitution, or ill-treated. It had its own detective agency and it established homes for the victims, mainly women and children. This relieved the British from taking action. The society's aim was not to end the mui tsai system but to uphold the patriarchal system, and prevent, for instance, persons from fleeing from their legal guardians or wives running away from their husbands.[36]

In 1917 after a member of Parliament, John Ward, asked the government to explain the position, the governor denied that mui tsai was slavery, and objected to interference with an institution that was widespread in China.[37] By 1920, however, a campaign against it was spearheaded by European missionaries and Christian Chinese. When the wife of a British naval officer, Mrs. Haslewood, denounced it in the press and her husband refused to restrain her, he was forced to resign. Like Diggle in the Sudan, they returned to England and embarked on a personal crusade.[38] Although not always accurate in their accusations,[39] they enlisted wide support and broadened their campaign to include abusive child labor and the sale of girls to brothels, which were legal and licensed in the colony. The League of Nations was just taking up the question of trafficking for prostitution and their protests fell on fertile ground. They sent information to the nascent ILO.[40] The Anti-Slavery Society took up the cause with enthusiasm.[41] They organized a spate of parliamentary questions and demands for the publication of reports, spearheaded by Ward. They enlisted the support of various feminist organizations, the National Society for the Prevention of Cruelty to Children, and the League of Nations Union. Representatives called at the Colonial Office. The archbishops of Canterbury and York were among the people who wrote to it. Constituents wrote to their members of Parliament.[42]

The matter became even more embarrassing when Ward announced that the buying and selling of people even for adoption had been banned in China when the Republic was established in 1911. This was misleading, as children could still be hired to strangers up to the age of twenty-five and parents could be paid at the time of hiring.[43] Moreover, selling of mui tsai was widespread in China in the 1920s.

The Colonial Office suggested various reforms, including forbidding further transfers of children without their parents' consent, and the registration and visiting of mui tsai. The Secretary for Chinese Affairs protested that families constantly moved in and out of the colony, that visits would alienate the Chinese and require numerous inspectors, and finally that the number of abused girls was probably large and neither the government nor charitable institutions had the resources to look after them. He wanted policing left to the Chinese community and the Po Leung Kuk.[44]

The number of mui tsai was unknown. The 1921 census had identified only some eight hundred. The Chinese guessed there were ten thousand. The population, estimated at about six hundred thousand, fluctuated constantly as thousands of people entered and left the colony every day, unrecorded. To sort out natural from "adopted" children would pose a major problem. The Anti-Slavery Society recognized that it might be impractical to free all mui tsai at a stroke and put them in homes. To defuse the situation, some Hong Kong Chinese established the Anti-Mui-Tsai Society, and their opponents founded the Society for the Protection of Mui Tsai. The Colonial Office used them as a further excuse for delaying action.[45]

In February 1922, the Anti-Slavery Society organized a conference of twenty-two societies. They called for a commission to discuss the matter. A week later the colonial secretary, Winston Churchill, faced with another barrage of parliamentary questions, in defiance of all his advisors, decided to end the impasse:

> "I am not prepared," he wrote, "to go on defending this thing. . . . no compulsion of any kind will be allowed to prevent these persons from quitting their employment at any time they like. I do not care a rap what the local consequences are."[46]

He commanded the governor to issue a proclamation stating that the status of mui tsai was no longer recognized and girls who were grown up might leave. He hoped the institution would end in a year.[47]

Needless to say, the governor watered down the proclamation. Mui tsai who had reached "years of discretion" might apply to the Secretary for Chinese Affairs to leave—but they must have a job to go to in order not to fall into the hands of procuresses.[48] They were not told of their rights. The proclamation was simply posted on government notice boards, but mui tsai were not normally allowed out unescorted and most could not read. Not surprisingly, no applications were received and the governor took this as proof that most were happy with their lot.[49]

To placate Churchill, however, he proposed a bill in the Hong Kong legislature that would have ended the acquisition of new mui tsai and allowed existing ones to leave or be paid wages. This provoked an outcry from the Chinese community. They argued that it would turn the girls into servants, ending genuine adoption, and would lead to infanticide, kidnapping, and forced prostitution. The governor took fright, envisaging the end of British rule in Hong Kong on the one hand, and the government having to support hundreds of destitute girls on the other. The removal of Churchill from the scene as the result of a change of government enabled a compromise to be reached. The Female Domestic Service Ordinance of 1923 reaffirmed that mui tsai status was not recognized by law. It forbade the acquisition of new mui tsai, and the employment of any children under ten, and their transfer without permission. Employers were bound to provide food, clothes, and medical treatment. Moreover, they were not to be overworked and the discontented could appeal to leave. Part III of the ordinance, providing for the registration of the children, the payment of wages, and inspections was withheld to placate the Chinese. Hence, the ordinance could not be enforced.[50] The British public was not told of this, nor was Lugard, who informed the TSC that mui tsai had been abolished in both Hong Kong and the Straits Settlements.[51]

In 1928, however, the agitation began again, fermented by the Hong Kong Anti-Mui-Tsai Society and spurred on by the outlawing of the practice in neighboring Kwantung (Guandong) Province. The governor, Sir Cecil Clementi, certain that the laws would not be enforced in China, claimed that it would be impossible to end mui tsai in Hong Kong while families constantly moved between China and the colony. The Colonial Office, fearing that the failure to enforce the 1923 ordinance would arouse public opinion in Britain, issued a doctored blue book.[52] The next year, however, brought a Labor government to power and the new colonial secretary, Passfield, coming fresh to the fray, told Clementi to put Part III of the 1923 ordinance into immediate effect and send six monthly reports on progress. The governor, reluctantly, ordered all mui tsai to be registered before 1 June 1930 and forbade further imports.[53]

Eventually 4,368 girls were registered. Thousands of pamphlets were issued to publicize this requirement, but little was done to make the ban on imports known, and no attempt was made to find unregistered girls. The Anti-Mui-Tsai Society claimed that four thousand were passed off as adopted daughters. Passfield, under humanitarian pressure, insisted on the appointment of a police inspector and two Chinese women inspectors in 1931. Although prohibited from making random calls or looking for unregistered girls, they had an impact. They made over five thousand home visits in 1932, and by mid-1933 had prosecuted some ninety owners, mostly for nonpayment of wages. Subsequently the numbers of registered girls dropped rapidly as they grew up, married, left the colony, returned to their parents, died, or just disappeared.

Passfield demanded that similar steps be taken in the Straits Settlements, the Malay States, where laws on the Hong Kong model had been passed in 1925 but not enforced, and in British North Borneo, Brunei, and Sarawak. These came into effect in the mid-1930s by which time the whole question, as will be seen, had been brought to the fore again.[54]

To do them justice, British administrators genuinely believed that infanticide would rise with the end of mui tsai. Whether they were right in claiming that it had caused a rise in the number of infant corpses found in Hong Kong in 1929 cannot be proved.[55] The prophets of doom were wrong, however, in their predictions that hundreds of children would be thrown onto the streets and that the Chinese would no longer cooperate with the government. Many continued to regard mui tsai as an ancient and justifiable institution but registration proceeded smoothly. The humanitarians, however, rightly believed that Chinese girls were still imported, sold, and abused in British colonies. Odd cases, as will be seen, still came to light in Hong Kong and Singapore in the 1950s.

At the grassroots level, there is all too little information on the impact of the new laws. To have been a mui tsai was considered a disgrace and most girls as they grew up tried to hide their former status. Fortunately, we have a notable exception in Janet Lim, who published the heartbreaking story of her sale by her penniless mother in China, her resale to a dealer who brought her, together with other children, to Singapore, her

abuse at the hands of her owner, and her escape.[56] What emerges clearly is that no attempt was made by customs officials to check their import into the colony, although
trafficking for prostitution was illegal and the prettiest of her companions ended up in
brothels. On the other hand, once registration was introduced, she became aware that
the authorities might help her. Moreover, the authorities, instead of prosecuting her
owner, made him pay for her education at a convent school in Singapore. She became
a nurse and ultimately matron of a hospital. Hers is a rare success story; most former
mui tsai remained low in the socioeconomic scale, and only recently, if at all, have they
divulged their origins even to their children.[57] As usual, governments could free those
in servitude but only rarely could they help them to improve their social standing.

Mui tsai have disappeared from the modern world, but the sham adoptions and
outright sales of children for domestic service, brothels, and other employment continued on a large scale into the twenty-first century. They differed, of course, from the
chattel slavery of the past in that the children were theoretically free and might become so when they grew up.

SLAVES OR SERVANTS IN THE BECHUANALAND PROTECTORATE?

"Slavery is not known to exist in the Bechuanaland Protectorate," wrote the resident commissioner in 1923 in reply to the League questionnaire. There was, he subsequently conceded, "a modified form of hereditary service."[58] Finally faced with the League's definition
of slavery as "a person over whom all or some of the rights of ownership are exercised,"
he had to admit that there were people regarded as personal property. However, their
work was not "strenuous" and they were happy with their lot.[59]

In fact, the form of servitude, sometimes called predial serfdom, was far from mild.
The Tswana were primarily a pastoral people. They lived in towns but moved out in
summer to their farmland. Beyond this were their cattle posts and still farther out their
hunting grounds, which they claimed, but did not occupy. As their kingdoms expanded
in the nineteenth century, they absorbed indigenous groups, each of which remained endogamous and occupied its own social stratum. The stratum that concerns us here was
called *malata* by the Ngwato, whose state was the most powerful of the Tswana kingdoms. Most malata were drawn from a hunting-and-gathering people known today as
the Sarwa.[60] The system of servitude was known as *bolata*. It was called by different
names and took different forms in each kingdom, but the main features were the same.

Malata (singular: *lelata*) were occasionally sold but there was no slave trade. They
were nonetheless considered as possessions by their owners, who were mainly members of the royal family, officials, and rich commoners. They could be transferred,
inherited, paid as tribute, or given away. Their status was hereditary. Their children belonged to their mother's owner and could be taken from them by force. Some did domestic work in return for food and clothing. Others, often families, looked after the
cattle posts in return for milk. The women might be taken as concubines. Malata had

no rights to land or property and no way to improve their social standing. They were a fully controlled hereditary labor force over whom masters had powers of life and death. They performed menial tasks in return for the bare necessities of life. The actual arrangements with their masters varied greatly and some may have been contented, but there were many documented cases of cruelty.

The British ruled through the Tswana kings, whom they called chiefs. These ruled native reserves in accordance with "native law and custom." No effort was made to find out what this meant until the 1930s. Theoretically, all groups had a voice in the *kgotla*—an assembly of adult men who dispensed justice and made all political and administrative decisions—but power lay with the Tswana elite, who, together with the rulers, owned many malata. The chiefs provided a cheap form of administration for the British who took no responsibility for the economic development of the reserves. The Tswana introduced some elements of capitalism—private property, production for export, and a money economy—but retained precapitalist land tenure systems and a servile labor force. Malata increased in numbers with the spread of cattle posts. Prosperous Tswana employed them and sent their own sons to school. No one could leave the reserve without permission from the chief. Malata also needed permission from their owners.

A mere handful of British policemen and resident magistrates with judicial and administrative functions were scattered around the protectorate to keep the peace, collect taxes, and keep out of trouble. The total forces were too small to risk alienating the Tswana elite. Fugitive malata were routinely returned. Missionary protests and denunciations that the system was slavery were ignored. An increasingly ossified administration was unwilling to provoke even minimal resistance and did not want attention drawn to bolata.[61] The Colonial and Dominions Office only became aware of the situation as the result of the League enquiries and the correspondence over the Slavery Convention. Bolata had been legalized in 1891 as part of native law and custom, and the legal status of slavery had never been ended.[62] At the very moment when the home government was preparing to sign the Convention without reservations, slavery in the protectorate made headlines as the result of a quarrel among the Ngwato elite over ownership of some malata girls.[63]

To maintain their antislavery image, the high commissioner, the Earl of Athlone, went to the Ngwato capital and declared that compulsory service must end and called on the chiefs and headmen to encourage the Sarwa (Basarwa) to "stand on their own feet." The Tswana were already suffering from taxes, laws limiting their commercial activities, and other difficulties. They gave malata just enough food and clothing to keep them working and ensure their reproduction. To pay them, to help them build up herds of their own, to give them land and tools, to dig wells and to allow them to market their own hunting products would cut into owners' profits and increase competition for scarce resources. Athlone had passed the buck to them. They were to bear the cost of helping the malata and the blame for further scandals. The Athlone Declaration cost the British nothing and enabled them to sign the Slavery Convention without reservations for Bechuanaland. They had taken "preliminary steps" to end slavery and this was all that was required.

The Tswana chiefs, led by the Ngwato regent, Tshekedi Khama, protested—once freed the malata would steal Tswana cattle or revert to foraging—a fate that both he and the British regarded as a return to barbarism. Athlone assured them that there would be no "sudden change."[64] Indeed nothing might have happened if the Dominions secretary, Leopold Amery, had not sent out a new resident commissioner in 1930, Charles Rey, to develop and "breathe new life" into the Protectorate.[65] Neither of them believed in indirect rule, and Rey decided to limit the power of the Tswana chiefs and codify native law and custom, incidentally ending all forms of servitude. Tshekedi Khama feared this was an attack on his independence, which would reduce the Tswana to the same level of poverty and impotence as Africans in South Africa. Slavery became a pawn in a bigger game.

A horrendous case in which two Ngwato seized some malata who had absconded, and beat one to death—and the revelation that the culprits had never heard of the Athlone Declaration—decided Rey to ask for a "cocked-hat official enquiry" into the whole question. A parsimonious treasury authorized a one-man inquiry to ensure that it would be cheap and return a unanimous decision. E. S. B. Tagart spent two months in the protectorate, interviewing Basarwa, as well as officials and Tswana leaders. He called the malata serfs rather than slaves because their duties were defined by custom and they usually changed hands only by inheritance within the owning family. Rey insisted they were slaves because they were chattels. Tagart thought they were treated reasonably well, but were anxious to be rid of their owners. He recommended that they be given the same rights as the Ngwato, that a proclamation should affirm that slavery was illegal, and that a census should be taken by a European officer, who would also help malata get wage labor, and set aside land for them. He also suggested that native demonstrators should teach them farming. He advocated master and servant laws to establish contractual relationships for all Africans and curbs on corporal punishment.[66]

Rey decided to delay action until he had introduced measures to curtail the powers of chiefs. The slavery question helped to give weight and urgency to his proposals.[67] A further inquiry and the appointment of another League committee kept the slavery question alive. In 1935, a "Masarwa Officer" was finally appointed to take the census of the Sarwa and inquire into their condition. This revealed that some were in wage labor and free of their owners but others were still tied to the cattle posts and were exploited and sometimes abused. They were paid in milk, which was only available half the year. In 1936, a proclamation declared slavery illegal and required payment for all labor in cash or kind—but no minimum wage was set.

The departure of Rey in 1937 ushered in a period of cooperation between the new resident commissioner, Charles Arden-Clark, and Tshekedi, who aimed at integrating

Sarwa into the community on an equal basis. Schools were started for them. An agricultural demonstrator was sent to teach receptive groups farming, and numbers were recruited to work in the South African mines. The British now considered them free since, theoretically, they could now dispose of their labor in the best market, pay their own taxes, own property, complain to the *kgotla*, were no longer subject to arbitrary punishment, and could keep and control their own children. Here again, however, "freedom" failed to improve the condition of the majority of the freed. Studies in the 1970s and 1980s showed that for many in the reserve their incorporation into the Bangwato had turned them into a landless, cattle-less proletariat. Without ploughs, oxen, wells, access to Western education, and earning only minimal wages, they were economically worse off then in the late 1930s.[68] They were not the only poor. Many Ngwato and other Tswana were equally poverty-stricken but the Basarwa were also socially despised.

SLAVERY IN THE ADEN PROTECTORATE AND
BRITAIN'S SATELLITES ON THE PERSIAN GULF

The Achilles' heel in Britain's antislavery campaign was in South Arabia and the Persian Gulf. In the colony of Aden, slavery had been outlawed, but in the Aden Protectorate there were a few outdated treaties against the slave trade with some rulers in the northeast and along the coast up to the frontiers of Muscat, but there was little or no contact with large areas of the interior, where the situation was unknown. The question will be discussed later since it received little or no attention in the Foreign and Colonial Offices until, as will be seen, it was raised at the League in 1932.[69]

In their satellites in the Persian Gulf, however, the British were well aware in the 1920s and early 1930s that chattel slavery continued on "a fairly considerable scale" and that there was an active slave trade. They were anxious to keep the matter from attracting international attention. Their legal powers acquired by treaties made with the rulers over many years and containing different provisions were surprisingly weak.[70] Bahrain and Kuwait were described by the Foreign Office as independent states under British protection—but they were not ordinary protectorates and were thus not bound by British treaties with other powers. Qatar and the Trucial States—Abu Dhabi, Ajman, Dubai, Fujairah, Ras al-Khaimah, Sharjah, Umm al Qaiwam—were described as "independently administered tribal principalities" ruled by their own shaykhs. Relations with all the rulers were handled by the India Office, which took no responsibility for their internal affairs. Its interests were limited to ending the maritime slave and arms trades, protecting British subjects, and preventing naval hostilities between the rulers. The rulers' foreign relations were controlled by the Foreign Office. They could not deal directly with foreign powers or sign treaties on their own. To avoid complications with other powers the British tried to ensure that they complied with treaties signed by Britain. Muscat and Oman was an independent state "in special treaty relations" with Britain. It was free to conduct its own foreign relations although the British tried to control them. The sultan relied on British protection and Britain paid him a subsidy. All these states were considered British satellites.

With all of them, except Kuwait and Fujairah, the British had treaties against the slave trade granting them the right to search their shipping on the high seas and in territorial waters.[71] Slavery, however, was not interfered with. It was practiced in accordance with Muslim law and slaves could legally be bought and sold within the states themselves.[72] British agents were stationed around the Gulf and if escaped slaves reached them, they would ask the rulers to free them, or they would issue manumission certificates. If relatives of persons enslaved appealed to the British, they would try to track them down. Sometimes a ruler would spontaneously free a runaway.[73] Each case was investigated to ensure, for instance, that the applicant was a slave and not a pearl diver trying to escape his creditors.[74] Until 1932, the British did not automatically give manumission certificates to *muwallid*—persons born of slave parents (domestic slaves)—for fear of causing unrest on the Trucial Coast. However, a minute, dated 1932, shows there were no legal grounds for distinguishing between domestic slaves and others and that this regulation had recently been waived.[75] The many instances of slaves taking refuge with British officials or on warships show that not all were, as the authorities so happily insisted, content with their lot.

There was still an active, if comparatively small-scale, traffic in slaves. Some were kidnapped locally, but most came across the Gulf from Baluchistan to the Batinah coast of Oman, and some ended up in the Trucial States or elsewhere in Arabia.[76] Baluchistan was divided between Persia and India. Persia had not established control over the Makran coast and British Baluchistan consisted of settled areas under direct administration, of princely states including Kalat, and "tribal areas" under indirect rule. Most victims were enslaved by khans or tribal chiefs in Persian territory. Some were kidnapped, others were promised jobs in Arabia. There was even a racket reported in 1923, by which parents sold their children to dealers or creditors in bad times and later asked the British to trace and free them. Thus, poor families used the traffic as a source of income. The numbers of slaves crossing the Gulf fell when Baluchi harvests were good and rose when they were bad. The British resident believed that most of the victims, particularly women, fared better in Arabia as slaves than as free people in Baluchistan.[77]

A trial in 1927 revealed the existence of an organization that lured Indian boys from Karachi to Gwadar, at that time administered by the sultan of Muscat. The boys were then smuggled into Persia for shipment to the Omani coast. The most unfortunate ended up as pearl fishermen in Dubai, where conditions were particularly harsh. In 1928, the Hindu community there denounced a dealer for importing Indian children of both sexes. However, the British political agent in Kalat claimed most had been freed and the route was no longer active.[78]

By 1930, there was promise of improvement. The khan of Kalat had outlawed slavery and was policing his state, and Reza Shah Pahlavi was laying the foundations of a modern state in Persia and had outlawed slavery the previous year. However, when Persia signed the Slavery Convention it announced that it would no longer be bound by any treaty which imposed the special rules on its shipping required for "native vessels." The Persians were anxious to replace their treaty with Britain, signed in 1882, with a new treaty giving them reciprocal rights to search. The British refused because it would have given them the right to search the dhows of British protected states in the Gulf, dealing a blow to British prestige and perhaps interfering with their commerce.[79] As the shah had still not established control over the Makran, and had only one gunboat, it was unlikely he could police his waters.[80] The British decided to continue searching Persian vessels between the Makran coast and Arabia and in the territorial waters of their satellites. If the Persians proved "unreasonable," the India Office proposed to take the case to the League.[81]

However, they had no desire to attract attention at the League to the slave traffic or slavery in their Gulf satellites. In 1928, the India Office warned the Foreign Office not to raise the matter:

While there is undoubtedly a certain amount of slaving, it would be unwise to magnify its importance, having regard for the fact that it is quite impossible for us to interfere in the hinterland of Muscat and the Trucial Coast, and that, short of doing so, little more can be effectively done at present. The results that have been achieved by our preventive measures are very substantial and . . . it would be a pity to give the League the impression that the problem in this particular area is in any way a really serious one.[82]

THE OFFICIAL MIND OF COLONIALISM

As these examples show, left to themselves, colonial administrations would have continued to ignore the problem of slavery. With few exceptions, the men on the spot had concluded that it should be tackled slowly with minimal disruption to the status quo. The Anti-Slavery Society, the missionaries, and other people who took up the cudgels on behalf of the slaves were seen at best as misguided do-gooders whose well-intentioned efforts were likely to do more harm than good—even to the slaves. At worst they were considered troublemakers satisfying a private grudge, or in the case of Harris, anxious to keep the Anti-Slavery Society going. The administrators were not impervious to the injustices of slavery, but as a matter of practical politics, they were content to pass laws allowing slaves to leave their owners, without taking steps to enable them to turn legal manumission into reality. The policy was self-sustaining in the sense that when few slaves left, governors chose to believe that they were contented with their lot and there was no need for further measures, or even for the strict enforcement of existing laws. Their attitude is hardly surprising since they were forced to operate on limited budgets and to rely on the cooperation of the local elites.

For the local governments, the trouble arose when one of their own, imbued with the idea that Britain was spearheading an antislavery crusade, criticized their policies, as Diggle did in the Sudan, or Haslewood in Hong Kong. Such people risked their careers since officials in the Colonial, Dominions, and India Offices usually agreed with the men on the spot. For the ministers who ultimately decided policy, the prime concern was usually to avoid scandal—some, however, such as Labor ministers, who depended on the support of labor unions, were more anxious to end slavery than others.

Moreover, imperial policy did not exist in a vacuum. Policy in Sudan, for instance, was conducted with one eye on Egypt and the other on Ethiopia. Action in Hong Kong was influenced by events in China. The belief that Bechuanaland would one day become part of the Union of South Africa played an important role in decisions affecting the Protectorate. Treaties with native rulers who administered large areas on the cheap had also to be factored in.

By the early 1930s, however, the contradictions of colonial rule, with its changing economic and political conditions, had dealt slavery a deathblow or at least ended it as an important method of marshaling labor. Events among the Igbo of Nkanu in southern Nigeria, where slavery was particularly harsh and immutable, furnish a rare and detailed example of the gradual empowerment of the slaves to settle their own future.[83] Here, colonial rule increased the opportunities for chiefs to exploit their slaves by sending them to work on the railways and in the mines and pocketing their earnings or forcing them to produce cash crops for owners to sell, but it also gave the slaves the opportunity to earn money and enabled them to resist these exactions. In 1922, when they were still denied access to land, and control over their children, and suffered ritual and social discrimination, when their children were still being sold, and they were still liable to be sacrificed at a funeral or other ceremonies, they rebelled. Their owners responded with violence. Disturbances continued for seven years. The British tried repression and conciliation. They suggested that slaves pay rent for land, then that they redeem themselves. They appointed slaves as chiefs to sit in native courts, and offered them control over their labor. They believed that they had freed them. But for the slaves, freedom meant having the same social, religious, and ritual rights as the free—as well as political and economic rights. This, the British could not give them. Ex-slaves remained a despised, endogamous group, although they became a cohesive political force, and some established their own villages.

The Nkanu case is but one example of the struggle for acceptance, equality, and integration by slaves which continued throughout the colonial period and worked itself out in a myriad different ways depending on ex-slaves' access to wage labor, Western education, and land. These grassroots struggles, in many instances peaceful and not discernable to administrators, were not reported to the League of Nations. Even when they were more obvious, the tendency was to say nothing. Thus the violent uprising in Nkanu, which lasted for most of a decade, was not reported until the late 1930s.[84]

To the British government, the League was a two-edged sword. On the one hand, it could be a threat—a body to which complaints, such as Diggle's, could be taken. On the other, the requirement in the 1926 Convention that signatories should inform each other of their antislavery legislation provided, as Cavendish Bentinck pointed out, a heaven-sent opportunity to effect "an excellent piece of propaganda which would be printed and published at the expense of the League." It was, however, an opportunity often missed. In 1927, Bentinck complained that the Government of India had missed a golden chance to turn the expeditions into the Hukawng Valley into a "thrilling tale" of "slave releasing expeditions" in the "wilds of Burma," including a "fight with the aborigines," in which a British officer had died. He urged the government to submit reports that would be widely read and inspire favorable comment in the press, rather than "dry as dust" lists of laws and freed slaves.

He wanted them, for instance, to show up the contrast between the British, who had freed the slaves in Tanganyika "at the stroke of a pen" and "at no cost to the British tax-payer," and the Germans, who had balked at the expense of compensating owners. His reasons were political. A few items of information of this nature "tactfully inserted" into the report might have more than humanitarian value—they could fend off any future agitation for the return of the German colonies.[85] However, his colleagues pointed out that Britain had simply ended the legal status of slavery without compensation and only when it was discovered that the number of slaves had been much reduced since 1914 and hence, although unpopular, the move would not be dangerous.

Nevertheless, Bentinck had made the important point that the League might now be used to combat criticism both at home and abroad by publicizing British antislav-ery efforts in this new international forum. This, however, required setting their own house in order. The Colonial Office asked governors whether the legal status of slav-ery had actually been abolished in their territories. They found a veritable hodgepodge of laws, different in every possession. For practical purposes the laws were adequate and the usual arguments for doing nothing—domestic slaves were all happy, chiefs would lose authority if deprived of them, and so on—were all put forward. The Colo-nial Office, however, decided that it was politically desirable if not legally necessary to issue new ordinances. To avoid implying that existing legislation was inadequate these reaffirmed that slavery had no legal standing.[86] They were promulgated in the Gold Coast, British Togoland, Gambia, Northern Rhodesia, Uganda, Somaliland, and Nyasaland. Elsewhere it was not thought necessary. The new laws were reported to the League to show that Britain was living up to its antislavery principles.

The impact of the League is difficult to evaluate, as other factors, such as parlia-mentary pressure or imperial imperatives also determined policy, but it is safe to say that throughout the empire, once the League had taken up slavery, colonial adminis-trations, under pressure from the home government, took, or at least reported that they had taken, steps against it. For the Foreign Office the League was useful not just to enable the British to demonstrate their antislavery zeal but as a tool for putting pressure on countries such as Ethiopia and Liberia whom they could not call to account themselves without diplomatic repercussions. Hence as will now be seen they began to pressure for a permanent League slavery committee.

NOTES

1. For the history of this, see AS MSS. Brit.Emp. s.22.G 352. Before the war, they had been afraid of antagonizing the chiefs and had expelled a missionary from the area for his efforts to free them.

2. See chapter 17.

3. A description of chattel slavery in the valley and adjacent areas and British actions is in IO L/E/7/1415.

4. Memorandum Regarding Slavery in the Hukawng Valley in Upper Burma, enclosed in India Office to the League of Nations, 27 August 1925, LON A.50.1925.VI. FO 371/10617. Slaves had already been redeemed in the neighboring administered area of Khamtilong, Putao District. See also chapter 17.

5. The discussion that follows is mainly based on Hargey 1981 and 1998, but see also Sikainga 1996.

6. Diggle to ASAPS, 21 May 1925, enclosed in ASAPS, to League 22 May 1925, LON. TE.38.

7. See above, chapter 6.

8. Hargey 1981, 274.

9. Minute by Murray, 3 June 1925, FO 371/10901 J1514/172/16.

10. Chamberlain to Allenby, no. 543, confidential, 26 May 1925, and minutes, FO 371/10901 J1197/172/16. Henceforth, the governor general acceded to or ratified conventions for Sudan, Reading to Campbell, no. 999, 19 October 1931, FO 407/214.

11. Murray to Lugard, 4 June and 10 July 1925, Lugard Papers.

12. Hargey 1981, 280–90. The British also restricted movement between northern and southern Sudan by the Closed District Ordinance.

13. Harris to Raglan, 11 December 1925, AS MSS. Brit.Emp. s 19, D3/39.

14. In Darfur, the date was 1916 when the British established their rule. For a while officials there, worried at the exodus of servile persons from the province, classified some as "serfs" and returned them to their owners.

15. Hargey 1981, 288 ff.

16. Hargey, 340. For the manumission and repatriation of slaves in Arabia, see above chapter 7 and below chapter 12.

17. This section is based primarily on the papers of the late Anthony J. Arkell, who as district commissioner, Southern District, investigated the traffic in the Upper Nile Province in 1928. See also Hargey 1981, 395 ff.; Spaulding 1988. The Watawit were of mixed Sudanese Arab and Berta descent. They had established themselves as rulers in Walaga. For a discussion of Shaykh Khojali's operations and his sending of slaves as tribute to Addis Ababa, see Ahmad 1999.

18. Question of Slavery, Maffey to secretary-general, 12 April 1927, LON VI B C.235.M.95. 1927. VI.

19. Hargey, 398, citing Maffey to high commissioner, 24 May 1928.

20. Sitt Amna was sentenced to fifteen years, but was released and repatriated in 1935.

21. Hargey 1981, 391 ff.

22. Hargey, 355.

23. Hargey, 336–44, 357–58.

24. Sikainga 1996, 112–15.

25. Sikainga, 116–19.

26. Rashid 1998. For early policy, see chapter 3 above.

27. Ordinance no. 9, 1926.

28. Rashid 1998.

29. Hansard 69, vol. 210, 199–214, cols. 615, 616, 23 November 1927.

30. Enclosures in Byrne to Amery, confidential no. 1, 14 February 1929, FO 371/13481.

31. Grace 1975, 251–53.

32. LON A.17. 1929. VI. 15 July 1929.

33. See examples in Grace 1975, 206–208, 252. For the modern trade, see below chapter 24.

34. Quote in heading comes from *John Bull*, 30 March 1929, copy in CO 129/514. Mui tsai means "little younger sister" in Cantonese. The girls were called by different names in different parts of China. The British used mui tsai to denote both the children and the system. Spelling varies. I have used the form found in the League of Nations and British documents. The main sources for this section are Jaschok 1988, Miners 1987, and Jaschok and Miers 1994.

35. See Sinn 1994, 146.

36. See Sinn 1994 for the work of Po Leung Kuk.

37. Miners 1987, 158.

38. See, for instance, letters from the Haslewoods to CO, 1920–1921 in CO 129/465 and 466.

39. See draft memorandum Notes on Lt. Cmd. Haslewood's Case, CO 129/473, pp. 182–87.

40. Delevingne to Lambert, 23 May 1921, enclosing information from Haslewood, 18 February 1921, CO 129/465.

41. Travers Buxton to Mrs. Haslewood, 1 April 1920, AS MSS. Brit.Emp.s.22. G361. See also the articles in *Anti-Slavery Reporter.*

42. Miners 1987, 160. Lugard, who had been governor of Hong Kong from 1906–1913, refused to see Mrs. Haslewood, whom the governor claimed was "unbalanced." Lugard had made inquiries when governor and decided the question was "difficult." He could not remember the upshot, Buxton to Lugard, 10 November 1920, Lugard to Buxton, 13 November 1920, AS MSS. Brit.Emp. s.22. G361.

43. Sales of persons were outlawed in 1910 by the Qing government and enforcement began when the Republicans took over the next year. Minutes 25 April 1921, CO 129/470 18914 p.534; minute 31 May 1921, CO 129/473 29711.

44. Memorandum on the Mui Tsai System by Halifax, November 1921, enclosed in Halifax to CO, 30 November 1921, CO 129/473, p. 264.

45. Churchill to ASAPS, 22 August 1921, CO 129/472 40065, p. 616.

46. Minute by Churchill, 21 February 1922, CO 129/478 p. 297, 8660.

47. Miners 1987, 162. Note by Churchill to Grindle, 30 March 1922, re Stubbs to Churchill, telegram 28 March 1922, ibid., 15196.

48. Miners 1987, 163.

49. Miners, 164.

50. Miners, 167.

51. Report of TSC chapter V, para.53; Lugard notes in Annex 2 to TSC Report.

52. The colonial secretary, Amery, unwisely promised to publish the documents on Hong Kong since 1923. Clementi to CO, 22 February and 16 May 1929, CO 129/514/2; summary of questions from Amery and replies from Clementi, nos. 32, 46, CO 129/514; minutes by G. G., 10 April, 25 May and 3 August, 1929, ibid.; Blue Book Cmd. 3424.

53. Passfield to Clementi, 22 August 1929, Cmd. 3424, p. 75, Ordinance no. 22, 1929.

54. See below, chapter 17.

55. Numbers jumped from 1,185 in 1927 to 1,851 in 1929, Miners 1987, 173.

56. See Lim 1958; Miers 1994; the latter was based on interviews with Janet Lim.

57. See inter alia Choo Chin Koh 1994.

58. Resident commissioner to high commissioner, telegram, no. 67, 14 May 1924, and resident commissioner to high commissioner, no. 188, 13 May 1924, BNA S.43/7. For the discussion that follows, see Tlou 1977; Miers and Crowder 1988.

59. Resident commissioner to high commissioner, 21 April 1926, BNA S 43/7.

60. The British called them Masarwa. They will be referred to here as Sarwa, with the Bantu prefix dropped.

61. See, for example, Stigand to May, 28 October 1912, enclosed in Stigand to Dutton, 7 March 1927, BNA S.43/7.

62. Crown prosecutor to resident commissioner, 13 May 1924 and resident commissioner to high commissioner no. 188, BNA S 43/7.

63. For a brief outline of this quarrel, see Miers and Crowder; for full information see BNA S 43/7. For press cutting, see DO 9/2 D 6951 and D 7566.

64. High commissioner's reply to Tswana chiefs, 22 November 1927, BNA S 6/1.

65. They hoped to build up the white farming community and then turn the Protectorate, together with Swaziland and Basutoland, over to the Dominion of South Africa, where they would be counterweights to Afrikane influence.

66. Tagart's original report and evidence is in BNA S 204/8, S.204/11. His amended report was issued in October 1931 and published with a Memorandum by the Bechuanaland Protectorate in March 1933. It was published by the League as LON ACE Report C.159.M.113.1935.VI, appendix 2, pp. 30–45.

67. Resident commissioner to high commissioner, 9 February 1932, BNA S 204/9 and confidential letter of the same date, in S 204/10.

68. Hitchcock 1978; Wilmsen 1989.

69. See below, chapter 16.

70. For a brief resume of their relations with Britain and the origins of the treaties, see Balfour-Paul 1991, 96 ff.

71. There was a treaty with Kuwait but it did not have specific clauses against the slave trade. For the treaty position with the various states in regard to the slave trade, see "Treaty Position in the Persian Gulf as regards Slavery," Fowle, 22 February 1937, IO R/15/6/414.

72. See Criminal Case no. 230 of 1932, in the Court of the Political Agent, Bahrain, IO R/15/1/205.

73. See, for instance, Biscoe to shaykh of Qatar, 20 August 1930, and reply in IO R/15/1/205.

74. Slaves were also sometimes forced to bond themselves to the owners of pearling boats to turn them into indebted divers, minutes in IO R/15/1/205, pp. 133–34.

75. Minutes on pp. 222–23, dated March and April 1932, IO R/15/205; memorandum no. 1200/v.o, 13 September 1932 from political agent, Bahrain, and minutes, ibid., pp. 279–80, 286.

76. Senior naval officer, Persian Gulf Division to commander in chief, East Indies Station, no. 27G/56/1, confidential, 12 September 1929, FO 371/13792.

77. Trevor to Howell no. 2060, 16 December 1923, FO 371/9531.

78. IO to FO, no. P.470/28, 9 February 1928 and enclosures, and political resident, Persian Gulf to Indian foreign secretary, no. 1095, 10 June 1928, FO 371/13007.

79. Minute on Slavery in the Near and Middle East, 5 December 1929, FO 371/13756 E 6340/6340/65; Clive to FO, no. 34 telegram, 28 January 1929, FO 371/13791.

80. Viceroy of India to IO, telegram, 20 April 1928, enclosed in IO to FO, P.1971, 21 April 1928 and FO minutes, E 2100/2100/34, Baxter minute, 6 June 1928, E 2980/2100/34, minutes on IO to FO, P.3591, 12 July 1928, E 3471/2100/34, FO 371/13068. Government of India to resident, Persian Gulf, 22 August 1928, FO 371/13007.

81. Cushendon to Clive, no. 557, 21 November 1928 and enclosures, FO 371/13068 E 5464/2100/34.

82. IO to FO no. P.1468/30, 7 March 1930, FO 371/14475 E 1251/1054/91.

83. Carolyn A. Brown 1996.

84. See below, chapter 17.

85. Minutes by Cavendish Bentinck, 18 March 1927, FO 371/11988 A 1730/16/52, and 2 June 1927, ibid., A 3942//16/52.

86. The voluminous correspondence on this subject is in CO 323/1027.

The Problems of a Moral Foreign Policy 1925–1932

SLAVERY IN ETHIOPIA

Britain's continuing dilemma about how best to handle slavery in foreign countries was most serious in relation to Ethiopia where, in spite of the edicts of 1925, reports indicated little change. In Maji, Consul Hodson estimated that only a few hundred people remained out of a population of "thousands and thousands" and they were hiding in the forest. The others had been taken as *gabbar* by Ethiopians, who demanded taxes from them. When they could not pay, they took their children as slaves. Every household now had three or four of them. Raiders were still attacking villages at night. With bloodcurdling yells and blaring trumpets, they set fire to the huts, killed the old, and seized the young. After a raid near the consulate in March 1925, the authorities sent troops to fight the raiders. They captured 300 people, but then gave them to their soldiers as slaves. The large number of captive women and children had so depressed prices that they could be bought for $15MT. To make matters worse, survivors of the devastated Tishana had acquired arms and were now raiding far and wide themselves, selling their captives. A *fusil gras* bought one slave, a mauser four, and a child and an adult could be had for fifty cartridges.

Like Darley, whose evidence he corroborated, Hodson was horrified at his inability to prevent the horrors perpetrated daily around him. He believed the edicts were intended to deceive and that judges who tried slavery cases would simply share the slaves they released with the provincial governor. The European powers were being "hoodwinked."[1] Miles away in Gojam, the only change reported was that the price of slaves had risen slightly.[2] In Addis Ababa, the Italian representative maintained that he could buy all the slaves he wanted at any time. He claimed the worst offenders were the empress and the head of the church, the *abuna*.[3]

The British urged British and American missions to open schools to try to change Ethiopian attitudes, but they were cutting back for lack of money. The Anti-Slavery Society offered £250 and an annual subsidy of £100 for a school for freed slaves to be run by Dr. Martin (Warqenah Eshete). The empress gave money and Ras Tafari gave land. But the plan was put on hold in 1928, as Martin had not had time to get it going.[4] The British also tried in vain to get France and Italy to join them in asking the League to appoint a commissioner or open an inquiry.

In May 1927, Consul Home reported that Shaykh Khojali el Hassan in Bela Shangul had enslaved some thirteen thousand young people less than a year before and eight hundred of them had been sold in Sudan.[5] The worst news was that Ras Tafari's wife, Waizero Menen, had paid Khojali $30,000 for 600 "young blacks" aged between seven and thirteen. Tafari was to claim in his autobiography that Khojali told him the children were freed slaves, and that he gave them certificates of freedom and enrolled them in military school and that some became musicians.[6] However, Khojali was reported to be regularly sending slaves and gold to Tafari as tribute,[7] making it likely that these children were enslaved for the purpose, and Tafari seems to have made no effort to send them back to their parents. Moreover, he had not freed the numerous slaves in his household.[8] The news that he might be directly implicated in the traffic was a blow to those who wanted to believe in his sincerity.

Ironically, Tafari now demanded the recall of Philip Zaphiro, the Oriental secretary to the British legation, because of press reports that he had told a visiting bishop that slaves could be bought in Ethiopia for £10 Egyptian. Relations were already strained and the foreign secretary, Austen Chamberlain, fearful of jeopardizing the Tana negotiations, was afraid of recalling Zaphiro, in case Parliament demanded an explanation, forcing him to publish the damaging reports from Ethiopia. After endless machinations, it was agreed that Zaphiro would go on leave and that Tafari would receive him on his return.[9] No one disputed the truth of his allegation—Tafari merely said he did not deal in slaves himself.[10]

The Zaphiro affair caused much soul-searching in the Foreign Office. Officials worried that their "deferring to Abyssinian sensibilities" was immoral and counterproductive. The Italian envoy made no secret of the fact that he planned to use evidence of slaving, supplied by Italian Roman Catholic missionaries in Kafa and Maji,[11] to blackmail Ethiopia if it rejected Italian plans to build a railway linking their colonies of Somalia and Eritrea. The British decided not to resort to blackmail to further their Lake Tana project. Instead, they made another effort to shelter behind the League. They tried to get another power to accuse Ethiopia of not carrying out its slavery obligations.[12] The Norwegian delegate agreed to ask a question about slavery in Sierra Leone and at the same time express regret that Ethiopia had not furnished information. Thus, Britain gained credit for the new laws in Sierra Leone, and called attention to slaving in Ethiopia without risking the repercussions of a direct attack.[13] However, much force was lost when the Ethiopians produced a list of recently freed slaves and convicted slavers. The British did not complain about continuous slave raids into Sudan and

Kenya, in case Ethiopia referred the frontier question to the International Court. They were afraid they would lose Moyale, to which their claim was weak.[14]

The next years brought some hope of improvement. Martin had been instrumental in founding an association—Fekerna-Aeguelguelot—for emancipating slaves. It was patronized by the empress and by Tafari and had some fifty members, one of whom had freed between five hundred and six hundred slaves. By 1929, there was even some good news from Maji.

There, a new consul, W. Pennefather Holland, discovered that the ivory poaching and raiding into British territory was run by some four hundred retainers of former governors. They had remained in Maji and controlled a hundred or so "Swahili"—a motley collection of Baluchi, Swahili, and Ganda hunters. They had arrived in 1911 and been given guns and credit by Ethiopian merchants for whom they hunted. Rates of interest were so high that they were in debt-bondage, forced to poach ivory in British territory where they were considered outlaws. Those who refused were put in chains and if they absconded, their families in Maji risked death or enslavement.

Holland broke the hold of this "conservative party" by taking the "Swahili" families under his protection, arresting the ringleaders, and forcing the Ethiopians to annul the loans. Most of the hunters were on the Boma plateau, which was claimed but not occupied by Sudan. Holland offered them generous terms of surrender, collected their wives and children in Maji, and marched them to the plateau to rejoin their husbands, most of whom were profoundly grateful to be extricated from their bondage. In an epic journey, he walked with his ragtag band of 250 British subjects to Mongalla in Sudan, and sent them on to their homes in Uganda, Kenya, and Tanganyika.

Holland then returned to Maji and with the help of the governor, who was no longer intimidated by the "conservatives," he expelled the troublemakers from the town, and freed their slaves. He had exceeded his powers in making arrests himself and in demanding the expulsion of officials, but he had gained the support of the governor, whom he considered an ideal partner—not strong, hence ready to accept a guiding hand. He reported that confidence was returning and people were farming again. He believed the frontier raids would end, particularly as Kenya now had a post at Labur Mountain. He recommended moving the consulate to the Boma plateau, to forestall its occupation by the Ethiopians.[15]

The Foreign Office received his euphoric reports with skepticism. Slaving was still reported from Addis Ababa and Arabia. Investigations in Sudan revealed that raiding was a system of government in Bela Shangul. In Gore in 1929, a number of slave dealers "escaped" from jail, and in 1930 a new governor arrived with a retinue of several thousand "active" buyers driving up the price of victims. Tafari's forces were reported to be selling the slaves of the defeated rebel Ras Gugsa, while the rebels were selling slaves captured from Tafari's soldiers to the Danakil who sent them to Arabia from French Somaliland.[16]

There were also indications of a disguised trade in Ethiopian boys and girls going to Egpyt. Ostensibly, they went for education, and traveled with passes issued by the British legation in Addis Ababa, which had also unwittingly issued passes to slaves traveling as servants. Such trafficking was normally only discovered if a victim escaped.[17]

The death of the Empress Zauditu in April 1930 brought renewed hope, as Ras Tafari now became the Emperor Haile Selassie I. He accelerated efforts to weld the country into a unitary state under a strong central government, and promulgated a constitution giving him control. Starting with "model provinces" he planned to replace gradually the unpaid hereditary provincial administrators, and their numerous retainers living off the land, with salaried officials chosen for merit and loyalty. The *neftenya-gabbar* system was to be abolished and a new system of taxation introduced. A national army was to replace the private forces of high officials. Communications were to be developed to ensure central control and develop the economy. More foreign advisors were to be hired, and schools were started to produce the trained, Western-educated administrators of the future. To the gratification of the British, an Englishman, Frank de Halpert, was appointed to advise the Ministry of the Interior on the new system of local government.[18]

The emperor was crowned with great pomp in the presence of representatives from the Western world. He hoped to project himself as a modern reformer. However, the very next month, Max Grühl, leader of a German expedition, described naked, heavily laden slaves, dragging small children through the sodden forests between Kafa and Jimma, "dying like flies." They had been seized by the soldiers of an outgoing governor and were probably destined for sale in Jimma.[19] In Britain, members of Parliament suggested that Ethiopia might ask for assistance similar to that requested by Liberia.[20]

Haile Selassie had been deeply disturbed to hear that Liberia had asked for a League inquiry into slaving, and he now made a shrewd move to diffuse criticism. He told the British minister, Barton, he would consider any antislavery measures the Anti-Slavery Society might suggest.[21] Although the Society was his greatest critic, their help, unlike that of the League, would not arouse the suspicion that he was jeopardizing Ethiopian independence. The Society offered to send out a deputation. At Lugard's suggestion, Daniel Sandford, a British settler in Ethiopia, asked the emperor what help he would accept. His greatest need, he said, was money to free the slaves, and his concern was what to do with them if they were all freed at once. Sandford suggested he needed a practical man as an advisor for five years to help carry out the reforms. Haile Selassie asked if Lugard would accept the job. Lugard, however, urged Sandford to put himself forward. Sandford's finances were in poor shape and he would have relished the job, but he felt someone with more prestige was needed to whom he could be a "staff officer."[22] The task was daunting as after the expenses of the coronation, there was little money to pay judges, or police, or to compensate owners. After considerable discussion, the emperor agreed to receive one member of the Society to offer advice and tell him what they could contribute.[23]

What the emperor really wanted was for someone to come out for a month or so to discuss financial help without traveling around the country. Advice poured in to the Society as to the kind of person it should send. To the chagrin of the Foreign Office, it chose Lord Noel-Buxton, a recently created Labor peer, who had been minister of agriculture, and now became a joint president of the Society.[24] He was the grandson of Thomas Fowell Buxton, and was a politician and philanthropist. But he knew nothing about Ethiopia and had no firsthand experience of slavery. He thus, as Lugard told him, had no expertise to offer and could not promise the financial help from the Society that the emperor expected. The Foreign Office, for its part, offered only its "blessing."[25]

While the mission was being discussed, reports of slaving continued to arrive. In Gore, slavers were punished according to their rank. The judge of the slavery court, who had been imprisoned for selling slaves, "escaped." Thousands of slaves were traded in the semi-independent states of Jimma, Wallaga, and Bela Shangul. The people of the lowlands were selling their children to buy ammunition from Ethiopian soldiers. Officials were afraid to tackle the traffic and the consul thought the emperor was either ignorant of the facts or deliberately misrepresenting them.[26] Barton believed that Haile Selassie wanted to end these abuses but had not the power to do so, and dared not admit it in case it led to an attack on his country's independence. "Independence," he wrote, "means a great deal [to him], slavery much less, except in so far as it may endanger independence."[27]

Haile Selassie regarded loans and foreign advisors as a threat, the more dangerous because just at this moment his relations with France were cool. He wanted quiet talks with a discreet delegate, but the Anti-Slavery Society, eager for publicity, arranged that Noel-Buxton would write to the *Times* and it organized other coverage. Moreover, Noel-Buxton, accompanied by his daughter and brother-in-law, Lord Polwarth, brought presents solicited by Harris from well-known firms—chocolates from Rowntrees, slippers from Clarks, blankets from Early's of Witney. He was also armed with copious advice from Lugard, as well as information from the Foreign Office and proposals from the Society.

He spent five weeks in the country in February and March 1932, mostly in the capital. He interviewed a great many people and collected much information. He had three formal audiences with the emperor and long discussions with ministers. He urged them to set a date for the end of slavery,[28] but they were afraid of alienating owners and could not pay compensation. Finally, they agreed to establish a slavery department in the Ministry of the Interior to supervise the working of the laws, to appoint slavery judges, to enforce court decisions, to establish a special police force, to register slaves, and to look after those they freed. Frank de Halpert was to be the slavery advisor. As an employee of the Ethiopian government, he did not pose the same threat as a League advisor. The Ethiopians rejected all idea of an investigator to travel around the country, but they asked to be given British consular reports to help them track down slavers. Haile Selassie also balked at setting a date for ending slavery. Since in theory no one could now be born into slavery or legally enslaved, he wanted the institution to simply die out. Eventually he agreed that it might be ended in about twenty years. He asked the Society to help him to secure a loan of £50,000 for schools and land on which to settle freed slaves.

Sandford, Barton, and the Foreign Office all pronounced the mission a success.[29] The Ethiopians had come up with a sensible plan and Noel-Buxton described the emperor as a "genuine abolitionist and an extremely able man," but thought he would have to be kept up to the mark.[30] In his efforts to keep up the pressure, he proceeded to sour relations with tactless talks and articles, and by failing to send Haile Selassie his report before it went to the League. At a meeting of the Society in April, he and Polwarth intimated that Ethiopia was uncivilized and Lugard talked about "great caravans of slaves" going to the sea. Sandford protested that such "inaccurate propaganda" was interfering with his own "quiet campaign" to get the emperor to follow advice.[31] Worse still, Noel-Buxton mentioned the possibility of an Italian mandate over Ethiopia—raising Haile Selassie's worst fears.[32]

Thus, when a new League committee of experts on slavery met at Geneva in May 1932, much of the goodwill generated by the mission had been lost. The Ethiopians were on the defensive, their image further damaged by a raid into Sudan in which twenty-seven Beir women, fifty-five children, and eight hundred head of cattle had been seized. Harris called this a slave raid. Sandford dismissed it as "intertribal" fighting. Whatever it was, it did nothing to raise trust in the emperor's ability to end slavery.

SLAVERY IN SAUDI ARABIA

While the British were becoming more involved in trying to end slavery and the slave trade in Ethiopia, they were trying to disentangle themselves from the problem in Hijaz and Nagd. Its ruler, Ibn Saud, who renamed the kingdom Saudi Arabia in 1932, was the rising power along the shores of both the Red Sea and Persian Gulf, and was in a position to threaten Britain's satellites on the Persian Gulf, as well as its protégés, Iraq, Trans-Jordan, and Muscat and Oman.[33] Consular manumission posed a threat to the good relations that both the king and the British wished to maintain. Ibn Saud saw it as an infringement of his sovereign rights and, barely a month after the fall of Jiddah, he asked if Britain would renounce manumission if he stopped imports of slaves. "Slavery," he said, was "barbarous," but he could not attack it for fear of rebellion. But the British were unwilling to give up what they considered a valuable antislavery weapon, particularly as they soon received reports that the king and his followers were involved in an increasing traffic to the Gulf States and Oman.[34]

Ibn Saud then suggested that the British should compensate owners of slaves they manumitted. This was dismissed as liable to fraud. He proposed a secret agreement to end the slave trade in return for the end of consular manumission. The British feared the secret would be leaked and they would face a storm at home. Moreover, Cecil, in his report to the League on the 1926 Convention had urged other powers to insist on consular manumission in treaties with the Saudis. A volte-face would be hard to explain, especially if the king was unable to end imports.[35]

Eventually a compromise was reached. By the Treaty of Jiddah, signed in May 1927, the British recognized Ibn Saud as ruler of Hijaz and Nagd. The slave trade figured only in article seven, which bound him to cooperate against it by all the means at his disposal. In an exchange of Notes the British stated that they would not give up consular manumission until it was clear that article seven was being carried out. Meantime they would not infringe the king's sovereignty or interfere in his affairs. Ibn Saud's Note asked that the British in Jiddah act in accordance with the spirit of the agreement. It was understood that this meant that manumitted slaves should be shipped out immediately so that they could not flaunt their freedom in Hijaz.[36] The king may have believed that this also implied that the British had accepted two further requests. One was that they would not seek out slaves to manumit—a point their Note made clear they accepted. The other was that they should not ask for the manumission of his personal slaves. This was not included in the Notes, although the British negotiator, Sir Gilbert Clayton, had mentioned in reports that the king had made the request. Ibn Saud wanted the Notes kept secret but the British insisted on publishing them with the treaty, which was to run for seven years.[37]

The treaty was a breakthrough for both parties. It recognized Ibn Saud as an independent ruler, whereas his previous treaty with Britain, the Treaty of Nagd of 1915, had bound him to conduct his foreign relations through the British.[38] It also offered him some protection against possible Italian aggression. He had designs on Asir that were opposed by the imam of Yemen, with whom Italy had a treaty. As for the British, they now had a basis for complaint if he did not stop slave imports, and virtual recognition of their right to consular manumission.

Ibn Saud imposed peace and order and, by 1927, pilgrims were coming in numbers not seen since the days of the Ottoman Empire. Two years later, the British consul believed that the kidnapping of pilgrims had virtually stopped and imports of slaves were declining. In March 1930, however, a new consul, W. L. Bond, sent a disturbing report.[39] Slaves were well treated and many came and went freely on trading expeditions to the African coast, and even came to the British legation, well aware that they could claim manumission if they wished. But public attitudes had not changed. Slaves were still the most desired investment. They were still imported and the king was charging customs duties on them. African pilgrims were sold by the very shaykhs appointed to protect them. Slave dealing no longer took place in the open market, but continued undisguised in brokers' houses in the towns, and was conducted by retailers in the countryside. Bond believed the king had taken no action because slavery contributed to his "comfort, prestige, and influence." A hundred slaves had been sent to his palace in Riyadh from Lith and Asir in 1928. When told that West Africans (Takruni) were being imported illegally or sold during the pilgrimage, he replied that they "lived like beasts" in their homelands and were better off as slaves. If he had his way, he would enslave all Takruni pilgrims to raise them out of their "depraved state" and turn them into "happy, prosperous and civilized beings."

Bond attributed a drop in imports to the closer control of the pilgrimage by the colonial powers, to the protection of pilgrims by Ibn Saud, and to a drop in demand caused by political and economic changes. The imposition of peace meant that slave retainers were no longer needed for defense. Cars were replacing slave camel drivers. Ordinary Hijazi could not make as much money off the pilgrimage as in the past, and prices were high.[40] Some well-known dealers had even gone out of business. Bond speculated that consular manumission might also be depressing the market, although fewer slaves were now claiming it—twenty-one had been freed in 1929 in contrast to forty in both 1926 and 1927, and thirty-nine in 1928. Nevertheless, it might be inducing owners in Jiddah and Mecca to hire paid servants rather than invest in slaves. This process would be stepped up if other powers would cooperate, but usually only the Dutch did so. The French had manumitted a slave in 1927 for the first time in five years.[41] The Italians gave the Ethiopians free passage home, but insisted that the British escort them to the ship, and thus take the blame for this unpopular proceeding. Bond made it clear that Arabia would provide a market as long as slavery continued.

In December 1931, a slave named Bakhit appealed for manumission.[42] He had been kidnapped when he was about six, on pilgrimage to Mecca, from, he believed, Baghirmi in French Equatorial Africa. After changing hands several times, he was given as a present to Abdullah Suleiman, who procured slaves for the king. After eighteen months without setting foot in the royal household, he fled to the legation. Ibn Saud claimed him as a "royal slave" and refused to let him leave the country, insisting that Clayton had given him oral assurances that his slaves would not be given refuge. Clayton had died in 1929, and the British believed there probably had been a tacit understanding on the subject, but were not sure of its scope.[43] An earlier case in 1929 had been tactfully resolved by the British handing over the fugitive to the Saudis who, by arrangement, returned him to them for disposal. Now, however, the king seemed determined to make a test case.

The British minister, Sir Andrew Ryan, faced a dilemma. To refuse to recognize Bakhit as royal property would be an insult to the king, but giving him up would open the way for the Saudis to make claims in other cases based on the "dubious" agreement with Clayton. Moreover, he could not be sure that the slave would not be punished or even killed. The foreign secretary, Sir John Simon, fearing trouble if the British allowed themselves to be "bullied into wrongdoing by so primitive a person as Ibn Saud," decided that even if a fugitive had actually served in the royal household he should not be returned. At risk of a serious diplomatic incident, he was prepared to send a ship to embark Bakhit by force. "I could not possibly justify," he wrote, "the return from what is really British territory of a slave who has escaped and might receive condign punishment."[44]

A crisis was averted because a British sloop happened to be in Jiddah and Ryan resorted to subterfuge. He informed the Saudis that he proposed to embark Bakhit, and sent him to the quay in the legation car with three British officials. One walked behind him, one in front, and the third distracted the authorities. Only when he was safely aboard the legation launch did the Saudi police shout to them to return. Hope Gill, in charge of the party, asked angrily if they knew who he was. "While they were scratching their heads," he reported, " the slave was put on board HMS *Penzance*."[45]

This bit of gunboat diplomacy was bound to be resented. The Saudis had already been making difficulties about manumitting other slaves and, since none could leave Jiddah without the governor's express permission, the embarkation of Bakhit had been in flagrant disregard of their authority. Not only had the king had been treated "like any little Trucial Sheikh," but the telegrams between the legation and the Saudi authorities in Mecca had not been in code, and the episode was common knowledge. It had caused a "considerable local flutter" in the newly conquered Hijaz, where discontent with Ibn Saud's rule was widespread and his humiliation apparently welcomed. The Saudis reacted by issuing stringent new instructions to prevent slaves reaching the legation.[46]

This was already difficult, as Hope Gill reported:

> A slave arrives at the Legation, usually in the very early morning and by stealth, having succeeded in entering the town by the guarded Mecca gate disguised as one of the West African day laborers who live outside the wall. Occasionally a slave arrives in broad daylight and actively pursued, having run away from a local household. Pursuit generally stops at the Legation gate. . . . although Bedouin have been known to carry it into the Legation itself, and have had to be turned out.

Strict procedures were then followed. Fugitives were cross-examined and searched to ensure they were not carrying stolen goods. If the consul was satisfied that the case was genuine, the slave was given a room, and was fed for a shilling a day. No work was required. A check was made with the local authorities to ensure that the runaway was not fleeing from justice. Sometimes a master tried to persuade his slave to return, particularly if it was a woman, but he was only allowed to speak to the fugitive in the presence of the consul. Sometimes the owner agreed to manumit the slave, and they would leave together. In most cases, masters made no claim and the authorities were given seven days to investigate the case before the legation asked for permission to embark the runaway on the next ship. If they refused, embarkation was delayed pending negotiations with the Ministry of Foreign Affairs. Normally permission was received and the necessary documents issued. A legation official then escorted the slaves to the ship.[47]

Most of those freed had been brought to Arabia as children, and spoke only Arabic, and did not know where they had come from, so those believed to be Sudanese or central African were sent to Sudan. Those who looked Ethiopian were shipped to Massawa. Of eighty-one manumitted in the three-and-a-half years from 1928 to the middle of 1931, forty-six went to Sudan, twenty-five to Massawa, and ten were settled locally.

By 1931, the Sudan government was reluctant to accept them. Jobs were scarce, and settling them on the land entailed providing shelter and food until their first crops were harvested.[48] The Italians, who had hitherto given Ethiopians free passage to Massawa, now announced that it was difficult to find employment for them, and their lives in Eritrea as destitutes were so miserable as to defeat the purpose of manumission. Henceforth, they would only accept those who came from north of the 12th parallel, spoke an Ethiopian language, could name their home village, and had enough money for fifteen days to make their way home.[49] Since these conditions were usually prohibitive, the British appealed to Haile Selassie to pay for sending Ethiopians to Jibuti and escorting them to Addis Ababa, where the British minister could ensure they remained free. Two slaves were duly repatriated before Haile Selassie realized that, if others heard of it, he might be faced with considerable expense, and he refused to pay for any persons enslaved before his decree of 1924. Those captured earlier were, therefore, sent to Jibuti at the expense of the British legation and there handed over to the Ethiopians.[50]

By this time, the British treasury, also hit by the world depression, was refusing to pay for the keep of fugitives in the legation. The minister was forced to draw on a private charity founded to help destitute Indian pilgrims.[51] The British began to hope that they might negotiate an international agreement to cover the costs of receiving and repatriating slaves, and of establishing a reception center and home for them on the western shores of the Red Sea—a point they hoped to raise at the next League Committee.

THE MARITIME SLAVE TRADE

The Slavery Convention had bound signatories to negotiate a general convention against the maritime slave trade and envisaged that the colonial powers on the Red Sea coast would conclude special agreements between themselves. To be effective, these required the registration of native vessels, control of passengers at ports of embarkation and disembarkation, as well as joint naval patrols or the granting of mutual rights to search in each other's territorial waters, as well as the exchange of information. These agreements were never concluded. They fell victim to colonial rivalry and the British fear that their long exercised rights to search might be challenged by rising local powers. Saudi Arabia and Persia both made it plain that they were not happy with British claims to the right to search their shipping. There were indications that both powers were planning to form their own navies, and the British feared they might hire foreign officers.

On the high seas, the British had assumed the right to search all "native vessels" irrespective of the flag they were flying.[52] They had no treaties authorizing them to search Hijazi vessels in the Red Sea, but claimed they had a right to do so because the Turks had been parties to the Brussels Act. Since the Turks had not adhered to the Treaty of

St. Germain, which annulled this Act, they maintained that it was still in force for the successor states of the Ottoman Empire. Ibn Saud soon made it clear that he did not consider himself bound by Turkish treaties. The only other legal ground for exercising the right to search was "long usage," and, from 1926, article seven of the Treaty of Jiddah binding Ibn Saud to cooperate against the slave trade. The British recognized that their legal grounds were weak and feared that if the question went to arbitration they would lose. This put them in a cleft stick. If they decided not to search Saudi vessels, to avoid an incident with Ibn Saud, there might be a recrudescence of the slave trade, which would certainly provoke an outcry in Britain.

However, in practice, few dhows flew the Hijazi or Asiri or Yemeni flags. Most local craft flew no authorized flag at all. At best, they put up red and white cloths decorated with stars, crescents, or daggers. At worst, they flew purple checked loincloths. The name of the dhow, if shown at all, was likely as not roughly painted on a piece of soap box nailed to the stern.[53] This suited the Royal Navy. If the nationality of a dhow was not clear, it could be stopped to verify it, and could then be searched if it was suspected of carrying slaves. Any agreement requiring that dhows be registered and issued with identity papers would end such searches. The British decided to leave well enough alone. Since the risk of an incident was slight, they determined to continue searching Saudi shipping in the Red Sea, and to tow any vessels with slaves aboard to a British port.[54]

They reached a similar decision with regard to Yemen, where their right to search rested on equally weak grounds. This case was the more difficult because relations with the ruler, the isolationist imam, were unfriendly and Britain did not even have a permanent representative in Sana'a. The imam was infiltrating into areas claimed by the Aden Protectorate where British control was tenuous, and he was suspected of having designs on the Hadhramaut, which the British did not administer and merely visited from time to time. Actual fighting with Yemen had broken out in 1928 and the British had used air power to force the imam's followers to retreat. They then began to consolidate their position in the Protectorate by arming loyal chiefs, and raising local levies commanded by British officers. Imam Yahya had been forced back into his own territory and negotiations were opened for delimitation of the frontier, so far without result.[55]

In sum then, in 1931, when discussing action to be taken at the League, it was clear that British rights to search in the Red Sea and Gulf of Aden rested on weak legal grounds. The Admiralty did not want to provoke any incidents or try to negotiate agreements with France and Italy that might call these rights into question or raise any challenge to their naval supremacy in these waters. Naval patrols were believed to be having a deterrent effect on the slave trade but could not end without more efficient methods of policing. These could not be introduced without risk of provoking hostile reactions from local powers and the other colonial powers in the area. Sea and air patrols in the territorial waters of Hijaz, Asir, or Yemen would clearly be resented.[56] No support was expected from the French, although most slaves were believed to be shipped through their territory.[57]

As for the Italians, the British feared that any further action might enable them to take advantage of the local resentment that was building up against British naval operations. Naval officers noted that their patrols were the subject of Italian anti-British propaganda. Owners of dhows fishing for pearls in the Red Sea would ask them whether they were British or Italian, and on being told the former, the conversations would end abruptly "not infrequently . . . with expectoration."[58] A particular cause of friction was the acceptance of fugitive slaves on British ships. The harboring of runaways thus remained a potentially explosive issue at sea as well as on land.

This delicate situation led to the issue of new and cautious instructions to naval officers in 1931. Admitting that treaty rights were limited or nonexistent, these stated that "by custom" all native vessels, irrespective of the flag they were flying, could be searched in the Red Sea and Persian Gulf, outside French and Italian territorial waters. However, searches in Hijazi territorial waters proper (not including Asir) were to be conducted "with great discretion" and away from the main ports. In the Persian Gulf, Nagdi vessels were not thought to be active in the slave traffic, hence they were not to be searched in Saudi territorial waters. On the high seas, the British decided simply to stop searching them without announcing that they had given up their right. They hoped this would pass unnoticed. Care was to be taken to avoid giving offense to dhows legitimately flying the Italian and French flags. Runaway slaves were to be taken aboard, but consular or political representatives were to be consulted at the first opportunity. Since Persia was already objecting to the terms of the 1882 treaty, its vessels in the northwestern Gulf were only to be examined if there were strong grounds for suspicion.[59]

This British retreat took place in spite of evidence of an active trade, across the Persian Gulf and the Red Sea, particularly through French Somaliland. In 1925, a Muslim trader was reputed to have arrived from Jimma with over eighty girls, young men, and elderly women. They were smuggled into Tajura in Arab dress and the sultan was paid a rifle for each one exported.[60] Four years later, Zaphiro believed that over a thousand slaves a year, mostly small children or pubescent girls, were still shipped to Arabia, although naval officers put the figure at only three to four hundred. Whatever its dimensions, the traffic was profitable. A slave costing £2 in Ethiopia could fetch £70–80 in Arabia and slavers could afford an intelligence service enabling them to steer clear of British naval patrols.[61] The French insisted they were taking effective measures and that the slaves must be coming from Sudan, British Somaliland, or Eritrea, or through the pilgrimage.[62] The governments of both British territories refuted this. Sudan now required all pilgrims to carry passports and pass through Suakin, and merchants traveling through Port Sudan with black servants had to give a bond of £50E. as guarantee for their return.[63] The Italians were believed to be effectively policing their coast, except for the far south near Raheita.[64]

Once at sea, the traffic was becoming harder to detect, as the number of legitimate passengers traveling to Arabia by dhow increased. Five or six slaves could easily be slipped in amongst them—the men disguised as sailors, the women as their wives, and the children as family members or apprentices. Children were often too young to give reliable evidence and the Royal Navy had no interpreters who could talk to them. In the changing conditions of trade in the Red Sea, the old indicators that a dhow was carrying slaves, such as large numbers of children on board or excessive quantities of food and water, were no longer useful. Medium-sized dhows engaged in fishing for pearls or sharks' fins now carried as many as forty men and thirty small boys, some only three years old, who were being trained as apprentices. They also carried supplies for three or four months.[65] Given these problems and the perennial difficulties of patrolling in uncharted waters, 10,000 square miles of which were inside the reefs, the odds were still on the side of the slavers.

The operations of the Royal Navy were admittedly not cost-effective. Two sloops, for instance, had spent sixty-nine days on slave trade operations and examined fifty dhows, without finding a slaver. During the winter of 1927–1928, the Admiralty had sent two destroyers to reinforce them. The fuel alone cost £6,583.10s, and not a single slave had been freed.[66] Since ships were plainly visible, the most the navy could hope for was to close down the traffic temporarily, especially as their antislavery patrol normally consisted of two sloops, only one of which was in the Red Sea at a time.[67] Stationing an additional sloop in the Red Sea would cost another £35,000 a year, and was not likely to improve results. Moreover, the navy objected that it would interrupt the training of its Mediterranean flotillas.[68] In 1930, the French had merely detached one sloop from their Mediterranean fleet to cruise in the Red Sea twice a year, while the Italians usually employed a sloop they kept at Massawa for survey work.

Between 1926 and 1931, the British toyed with a number of suggestions for increasing the effectiveness of their patrols. The most promising was the establishment of an intelligence service on the Arabian and African coasts. Its value was shown in 1928, when the resident in Aden had an intelligence agent in Tajura, who obtained details on the dealers, their dhows, the flags they flew, the ports of embarkation and landing, and the complicity of the sultans of Lohoita, and Raheita. In 1930, although this source was no longer operating, the British vice-consul in Jibuti, E. Lowe, easily established that the slaves captured during the Oromo rebellion in northern Ethiopia had been employed near Tajura as goatherds until they could be shipped to Arabia. He also discovered that women were being smuggled into Jibuti by train, singly, disguised as the wives of the dealers, and that the governor would not allow trains to be searched for slaves. He thought the French were afraid of the "savage and lawless Danakils," whose country they only ventured into with a strong guard.[69]

In interviews on the Arabian coast, the commander of HMS *Dahlia* pieced together a picture of operations in Ethiopia.[70] Dealers left Addis Ababa in May and headed west, where they bought children of both sexes. They returned through Wallo, selling them off as they went. At Dessie, they sold the remainder to Danakil merchants, who took them to a collecting point inland from Tajura and exchanged them for rifles. They were then shipped from Obock or small harbors along the coast, passing through the Kamaran passage in groups of about twenty, making landfall near Dhubab, and then sailing to Gizan, the main trading center.

An ambitious plan for an intelligence service to be run by the British vice-consul in Jibuti with Italian and French cooperation was given up because it would have cost £40,000 a year, and it was thought unlikely that France and Italy would agree to it. A more modest plan for an intelligence service run by the resident in Aden was also ruled out because of expense, fear of French objections, and because the navy thought its sloops could not be contacted in time to intercept slavers.[71] In 1931, the British gave up the idea of an intelligence service.

Other proposals for more effective policing of the Red Sea and Gulf of Aden were also rejected. "Mystery ships"—armed dhows manned by sailors disguised as native crewmen—had been used to police the arms traffic on the Somali coast, but were withdrawn because the slavers soon identified them and the sailors were demoralized by the poor living conditions.[72]

The commanding officer of the Red Sea patrol made the revolutionary suggestion that the League should take over the antislavery patrols, using four or five shallow craft capable of fourteen knots, equipped with light guns, and operating from Perim, supported by amphibious planes. It might even employ the Royal Navy, which would then be properly equipped and relieved of expense. The Foreign Office and the Admiralty both balked at the very idea of foreign control over British ships. The latter also turned down various suggestions for using small craft inside the reef, claiming they had no suitable vessels or large-scale charts, and if a native pilot were needed, secrecy would be lost.[73]

Airpower was playing a vital role in the control of the Aden Protectorate at this time, but the air force objected to patrolling for slavers. There were no suitable planes, and one dhow looked much like another from the air and so did the passengers.[74] The aircraft would need a boat for boarding dhows, and if the crew resisted, the pilot could hardly hold a slaver until the slow-moving parent ship arrived.[75]

Added to these technical problems were political ones. The suggestion that the Royal Air Force might track caravans heading for the coast in French Somaliland was rejected because the French would object to British planes in their air space.[76] The idea that the island of Kamaran, off the coast of Yemen, might serve as a base for patrols by small, armed vessels aided by sea planes was turned down because the navy and air force opposed any action which might provoke the Italians into increased activity in the Red Sea. They were already supplying the imam of Yemen with planes and arms, and might offer to cooperate in the patrols in order to have a pretext for increasing their forces in the area.[77]

The abortive discussions over maritime policing revealed some interdepartmental disagreements. Where the Foreign Office regarded the Red Sea patrol as primarily as an antislave trade operation, the Admiralty insisted its main duties were to protect British interests and show the flag.[78] The navy thought the slave trade was negligible because they examined hundreds of dhows a year and scarcely found any slaves, whereas the Foreign Office believed this was because slavers waited until the ships had gone to ship their cargoes. Similarly, while the Foreign Office proposed an aerial patrol from Kamaran in order to police the slave traffic, the air force wanted it only for a year to study weather patterns as part of the search for bases for an all-British flying route to the East.[79]

Thus, by 1932, plans for better policing of the Red Sea by Britain had foundered for political and technical reasons, and, of course, because they would have cost money.

LIBERIA, THE LEAGUE OF NATIONS, AND PRACTICES AKIN TO SLAVERY

While the British were wrestling with these problems, the League, at the request of the Liberian government, was conducting an inquiry into practices "akin to slavery." As has been seen, Liberia was trying to ward off American charges of slave trading.[80] A commission appointed by the League, the United States, and the Liberian government carried out investigations in 1930. Its report confirmed the existence of slavery, pawning, and forced labor, and accused the Liberian Frontier Force of forcibly recruiting workers for the Spanish island of Fernando Po and the French colony of Gabon. It recommended replacing a number of high officials with Europeans or Americans.

The government outlawed slavery, pawning, and forced labor. It also stopped labor exports. It asked the United States for assistance. This caused such outrage that the president and vice-president both resigned. In 1931, Liberia asked the League to help it carry out the recommendations. The League formed the Liberia Committee and sent out experts to study the situation. They confirmed the original report, and suggested restricting forced labor to local communal work, and the establishment of "liberty villages" for freed slaves. After discussing these proposals the Liberia Committee decided to await the reactions of the Liberian legislature before issuing a final report.

Thus, by 1932, Liberia was the only country that had asked for League assistance in suppressing slavery and related practices. The fact that the League was involved removed any pressure on Britain to take action.

THE ABOLITION OF SLAVERY IN NEPAL

The British were pleasantly surprised when Nepal abolished slavery at the very time the TSC was meeting. Until 1923, the British had treated this small Himalayan kingdom on the northeast border of India virtually as an Indian princely state. They had approached slavery here and in the other frontier states and unadministered areas with extreme caution, taking little action even against the slave trade.[81] In that year, however, they acknowledged Nepalese independence in a Treaty of Friendship. The next year the de facto ruler—the prime minister, Maharajah Chandra Shumsher Rana—took steps to end slavery itself.[82]

There were some sixty thousand slaves in a population of over 5.6 million. They were hereditary chattels, who were traded, inherited, and transferred. Families were split up, and fugitives were returned to their owners. The institution was deeply rooted.[83] By the beginning of the twentieth century, people were no longer enslaved through wars or as punishment for crime, but were still kidnapped and sold to dealers, or forced to sell themselves or their children to pay off debts to landowners and moneylenders. Slaves were valuable assets and most were well treated. Some owned land or other property. It was a master's duty, and to his benefit, to find them spouses, as he owned their children. However, there were few constraints on treatment and many fugitives fled to India.

Chandra Shumsher had already stopped new enslavements, freed all state-owned slaves, and made it easier for others to ransom themselves.[84] In November 1924, at a big public meeting, he made an impassioned plea for ending the institution. A plan was agreed by which all slaves were to be freed and their owners compensated, but they were to remain with their masters for seven years, during which the paying of wages was encouraged, but not mandatory. These measures came into effect in 1925. An antislavery office was established, and officials traveled around the country settling disputes. The government eventually paid £375,000—15 percent of its annual revenue—to over fifteen thousand owners and freed 59,873 slaves. Compensation varied with their age and sex. Women, particularly those between thirteen and forty, were rated higher than men.[85] Some owners refused compensation. Disruption was minimal. There were no complaints about a labor shortage. A third of the slaves elected to work as wage labor for their masters. Others were offered empty land and government loans.[86]

Nepal was not a member of the League and the prime minister denied that these measures were the result of its "moral influence."[87] His aim may have been to project the image of modernization. He certainly attracted wide attention in the press. Questions were asked in Parliament about the role of the Government of India, which, to its chagrin, had been taken by surprise. At the annual meeting of the Anti-Slavery Society in 1925, Lugard suggested that the measures taken in Nepal might serve as a model for other states—such as Ethiopia.[88] However, all was not as it seemed. The freed were not systematically rehabilitated. The land they were given was infested with malaria, and many were believed to have drifted back to their former owners.[89] Moreover, as will be seen, at the end of the twentieth century, Nepal was notorious for other forms of labor abuse, including child labor and debt-bondage.[90]

NOTES

1. Hodson to Bentinck, 22 March 1925, enclosed in Bentinck to Chamberlain, no. 176, confidential, 28 October 1925, FOCP 12911 J 3429/673/1 (FO 401/19 p.82); Bentinck to Chamberlain, confidential, no. 37, 1 June 1925, FO 371//10873 (FO 401/18, pp. 74–75). The

Foreign Office tried to discredit Darley after he published *Slaves and Ivory* in 1926 but dropped the attempt on discovering that slavery was widespread in Sudan; see Notes on Major Darley's Book and minute by Ronald, 7 September 1926, on Cairo Chancery to FO, 29 August 1926, FO 371/11572 J 2490/148/1.

2. Home to Bentinck, no. 134, 15 August 1925, enclosed in Bentinck to Chamberlain, no. 103, 17 August 1925, FO 371/10873 J 2756/673/1 (FOCP 12911 p.75). A ten-year-old girl cost $MT55 and a woman of twenty, $MT95. $MT8 = £1.

3. Bentinck to Chamberlain, no. 160 confidential, 15 October 1925, FOCP 12911 p. 81 (FO 401/19).

4. Bentinck to Murray, 23 July 1926, FO 371/11571 J 2047/148/1; ASAPS to FO, 25 October 1926, AS MSS. Brit.Emp. s.22 G 448 file 5; Bentinck to Chamberlain, no. 34, 7 February 1928, FO 371/13104 J 901/31/1.

5. Note on Slave Raiding by Home, 2 May 1927, secret, enclosed in Bentinck to Chamberlain, no. 129, very confidential, 5 May 1927, FO 371/12344 J 1441/55/1, Note on Abyssinian Slave Trade, 27 May 1927, enclosed in Bentinck to Chamberlain, no. 157 secret, FO 371/12345, J 1754/55/1. For Khojali's raiding, see Ahmad 1999.

6. Ullendorf ed. 1977, 79. Other reports state that Tafari's famous "Negro band" consisted of slaves sent to him as tribute by Khojali.

7. Erskine to Eden, no. 3, 3 May 1936, FOCP 15031 (FO 401/36) and Bell to Kelly, 22 September 1936, enclosed in Kelly to Eden, ibid.

8. Bentinck to Chamberlain, no. 223, 26 November 1926, FO 401/21, p. 45 J 3445/148/1.

9. See correspondence and minutes in FO 401/22.

10. Bentinck to Chamberlain, no. 152, 31 May 1927, FO 401/22, p.102, J 1751/55/1.

11. Bentinck to Chamberlain, no. 223, 26 November 1926, FO 401/22, p.105, J 17/3445/148/1.

12. Minutes on Bentinck to Chamberlain, no. 129, 30 May 1927, FO 371/12344 J 1441/55/1, and no. 93 telegram, 30 May 1927, ibid., J 1485/55/1; memorandum on Slavery in Abyssinia by Hamilton-Gordon, 27 August 1927, FO 401/23, pp. 63–64, J 2405/55/1; minute by Chamberlain, 11 August 1927, on Bentinck to Chamberlain, no. 206 confidential, 29 June 1927, FO 371/12345 J 2024/55/1.

13. Cavendish Bentinck to Murray, 18 September 1927, FO 371/12345 J 2613/55/1.

14. Minutes on Bentinck to Chamberlain, no. 204 telegram, 21 December 1927, FO 371/12347 J 3651/114/1. For the documents on the raids, see FO 401/22.

15. Holland told a complex story in successive reports. The most comprehensive are Holland to Dunbar, no. 122, 8 July 1929, and no. 130, 14 July 1929, both enclosed in Barton to Henderson, no. 201, 23 September 1929, FO 401/27, pp.163–75. Earlier reports, which he later described as inaccurate, provide details; they are in FO 371/13103 and his reports on outstanding cases in 1929 are in FO 371/13837 and 13838.

16. Barton to Henderson, no. 124, confidential, 29 August 1930, FO 371/14589 J 3265/22/1; memorandum by Zaphiro, 16 May 1930, and paraphrase of telegram from Barton to resident, Aden, no. 5, 3 July 1930, enclosed in Barton to Henderson, no. 87, confidential, 8 July 1930, ibid., J 2558/22/1.

17. See documents in FO 371/12344, pp.171–76, enclosed in Addis Ababa to FO nos.1 and 3, January 1927.

18. For these reforms, see Marcus 1995, 97 ff.

19. *News Chronicle*, 1 December 1930, *Daily Express*, 12, 13, 15 December 1930, extracts in FO 371/14590 J 4069/22/1.

20. Question by Mander, 11 February 1931, Hansard. For Liberia, see below.

21. Troutbeck to Henderson, no. 51, 4 March 1931, FO 371/15387 J 960/33/1; minute by Barton of conversation with Harris, 18 April 1931, FO 371/15387.

22. Sandford to Lugard, private and confidential, 16 June 1931 and 23 August 1931, memorandum 11 September 1931, enclosed in Lugard to Sandford, private, 12 September 1931, Lugard Papers.

23. Intelligence Report for quarter ending 31 December 1930, enclosed in Barton to Henderson, no. 24, 3 February 1931, FO 371/15389 J 571/571/1; Barton to Henderson, no. 121, 6 July 1931, FO 371/15387 J 2397/33/1, and no. 130, 21 July 1931, ibid., J 2502/33/1 enclosing Haile Selassie I to ASPS, 12 July 1931.

24. Noel Edward Noel-Buxton, first Baron Noel-Buxton, 1869–1948.

25. FO minute of telephone conversation with Harris, 2 October 1931, and subsequent minutes, FO 371/15387 J 2933/1; minutes on Peterson to Harris, 12 November 1931, ibid., 217–28; memorandum by Peterson, 13 November 1931, and minutes, ibid., J 3292/33/1.

26. Erskine to Barton, no. 54, 11 September 1931, enclosed in Barton to Reading, no. 193 confidential, 2 November 1931, FO 371/15887 J 3346/33/1 [FO 401/31 no. 23, p. 48].

27. Barton to Reading, no. 193, confidential, 2 November 1931, FO 371/15387 J 3346/33/1.

28. For these negotiations see Report on Abyssinia by Lord Noel-Buxton and Lord Polwarth, enclosed in FO to secretary-general, League of Nations, 26 April 1932, FOCP 14116 (FO 401/32) no. 61, J 1081/3/1, and memorandum enclosed in emperor of Ethiopia to the president of the Anti-Slavery Society, 11 March 1932, ibid., no. 60.

29. Sandford to Lugard, 21 March 1932, Lugard Papers; Barton to Simon, no. 46, 22 March 1932, and FO minutes, FO371/16096 J 950/3/1.

30. Record by Peterson of conversation with Noel-Buxton, 14 April 1932, FO 371/16096 J 991/3/1.

31. *Anti-Slavery Reporter and Aborigines Friend*, series V, 22, 2. pp. 62–70; Sandford to Lugard, 18 May 1932, Lugard Papers.

32. *The Times*, 7 April 1932, column 1, line 26, article by Noel-Buxton. The Italian Charge in Addis Ababa had asked to join Noel-Buxton's mission and had offered money for a slavery commissioner. The Society said an official could hardly join a private British mission, ASAPS to FO, 17 February 1932, and minutes, FO 371/16096 J 489/3/1; Barton to Simon, no. 28, 25 February 1932 and enclosure Scammacca to Barton, 25 February 1932, and enclosed communication from the Italian Anti-Slavery Society, 23 February 1932, ibid., J 794/3/1.

33. Iraq (until 1932) and Trans-Jordan were British mandates. For British relations with Muscat and Oman, see below. This state was known at the time as Muscat. It later became Muscat and Oman. Although the sultan of Muscat claimed it all as his territory, much of the interior was under the control of the imam of Oman. For convenience, I will call it by its present name of Oman.

34. Mayers to Chamberlain, no. 114, confidential, 28 September 1926, FO 371/11446, E 5859/900/91; CO to FO, 23 July 1926 and enclosures, ibid., E 4388/900/91.

35. Jordan to Chamberlain, no. 4, telegram, 30 November 1926, and minutes, FO 371/11446 E 6638/900/91; IO to FO P 4266/21, 9 December 1926, and minutes ibid., E 6759/900/91; CO to FO C.22515, 11 December 1926, ibid., E 6790/900/91.

36. For the notes and explanatory minutes, see Clayton to Chamberlain, confidential, 6 June 1927, FO 371/1225 E 2582/119/91; for the negotiations see Record of Conversations with H.M. King Abdul-Aziz ibn Abdul-Rahman al-Faisal Al Saud, enclosed in Clayton to Chamberlain, 6 June 1927, ibid., E 2583/119/91.

37. Stonehewer-Bird to Chamberlain, no. 49, telegram, 17 September 1927 and minutes, FO 371/12246 E 3994/119/91.

38. Memorandum of British Commitments to Ibn Saud, FO 371/12244 E 594/119/91.

39. Bond to Henderson, no. 60, 6 March 1930, FOCP 13886 (FO 371/14475) E 1541/1054/91.

40. A young female cost from £70 to £200 and a male from £20 to £150.

41. Jeddah Report in Stonehewer-Bird to Chamberlain, no. 65, secret, 1 June 1927, FO 371/12250 E 2849/644/91.

42. For this incident, see voluminous correspondence in FO 371/16020, some of which is printed in FOCP 14285 (FO 406/68). See particularly Ryan to Simon, no. 1, telegram, 22 January 1932, FO 371/16020 E 622/314/25, and no. 58, 29 January 1932, ibid., E 793/314/25 and enclosed correspondence with the Saudi government.

43. Minute by Rendel, 23 January 1932, on Ryan to Simon, no. 11, telegram, 22 January 1932, FO 371/16020 E 366/314/25.

44. Minutes by Rendel, 23 January 1932, and Simon, 27 January 1932, on Ryan to Simon, no. 11, telegram, 22 January 1932, FO 371/16020 E 366/314/25.

45. Ryan to Simon, no. 62, 1 February 1932, FO 371/16020 E 795/314/25 and enclosing correspondence with Minister for Foreign Affairs, and memorandum by Hope Gill, 30 January 1932, also in FOCP 14285 (FO 406/69).

46. Ryan to Simon, no. 62, 1 February 1932, FO 371/16020 E 795/314/25; Hope Gill to Warner, no. 506/64/35, 8 February 1932, ibid., E 798/314/25.

47. Memorandum by Hope Gill, 3 February 1932, enclosed in Hope Gill to Simon, no. 66, 3 February 1932, FO 371/16020, E 798/314/25 (FOCP 14285 no. 19).

48. MacMichael to Mack, 27 August 1931, FO 371/15301 E 4416/4182/1.

49. Hope Gill to Simon, no. 302, 21 July 1931, and enclosed Record of Conversation with Solazzo, 12 May 1931, and minute by Ryan, 6 July 1931, and FO minutes, FO 371/15301 E4182/4182/25; Hope Gill to Simon, no. 335, 16 August 1931, ibid., E 4594/4182/25.

50. Henderson to Barton, no. 256, 13 October 1931, FO 371/15301 E 5045/4182/25; Barton to Henderson, no. 142, 17 August 1931, ibid., E 4612/4182/25; Barton to Reading, no. 192, 2 November 1931, and minutes, ibid., E5780/4182/25; Hope Gill to Henderson, telegram, no. 221, 6 October 1931, and minutes, ibid., E 5045/4182/25; Barton to Simon, no. 131, 8 September 1932, FO 371/16020 E 5073/314/25. First Annual Report on Slavery in Ethiopia for 1932, enclosed in Barton to Simon, no. 15, 31 January 1933, FOCP 14384 J 444/429/1. Broadmead to Simon, no. 109, 18 July 1933, ibid., J 2013/409/1; Annual Report on Slavery in Abyssinia for 1933, enclosed in Barton to Simon, no. 84, 35 May 1934, ibid., J 1529/288/1.

51. Hope Gill to Simon, no. 302, 21 July 1931, FO 371/15301 E 4182/4182/25.

52. Jakins to Seymour, no. 385/99/20, 18 March 1929, minutes and memorandum by Orchard, 22 April 1929. FO 371/13735 E 1793/1484/91.

53. Report on the Slave Trade in the Red Sea, no. 5, enclosed in Commander, HMS *Dahlia* to C. in C. Mediterranean, 4 December 1928, in C. in C. to Admiralty no. 2314/668/121, 21 December 1928, FO 371/13837.

54. Minute by Cavendish Bentinck, 25 May 1928, on Admiralty to FO, M.0871/28 confidential, 10 May 1928, FO 371/13104 J 1565/31/1.

55. Barton to Henderson, no. 87 confidential, 8 July 1930, FO 371/14589 J 2558/22/1. For relations with Yemen, see Gavin 1975, 277 ff.

56. Minute on the 18th Meeting of Foreign Office Committee on Disarmament and Arbitration held on 11 April 1930, FO 371/14958 W 3823/31/98.

57. Minute by Noble on Barton to Henderson, no. 87, confidential, 8 July 1930, FO 371/14589 J 2558/22/1.

58. Report of Proceedings of HMS *Dahlia* for May 1927, enclosed in Admiralty to FO, confidential 2 September 1927, FO 371/12246 E 3802/129/91.

59. Instructions Concerning the Search of Dhows by H.M. Ships for Slaves and Arms, enclosed in Admiralty to FO M.0477/31, secret, 10 April 1931, FO 371/15275 E 1912/16/91.

60. Notes by Zaphiro, enclosed in Bentinck to Chamberlain, no. 137, very confidential, 28 September 1925 FO 401/19, p.77 J 3076/673/1.

61. Extract from Report of the Proceedings of HMS *Dahlia* for June 1929, FO 371/13838 J 2156/130/1; memorandum by Zaphiro enclosed in Bartlett to Henderson, no. 228 confidential, 25 November 1929, ibid., J 3529/130/1. Commander Cotton did not agree that slavers had an effective intelligence service since naval movements could not be predicted, Cotton to Admiralty, 30 July 1929, ibid.

62. Bentinck to Chamberlain, no. 245, 18 December 1926, FO 401/22 J 55/55/1. Intelligence reports enclosed in Bousfield to senior naval officer, Red Sea, 11 December 1928, enclosed in Admiralty to FO, M.0871, 10 May 1928, FO 371/13104 J1565/31/1; enclosures in Admiralty to FO, M.1759/28, 31 May 1928, ibid., J 1746/31/1.

63. Note enclosed in Berthelot to Phipps, 25 January 1926, enclosed in Crewe to Chamberlain, no. 165, 26 January 1926, and Chamberlain to Lloyd, no. 150, 9 February 1926, FO 371/11570 J 226/148/1; Huddleston to Lloyd, 3 April 1926, enclosed in Chamberlain to Crewe, no. 1322, 3 May 1926, FO 401/20, pp. 56–57.

64. Jackson to C. in C. Mediterranean, no. 913, 9 June 1930, enclosed in Admiralty to FO. M.3099/22/1, 16 October 1930, FO 371/14589 J 3452/22/1.

65. Report on the Slave Trade in the Red Sea, by commanding officer, HMS *Dahlia* to C. in C. Mediterranean, no. 5, 4 December 1928, enclosed in C. in C. to Admiralty, no. 2314/668/121, confidential, 21 December 1928, FO 371/13837.

66. C. in C. Mediterranean to Admiralty, no. 340/668/392, confidential, 29 February 1928, enclosed in Admiralty to FO, M.0871/28, 10 May 1928, FO 371/13104 J 1565/31/1.

67. One was a converted minesweeper making only eleven knots, and carrying only rowing boats and a twenty-foot motorboat of moderate speed. Waterlow to Chamberlain, no. 279, 3 December 1928, FO 371/13104 J 3615/31/1.

68. Admiralty to FO, M.0871/89 confidential, 10 May 1928, and FO minutes, FO 371/13104 J1565/31/1.

69. Jackson to C. in C. Mediterranean, 1 November 1930, confidential, no. 12/1163/6, enclosed in Admiralty to FO, confidential, no. M.03828/30, 16 December 1930, FO 371/14590 J 4055/22/1.

70. Jackson to C. in C. Mediterranean, confidential, no. 913, 9 June 1930, enclosed in Admiralty to FO confidential, M.03099/221, 16 October 1930, FO 371/14589 J 3452/22/1; Jackson to C. in C. Mediterranean, 1 July 1930, ibid.; Jackson to C. in C. Mediterranean, 1 November 1930, enclosed in Admiralty to FO, confidential, no. M.03828/30, 16 December 1930, FO 371/14590 J 4055/22/1.

71. Barton to Henderson, no. 87 confidential, 8 July 1930, with minutes and memoranda by Noble of conversation with Barton, 10 April 1931, FO 371/14589 J 2558/22/1. Memorandum by Noble, 12 December 1930, filed with Admiralty to FO M.03099/30, confidential, 16 October 1930, FO 371/14589 J 3452/22/1.

72. Admiralty to FO, 24 June 1926, FO 401/20, pp. 61–62.

73. Proposal by Woodward communicated by Bentinck, 12 July 1926, and minutes, FO 371/11571 J 1917/148/1; minute by Ronald, 17 June 1927, on Bentinck to Chamberlain, no. 129, 5 May 1927, FO 371/12344 J 1441/55/1; memorandum by Noble, 12 December 1930, filed with Admiralty to FO, M.03099/33 confidential, 16 October 1930, FO 371/14589, J 3452/22/1.

74. Admiralty to FO, 29 September 1927 and minutes, FO 371/12345 J 2700/55/1; Admiralty to FO, M.0871//28, confidential, 10 May 1928, minutes and naval reports, FO 371/13104 J 1565/31/1; Waterlow to Chamberlain, no. 4, 2 January 1929, and enclosed memorandum by Ratsey, FO 371/13837 J 237/130/1; memorandum by Noble, 12 December 1930, filed with Admiralty to FO, M.03099/33 confidential, 16 October 1930, FO 371/14589, J 3452/22/1.

75. Report on the Red Sea Slave Trade by commander HMS *Dahlia* to C. in C. Mediterranean, no. 5, 4 December 1928, FO 371/13837, pp. 209–15.

76. See inter alia Dunbar to Chamberlain, no. 195, 18 August 1928, FO 371/13104 J 2667/31/1; Holman to FO, no. 33/18/1928, 19 September 1928, and minutes, ibid., J 2704/31/1; memorandum by Behrens, 29 October 1928, ibid., J 3088/31/1; Waterlow to Chamberlain, no. 279, confidential, 3 December 1928, and minutes, ibid.

77. The British suspected them of planning to establish sovereignty over the islands of Hanis and Zukur in spite of an agreement that posts in the Red Sea would not establish claims to sovereignty. Reading to Murray, no. 1150, 25 September 1931, FO 371/15280 E 4794/3053/91.

78. Admiralty to FO, no. M01027, 2 June 1931, and minutes, FO 371/15387 J 1798/33/1.

79. Minutes of interdepartmental meeting on the traffic in arms and slaves in the Red Sea and Persian Gulf, 24 April 1930, FO 371/14475 E 2218/1054/91 with corrected versions in FO 371/14476; and minutes of interdepartmental meeting, 6 July 1931, FO 371/15279 E 3602/2756/91. At the time, the British were using a base in Eritrea.

80. See above chapter 10. The Liberian question cannot be entered into in detail here. There is a voluminous correspondence on Liberia in the British Foreign Office archives and the papers of the League Liberia Committee available in the League archives in Geneva. Its report was published as Report of the Liberian Commission of Enquiry, LON C.658.M272 June 1930. Secondary works include Buell I, Sundiata 1980, 1996.

81. See above chapter 11 for action in Assam and Burma.

82. O'Connor to Parsons, no. 140-C., 11 January 1925, IO L/PtS/11/256 file 536. Nepal had a king, but real power lay with Chandra Shumsher of the Rana family.

83. Caplan 1980, Levine 1980, Sever 1993, 219–23, and the press cutting in IO LPts/S11/256, file 536.

84. Sever 1993, 274–77.

85. Note of the Emancipation of Slaves and Abolition of Slavery in Nepal, issued by the Nepalese Anti-Slavery Office, enclosed in Wilkinson to Parsons, 20 August 1926, IO L/PtS/11/256 file 536. Figures on the compensation paid vary from £322,500 to £375,000. For the amounts paid to each category of slaves, see *Times of India*, 4 September 1925.

86. Wilkinson to Parson, no. 49, 20 August 1926, IO L/PtS/11/256/536.

87. Wilkinson to Howell, no. 2, 17 November 1926, IO/PtS/11/256/536.

88. *Pioneer Mail*, 3 December 1926, and other cuttings in IO/PtS/11/256 file 536.

89. Chalise et al., 2001.

90. See below, chapter 24.

The Committee of Experts on Slavery

THE BATTLE TO REVIVE THE LEAGUE'S SLAVERY COMMISSION

In 1929, Harris reckoned there were still four to five million slaves in the world. Public interest in slavery had been stimulated by the revelations over mui tsai in Hong Kong, Ethiopian raids into Kenya, slave trading in Sudan, and by the perennial campaign of the Anti-Slavery Society. Riding on the crest of the wave, and encouraged by the advent of a Labor government, Harris urged the foreign secretary to revive the Temporary Slavery Commission. The government agreed for a number of reasons. Britain was almost the only power sending information to the League, creating the "regrettable" impression that slavery only existed in the British Empire.[1] If the TSC were revived, Britain could send it information on countries such as Arabia and Ethiopia without fear of diplomatic repercussions. Cecil decided it might even help the Tana dam negotiations, which he believed the Ethiopians were delaying in order to keep the British quiet on slavery.[2] Finally, it might relieve Britain of the expense and odium of naval patrols so disliked by the navy.

Thus on 5 September 1929, in the Sixth Commission of the League Assembly, Cecil proposed that the commission be revived because the Slavery Convention had not been effective. Only twenty-eight of the forty-five signatories had ratified it, and few of them had sent the League the required information on their antislavery measures.[3] Predictably, the other colonial powers opposed the proposal, fearing it might become a permanent commission with powers to investigate and supervise colonial affairs. It was, therefore, shelved for a year, to give the League time to urge signatories to ratify the convention. In an important new departure, however, it also asked them to send it information on slavery from private sources. Harris, joined by the Society of Friends, and the Council for the Representation of Women in the League of Nations, kept up the pressure on the government with parliamentary questions.[4] In 1930, Britain took the bull by the horns and proposed a *permanent commission* with powers to call government representatives to give evidence, and conduct on-the-spot investigations.[5] This would have given it more power than the Permanent Mandates Commission,[6] and, as well as frightening the other colonial powers, it rang alarm bells at the Colonial and India Offices. The former feared that "slavery" would be so widely defined that the commission might try to interfere with marriage practices and other native customs. The latter worried that Indian princes might be called on to defend their labor policies. Cecil tried to calm them by emphasizing that the commission would be composed only of experienced colonial administrators, who would appreciate such problems.

Portugal, Belgium, Liberia, Ethiopia, and France all rejected the proposal. The French thought it would not only infringe the sovereign rights of states, but it would be a precedent for the establishment of League bodies to inquire into questions such as the protection of minorities. They also objected to financing another League committee at a time of world depression. The question was shelved for another year to allow time for the existing system to work. Eleven more countries had now ratified the Slavery Convention.

At the 1931 Assembly, the British asked for the revival of the TSC for one year, in hopes that it would recommend a permanent committee.[7] They sent the League their own information and asked the Anti-Slavery Society for a memorandum showing the widespread persistence of slavery. The Society's document contained lurid descriptions of slavery and the slave trade in China, Ethiopia, Saudi Arabia, the Gulf States, and Muscat. The Colonial Office worried that mui tsai was described as slavery, and the India Office feared repercussions in India and the Persian Gulf.[8] The Foreign Office, therefore, forwarded the memorandum, but disassociated itself from its contents.[9] It also refused to send in its information on child labor in Morocco and Algeria, for fear that France would oppose the revival of the commission.[10] The British thus sidetracked complaints about child labor, which were to become a vital part of the campaign against contemporary forms of slavery in the future.

This time, the British proposal met with a more positive response. The French had been embarrassed in May and June 1929 by the appearance in *Le Matin* of a series of articles on the slave traffic in Ethiopia, Arabia, and Jibuti. The series included the story of a dhow captain who avoided capture in the Red Sea by throwing three slaves overboard at intervals, knowing that the warship pursuing him would stop to pick them up. In 1930, *La Ligue Française pour la défense des droits de l'homme et du citoyen* urged the government to take action. Faced with a wealth of evidence that slavery and the slave traffic still existed, France, therefore, agreed to revive the commission—but only if it was temporary, and did not conduct investigations.[11]

A rearguard action was then fought at the League on the grounds of expense.[12] This was foiled by Harris, who was working so closely with the British delegation that the French believed he was directing it.[13] He arranged for the Society to offer 10,000 Swiss francs (£400), seriously stretching its budget.[14] The Italian *Societa Antischiavista d'Italia* offered a further 2,630 Swiss francs (10,000 lira). The offers were accepted on the understanding that the donors would not influence discussions. The League provided

11,500 Swiss francs, half the 23,000 Swiss francs needed for the committee.[15] Various ways to cut costs were discussed during the winter of 1931–1932, but with the main battle won, attention now centered on the composition and terms of reference of the commission, which came to be called the Committee of Experts on Slavery (CES).

CHOOSING THE EXPERTS

As Delafosse, Freire d'Andrade, and Grimshaw had all died since 1925, a new committee was appointed. Its size was determined by the amount of money available and the number of powers wanting representation. Harris wanted a small group chosen for their expertise on African, Arabian, and Asiatic slavery, or for their knowledge of Christian, Muslim, or "pagan" practices—rather than for the nationality.[16] Colonial rivalry precluded such an apolitical solution. When the Foreign Office, mindful that other colonial powers would resent not being represented, suggested a body of five without a British member, he was alarmed. A committee without Lugard would be "valueless." He was even more concerned when Lugard suggested that Lady Simon would "carry much weight" and was an "infinitely better speaker" than he was.[17]

All agreed that a woman delegate was needed to placate women's groups.[18] In 1930, the Council for the Representation of Women in the League of Nations had sent a deputation to the Foreign and Colonial Offices demanding representation on the proposed committee on the grounds that slavery was of particular concern to women, in the belief that in many African societies they were regarded as the property of their husbands.[19]

In the end, a committee of seven was chosen, all appointed at the request of their governments, except Lugard, whose membership was taken for granted.[20] The ILO sent only an observer. Gohr again represented Belgium. The Italian, Tulio Zedda, had been secretary to the government of Eritrea. He was later replaced by Ercole Vellani, head of the Office of Studies and Propaganda in the Ministry of the Colonies. The Dutch delegate, Neytzell de Wylde, was the former president of the Legislative Assembly of the Dutch East Indies and an official of the ministry of the Colonies. Spain sent Julio Lopez-Olivan, minister plenipotentiary at the Foreign Ministry, and formerly director general of the Protectorate of Morocco and the colonies. The token woman, a Portuguese, Virginie de Castro e Almeida, was a delegate to the League of Nations International Institute for Intellectual Cooperation. Her appointment killed two birds with one stone, satisfying the Portuguese who wanted a place on the committee,[21] as well as women's groups.

The French member was Gabriel Angoulvant, who had been governor of the Ivory Coast and governor-general of French West Africa. He was an authoritarian technocrat. Unlike Lugard and Delafosse, he had little respect for African institutions or indirect rule, and advocated concessionary companies, compulsory crop growing, and forced labor for the large-scale development projects he thought essential for "progress." A confirmed nationalist, he believed his policies were for the benefit of Africa as well as France. The Ministry of the Colonies sent the head of *Direction des*

Affaires Politiques to Geneva, at their own expense, to keep him properly briefed.[22] Lugard, with whom he quickly came into conflict, was given no such help because he was an "independent expert." The Foreign Office was later to regret its adherence to this principle, which was not respected by other powers.

THE ANTI-SLAVERY SOCIETY AND BRITISH POLICY

In November 1931, Sir John Simon became foreign secretary in the new coalition National government. For the Anti-Slavery Society this was a great opportunity. Simon, a distinguished politician and founder of the National Liberal Party, had been a vice-president of the Society since 1928 and his wife, Kathleen, had been on its committee since 1927.[23] With Harris's help, she had published a book on slavery in 1929. Simon had written the preface and sent a copy to every ambassador and minister in London with a personally signed letter.[24] Harris thought this had been an important factor in the establishment of the CES.[25] Simon believed that slavery could be "swept away" with public support and leadership from the League.[26] Where in the past the government had usually considered the Society a thorn in its side, it now began cooperating in a common cause. In January 1932, for instance, the Society sent a deputation to Simon to discuss policy. He listened sympathetically, promising full consideration for their concerns. Since his wife was one of the delegates and he was a vice-president of the Society he could hardly do otherwise.[27]

By this time, the Society had also enhanced its parliamentary position by a drastic reorganization of its officers. Three peers, Lords Noel-Buxton, Lytton, and Meston, one from each of the main political parties, were now joint presidents.[28] There were six members of Parliament on the General Committee and the twenty-six distinguished vice-presidents included the archbishops of Canterbury and York, the bishop of Durham, Lord Astor, and a number of prominent reformers, as well as Cecil, Simon, and Steel-Maitland.[29] Before leaving for Geneva, Lugard sought guidance from Simon as to what the CES was expected to achieve. They agreed that the aim was to get it to recommend the establishment of a permanent commission that would examine evidence and submit annual reports.[30]

FRICTION AMONG THE EXPERTS, MAY 1932

The terms of reference of the new Committee of Experts on Slavery were more restricted than those of its predecessor. It was not to deal with forced labor, which was now the province of the ILO. It was only to examine material "supplied or transmitted by governments" since 1926, and only to report on the effectiveness of the convention, identify obstacles to the eradication of slavery, and suggest modifications needed in the machinery of the League. Finally, it was to study how best to help states requesting assistance.

At its first meeting on 4 May 1932, the Belgian delegate Gohr was elected chairman, and Lugard vice-chairman.[31] Following precedent, the committee decided to meet in private and keep its proceedings confidential. An important departure was that it could take evidence in person, but only from members of organizations vouched for by their governments as reliable and authoritative. To protect governments, however, as in the past, evidence from private sources was to be shown to them, and, if they disputed its accuracy, the committee could mention it in its report without vouching for its accuracy. The report was to be published without the minutes.[32] Gohr was elected rapporteur and the session was adjourned on 11 May for him to prepare his report. This was debated and finalized at the second session held from 22 August to 30 August. For convenience, only the main issues and points of conflict will be summarized here.

When the CES reviewed progress against slave raiding since 1926, both France and Italy continued the ploys made at the TSC in order to get agreements to pursue raiders into neighboring territories.[33] Thus, Angoulvant claimed that France needed to pursue raiders over the frontiers of Spanish Rio de Oro. The French had a special Camel Corps to hunt down slavers, and if the Spanish did not want the expense of forming similar mobile units, he suggested that they allow the French to cross their border. The Spanish delegate, who took little part in the proceedings, weakly said that Spain had strengthened its frontier posts, but he would be glad to recommend more cooperation with the French. Zedda sought to make capital out of the Italian conquest of Fezzan and Kufra saying there was now no slavery in Libya, or in Eritrea and Somalia. The report duly praised France, Italy, and Spain for their efforts in the Sahara; and Britain for finally establishing the long overdue frontier posts and border patrols in Sudan, Kenya, and Uganda to protect their subjects against Ethiopian raiders. It recommended that the powers conclude agreements allowing the pursuit of slavers across frontiers, provided that the culprits were handed over to their own territorial officials for trial. It also advocated prohibiting the possession of arms, especially precision weapons. Control of the arms trade was an objective of the colonial powers, but they had not succeeded in negotiating a general treaty on the subject.

At its first session, the commission discussed Noel-Buxton's report. This duly noted that Ethiopian slavery was usually benign, and slaves were being freed by the courts, but painted a distressing picture of endemic raiding, caravans of slaves crisscrossing the country, an export traffic through French Somaliland, lack of imperial control over the provinces, and deep-seated opposition to reform.[34] Haile Selassie was described as enlightened, shrewd, humane, and hardworking—a "godsend" but lacking in "commanding presence." Noel-Buxton still recommended constant pressure to keep him up to the mark and strengthen his hand against opponents, and advocated a League inquiry. Lugard used this report and the recent raids into Sudan as "lamentable proof" of the inability of the emperor to establish control. He proposed that the League remind him of his obligations and offer to appoint an officer with antislavery experience to assist him, without interfering in internal administration. He urged his colleagues to consider what measures to recommend and whether the League should offer financial help.

Angoulvant leapt to the emperor's defense, making the incredible claim that there was no slave trading in Ethiopia, and maintaining that such slavery as existed was not inhuman, and should only be attacked gradually.[35] Yet, the French were as aware as the British of the state of affairs in Ethiopia. Informed by missionaries, Lebanese traders and prospectors, their representatives in Addis Ababa reported in 1931 and 1932 that the emperor's regulations were not even obeyed in the capital, whereas the slaving areas were depopulated. People were hiding to escape *razzias.* Parents were selling their children to pay taxes. Slave courts returned fugitives to their masters, and the decrees against the slave trade were merely window dressing for the benefit of the League. Improvement, however, would require complete reorganization of the government, which the Negus had not the power to undertake. Just before the CES met, the French minister reiterated this information but warned that sudden emancipation would precipitate a crisis. Slave owners would not work and had not the money to pay wages, freed slaves would die of starvation, owners would revolt, and Haile Selassie would need large funds to raise an army, improve roads, employ advisers, and introduce a new tax system as well as other reforms.[36]

Angoulvant tried to prevent Noel-Buxton's report from being considered by the CES until the emperor had had a chance to refute it, and objected strenuously to hearing evidence from Noel-Buxton and Harris. When he was outvoted, he insisted that their statements and the report, edited for the purpose, should be sent to the government of Ethiopia.[37] He pointed out that in northern Nigeria Lugard had only applied antislavery laws when it suited him, and asked how one could praise Lugard and criticize Haile Selassie "in the same breath." He tried to maneuver Noel-Buxton into agreeing that cross-border raids had practically ceased, and succeeded in getting him to retract his statement that the French were lying when they denied there was an export traffic through French Somaliland. He asked what an advisor could possibly achieve in the face of the great obstacles faced by the emperor.

He was determined that the CES report should pay tribute to the latter's efforts, and tried to alter the tenor of Noel-Buxton's report by including all the favorable remarks and omitting the others. He categorically rejected its recommendations. He maintained that Ethiopia, whose government was genuinely starting to abolish slavery and serfdom, was in a different category from countries like Liberia, where the authorities themselves were involved in "the gravest irregularities," or China, which was in a state of chaos, or the Arabian states on the Red Sea "more or less under European influence" which had not abolished slavery or the slave trade—a dig at Britain's policy in the Gulf and the Aden Protectorate. He insisted that praising Haile Selassie would strengthen his authority, whereas the criticism and pressure advocated by Noel-Buxton could only weaken it. Moreover, the League should assure the emperor that he could count on its support and willingness to provide financial assistance, as well as a

European advisor—if he applied for one "through his friends in France." Faced with this, and knowing that the secretary-general of the League was averse to offering Englishmen such appointments, Lugard had second thoughts about pressing for a League advisor in case a Frenchman or an Italian was selected.[38]

When Lugard's criticisms of Ethiopia were supported by the Italian delegate,[39] Angoulvant and his government were convinced that Britain and Italy were acting in concert. He believed that they were using press campaigns, official protest, and veiled threats of expulsion from the League in order to force the emperor to accept a permanent advisor who would impose administrative and financial reforms, thus establishing a system of tutelage which would infringe Ethiopian sovereignty, and which France must resist at all costs.[40]

In the second session of the CES, however, Lugard upstaged Angoulvant. The Foreign Office sent him a copy of de Halpert's proposed reforms,[41] and Sandford, who at Lugard's request rode the thirty or so miles from his farm, through mud and rain, to discuss plans with Haile Selassie, reported that these had been accepted and would probably be implemented. There was, therefore, no need for another advisor, or for a League loan. The decree establishing the slavery department as an independent office under a young energetic director with de Halpert as advisor came out early in August. Sandford's letter with full details arrived on the last afternoon of the second session of the CES—just in time for Lugard to tell his colleagues the good news, assure them that the emperor was taking effective action, and incorporate the information in an annex to the committee's report.[42] The report, therefore, dealt favorably with Ethiopia, stating that slavery could only be ended gradually, and recommending measures to speed up the process, such as registering slaves and allowing them to ransom themselves, and taxing slave holdings. It noted that some of these recommendations were already being carried out. Haile Selassie was delighted,[43] and Lugard got what he wanted—action from the emperor, without losing his confidence, or risking the appointment of a French or Italian advisor. Angoulvant, unaware that Lugard was playing his own game, was incensed at this British volte-face. France's role as the emperor's defender had been usurped by perfide Albion. He attributed this wrongly to the Ethiopians having at last agreed to the Tana dam.[44]

In the discussions on Arabia, however, Angoulvant carried off the honors by attacking Britain for allowing slavery in the Aden Protectorate, in their satellites on the Persian Gulf, and, unreasonably, in Saudi Arabia. Lugard, to his mortification, knew nothing about Oman or the Hadhramaut, and could not answer questions, raised by his Italian colleague about the arrangements with the Gulf shaykhs. Britain, unwilling to call attention to them, had sent no reports to the League on any of these territories. Under its rules, the CES could only ask governments for information through the League Council. Since this would preclude receiving a reply while the commission was in session, the chairman asked Lugard to find out privately whether Britain could force Yemen, the Hadhramaut, Kuwait, and Bahrain to suppress slavery and slave dealing, and whether slavers could be pursued over land frontiers and in territorial waters.[45] Anthony Eden, parliamentary undersecretary to the Foreign Office, was in Geneva, but he was as ignorant as Lugard. When the latter told the CES that Britain could not insist on the abolition of slavery in Muslim states, Angoulvant retorted that this was temporizing, a "very wise policy," exactly what Ethiopia was doing![46] He was sure Lugard was deliberately avoiding discussion of areas under British control where slavery was still legal.[47]

He consulted his government and was told that the British had notified France of their "special position" in the Hadhramaut on four occasions between 1894 and 1896; and that in 1891 the sultan of Muscat had bound himself and his successors not to cede territory to a foreign power other than Britain. France had not officially accepted this, but in fact had recognized Oman as within the British "orbit." Angoulvant held Britain responsible for ending slavery in the region except in Yemen, which was genuinely independent.[48] Lugard was forced to ask Simon for full information before the second session of the CES in August.[49]

The Foreign Office was far from happy to find that its much-vaunted expert on slavery was so ill informed about Arabia and the Persian Gulf that he did not know that Oman was under the sovereignty of the sultan of Muscat or that the Makran coast was part of Persia. Officials decided that he was "badly out of contact" with British policy in Arabia, and wanted to discuss this admittedly complex question with him, but he was too busy to see them.[50] However, they themselves had to ask the India Office to explain the position in the Persian Gulf. The latter confirmed that there were slave trade treaties granting rights to search with Bahrain, Muscat, and the Trucial States. The India Office also confirmed that there were political agents in Muscat, Bahrain, and Kuwait, and an Arab agent in the Trucial States, all of whom, except the one in Kuwait, had the power to manumit slaves. They claimed that their vigilance had reduced the slave trade to a "steady trickle" of "insignificant dimensions." The trade in Kuwait was "nonexistent," although there were a number of domestic slaves there. In Bahrain, slavery was almost extinct and not recognized by the courts, although again there were still some domestic slaves, forty-six of whom had been manumitted by the agent in 1929 and 1930. The sultan of Muscat was well disposed, but had not the means to control the semi-independent "warlike and uncivilized tribes" of the Omani hinterland and coast, particularly the Batinah region. However, British ships policed the coast, and a road was being driven from Muscat along the shore to help the sultan extend his rule.

The India Office claimed that the maritime slave trade in the Persian Gulf had been almost stopped by naval action and offenders severely punished. In Dubai in 1928, a dhow had been publicly burnt as a warning, and the rulers had been impressed with the dire consequences of conniving at the traffic. The shaykh of Qatar had recently rescued and repatriated a Persian boy and was ready to carry out his treaty obligations, but the Trucial shaykhdoms as a group, though nominally under individual rulers, were controlled by juntas, and their inhabitants were described as "fanatical, backward, and intensely suspicious of any European interference, which they regard as a threat to their liberties." A few slaves were manumitted annually—twenty-seven, for instance, in 1929 and twelve in 1930.

All in all the British felt they had almost eradicated the seaborne trade and brought about a decline in the numbers of slaves in the areas actually controlled by the Gulf rulers, but in the hinterland of Muscat and the Trucial Coast, only time could erode the institution. Further action, the India Office warned, would provoke economic and political reactions since slavery was "deeply rooted in religious and political history." However, they insisted that slaves were usually well treated and few sought manumission, although it was well-known that British officials had the power to free them. The India Office recommended that Lugard emphasize Britain's solid achievement in almost suppressing the maritime traffic and substantially reducing slavery itself in areas where British influence was most felt, such as Bahrain and Kuwait.[51]

The question of the Hadhramaut was referred to the Colonial Office, which controlled the Aden Protectorate. Lugard was informed that slavery was illegal in the colony of Aden, an area of some seventy miles in and around the town, and including the island of Perim. Cases that came to light, there, were dealt with under the Indian penal code. In the Protectorate, there were treaties against the slave trade with the "Arab tribes" in the northeast and south along the coast as far as the frontiers of Muscat. Every effort was being made to end the traffic in Lahej. There was "no reason to believe" that there was a regular traffic in slaves along the coast. Slavery still existed, but the discontented could easily flee into British territory. Most, however, were "happy and content" and would resent any attempt to free them. The sultan of Shihr and Mukalla actually found his slaves a "heavy burden on his exchequer" and was proposing to free them as soon as he felt he could deal with the disturbance it would cause.[52] The Colonial Office did not add that they had no contact at all with the Hadhramaut interior.

Angoulvant, with much less justification, claimed that since only the British had a treaty binding Ibn Saud to cooperate against the slave trade, and only they practiced consular manumission, they alone were in a position to "further the suppression of slavery in Hijaz."[53] This was a low blow given that neither France nor Italy had responded to British appeals to cooperate over manumission and neither had insisted on articles against the slave trade in their treaties with Ibn Saud in 1931 and 1932.[54] In response to pointed questions from Lugard, however, his French, Italian, and Dutch colleagues all claimed that their consuls would free any fugitives who came to their consulates, although British reports from Jiddah were full of complaints that they rarely if ever manumitted or repatriated fugitives, and did not support British representations to the Saudis.[55]

When the CES discussed the British proposal to establish a refuge in Sudan for slaves freed in Arabia, Angoulvant objected. France would welcome the few who did not know their country of origin and turn them into "good and loyal French subjects."[56] Lugard thought the refuge impracticable and the proposal was dropped. The CES recommended instead that the countries of origin should pay the cost of repatriation, and that slaves of unknown origin should be allowed to settle wherever they could be sent from Jiddah.

In keeping with its general policy, the CES report on slavery in the Arabian Peninsula was calculated to avoid offense. Slavery, it said, was upheld by Muslim law and public opinion, which rulers could not flout, but states should not be admitted to the League unless they agreed to begin the process of emancipation. Powers signing treaties with them should try to include a clause on the abolition of slavery.

As for the slave trade, private sources indicated that slaves were still imported into the Arabian Peninsula, but Angoulvant denied that any came through French Somaliland. Zedda claimed that Italy was "relentlessly pursuing" slave dhows in Eritrean waters. The British reported that the traffic was now very small. The committee decided they did not have enough evidence as to its scale. Their report naturally praised the efforts of Britain, France, and Italy on land and sea, but urged them to conclude the maritime treaty envisaged in the 1926 convention in order to coordinate their efforts and allow mutual rights to pursue suspects into their territorial waters—a proposal none of them welcomed.

As for the enslavement of pilgrims, the CES agreed that this continued, although all the countries concerned tried to make them travel by steamer from designated ports, and had agents in Mecca to look after them. The numbers were daunting—84,821 reached Arabia in 1930.[57] Those who came from the east by ship were easier to protect than those who came overland to the Red Sea coast. The British had protested to Italy that many of the latter boarded dhows in Eritrea and landed at small ports to avoid steamer charges and the cost of quarantine in Jiddah. The Italians had promised to stop this traffic in 1928, but protests in 1932 merely elicited denials that it continued.[58] At the CES, Zedda claimed that Italy was doing all it could and accused Britain and France of not exercising sufficient supervision over the Takrunis (West Africans), many of whom came across Africa on foot without passports. Lugard pointed out that they came by many routes, often taking years, and that once in Arabia they could hardly be denied access to the pilgrimage because they had no passports.[59] Angoulvant suggested that Britain and Italy should adopt the French method of having them travel in batches under the supervision of interpreters with collective passports. The CES recommended the issue of passports to all pilgrims, and checks to see that they returned home. They also suggested imposing heavy penalties on vessels boarding them at unauthorized ports, transporting them without permission, or not verifying that they were genuine pilgrims.

THE DEFINITION OF SLAVERY

An acrimonious discussion concerned the vital question of the definition of slavery.[60] Angoulvant, like Delafosse, maintained that persons who remained with their owners, but could claim their freedom at any time, were not slaves. He called them serfs, *captifs de case*, or praedial slaves, occupying an intermediate status between slaves and free people. These were called "domestic slaves" by the British. They were usually slaves of the second or later generations, born in their masters' households. They were often protected by native custom against sale and the harsher treatment of first generation or "trade" slaves. By colonial law, they could not be sold, forcibly detained, or made to work. As in the past, however, Lugard maintained that they were still slaves by the League definition since all or some of the rights of ownership were exercised over them. Moreover, they sometimes asked to be freed by officials and even paid a ransom in order to be free in their own eyes and the eyes of their communities.[61] Angoulvant countered that in French colonies this was not necessary as they had "sufficient reliance" on the manumission bestowed by the authorities,[62] and Zedda made the same claim for the Italian colonies.

The disagreement could not be resolved in spite of the valiant efforts of the chairman. In the end the Portuguese and Italian delegates sided with the French, while the rest agreed with Lugard that slaves who stayed with their owners came under the League definition of slavery. The participants insisted that their divergent views be recorded in the CES report.

Why was this so important? Angoulvant explained to his government that it affected the estimates of the numbers of slaves in the world. If these serfs, praedial, or domestic slaves (all the terms were used) were counted as slaves, then the numbers were high. Slavery would appear to be more widespread and important than he believed it to be. Moreover, persons who had remained with their masters in French West Africa would have to be called slaves, making it appear that France had not kept its agreements to suppress slavery. Like Delafosse, he insisted that these "serfs" enjoyed a benign form of servitude with greater security in old age and sickness than many European workers. France was therefore justified in tolerating it.[63] Classing them as slaves also diverted the League's attention away from the plight of real slaves in the Muslim world, Ethiopia, and elsewhere, and from others who suffered from greater disabilities, for whom it was more important to free.[64]

The discussion was confused, hampered by lack of precise data on native institutions, and consensus on terminology. The CES suggested that the League's definition of slavery might be revised, but it did not attempt the task, nor did it draw any real conclusion as to whether or not there should be a distinction between these so-called serfs and "real" slaves, merely noting that the colonial powers had passed laws abolishing the legal status of both institutions. To Angoulvant's gratification, however, the report stated that this "serfdom" (*servage*) helped to maintain political, economic, and social equilibrium and should be left to die a natural death. This meant that the so-called "vestiges of slavery" could continue without interference. The discussion begged the question of what had been done to actually make it possible for these so-called serfs to leave—a question that was to be raised in subsequent League committees.

However, the CES did discuss how the transition from slave to free labor might be achieved and in doing so furthered the interests of the colonial powers by stating that wage labor promoted the spirit of freedom among former slaves. Angoulvant went further, insisting that military service, including forced labor on public works performed by the Second Contingent, was more beneficial than employment in colonial commercial and industrial enterprises.[65] "The wearing of a soldier's uniform," he said, gave freed slaves "very strong feelings of freedom, and after discharge from military service, they considered themselves entirely free." Lugard objected that this forced recruitment broke up traditional life, and argued that independent production was a better way to speed up emancipation. To please them both, the CES report included military service, farming, and other independent activities among the occupations to be encouraged.[66]

PRACTICES RESTRICTIVE OF THE LIBERTY OF THE PERSON

The CES admitted that it knew little about various other practices "restrictive of the liberty of the person." One of the papers submitted to the committee had come from three members of Parliament, the Duchess of Atholl, Miss Eleanor Rathbone, and Colonel Josiah Wedgwood, and dealt with what they called "female slavery within the family." This raised worrying questions for colonial governments since it covered the rights of males over wives, widows, and other female kin. It claimed that these sometimes amounted to slavery as defined by the League. Among the customs attacked were bride wealth, particularly if paid for a child, the inheritance of widows by their husbands' kinsmen, and the fact that mothers had no rights over their own children, or over earnings and property. The authors acknowledged that these practices had a good as well as a bad side and they suggested a piecemeal attack, such as limiting rather than banning payment of bride wealth, fixing a minimum age for betrothal, educating girls, and encouraging the employment of women by colonial governments. They complained that the Colonial Office had published a "very whitewashing paper" which showed that governors were complacent about the condition of native women.

Lugard believed the status of women could only be ameliorated over time, and he advised them that raising this vexed question at the CES might provide ammunition for opponents of a permanent commission on the ground that it would interfere with national sovereignty. It would be wiser, he cautioned, to await the appointment of a permanent committee. This advice was taken.[67] Gohr decided the practices at issue were not forms of slavery and the CES merely acknowledged the communication.[68] This question of women's rights in marriage was to be an ongoing struggle leading to investigations of "servile marriage" later in the century. The CES, however, did discuss slave dealing under cover of payment of bride wealth. It decided that there was a fine line between marriage and slave purchase, which could only be settled by law courts dealing with actual cases. This begged the question of the impartiality of Muslim and native courts when it came to such questions, particularly as they were all run by men.

The CES also considered that, in general, the distinction between adoption and child purchase could only be settled by courts. In the case of mui tsai, they faced a difficult problem. There were several governments in China, which was threatened by Japan and torn by civil war. The delegate to the League from the Nanking government had categorically denied in 1931 that there was any trafficking in children. Mui tsai, he said, were adopted in times of disaster to save their lives. However, the provisional government in Canton (Guangzhou) in March 1927 had prohibited the sale of mui tsai, and ordered that they be genuinely adopted, sent to school between the ages of thirteen and sixteen, and married before they were twenty-three, if they so wished.[69] Harris, in his testimony before the CES, claimed that girls were sold in China as mui tsai, or for work in opium dens and factories. The Anti-Slavery Society was financing a home, run by missionaries, for rescued mui tsai in Yunan-Fu (Kunming). He had plenty of evidence of ill-treatment, and wanted the institution condemned by the League.[70]

Only the Nanking government was represented at the League and the CES had no wish to offend it. In view of the chaotic state of affairs in the country, its report merely noted that there was a conflict over whether mui tsai were slaves or adopted children. It recorded the various ordinances issued in China, but suggested that the 1929 Hong Kong ordinance might become a model for the future. Harris was outraged, but his problem was a perennial one—if official denials are to be contradicted, the evidence has to be solidly based, and he could not reveal his missionary sources for fear of compromising them; hence, his information could not be given the weight it deserved.[71]

When it came to debt-bondage, the CES had little to add to the report of TSC. Members had no information on peonage or on debt-bondage in India. They merely recommended that neither should ever be sanctioned by law, and that penalties should be imposed for all pledging of children. Work in discharge of a debt should only be allowed if there was a contract stating the amount of the debt and the nature and value of the work, which should be paid at the going rate for free labor. No augmentation of the debt should be allowed. This was a start in the laying down of general principles for an international agreement. The various forms of debt slavery were to come under attack in later League and United Nations committees and to become a major issue by the 1980s.

THE ESTABLISHMENT OF A PERMANENT ADVISORY COMMITTEE OF EXPERTS ON SLAVERY

In pursuit of Britain's main objective in promoting the CES, Lugard suggested that it should recommend the establishment of a permanent slavery committee of five experts to meet biannually for a short session to examine evidence, to advise governments requesting help, and to decide whether financial aid could be offered. To quiet the fears of his colleagues, he ruled out any suggestion of on-the-spot investigations unless a government asked for it, and agreed that it should only receive information from NGOs approved by their governments, and that their evidence, as usual, should always be passed on to governments for comment.

It was clear to all members of the CES that their information was inadequate. Few of the signatories of the Slavery Convention had sent the League regular reports. The committee could not even answer the main question put to them: How effective had the 1926 convention been? Moreover, it had been convened in a hurry, and had not been given the time or resources to do a thorough job.[72] Members, therefore, agreed to recommend a new committee. Angoulvant set out to emasculate it, by suggesting it should only consider official evidence, and should meet every three years. He also rejected Lugard's suggestion that part of the cost might again come from private donors. The British and Italian antislavery societies had renewed their offers of funds and the League would only have had to pay about a third of the estimated cost.[73] Angoulvant insisted this would compromise its impartiality.[74] That the offer came from British and Italian charities made it all the more suspicious.

In the end, the CES recommended the establishment of a permanent commission of not more than seven members—six experts of different nationalities and a representative of the ILO. To disarm fears that it might infringe national sovereignty, it was to be purely advisory and to meet only every two years for a short session. It was to be disbanded as soon as the suppression of slavery had been achieved. As usual, it was also only to take evidence from private sources acceptable to their own governments.

Lugard's verdict on the CES was that it had wasted most of its time on a useless attempt to answer questions about which it had too little information, but he was well pleased at securing the required recommendation for a permanent commission.

NOTES

1. ASAPS to FO 27 June 1929, and minutes and memoranda A4343/225/52, and 18 July 1929, minutes and memorandum, A 4829/225/52, FO 371/13480; minutes of FO Committee on Disarmament and Arbitration, 29 November 1929, FO 371/14117 W 11645/50/98.

2. Minute by Murray, 22 August 1929, J 2507/130/1, and memorandum by Zaphiro enclosed in Barton to Henderson no. 228, confidential, 25 November 1929, J 3529/130/1, FO 371/13838.

3. States did not ratify the convention for a whole range of reasons. Venezuela, for instance, replied that its own constitution went further than the convention, and sent no documents to the League after 31 December 1929, maintaining there was no more to be said. The League wanted governments to ratify the convention even if there was no slavery in their territories, see correspondence with Venezuela in LON carton R2359/ 6B/17739/15219.

4. ASAPS to FO 15 May 1930, FO 371/15038 W 5002/334/52; minutes on replies to parliamentary questions, ibid. W 1267, W 1610; notes of meeting between the Council for the Representation of Women at the League of Nation and the secretary of state, 8 April 1930, FO 371/14992; Society of Friends to Henderson, 8 July 1930, FO 371/15039 W 7009/334/52.

5. For the British discussions, see documents in FO 371/ 14475, FO 371/14476, FO 371/14958, FO 371/14959.

6. LON A.29.1931.VI, 20 August 1931; Cecil to Henderson, no. 85, 2 October 1930, and FO 371/15036 W 10333/34/52.

7. This had been suggested by the secretary-general, Drummond to Cadogan, personal, 21 August 1930, ibid., W 8626/34/52.

8. Memorandum 11 June 1931 from the ASAPS to the British government, enclosed in British government to the secretary-general of the League of Nations, 5 August 1931, LON A.29.1931.VI. This included published information on Saudi Arabia, Oman and the Gulf States, and Ethiopia by missionaries, travelers, diplomats, and journalists, and correspondence on Ethiopian fugitives in Sudan, and with the Chinese on mui tsai.

9. Minutes in FO 371/15769, pp. 239–40, February 1931, pp. 247–49, June–July 1931 and 302–303; IO to FO E & Q 4952, 18 July 1931, and minutes, FO 371/15769. W8354/ 2634/52.

10. ASAPS to Henderson, 17 July 1931, and minutes, FO 371/15769 W8440/2634/52. This information had been gathered at an international conference on the treatment and enslavement of African children.

11. Massigli to FMAE telegram, 5 September 1929, FMAE SDN 941, folder IM4; Note for Massigli, 7 September 1929, FMAE SDN 943 Esc. 1929-31; *Ligue Française pour la défense des droits de L'homme et du citoyen* to FMAE, 20 August 1930 and enclosed letter; note for French delegate to the League Assembly, 25 August 1930, ibid.

12. Harris to Lugard, confidential, 15 December 1931, Lugard Papers.

13. For Harris's activities, see AS MSS. Brit.Emp. s.20 E2/7, p. 25, minute 4630, Committee meeting, 1 October 1931. Two of the British delegates, Lords Lytton and Astor, were to become joint-presidents of the Society. For the French view of Harris's influence, see note on TSC, 19 October 1931, FMAE SDN 943 Esclavage, 1929–1933.

14. AS MSS. Brit.Emp. s.20 E2/7, p. 25, minutes 4630, Committee meeting, 1 October 1931.

15. For the budget correspondence, see LON 6/B 34172/14790 carton R 2357; Cecil to Reading no. 89, 27 September 1931, FO 371/15769 W 11537/2634/52. For the estimates of expenses and suggestions as to how they might be cut, see memorandum by Catastini, enclosed in Drummond to Cadogan, personal, 21 August 1930, FO 371/15036 W8626/34/52; minutes and memoranda on League to FO, 21 October 1931, particularly memorandum of 21 September 1931 and Lytton to Astor giving estimate by Catastini, FO 371/15769 W12246. Travel costs could be cut if delegates lived in Europe, especially Geneva, and if the Secretariat provided secretarial help,

estimated at a disproportionate 12,000 Swiss francs a year. There were also printing and other expenses.

16. For Harris's suggestions, see memorandum enclosed in FO memorandum, 24 September 1931, FO 371/15769, pp. 377–82; minute by Cadogan, 12 January 1932, minute of conversation between Harris and Cecil, FO 371/16503, p. 17, W 5/5/98; minutes on a proposed deputation from ASAPS to the Foreign Office, 5 January 1932, FO 371/16504 W 169/169/52; Harris to Lugard, confidential, 15 December 1931, Lugard Papers.

17. There were "several other reasons" against Lady Simon which sadly Harris said he could not "put in writing," Harris to Lugard, 16 and 17 December 1931, Lugard Papers.

18. Memorandum by Harris enclosed in memorandum, 24 September 1931, FO 371/15769, pp. 378–80. The secretary-general received petitions from the International Alliance of Women for Suffrage and Equal Citizenship, 6 September 1929, and the British Commonwealth Organization, and a deputation from the Joint Standing Committee of Women's International Organization, LON 6/B14790/14790 carton 2357.

19. They also argued that bride price was sometimes paid in installments with borrowed assets so that the wife became at least temporarily the property of the creditor—or even of a series of creditors. Notes of a meeting of the secretary of state and Lord Cecil, with a deputation from the Council for the Representation of Women in the League of Nations, 8 April 1930, FO 371/14992.

20. See correspondence with the various governments in LON 6/B33536/14790, 6/B34525/14790, 6/34693/14790.

21. De Andrade to Drummond, 22 December 1931, de Haller to Wilson, 30 December 1931, LON 6B/33536/14790 carton R2357.

22. Ministry of Colonies to FMAE, 15 and 18 December 1931, FMAE SDN 1 M4.

23. Sir John Simon 1873–1954, foreign secretary 1931–1935, home secretary 1935–1937, chancellor of the Exchequer 1937–1940, lord chancellor 1940–1945, vice-president of ASAPS from 1928–1953.

24. AS MSS. Brit.Emp. s.20 E2/17, p. 21, minute 4622, Committee meeting, 6 August 1931.

25. AS MSS. Brit.Emp.s.20 E2/17, p. 25, minute 4630, Committee meeting, 1 October 1931.

26. Kathleen Simon 1929, x–xi.

27. AS Mss.Brit.Emp.s.20 E2/17, p. 49, minute 4669, Committee meeting, 4 February 1932.

28. For Noel-Buxton, see above chapter 12. Victor Alexander Robert Bulwer-Lytton, 2nd Earl of Lytton 1876–1947, a Conservative, he was an idealist interested in promoting social services, was governor of Bengal 1922–1927, and held a number of government appointments. James Scorgie Meston, 1st Baron Meston 1865–1943, a Liberal, had had a distinguished career in the Government of India and had been one of the designers of the Royal Institute of International Affairs. With this reorganization, the long time president of the ASAPS, Charles Roberts, became

chairman of the General Committee, which oversaw the two executives—the secretary, Travers Buxton, and the parliamentary secretary, Harris.

29. *ASR* series V, 22, 2 July 1931.

30. Lugard to FO, confidential 15 April 1932, and FO minutes, and FO to Lugard, confidential, 26 April 1932, FO 371/16503 W 4386/5/52.

31. Minutes of the Committee of Experts on Slavery (CES), May 1932, LON C.E.E./1st session, P.V.1, confidential. The minutes of the first session are filed in LON carton 2358, 6B/37465/14790. Those of the second session are in LON carton 2359 6B/40347/14790. The minutes of each meeting are filed under a PV (process verbale) number corresponding to the order of the meetings. Henceforth, they will be referred by their PV number.

32. The Report of the CES was published by the League as A 34 1932 V1, 1 September 1932 (its number in draft was C.618. 1932. V1). The various drafts of the report are filed in LON carton 2358 6B/37985/1490. Henceforth, it will be referred to as CES Report.

33. The British and French allowed this on the frontier between Equatorial Africa and Darfur in the Anglo-Egyptian Sudan and the CES suggested making a similar arrangement with Ethiopia.

34. Report on Abyssinia by Lord Noel-Buxton and Lord Polwarth, enclosed in FO to secretary-general, 26 April 1932, FOCP 14116, no. 61 J 1031/3/1 (FO 401/32). For simplicity, this will be referred to as the Noel-Buxton report.

35. LON C.E.E. 1st session, P.V. 2, P.V. 5, P.V. 9.

36. Chargé d'affaires, Addis Ababa, to FMAE, no. 147, 3 October 1931, FMAE SDN carton 943 Esclavage en Ethiopie 1935; FMAE to de Reffye, no. 31, 8 March 1932 and de Reffye to FMAE, no. 78, ibid.

37. The editing removed some of the personal remarks about Haile Selassie and others liable to give offense, as well as some of the conclusions. For the version given to the emperor, see Catastini to Simon, 23 August 1932, LON 6B/21943/2053. This had been edited by the ASAPS and further edited by Barton, Barton to Simon, telegram no. 38, 27 June 1932, FO 371/16096 J 1830/3/1, FO to Barton, telegram, no. 28, 6 July 1932, ibid., Barton to Simon no. 109, 19 July 1932, Simon to Barton no. 36, 12 August 1932, Ashley-Clarke to Catastini, 15 August 1932, and minute by Mack, 11 August 1932, ibid., J2289/3/1. See also corrections noted in ibid., J11081/3/1 ASAPS to FO, 20 April 1932 and minutes.

38. Lugard to Sandford, 1 June 1932, Lugard Papers.

39. LON C.E.E., 1st session, P.V. 10. Further research is needed to unravel Italian objectives but it may simply have been because Zedda was ill and his replacement, Verlani, was noticeably less pugnacious.

40. Report by the French Delegates on First Session of the CES (no date as first page missing) SDN carton 943 Esclavage Général 1932–1937; FMAE to Reffye, 4 June 1932, no number, FMAE SDN 943 Esclavage en Ethiope.

41. This and the information that follows is based on Sandford to Lugard, 18 May, 9 July, 1 August 1932; Lugard to Sandford, 1 June, 9 August and 2 September 1932. For the proposals and their results see below, chapter 15.

42. Sandford also sent the *Times* the same information on the proposed reforms as he sent to Lugard, Sandford to Lugard, 12 October 1932, Lugard Papers.

43. Lugard to Sandford, 21 November 1932, Lugard Papers.

44. Report on the Second Session of the CES, 22–30 August 1932, FMAE SDN 943.

45. LON C.E.E. 1st session, P.V. 2; P.V. 6; P.V. 7.

46. LON C.E.E. 1st session, P.V. 10.

47. Reports of 1st and 2nd sessions of the CES, FMAE SDN, Esclavage Générale.

48. LON C.E.E. 1st session, P.V. 11.

49. Lugard to Simon, confidential, 23 May 1932, FO 371/16503 W 5963/5/52.

50. Minutes on Lugard to Simon, confidential, 23 May 1932, ibid.

51. IO to FO P.z.3804/32, confidential and immediate, 9 August 1932, and enclosed memorandum, The Slave Trade in Muscat, Oman, the Trucial Coast, Bahrain, and Kuwait, FO 371/16503 W 9073/5/52.

52. CO to Lugard, 9 August 1932, Lugard Papers. Treaties against the slave trade had been signed in 1863 with Mukalla and Shihr, Hertslet, *Commercial Treaties*, XIII, p. 687, and these were renewed and made binding in 1873, Harold Ingrams 1966, 10. For further discussion of the position of these slaves, see below, chapter 18.

53. LON C.E.E. 1st session, P.V. 11.

54. Italy in an exchange of notes had gotten Saudi agreement to cooperate against the slave trade, but had been refused the right to manumit slaves. Sollazzo to Feisal, 10 February 1932 and Feisal to Sollazzo, 10 February 1932, enclosed in FO to Lugard, 17 August 1932, FO 371/16503 W 8971/5/52.

55. LON C.E.E. 1st session, P.V. 4.

56. LON C.E.E. 1st session, P.V. 4.

57. For statistics for 1930 and 1931, when the economic depression and other factors caused numbers to drop to 39, 346, see enclosure in Ryan to Simon, 26 November 1931, FOCP14088 (FO 406/68).

58. Hoare to Reading, no. 825 (73/7/31), 7 September 1931, minutes, enclosures, FO 371/15417 J2775/186/16; Graham to Simon no. 330, 27 April 1932, FO 371/16121 J1187/254/16.

59. LON C.E.E. 1st session, P.V. 3.

60. LON C.E.E. 1st session, P.V. 6; P.V. 7; LON C.E.E. 2nd session, P.V. 6, P.V. 8.

61. Lugard called this "permissive slavery" and made the extraordinary claim that it was only allowed by the British in Muslim societies during the period of transition. Angoulvant, with reason, told him that it was practiced on the Gold Coast and accused him of not having studied the question like Delafosse. On inquiry, Lugard found this to be true. LON C.E.E. 1st session, P.V. 7; Lugard to Slater, 30 May 1932, Lugard Papers; Jones to Slater, 21 May 1932, ibid.; Lugard notes for Gohr re CES, 27 June 1932, ibid.

62. LON C.E.E. 1st session, P.V. 7.

63. By Angoulvant's estimate, this reduced the numbers of slaves in Ethiopia to 400,000–500,000 from the 2,000,000 claimed by the ASAPS—a figure disputed by Haile Selassie and other authorities. For the discussion, see LON C.E.E. 2nd session, P.V. 9.

64. For Angoulvant's views, see Report on the Second Session of the CES, FMAE SDN 943, 1932–1937; his carefully worded final statement on the subject, and those of his colleagues, are in the CES report.

65. Report of the French Delegates on the Second Session of the CES, ibid.

66. LON C.E.E. 1st session, P.V. 7; 2nd Session, P.V. 1, 8.

67. Rathbone to Lugard, 19 and 26 May 1932, enclosing memorandum; Lugard to Rathbone, 23 May 1932, Lugard Papers.

68. LON C.E.E. 1st session, P.V. 10.

69. LON C.E.E. 1(c) 1932 VI, p. 27.

70. LON C.E.E. 1st session, P.V.C. For this home, see Jaschok 1994, and The Anti-Slavery Society's published reports in the 1930s in the *ASR*.

71. Catastini note for Walters, 29 August 1932, and Walters to Catastini, 29 August 1932, LON carton 2358, 6B/37985/14790; Harris to Lugard, 27 September 1932, and Lugard to Harris, 30 September 1932, Lugard Papers.

72. The commission was expected to meet in April, but Lugard first heard of his appointment when he read it in the *Times* on 1 February 1932, before the letter of appointment had even been sent out.

73. The estimated cost was £750 (35,000 Swiss francs) a year for a seven-member committee. The ASAPS had offered £250 and the Italians 10,000 lira, Lugard to Cecil, 8 September 1932, ASAPS to Lugard, 3 August 1932, Brooks to Lugard, 6 August 1932, Lugard to Brooks, 8 August 1932, Lugard to Cecil, 8 September 1932, Lugard Papers. For the Italian offer, see president of the *Societa Antischiavista* to secretary-general, 4 May 1932 LON R 2357 6B/36004/14790.

74. LON C.E.E. 1st Session, P.V. 11, P.V. 12.

The Advisory Committee of Experts on Slavery

THE ESTABLISHMENT OF A PERMANENT SLAVERY COMMITTEE

Although the Committee of Experts on Slavery had unanimously recommended a permanent slavery committee, France and Portugal objected to the expense, but ruled out private funding.[1] Eventually, however, they agreed to a committee funded by the League, to meet only every two years *if it was necessary*. It was to be purely advisory, could not conduct investigations, and could only receive documents transmitted by governments. Its proceedings were to be confidential. Governments could vet the communications that concerned them and the Council was to decide whether to publish its report. To cut costs, instead of having its own bureau, an official from the League Secretariat was to do the secretarial work. Moreover, the first meeting was delayed until 1934 on the excuse that it was too late to fund it from the 1933 budget.[2]

The body, known as the Advisory Committee of Experts on Slavery (ACE) consisted of seven "independent" experts, appointed for an indefinite term, but subject to review every six years.[3] They were to study the documents sent in by governments and submit reports on measures to end the slave trade and ameliorate slavery. If a state asked for financial assistance, they could decide, at the request of the Council, on the sum needed and the guarantees to be required. They were on no account to discuss forced labor. The Secretariat was to collect published information on slavery for them. This fell far short of Lugard's hope that the committee would be a research center, able to collect evidence, correspond with societies and individuals, offer advice to governments, and receive contributions for such things as homes and schools for ex-slaves.[4]

At the public meetings of the Assembly, the proponents all sought credit for establishing this committee they had tried so hard to prevent, and had succeeded in emasculating. The French said they "wholeheartedly" supported the League's "noble struggle," and pointed out that Emperor Haile Selassie was already participating in this "campaign." Cecil, with a different axe to grind, deplored the delay in establishing the committee, and regretted that its proceedings were to be confidential, and was more voluble than the French in his praise of Haile Selassie. The Portuguese joined the chorus but warned that the committee must never infringe on national sovereignty.[5]

Humanitarians were euphoric. This first permanent slavery committee was established in 1933—the centenary of the Emancipation Act. In celebration the Anti-Slavery Society had launched an appeal for £20,000 for a fund to rally public opinion, create sister societies abroad, and collect evidence on slavery.[6] Clergy, ministers, and teachers were asked to speak on the subject, and the public was invited to join the society.[7] A series of lectures by eminent people on "progress" for "backward races" was inaugurated. Simon spoke at a "Celebration Meeting" in York Minster. A lantern lecture could be borrowed, and a pageant play on abolition was hired out to dramatic societies, schools, churches, and social institutions. Lugard launched a performance of the pageant at a League of Nations Union rally on Empire Day, and pronounced some of the scenes "quite affecting."[8]

The Society hailed the ACE as heralding the end of slavery and forced labor. Reginald Coupland, professor of colonial history at Oxford University published *The British Anti-Slavery Movement*—a short book timed for the centenary. His final chapter, optimistically entitled "The Last Phase," proclaimed that "the appropriate machinery" to ensure the execution of the 1926 Convention had finally been created. He had little doubt that "except perhaps in remote and unsettled regions of the world beyond the reach of civilized opinion the final eradication . . . of slavery" was assured.[9]

Thus, when the ACE finally met in Geneva over a year after the Assembly had agreed to its appointment, and nearly a decade after it had been suggested by the Temporary Slavery Commission, humanitarians confidently predicted that the final stage of Britain's great crusade was at hand. It is sad to turn from their confident, fanciful rhetoric to the reality of this emasculated and undistinguished committee.

CHOOSING THE EXPERTS

The members of the ACE were selected by their governments. Lugard was ruled out. He was seventy-five, quite deaf, and "a good way past his best."[10] The British choice was between someone with administrative experience, which no woman had, and someone without such experience, who knew a great deal about the subject, like Lady Simon. She was suggested by the Anti-Slavery Society, the British Commonwealth League, and the Council for the Representation of Women in the League of Nations.[11] Simon, however, decided it would not be appropriate to name his own wife, and chose Sir George Maxwell, a barrister who had served in the colonial service in Malaya. He had risen to be chief secretary to the Federated Malay States, but had been passed over for governor, and had retired in 1926. He was described as "self confident and obstinate on Malayan questions," but "friendly and amenable" on others.[12]

A month went by before Simon explained to Lugard that he had not been chosen because it was felt that he was too heavily burdened with the Mandates Commission and
other work.[13] He was deeply wounded. The suppression of slavery, he told his friends,
was always his first priority. He had not been consulted about the candidate, and realized that Maxwell was not someone he could "work with." He lost no time telling all and
sundry that the latter knew nothing of Africa, little about slavery, and would have no influence.[14] To keep the reins in his own hands, he maneuvered Simon into sending him
the official reports sent to the ACE,[15] and he arranged to "work privately" with Gohr,
"just as though I were a member [of the committee] only that my name will not appear."
Gohr, reappointed by the Belgians, duly kept him informed and Lugard sent him copious instructions, exhorting him to stick to the lines of the earlier commissions, and offered to help write his report—an offer Gohr accepted with gratitude.[16] This interference, coupled with Gohr's failing health, were to hamper the committee's work.

Angoulvant had died suddenly and the French replaced him with a less distinguished but less abrasive delegate, Th. Marchand, who had been governor of
Cameroon. Like his predecessor, he was accompanied by Maurice Besson of the Ministry of the Colonies to ensure that French interests were defended. The Dutchman,
Neijtzell de Wilde, and the Italian, Zedda, were reappointed. Women's organizations
had been disappointed by the little part taken at the CES by de Castro e Almeida, and
the Portuguese replaced her with José d'Almada, Colonial Advisor to the Ministry of
Foreign Affairs, who had accompanied her to the CES meetings. He was on the ILO
Committee of Experts on Native Labor, and had good grasp of Anglo-Portuguese relations.[17] This time the token woman, Isabel Oyarzabel de Palencia, a delegate to the ILO
and the League Assembly, was nominated by Spain, on a hint from the League Secretariat. Thus, there was considerable continuity with the CES. Gohr, Zedda, and de
Wilde had served on it. D'Almada and Besson had attended it. De Palencia was new but
was familiar with the League. Maxwell, on the other hand, had never been to Geneva,
and knew nothing of League procedure, but he soon made his presence very much felt.

THE RULES OF PROCEDURE
The new committee met in Geneva for a mere two days in January 1934 to discuss the
rules of procedure, which had been drawn up by the Secretariat in strict accordance
with the limits set by the Assembly. Gohr was elected chairman and Neijtzell de Wilde
vice-chairman.[18] As a harbinger of what was to come, members already had before
them a memorandum from Maxwell, who suffered from the misapprehension that the
members of the League of Nations really wanted the committee to achieve results.

What, he asked, would public opinion make of a body that might not even need to
meet every two years? He wanted annual meetings and the right to call extraordinary
ones when and where they were required, so that decisions could be reached quickly

and recommendations sent to the Council. Most important, he wanted to be able to collect information from all sources.[19] Whether he was as naive as would appear from his proposals remains a mystery. The French believed he was inspired by Harris, but Maxwell was very much his own man.[20]

Predictably, the Portuguese delegate objected to any deviation from the existing rules.[21] Marchand voiced the French and Italian fear that if the ACE met more than once every two years or even deliberated by correspondence between meetings, it might acquire powers of supervision. Moreover, biannual meetings would give administrations time to carry out the reforms it suggested and would prevent it from hampering them with too many proposals.[22] Even the suggestion that members might correspond on urgent matters between sessions and report on them to the Council was not accepted.[23] In the end, Maxwell backed down. Gohr reported to Lugard that he was "amiable" and judging from the minutes, discussions were amicable. However, Maxwell had changed his tactics not his aims.

He persuaded his colleagues to slip into their report carefully worded changes in the rules to give them more latitude.[24] Article 2 reiterated that they would only meet every two years "if necessary," but added "*without prejudice to such extraordinary sessions as the Council might decide to convene*" at the committee's suggestion. This opened the way to more frequent meetings. Article 16 allowed them to ask the Council to invite governments to throw "*further light*" on the information they had supplied, and to decide how long a government might be given to reply to such a request, thus precluding obstruction by delay.[25] At Maxwell's insistence, the changes also included the provision that the committee could consult "native labor experts" at the ILO, and most important, could consider evidence arising from "*the special knowledge of its members.*" This enabled him to bring the fruits of his own research to the ACE, thus establishing a chink in the armor set up by the Assembly to protect governments from information from unofficial sources.[26] To defuse opposition, the remaining rules stressed that the committee was advisory, that meetings were to be private, and all documents were to be confidential.[27]

Simon introduced the report to the Council of the League in January 1934, with an appeal to members to send in information for the next meeting, and a warning that, if governments did not do so, the rules of procedure might have to be widened to give the ACE more authority. The report was accepted.

MAXWELL'S STRATEGY: DEFUSING OPPOSITION BY REDEFINING SLAVERY

Long before the second session of the ACE met in April 1935, Maxwell began collecting information, writing to British government departments and colonial officials, and welcoming evidence from nongovernmental organizations. He produced long memoranda not only on perennial problems but also on hitherto ignored or barely explored questions. His efforts were part of a coherent plan to make the ACE more effective by defusing the opposition. Many of the practices considered by the Temporary Slavery Commission of 1924–25 were not slavery according to the definition in the 1926 Convention.[28] No ownership rights were normally exercised in cases of forced labor, for instance, or in some of the practices "restrictive of the liberty of the person." Even if there were such rights, he proposed a reclassification distinguishing between "absolute slavery" and "modified slavery." By the former, he meant the chattel slavery, formerly practiced in the New World, and Africa, and still practiced in his day in Ethiopia and parts of Arabia. He classed all first-generation slaves—those who had themselves been enslaved—in this category and called them "captive slaves." Like Angoulvant, he argued that they should be the first concern of the ACE. Persons born into chattel slavery where the institution was still legal were also "absolute" slaves, but since they had never known freedom, and were, in his view, as different from the captive slave as "a forest-bred animal" from an animal born in a zoo, their case was less urgent.

A third category was persons in "modified slavery." These were the praedial slaves, serfs, or domestic slaves in European possessions who could theoretically leave their owners—the people Angoulvant had so vehemently refused to recognize as slaves. Maxwell believed that much of the difficulty in securing international cooperation against slavery had arisen because governments were afraid that if they freed "captive slaves" they would also have to free the much greater number of persons in modified slavery. Colonial administrations feared that this would precipitate social and economic disruption. They, therefore, insisted that the institution, now deprived of legal recognition, was dying out peacefully.

Mui tsai and children in other forms of bondage were also in "modified" slavery, because their servitude ended when they grew up. In the same category were practices connected with "tribe," "caste," or "custom," such as the domination of the Sarwa by the Ngwato in Bechuanaland. Debt bondage and peonage were also modified slavery because they ended with the payment of the debt. Nevertheless, Maxwell wanted these practices discussed at the ACE in order to establish that they were not slavery. He hoped that once this was understood, states, such as those in Latin America where peonage existed, would support the antislavery campaign and sign the 1926 Convention.

As for the problem of bride wealth, the CES report had said that in some cases, such as *lobolo* in South Africa, this might cover a trade in females. This had upset women's organizations bent on combating prostitution and pitted them against colonial administrators, who were afraid of interfering in marriage customs and denied that these in any way approximated to slavery. Maxwell proposed that "tribal and marriage customs" be left to governments to tackle as they thought fit, and that anything that savored of prostitution should be passed from the ACE to the League committee which dealt with trafficking in women.

As for forced and compulsory labor, he thought the whole question and all labor contracts should be dealt with by the ILO after consultations with the ACE to decide where to draw the line between slavery and compulsory labor. This would allay the fears of the colonial powers, particularly Portugal, which had been the most active in blocking the cause at the League. In 1932, the Portuguese had sent the CES a letter going over the entire history of their colonial labor legislation, ending with a new Labor Code issued in 1928 and the Colonial Act promulgated in 1930.[29] Their new laws followed the lines laid down in the Convention of 1926. On paper, their legislation seemed admirable, but d'Almada told Maxwell confidentially that the Portuguese believed that their slavery record was now good, but were afraid the ACE might launch inquiries into the actual labor conditions in their African colonies.[30] Maxwell, therefore, had reason to hope that by narrowing the definition of slavery, he could gain their support on the committee.

His plan to shrink the definition of slavery was in direct contrast to the efforts of the Temporary Slavery Commission, encouraged by the Anti-Slavery Society, to include the most exploitative practices of the colonial powers and to protect women and children from disguised forms of slavery. He was not insensitive to these questions but believed in making haste slowly, attacking the worst abuses first, one at a time, and gradually educating the public to accept change. He wanted the ACE to give priority to ending chattel slavery and ameliorating the lot of persons in modified slavery. He then wanted it to decide which other practices were not slavery and could be passed to more prestigious League bodies, which could deal with them more effectively. He was thus raising a question which, as will be seen, was still a matter of debate at the outset of the twenty-first century—what institutions fall properly into the purview of a body dedicated to the eradication of slavery?

For the next few years, Maxwell dominated the ACE. His ideas were gradually refined, but he worked indefatigably to defuse opposition and looked forward confidently to the day when the committee could be disbanded, its work completed.

MAXWELL'S ATTEMPTS TO EXTRACT HONEST BRITISH REPORTS

In pursuit of these aims, Maxwell maintained that to gain the cooperation of his colleagues, disarm suspicion of British motives, and kill any thought that Britain had something to hide, the ACE must be sent full, up-to-date, and irrefutable information on all practices in the empire that might be considered slavery. His relentless quest to extract such information pitted him against officials who had no desire to call attention to many of the practices he wanted to bring before the committee.

Throughout 1934 and the early months of 1935, he kept government departments busy producing material. He burrowed through all the published information he could find, and then sent them the draft memoranda that he proposed to submit to the ACE based on his research—including criticisms. This usually jolted officials into a response.

When they complained, he rewrote his drafts, praising their policies, if he thought they merited it. In this way, he extracted fuller and more up-to-date information from the Colonial, India, and Dominions Offices than they had wanted to furnish. His tactics must be seen against the background of his long and only recently ended career as a colonial official. He understood the mind of imperial civil servants. He did not trust governors to produce accurate reports. He deplored what he called the "non-recognition attitude" of British officials—their unwillingness to face up to unpleasant facts—in this case the existence of any form of slavery in the British Empire.[31]

Maxwell was highly critical of the first reports officials prepared for the ACE.[32] He demanded solid facts, rejecting loose or misleading statements. When the Colonial Office proposed to say that antislavery legislation had been passed in all its territories, he searched the records to see if this was true, demanded copies of laws not references to them, as well as information on their impact. When they stated that the number of mui tsai in certain Malay States was "negligible," he demanded actual figures.[33] When they said that no report on mui tsai was needed because it was not slavery, he insisted that, as the girls were owned and sold, they were in modified slavery.[34] He complained that ordinances on the Hong Kong model only came into force in the Straits Settlements and Federated Malay States in 1933, and had still not been promulgated elsewhere in Malaya or the British possessions in Borneo. He pointed out the need for more inspectors in Malaya. He discussed the defects in the Hong Kong legislation, and won a major point—the appointment of a local committee composed of Chinese and Europeans—who were neither "enthusiasts nor experts," to inquire into the impact of the laws at the grassroots level. Known as the Loseby Committee, this body was appointed late in 1934 and reported in September 1935.[35] He suggested that a better tactic for the Colonial Office would be to stop denying that mui tsai was slavery and instead to send a full report to the ACE stating that former abuses had virtually ended owing to the enforcement of adequate laws, and that the practice would disappear when the last registered girls reached eighteen.[36]

He raised the question of the sale of Chinese boys, pointing out that when he was serving in Penang, his son's nurse had suggested that he buy him a playmate—a sturdy, healthy boy could readily be bought for fifty or sixty dollars.[37] The Hong Kong and Malaysian governments replied that boys were bought for adoption as heirs by families in need of male descendants and were not abused. However, the secretary for Chinese Affairs in Singapore admitted that theatrical groups bought Teochiu boys as actors. This was forbidden in the Federated Malay States in 1931 and in the Straits Settlements in 1934. Thereafter, boys whose voices had not broken were not allowed to perform.

Maxwell raised politically sensitive questions such as child labor in Ceylon (Sri Lanka). A bill in the Legislative Council in 1930 to protect children from poor families being bought as servants and sent to work far from home had been resented because it was introduced in response to criticism in Britain. It had been dropped, but a new Legislative Council had initiated a new bill,[38] and the Colonial Office feared that if Maxwell raised the question, offense would again be taken and it would not pass. When he insisted that "as a matter of conscience" he must explain to the ACE what had happened in 1930,[39] they complained to the Foreign Office. Maxwell was astonished, but rewrote the memorandum quoting the new report,[40] explaining that Singhalese parents did not sell or give up parental rights to their children, and that under the new bill, any who could not be protected by their parents were to be registered, inspected, and paid.

He was soon regarded with dread, particularly in the Colonial Office, which had responsibility for a far-flung empire, and owing to the world depression was short of funds and manpower. Officials complained to the Foreign Office that colonial administrators had to spend so much time producing reports and answering questionnaires for the League and the ILO that they could not get on with "their real job of governing."[41]

Maxwell also raised questions that the government of India had no wish to see discussed. He almost persuaded the India Office that the reservations exempting the princely states from the slavery and forced labor clauses of the 1926 convention should be withdrawn,[42] suggesting artfully that the Indian rulers might prefer to take action of their own accord rather than have the matter raised at the League. Revision of the treaties with the Indian states was being considered,[43] and at first, the India Office agreed with him. It was an anomaly that the Indian Princely States, covering some two-fifths of the subcontinent, with some eighty million inhabitants—over a fifth of the population—were not bound by the same treaties as British India. However, there were around five hundred and sixty rulers, fifty-two of them in Burma, and the India Office began to worry about how they could ensure that these clauses of the convention were enforced.[44] But the main reason they did not want the princes to be asked to accept the whole convention was because it might encourage their efforts, already under way in the case of Mysore and Travancore, to deal directly with the League and negotiate their own treaties, thus bypassing British control of their foreign relations and establishing their independence.[45] The Government of India claimed that the states had adequate laws. Many had criminal legislation based on the Indian penal code, which forbade slavery, the slave trade, and forced labor. The India Office, in spite of considerable misgivings, decided not to withdraw their reservations.[46] Not to be defeated, Maxwell sent the ACE a memorandum calling attention to the fact that the British had stated in 1926 that slavery no longer existed in the Indian states and asking why, in that case, they could not adhere to the convention, and how was it that Rewa and Kalat had recently outlawed it.[47]

He also produced memoranda on a question of particular importance for the future, debt-bondage in the Indian subcontinent. As the first British Resident in the Malay state of Kedah, he had ended debt-bondage by registering all debt-slaves, freeing those who were ill-treated, prohibiting the acquisition of new ones, and providing for the gradual liquidation of existing debts. This method gave creditors time to adjust. The debtors had been freed quickly and the treasury had taken over the last portions of remaining debts. This system had been introduced in the other Malay states and in Siam (Thailand).[48]

Maxwell sent the ACE four memoranda on the subject. One dealt with the *kamiauti* system by which in theory a laborer *(kamia)* received an advance of pay from a landlord in return for giving him first call on his labor. Wages were so low that the debt could never be repaid, and, although it was theoretically not hereditary, new debts were usually contracted by the debtor's sons on marriage, and the bondage continued. In 1920, legislation had been passed requiring the payment of an adequate wage, limiting the period of engagement to one year, forbidding inheritance of debts, and allowing *kamias* to leave at will. However, in some areas little had changed. The government admitted the situation was unsatisfactory but felt that further legislation would be counterproductive.[49] In other communications to the ACE, Maxwell pointed out similar systems elsewhere. They had been noted by the Royal Commission on Labor in India of 1929 and denounced as slavery by Mahatma Gandhi.[50] In the Princely State of Hyderabad there were *baghelas*—persons bound by debts to masters who had the power to keep them by force and "punish, starve or confine" them. In many cases, their position was hereditary.[51] "Possibly," Maxwell warned the Foreign Office, "there is more human misery in British India and the Indian States as the result of the 'debt-slavery' system than there is in Ethiopia, Arabia, and Liberia combined as the result of 'domestic slavery.'"[52]

Maxwell's intentions seem to have been above reproach, and he was surprised and offended at the anger he aroused among government officials. His problems with government departments illustrate how difficult it was to extract information on sensitive subjects even for someone in his semiofficial position. His relations with the Foreign Office, however, were more amicable. He asked for guidance, made valuable suggestions, and kept officials privy to all his plans. He had interviews with Simon, who was equally anxious to furnish the ACE with accurate information. "I should deplore," Simon wrote, "that we should make to Geneva too flattering a report and then find it is the subject of a well-informed challenge."[53] Foreign Office officials took their cue from him. "We like to do all we can to obtain information for Sir George Maxwell in particular and for the Slavery Committee in general" they minuted.[54] They sent for reports on peonage in Latin America, and discussed the situation in Arabia and Ethiopia with him. They realized they could use him to bring to the League questions they wanted discussed. For the first time, Britain's reports to the League were drawn up in close collaboration with its delegate to the slavery committee and were altered to meet his criticisms.[55]

Where Lugard had bumbled his way through the CES, insufficiently briefed by his government, displaying surprising ignorance in some fields, and inviting attack, Maxwell dominated the ACE, and tried hard to turn it into an effective body.

THE COMMITTEE GETS TO WORK

He arrived in Geneva for the second session with high hopes. As well as the memoranda already mentioned, he had prepared others on debt-bondage in the Malay States, mui tsai in China, and slavery in Mongolia, Tanganyika, and Sudan.[56] He

warned the Secretariat that he had enough material for at least three weeks[57] and suggested a preliminary meeting with Gohr and Castatini of the League Secretariat to
plan strategy. Gohr refused on the grounds that it might offend the other members of
the committee.[58] He had a more serious reason. He had already drafted the ACE report, following the format used in 1932, and Lugard had corrected and returned it. He
could not admit this because at the first session, when he had suggested that the rapporteur come armed with a draft report and use the meetings to revise it in the light
of his colleagues' comments, the committee had objected that this would give the rapporteur too much influence. He now planned to revise his draft during the session,
incorporating his colleagues' suggestions so that they would think he had written it
between meetings.[59] He apparently merely wanted to save time, but, by trying to keep
to his format, he caused confusion.[60] In view of his subterfuge, it was probably fitting
that the ACE began deliberations on April Fools' Day 1935.[61]

The government reports provided its core information, although many countries
had sent in little or nothing.[62] The British report, thanks to Maxwell, was over seventy
pages. It explained that slavery was no longer legal in areas "administered under the
authority" of the government in the United Kingdom—thus neatly ruling out the Arabian satellites and the Aden Protectorate. New legislation had recently been passed as
a precaution to ensure that the laws were correct, and former slaves had been informed
of their right to leave. Those who did not do so—the so-called "voluntary slaves"—
were no longer considered slaves. There was no slave raiding. Details followed on measures to control the slave trade to Arabia, and on the numbers of slaves manumitted
by the Jiddah legation. The legislation against the mui tsai system in all British Southeast Asian territories was outlined. A wealth of detail was supplied for Hong Kong, including lists of convicted offenders, lists of girls registered, or freed, and the methods
of the inspectors. As for the status of women in British African possessions, there were
reports from all the governors denying that they were in any way slaves, insisting that
paying bride wealth was not slave dealing, but was a method of cementing family relationships and protecting the bride.[63]

The information on Bechuanaland included the Tagart report and a description of
plans to settle Sarwa on the land and teach them farming. Sudan sent its own report, to
show that it was not under Egyptian control. This stated that the slave trade had ended,
that over two hundred slaves, mostly Ethiopian fugitives, had been freed, and there were
no longer border raids over the frontier. "Ex-serfs" were now integrating into the general population and it was expected that intermarriage and the working of Muslim law
would lead to their disappearance as a servile class. The India Office reported that antislavery operations in the Hukawng Valley and the North and South Triangle were no
longer necessary because the government of Burma was now administering the area.
The Naga Hills, however, were still not administered and the reservation made for this
area at the time of the signing of the 1926 convention remained in force.

By comparison with the British report, those from other powers were meager. The Italians sent in an eight-page summary of a recent inquiry. In Tripolitania, they reported that all former slaves were free to leave, although some remained with their masters and were a socially depressed group. In Cyrenaica, they recorded that their conquest of the oases of the interior and the breakup of the Sanusiya had led to the end of slave raiding and trading and the freeing of all the slaves—over nine hundred in Kufra alone. Those who had remained voluntarily with their owners were well treated. In Eritrea, "serfs" were now paid and the only slaves were recent fugitives from Ethiopia, who had been freed and resettled. Slavery and the slave trade had been totally abolished in Somalia, causing a temporary decline in agricultural production. However, some former "serfs" remained with their owners, and the communities of runaway slaves which had preexisted Italian administration were now settled in "colonizing villages" as farmers. As for the Red Sea slave trade, Italian vigilance and control was such that no slaves could possibly be shipped from Eritrea.

The French, who had sent in a long report in 1932, provided only three pages saying that slavery no longer existed in their territories, although some former slaves remained with their owners. Even in Mauritania, they claimed that there were only "a few household serfs" who could "easily claim their emancipation" but preferred to remain having nowhere else to go.[64] The depression had led to a recrudescence of pawning in West Africa but they were taking adequate steps against it. There had been no cases of slavery in French Somaliland since 1931, and the export trade had almost disappeared owing to their increased surveillance, and would end completely when projected new police forces arrived in the colony. They had passed new laws against slavery in Indo-China, and against slavery and debt-bondage in Cambodia.

The Dutch provided a page and a half claiming they had eradicated slavery and debt-bondage in their territories except in remote areas of Borneo and New Guinea, where there were isolated instances about which they knew little, but which they hoped to end. The Spanish sent in a brief note stating that in the northern part of their North African territories they had eliminated slave raiding and trading. They did not say anything about slavery. As for the Rio de Oro, where they only occupied a few coastal points in the Sahara, they had asked the authorities for information but had not yet received it. The Portuguese said they had nothing to add to their reports for 1932. The Belgians said the same. They did not think that any natives of the Belgian Congo were now living in slavery but the Royal Colonial Institute had launched an enquiry into this in 1933, which they promised to send to the League in due course.[65]

The Ethiopian report merely listed the number of slavery courts established, the numbers of slaves freed, and the number of offenders convicted. The Chinese maintained that slavery no longer existed. Mui tsai was "recognized as an anomaly in the social structure," hence, the Republican government had prohibited it. The girls were now either paid employees, or had been returned to their families, or sent to charitable or relief institutions. There was no report from Liberia.

As well as these official reports, the ACE had before it Maxwell's voluminous memoranda, a memorandum by de Wilde, monographs, news clippings, and lists of antislavery laws collected by the Secretariat. There was also a communication from the Anti-Slavery Society transmitted by the British government, with the usual disclaimer. Harris had consulted both Maxwell and Lugard and had cleared it with the Foreign Office, hence it was much watered down. The Foreign Office, for instance, would not allow reference to consular reports on Ethiopia. Maxwell wanted Indian questions left to him, and he and Lugard objected to the material on Arabia. The Foreign Office rated it a poor production,[66] a harsh judgment when so much was eliminated for political reasons. It was of interest for the future, however, because it raised the question of peonage and quoted an article from the Italian antislavery society claiming that there were thousands of peons in Latin America who were slaves in all but name.[67]

The session began amicably. Gohr was elected chairman and rapporteur and Marchand was vice-chairman. There were two disagreements on questions of principle. The first was the extent to which the committee could consider information from unofficial sources, including some of Maxwell's memoranda, and whether these could be appended to the report. It was agreed that documents that had not been commented on by governments could be referred to in the ACE report, but could not be annexed to it.[68] The more serious and unresolved disagreement was whether the committee could propose action, as Maxwell wanted, or whether, as Zedda and Marchand insisted, it could only record facts without making any proposals which might be taken as violating national sovereignty. For example, the maritime powers on the Red Sea coast had not followed up the recommendation in the Slavery Convention that they should negotiate a treaty to cooperate against the slave traffic. The question now was whether the ACE should simply note this as a fact or whether it could ask the powers to conclude an agreement. The principle was not resolved, but was solved for the present by cautious wording of the report which simply said that:

> It might perhaps not be too much to hope that, in order to more effectively prevent the slave trade across the Red Sea, the three European powers . . . should consider the possibility of concluding a special agreement . . . such as that envisioned in . . . the Slavery Convention.[69]

As in the past, delegates praised national efforts where possible. Marchand claimed that slave raiding in the Sahara was now being brought under control, and dealers could no longer buy slaves in Algeria, Morocco, or Tripolitania. The camel corps was intercepting raiders. France and Britain were cooperating against the trafficking in children along the Cameroon border. As for the slave trade in the Red Sea, the French had a camel corps in Somaliland and a squadron of planes to control shipping. Maxwell discussed the British naval patrol and the difficulty of suppressing the small maritime traffic. Zedda stated that Italy kept two large naval units in the Red Sea. He explained that pilgrims traveling in dhows from Eritrea had to have return tickets, and could only embark on approved native vessels, and had to land at Jiddah or Yanbu al Bahr, where they could be protected. Moreover, like the French in Algeria, Italy also sent a high official to accompany pilgrims.[70] In view of these claims and the fact that there had been no captures of slavers for many years, the ACE barely dared to mention that the Red Sea slave trade still existed. Its report simply stated that: "[i]t is not impossible, in spite of the measures taken, that human beings in limited numbers are still introduced into Arabia as slaves."[71]

The Ethiopian question threatened to cause the usual difficulties. Maxwell read a draft statement condemning the government for not ratifying the Slavery Convention, not suppressing the traffic, and not supplying adequate reports. He called for a "special international commission" to investigate the situation and advise the government on how to proceed, but the Italian delegate objected that it would infringe national sovereignty. When he suggested asking for information on the *gabbar* system, Zedda and Marchand threatened to make reservations. Italy, it seemed, had now joined France in defense of Ethiopia. Maxwell, anxious to "keep in with them both," agreed to drop the subject.[72] All recognized that the situation in Ethiopia was deplorable but Gohr, primed by Lugard, claimed that Maxwell's criticisms were too harsh, and the French weakly called on the committee to have confidence in the emperor's good intentions, although Ethiopian raiders had recently carried off women and children from French Somaliland and killed a French administrator.[73] The committee decided, against Maxwell's wishes, that it was for the League and not for them to point out that Ethiopia had not fulfilled the conditions upon which it had been admitted.[74]

In spite of all his efforts to obtain full information from the British government, Maxwell was asked to provide more on, for instance, the antislavery laws in the Unfederated Malay States, and the Indian Princely States. Gohr, who had bombarded him with questions in the months before the meeting, was particularly interested in Britain's Arabian satellites and the Aden Protectorate. Only at the very last meeting was Maxwell able to tell his colleagues that he had given the League copies of the treaties with Bahrain, "Trucial Oman," Qatar, Muscat, and with Shihr and Makulla, and Aulaqi in the Aden Protectorate. He also assured them that slavery was decreasing in Lahej in the Aden Protectorate.[75]

Maxwell adjusted his tactics as the meeting progressed. He decided not to annex his memoranda on debt-bondage in India to the committee's report, but to refer to it in such a way as to "get the attention" of the government of India without actually condemning it for lack of action. Thus, the report merely stated that the committee had taken note of the criticisms of some of these systems of debt servitude, but had too little information to decide whether they were forms of debt-bondage or of serfdom. Similarly, he got the ACE to state that since no Latin American state had supplied information on peonage, it could not express an opinion as to whether it was slavery.[76] He wanted the ACE to consult the ILO on the dividing line between peonage, debt-bondage, and slavery, but his colleagues refused to agree.[77] However, the remarks in the report opened the way for discussion at subsequent sessions.

The minutes do little to convey the atmosphere of the meeting, or the fact that many of the official reports were sheer camouflage. For instance, the rosy picture of the decline of mui tsai painted by the Chinese was completely at odds with the facts, although not with the laws.[78] The French denial that there was slavery in Mauritania was untrue. Slaves were still traded there and in other parts of the Sahara and would be for many years to come. The committee's work was hamstrung because many documents arrived too late to be read. Its effectiveness was diluted because most members were afraid of offending governments. Gohr, in particular, was "a very nervous and timorous old gentleman" who found everything "very difficult" and "very delicate."[79] Moreover, since he had already written his draft report based on that of 1932, he insisted that discussions follow the same order, precluding any new approach. He took Maxwell's suggestions for a new classification of slaves as personal criticism, and it could not be put to the vote without implying lack of confidence in him. He was also in a hurry to leave and tried to crowd the work into six days, which did not even give time to cover all the documentation, as he found to his distress. He had a heart ailment, and because he was ill, and they liked him, his alarmed colleagues gave in to him, but refused to let him revise his report alone, insisting they should do it together.[80] He was much upset by this and left before the work was finished. Marchand took the chair, and the committee struggled to fit their proposals into his draft in the short time left to them. They feared he would change the report if they were too bold.[81]

The report listed the states that had not acceded to the 1926 convention.[82] The most important of these was Saudi Arabia. The ACE asked all powers to ratify the convention and furnish it with full information—a plea that was to be made in all subsequent reports of the League committees and its United Nations successors. At Maxwell's instigation, it asked the government of India to withdraw its 1926 reservation for Burma, and to sound out the Indian princely states about the action they had taken or intended to take, over slavery. It suggested that Nepal, and, unrealistically, Yemen, might be asked to adhere. It regretted that slavery was still legal in Arabia and Ethiopia. It recommended that owning anyone who had been enslaved (Maxwell's captive or real slave) should be an offense. It noted that efforts were being made to improve the status of former slaves and serfs in, for instance, Bechuanaland, Burma, Sudan, and the Okavango River area in South West Africa (Namibia). Italy was praised for freeing the slaves of the Sanusi, and ending slave raiding and trading in Cyrenaica; and the French for taking action against slave raiders in the Sahara. In hopes of rallying Muslim opinion, a special point was made that Islamic law provided for the manumission of slaves, and forbade the enslavement of Muslims.

On Ethiopia, the report could only say weakly that the ACE had no information on slave raiding, but there was a "strong presumption" that unpaid soldiers in the west and southwest might be seizing and selling local peoples. The emperor's efforts to open up the country and the arrests of dealers were praised, but he was urged to supply more information. The British were taken to task for not providing more details on the slave trade and slavery in their Arabian protectorate and satellites, or updating their report on naval patrols in the Red Sea. The efforts of France and Italy to prevent the trade from their coasts, and of all the powers concerned to protect pilgrims, were noted.

Not surprisingly, the ACE asked the Chinese for more information on mui tsai, and pointed out the contradictions in their report. Their 1932 edicts were praised but the committee wanted to know the results and what was being done to help parents who could not support their children. The measures taken by Hong Kong, the Straits Settlements, and the Federated Malay States were considered effective but the British were asked to supply more information on their results in the Unfederated Malay States. Liberia was to be asked for information on the result of its proclamations of 1930 against slavery and pawning.

Payment of bride wealth was ruled out of the discussions, as it was not slave dealing. On pledging, or pawning, and peonage the ACE reported that it had too little information to comment, but suggested measures to protect debtors. The report recommended that other powers should launch an investigation similar to the Belgian one into the status of those slaves who remained with their owners although they were legally free, and who were variously called voluntary slaves, semi-slaves, domestic slaves, or praedial serfs. The Belgians had drawn up a far-reaching questionnaire and had invited officials, magistrates, and missionaries in the Congo to compete for a prize for the best response.

The only document appended to the report that did not emanate from a government was a memorandum by Maxwell on mui tsai in the International Settlements in Shanghai and Kulangsu, where the system was widespread but was not legally recognized. Theoretically, it was possible for girls to obtain their freedom by applying to the authorities. In practice, this was virtually impossible. In Shanghai, there were some one hundred prosecutions a year for dealing in girls and for "gross cruelty." Heavy penalties had been inflicted but trafficking had not declined and neither settlement had issued regulations to control the institution. Maxwell suggested that they emulate the measures taken in Hong Kong for its gradual elimination.

Child labor in Ceylon was not mentioned in the report. The Colonial Office had sent Maxwell the report of the subcommittee investigating the question and, as he told his colleagues, it had decided that the system, which it called "quasi-adoption," was not slavery. Maxwell considered its recommendations satisfactory and wanted to mention them in the ACE report. But Gohr cut his draft down to such an extent that, to his colleagues' applause, he decided to drop the subject and bring it up again at the next ses-

sion of the committee, by which time there might be information on the measures actually taken in Ceylon.[83]

MAXWELL'S FAILURE TO CHANGE THE RULES OF PROCEDURE

Difficult and disappointing as the session had been, Maxwell was encouraged by the
friendly atmosphere that had prevailed. The Italian, French, and Spanish members
had supported his efforts, and even Gohr had been "perfectly charming." He believed
he had dispelled Portuguese fears of the ACE's intentions. He had established his leadership as the "forward" member of the group, and some of his ideas had been mentioned in the report and could be raised in future sessions.[84] On his return to England,
he immediately called for a special session to be held in 1936 for six days to discuss the
outlines of the report and then adjourn for a month or so before meeting to finalize
it. The Secretariat advised him to get the British to suggest this at the next meeting of
the Sixth Commission of the League Assembly. Foreign Officials were not pleased with
the report. "Confused" and "colourless,"[85] it gave the impression that slavery was "peculiarly a British problem," whereas in their view the British were the only ones taking
action against it. Moreover, the report did not ask for an extra session in 1936.[86] However, Maxwell assured the Foreign Office that he and his colleagues were "secretly
ashamed" of the report and would welcome the extra session to try "to do better." In a
debate in the House of Lords, engineered by Harris, Noel-Buxton asked the government to propose that the League fund annual meetings. With this prodding the British
raised the matter in the Council and surprisingly carried the day.

Maxwell also proposed asking the League to change the rules to allow the ACE to receive material from private sources. The Secretariat thought this might be accepted if
all that was called for was information on the ownership of "one black man" by another.[87] To rally support, Maxwell, suggested that this material should be confidential
and be limited to slave trading and pawning.[88] This would shield the Portuguese and
Spanish from criticism of their labor policies, the Chinese from evidence on mui tsai,
and the Latin American states from a discussion on peonage. The Foreign Office, however, feared it would increase the focus on Ethiopia and Arabia, where important
changes were taking place and which they did not want to become subjects of a slavery
inquiry.[89] It insisted that any proposal to change the rules must come from the ACE,[90]
but the committee believed it could not ask for such changes unless told to do so by the
League Council. Its report had merely said that it did not have enough experience to request a change in the rules, because Gohr had thought this would be "a delicate way of
hinting" at the need for unofficial information. Maxwell had protested that a committee of experts "bleating about its inexperience" would not achieve its aim.[91]

Simon hoped that in the future Maxwell would be able to "ginger up" the committee to challenge both the prohibition on private information and the proviso that governments must vet all documents that criticized their policies.[92] In the House of Lords,

Noel-Buxton pressed Britain to ask the League to allow the committee to take private information.[93] The British, therefore, proposed to the Sixth Committee that the ACE, at its next meeting, should consider how far it could be effective under the existing restrictions and hinted that the Assembly might have to review its mandate. This raised such strong objections from Belgium, France, and Portugal that the Foreign Office concluded the change was impossible, and Maxwell had to drop the proposal.[94]

He had to rest content with having engineered an extra session for 1936, and hope that this would lead to annual meetings. He now focused on his grand design—whittling down the committee's agenda so that it dealt only with slavery proper. He was more certain than ever that defining slavery so broadly in the 1926 Convention had defeated its object. It had antagonized Portugal, prevented the Latin American states from acceding to the treaty, and embroiled the TSC and ACE in debates on marriage customs. He decided to try to get the ACE to recommend that practices "analogous to slavery" should be passed to other organizations. He had sounded out the ILO and believed it would take up peonage and problems such as the indebtedness of migrant labor.[95] He had discussed mui tsai with the Chairman of the Women and Children Protection Committee who had agreed it was within its province.

His priorities now were to free those slaves who had themselves been reduced to bondage, to improve the lot of those born into slavery in Arabia and elsewhere, and to clear away whatever vestiges of slavery remained in colonial territories, focusing particularly on "voluntary slaves" who remained with their owners. Fortified with the requests for information in the ACE report, he once more bombarded government departments with memoranda and queries in preparation for its 1936 session.

NOTES

1. Observations of Besson on the Report of French Delegates on the CES 1st session, FMAE SDN 943 esclavage générale; Ministry of Colonies to FMAE no. 543, 15 September 1932, enclosing conclusions of an interministerial committee to examine the work of the 1st session of the CES; Note for French delegation to the 13th Assembly, no. 13, 28.9.32, FMAE Folder marked SFSDN.

2. For the report of League proceedings see Slavery: Report of the Sixth Committee: Resolution at the 13th Assembly, 12 October 1932 LON R 2361 6B/40209/36952; for the British report see Hilton Young to Simon no. 303, 12 October 1932, FO 371/16504 W 11310/5/52.

3. On 13 May 13 the Council considered that a rule limiting the term of office to three years, but to be renewable, was consistent with this, Resolution of the Assembly of 12 October 1932, interpreted by the Council's decision of 13 May 1936, LON C.C.E.E. 138, 18 December 1936.

4. Lugard to Simon, 2 September 1932, and minutes, and Lugard memorandum, 17 September 1932, FO 371/16504 W 9885/5/52.

5. Proceedings of the 13th Assembly, 12 October 1932, LON R 2361 6B/4029/36952.

6. *The Centenary of Abolition within British Possessions: Statement Issued by the Committee of the Anti-Slavery and Aborigines Protection Society*, 1933.

7. A thousand "celebration members" were called for at a subscription of 10s. 6d., the normal cost of membership, and ten thousand "associate celebration" memberships were offered at the reduced rate of 2s.6d.

8. Lugard to Harris 15 June 1933, Lugard Papers.

9. Coupland 1933, 250.

10. Drummond to Cadogan, private and confidential, 1 May 1933, LON s.1670 file 7.

11. Ashley Clarke to Leeper, 2 October 1933, FO 371/17423 W 11222/197/52. Alternatively, the League suggested Dame Rachel Crowdy, a well-known social reformer, who had been chief of the League's Social Questions and Opium Traffic Section, Council for the Representation of Women at the League of Nations to Simon, 18 March 1933, and minutes FO 371/17423. The ASAPS also suggested Lugard, Sir Robert Hamilton, M.P., Noel-Buxton, and their own chairman and vice-chairman, Charles Roberts and Charles Roden Buxton, neither of whom had colonial administrative experience and who would have been anathema to other powers, ASAPS to Simon, 27 September 1933, ibid.

12. Harris to Lugard, 17 January 1935, Lugard Papers.

13. Simon to Lugard, 16 November 1933, Lugard Papers.

14. Lugard to Coupland 15 October and 23 November 1933 and to Gohr, 18 November 1934, Lugard Papers.

15. Minute by Simon on Lugard to Simon, 20 November 1933, FO 371/17423 W 14015/197/52.

16. Gohr to Lugard, 11 December 1933, Lugard Papers.

17. Lugard to Gaselee, 4 June 1932, FO 371/16503 W 6527/5/52.

18. The draft showing revisions and the discussions in the Secretariat is in LON 6B/7382/2663/R 4150. The minutes are in C.C.E.E./1st Session/P.V.1 LON 6B/10483/800/R4152. Henceforth only the P.V. numbers will be shown.

19. Maxwell's comments are in his notes of 24 November and 22 December 1933, LON 6B/7382/2663/4150.

20. Confidential Note, 15 December 1933, FMAE SDN 943 Esclavage Générale, 1932–1937, 40/10.

21. Memorandum by Gohr, 12 December 1933, and d'Almada to Castatini, 31 December 1933, LON 6B/7382/2663/ R 4150.

22. Revised minutes of third meeting, 1st session, 9 January 1934, C.C.E.E./1st session/P.V. 3.

23. Gohr to Lugard, 17 January 1934, Lugard Papers.

24. The Report was accepted by the Council on 19 January 1934, see *Official Journal*, 23 January 1934. It was published as C.29 1934.VI. It was amended in 1936 and published as League of Nations Paper C.C.E.E. 138, 18 December 1936, see *Official Journal* June 1936, 557–60 and 731, and November 1936, 1174.

25. The loophole here was that if a government sent no information there would be no grounds for asking for further enlightenment, but Gohr stated that failure to send a communication would be of itself "an important fact," C.C.E.E./1st session/P.V.3, LON 6B/10482/8000/R 4152.

26. Maxwell to Simon, 10 November 1934, FO 371/18593 W 9951/485/52.

27. In 1936, this was amended to allow the attendance of "experts invited by the committee," see the Advisory Committee of Experts on Slavery, Rules of Proceedure, and Resolution of the Assembly of 12 October 1932, interpreted by the Council's decision of 13 May 1936, LON C.C.E.E. 138, 18 December 1936.

28. A Proposal for a Reclassification of the Various Forms of Slavery, enclosed in Maxwell to Stevens on, 23 March 1934, FO 371/18592 W 3109/485/52. A second was enclosed in Maxwell to FO, 28 July 1934, ibid., W 7100/485/52, refining his classifications. Further explanations were included in a letter he sent to Simon on 10 November 1933, FO 371/18593 W 9953/485/52. For his memoranda to the ACE, see LON C.C.E.E, 18, 6 September 1934, and LON C.C.E.E. 41, 25 February 1935, 6 B/13143/8598 R 4155.

29. Letter from the Portuguese Delegation, Geneva, 2 April 1932, LON C.E.E. 1 (b) 6 April 1932, 6B/35277/31717/R 2361.

30. These, however, had done little to change conditions at the grassroots level. Africans were still under a "moral obligation" to work. They had to pay taxes and show they were earning cash income, or risk being declared vagrants and forced to work for the state. The rules against compulsory labor and those allowing them to choose their occupations were evaded, and officials still forced people to work for private enterprises. Compulsory crop cultivation, particularly of cotton, continued. Portugal did not sign the Forced Labor Convention of 1930 until 1956. For labor policies see inter alia Clarence-Smith 1985, 181–86; Vail and White, 249–371.

31. Maxwell to Croft, 6 February 1934, enclosed in Maxwell to Simon, 10 November 1934, FO 371/18593 W 9952/485/52.

32. See, for instance, Maxwell to Stevenson, 23 December 1934, FO 371/18593 W11126/485/52.

33. See, for instance, his notes enclosed in Maxwell to Stevenson, 23 December 1934, FO 371/18593 W 11126/485/52.

34. He had made proposals in 1929 for ending mui tsai, which the Colonial Office had rejected.

35. Maxwell to CO, 20 April 1934, no. 30231/7/34 (no. 15) and Maxwell to CO, 1 December 1934, no. 30231/7/34 (no. 49) FO 371/19731, contain memoranda on Hong Kong, the other

Southeast Asian colonies and the replies from the Colonial Office, Hong Kong, and the Straits Settlements.

36. Maxwell to CO, 24 April 1934, FO 371/18592 W 5480/485/52; Maxwell to FO, 30 June 1934, ibid., W 6380/485/52.

37. Maxwell "Mui Tsai System in Malaya" in Maxwell to CO, 20 April 1934, 30231/7/34 no. 15, FO 371/19731, p. 24.

38. Maxwell to CO 28 February 1935 and enclosed memorandum "Child Labor in Ceylon," enclosed in CO to FO, 22 March 1935, FO 19731 W 2634/426/52.

39. CO to FO, 22 March 1935, no. 55540/35, and CO to Maxwell, 22 March 1935, FO 371/19731 W 2634/426/52.

40. Maxwell to Cowell, 23 March 1935, and enclosed memorandum, Maxwell to CO, 23 March 1935, Cowell to Maxwell, no. 55540/35, 28 March 1935, FO 371/19732. The Report of the Ceylon Committee was published as *Sessional Paper II 1935*.

41. Paskin to Stevenson, 30231/9/34, 18 January 1935, FO 371/19731 W 624/52.

42. The articles reserved were Article 2, committing signatories to the gradual complete abolition of slavery in all its forms, Article 5, which laid down the restrictions on the use of forced labor, and Articles 6 and 7, committing them to pass adequate laws and communicate them to the League. Forced labor was not a concern of the ACE.

43. Maxwell to Croft, 30 January and 6 February, enclosed in Maxwell to Simon, 10 November 1934, FO 371/18593 W 9952/8521/52.

44. Patrick to Glancy, confidential P.Y.157/34, 23 March 1934, enclosed in IO to FO, E. & O.8223/34, 6 February 1935, FO 371/19731 W 1126/177/52. The India Office was already concerned because Indian labor delegates to the ILO were complaining about forced labor in the Princely States, and India had not ratified the Forced Labor Convention of 1930.

45. Glancy to Patrick, confidential, D.O. no. D.2811-P/34, 22 December 1934, enclosed in IO to FO, E. & O. 8223/34, 6 February 1935, 371/19731 W 1126/177/52.

46. Minutes on IO to FO, E. & O. 8223/34, ibid.

47. Maxwell, "The Position of the Indian Native States in Regard to the Slavery Convention of 1926," December 1934, ibid. W 1126/177/52, and as sent to the ACE, 21 January 1935, LON, C.C.E.E. 33, 6B/15815/8598, R 4156.

48. Maxwell to Lunn , 2 September 1929, CO129/514.

49. Maxwell, "The Kamiauti System of Debt Bondage in British India," 16 October 1934, LON, C.C.E.E.23, 6B/14055/8598. The legislation was the Kamiauti Agreement Act of Bihar and Orissa.

50. Maxwell, "References to 'Debt Bondage' in the Report of the Royal Commission on Labor in India," 4 December 1934, LON C.C.E.E. 28, 6B/14055/8598/ R 4155; Maxwell's

"The Rajwars of Bihar and Orissa," 4 December 1934, LON C.C.E.E. 27, 6 B/14989/8598, R 4155.

51. Maxwell, "The Baghela System of Debt-Bondage in the State of Hyderabad," 4 December 1934, LON, C.C.E.E.29, 6B/14055/8548, R 4155.

52. Maxwell to Strang, 14 December 1934, FO 371/18595 W 10839/10839/52. See below, chapter 24, for debt-bondage in the Indian subcontinent at the end of the twentieth century.

53. Minute by Simon, 22 January, and minutes of discussions with Maxwell, 23 January and 1 February 1935, FO 371/19731 W 887/426/52.

54. Minute by Nicholls, 27 September 1934 on Maxwell to FO, 20 September 1934, FO 371/18592 W 8443/8443/52.

55. See, for instance, "Observations on Sir George Maxwell's Notes on the Draft Memorandum for the League of Nations," FO 371/19731, pp. 107–114.

56. For a list, see LON 6B/14944/8000/R 4152.

57. Maxwell to Catastini, 24 November and 14 December 1934, LON 6B/14944/8000/R 4152.

58. De Haller note, 21 March 1935, LON S1670/file 2.

59. Gohr to Lugard, 16 February 1934, and 18, and 28 February, and 13 and 22 March 1935, and Lugard to Gohr, 20 February and 29 March 1935, Lugard Papers.

60. Gohr to Lugard, 17 January and 16 February 1934, Lugard Papers.

61. The minutes of this second session were numbered by the League of Nations as C.C.E.E./2nd session P.V. 1–12. Henceforth, they will be referred to by their P.V. numbers. They are all in LON 6B/18319/8000/R 4152.

62. These were published as annexes to the ACE report for 1935, LON C.159.M.113. 1935. VI.

63. These had been published in "Papers Relating to the Health and Progress of Native Populations in Certain Parts of the Empire," published as Pamphlet Colonial, no. 65.

64. For the persistence of slavery in Mauritania, see below, chapter 24.

65. Financed by the International Institute of African Languages and Culture, the Royal Belgian Colonial Institute in 1933. It was published in 1949 by E. de Jonghe, ed.

66. The memorandum is in the form of a letter to Simon from the ASAPS to Simon, 21 March 1935, FO 371/19731 W 2596/426/52. For the correspondence over it, see Lugard to Harris, 14 November 1934, 25 January 1935, 4 March 1935; Harris to Lugard, 17 January, 1 and 26 February, Lugard Papers. For its reception in Geneva, and the Foreign Office view of it, see Maxwell to Makins, 17 April 1935, and minute, FO 371/19732 W 3352/426/52.

67. Journal of the Italian Anti-Slavery Society, August and September 1932. Peonage was to become an important issue in the 1950s; see below, chapter 19.

68. LON C.C.E.E./2nd session, P.V. 5, 3 April 1935.

69. LON C.C.E.E./2nd session, P.V. 2, 4, 6, 7. For the final wording, see LON C.159.M.113. 1935. VI, p. 14.

70. LON C.C.E.E./ 2nd session, P.V. 10, 9 April 1935, and P.V. 12, 10 April 1935.

71. LON C.159.M.113. 1935. VI, p. 14.

72. LON C.C.E.E. 2nd session, P.V. 9, 11; Maxwell to Makins, 7 January 1936, FO 371/20184.

73. LON C.C.E.E./2nd session, P.V. 6, 4 April 1935; LON C.159.M.113. 1935. VI, p.11.

74. LON C.C.E.E./2nd session, P.V. 9, 8 April 1935. LON C.C.E.E./2nd session, P.V. 9, 8 April 1935; Lugard to Gohr, 29 March 1935, Lugard Papers.

75. LON C.C.E.E./2nd session, P.V. 12, 10 April 1935.

76. LON C.C.E.E./2nd session, P.V. 9, 8 April 1935.

77. They said that only "native labor experts" of the ILO could be consulted, not officials, Maxwell to Lugard, 7 August 1935, Lugard Papers.

78. For a discussion of the laws as opposed to the reality, see Strang to Lugard, 15 August 1934, enclosing Peking to FO no. 883 (4/62/1934) 22 June 1934, Lugard Papers. The ASAPS also included information on this in its memorandum, based on a report of the British consul in Amoy 1929, in Cmd.3424 1929 p. 65 PP and the Third Annual Report of the Chinese Society for the Relief of Chinese Slave Girls, containing examples of ill-treatment and estimating that there were some three million mui tsai. European missionaries guessed there were two million, enclosed final draft of ASAPS memorandum for the ACE, in Harris to Lugard, 26 February 1935.

79. Maxwell to Dunbar, confidential, 23 October 1935, FO 371/19734 W 9249/426/52.

80. Maxwell described Gohr's behavior and its impact on the ACE in confidential notes to the Foreign Office dated 12 and 13 April 1935, encl. in Stevenson to Makins, 17 April 1935, FO 371/19732 W 3494/426/52.

81. Correspondence in LON 6B/16746, Jacket 2/8000/R 4152.

82. For the report, see LON C.159.M.113, 1935. VI, 10 April 1935. Afghanistan, Argentina, Bolivia, Chile, Guatemala, Honduras, Luxemburg, Paraguay, Peru, Salvador, Siam, the USSR, and Venezuela had not signed the convention. Albania, Columbia, the Dominican Republic, Iran, Lithuania, Panama, and Uruguay had also signed but not ratified it. Of the nonmembers of the League, Monaco, Syria, and Lebanon had also signed it. The United States had signed it but made one reservation. The nonmembers who had not signed or acceded were Brazil, Costa Rica, Danzig, Iceland, Japan, Liechtenstein, and San Marino.

83. Maxwell to CO, confidential, 14 April 1935, and enclosed memorandum, FO 371/19732 pp. 261–65; LON C.C.E.E. 2nd session, P.V. 11. The report sent to him was of an inquiry by the Joint

Subcommittee of the Executive Committees of Home Affairs and of Education for the State Council of Ceylon.

84. Maxwell's confidential notes to the Foreign Office dated 12 and 13 April 1935, encl. in Stevenson to Makins, 17 April 1935, FO 371/19732 W 3494/426/52.

85. Minute on Walters to Stevenson, 3 May 1935, FO 371/19732 W 3917/426/52.

86. Minute on Stevenson to Makins, 17 April 1936, FO 371/19732 W 3494/426/52; minute on Walters to Stevenson, 3 May 1935, ibid., W 3917/426/52.

87. Note for secretary-general of mission to London and Paris, 10–20 August 1935, 21 August 1935, LON S.1670, file 7.

88. Maxwell to Castatini, 18 May 1935, LON 6B/16746/Jacket 2/8000/ R 4152; Stevenson to Makins, 17 April 1936, minutes and enclosed note by Maxwell of the main points in the ACE report, 12 and 13 April 1935, FO 371/19732 W 3494/426/52.

89. See below, chapter 15.

90. Makins to Maxwell, 24 May 1935, FO 371/19733, pp. 28–30.

91. Maxwell to Dunbar, 23 October 1935, FO 371/19734 W 9249/426/52.

92. Maxwell to Makins, 30 May 1935, and Simon minute, FO 371/19733 W 4792/426/52.

93. Hansard, 17 July 1935. For the preparation for this debate, see correspondence between Harris and Lugard, Lugard and Noel-Buxton, Lugard and Stanhope, in June, July, and August 1935, Lugard Papers.

94. The correspondence between Maxwell and the Foreign Office on changing the rule continued until late October, see particularly Makins, "Observations on points raised in Sir J. Harris's memorandum for the debate in the House of Lords on Slavery," 11 July; note of 9 July, and note for Stevenson, 31 July, and minutes of 7 and 8 August 1935, FO 371/19733, pp. 84–87, 101–103, 107–109; Maxwell to Stevenson, 15 August 1935, and minute, ibid., W7315/426/52; Cranborne to Hoare, 1 October 1935, FO 371/19734 W 8637/4526/52; Maxwell to Dunbar, confidential, 23 October 1935, and minutes of conversation with Maxwell, 5 November 1935, ibid., W 9249/426/52. See also, Gohr to Lugard, 7 August 1935, Maxwell to Lugard, 7 August and 10 August 1935, Lugard to Maxwell, 9 August 1935, Lugard Papers.

95. Maxwell to Makins, 18 May 1935, FO 371/19733, pp. 35–36.

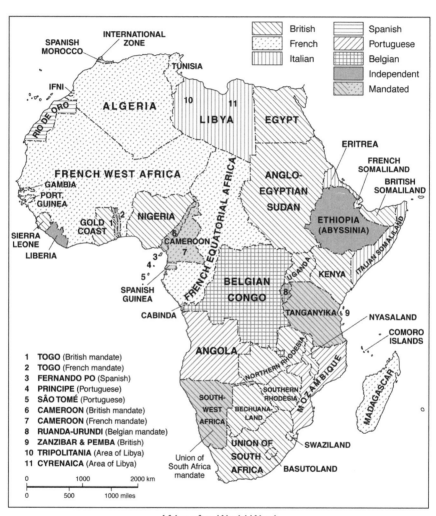

Africa after World War I.

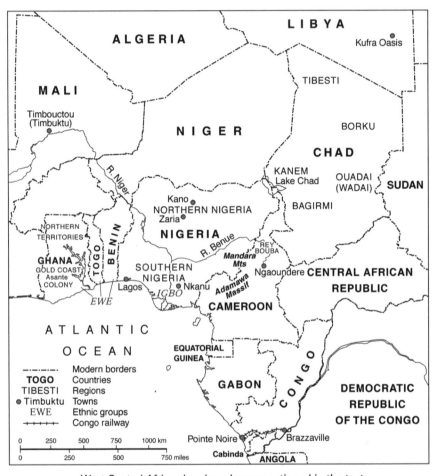

West Central Africa showing places mentioned in the text
in connection with slavery, the slave trade, and forced labor.

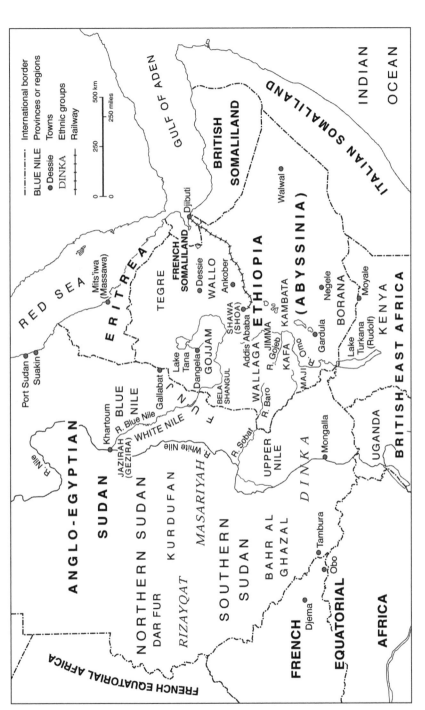

Ethiopia and Sudan after World War I.

Southwest Ethiopia and southern Sudan after World War I.

The Middle East after World War I.

The southern Red Sea coasts after World War I.

The Persian Gulf States in the 1950s.

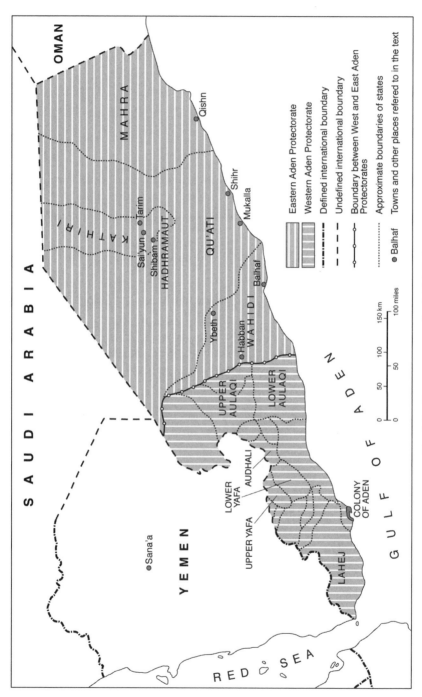

The Aden Protectorate under British Rule.

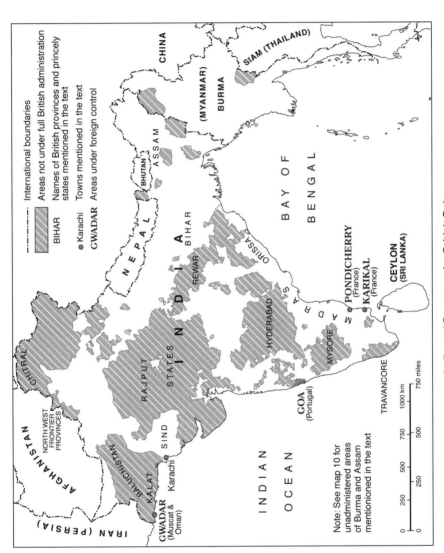

International boundaries

Areas not under full British administration

BIHAR   Names of British provinces and princely states mentioned in the text

● Karachi   Towns mentioned in the text

GWADAR   Areas under foreign control

AFGHANISTAN

IRAN (PERSIA)

GWADAR
(Muscat & Oman)

BALUCHISTAN

KALAT

Karachi

SIND

NORTH WEST
FRONTIER
PROVINCES

CHITRAL

RAJPUT
STATES

INDIA

NEPAL

BHUTAN

ASSAM

CHINA

(MYANMAR)
BURMA

SIAM (THAILAND)

BIHAR

REWAR

ORISSA

MADRAS

HYDERABAD

MYSORE

GOA
(Portugal)

PONDICHERRY
(France)

KARIKAL
(France)

TRAVANCORE

CEYLON
(SRI LANKA)

BAY OF

BENGAL

INDIAN

OCEAN

Note: See map 10 for
unadministered areas
of Burma and Assam
mentionioned in the text

0   250   500   750   1000 km

0   250   500   750 miles

India and Burma under British Rule.

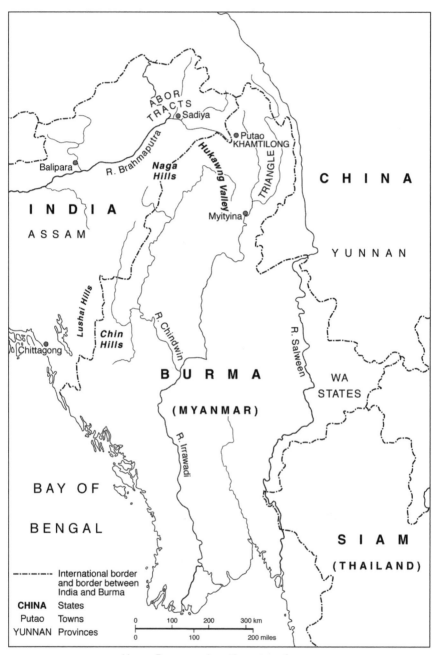

Upper Burma and north eastern Assam.

Sir George Maxwel. (Photographer unknown.)

*Sir John Harris, Secretary
of the Anti-Slavery Society (1910–1940). (Photographer unknown.)*

Freed child slaves (Mui Tsai)—China. c. 1930.

The boy Impongi of Illinga, Belgian Congo, mutilated by sentries of the ABIR
(Anglo-Belgian-Indian Rubber company) as his village failed to reach its
rubber quota. He was a witness before the Commission of Enquiry. 1905.

Congo atrocities: Men of the Nsongo District (ABIR concession) with hands of two of their countrymen Lingomo and Bolenge murdered by rubber sentries in May 1904. The two white men are Mr. Stannard and Mr. Harris of the Congo Balolo Mission at Baringa. (Photographer Alice Harris.)

West African boys taken by plane to Saudi Arabia by pilgrims allegedly to be sold as slaves. 1960. (Photographer Lars Holmberg.)

Slavery in a Changing World 1932–1939: Ethiopia

From 1932 to the outbreak of war in September 1939, crisis after crisis rocked the international community. In the past, the League antislavery committees had been bedevilled by rivalry between the European colonial powers; now the ACE was affected by the tensions created as Germany, Italy, and Japan embarked on imperial ventures. The event that did most to change the slavery picture was the Italian conquest of Ethiopia.

THE DETERIORATING SITUATION 1932–1935

In the early 1930s, Haile Selassie continued to consolidate his power, hiring foreign advisors to reorganize the army and police and setting up model provinces with salaried officials, and promoting economic development.[1] The Slavery Department was duly set up in August 1932 under Likamakuas Mangasha, an aristocrat of "relatively advanced views," who had been minister in Rome. As director general he had direct access to the emperor. Under him, the secretary- general, Lej Alemayu Tene, was a competent, energetic younger man who had spent some years in France, had translated *Uncle Tom's Cabin* into Amharic,[2] and had served as frontier agent at Mega.[3] The department was to supervise the implementation of the slavery laws, register slaves, look after those who were freed, and run the slavery courts assisted by a special police force. Since slave capture and trading were illegal, and slaves already had to be registered, and freed within a year of their owner's death, and no one could now be born into slavery, progress should have been swift.

The laws, however, had only been enforced sporadically. The only large numbers of slaves who had been freed—over two thousand—were those of the emperor's enemies.[4] De Halpert had no idea how many remained in bondage. Where the Anti-Slavery Society maintained there were some two million, he thought there might be three hundred thousand, out of a total population of eight to sixteen million.[5] Fearing that freed slaves had neither the will nor the ability to fend for themselves, he advised starting by registering slaves in only one area, Ankober.[6]

His plans were soon defeated by procrastination and internal feuding. His request for a budget of $MT338,000 was cut to $MT68,000. His proposals for the reorganization of the slavery courts and prisons, the raising of the police force, inspections in the provinces, the registration of slaves, the disposal of those freed, and the collection of statistics were not carried out. He went on leave in the autumn of 1932, leaving a list of measures to be taken. On his return, five months later, most had been shelved and the director general was not speaking to the secretary-general.

In May 1933, de Halpert warned Haile Selassie that the British were dismayed at continued raiding over the frontier, and by their reports from Maji. He urged him to send Aleymau to inspect Maji, Kafa, and other "bad provinces."[7] The orders were duly given but the director general, who rarely came into the office, had Aleymau arrested, ostensibly for bribery and corruption.[8] The British believed that Aleymau was too zealous. Henceforth, the department was paralyzed. De Halpert repeatedly sent the emperor notes urging action and requesting an audience.[9] Finally in October 1933 he asked Haile Selassie to appoint a new secretary-general. The emperor named a replacement, who soon announced that he could not "restore order in the confusion" caused by his predecessor's imprisonment.[10]

De Halpert resigned in despair on 20 December 1933.[11] His regulations had never been issued. The cashier had absconded with the department's cash eight months earlier. Owing to nepotism, there were ten clerks more than were provided for in the budget. The secretary-general languished in prison. The registration of slaves had not begun. No steps had been taken to resettle freed slaves. The school for them was "all but dead" and the pupils did not have enough to eat. Of the sixty-seven slavery courts, the one in Addis Ababa had been closed for five months because the judge was "in chains." Over half the judges of the provincial courts had failed to produce records in spite of repeated requests. Only one of the "good" judges, who were to be sent to the worst areas and paid salaries, had been appointed. The rest lived on bribes, or were paid in kind or in *gabbar* by the provincial governors. Judges were expected to come to Addis Ababa twice a year at their own expense to have their books inspected, and were often kept waiting there for months, while their courts remained idle. Dealers awaiting trial and slaves waiting to be freed were chained up together for long periods in appalling conditions. The controller of the department and his staff, who were meant to inspect the courts, had never left Addis Ababa. The police officers who were to be selected for the worst trouble spots in the west and southwest, and to the eastern frontier to stop smuggling to Arabia, had not been appointed.

De Halpert attributed the lack of progress to resistance to the emperor's reforms, aggravated by Haile Selassie's personal failings. In order to exert personal control over all details of government, he appointed ministers of the old school—nobles with no conception of their duties. Under them, he placed educated progressive young men of humble origin dependent on himself for promotion. When friction developed between the young men and their aristocratic superiors, he failed to support the former. He employed foreign advisors to institute reforms, but gave them no authority. The entire administration of the country was corrupt as the result of the failure to impose discipline. De Halpert believed that Haile Selassie understood the problem, but had not the strength of character to remedy it.[12]

While he was struggling to make the Slavery Department a reality, British consuls were sending in disturbing reports. There were some bright spots. The consul in Dangela reported that a new director of customs, Negadras Heltework, inspired by Haile Selassie himself, was arresting traders, freeing slaves, and refusing bribes. He was a "lowly man," looking for promotion and was supported by the progressive governor of Gojam,[13] Ras Emru, who came to be known as the "red ras" for his liberal views. But Heltework had only three police and an escort of nine rifles. Public opinion was solidly against him. Slave dealers burned down his house. The local authorities, ordered by the emperor to give him fifty riflemen, provided three old men with ancient rifles and no cartridges.

A beginning had been made in tackling the problem of resettling freed slaves. Initially many of those belonging to the disgraced governor, Ras Haylu, were either claimed by other owners, or "spirited away," but the slavery judge appointed by Ras Emru, and other officials, prodded by the British consul, freed quite large numbers, placed some in wage labor, settled others on the land, and took measures to ensure that they were not re-enslaved.[14]

In Gore, however, the consul reported in 1934 that after a temporary lull the traffic was reviving. When reluctant authorities prosecuted dealers, the trials were often a farce since the principal witnesses—the slaves—unable to speak Amharic, could not testify. When the consul, suspecting that some ten children were British subjects, insisted on an interpreter, the little captives were afraid to testify. Many slaves, chained up in disease-ridden prisons, died while waiting to be freed. Those who were "freed" simply passed to another master, often the judge who tried the case. Traders who did not bribe their way to acquittal were given light fines that were often not collected.[15]

In 1932, the consul in Maji, Captain Whalley, reported that in his twenty years in Africa and Asia, he had never seen such appalling conditions. By 1935, they were even worse. Maji had had fourteen governors in twenty-five years, each of whom had departed with slaves, sometimes numbering thousands. The population of Maji Mountain dropped from some two hundred thousand in 1925 to between eight and ten thousand. Up to 1930, produce had been sold in local markets and coffee, hides, and beeswax had been exported to Addis Ababa. The world economic crisis of the early 1930s had caused a fall in demand, and depopulation completed the decline of the economy. Money became increasingly scarce as each governor departed with all the cash in the treasury. As the numbers of gabbar dropped from some thirty or forty thousand to an estimated seven hundred in 1935, the taxes, tribute, and services demanded of them reached impossible levels. Their livestock and grain were seized. They were conscripted as porters when officials went on safari, and kept from their fields for months at a time. They eked out a living on *kotcho*, a type of banana. If they could not meet the demands, they or their children were enslaved. Officials expected to be presented with children, as well as ivory and other gifts. Every Amhara in Maji had at least one or two slaves to "carry his rifle, attend to his mule, wash his feet on trek and so forth." Officials from the governor down had many more, and exported them in defiance of the emperor's orders, bribing customs officials to let them pass. Even the consulate interpreter had taken slaves to the capital, one of whom had been given to him by the governor.[16]

The surrounding Tishana were willing to pay taxes or tribute, but not to become gabbar. They were selling their own or their neighbors' children to buy arms to defend themselves and attack their oppressors, who retaliated by destroying their huts and crops, and seizing them and their livestock. A vicious cycle of violence prevailed in the whole area. Whalley witnessed a typical punitive expedition in 1932 against the Tirma, who had killed an Ethiopian merchant and his retinue for enslaving one of their women. The soldiers torched homes and granaries, and marched the women, children, and old men back to Maji, where many died of exposure; some were ransomed by their relatives, and the young and fit were enslaved. Three years later, Tirma lands were still deserted.

Whalley actually showed Haile Selassie photographs of the depopulated areas, abandoned huts and terraced fields, and gave him details of captures, including some British subjects seized by poachers. The emperor promised action. But Whalley had not seen one imperial proclamation obeyed in five years, nor had he found any trustworthy officials. When the slavery judge died, having amassed some thirty or forty slaves, his successor did not arrive for fifteen months and then when he tried to take action, his assistant's house was burned down and all evidence was destroyed. Inevitably the judge soon worked out an arrangement by which he freed slaves and then sold them back to their owners. The emperor's own nephew, although heavily implicated in slaving, was transferred from Maji to become director general in the ministry of war. His successor, Ras Gestacho, was expressly chosen in 1933 to suppress the traffic in Maji and Kafa in spite of his notoriously bad record. He left Maji in the charge of the very deputy who had been responsible for the removal of some three thousand to five thousand slaves in 1926.[17]

These reports and the resignation of de Halpert caused consternation in Britain. Maxwell, the Anti-Slavery Society, and the Foreign Office all suggested different solutions. Maxwell proposed asking the Council of the League to call an extraordinary meeting of the ACE to discuss slavery in Ethiopia. The Society supported this and wanted a "publicity campaign" including publication of the consular reports, and agitation at the League to shame the Ethiopians into action and strengthen the emperor's hand against his opponents. They suggested that France and Italy might be asked to produce their material. The Foreign Office thought this typically unrealistic. Officials believed that most Ethiopians—"barbarous" and "warlike blacks"—cared "not a fig" for the League, and that Haile Selassie—"a reasonably enlightened native," genuinely interested in reform—would "lose his seat and possibly his head" if he acted too fast. France, having promoted Ethiopian membership in the League, persisted in denying that conditions justified criticism. Italy regarded slavery as a "pawn in the political game" and the British minister, Sydney Barton, believed the Italians would only support Britain to embarrass Ethiopia or annoy the French.

The British recognized that there were intractable logistical, administrative, and financial problems in asserting imperial authority. A letter to Maji from Addis Ababa still took at least four weeks. Telegraph and telephone lines were often out of order. All-weather roads were few and short. Slaving was almost entirely the work of the sedentary garrisons in the southwest, and removing them or paying and disciplining them would be expensive and difficult. Haile Selassie was also increasingly beset by fears of Italian aggression, and was frustrated by the French refusal to make Jibuti a free port, to promote economic development.[18] These concerns were leading him to closer relations with Britain. In 1934, in secret negotiations, the British offered him the port of Zeila, with a corridor providing access to Ethiopia, and a treaty of amity, in return for territorial concessions on the frontiers of Sudan, Kenya, and Somaliland, and—a sine qua non—an undertaking that he would end the slave trade and the legal status of slavery. The dam on Lake Tana, so much desired by the British in the past, was no longer a priority because schemes to expand cotton production in the Gezira had been shelved as the result of the world depression.[19] The Foreign Office hoped that the offer of Zeila would stir the emperor into action, and they refused to publish their reports, for fear, as always, of compromising their sources.[20] An alternative would have been to send them to the ACE—but under its rules they would have had to be sent to Haile Selassie for comment before the committee could discuss them. It was one thing to show him the consular reports confidentially, but quite another to have them reach him through the League.

Maxwell offered to go to Ethiopia at the expense of the British government to write a report for the emperor to send to the ACE, with his own comments.[21] Barton was enthusiastic, but the Foreign Office were unwilling to spend money, or risk their other interests in Ethiopia, by acting as " handmaiden" to the committee. Unrealistically, they urged Maxwell to get the ACE to throw off its restrictive rules and demand information from Ethiopia itself.[22] This was a vicious circle as the committee needed solid evidence to attempt such a thing and the Foreign Office would not produce the evidence. The result was frustration on all sides and when the ACE met in 1935, it only had information gleaned by Maxwell from published sources and previous Ethiopian reports, and a list from the Ethiopians stating that over three thousand six hundred slaves had been freed, and nearly three hundred offenders sentenced.[23]

REFORM AND THE ITALIAN CONQUEST

By this time, however, there had been important changes on the ground. Under its Fascist dictator, Benito Mussolini, Italy embarked on building an empire spanning the horn of Africa and offering new fields for colonization.[24] The preparations took over a year and, as the threat became more explicit, Haile Selassie's attention was diverted away from internal reforms and into preparations for war, which he made desperate attempts to avoid. Anxious to retain British support, by the fall of 1934 he talked of replacing de Halpert. Sandford angled for the job.[25] In November, as the result of the reports from Maji, the British made a strong protest.[26] In December, Mussolini demanded reparations and apologies for a small skirmish at Wel Wel, near the Somaliland frontier, and rejected arbitration. In January, Ethiopia appealed to the League to settle the dispute. Sandford warned the emperor that he would be wise to have a slavery advisor in place before the ACE met for its first session in April 1935.[27]

In March Haile Selassie finally sent Lej Alemayu—released from prison after a year without charges—to investigate conditions in Maji. In June he took the unprecedented step of asking Sandford to go there as advisor to a new governor. Maji was to become a model province, with a paid administration under the emperor's direct control. Taxes were to be light, trade was to be developed, and slaving stopped. Hitherto, foreign advisors had only been attached to ministries in Addis Ababa. Their duties had been general and largely theoretical, but Sandford was now given a practical task confined to one area.[28] The British welcomed the appointment. They felt that, in fairness to the Ethiopians, they should publicize it, but did not want it "splashed" in the press for fear of offending the Italians. Their dilemma—how to support Ethiopia without antagonizing Italy—was to become a recurring problem. They decided just to mention the appointment in Parliament.[29] Sandford tried to disarm criticism by asking Lugard to make it clear to the Anti-Slavery Society that his appointment was not "a sympathy catching stunt" to gain British support but was the result of Haile Selassie's concern at Alemayu's reports.[30]

Sandford and the new governor did not arrive in Maji until November, and war with Italy had broken out the previous month. The old garrison, which had caused such trouble, was recalled to Addis Ababa to fight, and the new governor brought several hundred fresh soldiers. At first all went well. Lej Alemayu had already abolished the gabbar system, freeing thousands, who now only paid a light tax. The population was returning. Long-abandoned fields were being cultivated. Women and children came out of hiding.[31] Early in 1936 Sandford reported that the slave trade had been driven underground and neighboring people, no longer subject to raids, had promised to give up slave dealing.[32] He hoped at the end of the war to extend his operations to Kafa and Gore, and believed that, given two or three years, he could suppress the slave trade altogether.[33]

Sadly, problems soon piled up. The governor, reluctant to take his advice without direct orders, withheld information, refused to tour the area, and was soon at loggerheads with Lej Alemayu. The latter sent poachers into Sudan and conscripted labor to bring back the ivory. Time was lost settling feuds between local peoples and recovering captives.[34] There was a chronic shortage of money. Sandford was not paid, and there was soon no cash to pay the soldiers, who resorted to selling their ammunition. The emperor, busy fighting the Italians, did not answer appeals for financial help. The years of devastation had rendered the area too poor to raise much in taxes and lack of roads prevented the development of trade. In desperation, the governor was forced to revive the gabbar system to pay his men.[35]

Reforms had also been introduced in Gore, where Haile Selassie had appointed a slavery inspector who publicly freed some one hundred and fifty slaves and paraded thirty-five dealers in chains. As in Maji, the disappearance of the old *neftenya*, conscripted to fight the Italians, led to immediate improvement.[36] But here, too, the war called a halt to reforms.

Haile Selassie had put his faith in the League, but its leading members, France and Britain, were unprepared for war and afraid of alienating Italy in the face of the much greater threat from Germany.[37] An interdepartmental committee reported in the summer of 1935 that the Italian conquest of Ethiopia would not threaten vital British interests. Although the British would have preferred the country to remain independent,[38] both they, and the French, who were vulnerable to attack in Europe, decided to sacrifice Ethiopia for the sake of friendly relations with Mussolini.[39] Only mild sanctions were imposed against Italy, while various abortive schemes were proposed to halt the conflict, all of which included reforming the government under international supervision—anathema to Haile Selassie. Finally the infamous Hoare-Laval plan, giving most of the country to Italy and establishing an Italian commercial monopoly over much of the rest, raised a storm in Britain where public opinion was strongly in favor of Ethiopia. Hoare resigned and the plan, rejected by Italy, was scrapped. While the League talked, the Italian armies swept forward, bombing and gassing defenseless civilians in a ruthless campaign of "total" war.

In May 1936, Addis Ababa fell. Haile Selassie fled, leaving his generals to continue the fight, and appointing a regent to carry on the government from Gore. He appealed in vain to the League not to recognize the Italian occupation and went into exile in England. The consulate in Maji was closed. Sandford retreated to Kenya. By August he was in England, broke and jobless.[40] The Oromo in Gore rose against the Amhara.[41] Slave dealers were released; slave raids and disorders were reported. The British, alarmed that their consul in Gore was being drawn into Ethiopian politics, withdrew him in September 1936.[42] The British forces in Sudan were minimal and, with the Italian advance, the defense of the border became a crucial issue.[43] To establish its position in the area before the arrival of the Italians, Sudan at last occupied the Boma Plateau, which had hitherto been subject to Ethiopian raids. The only good news was that Shaykh Khojali in Bela Shangul was overthrown by his own vassals.

The slavery question provided the Italians with a moral justification for their unprovoked attack on a fellow member of the League. In September 1935, before the invasion, they accused Ethiopia, which had still not ratified the Slavery Convention, of failing to carry out its obligations to the League, and declared it unfit for membership. On 2 March 1936, they sent the secretary-general a memorandum, with photographs of atrocities, to show that the laws against slaving had not been obeyed. They claimed to have abolished slavery in Tigre in October 1935, freeing some twenty thousand people. In April, proclaiming an "Easter of Liberation," they outlawed it in all occupied territories.

THE ACE AND ITALIAN ANTI-SLAVERY PROPAGANDA

The ACE met in Geneva in April 1936, just before the fall of Addis Ababa. Zedda had been replaced by Mario Moreno, inspector general and chief of the Office of Studies and Propaganda at the Ministry of the Colonies. He had served in Libya and Eritrea, been on missions to Yemen, and been colonial attaché at the legation in Addis Ababa from 1931–1934.[44] Unlike Zedda, who was respected for his "competence and objectivity,"[45] he was the mouthpiece of the Fascist regime. He tried to get the Italian occupation recognized by having the ACE, in its report, express satisfaction with Italy's antislavery measures and take note of the Italian accusations against Ethiopia. He added to these accusations other charges, including the castration of boys for sale as eunuchs.[46] He denounced the gabbar system, which Zedda had refused to discuss the year before, as an "iniquitous" form of slavery.[47] His colleagues pointed out that many of his charges were based on hearsay or on private sources that they were not meant to consider.[48] They recognized that if they accepted the Italian report on Ethiopia they would, indirectly, be recognizing the conquest—a step the League had not taken. They, therefore, claimed they could not take it into account as the Ethiopian government had not been able to comment on it.[49]

In the end they compromised. The ACE report for 1936 simply stated that Italy had announced that it had freed slaves in the occupied areas, and it summarized the Italian accusations without expressing an opinion on them. The accusations were included as appendices, theoretically to be sent to the Ethiopian government for comment.[50] Thus, to the irritation of the Foreign Office, the Italians got the publicity they wanted. However, their triumph was more theoretic than real as the League had already published the charges.[51] As for sending the Italian documents to Ethiopia for comment, the Council deferred the matter until 1937, while the League debated whether or not to recognize the Italian conquest.

In 1937, the Foreign Office feared Italy would raise the issue of recognition again by submitting information on Ethiopia. They were worried enough to consider postponing the ACE meeting. Alternatively, they suggested that the committee consider Italy as de facto not de jure ruler. This would also avoid having to ask the Council to forward the material to Ethiopia, raising the question of whether it was still a member of the League.[52] To their relief, however, neither Italy nor Ethiopia sent in a report. The Italians replaced Moreno by Enrico Cerulli, who had been advisor to the Italian legation in Addis Ababa for many years and was now at the Ministry of Colonies, but he did not even attend the session. In December 1937, Italy left the League and there was henceforth no Italian delegate at the ACE and no information or discussion of Ethiopian slavery. The subject, so important, from the inception of the League committees, now ceased to be an international issue.

BRITAIN'S CONTINUING DILEMMA OVER SLAVERY IN ETHIOPIA

For the British government, however, the dilemma continued. When the full reports of the situation in the southwest in 1934–1935 reached the Foreign Office in August 1936 after the emperor had left the country, officials concluded that the Ethiopians were "rotters" and the Italian occupation would be a "godsend" for the subject peoples. However, the government was under attack for accepting the Italian conquest. If they published the reports they would seem to be vindicating the Italian accusations and justifying their own failure to halt aggression. Moreover, publishing information on foreign countries was against their established practice and would give Harris a lever to demand publications in the future. They decided to let the Italians "do their own propaganda" and simply showed the reports to Harris, Maxwell, and a few others in strict confidence, or so they hoped.[53] However, Harris, outraged at the reports, proposed to state publicly that the sooner an effective Italian administration was established the better. To mollify him, the government engineered a parliamentary question in order to reply that their reports showed that the emperor had not been able to suppress the slave trade.[54]

This roused the supporters of Ethiopia, including the newly formed Abyssinia Association, which had influential members in the country and in Parliament.[55] They protested that slave raiding and trading had been abolished in Maji and any recrudescence was due to the Italian invasion.[56] They accused British officials of not giving Haile Selassie credit for successes over the previous decade, and claimed that this had weakened support for Ethiopia in the face of Italian aggression.[57] Maxwell joined the fray on the other side, writing to the *Times* that the peoples of the southwest had been systematically ravaged and would welcome the Italians.[58] This conflict between the supporters and opponents of the emperor continued. Haile Selassie kept in touch with his adherents from his house in Bath, as well as with the resistance movement in Ethiopia, and corresponded with the League. Harris, for his part, went on demanding publication of the reports and wanted assurances that any agreements with Italy would include antislavery articles. He even suggested that the Anti-Slavery Society might contribute to the cost of resettling freed slaves, perhaps working through the Italian antislavery society.[59]

British politicians were divided between those who wanted to appease Italy to wean it away from Germany and those who refused to accept Italian aggression. The conquest, however, had put Italy, with its large army in Ethiopia, in a position to threaten the British in Egypt, Sudan, and East Africa, as well as the Red Sea and even to threaten their communications in the western Mediterranean, where the Italians were helping the

Fascist forces of General Franco in the Spanish Civil War.[60] Hence the government moved to settle differences with Mussolini.[61] Britain virtually recognized the de facto conquest of Ethiopia in December 1936. Early in 1938 it negotiated a *bon voisinage* agreement with an exchange of notes, identifying potential areas of conflict and suggesting ways to resolve them. These included delimitating the frontiers of what was now Italian East Africa, guaranteeing the independence of Saudi Arabia and Yemen, exchanging information on naval forces in the Mediterranean and Red Sea, Italian recognition of "obligations" to Britain and Egypt in respect to the waters of Lake Tana and the Blue Nile, and an end to anti-British propaganda.[62]

After their conquest, the Italians continued to vaunt their antislavery efforts and Lady Simon, who had been assured by Mussolini that he would suppress slavery, urged Halifax, now foreign secretary, to encourage this propaganda in order to counter British public support for Haile Selassie.[63] Count Ciano, the Italian foreign minister, needed no prodding. The Italians claimed to have freed some thirty-five thousand slaves by 1937. They said they had settled some in villages, sometimes under the care of missionaries, and had given them land, tools, and animals. Others were enrolled in labor detachments building roads, or were employed in other occupations. They could remain with their owners if they wanted to, but had to be paid, and there were severe penalties for ill-treatment. The gabbar system was ended without difficulty by enrolling the neftenya in the Italian forces. Chiefs now received regular salaries. In Bela Shangul and Ometo, slaves had been turned into sharecroppers—ending slavery without dislocating the economy.[64] A representative of the firm of Gellatley, Hankey and Co., in Gambela brought the good news that coffee production had decreased because slave pickers were no longer available.[65]

The British consul in Addis Ababa, however, was sceptical. He had no information on slavery and suspected the Italians were too occupied to pay much attention to it. He did not doubt that it had diminished, but attributed this as much to the fact that many of the nobility had fled or been killed as to Italian actions. He suspected that large numbers of Ethiopians were now being forced into labor gangs or into the armed forces. Halifax was warned that Italian claims might not stand up in the face of informed criticism from the emperor's supporters.[66]

Indeed, in 1937, reports from Whalley, the former consul in Maji and a bitter critic of Ethiopian rule, now established on the Boma Plateau, bore this out. Informants from Maji told him that the population had initially welcomed the Italians, but soon found them worse than the Ethiopians. They requisitioned food, paying little or nothing for it. They had disrupted the agricultural cycle and caused a food shortage by conscripting all males over fourteen for military service. The recruits were paid irregularly and badly fed. The Eritrean and Oromo troops in the Italian army abducted and raped women. The Italian colonel himself had appropriated the wife of one of Whalley's consular guards. Children were being forced into domestic work. The thirty Italians in

Maji were so unpopular that they moved under armed guard and their native troops, as well as the local people, were disaffected.[67]

In the next years, little information on slavery reached the Foreign Office. Although Haile Selassie kept in touch by correspondence with the Ethiopian resistance—the Patriots—the British were inhibited by the *bon voisinage* agreement from intelligence activities, and were increasingly preoccupied with crises in Europe. It was not until September 1939, on the eve of the outbreak of the Second World War, that Sandford was sent to Cairo and Khartoum to lay plans for contacting the Patriots in the event of war with Italy.[68] When this broke out in 1940, the question arose of whether or not Haile Selassie should be restored to his throne, and the conflict between the Anti-Slavery Society and his supporters again came to the fore, as will be seen.

NOTES

1. De Halpert summarized his part as advisor to the Ministry of the Interior in suggesting and promoting these reforms in Report of Mr. de Halpert on his period of service with the Ethiopian government, 22 May 1934, enclosed in Barton to Simon no. 94, 18 June 1934, FOCP 14384 (FO 401/34) J1625/288/1 (henceforth de Halpert Report). For an overall discussion of the emperor's policies, see Marcus 1995, 96–147.

2. De Halpert Report.

3. Barton to Simon no. 117, August 16 1932, FOCP 14226 (401/33) J 2518/3/1.

4. These were the slaves of Ras Gugsa Wele and Ras Haylu of Gojam, who had conspired against the emperor, and those of the hereditary sultan of Jimma, which lost its autonomy in 1933.

5. Memorandum 1931, and audience with Emperor 20 May 1933, de Halpert Papers, Rhodes House, Oxford, 1 (henceforth HPR).

6. Memorandum 1931, "Registration of Slaves" 28 July 1933, ibid.

7. "Regulations of the New Slavery Department which was established in August 1932," 1 August 1933, and Notes of an audience with the Emperor 20 May 1933, ibid.

8. Barton to Simon, no. 109, 18 July 1933, FO 371/16878 J 201/429/1.

9. Diary, 4 August 1932 to 14 August 1933, HPR 1.

10. Summary report 22 May 1934, HPR 1, pp. 36ff.; copy in FO 401/34 pp. 77 ff.

11. This and the information that follows is compiled from the de Halpert Report and memoranda in HPR 1 and 2.

12. De Halpert Report.

13. The only other governor credited with making a sustained attack on slavery was Dr. Martin (Werqneh Eshete), who was Governor of Chercher from 1930 to 1933.

14. Extracts from Reports by HM's Consul in Dangela, 31 May 1933, confidential, FO 371/16997 J2421/429/1; and 21 October 1931, enclosed in Barton to Simon no. 15, 31 January 1933, J 444/429/1, FOCP 14384 (FO 401/34); Report on Slavery in North-West Ethiopia, enclosed in Cheesman to Barton 31 May 1933, enclosed in Barton to Simon, no. 78, June 6 1933, J 1539/429/1, ibid. Extract from HM's Consul in Dangila no. 12, 11 April 1934, enclosed in Barton to Simon no. 129, 25 May 1936, FOCP 15215 [FO 371/20185].

15. Consul, Gore, to Simon no. 35, 19 September 1933, FO 371/16997; Extract from Report of the HM Consul, Gore, 3 April 1934, enclosed in Barton to Eden no. 129, 25 May 1936, FOCP 15215 (FO 371/20185).

16. Whalley to Barton no. 44, 6 June 1933 enclosed in Broadmead to Simon, no. 142, 4 September 1933, J2334/429/1, F0CP 14384.

17. Annual Report on Slavery in Ethiopia for 1933, enclosed with consular reports, in Barton to Simon no. 84, 31 May 1934, and minutes, FO 371/ 18030 (FOCP 14384); General Slavery Report of HM Consul at Maji, 8 July 1935, enclosed in Barton to Eden, no. 129, 25 May 1936, FOCP 15215 (FO 371/20185); Barton to Simon no. 13, 21 January 1935, enclosing correspondence on slavery in Maji, FO 371/ 19187 J865/524/1.

18. Italy was at this time pressing for permission to build a road to link Eritrea with Italian Somaliland.

19. Barton to Simon no. 174, secret, 22 November 1932 and minutes, FO 371/16101 J3314/103/1; Minute by Peterson, 28 March and by Simon, 29 March 1933, on Barton to Simon no. 20, 13 February 1934, FO 371/18030; Barton to Simon no. 53, secret, 16 April 1934, FO 401/28–34, p. 51. The session or leasing of Zeila had been discussed in 1919 and was then strongly advocated by Lugard.

20. This question was debated over a number of months, but see particularly Maxwell to Simon, 28 July 1934, and minutes, FO 371/18030 J 1811/288/1, and ASAPS to Simon, 2 August 1934, and minutes, ibid., J 1842/288/1. The consuls were paid by the governments of Uganda, Kenya, and Sudan.

21. Maxwell to Stevenson, 2 March 1934, and minutes, FO 371/18030 J586/288/1.

22. Minutes on Maxwell to Stevenson, 2 March 1934, FO 371/18030 J 586/288/1; Barton to Peterson no. 113, 30 April 1934 and minutes, and Peterson to Barton, confidential, 14 June 1934, ibid., J 1282/288/1; Stevenson to Maxwell, 25 May 1934, ibid., J 1325/288/1; Wallinger to Maxwell, 12 June 1934, ibid., J 1325/288/1.

23. The Ethiopians wanted to send an observer to the ACE, but were told it was not possible, Note by Catastini, 8 April 1935, LON s.1670 file 7.

24. For a resumé of Italo-Ethiopian relations from 1928 to 1935 see Barton to Hoare, no. 85, 10 July 1935, FOCP 14810 J 3471/1/1. For Italian policy, the war and its legacy, see Sbacchi 1997. For Haile Selassie's policy see Marcus 1995.

25. Sandford to Lugard, 21 September 1934, Lugard Papers.

26. Barton to Simon no. 13, 21 January 1935, and enclosures FO 371/19187 J 865/524/1.

27. Sandford to Lugard, 17 January, and 6 February 1935, Lugard Papers.

28. Barton to Simon, tel. no. 165, 9 July 1935, FO 371/19187 J 2761/524/1; Barton to Thompson 13 September 1935, ibid., 147.

29. Minutes on Barton to Hoare, tel. no. 165, 9 July 1935, FO 371/19187 J 2761/524/1.

30. Sandford to Lugard, 20 July 1935, Lugard duly complied, see Lugard to Sandford 14 August 1935, Lugard Papers.

31. Sandford to Lugard, 24 January 1936, Lugard Papers.

32. Sandford to Gillan, 13 March, and to McMichael, 15 April 1939 precis; Sandford report of tour among the Gaisha, Beru, Tid, and Tirma, 21 February 1936, Sandford Papers.

33. Sandford to Lugard, 19 February 1936, Lugard Papers.

34. Sandford papers, Maji 6; for details of these raids see Symes to High Commissioner for Egypt and Sudan, no. 107, 26 May 1936, and enclosed note on Boma plateau, FO 371/20176.

35. Sandford to Lugard, 24 January and 19 February 1936, Lugard Papers; Sandford Papers, Maji 2, 3, 5.

36. Barton to Hoare, tel. no. 20, 10 January 1936, FO 371/20184, p. 224. The emperor asked de Halpert to go to Gore as Slavery Advisor but he had joined the Red Cross and was serving with the Ethiopian army, see Miers 1997.

37. For a discussion of the policies of the powers and events at the League see inter alia Sbacchi 1997; Marcus 1995, 148 ff.

38. Sbacchi 1997, 279–81.

39. Report of Inter-Departmental Committee on British Interests, enclosed in Maffey to FO, secret 18 June 1935, FOCP 14810 (FO 401/35) J 2381/97/1.

40. Sandford to Lugard, 8 June and 16 August 1936, Lugard Papers.

41. The Oromo in Gore hoped to create an independent state under League Mandate.

42. Eden to Kelly, tels. nos. 314 and 315, 5 June 1936, FOCP 15031 (FO 401/36) J 5094/4044/1; Bell to Kelly, no. 182, 22 September 1936, enclosed in Kelly to Eden, no. 1150, 3 October 1936, ibid., J 7978/100/1; Erskine to Eden, no. 17, 1 October 1936, ibid., J 8096/4044/1.

43. The British in Sudan had only 4,700 African troops, two British battalions, a small air force and one field battery, minute by Thompson, 25 May 1936, on Lampson to Eden, tel. no. 462, 22 May 1936, enclosed in governor-general Khartoum to Lampson, no. 70, 18 May 1936, FO 371/20176 J 4656/100/1.

44. LON 6B/23123/2185 R4149.

45. Catalini to secretary-general, 6 November 1935, LON 6B/7410/2186 R4149 1933–1946. Zedda was said to be ill, but Maxwell thought he had been replaced because the line he had taken in the 1935 session had been "somewhat peculiar," Makins's record of conversation with Maxwell, 25 March 1935, FO 371/20517 W 2741/154/52.

46. C.C.E.E. 3rd session/P.V. 8, 21 April 1936, LON 6B/25052/8000 R4153.

47. The memorandum is LON C.C.E.E. 127, the minutes of the discussion are in C.C.E.E./3rd session/P.V. 11, 24 April 1936.

48. Maxwell's notes on the Report of the Slavery Committee 1936, 28 April 1936, FO 371/20517 W3735/154/52.

49. LON C.C.E.E./3rd session/P.V. 4, 16 April 1936.

50. See p. 7, Report of 1936, LON C.189 (1). M.145.1936.VI.

51. FO minutes on Report of the ACE, FO 371/20517 W3874/154/52.

52. Foreign Office 3–16 February 1937, FO 371/21280 W 2452/1006/52; notes for conversation with Maxwell, 5 March and 12 March 1937, and record of conversation with Maxwell, 12 March 1937, ibid., W 4530/1006/52 and W 5085//1006/52.

53. Barton to Eden, no. 129, 25 May 1936, enclosures and minutes, FO 371/20185 J 6921/273/1; minutes on ASAPS to Eden, 10 December 1936, FO 371/20185 J 8969/273/1; Patrick to Oliphant, 10 December 1936, and minutes, ibid.

54. Parliamentary question by Cazalet, 18 December 1936, Hansard 318, no. 35. Col. 2815.

55. Sbacchi 1997, 27–28.

56. The Abyssinia Association had the support of a number of prominent people including members of Parliament.

57. Abyssinia Association to Eden, 19 December 1936, FO 371/20927. The association claimed that its sources were impeccable, but could not be named.

58. The Times, 22 December 1936.

59. Minute on Harris to Harvey, 25 March 1938, FO 371/22029 J 830/537/1.

60. The war lasted from 1936–39, for its impact on the ACE, see below, chapter 17.

61. For a detailed discussion, see Sbacchi 1997, 269–308.

62. This agreement, also called the Easter Accord, was never really put into operation since it was overtaken by events as Europe moved towards war. For a discussion of it with text and correspondence, see Sbacchi 1997, 295–308, 337–93. See above, chapter 9, and below, chapter 16 for British fears of Italian designs in Arabia. See inter alia chapter 6 above for the Tana dam issue.

63. Lady Simon to Halifax, 5 April 1938, FO 371/22029 J 1385/537/1.

64. Perth to Halifax, tel. no. 318, 6 April 1938, FO 371/22029 J 1409/5/537/1; Drummond to Eden tel. no. 240, 20 April 1937, FO 371/20927; Summary of Section on Slavery in Report on Estimates for Italian Africa, Presented to the Chamber of Deputies, 16 March 1938, enclosed in Perth to Halifax, no. 356, 8 April 1938, FO 371/ 22029, pp. 157–59, and Perth to Halifax, tel. no. 66, 5 April 1938, ibid., J 1422/537/1.

65. Foreign Office minute on Perth to Halifax, tel. no. 66, 5 April 1938, FO 371/ 22029 J 1422/537/1.

66. Minutes on Lady Simon to Halifax, 5 April 1938 and Halifax to Perth tel. no. 182, 4 April 1938 and minutes, FO 371/22029 J 1385/537/1; Perth to Halifax tel. no. 66, 5 April 1938, ibid., J 1422/537/1; Stonehewer-Bird to Halifax, tel. no. 60, 11 April 1938, ibid., J 1560/ 537/1.

67. Whalley to Civil Secretary, Khartoum, no. F.A.B. 1/37, 24 April 1937, enclosed in Lampson to Eden, no. 24, 30 May 1937, FOCP 15544 (FO 401/37) J 2591/43/1; Whalley to Governor General, Khartoum, 17 November 1937, enclosed in Lampson to Eden no. 1457, 22 December 1937, FOCP 15758 J 24/24/1.

68. For Sandford's activities and the operations which followed, see Shirreff 1995; Casbon 1993, 115–26.

16

Slavery in a Changing World 1932–1939: Arabia, the Red Sea, and Persian Gulf

SAUDI ARABIA AND THE RENEWAL OF THE TREATY OF JIDDAH

In 1932, the League of Nations asked all members to include an antislavery commitment in treaties with Arab states.[1] The next year the Saudis asked the British whether they would support them if they applied for membership in the League of Nations. The latter, although anxious not to upset Ibn Saud, decided they could not encourage him to apply as, among other reasons, slavery was still legal in his kingdom.[2] From March 1934, the Treaty of Jiddah could be denounced by either party, and the British feared the king might do so largely because of the article binding him to cooperate against the slave trade, and the notes about consular manumission. The British themselves were now having second thoughts about the value of both of these as antislavery measures. Article 7 merely made it more difficult for the Saudis to block British efforts against the traffic, while consular manumission only affected small numbers of slaves, and the Saudis could always end it by refusing to allow fugitives to be repatriated. However, Britain could not denounce these agreements without precipitating a humanitarian outcry.

The prospect of having to reopen discussion on the treaty of Jiddah led to a review of slavery in Saudi Arabia and of British policy.[3] Furlonge, an official of the British legation, informed the Foreign Office that there were probably not more than forty thousand slaves in the country and numbers were declining, as more were freed or died than were being born or imported. Imports came mostly from Yemen and consisted of Africans or Yemenis who had either been born into slavery or been enslaved as children. Girls from Malaya, Java, and China were no longer enslaved. The European powers had greater control over the pilgrimage, and the depression had curtailed the numbers of pilgrims, and eroded the purchasing power of the Hijazi. Very few slaves were believed to be smuggled across the Red Sea. Economic and political change was also eroding slave holdings. As well as the reduction of slave soldiers and camel drivers already noted,[4] improved communications had "swept away . . . the semi-independent robber-barons and their slave retinues," and Hijazi women were now objecting to their husbands taking concubines. The depression had caused a big drop in sales and prices. Thus where a "town-trained" marriageable girl had sold for up to £150 in gold in 1931, she commanded at most £50 in 1934. Internal slave trading was mostly in the houses of brokers and the *dekka* or open market in Mecca was just a small shop in a side lane.

The royal family were the largest slave owners. The king was reputed to have three thousand, nearly half recently acquired by purchase or gift. He did not sell them but gave some as presents to notables. Slaves were an essential accoutrement of his power since prestige still depended on the number of a man's followers. His slave bodyguard, "arrogant, well provided with food, clothes and even money, well contented with their lot," formed a "striking contrast" to his free lower class subjects. He had not attempted to change attitudes to slavery, and could not do so without alienating his followers. The British minister Sir Andrew Ryan had been told that Emir Faysal[5] did not "really like slavery," but most people had an interest in maintaining it and had little knowledge of, or regard for, the attitude of other powers or the League of Nations. Ibn Saud was thought to be enforcing regulations against imports, and was readier to free persons recently captured, and had virtually ended the enslavement of pilgrims. All but fifteen of the two hundred slaves manumitted through the legation since 1926 had been born into slavery or been in bondage at least ten years. Since the British had undertaken to give up the right of manumission as soon as Saudi cooperation against the slave trade rendered it unnecessary, Ibn Saud might now claim that this stage had been reached.

Relations continued to be bedevilled by the arrival at the legation of fugitive royal slaves, including, early in 1934, a personal slave of the king. The British had little hope of spiriting him away as they had done Bakhit. After difficult negotiations, he was returned to the Saudis on condition that he would be manumitted in two weeks and repatriated.[6] He was duly shipped off to Jibuti. But the problem threatened to grow worse each time a slave arrived panting on the doorstep. The Saudis complained that the newly concluded treaty of Sana'a with Yemen contained no articles against the slave trade.[7] They accused the British of encouraging slaves to demand manumission and of rejecting Saudi evidence and decisions of the Shari'a court. They also began denying that the fugitives were slaves. A dark African youth, for instance, was claimed as a son by a light-skinned Arab couple, and subsequently enticed from the legation and then arrested as a slave.[8] Further difficulties arose when a man claiming to be the slave of a Saudi diplomat claimed asylum at the British embassy in Baghdad. Slavery was illegal in Iraq and the man was therefore free by law, but the case showed that manumission might cause friction even outside Arabia.[9]

The British recognized that Ibn Saud's standing throughout Arabia would be diminished if he continued to allow them to free members of his own household. He was in a much stronger position at home and abroad than he had been in 1927, and would find foreign support if he renounced the treaty of Jiddah. A major conflict with him would also risk "incalculable" repercussions in the British satellites on the Persian Gulf and among Muslims in India. Ryan advised replacing the treaty of Jiddah with a new agreement settling all outstanding differences and, as a quid pro quo, renouncing consular manumission. He stressed that Ibn Saud was an enlightened ruler, anxious for good relations with Britain, who had himself broached the idea of a new treaty.

There was the danger, however, that the return of prosperity to the kingdom in the shape of oil revenues and a rise in the numbers of pilgrims might lead to a revival of the slave trade. The British believed that they were the only power interested in preventing this and their options were strictly limited. Their main problem was that the kingdom's eastern and southeastern frontiers had not been defined, and the search for oil had brought this question to a head. In 1933, Ibn Saud had granted an oil concession in Al-Hasa to an American company, and in 1934 a mainly British company was angling for a concession in the British satellite state of Qatar. Hitherto the British had not taken any steps to establish claims to the area east of a "blue line"—the border agreed with the Turks in 1913 and 1914. Much of the region was sparsely populated desert, but Ibn Saud had been slowly establishing "unofficial suzerainty" over its nomadic inhabitants and had planted settlements of his followers east of this line. He was very upset when told of the British claims in the spring of 1934 and the British, who knew their legal case was weak, recognized that if he were forced to retreat his prestige would suffer. They were bound, however, to protect their own interests and those of their protégés on the Persian Gulf, as well as Muscat and Oman, by limiting Saudi expansion. To keep Ibn Saud's friendship, they would have to make territorial concessions, and they believed this would be less damaging to their own prestige if they were made as part of a general settlement. The Saudis were also virtually blockading Kuwait, and there was a dispute over transit dues through Bahrain to the Al-Hasa, and a number of other problems, which both sides were anxious to resolve.[10]

After putting out feelers, the Saudis made it clear in September 1934 that they would be prepared to limit the import of slaves, as well as to take measures to decrease the numbers of those already in the country, and alleviate their lot by, for instance, manumitting those who were ill-treated. But such measures would have to seem to be spontaneous gestures, and in return the British would have to give up consular manumission.

Maxwell, marshalling information for the ACE, decided that manumission was an irritant, and now that slavery was a matter of international concern, Britain should not "retain special powers." He suggested giving them up if Ibn Saud acceded to article 2 of the Slavery Convention of 1926, which pledged signatories to end the slave trade and make other concessions, including freeing all captured slaves. He thought owners might be compensated by the League—a suggestion the Foreign Office considered unrealistic. But they, and Ryan, were much impressed by "the practicality of Maxwell's attitude"[11] and because he was so helpful, sensible, and reliable, they showed him the Furlonge report, which they did not send to either Lugard or to Harris.[12]

Ryan and Maxwell agreed that more might be achieved by extracting a serious Saudi commitment against slavery than by continuing to insist on a "right" which had little overall impact on the institution and seemed to be a fast-fading asset. Ryan thought that condemnation of the slave trade by Ibn Saud—the principal independent Arabian ruler—would be more valuable.[13] Simon, however, "on grounds of policy and principle" would only renounce manumission in return for specific antislavery measures. Manumission was not to be traded for what it would "fetch" in the settlement of other issues. He instructed Ryan to ask Ibn Saud to adhere, as Maxwell had suggested, to the article in the Slavery Convention binding signatories to suppress the slave trade, or to agree to an exchange of notes to this end, and to inform the British of the precise steps he would take to enforce this undertaking, and how he proposed to help existing slaves.[14] Long negotiations followed which were still in progress when the ACE met in 1935 and hence Maxwell was warned to say as little as possible for fear of jeopardizing them.

They were still in progress when the Italians conquered Ethiopia. This made it even more desirable for the British to settle differences with Ibn Saud to prevent his being "wooed" into the Italian "camp." Italian propaganda in Arabic newspapers published in Libya was vociferously anti-British, and Italy offered Ibn Saud arms and money and sold him airplanes. Ryan believed the king regarded the Ethiopian war as a conflict between Britain and Italy, and at one point he seemed to be holding up the negotiations while he watched events. He also signed a Treaty of Arab Brotherhood and Alliance with Iraq and opened negotiations to settle differences with Egypt, raising suspicions that he aspired to lead the rising Pan-Arabian movement and form an Arab block to take advantage of the difficulties in Europe.[15] However, Ibn Saud wanted British assurances that they would protect his country should Italy also attack him,[16] and by April 1936 he was anxious to conclude the negotiations.

Consular manumission was only one of a wide range of issues to be settled, but the Saudis attached much importance to ending it, whereas the British were more concerned with the frontier question, particularly the ownership of the Buraimi Oasis claimed by Ibn Saud, and with raising the long blockade of Kuwait.[17] Appearances were important to both powers. The king would only agree to unpopular measures against slavery if they seemed to be spontaneous gestures on his part; while the British, to placate the humanitarian lobby, could only give up manumission in return for "really reliable and solid" regulations which they could claim to be of greater benefit to slaves.[18] Long before the negotiations came to fruition the participants agreed to a face-saving strategy. Once they had agreed on the regulations, the Saudis would issue them—apparently spontaneously—and shortly afterwards the British would publicly renounce consular manumission on the grounds that it was no longer needed.

The negotiations took months. The British tried to get all imports of slaves and all new enslavement prohibited. The Saudis agreed to ban imports by sea, but claimed they could not stop them overland while slavery continued in adjacent territories, nor could they deny entry to foreign visitors with slave retinues. As a compromise, they agreed to allow importers only to bring in persons enslaved on or before 2 October 1936, the date on which the new regulations were to be published. The British tried to get this date put back first to 1925 and then to 1934.[19] The Saudis refused. This nearly derailed the negotiations early in 1936 when Anthony Eden, the new foreign secretary, realized he would have to defend the agreement in Parliament. However, he eventually gave way, realizing that at least there would be no legal imports of slaves after 1936.[20]

The British also wanted all persons who had themselves been enslaved (Maxwell's captives), to have the right to claim their freedom. This would have meant liberating many existing slaves. The Saudis would only agree to give the right to those who could prove they had been born free and had been enslaved contrary to the principles of Islam since 1925, when they had conquered Hijaz. This was not really satisfactory as persons enslaved before that date, which included most of those manumitted by the legation since 1930, would be worse off than they had been while consular manumission offered them an avenue of escape.[21] Moreover, proof of enslavement, particularly in childhood, would be hard to obtain. But, again the British gave way.

They also failed to get agreement that ill-treatment would automatically lead to manumission. Saudi practice was to give an owner two months to mend his ways. After that if complaints continued, he had to dispose of his slave by sale or other means. However, the Saudis agreed to state in the projected regulations that slaves had the right to good treatment. They also agreed to forbid the separation of minor children from their mothers. They could not do the same for married slaves because owners normally reserved the right to separate them at the time of the marriage, but they agreed to ban the separation of spouses if the owners had not made such stipulations.

The British discovered during the negotiations that manumitted slaves did not become free in the Western sense. The Saudi negotiator explained to Ryan that under Muslim law an ex-owner remained the slave's guardian or *wali*. His consent was necessary, for instance, before a freed slave woman could marry. Free women also had to have the consent of their male guardians to marriage. However, a woman could appeal to the court and the judge could become her guardian. Owners, as the guardians of manumitted males, had the right to inherit two-thirds of their property if they died without heirs.[22]

The Saudis undertook to ban all slave trading within the country except under license. Slaves were to be registered and given identity papers within a year of the publication of the regulations. All transactions were to be registered. Unregistered slaves could apply for manumission and unlawful transactions were to be punished by a fine and up to six months in prison. Slaves were to be entitled to buy their freedom, and any born outside the country could return home. The Saudis also undertook to lay down penalties for taking any part in slave dealing. They were to appoint inspectors to see that the regulations were carried out, and local authorities were to report on progress every six months.[23]

On 1 October 1936, after some two years of negotiation, confidential notes were exchanged by which the Saudis undertook to issue the new regulations and the British agreed to end consular manumission. The next day the Saudis published the new regulations, and on 3 October the two governments exchanged notes for publication. They renewed the Treaty of Jiddah for seven years. The British then duly renounced consular manumission.[24]

The last slaves to take refuge in the legation were manumitted in December.[25] Consular manumission in Saudi Arabia now passed into history, just before the charity fund, which had been raided to pay for repatriations, ran out of money. The suppression of slavery was henceforth purely an Arabian matter.

Since the 1936 session of the ACE took place before the treaty was signed, its report merely contained details of the slaves manumitted by the legation. The committee expressed a wish to know whether there had been prosecutions for slave trading and whether the import of slaves from Africa was being prevented as the result of Ibn Saud's undertaking of 1927 to cooperate with the British. In the discussions, Maxwell, who was privy to the ongoing negotiations with the Saudis, fended off suggestions that other powers might try to get rights of consular manumission.[26] He also persuaded Moreno, intent on calling attention to Italy's antislavery measures in Ethiopia, to drop his efforts to get the ACE to recommend the abolition of the legal status of slavery everywhere, arguing that neither Saudi Arabia nor Yemen would agree to this and it could only do harm.[27]

In 1937, the British reported the renunciation of consular manumission to the League and sent copies of the notes exchanged with the Saudis and of the new regulations. There was some criticism, particularly from the Belgian member of the ACE, because no information was ever received directly from Saudi Arabia. He wanted it made clear that the new regulations were only the beginning of the attack on slavery.[28] However, Maxwell had been so impressed by the regulations that he had wondered if the Saudis understood their implications! In the end, the report merely expressed gratification at the news,[29] to the relief of the British who had feared they would not be pleased,[30] and called attention to the fact that Islam encouraged manumission.

In 1938, with the end of consular manumission, the ACE received no information on slavery in Saudi Arabia. Its report contained only the usual forlorn reminder that Islam encouraged manumission, and the vague statement that "the beneficial effects" of the new regulations "should be known." Since the ACE was precluded from seeming to be making a direct request for information this was as far as it could go.

Thus the largest nation in which slavery was still legal was sheltered from further scrutiny by the League committee. The British were from the outset sceptical about the value of the regulations. At first, however, all seemed well. The Saudis appointed the inspector general of police in Mecca as slavery inspector and put the police in charge of the registration of slaves. Six months later, in the summer of 1937, the British minister, Reader Bullard, reported that although the regulations for the registration of slaves were being called to public attention, he feared the king could not risk fanning the existing discontent in the Hijaz by freeing unregistered slaves at the end of the first year.[31] By the end of the year, he believed some slaves had been registered and some brokers had bought licenses for £1 in gold.[32] However, in February 1938, the director of customs at Ujair told him he had never heard of the regulations, that they were unknown or ignored in eastern Arabia, and that slaves from the Makran coast were being imported with impunity by dealers from Dubai. They sailed by night to avoid British patrols, and, in their letters, referred to slaves as "carpets."

The political resident in the Persian Gulf agreed that slaves were being imported but thought the dhows were from Abu Dhabi not Dubai. He warned the shaykh that he would lose British "good offices" if it continued and ordered the navy to patrol near Abu Dhabi. Direct traffic from Persia to the Arabian Al-Hasa coast was said to have fallen off due to British vigilance.[33] The news was discouraging, but the British were reluctant to become once more watchdogs over Saudi slavery. However, as will be seen, their representatives in the Persian Gulf took strong action.[34] By the end of 1938, after a man manumitted by the legation some years earlier returned to Jiddah and was re-enslaved, the British concluded that the regulations were not observed even in Jiddah,[35] and Bullard commented acidly if the Saudis turned "Philby [an Englishman living in Arabia and advisor to Ibn Saud] into a harem eunuch . . . we should have to remain silent."[36]

Further research is needed to establish the actual impact of the regulations, but certainly by 1938, the British, while glad to be rid of the annoyance and expense that consular manumission had caused them over many years, did not think that the Saudis were seriously enforcing them and, as will be seen, the slave trade remained active during the ensuing decades.

BREAKTHROUGH IN YEMEN

With Yemen there had been a breakthrough since 1932. On the one hand Imam Yahya's relations with Ibn Saud had become increasingly strained after the latter occupied, and then, in 1930, annexed, Asir, and hostilities were expected. On the other, the use of air power was having an impact on the imam's influence in the Aden Protectorate and his willingness to evacuate areas he claimed. In need of British friendship and recognition of his independence, he signed the treaty of Sana'a in 1934. This ended long and tortuous negotiations dating from 1921. Several draft treaties had included articles against the African slave trade, but attempts to include them were dropped in 1926. Negotiations for the treaty were well under way when the Anti-Slavery Society reminded the Foreign Office that the League had asked members to include commitments against the slave trade in their treaties with Arabian rulers. The Colonial Office was reluctant to jeopardize a long hoped for treaty of friendship and mutual cooperation for the sake of a probably illusionary cause. The Foreign Office pressed the point. Not only would it establish a valuable principle, but it was also a League requirement. Eventually in a separate exchange of notes the imam agreed to prohibit the import of Africans by sea and stated that he would instruct his governors to prevent it.[37]

He then retired once more into splendid isolation. British fears that he might be drawn into close relations with Italy were laid to rest, first by their own agreement with Italy in 1927 binding them to consult each other over their Arabian policy and then by the imam's determination to keep his kingdom insulated from the outside world. The British had no means of monitoring the effectiveness of their treaty, but the imam had impressed them with his establishment of law and order in his now highly centralized state and the fact that caravans could travel safely in his territory. Even if he did not fulfil his obligation, they had at least met the League's requirement and the wishes of the Anti-Slavery Society. They hastened to give the notes publicity at home and at the League.[38]

In preparing their information for the ACE's session in 1936, the British considered whether or not to supply information about Yemen. Strangely the Colonial Office thought they should, but the Foreign Office did not want to depart from their practice of not sending information on foreign countries. They were even wary of giving Maxwell, upon whose discretion they felt they could rely, the very scanty information they had.[39] This came from the frontier officer in Aden, who visited Yemen, but found people reluctant to discuss the question without permission from Zeidi officials.[40] The imam was described as "too suspicious and fanatical" to pass on details of an institution which was part of the social, religious, and economic system and was permitted by Shari'a law. Their information was thus sketchy. Out of an estimated population of three million, there were believed to be only some four thousand, five hundred members of the slave class, and of these only 50–60 percent were still legally slaves. The rest had been freed. Ninety percent of them lived among the Sunni Shafeis of the coastal belt or Tihama. The remainder were slaves of the highland Shia Zeidis. The majority were Africans born in Yemen, and the rest mostly Africans who had been imported. A very small number were of mixed descent, and a very few were Caucasian. None were pure Arab. Most were farmers, but some were soldiers, shepherds, porters, fishermen, and laborers, and a few managed their owners' businesses. Their lot was not considered particularly hard. Little was known of the incidence of manumission, but it was perhaps decreasing as the decline in imports in the previous five years had increased slave values. There was no known public slave market. Transactions took place privately in secret. No cases had recently come to light of slave trading to the Aden Protectorate and imports were thought to have declined due to lost purchasing power as the result of the depression and of naval vigilance.

Since Yemen was an independent country, this information was not sent to the ACE and its report merely stated that the committee would like to know more about the steps taken to end the slave trade in view of the undertaking given by the imam at the time of the Treaty of Sana'a. It also commented on the fact that Yemen had not acceded to the 1926 convention.[41] Similarly, no information was furnished and thus no comments of note could be included in the reports for 1937 or 1938.

THE RED SEA SLAVE TRADE AND THE PILGRIMAGE

As far as the slave trade across the Red Sea was concerned, the navy continued to visit native craft, cruising thousands of miles without finding slaves. Officers were often suspicious that the small children on board might be captives, but, even though they now had interpreters, they could not be sure. From time to time the navy was given tips that slaves were about to be embarked or had landed, but no captures were made. The French and Italians still insisted that they were supervising their coasts adequately, but the navy complained that they were not cooperating. Although they had not caught a slaver since 1922, officers were convinced that their patrols deterred slavers. The British memorandum for the ACE emphasized this and the need for a joint intelligence service on the Red Sea coast.[42]

Maxwell tried to get information on slavery in Egypt and pressed for Egyptian cooperation against the Red Sea slave trade and for an Egyptian report to the League. However, he was assured that slavery and the slave trade no longer existed in Egypt therefore there was no need for reports and that Egypt, while not specifically mounting slave trade patrols, policed water holes along the coast which slavers would have to use and this was enough to prevent the traffic.

As for pilgrims, various measures had been taken to ensure they were not enslaved. Nigeria, for instance, had instituted an elaborate system of passports in 1933 and required them to deposit funds to cover their expenses and return fares. The Inter-Sanitary Conference held in Alexandria in 1927 had ruled that they should only travel in steamers or motorboats. The British tried to force them to go through Suakin and take a steamer to Jiddah. Many, however, still came by dhow from Massawa to small ports on the Arabian coast that could not be supervised. The Italians were reluctant to force them onto steamers, as it would affect the ferryboat industry from Eritrea to Arabia. They insisted pilgrims should have the right to travel by dhow provided they landed at specified ports in the Hijaz that could be supervised.[43]

The Italo-Ethopian war had its impact on the situation in the Red Sea. Any discussion of cooperation with France and Italy as suggested by the ACE, together with ideas of a joint intelligence service or mutual patrolling of territorial waters were ruled out by the Foreign Office.[44] From September 1935 to the spring of 1936, ships were withdrawn from the antislavery patrol for more urgent duties connected with the war. Patrolling was partially resumed in the early summer of 1936. In the nine months ending on 31 December 1936, only one sloop had been on duty. It had covered over eight thousand miles, examined only eight suspects, and found no slavers.[45] In 1937 patrols covered over fourteen thousand miles, and examined thirteen suspects, again without results. By 1938, Harris, with typical lack of realism, was asking the Foreign Office to suggest that Italy should declare the slave trade piracy and be invited to join Britain in antislavery patrols.[46] Patrolling continued through 1938, but since no slaver had been caught since 1922, the Royal Navy asked and received permission merely to send its slave patrol reports to the Foreign Office annually instead of quarterly.[47]

The lack of captures, the fact that Italy was now in control of Ethiopia and presumably would cut off this once fertile source of slaves, the new Saudi regulations and the undertaking of the imam of Yemen to prohibit imports of Africans, all fuelled hope that this traffic was now moribund. At the ACE in 1936, the French again emphasized that they were keeping a close watch on the Somali coast and were now using aerial patrols. Moreno said that even if it was established that a small-scale traffic still existed, "not the slightest portion of it came from Italian territory." The committee duly noted the information sent in by the British about the miles they patrolled and suggested again that it would "welcome special agreements . . . for still closer cooperation" between the European powers, without actually recommending an international convention. As Moreno said, local authorities could agree to cooperate without raising the legal and other questions that made it difficult for governments to negotiate treaties. In 1937 the ACE "contented itself" with merely inviting attention to the matter and it did not mention it in its report for 1938.[48]

BRITAIN AND SLAVERY IN THE PERSIAN GULF

Before the first session of the ACE in 1935, Gohr wrote to Maxwell asking if the British intended to send the ACE official information on the Persian Gulf and the Aden Protectorate.[49] Maxwell, anxious not to convey the impression that he or his government were concealing anything,[50] sent the Foreign Office a memorandum he had prepared for the ACE on slavery in the whole Arabian Peninsula, based on previous League reports and published sources.[51] Perhaps by covering the entire subject he hoped to put the question of the British "satellites" into a larger perspective.

He estimated the total numbers of slaves at around seventy thousand, of whom forty thousand were in Saudi Arabia. He suggested trying to persuade Arabian rulers to forbid all imports of first generation ("captive") slaves, and set a date for freeing those already in the country. Compensation, if necessary, might be negotiated by the League. As for domestic slaves (those born into or enslaved in early childhood), he hoped the *ulama* (religious leaders), might issue a *fatwa* (religious pronouncement) urging owners to treat them in accordance with the dictates of the Qur'an. He suggested that allowing them to ransom themselves might be an acceptable way to free them and their children gradually. Foreign Office officials rejected his proposals. They believed that Arabian rulers had no desire to end slavery and would resent suggestions from the League, particularly on Muslim law, and would be offended at Maxwell's remarks on the moral degradation and inefficiency of slavery, and the poor treatment of slaves, much of which they believed to be untrue. Maxwell pointed out that no reports had been submitted by the government on "Trucial Oman" whose shaykhs he said were "protected and subsidized" by Britain and regretted that Britain had not done more to end slavery in these states or the Aden Protectorate.

The Foreign Office persuaded him not to send his memorandum to the ACE, but when he insisted on accurate information in case of attack, they corrected it for his use only.[52] Neither the India Office nor the Colonial Office would give him a written description of the situation for the ACE. Their problem was that their policies were in a state of flux as the result of the fast changing world order.

By the beginning of 1935, geopolitical considerations were forcing them to rethink their policy in the Persian Gulf, which was still based on principles laid down in the nineteenth century when Persia was weak and divided and gunboat diplomacy prevailed. The India Office was still responsible for local policy and the British resident, dubbed jokingly "governor of the Gulf," was still stationed at Bushire in Persia—a relic of the gunboat diplomacy of the past. Now, with Persia a rising and increasingly nationalistic power, the Foreign Office considered his position would soon become untenable. Rather than wait until he was forced to withdraw, they wanted to move the residency to Bahrain, to which the Royal Navy had already transferred its base. They were also anxious to tighten control over the shaykdoms on the western shore of the Gulf, where their treaty rights were so indeterminate as to baffle even the Foreign Office. But the India Office, with limited resources in the area, still insisted it could only take responsibility for preventing maritime hostilities between the shaykhdoms, suppressing the slave and arms trades, and protecting British subjects.

The Foreign Office and the Air Ministry were challenging this, realizing that they might have to protect their fast developing air routes to the east, and defend the shaykhdoms from overland attack if Saudi Arabia should extend its frontier claims. Moreover, the legal officers of the Crown pronounced that in international law these states were as much under British sovereignty as the rulers of the Aden Protectorate with whom the same kind of treaties existed. By 1935, the prospect of oil concessions for largely British-owned companies in Abu Dhabi and Dubai as well as Qatar made it desirable for Britain to assume responsibility for the internal affairs of all these little states and to define their frontiers.[53]

If the British assumed such responsibilities, they would have to acknowledge that they were countenancing slavery as a legal institution in areas under their domination. It was clear that any attempt to end it would be resisted. When, for instance, the British political agent in Kuwait was negotiating for an airport in Sharjah in 1932, he found the shaykh and his neighbors fearful that this would open the way to interference in their internal affairs and particularly with slavery. Slaves were common, were widely used as pearl divers, and were said to be more harshly treated on the Trucial Coast than elsewhere on the Arabian littoral.[54]

When the ACE met in April 1935, the India and Foreign Offices had not reached agreement on future policy and, as in 1932, they did not want attention drawn to the status of these states, for fear it might raise questions of sovereignty, and of rights of interference in their internal affairs. They refused to give Maxwell a memorandum explaining the position to the ACE. They only authorized him to tell his colleagues that there were treaties against the slave trade with all the Gulf States except Kuwait, copies of which were only sent at the last minute, together with maps showing "tribal boundaries" insofar as these were known.[55] He was asked to resist suggestions that a treaty might be negotiated with Kuwait, and to assure the committee that the presence of the British political agent was sufficient to check internal slave trading.

The same problems arose over Muscat and Oman. It was always described as independent, but, as has been seen, it had its own "special treaty relations with Britain." There was also a slave trade treaty binding the sultan to end all slave imports and public sales, and protect freed slaves. However, the India Office acknowledged that there was still "a small trickle" of imported slaves,[56] and wanted minimal attention called to it.

By 1936, however, the Foreign Office had overcome the reluctance of the India Office to admit responsibility for the internal affairs of the shaykhdoms,[57] and to send an official report to the League. The Foreign Office feared that the Italian member of the ACE might suggest that, if the Gulf States were independent, they should be given a chance to reply to the British reports, in the same way that the ACE had insisted that Ethiopia must comment on the Italian report before it could be considered. If the British wanted to retain influence in the Gulf and "keep foreign powers out" they had to admit ultimate responsibility. The Foreign Office now informed the League secretariat that Britain controlled the foreign relations of the shaykhdoms and they could only be communicated with through British channels.[58]

This removed some of the smoke screen over the Gulf, but did not lead to honest reporting. The Foreign Office stressed that Britain had virtually stamped out the slave traffic in the Gulf,[59] omitting the India Office's cautious admission that one or two slaves were occasionally imported on ordinary trading dhows from Baluchistan, or slipped in from Saudi Arabia. They claimed that the shaykh of Kuwait, with whom there was still no treaty, had "completely stamped out the sale of new slaves, however secretly imported," a caveat to which Maxwell objected. They said no slavery or slave trading existed in Bahrain. Slaves recently manumitted there had been recently imported. In "Trucial Oman" and Qatar, where the India Office admitted that the rulers had only "very limited" control and there "might" be a "small and intermittent traffic," the report stated that since no slaves had been discovered in recent naval searches, the seaborne trade must be negligible. At the ACE, Marchand commented that if he had not shot a tiger in the jungle it did not mean there were none. There had been no captures in Muscat waters, and the sultan was "well disposed to the suppression of the traffic." The admission that he had no "effective control" over the Batinah coast was left out.

Replying to the questions asked by the ACE in 1935 about the condition of slaves in the Gulf States, the report maintained that household slaves, who included bodyguards, coffee makers, and domestics, were often better off than the free poor, but the condition of industrial slaves—the date gardeners and the far more numerous pearl fishermen—was less satisfactory because the pearl industry had been hit by the depression. However, slaves were better off then free divers, who had to provide for themselves for eight months of the year between seasons. Conditions in general were improving. There had been around two thousand slaves in Kuwait in 1930, mostly household slaves born in captivity, but numbers had dropped because the shaykh—an enlightened and humane ruler—protected them and bought their freedom if he could not solve their grievances. Only about a hundred were pearl fishermen and these could keep their profits like the free.[60] In Bahrain, pearl divers were no longer in hereditary debt-bondage to the captains of fishing boats.[61] In the Trucial shaykhdoms and Qatar, slavery was common and several thousand were pearl fishermen. There was no public market but slaves sometimes changed hands. However, they could apply for manumission to the agent of the British at Sharjah. In the independent state of Muscat, there were unknown numbers of domestic and industrial slaves, of whom perhaps five hundred were pearl fishermen, half the estimate of five years earlier.

The report ended with the doubtful assertion that no one needed to remain in servitude. There were no gangs, no overseers, and opportunities for escape were frequent. A fugitive had only to reach the British authorities in Muscat, Bahrain, or Sharjah, or clamber onto a British sloop. That the numbers requesting manumission were small and declining showed that most slaves were content. The presence of British agents and the possibility of manumission was said to be ameliorating the lot of the remaining slaves.[62] No information was included on the total numbers in captivity.

Maxwell thought it "a little optimistic" to believe that no slave need remain in captivity.[63] He was suspicious of the report and embarrassed by his colleagues' criticisms of British policy and requests for more information. Before the 1937 session of the ACE, he pressured the India Office for more details on the origins of manumitted slaves, on the condition of born slaves and pearl divers, and on the prosecution of slavers. He wanted the shaykhs to declare that the buying, selling, and possession of captured slaves were criminal offenses. He asked why, if there was no slavery in Bahrain, they could not issue a proclamation to that effect.[64]

He made little headway in 1937, but the next year, the India Office provided figures showing that most recently manumitted slaves were domestic slaves, who had not been captured themselves, and claimed this proved that "the slave trade as such in the Persian Gulf *practically no longer exists*,"[65] just the kind of qualified statement that infuriated

Maxwell. They reported, however, that the child of a slave in Umm-al-Qawain had been sold to a Nagdji in Dubai in 1937, and had been recovered with the help of the rulers of the two states. This highlighted the unsatisfactory legal position in the Gulf States, where, except for Muscat, existing treaties merely bound the rulers to prohibit the import of slaves and agree to their shipping being searched at sea.[66] The British could not legally take direct action against enslavements or sales in or between the Trucial States.

The India Office considered the problem in 1937, but decided that the rulers would not want to negotiate new treaties and that slaves could always apply to British officials for manumission. The suppression of the internal traffic, therefore, continued to depend on the cooperation of the shaykhs. The Foreign Office worried that, since they were British "vassals," other powers would regard it as Britain's duty to end the trade. The India Office report, moreover, did not mention that slave traders were only fined and/or deported, because there were no prisons on the Trucial Coast and rulers normally kept offenders in the stocks or in irons for a few days. They considered the fines adequate punishment.[67]

On one point Maxwell won a handsome victory. The shaykh of Bahrain issued a proclamation reminding the public that owning slaves was forbidden. Officials had decided that a mere reminder would not damage his standing, and would please Maxwell. There was also a sentence or two on pearl divers and on the various forms of manumission in the shaykhdoms. The political resident in the Gulf was now taking the ACE seriously enough to prepare the 1938 report himself, but he made it clear that, together with earlier reports, the ACE now had all the information that he could produce, short of testing the waters by becoming a slave himself.[68]

However, at the very time the ACE recorded in its 1938 report that the slave trade in the Gulf "practically" no longer existed,[69] evidence was received in London showing that it was not as moribund as the India Office claimed.

SLAVERY IN THE ADEN PROTECTORATE

In 1935 Aden and its surroundings were under the dual control of the Colonial and India Offices. Much of the Protectorate was still not administered or even visited although it stretched from Perim to the border of Muscat and Oman, and northwards to Yemen and the edge of the Rub' al Kali desert; its northern frontiers were not defined, and little was known about its people. In fact the Hadhramaut had only recently been considered as British territory. The Royal Air Force had taken over the defense of Aden in 1927 and air strikes now provided a powerful weapon against recalcitrant rulers, opening the way to closer control. In Lahej, the sultan was willing to forbid the import of new slaves. Elsewhere there were treaties against the slave trade with some rulers, including the Qu'ati shaykh of Mukalla and Shihr, but they were out of date and there was no British presence to see that they were enforced. The resident in Aden did not want to negotiate new ones that he could not enforce, especially as he thought there was no significant slave trade, or import traffic. Slavery was pervasive, but slaves were, he insisted, generally well treated and rulers relied on slave soldiers to control "refractory tribesmen." The most disturbed and backward areas were those whose chiefs did not have slave armies, and slaves were reliable governors of outlying areas.[70] These royal slaves were highly privileged and would resent any change in their status. The sultan of Shihr and Mukalla had wanted to free his slave soldiers and officials in 1924 because they were expensive to feed and house. However, he needed their support and could not afford to compensate them for their freedom. The Colonial Office had refused to give him a loan for this purpose and in 1935 he still could not afford to free them.

In parts of the Hadhramaut the inhabitants were locked into local vendettas and warfare was chronic. It was 1934 before the first British official, Harold Ingrams, was sent there to study political conditions and pacify the country. His first report on slavery had not been received when the ACE met in 1935.[71] Maxwell was told that he could inform the ACE orally that there was no regular slave trade in Lahej, that the sultan was determined to end the import of slaves, and that domestic slavery was decreasing.[72] He was to emphasize that Britain had only just sent the first officials to visit the remoter parts of the Hadhramaut. If the ACE were critical, he could suggest that it might recommend that Britain "bear in mind the possibility of negotiating treaties against the slave trade" in the Protectorate.[73] He protested that his colleagues would not be satisfied with anything less than a statement that the British intended to negotiate treaties with all the Protectorate rulers in order to comply with the 1926 Convention. He could hardly comment on Ethiopia's failure to carry out its obligations if his own government had not done so. The Colonial Office, irritated at the idea of criticism, would only say that, if it appeared as a result of consultations with the resident in Aden, further steps were required, they would take them. The Foreign Office thought Maxwell's remarks justified and foresaw that the Colonial Office would have to take action.[74]

The British, with some embarrassment, produced the first detailed reports on the slave trade and slavery in the Aden Protectorate only in 1936. Harold Ingrams reported that slave imports by sea had virtually ceased, except perhaps for an occasional victim kidnapped in East Africa.[75] The only treaties against the import trade—those with Shihr and Mukalla, and the Lower Aulaqi sultan, were dead letters, but he was sure that treaties could be negotiated with the various rulers. This would put the matter on "a legal basis" and set an example for other Arab powers. There was a problem, however, for which he did not suggest a solution. In the Hadhramaut there were several wealthy men who had Chinese and Javanese concubines, who by definition had to be slaves.

Overall he estimated that there were between five and ten thousand slaves—three thousand of them in the eastern protectorate. The spread was uneven. Some peoples had none.[76] Others used them mainly as soldiers, but some were domestics and farm hands. The soldiers and officials—royal slaves—were so expensive that the ruler of Lahej had freed all but a hundred. The sultan of Shihr and Mukalla still had several hundred he wanted to liberate, and a cadet corps for their sons.[77] Slaves were not the lowest social category, were not liable to be killed in the endemic blood feuds, and were generally well treated. Possibly, however, they suffered worse penalties than the free. Three had been tortured in Lahej and a twelve-year-old boy had been saved from burning by a political officer. Moreover, they were traded. In the Hadhramaut they were sold at fairs along with livestock.

The resident in Aden forwarded this report and proposed to discuss treaties against the slave trade with the various rulers.[78] He particularly wanted to end sales at fairs, and give slaves the right to claim manumission. The sultan of Lahej warned that the *ulama* would claim that this was illegal under Shar'ia law, and rulers would have to protect themselves by saying they were being forced to take action by order of the British government.

The Colonial and Foreign Offices were dismayed by this report. They had not realized that there were so many slaves or that they might be ill-treated. "No amount of re-drafting," minuted one official dismally, "can gloss over the fact that the situation is unsatisfactory" and when published may produce "a small but embarrassing storm in humanitarian circles."[79] The Foreign Office, therefore, edited its report,[80] cutting the estimated number of slaves to four to five thousand, stressing that they were well treated, and stating that they now proposed to end abuses and gradually attack slavery itself. This would take time because the rulers were "semi-independent" and the area was not directly administered.

In 1937, the Colonial Office reported the good news that the leading sultans in the Aden Protectorate had agreed to issue proclamations against the import of slaves by sea.[81] Lesser rulers had been asked to follow suit and those inland were to be requested to prohibit overland imports. The leading rulers had also agreed to end sales at fairs and to grant slaves manumission on demand. To Maxwell's gratification, negotiations were under way to make the buying or owning of captured slaves a criminal offense, carrying heavy penalties. The Colonial Office also reduced its estimate of the number of slaves from five to ten thousand to four or five thousand, claiming that the higher figure was the result of the frequent use of the term "slave" to cover people of slave descent. Freed slaves were said to be easily absorbed into the free population.

In this year, the Colonial Office, hitherto in charge only of the Protectorate, took over the colony of Aden from the India Office, and stepped up the pace of integration between the two. Relationships with protectorate rulers were strengthened and their powers boosted. Their forces were reorganized as "Tribal Guards" armed and financed by the British. Recalcitrant "tribes" were bombed into submission. New airfields increased the strategic importance of south Arabia. Ingrams persuaded the leaders of the Hadhramaut to end their endemic blood feuds and agree to a truce known as "Ingram's peace." He became resident advisor with powers of manumission. This "forward policy" was facilitated by the fact that, particularly in the barren Hadhramaut, many leaders had business and other links with South and Southeast Asia and were anxious to introduce reforms.[82]

In June 1937, Ingrams sent home the first detailed report on slavery in the Hadhramaut. Slaves were owned by all classes, hence their lifestyles were varied. He still believed most were well treated.[83] However, the daily requests for manumission he received and the case histories of those he freed showed that not all were contented and, as the following testimony shows, their lives were precarious:

> Sherif Ahmad sold me to Sheikh [sic] Sali . . . [84]when I was about 13 . . . [He] changed my name to Marbruk and . . . sold me to Sheikh Salim . . . with whom I remained for three months. I was then sold to Sheikh 'Abdullah 'Ali . . . and I remained with him for nine years. He sold me to a broker . . . and after 15 days the broker sold me to Sheikh 'Abdullah bin Salih . . . with whom I remained for three years. During that time I was treated very harshly for no cause . . . [this] compelled me to ask . . . [him] to sell me. He threatened to shoot me, and kicked me and beat me so badly that I was unable to move for four days. When I recovered . . . my master continued his ill treatment of me. . . . Finally I decided to run away in order to save my life. Bin Ja'fer accepted me and treated me like one of his own sons. . . . My mother . . . lived at Wadi al Ashraf . . . but God knows whether she is still there . . . I had a stepbrother . . . but I do not know . . . whether he is alive or dead.[85]

Even more disturbing was evidence that the slave trade continued. Indian children sent to the Hadhramaut for religious education had been recently enslaved on arrival. Chinese concubines had been brought from Singapore. Indian women had been sold by their husbands. Africans had been imported as servants and then sold. Free Arabs in the protectorate had been abducted. A dealer brought victims from Habban twice a year to sell in Mukalla.

By August 1937, Ingrams was worrying about what to do with the increasing numbers who were likely to ask for manumission. Wage labor in the colony was limited, and many were not strong enough to load ships.[86] He suggested establishing a clearinghouse for them in Aden, from which the soldiers could be absorbed into the Tribal Guards, and the cultivators sent to other British territories.[87] Funds were earmarked for this, but, as will be seen, sending ex-slaves to Africa was to prove more difficult than repatriating Indians.

The Colonial Office was not as dismayed by this report as the last one for the simple reason that it suited them. Their "forward policy" had been attacked in the press,[88] and, as an official minuted:

> The widespread existence of slavery in the Protectorate, and in particular the instances here given of child slaves being introduced from India and Malaya, add an additional ar-

gument in favor of our policy of extending our influence in the Protectorate, and of securing where possible, the acceptance of British Advisors by the more important rulers. We cannot long continue to plead before the League of Nations our inability to enforce the gradual extinction of slavery throughout the Protectorate. We have secured the issue by certain Rulers of salutary laws; but except through fairly close supervision we cannot guarantee that those laws are strictly observed.[89]

Supported by the Foreign Office, they requested £50 from the Treasury for an inquiry in the Mahra and Wahidi regions in the far east of the Protectorate, where Ingrams suspected there was a considerable slave trade.[90]

Ingrams's report was not communicated to the ACE in 1938, although Maxwell was kept in close touch with developments. The committee was told that progress was being made in getting the rulers to impose severe penalties for owning captured slaves; and they were informed of proposals that Ingrams had discussed with the leading sultans. These included outlawing the slave trade, registering slaves, manumitting them on demand, accepting fugitives, and stipulating that the children of slaves "belonged" to their parents. Ingrams believed that since most victims had been illegally enslaved, as they were not infidels taken in war, the rulers would accept these proposals, especially as Islam favored manumission and the "enlightened classes" regarded the splitting up of families as "contrary to the Shar'ia."[91] A new era seemed to have begun in South Arabia, and the ACE in its report proposed to follow developments with the "greatest interest."

By 1938, the British were no longer manumitting slaves in Saudi Arabia, and the Saudis and Yemen had given undertakings to suppress the African slave trade. The Red Sea traffic was believed to be minimal. On paper at least much had been achieved since the League had taken up the question. However, in the British satellites on the Persian Gulf and in the Aden Protectorate the position was far from satisfactory, and was to remain so until the 1960s.

NOTES

1. Ryan memorandum, 17 October 1933 and minutes, FO 371/16878 E 6284/5485/25; minutes on Maxwell to Stevenson, 22 February 1934, FO 371/17822 E1251/1251/91. Minutes on Blaxter (CO) to Warner, no. 37957/34, 18 January 1934, FO 371/17796 E452/22/91; Ryan to Simon no. 123, 23 April 1934, FO 371/17822 E 3121/1251/91. For the League recommendation, see W 10431/5/52 1932.

2. FO Minutes in FO 371/16875 E 1210/840/25; Simon to Ryan no. 124, 17 May 1933, and minutes, FO 371/16875 E 2491/840/25. Other problems were the lack of defined frontiers, the "primitive" organization of government, the risk of irritating Egypt, which was still excluded, and fears that it might open the way to interference by other powers, notably Italy, and lead to commissions of inquiry.

272

CHAPTER 16

3. Memorandum on slavery in Saudi Arabia by Furlonge enclosed in Ryan to Simon no. 149, 15 May 1934 and minutes, FO 371/17935 E 3764/722/25.

4. See above, chapter 12.

5. Ryan to Simon no. 14, 14 January 1935, FO 371/19009 E 760/325/25. Prophetically, Faysal was to be the ruler who abolished slavery in 1962, see below, chapter 20.

6. Many documents deal with this case, between 11 April and 19 May 1934. They are filed in FO 371/17935, beginning with E 2270/722/25 and ending with E 3287/722/25.

7. See below.

8. Calvert to Simon no. 283, 17 September 1934 and enclosures, FO 371/17936 E 6088/722/25.

9. Ogilvie Forbes to Simon, tels. nos. 28, 38 August 1934, and no. 34, 26 September 1934, FO 371/17936 E 5585/722/25 and E 6144/722/25.

10. See inter alia "Memorandum respecting Anglo-Saudi Relations as seen by Sir A. Ryan" in July 1934, and minute by Rendel for Sir George Mounsey, 5 September 1934, FO 371/17940 E 5064/2429/25; memorandum "Proposed New Comprehensive Anglo-Saudi Settlement and Question of South-Eastern Frontier of Saudi Arabia" by Rendel, 15 November 1934, ibid., E 6928/2429/25. Conversations were protracted and there are many documents on the subject in ibid., and also in FOCP 14717 (FO 406/72).

11. Minute by Warner on Maxwell to Warner confidential, 25 June 1934, FO 371/17822 E 4194/1251/91; minute by Ryan on Maxwell to Warner, 5 July 1934, FO 371/17936 E 4437/722/25.

12. Minutes on Maxwell to Warner, 5 July 1934, FO 371/17936 E 4437/722/25; minutes on "Memorandum on Slavery in Saudi Arabia" by Furlonge, enclosed in Ryan to Simon no. 149, 15 May 1934, ibid., E 3764/722/25.

13. Minutes by Simon, 1 August 1934, FO 371/17936 E 5031/722/25; memorandum and note by Rendel, 23 October 1934, minute by Simon, 3 December 1934, and Simon to Ryan no. 452, 13 December 1934, ibid., E 6510/722/25; note by Ryan, 23 October 1934, ibid., E6522/722/25.

14. Simon to Ryan no. 452, 13 December 1934, FO 371/17936 E6510/722/25.

15. Ryan to Eden, no. 131, 4 May 1936, FO 371/20062 E 3186/486/25.

16. Ryan to FO, tel. no. 8, 9 January 1936, and minutes, FO 371/20058 E 131/131/25; Ryan to Eden tel. no. 23, 11 February 1936, and minutes, ibid., E 767/131/25; Ryan to Eden, tel. no. 28, 24 February 1936 and minutes, ibid., E1035/131/28. The Anglo-Italian *bon voisinage* agreement of 1938 actually guaranteed Saudi and Yemeni independence.

17. Minutes by Rendel 1 and 2 January 1936, on Ryan to Hoare, no. 228, 28 December 1935, FO 371/19010 E 7546/325/25.

18. Vansittart minute, 23 July 1935, FO 371/19009, E 4639/325/25.

19. They suggested 1925, the year the Saudis came to power, and then 1934, the date of the treaty with Yemen.

20. Eden to Simon, immediate, 26 February 1936, and Ryan to Eden tel. no. 26, 24 February 1936, and minutes, FO 371/20058 E 1035/131/25.

21. Of the 130 slaves manumitted by the legation between 1 January 1930 and 30 April 1935, 29 were locally born as slaves. The most recently enslaved was an Ethiopian pilgrim sold in 1931. Most of the rest had been in slavery for many years and came from as far away as Wadai and Nigeria. Calvert to Hoare, no. 203, 13 July 1935, FO 371/19009 E 4749/325/25.

22. Memorandum by Ryan on Anglo-Saudi negotiations, enclosed in Ryan to Eden, no. 122, 27 April 1936, FO 371/20058 E 2832/131/25; Calvert to Eden, no. 198, 4 July 1936, FO 371/20059 E 4596/131/25.

23. All important documents on these long negotiations cannot be cited, but see particularly the following: Ryan to Simon, no. 137, 6 May 1935, enclosing notes exchanged with Fuad Hamza, FO 371/19009 E 3296/325/25; record of private conversation between Ryan and Fuad Hamza, 4 July 1935, ibid., E 4163/325/25; Ryan memorandum, 13 July 1935, enclosed draft agreement and minutes, ibid., E 4217/325/25; draft Saudi Regulation on Slavery, 19 July 1935, and Ryan comments, 9 August 1935, ibid., E 4644/325/25; Ryan to Eden tel. no. 23, 11 February 1936, and minutes, ibid., E 767/131/25; Ryan to Eden, tel. no. 28. 24 February 1936 and minutes, ibid., E1035/131/25. A useful summary is in a memorandum in FO 371/20069 E5053/131/25. Further documents are in FO 371/19009, FO 371/19010, FO 371/20058, and FO 371/20059.

24. Bullard to Eden, no. 278, 6 October 1936, and enclosures FO371/20059 E 6720/131/25.

25. Bullard to Eden, no. 333, 31 December 1936, FO 371/20838 E 579/92/25.

26. ACE Report LON C.189 (i). M.145.1936.VI; p. 15, and annex 4; ACE minutes, pp. 19–22, C.C.E.E. 3rd session, P.V. 2, LON 6B/25052/8000 R4153.

27. Notes by Maxwell on the Report of the Slavery Committee, 28 April 1936, FO 371/20517 W 3735/154/52; ACE minutes, C.C.E.E. 3rd Session, P.V. 2, p. 1, LON 6B/25052/8000.

28. ACE minutes, C.C.E.E./4th session, P.V. 2 LON 6B 29848/8000.

29. LON C.188.M.173.1937.VI, annexes 1 and 6.

30. Minute by Rendel, 7 July 1936, on Maxwell's notes on the Report of the Slavery Committee, FO 371/20517 W 3735/154/52.

31. Bullard to Eden, no. 102, 24 May 1937, FO 371/20840 E 3205/202/25.

32. Bullard to Eden, no. 173, 29 November 1937, and minutes, FO 371/20840 E 7445/202/25.

33. Bullard to Eden, no. 34, 22 February 1938, FO 371/21907 E 1403/1403/25; Fowle note, 11 April 1938, enclosed in IO to FO no. PZ 2044/38, 16 April 1938, ibid., E 2208/1403/25.

34. IO to FO no. PZ 2044/38, 16 April 1938, and minutes and FO to IO, 9 May 1938, FO 371/21907 E/2208/1404/25.

35. Minute on Bullard to Halifax, no. 207, 1 November 1938, FO 371/21907 E 6915/1403/25.

36. Bullard to Baggallay, 4 September 1938, FO 371/21907 E 5061/1403/25, referring to H. St. John Philby.

37. Note by Rendel, 2 January 1934, FO 371/17796; Blaxter to Warner, 18 January 1934, ibid., E 452/22/91. The text of the notes exchanged on 10 February 1934 are in FO 371/17936 E 6510/722/25.

38. Reilly to CO no. 50 secret, enclosed in CO to FO no. 37957/1/34, 23 March 1934, and minutes on treaty, FO 371/17796 E 1920/22/91.

39. Blaxter to Brennan, 12 February 1936, and minutes, FO 371/19969 E 819/33/91.

40. Replies to the questionnaire relating to the system of slavery in the Yemen enclosed in resident Aden to CO, 26 May 1936, no. 236, enclosed in CO to FO, 4 November 1936, FO 371/19969 E 6934/133/91 and minutes.

41. ACE Report 1936, LON C.189 (i). M.145.1936.VI., pp. 15, 22.

42. ASAPS to FO, 21 March 1935, enclosed memorandum for the ACE and minutes, FO 371/19731 W 2596/426/52.

43. Graham to Simon, no. 330, 27 April 1932, FO 371/16121 J 1187/254/16; Ryan to Simon no. 286, 8 July 1932, ibid.; Report of Pilgrimage Commission of meeting October 1933, enclosed in Ministry of Health to FO, 30 November 1933, FO 371/17028 J 2808/854/16. Minutes of the ACE, LON C.C.E.E./2nd Session/P.V. 3, 2 April 1935.

44. Admiralty to FO, 17 September 1935 and FO minute, FO 371/19734 W 8191/426/52.

45. Admiralty to FO, 3 April 1937, FO 371/20927 J 1575/22/1.

46. Harvey minute for Halifax, March 1938, and minute by Lampson, 7 March 1938, FO 371/22029 J 830/537/1.

47. Admiralty to FO, 14 November 1938, FO 371/22029 J 4253/537/1.

48. See ACE reports for 1936, p. 4, LON C.189 (i). M.145.1936.VI; for 1937, LN C.188.M.173. 1937.VI, p. 9.

49. Gohr to Maxwell enclosed in Maxwell to FO, 4 February 1935, FO 371/19731 W 1083/426/52.

50. Maxwell to FO, 9 March 1935, FO 371/18915 E 1618/280/91.

51. Note upon slavery in Arabia, enclosed in Maxwell to FO, 30 January 1935, FO 371/18915 E 703/280/91. This was a second version, the first having been amended after consultation with the Foreign Office.

52. Observations on Sir George Maxwell's draft memorandum on slavery in Arabia, enclosed in FO to IO, confidential, 21 March 1935, FO 371/18915 E 1618/280/91; Maxwell to FO, 30 January 1935, ibid., E 703/280/91. IO to FO immediate, 23 March 1935, ibid., E 2038/280/91; Ryan to Simon no. 14, 14 January 1935, FO 371/19009 E 760/325/25.

53. See inter alia Knatchbull-Hugessen to Rendel, private, 26 February 1935, and minutes, and Rendel to Knatchbull-Hugessen, 18 April 1935, FO 371/18911 E 1891/247/91; Fowle to foreign secretary, Government of India, 16 November 1934, and Government of India to secretary of state for India, tel. 22, April 1935, ibid., E 3802/247/91.

54. Dickson to IO, 4 August 1932, FO 371/16504 W 9759/5/52.

55. See above, chapter 14.

56. IO to FO 7 January 1935, FO 371/18915, pp. 100–104.

57. IO to FO, 27 February 1936, and minutes and enclosures, FO 371/20517 W 1832/154/52. For the history of this question, see above, chapter 11.

58. FO minute recording conversation with de Haller, 27 March 1936, FO 371/20517 W2844/154/52. For the Italo-Ethiopian problem, see above, chapter 15.

59. Annex 8 to Report of the Advisory Committee of Experts on Slavery, LON C.189 (1). M.145.1936.VI.

60. This information was based on an express letter from the political agent in Kuwait to the political resident in Bushire, no. C-343, confidential, 5 December 1935, FO 371/19969, pp. 111–12. The resident had added that only the nobility had slaves and they were trusted members of their families and would not dream of exchanging their positions for the uncertain lot of a free man.

61. This information came from the political resident in Bahrain who said that the pearl fishermen had indeed been virtual slaves until some fifteen years earlier. Descendants of slaves formed a large and useful part of the community and, although free, were still called "Abd" to distinguish them from other groups. Political resident, Bahrain, to political resident, Bushire no. C/606-20/1, 14 December 1935, FO 371/19969, p. 113.

62. Manumission statistics for the whole area from 1929 to 1934 showed a high of seventy-seven in 1929 declining to between fifty and sixty in subsequent years, with a low of forty-two in 1933. These figures do not include manumissions on the Persian side of the Gulf; see note for Sir G. Maxwell, enclosed in IO to FO, 27 February 1936, FO 371/20517 W1832/154/52.

63. Maxwell to FO, 28 April 1936, FO 371/20517 W3735/154/52.

64. Maxwell to Walton, 30 July 1936, enclosed in IO to FO, 14 October 1936, FO 371/19969 E6505/133/91.

65. Italics are mine.

66. The provisions of these treaties are reviewed in Treaty Provisions in the Persian Gulf as regards Slavery, by Fowle (political resident, Bushire), 22 February 1937, enclosed in IO to FO, PZ2603/37, 22 April 1937, FO 371/20775 E 225/68/91; see also Fowle to Walton, 12 June 1937, enclosed in IO to FO, PZ 4248/37, 14 July 1937, ibid., E 4039/68/91. Muscat was an exception because in 1873 the sultan had issued a proclamation forbidding all traffic in slaves

and hence he could be pressed "to make good this proclamation." In Bahrain, the situation was satisfactory because slavery was not recognized by law. There was still no treaty with Kuwait.

67. IO to FO, PZ 4248/37, 14 June 1938, enclosure and minutes, FO 371/20775 E 4039/68/91; Fowle to Walton, 12 June 1937, enclosed in IO to FO PZ4248/37, 14 July 1937, ibid. The money was subsequently returned to the sheikhs as it was considered that it rightfully belonged to the local administration

68. Fowle to IO, confidential, 16 August 1937, enclosed in IO to FO, 28 August 1937, FO 371/20775 E 5049/68/91.

69. ACE Report 1938, LON C.112.1938.VI, p. 7.

70. CO to FO, 7 February 1935, and Reilly to CO, 28 November 1934, FO 371/18915 E 893/280/91; CO to Maxwell, confidential, 27 March 1935, ibid.; Reilly to Cowell, confidential, 6 March 1935, ibid.; Freya Stark, however, describes a slave governor who was despised and ignored because he was a slave, see Stark 2001, 131.

71. For a discussion of British policy in Aden see Gavin 1975, 276 ff. For Ingrams tours of the Hadhramaut, see Harold Ingrams 1966, and Doreen Ingrams 1970.

72. This was because the children of a male slave by a free wife were free and the male slave was often also freed. Reilly to Cowell, 6 March 1935, FO 371/18915, pp. 218–21. Under Muslim law the children of a free man and a concubine were usually also free.

73. CO to Maxwell, confidential, 27 March 1935, FO 371/18915.

74. Maxwell to CO, confidential 29 March 1935, and CO to Maxwell, confidential, 8 April 1935, enclosed in CO to FO, 8 April 1935, and minutes, FO 371/18915 E 2335/280/91.

75. Ingrams made the first visit to study conditions in the Hadhramaut in 1934. For his report, see Memorandum on Slavery and the Slave Trade in the Aden Protectorate by Harold Ingrams, enclosed in Thomas to CO no. 3, 8 January 1936, in CO to FO, 12 February 1936, FO 371/19969 E 189/133/91.

76. The report lists tribes with and without slaves and gives estimated minimum numbers.

77. A detailed breakdown of these numbers was not supplied by Ingrams until 1937, see Memorandum on Slavery and the Slave Trade in the Hadhramaut, 16 June 1937, enclosed in IO to FO, 11 August 1937, FO 371/20775 E 4703/68/91.They cost him 7.1/2 annas a day as against 3.1/2 for free soldiers.

78. Reilly to CO no. 3, 8 January 1936, in CO to FO, 12 February 1936, FO 371/19969 E 189/133/91.

79. Minute by Makins, 27 February 1936, FO 371/20517 W 1949/154/52.

80. The Colonial Office sent in a long report incorporating information from the various colonies as well as a few separate reports.

81. These were the sultan of Lahej, the Qu'ati sultan of Shihr and Mukalla, and the Kathiri sultan of Sai'yun. For a map and information on the divisions of the Aden Protectorate see Western Arabia and the Red Sea, Geographical Handbook Series, Naval Intelligence Division, June 1946, B.R. 527.

82. Gavin 1975, 295–306; Ingrams 1966.

83. Some doubt had now been thrown on the cases of torture and ill-treatment of slaves reported earlier by Ingrams, Reilly to colonial secretary, no. 238, 26 May 1936, enclosed in CO to FO, 4 November 1936, FO 371/19969 E 6934/133/91.

84. I have omitted the full names in the interests of brevity.

85. Slavery and the Slave Trade in the Hadhramaut, by Ingrams, 16 June 1937. Appendix II case C. enclosed in Reilly to Ormsby Gore, confidential, 30 June 1937, CO 737/78/7980.

86. Reilly to Ormsby Gore, confidential, 1 September 1937, CO 732/78/7980.

87. Memorandum by Ingrams, 23 August 1937, enclosed in Reilly to Ormsby Gore, 1 September 1937, CO 732/78/79080.

88. Warner minute, 25 August 1937, on Cowell to Baggallay, 20 August 1937, FO 371/20775 E 4930/68/91.

89. CO minute 23 July 1937, on Ingrams Report, enclosed in Reilly to Ormsby Gore, confidential, 30 June 1937, CO 732/78/79080.

90. Reilly to Ormsby Gore, 27 July 1937, CO 732/78/79080; Warner to Blaxter, 3 September 1937, FO 371/20775 E 4930/68/91.

91. Slavery and the Slave Trade in the Hadhramaut, by Ingrams, 16 June 1937, enclosed in Reilly to Ormsby Gore, confidential, 30 June 1937, CO 732/78/7980.

The Advisory Committee of Experts on Slavery 1936–1939

MAXWELL TAKES THE LEAD

The main issues discussed at the next three meetings of the Advisory Committee need only be summarized here. Normally the committee would not have met in 1938, but Maxwell engineered another extraordinary session.[1] It, therefore, met annually from 1935 to 1938.[2] It was typical of the petty economies forced on the operations of the League by the penny pinching of its supporting governments that in 1936 all committee sessions were reduced to one sitting a year. The ACE could now no longer examine its information at one meeting and prepare its report at a second one. Since discussion by post had been ruled out, members could not get through all the material, and the 1936 report, to quote Maxwell, "was knocked together in four sittings of a drafting committee of three—Marchand, Moreno, and myself, and then raced through in a final meeting."[3] In subsequent years, the sessions were even shorter but thanks to Maxwell, they were better organized and more focused.

Before all three meetings, Maxwell flooded his colleagues with summaries of the documents, and with new proposals, which he revised in the light of their comments.[4] Gohr died unexpectedly on 7 April 1936 and was succeeded by the amenable Octove Louwers, colonial advisor to the Belgian Ministry of Foreign Affairs.[5] The removal of Gohr, and hence of Lugard as the power behind the scene, enabled Maxwell to assert his leadership. He persuaded his colleagues to revise the format of their reports to reflect his classifications and recommendations.[6] His primary aim remained the freeing of "captive slaves," and at his instigation the ACE recommended setting a definite date after which it would be a criminal offense to own them. If necessary, the League might be asked to compensate owners.[7] The reports continued to advocate the manumission and good treatment of born slaves in accordance with the dictates of the Qur'an. Maxwell called other institutions "practices restrictive of the liberty of the person." He hoped to define them, and then transfer them to more powerful League bodies. These institutions included child slavery, including mui tsai, debt bondage, and serfdom. Bride wealth and other questions about the status of women and discriminatory marriage customs were ruled beyond the competence of the ACE in 1936 since they were not forms of slavery, but the way was left open to return to this if new material was presented.

In colonial territories where slavery was not recognized by law, Maxwell refused to accept the concept of "voluntary" slaves. If they had not left their owners, there must be something wrong with government policy. They must need protection, access to land or employment, or credit. He urged the Colonial Office to order a census of all former slaves in British Africa to establish how many had stayed with their owners, why they had done so, and what had become of those who had left. Before the 1937 meeting, he warned officials that the ACE—meaning himself—would make "a special feature" of the fate of former slaves. He gave notice that he would not be satisfied with vague statements such as slavery no longer exists "in the normal sense." He wanted an unequivocal declaration from each territory that there were no "persons in any status or condition resembling slavery." If a census was considered too expensive, he was prepared to accept estimates of the numbers of voluntary and freed slaves, with details of their ages, sex, and occupations,[8] and copies of all antislavery legislation. The Colonial Office, acutely aware of his ability to embarrass them, ordered governors to provide the information and take note of his recommendations. Henceforth, British reports were fuller and less evasive.[9]

SLAVERY AS REPORTED TO THE ACE: COLONIAL AFRICA

The last slave raids mentioned in the ACE reports were raids into Sudan from Ethiopia in 1936. Thereafter no raids were reported. In the Sahara, Spain and France agreed in 1937 that they were cooperating to suppress them.[10] In 1938, the French added that they were now in effective occupation of the "Algerian-Morocco confines" and had suppressed kidnapping.[11]

As for slave trading, Nigeria admitted in its 1936 report, that there was still a small-scale traffic, mainly in children, many of them sold by their parents in times of famine. In the Cross River area they were treated as adopted children and it suggested that this was really "adoption by purchase."[12] Slaves were also exported to Wadai, Kanem, and Tibesti, in French territory.[13] The French admitted reluctantly that children had indeed been exported from Mandara, on the borders of Cameroon and Northern Nigeria. A branch of the Sanusi in Borku had been a center of the traffic, which they claimed had been suppressed.[14] French and Italian soldiers and British airmen were now watching the watering places along the caravan routes.[15] The next year small-scale slave trading was still reported in Nigeria and Cameroon, but both the British and French claimed that it was declining as the result of their vigilance. The Belgians reported no convictions in the Congo since 1933.[16]

This good news led the ACE to conclude in 1937 that, apart from occasional "frontier forays" and isolated cases of kidnapping, mainly of children, slave raiding and organized trading were a thing of the past in Africa. Moreover, as has been seen, the Red Sea slave traffic was also apparently virtually at an end and the pilgrimage was better controlled.[17] The committee praised the colonial powers for their vigilance and cooperation.

As for slavery itself, the Italians and Portuguese denied that it continued in their colonies.[18] The Belgians, still busy with their inquiry, reported that it was dying out in the Congo, where only voluntary slaves remained. The French noted that in Equatorial Africa few slaves had asked for freedom in spite of offers to waive their taxes for a year and the fact that former owners had to pay them a gratuity. Some British colonies, in response to Maxwell's inquiries, produced estimates of the numbers of their "servile population."[19] In the Gambia, for instance, they were believed to number twenty to forty thousand. The Gold Coast could not give an estimate for the novel reason that neither the former slaves nor former owners would admit that they were not free!

Maxwell's vigilance paid off in the case of Northern Nigeria. Once slavery had lost its legal status, anyone born or arriving in the protectorate after 31 March 1901 had been declared free.[20] He now asked whether slaves born earlier were still slaves and had to ransom themselves if they wanted their freedom. The administration had to admit that older slaves did still have to take their cases to Islamic courts and that some were still paying ransom to former owners. As the result of his inquiries, in 1936 the government amended the original proclamation to state that everyone was free. In reply to Maxwell's request for a census, it estimated that there were 119,030 voluntary slaves,[21] but claimed that they probably remained in servitude because their lives were the same, or better, than those of the free, except for some "social stigma."

The ACE had to accept this estimate, but a recent study suggests that the real number was closer to four hundred thousand,[22] and that the new proclamation did not necessarily improve their condition. In Zaria, for instance, owners kept control of the land, and, unknown to the British, former slaves were forced into sharecropping arrangements, which were still in operation in the late 1940s.[23] How far owners elsewhere in the north were able to retain their privileges varied with local conditions.[24] The retention of control over land, employment, or other attributes of power was not unique to Nigeria. It happened in many other areas.[25]

The gist of all these reports was that in European colonies in Africa only voluntary slaves remained and that all they suffered was "social discrimination," which, the colonial powers believed, could not be eradicated by government action. Social discrimination, however, could mask serious disabilities. Southern Nigeria reported in 1938 that in some areas former slaves could not attain the highest chieftaincies, or the top ranks in societies, or take part in community councils. They could not marry the free, or perform the same rituals, or dance the same dances. They did not have the same rights to land, and some still performed labor services for their owners. The government admitted that in parts of Onitsha province there had been "minor troubles" from time to time because the free were jealous of the increased influence of the "liberated Awbia" or "strangers," the euphemism for slave (a word now outlawed, to appease the slaves). In fact, there had been serious disturbances in South Nkanu, where by 1938 an uneasy peace had been restored. Some slaves had been settled in their own villages, or on designated areas of village land. Others had paid their owners a fee and moved away or taken up land of their own. Slave chiefs had been appointed to native courts. In some places, ex-slaves formed a group apart with their own political organizations. Friction, however, continued. Those who settled in their own villages suffered harassment as late as the 1970s, and in the 1990s were noticeably poorer than the descendants of their freeborn neighbors.[26]

This raises the whole question of whether administrators after more than thirty years of colonial rule really understood the situation at the grassroots level, or whether they turned a blind eye to it, or decided to accept the position rather than rock the boat. Doubtless, all three factors came into play. Officials, as well as the members of the ACE, thought such discrimination acceptable. They themselves came from stratified societies in which it was a fact of life, where marriage between classes was rare, and disparities in wealth were taken for granted. Moreover, by the 1930s they could sometimes point to cases where slaves were richer than their owners. In Itu and Ijebu in Nigeria, for instance, masters had sent slave children to school rather than their own sons, and these had become the richest and most prosperous members of the community. This did not necessarily make them the social equals of the free in Africa, any more than education and wealth conferred equal status in Britain at the time, but it made it easier for colonial officials to maintain that all necessary steps had been taken to end slavery, that the freed were being absorbed into the general population, and that it could now be left to education and missionary activity to end all "vestiges" of the institution.[27]

Overall, however, by the late 1930s a great deal had changed, partly as the result of the political and economic changes that accompanied colonial rule, but also because in many cases the slaves themselves had taken action. Slave action as an agent of change does not emerge in the ACE reports as an important factor, although, as has been seen, thousands of former slaves had taken advantage of their newfound freedom to establish themselves as independent farmers or workers. Some had rebelled, forcing administrators to take action as in South Nkanu. Some had stayed in place but had renegotiated their terms of service.[28] In French territories, many had served in the army and returned, determined not to return to slavery.[29] Nevertheless much remained to be done and it was only due to Maxwell's incessant pressure that a semblance of the real situation, including the troubles in South Nkanu, were reported to the League at all, and then only long after they began. Maxwell could and did ask searching questions, but he could not get at the truth without taking evidence from slaves themselves and this the ACE could not do.

One form of slavery, which might have held the attention of the ACE, had it been able to take such evidence, was cult slavery—the dedication of children to a deity by their families, usually to atone for a crime. The girls often became the wives of the fetish priest. Nigeria described this form of servitude in its 1936 report, but claimed it was not slavery as the persons dedicated did not "perform services of a servile nature" and could run away. It admitted, however, that their families would not receive them back. The practice varied in different areas but in some forms it was to be denounced as a type of contemporary slavery at the end of the twentieth century.[30]

In view of these optimistic reports it was small wonder then that the ACE concluded in 1938 that:

> In Africa, the age-old home of most slaves of the world, there is no disquietude concerning any of the colonies of the Europeans. In most of them, slavery in any form has now ceased to exist: in some it lingers on, without legal status, as a social tie. Even as such, it is dying rapidly and painlessly.[31]

SLAVERY AS REPORTED TO THE ACE: BURMA AND INDIA

The eradication of slavery was also reported to be proceeding smoothly in Burma. As has been seen, the government of India had reported in 1925 that it had arranged a system by which slaves in the Hukawng Valley could ransom themselves.[32] In 1935, it reported that these areas were now administered and slavery had ceased. The Naga Tracts, however, area that it had exempted from the provisions of the 1926 convention, were still not administered. It believed in 1935 that there were only a small number left.[33]

In 1937, the India Office, stung by the reminders from the ACE, inspired by Maxwell, that it was responsible for ending slavery throughout India and Burma, sent in a long historical account of the measures taken against it in the remoter parts of northern Burma from 1910.[34] At that time, slaves had been freely bought and sold, could not be redeemed, and suffered severe discrimination. The government had dealt with the matter differently in each area. In Khamtilong, slavery was at first not interfered with and runaways were returned unless their lives were in danger or they had been recently captured. As the administration was established, ill-treatment was punished and fugitives were no longer returned. In the Hukawng Valley and Triangle, annual expeditions had been dispatched, first to explore the territory, then to register, and finally to release, slaves. Once the government was ready to tackle the question, the abolition of slavery was announced. Children born after a certain date were declared free, and able-bodied slaves were given loans to redeem themselves. Land was reserved elsewhere in the Myityina District for those who insisted on leaving. The expeditions were not without cost—several officers had been killed in the Triangle in

1926–1927. Many loans were never recovered. Eventually, however, more than nine thousand, five hundred slaves were released at a cost of some five million rupees. The government congratulated itself on the fact that there had been minimum economic disruption. Owners had been compensated and most slaves had remained in place and settled down as ordinary members of their communities—at least so the administration believed.

In the Naga Tracts (Upper Chindwin) west and south of the Hukawng Valley, on the border with Assam, the number of slaves had been reduced by annual expeditions sent to free them between 1925 and 1931. At first they had concentrated on ending human sacrifice, the victims being nearly all slaves. In 1932, these expeditions had ceased owing to government retrenchment, but the India Office reported that it was corresponding with the governments of India and Burma on the subject. To Maxwell's gratification the reservations for the tracts were withdrawn in 1936, ending the reservations for Burma.

The only remaining reservations were for part of the Sadiya and Balipara frontier tracts in Assam. Slavery was said to be no longer practiced in the administered portions of these tracts, but it continued in the unadministered areas, which were inaccessible most of the year and inhabited by "intractable" peoples. The government was "contemplating" sending an officer on tour to explain that it wanted to end slave trading. Maxwell saw to it that the ACE Report for 1937 again contained the reminder that since Assam was part of the Empire, the British were bound to end slavery there.[35] In 1938, he won the point when the India Office withdrew the exemption for the tracts. The question had been brought to a head by raids. Some villages had enslaved their captives and were terrorizing their neighbors. An expedition was sent to free the slaves and punish the culprits. A handful of slaves were freed and the headmen were told that the government intended to end slavery.[36] However, this was only a first step towards establishing the administration. Not all villages had been reached and at least one slave child had not been freed.

Whereas in the remoter parts of Burma and Assam, ending slavery, or at least seeming to end it, had been a matter of extending British administration or influence, the reservation for the Indian Princely States remained a politically sensitive question. Maxwell pecked away at it in vain. The Government of India contended that it could not, as recommended in the 1935 report of the ACE, ask the rulers to declare their intention to take steps against slavery. However, it did ask them to bring their legislation into line with British India.[37]

"OTHER INSTITUTIONS" AS REPORTED TO THE ACE: UNFREE CHILD LABOR—MUI TSAI

The ACE's concern with child slavery continued to be almost entirely centered on mui tsai, although Maxwell produced some information on adoption in Ceylon, and on the terrible conditions under which children worked in the tin mines in Yunnan. In 1936, the Chinese again denied that mui tsai was slavery but sent copies of regulations prohibiting the acquisition of new mui tsai and providing for the registration and protection of existing ones. In 1937, the Dutch reported that before 1919 many "slave" boys and girls had been imported into the Netherlands East Indies by Chinese who claimed to be their parents in order to avoid a tax on unrelated immigrant children. After 1919, the administration had established closer control and raised the tax and such children were no longer imported. Those in the country had all been educated and when they reached puberty were offered the choice of remaining in the country or returning home.[38] In 1938, the Portuguese stated that mui tsai was not recognized by law in Macao and abused girls were either restored to their parents or sent to convent schools. There were no special laws but the girls could easily recover their freedom if they wished. The French reported a similar system in Cochin China. Not surprisingly, the ACE expressed the hope that they would supply more information.

The Colonial Office, anxious to mollify Maxwell on his favorite topic, sent in ever more detailed reports. They included new laws, information on registration in Malaya and Borneo, and descriptions of the work of the inspectors, down to details on why two girls in Hong Kong had committed suicide. The whole question was the subject of an ongoing campaign in Britain, led by Harris, Lady Simon, the Haslewoods, and others. Maxwell had joined the fray in 1934, suggesting measures to strengthen or clarify existing legislation, and recommending the appointment of a committee of Europeans and Chinese men and women to consider his proposals.[39] To his gratification, the governor of Hong Kong had appointed the Loseby Committee.[40] It reported in September 1935, advocating a comprehensive inquiry into the sale and adoption of Chinese girls. It revealed that sales continued and that the real number of mui tsai was unknown. Maxwell agreed that there should be another inquiry and wanted laws to protect all children (including boys) and young people of the "mui tsai class" transferred under the age of twelve. One of his aims was to end the concentration on mui tsai and stop the use of this pejorative term, which set them apart from other children.[41] His proposals, which were supported by the Anti-Slavery Society, were duly relayed to the governor of Hong Kong with instructions to take note of them.[42]

The Colonial Office was sufficiently concerned to appoint its own commission of inquiry, known as the Woods Commission, which sailed in April 1936 to take evidence in Singapore and Malaya and Hong Kong. It issued two reports. The minority one, largely inspired by Maxwell and supported by the humanitarian lobby, called for the notification of all transfers of children under twelve—not just mui tsai and not just Chinese [43]— and the registration, protection, and inspection of those who did not seem to have been genuinely adopted.[44] This would prevent girls who had been bought as mui tsai or for prostitution from being passed off as wards (genuinely adopted children), foster children, daughters-in-law, or relatives. Thousands of mui tsai were believed to have slipped through the net in this way or had simply not been registered. Moreover, there was no way to keep track of the girls who were registered. The report for 1938 showed that the whereabouts of nearly half the four thousand or so girls originally registered in Hong Kong were unknown. Constant population movements to and from the mainland, and the fact that many families lived on boats, exacerbated the problem.

The majority report of the Woods Commission recognized that the situation was not ideal but believed that the registration of all transferred children would have to be backed up by house-to-house visitation, which was not practicable. The governor of Hong Kong was afraid that registering wards would transfer the taint of mui tsai to "the honorable state of adoption" and end Chinese cooperation.[45]

Maxwell, women's groups, societies for the protection of children, and Christian organizations supported by the bishop of Hong Kong and the archbishops of Canterbury and York all lobbied for the minority recommendations. Questions were asked in Parliament. Petitions were presented. An Anti-Slavery Society delegation to the colonial secretary consisted of some fifty people representing eleven societies, including Harris, Lady Simon, Lady Astor, and the Haslewoods.[46] Finally, the scales were tipped in their favor by a letter from a Mrs. Forster enclosing evidence she had taken from prostitutes. These showed that little girls were bought by "pocket mothers," who brought them up and then sold them to brothels to provide for themselves in their old age. They were taught that prostitution was an acceptable profession, and were trained for the job. They had no other means of support. Procuring for prostitution was illegal, but adoption was not and was not subject to any particular legal procedure. Evidence was hard to come by as many of the girls accepted their fate, believing they were in honor bound to repay their pocket mothers or even the brothel owners who had bought them. This information finally convinced Colonial Office officials that more comprehensive measures were needed to protect all children.[47]

To their relief, in 1937, a governor of the Straits Settlements, new to Southeast Asia, accepted the minority report and ordered the registration of all transfers of girls under fourteen. The Malay States followed suit.[48] The following year the governor of Hong Kong, with the support of leading Chinese, merely required the registration of all adopted children, and gave the secretary for Chinese Affairs the power to make arrangements for their custody and inspection. Maxwell's hope of ending the stigma of mui tsai, however, was unrealized as, in both territories, they were registered separately from other transferred children, and hence remained a socially despised group.[49] However, the battle against the institution had been won in principle in the British possessions.

The heart of the problem, however, lay in China where unknown numbers of girls were sold as mui tsai, only a few of whom reached Hong Kong and Malaya. China, engulfed in war with Japan, sent no reports in 1937 or 1938, by which time the Japanese had occupied Peking, Nanking, and Shanghai and were advancing southwards. Thanks to Maxwell, however, the ACE received reports from the International Settlements at Kulangsu (an island in the harbor at Amoy, now Xiamen) and Shanghai.[50] The Municipal Council of Kulangsu registered all unpaid females under twenty-one who were not members of the families with whom they lived, except for those attending authorized schools, who were regarded as adopted children. By February 1937, five hundred girls had been registered and a search was under way for others. A hundred were in a hostel supported by the Municipal Council and charitable organizations. No information was received in 1938 when the town fell to the Japanese.[51]

The Municipal Council of Shanghai, which controlled only part of a large Chinese city, sent a report revealing the extent of the problem of unfree child labor in China. It had appointed a Protector of Mui Tsai in 1937 with a staff of social workers. Her report, transmitted to the League in 1938, showed that mui tsai were only a minority of the children transferred for money in China. For instance, girls were "mortgaged" into prostitution for three years in return for a lump sum paid to their parents or to traffickers. Middlemen bought children from their parents, mortgaged them to cotton mills and factories, pocketed their earnings, and paid them a pittance, and so it went on.[52] In accordance with the regulations of 1936, the Chinese had registered many mui tsai, but the existing homes could only take some two thousand females, and, as well as mui tsai they took in beggars, prostitutes, abandoned children, and fugitives from the war. Shanghai also soon fell to the Japanese.

Maxwell had decided that the mui tsai problem should be passed to the League's Advisory Committee on Social Questions as part of the problem of child protection generally. He began discussions with them in 1935.[53] But this committee was composed of the representatives of twenty-one states including China, and dealt only with general matters referred to it by the League or by governments. It already had two years' work on its agenda. Since mui tsai concerned mainly China, which was at war, it was agreed that it was not the moment to take up the question. Maxwell's colleagues also decided that, as a committee of experts, they had greater freedom than a committee of government representatives, and therefore they should continue to investigate the mui tsai system. The only joy for Maxwell was that the two committees agreed to keep in touch.[54] However, he saw to it that the ACE report for 1938 pointed out that the protection of children was a question for the Social Questions Committee, and only concerned the ACE if the child was a slave, as well as the "victim" of a transfer.[55] In June 1939, the Chinese agreed to put mui tsai on the agenda of the Social Questions Committee. They wanted it considered as a question of child protection in order to counter the charge that they countenanced slavery. The committee agreed also to cooperate with both the ACE and the ILO.[56] However, Maxwell's efforts were to be thwarted by world events.

OTHER INSTITUTIONS: DEBT-BONDAGE
INCLUDING PAWNING AND PEONAGE

Nigeria, French West Africa, and the Belgian Congo all reported taking steps to stamp out pawning. Maxwell defined it as the pledging by a debtor of someone else as security for the debt, as distinct from a debtor who was himself in bondage to his creditor. Pawning was distinct from slavery. Nevertheless, it had been attacked in all European territories. The most notable reports to the ACE came in 1938 from Southern Nigeria. These described self-pawning, child pawning, and the pawning of young girls with a view to their marrying the creditor. To protect children, the British had outlawed the pawning of anyone under sixteen, and pawns over that age had to give their consent. The pawning of girls with a view to marriage was difficult to prove. Pending outlawing pawning altogether, the government was considering legislation to prevent creditors from recovering their loans through the courts, and was encouraging debtors to have their terms of service regulated by a court.

The French had recognized that in spite of laws against it, pawning in Africa had revived as the result of the world economic depression.[57] Administrators had countenanced it because it enabled people to pay their taxes. The government decided to treat it as slave trading from 1938. They also took steps to prevent the pledging of girls under guise of marriage arrangements, and returned to their parents any who had not freely agreed to their marriage. They also reported their efforts to protect persons from falling into long-term debt bondage in Indo-China.[58] Liberia, in its first and only communication to the ACE, stated that when all pawns were freed in 1930, "intoxicated" with freedom, they had refused to work, but the "guiding hand of the government" had now settled them on their farms "in the happy pursuit of a livelihood." Louwers informed his colleagues that pawning existed in the Belgian Congo but was not particularly oppressive. In general, it was felt that pawning would disappear as the population became more mobile and had access to other forms of credit.

Maxwell agreed that it probably only caused real hardship if the creditor had control of land, cattle, and property, and the debtor belonged to a dependent "debased class."[59] This was nearer to the situation in the Indian subcontinent. In response to his requests, in 1937 the government of India supplied detailed information on debt servitude in Madras and Orissa. This varied from short-term engagements to vicious systems of lifelong hereditary bondage. The ACE asked what was being done to eradicate them. The answer was that in Madras the administration was considering giving victims land and housing sites, and introducing protective legislation. In Orissa, efforts to protect victims were hampered by the remoteness of the area, and the "mentality" of the hill tribes who were said to be unable or disinclined to help themselves. The government was considering limiting the length of service of the debtors, establishing debt conciliation boards, and extending other legislation.[60] The real hope, however, lay in the spread of education, communications, and the provision of other kinds of employment. The authorities were trying to bring this about but their resources were limited.

In 1937, India also described measures to end the *Bhagela* system in Hyderabad. All old agreements were declared void. New contracts were limited to one year. Wages were to be "fair" and the hours of work "reasonable." This was acceptable to the creditors because they could recover the debt plus up to six percent interest if the work was not performed. The Bhagela realized the benefits, but feared that, henceforth, they would not be able to borrow such large sums. The administration thought this was to the good, since it believed that most loans were spent on drink at weddings. In 1938, it reported problems of enforcement. The new agreements were often not properly recorded on "stamped" paper. The Bhagela were too timid to protest when powerful landlords tried to keep them to the terms of the old agreements. Some thought it dishonest or unlucky to leave their masters before their old debts were repaid. However, efforts were being made to enforce the new regulations. The ACE recommended these measures as a model for other countries in which agricultural debt slavery persisted.[61]

Maxwell tried to get the ILO to take up the question of debt bondage. At this time, however, it mainly concerned small farmers in debt to their landlords and the ILO was primarily interested in protecting industrial workers in Europe. It had not tackled agricultural problems even in Europe, let alone in "complicated marginal cases in distant countries." It had also not pursued its promised inquiry on peonage.[62] Hence, the ACE had no information on that subject in 1937 or 1938. As will be seen, debt-bondage in the Indian subcontinent was not only still a problem at the outset of the twenty-first century, but it was increasing in many parts of the world and taking new forms.[63]

OTHER INSTITUTIONS: SERFDOM

Discussions on serfdom were bedevilled because there was no agreement on what the term meant. The 1936 report, quoting Maxwell, admitted that: "[I]t is fairly possible to have a clear impression that 'serfdom' is quite different from 'slavery' without having any idea where the difference lies." Broadly speaking, the committee defined a slave as the victim, or descendant of a victim, of an act of personal violence, who was used as an article of property; whereas a serf's position was the result of his connection with the land, or his "employment in or around a householder," or of the relations between "tribes" or even sometimes perhaps "a curious medley of all three." Moreover, some born slaves were treated so mildly as to be "almost indistinguishable from serfs." Treatment was thus confused with legal status, and serfdom seemingly could often not be distinguished from slavery.

In its 1936 report, the ACE appealed for information on serfdom,[64] but the only serious case reported was that of the Sarwa in the Ngwato Reserve in Bechuanaland whom Maxwell called "tribal serfs." The British submitted long reports on their attempts to integrate them into the Ngwato. In 1936, a "Masarwa Officer," J. W. Joyce,

had been put in charge of their interests, a census had been authorized, and a proclamation had declared slavery unlawful.[65] The report of an inquiry by the London Missionary Society, based mainly on evidence from Tshekedi, asserted that the Sarwa were
neither slaves nor serfs, since any one of them could at any time "take his bow and ar-
row and go straight to Central Africa."

Maxwell demanded a "full report" for 1937, although he admitted that he and his colleagues felt that this "tribal serfdom" was not a matter for a slavery committee.[66] This
elicited the information that the Sarwa had been told they could dispose of their services
as they wished. Missionaries were being encouraged to work among them, and the administration planned to open a school, provide them with land, and appoint agricultural
demonstrators to ease their transition from foragers to farmers. This was held to be a
necessary step in their evolution towards a "higher" form of life. In 1938, the ACE received Joyce's report, showing that there were over ten thousand Sarwa. He described
their relations with their masters, their work and living conditions. The ACE decided
that it "seems possible to say that the status of the Masarwa is not one of slavery."[67]

Maxwell could not persuade his colleagues that serfdom was never slavery, but
since they were unlikely to get other reports on the institution, he felt that this section
of their work had ended,[68] and he tried, although in vain, to get the ILO to take up the
matter.

The confusion over terminology, which had bedeviled earlier League committees,
was not resolved by the ACE. It was merely ignored. The French continued to describe
what Maxwell called "voluntary" slaves as serfs in Mauritania. They referred to tenants
who performed unpaid labor for their landlords in Indo-China as being in a voluntary
form of serfdom. Sudan called freed slaves serfs. Both used the terms "domestic slave"
and serf interchangeably in their reports.[69] This reflected the fact that the people whose
various conditions they described did not fit neatly into any clear European category.

THE DEMISE OF THE ACE

When the 1938 meeting ended, the ACE agreed to meet again for its normal biannual
meeting in the spring of 1939, provided there was enough material to justify it. If not,
the chairman was to consult members by mail before deciding whether to meet later
in the year or not at all. As it turned out, the 1938 meeting was their final one.
Maxwell, however, had been planning the committee's demise since 1937. He believed
that slave raids were now almost nonexistent, that slave trading had been reduced to
petty dealing, that slavery in the Aden Protectorate and the Persian Gulf was "well in
hand," and that nothing more could be expected from either Saudi Arabia or Yemen.
He regarded voluntary slavery as a social and economic problem to which governments were now giving serious attention, and which was anyway disappearing in the
face of changing labor conditions, new forms of transport, and modern ideas. He was
angling to pass it to the ILO, together with debt-bondage, peonage, and serfdom. He

hoped the Social Questions Committee would take up mui tsai as part of the larger problem of transferred children. He had already decided that customary marriage was not slavery. He was sure that little more material would be sent to the ACE, and hence there was not much more for it to do. However, he wanted the transfer of its functions to other bodies to be part of a "carefully designed" plan, and believed it could be done in the course of a session in 1939, and, perhaps, a final one in 1941. The committee would then wind up its affairs "honorably" and the Council of the League could dissolve it.[70] This would avoid an outcry from the humanitarians.

Colonial Office officials were astonished to hear of these plans. The ACE had been a "great nuisance" to them. Maxwell had left the Malayan Civil Service with "bitter recollections" which were "heartily reciprocated," and they had frequently had to soothe the ruffled feelings of governors whom he had criticized in ACE reports, in the press, and in letters to government departments. They had learnt to treat him with caution—to the point of not defending themselves too vigorously, knowing that he never forgave those who proved him wrong. He had assiduously shown up British failings and tried to force acceptance of his pet projects. Nevertheless, during the last two years, he had been "helpful,"[71] and by 1938, he had more or less squeezed out all the information he wanted on the British Empire.[72] Moreover, they had mixed feelings about some of his plans. For instance, they heartily endorsed turning mui tsai, which they had always denied was slavery, over to the Social Questions Committee, but did not want the ILO to take on voluntary slavery or debt-bondage. It had already proposed a convention to regulate the recruitment and terms of service of native labor, and they feared it might become an "inquisitive body" demanding information already sent to the ACE. Most importantly, they feared a humanitarian storm if the ACE was dissolved before slavery had been completely eradicated, and warned the Foreign Office that the proposal must come from the committee itself, and not from the British government.[73]

The Foreign Office had wanted the ACE in order to avoid the diplomatic embarrassment of sending the League information about slavery in other countries, as well as to deflect humanitarian pressure away from itself. The ploy had failed. The humanitarians still urged it to pressure other nations into action. Maxwell pressed it to ask for information from governments like Yemen and Liberia, which they had no wish to do.[74] Even worse, thanks to Maxwell, the ACE reports had given the impression that slavery was a "peculiarly British affair."[75] Over ninety of the one hundred and five pages of annexes to the 1938 report, and some fifty-one of the sixty-three pages of its predecessor, concerned the British Empire. By 1938, officials had hoped that other countries would be shamed into producing more material. They now realized that this was highly unlikely, except perhaps in the case of France,[76] but the French reports bore no comparison with their own. Far from holding up Britain's antislavery efforts as shining examples before an admiring world, the ACE had exposed its shortcomings, while powers with much worse records had escaped condemnation by the simple device of not furnishing information. Thus by 1938, the British agreed with Maxwell that it had done all it could, and that if it suggested its own dissolution, they would have a strong "card" to play against the Anti-Slavery Society, which was still demanding annual meetings.[77]

By February 1939, when little documentation had been received, the Secretariat suggested postponing the sixth meeting, scheduled for the end of March, to later in the year. Marchand readily agreed.[78] Maxwell objected strongly, assuring the Secretariat that material was en route from the Colonial Office and India Offices. Moreover, he anticipated an hour of glory since the latter had finally withdrawn its exclusion of the Indian Princely States from the 1926 convention—the "most important thing," he wrote, that had happened since the ACE had come into existence. He acknowledged that nothing could be expected from China or Spain, both in the throes of war. The Belgians were still mired in their inquiry and the Portuguese were unlikely to produce anything, but he hoped the French might do so and he was sure there was enough material for a short meeting.[79] Marchand, however, did not feel that it merited the journey, and both the British and French governments were ready to postpone it, provided the initiative came from the ACE itself.[80]

The committee was in any case dying of attrition. No Italian had attended its meetings since 1936. The Portuguese member had not come in 1938, as he was ill, although he promised to attend in 1939. The Spanish government that had appointed Palencia was losing the civil war, which had raged since 1936, and she failed to answer the Secretariat's query about her views on postponing the meeting.[81] The Dutch and Belgian members favored postponement.[82] Maxwell, however, was still assiduously collecting information. Hoping to conciliate him, the Secretariat urged Marchand to soothe him with an appreciative and sympathetic letter.[83] He was indeed "very much upset" when he was outvoted and the session was postponed.[84] The delay proved fatal.

By May 1939, the Secretariat was suggesting that the ACE should not meet until early in 1940. The Foreign Office anticipated an outcry from the Anti-Slavery Society, but hoped the brunt of it would be borne by the Colonial Office. There were no urgent questions to be discussed and postponement would save money at a time when League finances were shaky. More important, there were political reasons for not raising the question in the Assembly. Officials feared that the protagonists of Haile Selassie might try to show that the Italians had replaced slavery in Ethiopia with forced labor on the roads. At this critical juncture in Europe, with tensions rising and preparations under way for war, the British had no desire to antagonize Mussolini and drive him further into the German camp. Moreover, they were now aware of a revival in the traffic in Baluchi of slaves across the Persian Gulf. Raising this might cause "difficulties" with both Ibn Saud and the Trucial shaykhs in the strategically important Middle East.[85]

In August, Maxwell made a final plea for a meeting, to prevent the ACE from an ignominious "fade out" rather than the "honorable end" he had hoped to engineer. But the outbreak of the Second World War on 3 September sealed its fate. In October, the

Secretariat, as a matter of courtesy, asked the members if they wanted a meeting before the end of the year.[86] As expected, even Maxwell thought it was now impossible.[87] The committee was never officially disbanded. Because of the war, the Council renewed indefinitely the appointment of its members, which had been due to expire in January 1940, but it never met again.[88] The Dutch member died in October 1939. Marchand resigned early in 1940, leaving Maxwell, Louwers, and d'Almada as its only members. A few British reports continued to come in for a while and were duly filed, but early in the war, the various components of the League were transferred from Geneva to Britain, Canada, and the United States. In 1946, the League was replaced by the United Nations Organization (UN).

Some tribute must be paid to the forceful personalities whose hard work and persistence had brought the slavery question to the League and forced the colonial powers to discuss the issue. It was Harris who had gotten slavery raised at the League, and played an important role in stimulating the ILO to take up forced labor and the protection of native labor. His ability to arouse public opinion, to formulate questions in Parliament, and to muster support from other philanthropic bodies and finally from members of the government and the civil service, and his indefatigable behind the scenes pressure in Geneva, were vital factors in raising support for the formation of the League committees. His tendency to exaggerate and his refusal to be deflected from his goals added to his effectiveness. His death in April 1940 heralded the end of an era. Nearly a decade later he was remembered in the Foreign Office as "a very great figure in the slavery field" who "made a great nuisance of himself and goaded the Foreign Office and others into doing a lot of good which they would not have done otherwise."[89]

It was Lugard, assisted by Delafosse, and Grimshaw, who had set the tone of the first committee, and it was Lugard who forced the issue of the slavery convention of 1926. He also served on the ILO Forced Labor Committee. He proclaimed that ending slavery was the enduring interest of his life, and although his record in Nigeria was dubious, his work on the first League committee and the expansion of the definition of slavery proved enduring.

As for Maxwell, he was the life and soul of the ACE. He forced the British to confront questions such as mui tsai in Hong Kong, debt-bondage in India, and so on. He was understandably distressed at what he considered the quiet "blot out" of what had really been his committee, but his work was not forgotten. When the United Nations finally appointed a successor committee, he was "regretfully" ruled out as too old to serve at seventy-eight. Although his attempt to limit the definition of slavery was ultimately not successful, he did much to actually define the various forms of servitude included in the term "slavery in all its forms" by the first League committee.

SHORTCOMINGS IN THE INTERNATIONAL
ANTISLAVERY MECHANISMS

The proceedings of the ACE had highlighted defects in the League mechanisms for dealing with slavery and related institutions. There was little coordination between its various bodies—all differently composed and bound by different rules of procedure. The ILO, made up of representatives of governments, labor, and employers, was a powerful body, but it could only deal with questions referred to it by the International Labor Conference, whose priority was the protection of European industrial workers. Although it had dealt with forced labor and other native labor matters, it had not discussed, for instance, the problem of girls recruited by agents for work in factories in China. It could only deal with labor problems, and not child protection. Its interest in mui tsai was limited to the payment of wages.[90] The Social Questions Committee could only deal with matters placed on its agenda by governments, and it hesitated to take up the question of child protection. The League had a health section, which supplied technical help to governments that requested it. One of its experts had gone to Yunnan at the request of the nationalist government of General Chiang Kai-shek. He had reported in 1935 that some 50 percent of the fifty thousand workers in the mines were under fifteen, that their life expectancy was short and working conditions deplorable. Recruiting agents paid their parents ten to thirty dollars in advance, and the boys earned an average of ten cents a day carrying heavy loads from underground tunnels, an occupation so unhealthy that they turned green, were wracked with coughs, and suffered from eye inflammations and swollen legs. There was no sanitation, no washing facilities, and twenty workers slept in a small room in the same building as horses and buffaloes. This question was being investigated as a health issue.[91] Maxwell, seeing the potential of raising issues under the health rubric, toyed unsuccessfully with the idea of raising debt-bondage as a rural health question.[92]

The League Secretariat might have coordinated its various bodies, but it was the very first international civil service—less than two decades old—and was still feeling its way. Anxious not to alienate governments or overstep its powers, it was nevertheless sensitive to criticism, and this Maxwell exploited. He complained that the position brought the League into ridicule. He published an article pointing out that neither the ILO nor the Social Questions Committee had given attention to the general problem of the protection of children, boys as well as girls, yet boys were exploited as unpaid apprentices, servants, agricultural laborers, and worked, often in hazardous conditions, in factories, mills, mines, quarries, circuses, and theaters. He suggested that the Social Questions Committee could appoint a subcommittee with representatives of both the ILO and the ACE. He persuaded the Colonial Office to send its reports on child protection and mui tsai to both the ACE and the Social Questions Committee. He got the British delegate, Lord Halifax, to raise the problem when he introduced the ACE report to the Council in 1938, and he suggested that in 1939 the ACE should give special attention to the need for coordination. But it was all to no avail. As Marchand said, the ACE was not "expert in transferring its babies."[93]

Finally, there were the defects in the ACE itself. It suffered from its restrictive rules of procedure. Its reports contained only such information as governments felt they had to reveal, with the exception of the British ones, which, thanks to Maxwell, often contained more than his government wished to make public. Nevertheless they too must be read with a critical eye.[94] Its information was thus deficient and having no powers of enforcement, its only weapon was publicity, which could only be effective in countries in which public opinion could be mobilized and governments were responsive. Maxwell's vigorous efforts to bring about change led to a debate in the League Secretariat in 1936, as to whether the ACE itself would be more effective if it were composed of government representatives including delegates from countries where slavery was legal. Although the so-called "independent experts" were freer to criticize official policies, governments could ignore their recommendations more easily that they could those made by their own representatives. Nothing, however, came of the idea.[95]

For all its defects, however, the ACE had collected a great deal of material and forced governments to take some account not only of slavery, but of other forms of unfree labor. Some were more responsive than others, but nevertheless, it had consolidated much of the work of its predecessors and laid the groundwork for the United Nations committees that were to succeed it, in the very different circumstances of the postwar world.

NOTES

1. Record of Conversation with Sir G. Maxwell, 12 March 1937, FO 371/21280 W5085/1006/52.

2. It was Marchand who suggested the 1938 meeting during the 1937 session. ACE minutes, 7 April 1937, C.C.E.E./4th session/P.V. 6. LON 6B/29848/8000 R 4154. For the discussion over the ACE's right to ask for a change in the rules, see minutes, 9 April 1937, LON C.C.E.E./4th session/ P.V. 7, ibid.

3. Maxwell to Stevenson, 28 April 1936, FO 371/20517 W 3735/154/52. The ACE held eleven meetings and the session ended on 24 April 1936.

4. These notes are in the LON C.C.E.E. series in 6B/23167/8598/ R 4155, 6B/222306/8598/ R 4156, 6B/21563/2663 R4151, R4157, 6B/30374/8598 R4157, 6B/22171/8000/R4153, S 1670/2; 6B/1118/2663/R 4150; 6B/30224/2663/R4151.

5. He was also secretary-general of the International Colonial Institute.

6. See documents in LON 6B/22306/8598/R4156. For Maxwell's classifications, see above, chapter 14.

7. Note by Maxwell, 8 November 1935, C.C.E.E.63, LON 6/B/22171/8000/1 R4153; revised note by Maxwell, 4 April 1936, C.C.E.E.71 (1) 9 April 1936, LON 6B/22306/8598/R4156.

8. Maxwell to CO, 15 June 1936, confidential, enclosed in Circular Dispatch, 29 August 1936, to all colonial governments, CO 323/1431.

9. For instance, the governor of Tanganyika's report that it "may be asserted with a considerable degree of certainty that there are no persons in any status or condition resembling slavery" was altered by the Colonial Office to read: "[I]t may now be asserted that there are no persons. . . ." Minutes of 29 January 1937 in CO 323/1431.

10. Minutes of third meeting, 6 April 1937, C.C.E.E./4th session P.V. 3, p. 1, LON 6B/29848/8000 R4154.

11. Report from the French government, C.C.E.E. 201 (1), LON C.112.1938.VI.

12. For adoption by purchase in the late twentieth century, see below, chapter 24.

13. Kanem and Borku were in Chad, then part of French Equatorial Africa. The Tibesti region runs from Chad into Libya, which was then under Italian rule.

14. Minutes of ACE 1936, C.C.E.E./3rd Session/P.V. 5, and P.V. 6, LON 6B/25052/8000/R4153.

15. The British airmen were presumably stationed either in Sudan or northern Nigeria.

16. Minutes of ACE 1937, C.C.E.E./4th session/P.V. 8, p. 8, LON 6B/29848/8000 R4154. Figures for 1936 were not available.

17. See above, chapter 16.

18. For the Belgian and Italian reports, see ACE report 1936, LON C.189 (1). M. 145.1936,VI. The reports from the French, Spanish, and British and the communication of the Portuguese member of the ACE were published as annexes to the 1937 and 1938 reports, LON.188.M. 173.1937.VI, ACE report 1938, LON C.112.1938.VI.

19. The British claimed that there was no slavery in Gambia, Gold Coast, Togo, Kenya, Northern Rhodesia, Nyasaland, Sierra Leone, Somaliland, Tanganyika, Uganda, and Zanzibar.

20. See above, chapter 3.

21. According to the report, there were 71, 880 "voluntary" slaves; 46,060 persons who had been freed, or were born after 1901, were also still with their former owners, as were 1,090 in Cameroon, who had been freed by ordinance in 1925, annex 4 to Report of the Advisory Committee of Experts on Slavery, Fourth Session 1937, LON C.188.M.173.1937.VI.

22. For a discussion of this whole question, see Lovejoy and Hogendorn 1993, 274–84.

23. Lovejoy and Hogendorn 1993, 283, citing M. G. Smith 1960.

24. Lovejoy and Hogendorn 1993, 284. This subject invites further research.

25. See, for instance, Getz forthcoming, Klein 1998, Mbodji 1993.

26. Carolyn A. Brown, 1996. For this question, see also above, chapter 11.

27. See below, chapter 24, for further discussion of "vestiges" of slavery.

28. For examples, see inter alia chapters in Miers and Roberts, Miers and Klein, Klein 1998.

29. See inter alia Klein 1998, 216–19.

30. See below, chapter 24.

31. ACE report 1938, LON C.112.1938.VI, p. 9.

32. See above, chapter 11.

33. ACE Report 1935, LON C.159.M.113. 1935, VI, annex 10, C.C.E.E.32; ACE Report 1936. LON C.189 (1). M.145, 1936, VI, annex 15, C.C.E.E.65.

34. ACE Report 1937, LON C.188.M.173. 1937.VI, annex 15, C.C.E.E. 158.

35. C.C.E.E./4th Session/P.V.2, LON 6b/29848/8000 R4154.

36. ACE Report 1938, LON C.112.1938.VI, p. 7, and annex 10, C.C.E.E.173.

37. See above, chapter 9, for this exclusion.

38. C.C.E.E./P.V.3, LON 6b/29848/8000 R4154.

39. Maxwell to CO, 20 April 1934, and enclosed memoranda, COCP Eastern no. 169, CO 882/16 pp. 1–27, and FO 371/19731; Maxwell to CO, 1 December 1934, ibid., pp. 34–36; some Observations on the Report of the Mui Tsai Commission, by Maxwell, 26 March 1937, COCP 882/16 no. 21, p. 63.

40. All its members were on the executive committee of the Hong Kong Society for the Protection of Children.

41. Report of the Loseby Committee was published as Cmd.5121 *Mui Tsai in Hong Kong.* Maxwell's comments on it are in Maxwell to CO, 13 December 1935, CO 882/16, pp. 38–43.

42. CO to governor, Hong Kong, 20 January 1936, CO 882/16, p.12; Harris to CO, 11 February 1936, ibid.

43. Witnesses had told the commission that Indian, Malay, and Thai girls were also used as mui tsai.

44. For a discussion of the commission and its impact, see Miners 1987, 180–90. For the Reports of the Commission, see W. W. Woods, *Mui Tsai in Hong Kong and Malaya, Report of Commission,* HMSO Colonial 125, London 1937. For Maxwell's criticisms, see "Some Observations on the Report of the Mui Tsai Commission," 26 March 1937, no. 21, CO 882/16, pp. 63–78.

45. Caldecott to CO, no. 168, 18 March 1936, CO 882/16, p. 50.

46. For this delegation and other appeals to the CO, see CO 825/22/9 and CO 825/23/3.

47. Forster to Ormsby Gore, 2 June 1937, and enclosures and minutes CO 825/22/8. For further correspondence see CO 825/22/9. For further information on prostitution in Hong Kong and Malaya see Miners 1987, pp. 191–206; Warren 1994.

48. For his reasons, see Thomas to Ormsby Gore, private and confidential, 27 September 1937, and minutes CO 825/22/9.

49. Koh 1994; Miers 1994. See also above, chapter 11.

50. See ACE Report for 1935, p. 108, LON C.159.M.113.1935.VI. Contact with these settlements had been established through the foreign diplomatic corps with British help, and the reports were unofficially communicated to the League while awaiting their arrival through official channels.

51. For the 1937 report, see LON C.188.M.173.1937 VI., pp. 79–80. A report for 1938 was given to the Japanese consul to send to the League, but it merely said that Kulangsu had nothing to add to its last report, Miselj record of conversation between de Haller and Reilly (FO), 25 May 1939, LON 6B/38201/2663 R4151.

52. This was known as *pao fan* (guaranteed rice) system of "contract" labor; see ACE Report 1938, LON C.112.M.98.1938.VI., pp. 93–106.

53. Maxwell to de Haller, 7 December 1937, LON 6B/30224/2663/R4151; Miselj, note on liaison between ACE and Social Questions Committee, 15 January 1938, ibid.; question of liaison between the Slavery Committee and the Committee on Social Questions, summary of correspondence, ibid.; Maxwell to S.W. Harris, 28 February 1938, ibid.; Maxwell to de Haller, 22 March 1938, LON 6B/33281/2663/R4151.

54. Maxwell to de Haller, 22 March 1938, LON 6B/33281/2663/R 4151; ACE minutes, 1 April 1938, C.C.E.E./5th (extr) session/P.V.4.; Maxwell to FO, confidential, 9 April 1938, FO 371/22700 W 4746/890/52.

55. ACE Report 1938, LON C.112.1938.VI, p. 15.

56. De Haller notes of conversations with Ekstrand and Hoo, 11 January 1939, LON 6B/30224/2663 R4151; note by Miselj, of de Haller record of conversation with Reilly (FO), 18 January 1939, 19 January 1939, and 25 May 1939, LON S.1670, file 7, and note by Miselj, 19 May 1939, LON 6B/38201/2663 R4151; and Hoo to Ekstrand, 12 June 1939, LON 6B/30224/2663 R4151; de Haller to Maxwell, 4 July 1939, LON 6B/30224/2663 R4151; Report on the Work of the Advisory Committee on Social Questions, 15 July 1939, LON C.214.M.142.1939.IV, p. 14; the committee was already in process of establishing permanent cooperation with the League Health Organization.

57. Klein 1998, 231–33.

58. French report to ACE, LON C.112.1938.VI, pp. 80–81.

59. ACE minutes, 31 March 1938, C.C.E.E./5th session/P.V.1 and P.V.2, LON 6B/33398/8000 R4154.

60. The most oppressive systems in question were *Gothi* in Koraput district and the *Kamia* system in Sambalpur. The government was considering extending the Agriculturalist Loans Act to cover these.

61. ACE Report 1938, LON C.112.1938.VI, p. 11.

62. Note of interview with Weaver, 29 March 1938, LON 6B/16577/1864, S 1669 file 4.

63. See below, chapter 24.

64. See note by Maxwell on serfdom, 3 March 1936, C.C.E.E. 96, LON 6B/22697/8598/R 4156.

65. See above, chapter 11.

66. Maxwell to FO, confidential, 4 June 1936, FO 371/20517 W 5023/154/52.

67. ACE Report 1938, LON C.112.1938.VI, p. 16.

68. Note of interview with Weaver, 29 March 1938, LON 6B/16577/1864, S 1669 file 4; Maxwell to FO confidential, 9 April 1938, FO 371/22700 W 4746/890/52.

69. Sudan report, ACE Report 1937, LON C.188.M.173.1937.VI., pp. 75–78; French report, ACE Report 1938, LON C.112.1938.VI, pp. 79–83.

70. Minutes on Maxwell to FO 25, February 1938, FO 371/22700 W 2705/890/52; Maxwell to Stevenson, 11 March 1938, and enclosed notes, ibid., W 3331/890/52.

71. Minutes on Thomas to CO, 15 December 1937, CO 323/1431; minutes on Stevenson to CO, 16 March 1938, CO 323/1544/1901/1938; FO minutes re notes for conversation with Maxwell, 5–12 March 1937, FO 371/21280 W4530/1006/52 , pp. 67–76.

72. Note of discussion with Maxwell, 22 March 1938, FO 371/22700 W 3799/890/52, p. 177.

73. Minutes on FO to CO, 16 March 1938, CO 323/1544/1901/1/1938.

74. Minutes on CO to FO, 4 November 1936, and FO to CO, 9 December 1936, FO 371/19969 E 6934/133/91. For instance, they feared Yemen might turn to the Italians, and they did not want to sour relations with Liberia, which already had introduced reforms.

75. Minutes on CO to FO, 4 November 1936, and FO to CO, 9 December 1936, FO 371/19969 E 6934/133/91.

76. Minutes on the Report of the Slavery Committee enclosed in de Haller to Stevenson, 23 April 1938, FO 371/22700 W 5238/890/52.

77. Minutes on Maxwell to Makins, 25 February 1938, and Maxwell to Stevenson, 11 March 1938, FO 371/22700 W2705/890/52; Notes on Slavery, enclosed in Maxwell to Stevenson, 11 March 1938.

78. De Haller note to secretary-general, 14 February 1939, LON 6B/34020/8000 R4154; note of de Haller record of conversation with Reilly (FO) 18 January 1939, 19 January 1939, LON S.1670, file 7.

79. Maxwell to de Haller, 16 and 20 February 1939, LON 6B/34020/8000 R4154.

80. De Haller note to secretary-general, 8 March 1939, LON 6 B/34020/8000 R4154.

81. By May 1939, her government had lost the war to General Franco, and she was no longer Swedish minister in Stockholm.

82. Louwers also said he had nothing to report as the persons running the long Belgian inquiry would not send him any information until it was completed, but, in any case, he said it was of purely historical interest, Louwers to de Haller, 28 February 1939, LON 6B/34020/8000 R4154.

83. De Haller to Marchand, 7 March 1939, LON B/34020/8000 R4154.

84. De Haller record of conversation with Reilly (FO), 25 May 1939, LON 6B/38201/2663 R4151.

85. Minutes on UK delegation to Geneva to FO, 26 May 1939, FO 371/24107 W 8488/565/52.

86. De Haller note for secretary-general, 5 October 1939, LON 6B/34020/80 00 R4154.

87. Maxwell to de Haller, 21 October 1939, LON 6b/34020/8000 R4151.

88. The terms of its members had been due to expire in January 1940, but a League resolution of 14 December 1939 extended them, LON 6B/2891/2185/ R 4149.

89. Corley Smith to Boothby, 11 November 1949, FO 371/78977 UNE 4525/17319/96.

90. Minutes of ACE C.C.E.E./5th (extr.) Session/P.V.(5), LON 6B/33398/8000 R.4154.

91. Extract from the *Malay Weekly News*, 1 July 1937, p. 3, LON 6B/1118/2663/R 4150, file 2. For the correspondence between Maxwell and de Haller (League Secretariat), see LON 6B/30374/8598/R4150.

92. Maxwell to de Haller, 22 March 1938, LON 6B/30224/2663/R4151.

93. Maxwell to FO, confidential, 9 April 1938, FO 371/22700 W 4746/890/52; Maxwell to de Haller, 1 November, and 8 December 1938, and "The Problem of the Transferred Child," by Maxwell, *The Catholic Citizen* (journal of St. Joan's Social and Political Alliance) LON 6B/36008/8598, and 19 November 1938, LON 34020/8000 R4154.

94. These official reports are all published as annexes to the *Reports of the Advisory Committee of Experts on Slavery* for 1936, see third (extraordinary) session 1936, LON C.189 (1). M.145.1936.VI; for 1937 C 188.M 173.1937.VI; for 1938 C.112.1938.VI.

95. Notes by de Silva, 26 February 1936, and by de Haller, 5 March 1936, LON 6B/21563/2663/R4151.

The Slavery Question
from 1939 to 1949

THE END OF SLAVERY IN ETHIOPIA

One result of the Second World War was the demise of slavery in Ethiopia. In 1940, Italy declared war on Britain and the following year the British conquered all the Italian colonies in the Horn of Africa. Before the conquest was even complete, the Anti-Slavery Society reminded the foreign secretary, Anthony Eden, of the slavery scandals of the 1930s and asked how he proposed to prevent a resumption of slave raiding and trading once Haile Selassie was restored to his throne. "Had the emperor been told," asked Lady Simon, "that slavery must stop?"[1]

The opportunity was unique. The emperor returned to his capital in the wake of the British army. British military administrations were established in each area as it was conquered. Foreign Office officials agreed that a return to the old ways was likely, but they saw no alternative to restoring the emperor. Eden, taking his stand on the last-minute reforms of 1935 and 1936, declared that he had proved himself "an enlightened native prince," ready to modernize his country with outside assistance.[2] British resources were strained to the limit. The war was far from over, and they had no desire to take over the administration of the country themselves. Haile Selassie, however, feared that they wanted to establish a protectorate over it. He had been bitterly disappointed at not being given arms and troops to reconquer Ethiopia himself. Once back in Addis Ababa, he took every opportunity to assert his authority.

He had been forced to accept the appointment of British political officers to run the liberated areas until the Italians had been driven out and a treaty could be drawn up handing power over to him. The British provided money and advisors and agreed to consult him on all administrative measures. But he had no power to legislate or appoint officials, and no money to pay them. Nevertheless, he no sooner reentered his capital than he began to appoint his own cabinet ministers, officials, and governors, in an attempt to regain power.[3] Friction inevitably developed between the emperor, who was determined to assume control, and the British chief political officer, Philip Mitchell, determined to prevent the reestablishment of the old system.

In Britain, the antislavery society expressed its fears, while the Abyssinia Association and Sylvia Pankhurst, the editor of *New Times* and *Ethiopia News*, rushed to Haile Selassie's defense, fearful that he would not regain full independence. They tried to counter the propaganda emanating from what they called the "anti-slavery enthusiasts," the "welfare of natives group," and denounced them as Roman Catholics and Fascist sympathizers. They planned to submit their own proposals to the emperor for the abolition of slavery. The Foreign Office was happy to see these two groups at loggerheads, hoping it would give them a rest from their attacks.[4]

The task of reestablishing the administration in Ethiopia was daunting. Many of the old *rases* and Western-educated younger officials had been killed in the war. Much of the country had been devastated. The economy was in ruins. Armed bands roamed the countryside. Abandoned children flooded the towns. In some areas, the people, particularly the Oromo, had no desire to see the emperor restored. As each region was conquered, British officers began the task of rebuilding the government. All went peacefully until:

> the sudden arrival without warning of an Ethiopian governor or similar official accompanied by a rabble of armed men, asserting truthfully . . . that he had been appointed by the emperor. Murder and looting by these parties were widespread and from all sides political officers reported the disastrous consequences of this premature attempt on the part of the Emperor to establish an administration for which he lacked the necessary means and staff.[5]

However, they were not accused of slave raiding or trading. Haile Selassie was well aware that there would be an outcry in Britain if it were believed that subsidies were going to a government which countenanced slavery. He let it be known that he intended to abolish it. The question was how and when to do it.

In November 1941, as a first step, he proclaimed the *gabbar* system abolished. Henceforth, peasants were to pay taxes and officials were to be paid. Slavery was tackled more slowly. Lugard, Maxwell, and de Halpert all sent proposals to the Foreign Office.[6] Sandford, who was now British advisor to the emperor, consulted them.[7] On a brief visit to England, he visited the Society's committee, hoping to pacify them, but reported that they were a "set of ghouls positively slapping their lips on any spicy bit of information" he could give them.[8] In January 1942, the Anglo-Ethiopian agreement was signed, restoring the emperor to power, and providing a subsidy to set up his administration. In return, he had to appoint British advisors to both the central and local government, and, of prime importance, British judges, and police commissioners.

Sandford became advisor to the Ministry of the Interior. The emperor now had a golden opportunity to implement his prewar plans to establish a paid civil service and army, and attack slavery. Many owners had died during the Italian occupation and the war, and many had lost their slaves. Sandford believed that household slavery was already dying out and slave trading had greatly diminished.[9] The slavery proclamation was only held up while he discussed drafts with Lugard and others.[10] Questions in Parliament made it clear that the matter was not forgotten in Britain. By June, he reported that peace and quiet prevailed all over the country and the emperor was "pretty firmly in the saddle," but a vast number of new laws and regulations were waiting to be cleared through the Council of Ministers. Finally, on 27 August 1942, a proclamation announced that slavery was no longer a legal status and slave dealing was a capital offense.

However, the old structural problems of government remained. The emperor kept the details of administration in his own hands and the conflict between old-style *rases* and Western-educated officials continued.[11] More than a year after Sandford had declared Haile Selassie was in control, his writ did not run in much of the southwest. The British advisor in Jimma reported that the governor-general of the southwest provinces was "progressive" and carried out local reforms on his advice but had no control beyond the River Gojeb and did not have the means to gain it. Without an all-weather road all the way to Maji,[12] and the money to pay them, it was impossible to maintain a police force in the area.

Whalley returned briefly to Maji and reported a new situation. The local people, alienated by the Eritrean and Somali troops in the Italian army, had joined the Patriots—guerrillas who had fought the Italians during the war. They had cleared the way for the British entry into the town and had been won over to the emperor by his proclamations promising an end to oppression as soon as his administration could be established. However, his officials were unwilling to serve in the southwest, and the governor paid only a brief visit to the area. The countryside formerly ravaged by Amhara raids was now controlled by the local chiefs, well armed as the result of the war, and the few Amhara officials were pinned in the towns. They were still unpaid. Both the locals and the administrators used the same methods of extortion. Thus, the old abuses had returned, although Amhara control was much reduced.[13] Further south there were also raids into British territory, but although captives were sometimes taken, these were cattle raids by pastoralists. The emperor's new territorial army administered rough justice on the frontier, causing alarm in British circles. The courts in which cases were heard by British and Ethiopian judges were liable to be flouted. As soon, for instance, as the judges left Negele, the local authorities reversed their decisions.[14]

However, in October 1943, a question in Parliament on the impact of the antislavery decrees brought an encouraging reply. The British judicial advisor reported that he was impressed with Ethiopian efforts. Slaves were being freed. One hundred forty-nine people had been tried for offenses since June 1942.[15] In 1945, a new agreement was signed with the emperor, restoring more of his powers. It did not mention slavery. The Foreign Office explained that Haile Selassie would never admit in a treaty that slavery existed or that Britain had any right to interfere in internal policy.[16] Times were changing. Reports from Addis Ababa stated that no European had seen any signs of an organized slave trade, and that the authorities were dealing with the few cases of kidnapping and small-scale trading. However, the information was tenuous as Europeans found it hard to get solid evidence. The French denied that there was any export traffic through Somaliland.[17] The British were in control of Eritrea and although, as will be seen, some slaves were exported from there, the traffic was small. In spite of reassurances, the Anti-Slavery Society kept prodding for information and asked to see consular reports from both Ethiopia and Arabia. The Foreign Office refused.[18]

In 1949, Alexander Curle, who had been British advisor in Jimma some years earlier, returned on a visit and drove on into Kafa. Unfortunately, the road was so bad that he could not get to Maji. He reported that the governor-general in Jimma, who was in charge of the whole area, was corrupt and that, in Kafa, the Amhara still lived in villages along the road, while the local peoples lived far away from it. Ominously, the governor in Bonga had small "very black" youths as servants, who might be slaves. However, the roads were safe and he saw no signs of raiding. Most encouraging was the fact that the governor-general was proposing to open an airstrip in Maji. Thus the town, previously weeks by mule from Addis Ababa, would now become quickly accessible. Also encouraging, the emperor's private secretary asked him for his impression of the servants of officials in Kafa.[19]

Curle made a number of trips to Maji in subsequent years, but only once mentioned slavery in his private papers. In 1953, he said that children were abducted by passing mule caravans. A girl captured in Kambata was rescued in Jimma two years later, having changed hands three times.[20] He thought the local authorities turned a blind eye but that the central government "frowned" on slave dealing. The American embassy reported in 1951 that the sale of small children was "commonplace" outside of Shawa and Tegre.[21]

It seems clear that petty trafficking continued, but that slave raids, enslavements, and slave trading on any scale ended as the emperor extended his control. However, the British also distanced themselves from the question. After the 1940s, they ceased to ask for reports on slavery.[22] Perhaps because they thought it was being suppressed by the Ethiopian government but also perhaps because their influence was waning. By 1948, the minister in Addis Ababa wrote that he could no longer demand an audience with the emperor or "have a straight talk" with him—although there were a number of outstanding British grievances, including serious frontier raids. British protests were unlikely to bring results. The only weapon he could recommend was publicity. The Ethiopians were sensitive to any information that might damage their image at the United Nations, where they wanted to appear as a "virtuous little African state with a homogenous population and an enlightened government," a description he did not believe would stand investigation. Clearly, a new era had dawned in which Britain could no longer expect to exert pressure on small nations with impunity. The same changes in the world situation were, as will be seen, to affect British policy in Arabia.

SLAVERY IN THE ADEN PROTECTORATE

To the consternation of the Colonial Office, things moved slowly in the Aden Protectorate. By January 1939, coastal rulers had been asked to sign agreements to prevent further imports of slaves, but only a few had done so, and the inland rulers were only now addressed. Only one ruler, the Abdali sultan of Lahej, had proclaimed it an offense to own an imported or captured slave. The others were not even asked to do this, as they were too weak to enforce such a law.[23] As unsatisfactory reports came in, officials in London were divided as to what to do. Some thought that on principle, "Geneva or no Geneva," slavery should not be tolerated in the British Empire. Others were reluctant to "stir up trouble" and risk unpopularity in an area where their control was still "flimsy." Moreover, they did not want to create a "landless, masterless population" of freed slaves. Finally, they urged the governor to greater efforts, but left it to him to decide what pressure to put on local rulers,[24] and the position remained unsatisfactory.

For instance, Ingrams believed there was "a deplorable amount of slave trading" in Wahidi country, west of the Hadhramaut, an area he hoped to "pacify" and organize in the next year.[25] A decade later, it was still described as a "black spot." Similarly, in Mahra country, east of the Hadhramaut, the sultan of Qishn and Socotra had signed an agreement to end the import of slaves by sea, and an officer was finally sent to investigate the condition of the slaves and the state of the slave trade in 1939. He estimated that there were some eight hundred slaves in the region, eighty of whom had been imported—most having been kidnapped in East Africa. Some were Baluchis. None had been brought in recently. However, the slave traffic was active in the country itself and slaves cost between $200 and $350 each. Some were well treated but others were in a "pitiable condition"—overworked and underfed. Owners were obstructive and slaves afraid to talk to him, so his information was incomplete. He suggested that further investigations would have to be secret.[26] Nothing had been done by 1949.

Elsewhere, Ingrams ran into an unexpected problem over the disposal of freed slaves. In May 1939, penetrating into the Wahidi Ybeth, he freed an old Swahili slave, whom he found living miserably with his Bedouin owners. The man had been kidnapped long ago in Mombasa. His wife was of Ethiopian origin, and his daughter-in-law of Nubian descent. They and his children had all been born as slaves in Arabia. They were agriculturalists, but Ingrams was afraid that if he settled them on the land, they would be re-enslaved. He sent them to Mukalla, where they waited miserably for repatriation to Mombasa. The Protectorate budget included £500 for fares and help with resettlement. The young men of the family were willing and able to work. But the governor of Kenya refused to take them for fear they would not accept a status lower than the Arabs on the coast—a reflection on the fact that Arabs and Indians were treated differently from Africans. Ingrams tried Tanganyika and when there was no answer, he appealed to the Colonial Office. Tanganyika finally agreed to take a hundred freed slaves, provided that they were "genuine agriculturalists of African origin." The delay, the administration explained, had been caused by the need to find suitable land and climate in an area where the local population would accept them. In the end, the island of Mafia was suggested.[27]

If some slaves were clearly badly treated in the Protectorate, royal slaves were over-indulged. There were some two thousand troublemakers mostly in Mukalla, Shihr, Sai'yun and Tarim, employed on garrison duty and as tax collectors. They lived in idleness, enjoying "a privileged position." The soldiers did not show up for parades. They banded together in defense of their privileges, and felt they had "a sort of freehold of their jobs." They earned more than free soldiers, but refused arduous or dangerous postings. Some ran private businesses. Some sold their rations in the market. Those in charge of the gate in Tarim paid themselves from the collection of dues.

Unproductive and expensive as they were, rulers who, as has been seen, had long wanted to free them, were still reluctant to risk antagonizing them. Some of those belonging to the Qu'ati sultan refused freedom even when offered good land, rations, and money to build houses. In 1943, matters came to a head when under wartime regulations they were ordered to register their private rifles and put their government arms in the armory. Fearing loss of their privileges, they took over the government buildings in Mukalla, including the treasury, and refused to give up their weapons. They only surrendered when a detachment of Indian troops arrived from Aden. Subsequently they were disarmed and forcibly freed. The able-bodied were then enrolled in the state forces and the rest pensioned off.[28] The Kathiri sultan, however, still had slaves paid by the state treasury, who "imposed their will" on the sultan as well as his free subjects. By 1949, however, with the improvement in law and order, they were said to be no longer "a menace." Although still employed as irregular troops, their privileges had been curtailed to the point that many opted for freedom.

By this time, the import of slaves into the Protectorate by sea was believed to have ended. There were thought to be few slaves in the administered parts of the Western Protectorate, but trading continued in the less accessible Aulaqi sultanates beyond the range of British action. In Wahidi territory, there were a large number of slaves, many of whom absconded when faced with the prospect of being sold. The British hoped that the young and newly elected sultan of Balhaf would abolish the traffic, with their help, as he expanded his control. He was sympathetic but not yet strong enough to begin a policy of liberation. In the Qu'ati and Kathiri sultanates of the Hadhramaut, slave trading had been forbidden and, theoretically, all slaves had the right to claim their freedom. However, this was only a reality in the administered areas. Further east, conditions in the Mahra still could not be investigated. In the northern areas west of the Hadhramaut, the "semi-nomadic tribes" were said to be "inveterate slave traders" who kidnapped men, women and children, particularly in times of famine. Some were taken through the remoter areas of Yemen to Saudi Arabia. The encouraging news was that the Saudis had promptly set free those they heard about, and had repatriated some thirty victims since 1944.

The British agents in the Protectorate were "stretched to the limit" trying to improve conditions in the more accessible and populated regions. Advance into the remoter regions to the north and west of the Hadhramaut was not only hampered by lack of resources, but also by the fact that the internal frontiers with Yemen and Saudi Arabia had not been defined. Nomads crossed the frontiers freely and were not under the control of any government. Yemen had refused to agree to a definite borderline, and owing to the harsh desert conditions, the British had almost no contact with the local Saudi authorities.[29]

Thus, when reporting the position to the Colonial Office, the administration had to admit that the slave trade was still active in the remoter areas of the Protectorate and that unknown, but probably small, numbers of victims were exported to Saudi Arabia. As for slavery, they repeated the old chestnut about slaves preferring the security of slavery to the uncertainties of freedom. This was doubtless true but it surely reflected the fact that little had been done to give them the confidence to leave their owners, and that the lot of the free poor in this British protectorate was dismal in the extreme.

THE SLAVE TRADE IN ARABIA AND THE PERSIAN GULF

Saudi Arabia was neutral in the Second World War, but Ibn Saud was staunchly anti-German as well as anti-Soviet, and he suppressed anti-British propaganda, and let frontier and other sources of conflict "slumber." The British were, therefore, dismayed to hear that his slavery regulations of 1936 were "a dead letter" and that children were imported from Persian and British Baluchistan.[30] Unable to take action against the king, they attacked the traffic in the Persian Gulf.

In 1938, they had deprived the shaykh of Abu Dhabi of British "good offices," meaning that he and his subjects would not be issued with travel papers. They considered fining him eight thousand rupees to be returned if he stopped the slave trade. If he refused to pay, they proposed seizing part of his pearling fleet. This idea was dropped, as it would have engaged the whole of the Royal Navy's Persian Gulf squadron at a time of year when the crews would suffer from the heat. Instead officials suggested a naval bombardment of his fort. This tactic had been used in the past for slave dealing and other offenses, and strict rules had been drawn up to minimize casualties. The mere threat of bombardment had sometimes been enough to ensure compliance. The Foreign Office, worried that they "would never hear the end of it" if the traffic revived, favored strong measures.[31] For all this brave talk, however, the India Office decided to do nothing until the negotiations under way between the shaykh and Petroleum Concessions Ltd., came to fruition. "Oil," the Foreign Office commented dryly, "is considered more important than slaves."[32] The matter was shelved.

In 1939, a small traffic in Baluchis to Saudi Arabia was reported to be coming through Oman. Here again there were problems about taking action. After the outbreak of war, the British Royal Navy could no longer spare ships to search for slaves. For forty years, the British representative in Muscat had pleaded in vain for a suitable launch. He was expected to watch the coast but was not given the means to do so. The sultan, Said bin Taimur, who had with difficulty paid off his father's debts, claimed that he could not police the 300 or so miles of the Batinah coast. Part of it was uninhabited, while the area around Suwaiq and Al Musana'a was controlled by the half-Baluchi shaykh of the Yal Seed. He sheltered slavers and kept a private army of Baluchis. The villagers along the shore were either his adherents or his slaves. To help the sultan extend his control and ensure security, the British provided him with arms and a subsidy, but did not think the time opportune to urge him to tackle the Yal Seed. The shaykh of Fujairah was also suspected of complicity. He was anxious to enter into treaty relations with the British like his Trucial neighbors, but at this time they thought him "a man of no importance" and had no desire to extend their treaty commitments.[33]

There was, however, a side to this traffic that made it easier to ignore. The British political resident in the Gulf in 1940 reported that Persian Baluchis were "utterly destitute, and had left their country to get food to eat." They preferred "the security of slavery" to the "starvation of freedom" and willingly sold themselves or their children to caravans bound for Buraimi.[34] Two years later the traffic was increasing. The Iranian navy had been either sunk or appropriated by the British, and Iran was too weak to control Baluchistan, where life, already harsh, was made worse by disturbances encouraged by the active arms traffic across the Gulf. The British decided that they would once more search Persian dhows at sea.[35] They also put pressure on the Trucial shaykhs with varying degrees of success.

Since the main market for the slaves was in Saudi Arabia, they made representations to Ibn Saud. This yielded profuse professions of cooperation, which the British thought "worthless."[36] They knew the king was importing concubines from Syria,[37] that he had received a gift of twenty slaves from Qatar, and that British subjects from Baluchistan were still imported through Oman.[38] Baluchi girls were the concubines of choice, now that Circassians were not available. They sold in Mecca in 1943 for between £350 and £450. There was also a disturbing hint that the traffic had increased because the British had renounced their right of manumission—an idea the Foreign Office was eager to reject.[39] The war ended in 1945 and in the next years there were reports that this traffic was growing.

These were years of dramatic change in the Gulf. India and Pakistan became independent in 1947, and the Foreign Office took over the affairs of the Gulf from the defunct India Office, opening an era of increasing intervention in the internal affairs of the Gulf shaykhdoms. Already in 1946 the political resident had been transferred from Bushire to Bahrain where he could keep a closer watch on them. These states became more and more important to the world economy and to the sterling area as their wealth grew with the opening of new oil fields. Oil had been produced in Bahrain before the war, but output rose dramatically immediately after it. Production in Kuwait began in 1946, and in Qatar three years later. In the late 1940s, rival British and American oil companies were prospecting on the Trucial coast and in the sultanate of Muscat and Oman. Everywhere the rulers were patriarchal and conservative. The radical changes in the economy and standard of living that came with oil wealth were just beginning and were unevenly spread around the Gulf. Saudi Arabia, Kuwait, and Bahrain were being rapidly enriched, but the Trucial shaykhs and the sultan of Muscat were still poor and weak, and had little or no control over the peoples of the interior, who had always shifted allegiance according to circumstances.

This was possible because frontiers had neither been agreed nor demarcated and transhumant pastoralists moved freely in their eternal search for grazing. There had been no incentive to delimit borders in the past, but now every mile of formerly useless desert, and of offshore water, became a potential oil field of inestimable value, and sources of fresh water became all important. The frontier question, which had begun to be addressed before the war, became increasingly urgent as rival oil companies advanced into the interior and also cast their eyes on territorial waters. The British were faced with having to choose between supporting the claims of the coastal rulers, or dealing directly with the tribes of the hinterland. They chose to support the former and to encourage them to establish control over the latter. The slave trade complicated British policy. To an even greater extent than in the past, action or inaction was determined by the likelihood of political repercussions.

By 1948, British officials reported a "considerable traffic" in women and children abducted, or bought on the Makran coast, in the Batinah, and in the Trucial shaykhdoms. Hitherto, their efforts had been confined to preventing the import of slaves by sea. This overland traffic covered regions they had visited from time to time but about which they knew little. The slaves were taken to Buraimi and from there to Saudi Arabia.[40] Buraimi was an oasis of eight villages, six of them claimed by the shaykh of Abu Dhabi and two by the sultan of Muscat. The latter claim was disputed by Saudi Arabia. In 1948, much of the interior of Oman was controlled by local shaykhs and by the imam of Oman, an elected religious leader with temporal powers, whose authority was acknowledged by the people east and south of Buraimi. The sultan had agreed with the leaders of the interior in 1920 that he would not interfere in their affairs and would allow them access to the coast in return for their not raiding into the areas over which he ruled. In the late 1940s, relations between the sultan and the imam were stable—neither interfered in the affairs of the other. The sultan, however, had not given up his claim to all Oman.

Late in 1948, P. D. Stobart, the political officer in Sharjah, reported that the slave traffic was growing, and recorded the names of victims and dealers. He blamed its increase on escalating Saudi wealth and the depressed state of the coastal economy, which reduced people to kidnapping, or to selling themselves or their children. Forty-eight cases of abduction had been reported in the previous two years.[41] He believed many more went unreported because the victims had no relatives or because their relatives feared reprisals. The victims were mostly free Africans or Baluchis, but some were Arabs and Iranians. They were often seized at wells or while cutting wood outside Dubai or Sharjah, and their mouths were stuffed with dough or dates to prevent them crying for help. The kidnappers were Arab, Iranian, and Baluchi. The captives were assembled in known villages, and then taken by camel to Buraimi. There they were kept in newly built compounds in Hamasa, and were joined by slaves kidnapped on the Batinah Coast or imported across the Gulf.

In Buraimi they were bought by resident Saudi, Iranian, Qatari, or Baluchi traders. Prices ranged from 500 to 3,000 rupees for Arab or Persian girls. Buraimi shaykhs charged dealers Rs.20 to Rs.100 for documents stating that the victims had been born into slavery, so that they could be legally imported into Saudi Arabia. They were then taken to Salwa, on the Qatar-Saudi border, either by hired camels—a journey of 500 miles at a cost of one hundred rupees a head (about £8)—or shipped via the Trucial Coast to Qatar and then taken overland to Salwa, where the Saudi authorities readily accepted their false documents.

Stobart thought a caravan of fifty slaves had left Buraimi in December 1948, just before he arrived.[42] The explorer, Wilfred Thesiger, reported that the traffic was so "blatant" that he had seen forty-three slaves driven out of Buraimi "like cattle."[43] His Arab companions suggested, only partly in jest, that, with his fair skin, he would be safer if he posed as a Baluchi slave trader.[44] The shaykhs in Buraimi were equally blatant. In Hamasa, Shaykh Rashid bin Said had shown C. J. Pelly, the political officer in Bahrain, the stocks used to punish recalcitrant slaves.[45] Moreover, except in the areas that acknowledged the authority of the imam, there was no security for women, children, or indeed any unarmed persons. Even British officials had been fired on by hostile tribesmen.

Once in Saudi Arabia, the captives sold for between Rs.4,000 and Rs.8,000. Not all decried their fate. Many of the young concubines, who fetched the highest prices, lived in such comfort that they were thought not to want to be freed. Buyers included the heir apparent to Ibn Saud and his other progeny, including many sons, most of whom lived in idle luxury and had an appetite for concubines and domestics. Some were gifts. Thus in November 1948, the ruler of Dubai was said to have given the king and his sons a number of female slaves in return for a car and 10,000 ryals.[46]

The Red Sea trade was also reviving. In 1947, to the surprise and gratification of the Foreign Office, the Saudis freed and asked the British to repatriate eight Eritreans. Eritrea, conquered from Italy in 1941, was under temporary British military administration. Investigation showed that the slave traffic was taking a new form. The three women were prostitutes who had been enticed onto a dhow and sold at Maidi in Yemen. The five boys, all under twelve, had been promised a share of his fishing profits by a dhow captain. They testified that there was a "slave market" in Maidi, where there were other newly arrived Eritrean slaves.[47] This traffic was difficult to stop on the African coast since the victims left voluntarily and only knew their fate on landing in Arabia.

The fact that the Saudis had freed the victims, and promised cooperation in the future, encouraged the British to ask them to end the traffic from the Gulf into eastern Arabia. They did not mention Buraimi, however, for fear that Ibn Saud might think they recognized his claims to it.[48] They were also wary of giving the impression that the Trucial rulers were conniving at the traffic for fear that he might use the information to back up his claims to their territories.[49] He considered all the Persian Gulf shaykhs as his vassals and border tensions were rising.

The news from Aden that an important Saudi advisor to the king had recently bought two slaves in Al Hudaydah in the Yemen, led the British to reconsider their policy. They debated whether they had a moral obligation to protest to the Saudis, or whether for the sake of expediency they should do nothing. Their discussion of this relatively trivial episode shows how the unsatisfactory situation in Arabia was now merging with an increasingly volatile world situation.

Britain was faced with the Cold War with the Soviet Union, a growing challenge from the newly independent Asian nations, and the rising powers in the Middle East—Egypt, Iraq, Iran, and Israel. They condemned colonialism and blamed the British for their close relations with what they regarded as "socially reactionary and uncivilised" Arab rulers in Saudi Arabia and the Gulf States. In Britain, the Anti-Slavery Society claimed there were over a million slaves in Arab countries and demanded a United Nations slavery committee—a proposal that was under discussion.[50] In 1948, the United Nations, at the suggestion of the Soviets, had condemned slavery "in all its aspects" in the Declaration of Human Rights. The Russians were suspected of proposing this in retaliation for Western attacks on their forced labor camps. The danger was clear. As a Foreign Office official minuted:

> We have only to recall the Ethiopian invasion to realise how tremendously the revelation of the present situation would weaken the Arabs' moral position and what wonderful propaganda the U.S.S.R. or Israel could make with it. Slavery and oil are both dynamite in the hands of the propagandist. The same stories could be used to throw indirect discredit on those Arab states where there is no slavery, and unless we can show a clean bill of health, in the Hadhramaut and the Persian Gulf States—even when we are responsible only for their external relations—we ourselves shall not escape the breath of calumny. ... There are practical as well as moral grounds for taking a more vigorous attitude in this question generally. Inevitably we have tended to let things drift these last ten years but before that we could show a century of effort.[51]

This fear of propaganda attacks fomented by communists, "progressive" Arabs, and even sections of opinion in the United States, led the British to decide that they must do all they could to "root out slavery in Arabia." They toyed with the idea of trying to get the "more progressive" Arab governments, such as Egypt and Syria, to put pressure on Ibn Saud and the Gulf shaykhs. As a start, they decided to make sure their own hands were "clean" in Aden and the Gulf, and then to consider a "high level" approach to Saudi Arabia and perhaps to Yemen.

The need to take action was all the more urgent as more and more Europeans and Americans were coming to the Gulf, and oil prospectors were going into the interior and would soon spot evidence of slave trading.[52] As matters stood, the Gulf rulers had no means to suppress the traffic, even if they wished to do so. It was, therefore, difficult to call them to account. The navy had no craft able to patrol in shallow waters, and there was no military force to coerce the tribes of the interior.[53]

Moreover, there were important political reasons for creating a military force. Exploration for oil was drawing the British into the internal affairs of the shaykhdoms as well as into boundary questions and bringing them increasingly into contact with the peoples in the hinterland, where in the past they had been able to exercise "maximum political pressure" with little prospect of backing it with force. Now their bluff might be called. Boundary demarcations might cause disturbances between rival groups. Oil company personnel and property would have to be protected. Coastal rulers might foment trouble. Shaik Rashid bin Said of Dubai, for instance, had paid tribesmen to prevent the employees of an oil company from crossing their territory.[54] Also, interior peoples might follow the example of the Naim in Buraimi, who demanded that the oil company, to whom the sultan of Muscat had given a concession, should negotiate directly with them. A Pandora's box would be opened if tribes negotiated with rival companies.[55]

In 1948, the British began discussing the recruitment of a local force to protect British personnel and property. The chiefs of staff rejected this proposal, together with one to provide the sultan of Muscat with a subsidy to increase his existing army. British interests, they argued, could be protected by bringing in other forces when required.[56] By 1949, as reports showed that the slave trade was increasing, the Foreign Office decided they could make a good case for a local force to stop "slave raiding and enslavement." It could, of course, then be used, accidentally on purpose as it were, for the protection of British and foreign interests—notably oil installations and British political officers. As so often in the past, there was a convenient marriage between humanitarian and more mundane aims.[57]

The threat from Saudi Arabia now became more explicit. Relations had deteriorated with the creation of the state of Israel. The Saudis were rapidly increasing their wealth and they had the backing of the United States. Without British help, the small Gulf States, which, in the past, had bought the friendship of interior tribes with subsidies, could not defend themselves against the encroachments of so rich and powerful an adversary. In April 1949, a group of American geologists with armed Saudi guards appeared in territory claimed by Abu Dhabi. Stobart and Shaykh Hazza, brother of the ruler, ordered them to leave.[58] The shaykh appealed for British help in asserting Abu Dhabi claims. Ibn Saud, he declared, wanted to occupy "the whole world." He was astute enough to mention that the slave traders in Buraimi were "building houses like forts."[59] Diplomatic protests followed on both sides and Britain asked the United States to restrain the American oil company, Aramco, until the frontier question could be settled.

The Saudis claimed large areas of the Trucial Coast and Muscat and Oman, including Buraimi and everything south and east of it, as far as the coast opposite Masirah Island on the Arabian Sea. The British were particularly anxious at this time to encourage oil production in Muscat and Oman because, if there were a war, it would be easier to collect oil in the Indian Ocean than the Persian Gulf.[60] In the absence of settled frontiers and security in the interior, the oil companies would not begin operations.[61] The British solution was to build up the power of the sultan with his small levy and create a small British force to enable the Trucial shaykhs to control the regions they claimed.[62]

However, the force would take time to raise and train, and in the summer of 1949, the Foreign Office was anxious to take some action quickly as reports of the slave traffic involving some of the shaykhs continued to arrive.

"I do not think", minuted an official, "that the trouble that we may be in for in the United Nations or elsewhere if [the] slave trade is discovered in territories under our jurisdiction can be over-estimated. Clearly we must stop it and stop it soon."[63]

The question, of course, was how. The sanctions at their disposal, such as stopping courtesies or travel facilities, were hardly adequate. Fines were more serious, but the problem was how to extract them from recalcitrant rulers. A blockade and preventing the landing of supplies would affect the poor rather than the guilty. Stopping calls by mail steamers might prejudice the interests of the oil companies. The naval bombardments of the past were ruled out as likely to rouse public outrage at home and abroad. Naval landing parties might demolish the property of the guilty, but this could only be justified if it was to put down the slave trade, and the government wanted to conceal the fact that the traffic still existed in territories under British protection.

In the course of the discussions, the navy was asked to reinforce the four sloops it theoretically kept in the Gulf with three or four motor torpedo boats to enable it to search dhows in shallow waters. Such vessels could also be used to enforce boundaries as oil operations moved offshore. The navy, however, replied that it would have difficulty even supplying slow motor fishing boats. Although the question was left open, its response made it all the more imperative to establish the military force.[64]

It was October before the chiefs of staff agreed to the levy, as the force was called, and December before the Foreign Office asked the Treasury for the necessary £55,000 for 1950.[65] It was to consist of local people, but to be trained and staffed initially by men from the Arab Legion. By the time it came into being, the United Nations had agreed to establish a committee on slavery.

Although slavery had been a minor issue in the decade since the outbreak of war in 1939, there had nevertheless been important changes. It was now no longer legal in

Ethiopia and was certainly no longer practiced on any scale. In Saudi Arabia, however, it was not only still legal but there was an active import trade from the Persian Gulf states. Little had changed in the Aden Protectorate. A small numbers of royal slaves had been freed against their will, but unknown numbers of ordinary slaves remained in servitude in areas claimed, but barely administered, by the British.

The British were now drawn into the next round of the international antislavery campaign, orchestrated by the nascent United Nations Organization, in the knowledge that slavery was still legal in some of their own territories. In the eyes of the public, they were still the leaders of the great crusade, but their options were to be increasingly limited by their progressive political, military, and economic weakness as their empire disintegrated and their influence declined.

NOTES

1. Lady Simon to Eden, 16 April 1941, FO 371/27537.

2. Eden to Lady Simon, 2 May 1941, and minutes, FO 371/27537.

3. Shirreff 1995, 65–80; Casbon, 115 ff., Marcus 1997, 96 ff., Mitchell to Auchinleck, 15 September 1941, chief political officer's dispatch, CAB 106/356.

4. Pankhurst to Eden, 15 September 1941, and minute, FO 371/27537 J 2972/1026/1; H. Stanley Jevens to Sandford, 12 September 1941, Sandford Papers 1941–1942.

5. Mitchell to Auchinleck 15 September 1941, vol. 1, secret, para. 36, CAB 106/356; see also appendix, vol. II Lush report, secret, 127 ff., CAB 106/357.

6. See documents in FO 371/27537.

7. Lugard to Sandford, 13 September 1941, Sandford Papers; Greenidge (ASAPS) to Sandford, 17 and 25 September 1941, ibid.; Sandford to Lugard, 14 October, 5 November, 1941, Lugard to Sandford, 17 October, 27 October and 12 November 1941, Lugard Papers.

8. Sandford to Lugard, 18 October 1941, Lugard Papers.

9. Sandford to President of the High Court, 28 June 1942, Sandford Papers.

10. Sandford to Lugard, 17 June 1942, Lugard Papers.

11. Christine Sandford to Lugard, 22 January 1943, Lugard Papers.

12. Hope Gill to Howe, 30 June 1943, FO 371/35626.

13. Whalley memorandum, 3 May 1943, enclosed in Howe to FO, no. 73, FO 371/35605 J 2793/1/1; Whalley report on journey to Maji, 3 May 1943, enclosed in Howe to Eden, no. 74, 27 May 1943, ibid., J 2794. 1/1.

14. Notes on the situation in Borana, enclosed in Howe to Eden, no. 101, 28 June 1943, FO 371/35605 J3187/1/1 and many other reports in this volume.

15. Howe to Eden, telegram, no. 813, 9 October 1943, FO 371/35656 J 4232/4220/1.

16. Minutes on Parliamentary question, 17 January 1945, FO 371/46056 J 294/30/1.

17. Howe to Coverley-Price, 15 January 1945, FO 371/46056 J 458/30/1, and 26 January 1945, and enclosures, ibid., J 564/30/1; Cook to FO, no. 49, 7 March 1945, and enclosures, ibid., J 1062/30/1.

18. Greenidge to FO, 7 November 1945, FO 371/46056 J 4147/30/1; Baxter to Green, 3 December 1945, ibid., E 8623/8623/91; minutes on letter from Noel-Buxton, 15 February 1946, and on visit by Noel-Buxton and Greenidge to FO, 21 February 1946, FO 371/53478 J 762/762/1.

19. Report by Curle, enclosed in Lascelles to Attlee, no. 114, 30 November 1949, FO 371/73681 file no. 10111.

20. Curle Papers.

21. Rives Childs to Department of State, restricted, 24 August 1951, no. 100 (875.064/8-2451) United States National Archives (USNA).

22. The British documents for the late 1940s and early 1950s are disappointing. Some documents on the southwest are missing. Some have been destroyed.

23. Reilly to MacDonald, confidential, 11 January 1939, CO 725/63/15.

24. See minutes which begin on Reilly to MacDonald, confidential, 11 January 1939, and continue to May 1940, CO 725/63/15. MacDonald to acting governor, Aden, confidential, 17 August 1939, ibid.

25. Ingrams, memorandum no. C/122/2/38/2930, 20 December 1938, CO 725/63/15.

26. Secret Extract from Political Intelligence Summary, no. 88, for the week ending 18th March 1939, and Report by Nasir bin Abdulla Al Kathiri, enclosed in Reilly to MacDonald, 7 June 1939, CO 725/63/15.

27. Ingrams to colonial secretary, Nairobi, no. 106/5/39, 8 October 1939, and to chief secretary Dar-es-Salaam, no. 106/5/39/686, 15 February 1940, and to the political secretary, Aden, no. C/122/38/1199, 10 March 1940, CO 725/70/20; governor Tanganyika to Lloyd, confidential, 17 August 1940, ibid. The family could not be sent to Tanganyika at this time owing to lack of transport because of the war. Further research is needed to establish what happened to them and to other freed Swahili slaves.

28. Memoranda and minute dated 1943, in CO 725/82/1.

29. Champion to Reilly, 21 April 1949 and enclosed memorandum, CO 725/92/5; Thomas to Creech Jones, no. C/82/41, 1 June 1949, ibid.

30. Political review of events in Saudi Arabia for the year 1939, enclosed in Stonehewer-Bird to Halifax, no. 62 secret, 18 July 1940, FO 371/24589 E2720/1194/25.

31. Political resident, Bushire, to political agent, Bahrain, no. C/141 of 1938, PZ2456; political resident, Bushire, to IO, no. C/336, 19 June 1938 and FO minutes, Gibson

memorandum on resort to force in dealings with Arab Sheikhs [sic], 21 July 1938, FO 371/21825 E 4251/573/91.

32. Gibson to Fowle, no. PZ 6320/38, 27 September 1938, enclosed in IO to FO PZ6320/38, 28 September 1938, FO 371/21825 E 5669/573/91.

33. Prior to Gibson, confidential, P.Z. 4864/40, 31 July 1940; Gibson to Prior, confidential, P.Z. 7839/39, 1 January 1940, FO 371/24542 E 54/54/91; Brown to consul-general, Meshed, confidential, no 21, 10 February 1940, FO 371/24589.

34. Prior to Gibson, confidential, no.D.O. no. 562-S, 31 July 1940, FO 371/24542 E 54/54/91.

35. Bullard to FO, no. 475 tel., 13 April 1942, and minutes and tel. no. 476, 14 April 1942, FO 371/31348 1607/65.

36. See minutes on Stonehewer-Bird to FO, no. 48, 21 November 1942, FO 371/31348 E 7394/1607/65; and on Jordan to Eden, no. 79, 3 October 1943, FO 371/ 35165 E 6236/4587/25.

37. Minute 3 August 1942 on political agent, Muscat, to political resident, Bushire, no. C/683, 12 June 1942, FO 371/31348, E 4472/1607/65.

38. IO to FO, confidential, no. 4922/42, 16 September 1942, and enclosures FO 371/31348 E 5509/1607/65.

39. Jordan to Eden, no. 79, 3 October 1943, and minutes, FO 371/35165 E 6263/4587/25.

40. Hay to Donaldson, confidential no. 152-S, 16 January 1948, enclosed in CRO to FO, Ext. 248, 30 January 1948, 371/68774 E 1627/513/25; Hay to Burrows, no. 19, 21 April 1948, enclosing Jackson to Pelly DO no. 341.1317, 12 April 1948, ibid., E 5440/513/25.

41. Of these, twenty-six were women or girls, and twenty-two men or boys.

42. Stobart to Pelly, confidential, no. 1095–1370, 21 December 1948, enclosed in Hay to Bevin, secret, no. 10, 27 January 1949, FO 371/75034 E 1765/1731/91. Details of the prices are in Thesiger 1984, 282.

43. Semiofficial letter from Stobart to Pelly, 17 April 1949, enclosed in Hay to Burrows, secret, no. 207/49G, 4 May 1949, FO 371/75018 E 5773/1535/91. See also, Thesiger 1984, pp. 282, 310.

44. Personal communication from Sir Wilfred Thesiger, 21 July 1995.

45. Pelly to Hay, confidential, no. C/R-14, 13 January 1949, FO 371/75034 E 1765/1731/91.

46. Bahrain Intelligence Report for January 16–31, 1949, enclosed in Pelly to FO, secret no. 2, 15 February 1949.

47. Clark to Bevin, confidential, no. 125, 2 September 1947, FO 371/62109 E 8599/ 8393/25; Clark to chief administrative officer, B.M.A. Eritrea, no. 897/5/47, ibid., E 8458/8393/25.

48. Trott to Burrows, confidential, no. 359/10/48, 6 July 1948, minutes and drafts, FO 371/68774 E 9683/513/25. Trott to Bevin, no. 142, ibid., E 11523/513/25.

49. Jiddah Chancery to FO confidential, no. 482/2/49, 24 February 1949, FO 371/75034 E 2866/1731/93.

50. See below, chapter 19.

51. Minutes by Corley Smith, 13 December 1948, and on Clarke to Burrows, no.808/8/48G, 1 November 1948, FO 371/68774 E14854/513/25.

52. Minute by Burrows, 23 December 1948, on Clarke to Burrows, no 808/8/48G, 1 November 1948, FO 371/68774 E 14854/513/25.

53. Pelly to Hay, confidential, no. C/R-14, 13 January 1949, and enclosure Stobart to Pelly, confidential, no. 1095–1370, 21 December 1948, FO 371/75034 E 1765/1731/91; Hay to Bevin, secret no. 10, 27 January 1949, and enclosures, ibid.

54. Pelly to Hay, confidential, no. C/R-14, 13 January 1949, ibid.

55. Hay to Burrows, no. 35, 19 March 1939, and Burrows to Hay, 29 April 1949, FO 371/75018 E 4046/1535/91.

56. MOD to Burrows, top secret, c.o.s. 323/1/3/9, 1 March 1949, FO 371/75018 E 2892/1535/91G.

57. Burrows to Hay, top secret, 11 March 1949, FO 371/75018 E 2892/1535/91G. Burrows to Bowden, top secret, 6 September 1949, FO 371/75018 E 2892/1535/91G.

58. Chadwick memorandum, Frontier Dispute Between Saudi Arabia and Qatar, confidential 21 April 1949, FO 371/75018 E 5124/1535/91.

59. Pelly to Hay, secret, no. C/R-177, FO 371/75018 E 5835/1535/91.

60. Nuttall to Chadwick, top secret, 5 May 1949, FO 371/75018 E 6011/1535/91.

61. Longrigg to Burrows, 20 June 1949, FO 371/75019 E 7864/1535/91.

62. Burrows memorandum on the internal situation in Muscat, 26 May 1949, FO 371/75019 E 6631/1335/91.

63. Minute by Beckett, 27 May 1949, FO 371/75034 E 6723/1731/91.

64. Various drafts of Bevin to resident, Bahrain, secret, May 1949, and minutes, FO 371/75034 E 6723/1731/91; Hall to Bevin, 21 July 1949, and minutes, and draft McNeil to Hall, secret, September 1949, minute for Bevin conversation with Hay, 17 August 1949, and minute 13 October 1949, ibid., E 9087/1731/91; record of meeting at the FO on 16 August 1949, secret, ibid., E 1059/1731/91.

65. Extract from COS (49) 156th meeting, top secret, 24 October 1949, FO 371/75034 E12999/1731/91; FO to Treasury, secret, 7 December 1949, ibid.

The Cold War and the Supplementary Slavery Convention of 1956

THE STRUGGLE FOR A UNITED NATIONS SLAVERY COMMITTEE 1946–1950

In May 1946, less than a year after the end of the Second World War, Charles Greenidge, who had succeeded Harris as secretary of the Anti-Slavery Society in 1941, asked the Foreign Office to support a proposal for the establishment of a permanent United Nations slavery committee.[1] He had already started lobbying at the nascent United Nations Commission on Human Rights in New York.[2]

The UN was inspired by the same ideals as the League of Nations, made the more urgent by the prospect of nuclear warfare, and the horrific revelations of genocide and slave labor perpetrated by Nazi Germany. Its charter, issued in 1945, stated that one of its aims was to promote "universal respect for, and observance of, human rights and fundamental freedoms for all without distinction as to race, sex or language or religion." Slavery was not specifically mentioned, but its eradication was clearly implied.

The same structural problems that had paralyzed the League were passed to its successor. The UN Charter ruled out intervention in the domestic affairs of member states. With national sovereignty thus still inviolate, the question was, how were these noble principles to be implemented? Covenants could bind signatories to respect them, but nations could not be forced to sign or ratify them or to carry them out if they acceded. The ultimate sanction for the recalcitrant was expulsion from the UN, but it was only likely to be resorted to if there was an imminent threat to peace. As in the past, protests and the pressure of public opinion remained the only weapons in the international armory. Small powers might be bullied and shamed into compliance but great powers could break treaties with impunity.

The late 1940s and early 1950s were a time of intense activity at the United Nations. Its subsidiary bodies were taking shape in an atmosphere of rising tension, created by the Cold War between the Soviet and Western blocs. Where the League had been dominated by the leading Western colonial powers, France and Britain, the great powers were now the United States and the Union of Soviet Socialist Republics (USSR). They, with Britain, France, and Nationalist China, had permanent seats on the UN Security Council and the power of veto, but in the Assembly, every member nation, great or small, had an equal voice and vote. The battle lines had been drawn between the Western democracies and the communist bloc. Now the picture was complicated by the emergence from British domination of the newly independent states of India, Pakistan, Ceylon (Sri Lanka), and Burma (Myanmar), of Indonesia, which won its freedom from the Netherlands, and of the former French colonies in Southeast Asia. The Communists established the Peoples' Republic of China. North Korea and North Vietnam became communist states, and Soviet satellite governments were set up in Eastern Europe. Muslim, particularly Arab, opinion was inflamed by the proclamation of the state of Israel.

The United Nations became the forum for an intense propaganda campaign between the Soviet and Western blocs as they fought to influence world public opinion, not only in the new states which had no love for colonialism, but also in the Western democracies themselves, threatened from the inside by communist parties and their sympathizers. Colonialism was under particular attack, not just from the communist bloc but also from sections of the American public. The Labor government of Britain was already taking steps to give self-government by stages to many parts of the empire, but the British still believed it would be decades before many of the colonial peoples would be "ready" for independence. The pace was always too slow for their more restive subjects.

The Commission on Human Rights (CHR)—a subsidiary of the new UN Economic and Social Council (ECOSOC), which dealt with economic and social problems— was drafting the Universal Declaration of Human Rights as well as the covenants to implement it. There was a basic disagreement between the power blocs on the definition of human rights. In Western democracies, it meant a recognized set of freedoms, including freedom of expression, of assembly, of religion, of information, freedom from arbitrary arrest, the right to a fair trial, and other components of the rule of law. In the Soviet bloc, the main emphasis was on economic and social questions, such as freedom from want and discrimination, the right to employment, to education, and to equal opportunity. In the summer of 1946, the Soviet Union won an early victory when it proposed the establishment of subcommittees of ECOSOC to counter discrimination and protect minorities. The United States was particularly vulnerable on this point for its treatment of African Americans, Native Americans, and other groups, and so were the colonial powers for their treatment of subject peoples. The Russians prided themselves on their handling of minorities, and the British saw the proposal as a countermove to the American insistence on a subcommission for freedom of information—a strong point in the West.[3] Sadly, this rivalry for hearts and minds set the context for the antislavery game at the United Nations, and was to dominate the antislavery campaign until the end of the Cold War in the 1990s.

In 1946, slavery was the last thing on the minds of politicians. The Slavery Convention was not even among the treaties the UN took over from the League of Nations at its demise. It was generally believed that the institution no longer existed and the matter would surely have been forgotten, had it not been for Greenidge. He was a white Barbadian lawyer, who had served in the Colonial Service in the West Indies and Africa, becoming chief justice of Nigeria, and of British Honduras, and was secretary of the Colonial Advisory Committee of the Labor Party National Executive. The Foreign Office considered him a "moderate left-winger," with "few illusions" and a "sincere interest" in the gradual improvement of labor practices in less developed regions. He was in sympathy with the aims of the Labor government and, at this time, maintained "close official and personal relations" with the colonial secretary.[4] During the war, he had paid more attention to colonial problems, in which he was well versed, although he had been active in the campaign to end slavery in Ethiopia and he had attacked Osu cult slavery and pawning in Southern Nigeria.[5] Now, following Harris's example, he attended UN meetings, lobbied delegates, made speeches, wrote pamphlets, kept up an extensive correspondence, and generally drummed up support.[6]

In 1948, the Universal Declaration of Human Rights was being drafted. It defined fundamental rights in such a way as to meld the priorities of the communist and Western worlds. As has been seen, it was the Russians who proposed that it should specifically condemn slavery. Accordingly, article four declared that "no one shall be held in slavery or servitude: slavery and the slave trade shall be prohibited in all their forms."[7] The declaration was simply a statement of principles, and covenants were drafted to bind signatories to implement them.[8] It was to be nearly twenty years before these were even open for signature and another ten before they came into force. Meanwhile the declaration remained a pious hope and the Foreign Office had little faith that sanctions against recalcitrant states would ever amount to more than the time-honored and usually ineffectual publicity and moral pressure.[9]

Greenidge firmly believed that only the creation of a permanent advisory committee on slavery would prevent the slavery article from remaining a dead letter, but the Foreign Office opposed its establishment because it would cost money and encourage demands for other committees.[10] After two years without a response to his proposal, the director of Human Rights in the UN Secretariat advised Greenidge to ask delegates personally to propose a formal resolution, just as Harris had done in 1922. Unlike Harris, he warned the Foreign Office of his plans and sent them a memorandum stating that there were at least five million slaves in the world, as well as several million Amerindian peons in debt-bondage in Latin America, twenty million Russian slave laborers, and—to bring the point home—that mui tsai were still being sold in the British colony of Singapore.[11] Like Harris, he believed in sweeping estimates.

Foreign Office officials relying on the views expressed by Maxwell in 1938 believed that chattel slavery was virtually dead, and that the Anti-Slavery Society, to justify its existence was "straining the word" slavery to cover problems better dealt with by the ILO or other UN bodies.[12] However, unwilling to upset the Society, with its supporters in Parliament and proven ability to stir up trouble, they played for time. This allowed Greenidge to steal a march on them. He persuaded the Belgian delegate, Fernand De-housse, to propose that the UN establish a committee for three years to inquire into slavery in all its forms.[13] The French seconded the motion. Greenidge again appealed for British support.[14] At a talk in Paris to *Les Amis de l'Abbé Grégoire*, he explained that he hoped for a committee that would organize United Nations financial aid to member states wanting to eradicate slavery, direct them to establish a slavery suppression service, and furnish annual progress reports—proposals that alarmed the Colonial Office.[15]

His "intensive lobbying" forced the British to "collect" their "thoughts" on slavery. As a start, they persuaded Dehousse to change his proposal so that the Third Committee of the UN Assembly merely asked ECOSOC to study the problem of slavery at its next session. This delayed consideration of the committee until the late summer of 1949.[16] Meanwhile, they consulted other departments as to how far slavery and related institutions existed in the British Empire.[17] They wanted full information on their own "iniquities."[18] The Colonial Office duly sent out a circular asking for information.[19]

SLAVERY, FORCED LABOR, AND THE COLD WAR

As they mulled over their next moves, the British decided that tradition demanded that they support some kind of investigation into slavery, but they wanted it to include forced labor, peonage, mui tsai, and other forms of exploitation.[20] They hoped this would divert attention from the chattel slavery in their Persian Gulf satellites and the Aden Protectorate, and focus it on forced labor in Russia, peonage in Latin American, and mui tsai in China. Showing that chattel slavery was only one of a spectrum of exploitative institutions, many of which were more oppressive, would put it into "proper perspective" and avoid giving the impression—so regrettable in the ACE's 1938 report—that slavery existed almost entirely in the British Empire.[21] Their main interest, however, was to expose and attack the "new slavery" in the labor camps of the communist bloc.

A full discussion of the forced labor problem is beyond the scope of this study, which will only consider its impact on the antislavery campaign. In 1947, the American Federation of Labor (AFL) had accused the Soviet Union of arbitrarily sentencing dissidents and others to forced labor camps, where the conditions and the loss of life were appalling.[22] The numbers ran into millions and enabled great engineering projects, mining, and other works to be carried out more cheaply and quickly than if they were performed by free wage labor. Full information on the extent of the system was just emerging, mainly provided by persons who had escaped from the camps. As communist governments were established in Eastern Europe, the system was spreading and it was seen as a threat to free labor, and the whole trade union system. Exposing it, in all its horrors, became an important card in the Cold War.

In February 1949, the U.S. delegation to ECOSOC proposed an inquiry into forced labor everywhere. As the proposal developed it was to include on the spot visits to investigate complaints. The Soviet Bloc rejected it, and responded with countercharges of peonage in the United States, discriminatory labor practices in colonial possessions, and the plight of unemployed and low paid workers in capitalist countries.[23] They claimed that under their benevolent penal laws, they were reeducating criminals through labor. They proposed an investigation by some one hundred trade unions into all aspects of labor and unemployment worldwide, but particularly in non-self-governing territories.[24] Since many unions had strong communist affiliations, this was rejected by the Western powers, which had a majority in ECOSOC. Instead, ECOSOC asked the ILO to investigate forced labor, and instructed the secretary-general to ask member states if they would cooperate in an impartial inquiry. A joint UN-ILO investigation was necessary in order to include the USSR, which had not joined the ILO, claiming it was a capitalist organization.[25]

The Colonial Office was as opposed as the Russians to such an inquiry. Officials maintained they had nothing to hide, but feared it would stimulate the existing agitation against the "communal services" still exacted by chiefs.[26] The British decided for tactical reasons only to agree to an inquiry if the Russians and a majority of other countries did the same. They believed this would maneuver the Soviets into rejecting the proposal, thus giving the Western bloc a moral advantage in this game of "political warfare."[27]

By June 1949, the Foreign Office had decided to support the establishment of a UN slavery committee rather than the proposed alternative—an inquiry by the secretary-general. Costs would be about the same, £6,000—and by supporting the committee, they would appear to be more enthusiastic. Moreover, a committee of independent experts was more likely than the Secretariat to include forced labor in its discussions.[28] The British hoped to expose Soviet labor camps and support the antislavery movement at the same time, killing two birds with one stone. Anticipating that when this was debated in the Council, the Russians would turn the spotlight on slavery in colonial territories, they prepared to counterattack by producing the text of the Codex, Russian penal labor laws, which infringed the Declaration of Human Rights.[29] They hoped this would "burst like a bombshell" on a surprised ECOSOC.[30] To get maximum publicity, American trade unions and the labor press were warned to expect it.[31]

In July 1949, Dehousse duly introduced the agreed resolution on slavery in ECOSOC and, as predicted, the Russians supported it, taking it to apply only to chattel slavery in colonies and "backward areas." The British then introduced a new resolution instructing the secretary-general to appoint a small ad hoc committee for twelve months of not more than five experts to "survey the field of slavery and other institutions or customs resembling slavery," and suggest which UN bodies could best attack them. The Chinese and the Chileans were unhappy that mui tsai and peonage were equated with slavery, and there were attempts to define slavery more narrowly, but the British resolution was adopted by twelve votes to six. Predictably, China, the

USSR, Poland, and Byelorussia opposed it. So, more surprisingly, did Denmark and New Zealand.[32]

A few days later, when ECOSOC discussed the secretary-general's report on government reactions to the proposed inquiry into forced labor,[33] the British produced their "bombshell," the Codex. The United States called for an impartial investigation by a joint ECOSOC-ILO commission of independent experts, which could take evidence from nongovernmental organizations, and visit the areas about which complaints had been made. The Soviets, charging the West with conducting a malicious capitalist campaign, again called for a trade union investigation, putting the Western powers into the unwelcome position of rejecting it.

A problem now arose between the Americans who favored a separate inquiry into forced labor, and the British who wanted it conducted by the slavery committee. To the dismay of the colonial powers, the Americans introduced a resolution to hold the inquiry on forced labor even if the Russians boycotted it. The colonial powers feared that, if it could not investigate Soviet practices, the inquiry would turn its full attention on their colonies. As signatories to the 1930 convention, they already reported on forced labor to the ILO, and their only purpose in supporting a new commission was to publicize Russian iniquities. The Americans resisted their requests to withdraw the proposal, believing that of all the "Cold War themes," the attack on their labor policies caused the Soviet bloc the "most pain."[34] The Western powers, anxious to put up a united front, delayed further discussion until the 1950 session of ECOSOC.

As the question festered on, some Foreign Office officials began to have second thoughts. They feared that a new body, the International Confederation of Free Trade Unions (ICFTU), might launch its own inquiry into forced labor and include the colonies. Since it was not a communist organization, they would have to cooperate, but they preferred a UN committee, which would be more likely to show up Russian forced labor without embarrassing the colonial administrations. "Objective truth" was secondary to the maintenance of the initiative in the Cold War.[35] The Colonial Office and the Ministry of Labor, however, remained solidly opposed to any inquiry that did not include the Soviet bloc.[36] When ECOSOC met in February 1950, the Russians and their allies were boycotting the UN in protest at the Western refusal to admit the communist People's Republic of China, now in power on the mainland, in place of the Nationalist Chinese government in exile in Taiwan. The Soviets announced that they would not recognize any decisions taken in their absence, giving the British a welcome reason to support an American proposal to postpone the discussion on forced labor until 1951.[37]

However, in the spring of 1950, the ILO, at the request of the American Workers representatives, decided to investigate forced labor without waiting for ECOSOC,[38] and it was soon clear that the United States, pressured by unions, would have to support an inquiry. The British, anxious that it should be a joint UN-ILO investigation, asked the ILO to delay appointing a committee while the secretary-general appealed again to recalcitrant states to cooperate.[39] The outcome was still uncertain when the Slavery Committee was established, and it was not clear whether, as its British sponsors wished, it was to include forced labor in its deliberations.

THE AD HOC COMMITTEE ON SLAVERY 1950–1951

The Secretariat had had an "awful time" finding five suitable experts for the slavery committee. They had to be of "first class caliber" and, where the League committees had been composed of experts from the colonial powers, these had to come from different geographic regions of the world—a new principle for selecting UN committees. Intergovernmental agencies, nongovernmental organizations, and trade unions were invited to submit names. The Foreign Office was asked to approve Greenidge. They believed that he was sincere and sensible, but added prophetically that he could be "difficult" as a team member. The Colonial Office, afraid of his proposed slavery suppression service, was not enthusiastic, but by the time this was relayed to New York, he had been appointed by the secretary-general.[40] Women's organizations lobbied for a female member, and the token woman this time was Jane Vialle.[41] Half French and half African, she represented French Equatorial Africa in the upper chamber of the French parliament, and had done extensive social work on behalf of Africans in the French colonies. The third member was Professor Pablo Troncoso, a Chilean professor of law and social sciences in the University of Santiago and for years a correspondent of the ILO on labor questions in Latin America. The last member was Professor Bruno Lasker, a German-born American, who had been on the research staff of the Institute for Pacific Relations. He was the author of several works on social and economic problems and, most recently, of *Human Bondage in South-East Asia*. He was appointed when the Secretariat failed to find a suitable "full blooded Oriental." They were also unable to get a candidate from Eastern Europe.

Greenidge's three years of tireless lobbying had finally been rewarded. Not only had his long-sought committee been appointed, but, in a startling break with precedent, he was to be a member of it, giving the Anti-Slavery Society a unique influence. Sadly, however, this committee was to prove a shambles, for which he was held partly responsible.

The Society's status at the UN had now to be determined. Member states, like their predecessors at the League, sought to protect themselves from attacks by national NGOs by stipulating that NGO evidence would only be considered if they had "consultative status." For this they had to be vouched for by their own governments, and there had to be no international body covering the same field. In October 1949, the Anti-Slavery Society applied for consultative status with ECOSOC. The Colonial Office feared it would "stir up Colonial problems" but realized that refusal would be challenged in Parliament or, even worse, the Society might be nominated by some other state, "one of the Slavs!" for instance. This would certainly not "look good." The Foreign

Office considered a joint appointment with the French society *Les Amis de l'Abbé Gré-goire*, but dropped the idea when Greenidge told them it was mainly interested in the history of slavery, and that the only other French society was a one-man show.[42] The Anti-Slavery Society, described as "the only organization, national or international . . . of any weight" in its field, was duly accredited.[43] This vital privilege, however, could always be withdrawn. In the years to come, the Society worried that its small size might make it vulnerable to attack by those powers it criticized. This might not have completely silenced it as it could have made its submissions under the umbrella of an accredited society, but it would certainly have made it difficult for it to be regularly represented and would have been a great loss to the antislavery cause.

The Ad Hoc Committee was appointed in December 1949. Under its terms of reference, it was to "survey the field of slavery and *other institutions or customs resembling slavery.*"[44] These were not specified, but Greenidge and the Foreign Office had agreed they would include peonage, mui tsai, and forced labor.[45] It was to consider the "nature and extent" of these problems and suggest "methods of attacking" them, bearing in mind the fields of competence of existing UN bodies. At its first meeting, at Lake Success in February and March 1950, members discovered they had no common language. Troncoso and Vialle spoke no English and one of the others spoke no French. Troncoso was elected chairman, according to the UN custom of giving such posts to nationals of smaller countries. The Secretariat had collected information on slavery from League reports and published works, and the Trusteeship Division of the UN, which had replaced the League Mandates Commission, furnished a memorandum on non-self-governing and trust territories. Troncoso produced details on peonage—a step well within its brief but which was to prove fatal to its success.[46]

Members began by preparing a questionnaire asking all governments to furnish up-to-date information on their territories by 1 October 1950.[47] The questionnaire asked for information on the slave trade and slavery as defined in the 1926 convention; on serfdom, defined as the hereditary tenure of land accompanied by obligatory service; on peonage, defined as "traditional forms of involuntary unpaid service exacted by land owners and other employers of labor;" on debt-bondage, pawning, the exploitation of children under guise of adoption (including mui tsai), on forced marriage, and forced labor.[48] It also asked what measures had been taken to end these practices. It had great advantages over the ACE. It was able to solicit information from individuals and NGOs, including the communist-dominated World Federation of Trade Unions on the one side, and, on the other, the American Workers' Defense League. Jewish organizations claimed that there were still a million-and-a-half slaves in Arabia. Some information was collected on peonage in the southern United States. It was also allowed to interview members of the specialized UN agencies and the ILO, in order to determine which antislavery functions might be passed to them.

ECOSOC was in session at the same time and the committee, not anticipating trouble, submitted its questionnaire for approval. The colonial powers had all passed laws against slavery and had ratified both the Slavery and the Forced Labor Conventions. They were, therefore, prepared to accept the questionnaire, and in discussion assumed a confident, "self-righteous attitude," commending the committee for its work. Not so their critics, some of whom took fright at the prospect of a UN inquiry into their internal affairs. The Peruvian representative, incensed at the questions on peonage, demanded that the questionnaire be revised and approved by the Council before being circulated. His motion was defeated. The Committee also won a further point; it was agreed that it might hold two further sessions, one in November 1950 to prepare further questions for governments if needed, and a final one in the spring of 1951 to prepare its report. There were also two other significant changes made at the request of the United States. It was told to drop forced labor, which was now to be assigned to a special committee. Thus, this highly divisive issue was once more divorced from the slavery question. Secondly, it was directed to hold its next sessions in private.[49] However, it had already received considerable publicity. All but six of its thirty-three meetings had been closed, but it had held two press conferences, which got good coverage. Moreover, Vialle had given several interviews, Troncoso had lectured at Columbia University, and Greenidge had been on television.

The Committee had asked each member to report on particular areas of the world, and to send their information to Troncoso, who, as rapporteur was to produce a draft report to be discussed at the next session.[50] But, in August 1950, before this session could be held, the Peruvian delegate launched a violent attack in ECOSOC and succeeded in getting the Council to postpone the November session until April 1951 to give governments more time to reply to the questionnaire. An attempt by Peru, Columbia, and Chile to replace it altogether with a special commission of government representatives was defeated,[51] but they managed to cancel the second session. This meant that the Committee had only one further session for four weeks in April 1951. This was too little time to complete its work. Greenidge managed to get the Secretariat to give him money to do some extensive research in Geneva during the winter of 1950 and he superseded Troncoso as rapporteur.[52] Already pressed for time, the last session was hampered because the simultaneous translation system in the new UN building in New York where it met was not yet working and, without a common language, time was lost in consecutive translation. Moreover, there was dissension among its members. As a result, it submitted two hasty reports: a majority one agreed by the others before they left, and a fuller, minority one, which Greenidge produced after doing more research.[53]

Unfinished as their work was, their recommendations were to bear fruit. They accepted the definition of slavery in the 1926 Convention and suggested that the United Nations should take over that convention. This was duly done by a protocol executed in 1953, and all states were invited to adhere to it.[54] More controversial was their suggestion that the UN should negotiate a supplementary convention to forbid debt bondage, serfdom, forced marriage, and adoptions aimed at exploiting children. They recommended fourteen as the minimum age for marriage and that marriages should be registered. They wanted mutilation prohibited. They revived an old cause of conflict by suggesting that slave trading on the high seas be treated as piracy. Finally, they made two other unpopular suggestions—that signatories should furnish annual reports to the UN and that a permanent UN slavery committee should be established.

ECOSOC found their hasty reports too "full of undigested material" and too incomplete to form the basis for action. The committee had received sixty-four replies to its questionnaire and another nine came in after their session. No replies were sent by either Yemen or Saudi Arabia.[55] The British had stated that slavery was legal only in the Aden Protectorate, but had not sent in information on the Sudan, or on their Achilles' heel—the Persian Gulf states. Most replies simply stated the legal position without showing how the laws were applied or what the actual position was, and many answers were ambiguous. To provide a more solid basis for discussion the secretary-general was asked to solicit more information and produce a clearer report suggesting further action. But, when he produced it early in 1953, it added little to what was already known.[56]

DRAFTING THE SUPPLEMENTARY CONVENTION OF 1956
Greenidge now forced the issue, as Lugard had done in 1925. He submitted a draft supplementary convention that included the practices identified as analogous to slavery. ECOSOC asked member states if they would accept it. Only twenty replied but most of these were in favor, Britain among them. However, the Colonial Office, which did not want the convention, objected to some of Greenidge's proposals. As in the past, the Foreign Office, therefore, decided to submit a draft convention of its own, taking account of these objections. There followed months of discussion between the various ministries, the Anti-Slavery Society, and other NGOs.

The Colonial Office insisted that any commitment to attack these practices must be progressive, and be acceptable to colonial governments. They objected to providing annual reports, which might be debated in ECOSOC and become a form of supervision, exposing Britain to attack by "anti-colonialists," while powers that did not adhere to the convention would escape criticism. They wanted colonial governments to be free to decide whether or not to pass laws on such questions as the age of marriage and the protection of women and children. Education, they claimed, was more effective than legislation.[57] There was also a serious constitutional problem. Many of the colonies now had their own legislatures and, although there were no laws on the subject, the home government did not feel that it could sign treaties for them without their consent. The British, therefore, wanted to ensure that the convention would include a colonial application clause that would allow them to sign the treaty for the metropolitan government and its dependencies but not for "semi-independent" territories until they had agreed to it. It was April 1954 before the draft was finally agreed and sent to ECOSOC and to the ILO.[58]

To speed things up the British suggested that the Council appoint a rapporteur to summarize the "amorphous" information in the three existing reports, and present it as the basis for the debate on the draft convention. They proposed Greenidge for the job—a move bound to please the humanitarian lobby. The Secretariat objected that he was "difficult" and too imbued with "missionary zeal and enthusiasm" to produce a balanced report, and was not a sufficiently "prominent figure" to command universal respect. Other powers considered him discredited by the performance of the Ad Hoc Committee.[59] The Foreign Office, however, claimed that only he had "sufficient, distinction, ability, energy, and acquaintance with the subject to reduce the existing information into digestible form" in time for the 18th session of ECOSOC. Moreover, he was available and cheap, as only his expenses had to be paid. He arrived in New York blissfully unaware of the objections and sure that he would be appointed, but although his British sponsors lobbied hard on his behalf, their efforts were in vain.[60]

They had difficulty mustering support for a rapporteur at all, and had to persuade the Norwegian delegate, Hans Engen, to accept the job, and Australia, Belgium, and the United States to nominate him.[61] Discussion of the convention was put off to await his report to the nineteenth session of ECOSOC in 1955. That there would be a convention was by no means assured. Only Belgium and Australia had come out in favor of it. Ecuador vehemently opposed it. Venezuela was defensive. France, the United States, and a number of other delegates from both sides of the iron curtain opposed it.[62]

Discussions on the draft began in earnest in Britain as comments came in from the ILO, the UN Secretariat, from other governments, from the Anti-Slavery Society, and women's groups. The Colonial Office, the Ministry of Labor, the Home Office, and the Admiralty had second thoughts. Problems arose over the distinction between forced labor and slavery, over what constituted debt-bondage, and serfdom. The adoption clauses were reworded so as not to rule out transfers of children that might be to their benefit. The St. Joan's Social and Political Alliance wanted the articles against forced marriage, the inheritance of widows, and child betrothal strengthened, while the Colonial Office worried about their impact on customary law. All mutilation could not be banned because some Muslim countries punished certain crimes with the amputation of a hand and/or foot. The wording had to ensure that castration was forbidden, together with branding, but not bruising from a beating with a carpet slipper! There were fears that treating the maritime slave trade as piracy might offer an excuse for interfering with the freedom of the seas. If to avoid the right to search was limited to a zone as in the Brussels Act, the zone had to be defined. There were complex legal questions and every word was subject to scrutiny. Drafts went backwards and forwards, sometimes several times, between government departments and NGOs. The views of the Anti-Slavery Society were given considerable weight and changes were made to incorporate them.[63]

When the draft convention and the Engen report were presented to the Social Committee of ECOSOC in March 1955, it was soon clear that not all delegates were ready to undertake the complicated task of redrafting. Therefore, the British persuaded the Dutch, Norwegians, and Yugoslavs to introduce a resolution establishing a small drafting committee to present a revised version to the 21st session of the Council in 1956.[64] They then lobbied to get as many like-minded powers as possible included among the ten delegates elected to it by secret ballot. They succeeded in including the other colonial powers, France, the Netherlands, and Australia,[65] as well as themselves. Of the remainder, they welcomed Turkey as a staunch ally; and India and Ecuador, believing they would support "progressive" rather than immediate action against debt-bondage and peonage respectively. The USSR, Yugoslavia, and Egypt, whose delegate spoke for the Arab states, could not be excluded, but the British hoped they would be outvoted.

Charles Greenidge had tried and failed to get himself appointed to the British delegation. His honeymoon with the Foreign Office was over. Officials had decided that he was a busybody, a "menace" with a gift for alienating people. Worse still, he would "obstinately advocate views more extreme" than theirs.[66] He now tried, again in vain, to get himself appointed to the drafting committee as an expert.[67] He also angled to have the secretary-general appoint a slavery expert to his staff, doubtless hoping to be chosen.[68] As the representative of an accredited NGO, he was able to attend meetings, however, and voice his opinion if called upon, but he did not have the right to vote. He had resigned as secretary of the Society at the end of 1955, but had been nominated an honorary director and continued to represent it at the United Nations. He was to prove a thorn in the side of the British delegates, who were anxious to get the convention accepted by ECOSOC with as few changes and delays as possible and to draft it so that it was acceptable to the largest number of states. Like Lord Robert Cecil, thirty years earlier, they believed a minimal treaty was better than no treaty at all.

The drafting committee met in Geneva in January 1956. To Britain's disappointment, India and Ecuador joined the USSR, Yugoslavia, and Egypt to form an anticolonial block. The committee was thus split five to five, with Turkey voting with the colonial powers, and many issues were decided, not on their merits but by Cold War tactics. The mere mention of the word "colonies," the delegation reported, aroused "emotions which cloud all normal process of reasoning."[69] The main points of contention were predictable. The anticolonial bloc wanted immediate, not "progressive," elimination of all forms of servitude. They wanted the convention applied to all colonial territories at once, sweeping away British arguments that this would be a retrograde step for those on their way to self-government. As for the maritime provisions, the British had given up the idea of treating slavers as pirates and suggested search only in a designated zone, covering the Persian Gulf and Red Sea. This was criticized as pointing the finger at the Arabian countries in which slavery was still legal. Eventually, uneasy compromises were found and the British gained most of their desiderata.

However, the British delegates realized that if the convention went to ECOSOC or the UN Assembly for approval, they would be forced to apply it immediately to all their territories without consultation or reservations. They, therefore, proposed convening a conference of plenipotentiaries with powers to adopt a final version and open it for signature; they wanted it held in Geneva, rather than New York where all members had permanent delegations. They hoped that only really interested states would send representatives to Geneva and that they would be mainly lawyers and experts.[70] Moreover, only states that belonged to the United Nations and Specialized Agencies or were parties to the Statute of the International Court needed to be invited. This would exclude the new communist states such as East Germany, North Korea, North Vietnam, and the People's Republic of China, which had not yet been admitted to the UN. The fear was that if they came or even adhered to the treaty, they would be gaining recognition "by the backdoor."

The British tried to persuade "friendly" powers, such as the western European states, Turkey, Japan, and the "old" or "white" members of the Commonwealth, to send delegates in hopes of getting a sympathetic majority. It took some arguing to convince countries like Norway that a slavery convention could affect them in any way.[71] When the conference opened in Geneva on 13 August 1956, their hopes died. Over fifty delegations and some observers attended.[72] Even the tiny enclave of San Marino was represented. The communist bloc was there in force, as were the Latin American states. To make matters worse, the Suez Canal had just been nationalized by Egypt and attention was focused on the Middle East. The atmosphere was even more highly charged than it had been in the drafting committee. The meeting also attracted press attention, and a spate of misleading articles, particularly in the *Times*, often reflecting Greenidge's views, added fuel to the fire.[73] The British delegates, who had a small entertainment allowance to give semiformal lunches to those members whose votes they wanted, had an uphill struggle. Intense behind-the-scenes lobbying failed to prevent public wrangles over almost every article. In some cases, these resulted in useful changes of wording, but in others, the conflict was purely political.

The anticolonial powers, as expected, demanded immediate, not progressive, elimination of slavery and servitude. By a very close vote, however, the British won this point.[74] They had more trouble getting their way over the colonial application clause, and believed that the Russians opposed it simply to embarrass them by putting them in the position of not being able to sign the convention they had proposed. They eventually rallied support by agreeing to try to get the agreement of their semi-independent dependencies within twelve months. In order to get this accepted, however, they had to emasculate the maritime clauses, particularly the provisions for the search and seizure of suspects by warships and military aircraft in the specified zone and their subsequent trial.[75]

These clauses were violently attacked by the Saudi observer, who denounced it as "a match to set the Middle East on fire." Similar wild fears were expressed by the delegate from the newly independent state of Sudan, who feared it might furnish an excuse for "foreign powers" to revive imperialism in the area by establishing air and naval bases. Other powers had more limited concerns. The Pakistanis, for instance, were irritated by Greenidge's appeal to extend the zone to the whole coast of Baluchistan. They were engaged in negotiations with Oman over the session of Gwadar, an Omani enclave on their coast, and feared the sultan might break off talks because of the implication that slaves from the Makran coast were being imported into his territories.[76] The Portuguese worried that India might use the article to interfere with shipping between Beira in Mozambique and their colony of Goa, on the Indian coast.[77] Neither could state these reasons publicly but the delegation knew of them. The Soviet bloc and the Latin American states supported the opposition. In view of the ongoing Suez crisis, even "friendly" powers thought the article too provocative to support at this time. Moreover, it would have prevented the Arab states from signing the convention. In the end, all that was agreed was that the slave trade was a crime, and each signatory was to take measures to prevent its flag, or its ports, airfields, and coasts from being used by slavers. The powers were to exchange information and to cooperate, but policing was left to each individual nation.[78]

The British, "making a virtue out of necessity," struck a bargain. In return for scrapping the maritime zone and giving up the right to seize suspects, they got support for the colonial application clause and for limiting reporting to merely furnishing the secretary-general with information on laws and measures against servitude. This last article was carefully worded to prevent the reports being used by ECOSOC as a mechanism for supervision.[79]

The British delegation was pleased with the convention, which was signed on the spot by thirty-one powers, including the Soviet Union. They thought it a triumph to get a treaty Britain could sign, and their main objectives had been achieved. To their bitter disappointment, however, far from welcoming their triumph, the press labeled the treaty a failure. *The Times* commented that the conference had become the "occasion for shadow boxing" in which the communist powers and Egypt had tried to get credit as "leaders of anti-colonial opinion," that Britain had been put "on the defensive" and gained very little, "and the slaves nothing at all." Echoing Greenidge, it stated, "an organization which denounces slavery is useless unless it has teeth to enforce its denunciation."[80] These articles inflamed opinion further and the British delegation believed that they prevented Sudan, Egypt, Iraq, and Syria from signing the convention at once.[81] The Foreign Office tried to get *The Times* to write a more favorable editorial, but was not happy with the result.

There followed a spate of criticism in Parliament in the same vein. There were complaints at the failure to end slavery in the Gulf States, and the failure to include the original maritime articles.[82] On the latter point, the government claimed that Britain's slave trade treaties granting the right to search and seize suspects in the slave trade zone were all still operative—even the Brussels Act. This was highly debatable. In response to parliamentary questions, the instructions to naval officers were reviewed in 1957. The Royal Navy had not operated a slave trade patrol since the outbreak of war in 1939. Naval officers had simply been told to look out for slavers and take appropriate action if they encountered suspects. Now the navy, still theoretically operating under the instructions issued in 1932,[83] wanted these revised and brought up to date in case the right to search was challenged in the International Court. The Law Officers ruled that the Brussels Act could only be abrogated with the consent of all its signatories and was thus still binding on all except those who had acceded to the St. Germain Conventions, and even they were bound by the articles not covered in these conventions. This meant that the rights of visit and search acquired under the Brussels Act were still valid, as well as Britain's other slave trade treaties. [84] However, they were obviously out of date. There were no treaties, for instance, with the now independent Pakistan, or with Saudi Arabia, and Iraq. Since these rights had not been recognized in the new conventions, it was highly unlikely that they could be exercised without raising protests.

The Foreign Office, reviewing the situation, concluded that the only treaties that could stand up in court were those with Bahrain, Qatar, the Trucial States and Muscat and Oman.[85] In practice, only these vessels were being intercepted.[86] However, the Royal Navy was much smaller than it had been before the war, and the Admiralty now stated that it could not afford to keep vessels in the Red Sea to patrol for slavers, and it did not wish to do so in the Persian Gulf. Thus, what had once been a great pillar of the antislavery campaign was now fading into oblivion.

THE RESULTS OF THE SUPPLEMENTARY CONVENTION

The Supplementary Convention did not replace the 1926 Convention; it complemented it. The main result was that the definition of slavery now firmly included peonage, debt-bondage, forced marriages, and adoption for exploitation. International attention had been called to these practices and their eventual elimination had been agreed upon. The point had also been made in the various committees by the so-called underdeveloped or developing nations that the real problem which kept many of the practices going was poverty and that they would only end when living standards rose.

If there was no mechanism for enforcement, at least the groundwork for further treaties had been set in motion. A model had also been established for an attack on a wide variety of institutions, which would be denounced as slavery, however far-fetched the analogy. Moreover, the Anti-Slavery Society had now been firmly launched on a crusade to secure a United Nations slavery committee—a crusade that was to last for nearly twenty years. It was also to play a part in the ever-widening definition of "practices analogous to slavery."

The long discussions on forced labor also ended in the adoption by the ILO of the Abolition of Forced Labor Convention in 1957. This complemented the 1930 treaty

and took note of the two slavery conventions. As the British had wanted, it only outlawed forced labor as an instrument of political repression, economic advantage, and
labor discipline. The supreme irony was that the United States, which had initiated the
attack on forced labor as a weapon in the Cold War, was unable to sign either this convention or the one on slavery because of congressional efforts to control the president's treaty-making powers, and because both treaties dealt with practices that came
within the legislative spheres of individual states.

The long and acrimonious negotiations for the 1956 Slavery Convention had focused attention on Arabia. The British tried to downplay this, hoping for improved
relations with the Saudis, but Greenidge, to the irritation of the Foreign Office and
delight of the prime minister, Anthony Eden, had had a public altercation with the
Saudi delegate over whether his government had allowed slave trading to revive and
had licensed slave dealers.[87] This spotlight may have been among the stimuli for the
abrogation of slavery in Saudi Arabia a few years later. Ironically, it also gave a new
urgency to the British need to end the institution in the Aden Peninsula and Persian
Gulf. That slavery was still legal in these satellites became more and more of an
anomaly, whereas the other practices included in the convention soon ceased to be of
much concern to Britain for the simple reason that one after another of the dependencies in which debt slavery, pawning, and forced and early marriage were practiced
became independent. As for mui tsai, this ceased to be a problem in Hong Kong and
Singapore within a few years of the establishment of the People's Republic of China,
which suppressed it at home and cut off the supply to the British colonies. As will
now be seen, slavery in Arabia became the focus of the antislavery campaign for the
next few years.

NOTES

1. Greenidge to Noel Baker, 29 May 1946, FO 371/59739 UNE 482/41/78.

2. Greenidge draft report to the ASAPS, 30 September 1946. He had seen, for instance, Ralph
Bunche of the State Department, officials of the ILO, the American Civil Liberties Union, the
Rockefeller and Phelps-Stokes Foundations, members of missionary and philanthropic bodies,
as well as African American organizations. He tried and failed to see Mrs. Roosevelt, the
chairman of the Human Rights Commission.

3. Cadogan to FO, secret telegram, no. 407, 16 June 1946, FO 371/59739 UNE 254/41/78.

4. Minute by Duffy, 18 November 1949, on Corley Smith to Boothby, 11 November 1949, FO
371/78977 UNE 4525/17319/96.

5. See issues of the *Anti-Slavery Reporter*, which was published throughout the war, although its
volumes became slimmer after 1940. Osu were Igbo who were dedicated to shrines and were
both feared and ostracized. For cult slavery, see below, chapter 24.

6. For his activities, see Archives of the British Anti-Slavery Society and his own papers in Rhodes House, Oxford.

7. Universal Declaration of Human Rights, adopted by the UN General Assembly 10 December 1948, see inter alia, *HRI.*

8. Minute by Hebblethwaite, 1 March 1948, FO 371/72853 UNE 342/342/96. The International Bill of Human Rights included the Declaration issued in 1948 and the covenants or treaties designed to implement its provisions.

9. Minute by Hebblethwaite, 1 March 1948, FO 371/72853 UNE 342/342/96.

10. Greenidge to Bevin, 25 April 1947, FO 371/67618 B UNE 188/188/96; minutes on Grossmith to Maclean, no. 12351/7/48, FO 371/72853 UNE 342/342/96 and no. 12805/2/48, 31 March 1948, and minutes, ibid., UNE 1333/342/96.

11. Greenidge to Heppel, 30 August 1948, and enclosed memorandum, 18 August 1948, FO 371/72853 UNE 3622/342/96.

12. Minutes and memorandum on Greenidge to Heppel, 30 August 1948, FO 371/72853 UNE 3622/342/96.

13. Heppel minute 8 November 1948, FO 371/72853 UNE 4489/342.96. For the Belgian draft resolution see UN General Assembly, 3rd session, 3rd Committee, 22 October 1948 A/C.3/93.

14. Greenidge to Bevin, 12 November 1948, FO 371/72853 UNE 4455/342/96.

15. Address 23 October 1948, copy in FO 371/72853 UNE 4455/342/96.

16. Rundall to Galsworthy, restricted, 6 January 1949, FO 371/72853 UNE 4933/342/96.

17. Minutes in FO 371/72853 UNE 4489/342/96, and on Rundall to Matthews, confidential, 13 November 1948, and FO to Rundall, confidential, 17 November 1948, ibid, UNE 4490/342/96.

18. Rundall to Galsworthy, restricted, 6 January 1949, FO 371/72853 UNE 4933/342/96.

19. Burnham to Rundall, no. 12805/A/49, 10 February 1949, and enclosed circular, FO 371/78972 UNE 656/17319/96.

20. Boothby to Rundall, 29 November 1948, and Boothby to Greenidge, 29 November 1948, FO 371/72853 UNE 4455/342/96; Mayhew minute, 12 January 1949, of conversation with Judd, (UNA), FO 371/78972 UNE 247/17319/96.

21. Cabinet Paper, I.O.C. (49) 138, confidential, 29 June 1949, CAB 134/399.

22. For conditions in these camps, see inter alia Solzhenitsyn 1963, 1973; Conquest 1978, 1990.

23. UK delegation to UN to FO, confidential telegrams nos. 344 and 345, 14 February 1949, no. 359, 15 February 1949, nos. 389, 390, and 391, 18 February 1949, FO 371/78972; speech by Mayhew at ECOSOC 8th session, 18 February 1949, ibid., UNE 876/17319/96.

24. UK delegation to UN to FO, confidential telegram no. 80, 5 March 1949, FO 371/78973/UNE 1124/17319/96.

25. For a summary of these proceedings, see Cabinet Steering Committee on International Organizations, Forced Labor, draft brief for 9th session of ECOSOC, item 23, confidential IOC (49) 149, 10 June 1949, CAB 134/399.

26. It was allowed by the Forced Labor Convention of 1930 (see above, chapter 10) but was unpopular.

27. Minutes on Tennant to Cape, no. 0.164/1949, 26 May 1949, FO 371/78973 UNE 2334/17319/96; Cape minute on forced labor, FO 371/78974 UNE 3134/17319/96.

28. Minute by Salt, 8 June 1949, on memorandum by the secretary-general, FO 371/78974 UNE 2431/17319/96.

29. Corley Smith to Rundall, no. 699/2/49, 15 June 1949, and minutes, FO 371/78974 UNE 2637/17319/96.

30. Cape to Duffy, secret, 7 July 1949, and enclosed draft of statement to be made at ECOSOC, FO 371/78974 UNE 2883/17319/96. The information for these attacks is in "Forced Labour in the Soviet Union," in FO 975/23, and "The Forced Labour Codex of the RSFSR," FO 975/29 and in Cabinet Papers, I.O.C. (49), confidential, 29 June 1949, CAB 134/399.

31. Washington to FO, telegram no. 3562, 13 July 1949, FO 371/78974 UNE 3030/17319/96.

32. Cape to Greenidge, 26 July 1949, FO 371/78974 UNE 3161/17319/96, and enclosed provisional summary of the Council debate; UK delegation Geneva to FO, telegram no. 138. 21 July 1949, ibid., 3169/17319/96.

33. Only a third of those who responded fully supported the idea. Over half rejected it, ignored it, or qualified their agreement. For a breakdown, see minutes on UN Report by secretary-general on Forced Labor, 13 January 1950, E1588, FO 371/88869 UNE 4925/173/19/96 US2182/8.

34. Cape memoranda for Jebb on the attitude of the U.S. government on forced labor, 5 September 1949, and on the American proposal to hold an inquiry without Soviet participation, FO 371/88869; Corley Smith to Boothby, confidential no. 608/112/49, 23 November 1949, FO 371/78978 UNE 4666/17319/96.

35. Minute by Le Quesne on policy agreed at a Foreign Office meeting, 12 January 1950, on Huijman to Cape, no. 12252/49, 20 December 1949, FO 371/78978 UNE 4899/17319/96. For these discussions which took place over several months, see also other documents in this file and UK ECOSOC delegation to FO, restricted telegram nos. 181 and 182, 4 August 1949, FO 371/ 78976 UNE 3436/17319/96; minutes on Dallin to Hankey, 5 October 1949, FO 371/78977 UNE 4319/17319/96; Colonial Office to Cape, no. 12252/49, 20 December 1949, FO 371/78978 UNE 4666/17319/96. Corley Smith to Boothby, confidential, no. 608/112/49, 23 November 1949, and minutes and enclosed U.S. memorandum on its proposal, ibid., UNE 4666/17319/96.

36. Robertson to Cape, no. O.164/1949, 2 January 1950, FO 371/88869 UNE 4925/17319/96.

37. UK delegation to UN to FO, no. 38/8/50.E, 1 February 1950, FO 371/88869 US 2182/11 and no. 167, 8 February 1950, FO 371/88870 US 2182/12; FO to UK delegation, confidential telegrams nos. 153 and 213, 4 February 1950, no. 250, 10 February 1950, and minutes, FO 371/88869 US 2182/11.

38. ILO to secretary-general, 11 April 1950, circular from secretary-general 24 April 1950 E/1671, and minutes in FO 371/88870 US 2182/38. The ILO debate is enclosed.

39. FO to UK delegation, confidential, 16 June 1950, and minutes, FO 371/88870 US 2182/40.

40. Corley Smith to Boothby, no. 699/9/49, 11 November 1949, and minutes, FO 371/78977 UNE 4525/17319/96; Huijman to Duffy, no. 12805/A/49, confidential, 30 November 1949, FO 371/78978 UNE 4694/17319/96. Corley Smith to Boothby, no. 699/13/9, restricted, 22 December 1949, ibid., UNE 4925/17319/96. UK delegation to FO, no. 280/6/50 E, 25 March 1950. FO 371/88870 US 2182/33. The Colonial Office suggested Margaret Read or Victor Purcell.

41. The Liaison Committee of Women's International Organizations suggested Margaret Read among others, Peel to Jebb, 12 October 1949, FO 371/78977 UNE 4197/173/96.

42. Greenidge to White [UN], 4 October 1949, and reply 6 January 1950, and FO to delegation NY, confidential, 7 February 1949, FO 371/88869 US 2182/7; Greenidge to Rundall, 13 October 1949, Home Office to FO, 29 October 1949 and CO to FO no. 25114/49, 13 December 1949, and FO minutes, FO 371/78977 UNE 4189/17319/96.

43. This was formally approved by ECOSOC on 6 March 1950.

44. Italics are mine.

45. Cape minute of conversation with Greenidge, 24 June 1949, FO 371/78974 UNE 2496/17319/96.

46. These documents are conveniently collected in the UN library in Geneva under UN ECOSOC, ad hoc committees 1950. See particularly, memorandum by the secretary-general on the suppression of slavery and the slave trade in international agreements E/AC 33/3, 2 February 1950, and on the terms of reference of the ad hoc committee E/AC 33/4, 3 February 1950, and on slavery in non-self-governing territories, 16 February 1950, E/AC 33/8; Troncoso memorandum on slavery and similar practices in Latin America, E/AC33/6, 16 February 1950.

47. I have drawn here on Greenidge's draft report on the first session for the ASAPS, some of which was deleted from his final report, Brit.Emp.Mss.s.285. The summary records of both sessions of this committee were published as E/AC 33, first session SR 1–34, 2nd session SR 35–55.

48. Report of 1st session of Ad Hoc Committee, 27 March 1950, E/1660 E/AC 33/L.10. The practices named as peonage included *concertaje, servicio personal, pongage* or *ponguaeaje,* and *yanaconzazgo.*

49. UK delegation to FO, confidential telegram no. 142, 14 March 1950, FO 371/88870 US 2182/26 and no. 143, 14 March 1950, ibid., US 2182/27.

50. Greenidge was to report on Western Asia, Ethiopia, and Europe; Vialle on Africa and Madagascar; Troncoso on the American continent and the East Indies; and Lasker on Southeast Asia.

51. Jebb to FO, no. 439, telegram, FO 371/88775 US 17321/18.

52. Greenidge to Humphrey, 12 October 1950, AS MSS. Brit. Emp. s.22, G 516.

53. These reports are E/1988 and E/AC.33.B.14; see also Greenidge, 193–94. His draft report and comments on it by the Secretariat, Lasker, and others are in AS MSS. Brit. Emp. s.22, G.516.

54. Protocol Amending the Slavery Convention signed at Geneva on 25 September 1926, approved by General Assembly resolution, 794 (VIII) of 23 October 1953.

55. Other states that had not replied were Liberia, Cuba, Haiti, Nicaragua, Paraguay, and the Ukraine.

56. See UN SOA 317/10/03 and, UN E/2357, 27 January 1953.

57. For the interdepartmental discussions see draft convention, draft letters, and minutes in FO 371/112512 US 2181/ 4, US 2181/6, US 2181/8, US 2181/13; West CO to Warner, no. SSB 124/125/01, 19 February 1954, and minute, US 2181/7; Reading to Winster, 7 April 1954, FO 371/112513 US 2181/21.

58. See draft in FO 371/112513 US 2181/26.

59. UK delegation to Warner, confidential, no. 2183/7/54, 2 March 1954, FO 371/112512 US 2181/13; FO to Dixon, no. 311 confidential telegram, 19 April 1954, FO 371/112513 US 2181/27.

60. Warner to Meade [UK delegation], confidential, 9 March 1954, FO 371/112512 US 2181/13; Meade to Warner, confidential, 9 March 1954, ibid., US 2181/19; Dixon [UK delegation] to FO, confidential priority telegram no. 241, 6 April 1954, ibid., US 2181/24.

61. Ukdel to FO, confidential telegram no. 111, 3 May 1954, FO 371/112513 US 2181/37.

62. Ukdel to FO, confidential telegram no. 110, 3 May 1954, FO 371/112513 US 2181/36; Meade to Greenidge, 4 May 1954, enclosed in Ukdel to FO. 14 May 1954, ibid., US 2181/41.

63. See numerous documents in FO 371/117579.

64. UN E/Resolution (XIX)/6, 12 April 1955.

65. Dixon to FO, confidential telegram, no. 292, 1 April 1955, FO 371/ 117580 UNA 2182/24S; no. 48, 11 April, ibid., UNS 2182/30 and minutes; no. 50 restricted telegram, 11 April, ibid., UNS 2182/33. These were now called administering powers—Australia had a mandate over part of New Guinea.

66. Minute by Warner, 17 February 1955, FO 371/117579 UNS 2182/9; minute on Scott Fox to Murray, 9 May 1956, FO 371/123803 UNS 2183/79.

67. Minutes of AS Committee Meeting, 22 September 1955, FO.371/117582; Warr to Brinson, confidential, 23 November 1955, and minutes, ibid., UNS 2182.

68. Scott Fox to Murray, 26 April 1956, and enclosed letters from Greenidge, FO 371/117582 UNS 2183/69.

69. Report on the Drafting Committee, January 16 to February 6, 1956, enclosed in UK del. to FO, confidential, February 141956, FO 371/117582 UNS 2183/39.

70. Ibid. and minutes.

71. Scott Fox to Murray, confidential, 8 June 1956, FO 371/123803 UNS 2183/90; Scott Fox to Swann, confidential, 26 July 1956, ibid., UNS 2183/98. The Norwegians, for instance, were told that freedom of the seas should concern them.

72. The voluminous reports from this conference are too many to enumerate separately. They consist of a number of "reporting telegrams" discussing each article as it was drafted which are in FO 371/123804, FO 371/123805, FO 371/123806. A useful brief summary is in the report on the conference in CAB 134/1270 IOC (56) 82.

73. *The Times*, 16, 17, 30 and 31 August and 4 September 1956; Greenidge letter in *Manchester Guardian*, 15 August 1956; *Birmingham Post*, 14 August 1956; *Daily Express*, 10 August 1956.

74. See article 1, Supplementary Convention on the Abolition of Slavery, the Slave Trade, and Practices Similar to Slavery 1956, *HRI*.

75. The Russians had objected violently to trial by any but a suspect's own national court, and were insistent that if trial by another tribunal was necessary, the suspect's government should agree to it.

76. CRO to FO, no. WES.81/3 secret, 19 April 1956, FO 371/117582 UNS 2183/66.

77. Stirling to FO, no. 167, 31 July 1956, and minutes, FO 371/123804 UNS 2183/100.

78. See article 3 of the Supplementary Convention, *HRI*.

79. Scott Fox to Pink, confidential no. EC/SL/26, 30 August 1956 FO 371/123805 UNS 2183/7. These articles are numbered 12 (2) and 8 (2) and (3).

80. *The Times*, 30 August 1956.

81. Scott Fox to Pink, 30 and 31 August 1956, and minutes, FO 371/123805 UNS 2183/134 and 134 A.

82. Parliamentary questions 4 and 29 October and 1 and 26 November 1956 and replies, and draft replies for supplementary questions, FO 371/123806 UNS 2183/170, 2183/172, S2183/177, and 19 December 1956, with draft speech for debate, FO 371/123807 UNS 2183/191.

83. Extracts from Standing Instructions for the Guidance of the Commander-in-Chief, Mediterranean, and for Commander-in-Chief, East Indies. These go back to 1932 and are enclosed in Nairne to Denson, confidential, 11 January 1957, FO 371/127019 EA 2184/1.

84. Parliamentary questions 9 July 1956, minutes and correspondence, FO 371/120691 EA 2185/14 and EA 2185/15. The validity of the St. Germain Conventions was questioned, but it was politically impossible to invalidate them.

85. Treaties had been signed with Bahrain 8 May 1847, the Trucial States, and Qatar, 3 November 1916, with Muscat, 14 April 1873. For a discussion of the legal rights, see correspondence September 1956 in FO 371/120691 EA 2185/18.

86. Minute by Riches, 30 January 1957, FO 371/127019 EA 2184/3; Denson to Nairne, 31 May 1957, and minutes and revised draft instructions, FO 371/127019 EA 2184/5.

87. Scott Fox to Swann, no. 2223/50/56 confidential, 13 April 1956, and minutes, FO 371/117582 UNS 2183/64; UK del to FO, confidential telegram, no. 87, April 19, 1956, ibid., UNS 2183/67; Greenidge to Hogan, 21 April 1956, ibid.; Greenidge letter to *The Times*, 15 August 1956. Prime Minister's Office to Logan, 21 April 1956, ibid., UNS 2183/67A.

The End of Slavery in Arabia and the Persian Gulf 1950–1970

SLAVERY AND OIL WEALTH IN THE PERSIAN GULF STATES IN THE 1950s

While the United Nations was discussing slavery in the early 1950s, the British were wrestling with the problem of ending it in their Protected States in the Persian Gulf. Tensions in the Middle East were rising. In 1951, Iran nationalized the Anglo-Iranian Oil Company's installations. This stimulated oil production in Kuwait and Qatar and led the oil companies to increase both royalties and wages. Revenues in Kuwait alone were expected to top £50,000,000 a year. In 1952, Gamal Abd el-Nasr (henceforth Nasser) seized power in Egypt and set out to make himself leader of the Arab world, posing a challenge to the British in Aden and the Gulf, and to the patriarchal rulers in Arabia. Egypt was now seen as the fount of progressive political ideas, and the voice of nationalism and anticolonialism in the Middle East.[1]

The establishment of the Trucial Oman Levies (later Scouts) heralded growing British involvement in the hinterland, going beyond the role authorized in treaties with the rulers. The declared aims of this small force were to maintain peace and order, suppress the slave trade, and protect British political officers.[2] Under the control of the Foreign Office, its local commander was the political resident in the Persian Gulf stationed in Bahrain—the only diplomat in the world with a private army.[3] Originally intended to be a hundred strong by the end of 1951, thanks to a parsimonious Treasury it started with a mere thirty-five men from the Arab Legion in Jordan and twenty local recruits. Locals gradually replaced the Jordanians.[4] The shaykhs were not consulted when the force was planned,[5] but they received the news with enthusiasm, for it provided the means of establishing their claims in the interior. At the same time, the British appointed political agents to the Trucial States and urged the rulers to employ specialist advisors. What had been a British maritime umbrella sheltering them from the territorial claims of their increasingly powerful neighbors—Iraq, Iran, and Saudi Arabia—now became a force for social and political change, albeit a muted one.

In the richer states of Kuwait and Bahrain, particularly the latter, there were already demands for greater democracy, and development schemes in the shape of stronger administration, and the provision of schools and hospitals were under way. But in Qatar and the Trucial States, administration was rudimentary and facilities minimal. The rulers were weak and afraid of alienating their supporters. The British tried to prod them to introduce reforms, without letting in the forces of revolutionary change.

This policy was pursued with one eye on the international situation. Thus care was taken to inform Ibn Saud of the proposed Levies, and to assure him that the Jordanians— subjects of his old enemies the Hashemites, who now ruled Jordan and Iraq—would be replaced as soon as possible. Talks were opened with him on the boundary question in 1950 and the next year the London Agreement stipulated that neither troops nor oil company personnel would enter disputed areas until the frontiers had been agreed.

The attack on slavery began cautiously. In the summer of 1951, the Levies chased a robber to Buraimi. The small force could not police the whole area, and the resident stopped it from arresting the slave traders in Hamasa, deciding that the traffic was not serious enough to risk upsetting Muscat and the Saudis by operating in the disputed area. By the end of the year, however, the Levies were eighty strong, had done much patrolling, and were a "steadying" influence. No cases of kidnapping had been reported since they were established.[6]

A major breakthrough in the antislavery campaign now occurred in the little shaykhdom of Qatar. The political officer, M. B. Jacomb, estimated that there were some three thousand slaves, including men, women, and children, in a total population of fifteen to twenty thousand. Perhaps fifteen hundred owners were scattered through the towns and villages. Many had only one slave. Before the oil age, Qatar had had only two industries—pearling and slaving. The ruling family had been poor and deeply involved in the traffic. Jacomb reminded owners that the trade was forbidden, and made it known that slaves could appeal to him for help. On average, four did so each week. The ruler agreed to free those acquired in the previous ten years, but not those acquired before 1916—the date the treaty against the slave traffic had been signed with Britain, or those who had been in slavery for a long time.[7] Within a few months, Jacomb had broken through this barrier and was freeing slaves bought or born since 1916, and a few owners had begun to manumit their slaves voluntarily. Better still, the ruler was considering buying out all slaves when his oil revenues increased.[8]

Oil production was already changing relationships. The Foreign Office had been disturbed to hear that a British company was hiring slaves in Qatar and that their owners appropriated up to 90 percent of their wages. When reproached, the masters claimed that they were supporting their families—a specious argument, as the women usually worked for them. After Jacomb remonstrated with the ruler, owners dropped their demands to 50 percent of the wages. By July 1951, bolder slaves were refusing to pay them anything. As oil company jobs proliferated, and other sources of investment and income opened up, owners and slaves became less dependent on each other.[9]

At this point the discussions on slavery in ECOSOC and the spectre of a new convention led the Foreign Office to make it clear that they could no longer permit slavery in the shaykhdoms. The political resident in Bahrain tried to avoid action by raising the old cry that most slaves were content, and that they would lose their livelihood if freed.[10] Nevertheless, he was asked to press the shaykh of Qatar to make good on his promise.[11] The ruler was as good as his word. In March 1952, he freed all slaves from 10 April and offered to compensate their owners.[12] He originally proposed offering Rs.3,000 for every slave freed, but his advisors persuaded him that half the sum would do. Six hundred and sixty slaves were freed and their owners received a total of Rs.70,000, a quarter of which the ruler paid himself. The disparity between this small number and the original estimate of three thousand slaves has still to be explained. However, it is clear that some owners refused compensation. Others had already freed their slaves, and some slaves did not want to leave. Foreign Office officials considered the compensation high until they realized that the oil revenues had reached nearly £3,000,000 for the year. Compensation was paid to poor owners for one or two slaves, resulting in a wide distribution of the oil money.

Lessons were learned as a result of this operation. No proper registers of slaves or owners had been kept. The ruler had been confident that there would be no fraudulent claims but a charter aircraft full of supposed Qatar slaves and owners arrived from Bahrain. They were sent back empty-handed, but the British believed there had been many successful false claims. All former slaves could now claim wages, and many were expected to stay with their owners, particularly the women, for whom prostitution might be the only alternative.[13]

On the orders of the Foreign Office, the political resident in the Gulf reviewed the position in the summer of 1952. In Kuwait, slavery was not recognized by the courts, and the ruler freed any who applied to him. The British themselves could not issue manumission certificates for local slaves without reference to the ruler, because they had never concluded an antislave trade treaty with Kuwait. However, the ruler normally agreed to their requests and they found the procedure useful in that he "protected them" from claims for compensation from dispossessed owners. In difficult cases he was prepared to pay compensation himself.[14] Slaves received wages and their keep. Since no local slave had applied for manumission for three years, it was assumed that they were indeed contented. It was thought unlikely that the shaykh would issue a proclamation abolishing slavery since it was recognized by Muslim law. In Bahrain, slavery had been abolished since 1937 and freed slaves in danger of re-enslavement were often settled there.

In the Trucial States, oil had not yet begun to produce large revenues. The rulers were considered too weak to end slavery, and even the slave trade continued. In 1953, the British suggested to the newly established assembly of rulers—the Trucial Council—that they might follow the example of Qatar. They listened with incredulity and refused. Slavery, they said, was recognized by Islam, and they did not have the funds to compensate owners, who would argue that they should be reimbursed for the expenses of rearing slaves since childhood. The political agent saw no hope of emancipation without compensation. The British considered offering them the money.[15] At a guess there might be two thousand slaves in the Trucial States and Buraimi. At Rs.1,500 a slave, the cost would be around £225,000. But the rulers and their powerful relatives were the main owners, and it was thought unlikely they would even forbid slave trading. Although the Foreign Office thought it monstrous to kowtow to slave owners, the British decided merely to review the matter from time to time.[16]

Their main concern was to prevent oil riches from fuelling the slave trade.[17] They also worried that it might become known that a high percentage of oil workers in Abu Dhabi were slaves. The Foreign Office repeatedly asked the Iraq Petroleum Company not to employ slaves, but it replied that it depended on the shaykhs to supply labor.[18] The British considered asking the rulers to stop slaves from being sent to the oil fields, but slave labor was essential to production and they could hardly prevent a man from being employed because he was a slave.[19] Around one hundred former pearl divers in Qatar and perhaps two hundred in the Trucial States were chronically in debt, and forced to work for their creditors. In contrast, in Bahrain and Kuwait they could change employment and pay off their debts with a portion of their wages.[20] The news that there were people in debt-bondage was particularly upsetting to the British, who had insisted that it be included among the institutions to be outlawed by the Supplementary Slavery Convention under discussion at the United Nations.

SLAVERY AND THE BURAIMI CONFLICT

In August 1952, the Saudis, in contravention of the London Agreement, sent a small force to occupy Buraimi and Hamasa, the two villages in the Buraimi oasis claimed by Muscat.[21] They set out to win the allegiance of the local shaykhs and their followers with offers of money, food, arms, protection, and a share of oil revenues if oil was discovered in viable quantities. Initially, the imam of Oman and the local people reacted against them and the sultan of Muscat and the shaykh of Abu Dhabi mustered their forces to drive them out. But the British persuaded them not to attack and opened negotiations with Ibn Saud. This resulted in the "standstill agreement," leaving the Saudis in place until the frontier problem was solved. The Levies blockaded Hamasa. The question of sovereignty was submitted to arbitration in 1954, with the British acting on behalf of Muscat and Abu Dhabi. At stake was not simply control of a small oasis, but whether oil found in the area would be produced by the primarily American company, Aramco, under Saudi protection, or by the British company, Petroleum Concessions. It was agreed that neither side would undermine the arbitration process by bribing the local peoples.

Slavery, as usual, was a pawn in a bigger game. In 1953, the British had received details of the slave traffic in Hamasa, including a list of traders. Slaves were no longer abducted on the Trucial Coast. Although some were still kidnapped in Batinah, most were now bought from villagers, often using trickery. An agent would pay a high bride price to get the bride's parents to agree to his taking her to another part of the country. They would live there for a while until he sold her to Saudi traders and told her parents that she had been divorced for "immoral ways." The slaves, almost all female, were sent on to Al Hasa or Riyad. The Saudi commander and his followers in Hamasa were reported to be buying slaves.[22]

The Levies were ready to arrest slavers leaving the oasis with their captives, and initially the British hoped to capture a caravan heading for Saudi Arabia as proof that if the arbitration resulted in Buraimi being awarded to the Saudis, the traffic would increase.[23] However, when they heard that Omanis and Trucial tribesmen were also involved in the trade,[24] this idea lost its attraction. They decided just to insist that the Saudis would not tolerate the traffic.[25] The Saudis for their part continued, in contravention of the Standstill Agreement, to try to win over the local people and to suborn witnesses called by the arbitration committee.

Matters came to a head in November 1953, after the death of Ibn Saud, with whom the British had some rapport, followed in 1954 by that of the old imam of Oman. The new imam, supported by the Saudis, declared Oman an independent state, no longer owing any allegiance to the sultan of Muscat. The British withdrew from the arbitration proceedings and, in October 1955, sent the Levies to retake the Buraimi Oasis for the sultan of Muscat and the shaykh of Abu Dhabi.[26] They deported the Saudis and their leading supporters, who, with the new imam, took refuge in Saudi Arabia. They then arbitrarily selected a new frontier line, conceding some Saudi claims.[27]

The eviction of the Saudis from Buraimi was much criticized in America as well as in the Middle East. The British were urged in vain to return to arbitration or open negotiations with the Saudis. At stake was the whole British position vis-à-vis the Gulf rulers who looked to them for protection, not just of their territory, but of their existing and potential oil assets. The retaking of Buraimi proved the value of the British connection, but it also forced the British to face a growing dilemma. Although not legally responsible for the internal affairs of the shaykhdoms they were now too closely enmeshed in running them and protecting them to avoid being held responsible for them in the eyes of the world. Their position was one of responsibility without authority, since the rulers and their subjects were only prepared to accept the British connection as long as it did not impinge too obtrusively upon their independence, their convenience, and their conception of themselves as good Arabs.[28]

The negotiations for the Supplementary Slavery Convention focused attention on slavery. Thanks largely to the efforts of the Anti-Slavery Society, intent on getting a convention, articles about it appeared in the press and questions were asked in Parliament.[29]

British attempts to downplay the matter led to some ludicrous situations. For instance, documents found in Buraimi had shown that the Saudis were involved in the slave traffic and had sent slaves as presents to King Saud,[30] but Saudi protests about their expulsion from the oasis had been surprisingly muted, and rather than "blackening" them, the Foreign Office decided it would be better to try to deflect attention in Parliament away from the continuance of slavery in the Gulf States.[31] However, officials had given the Anti-Slavery Society information about the Saudi traffic when they wanted to prove their involvement. This came home to roost, when, in reply to parliamentary questions, the government stated that it had no evidence that the slave trade still continued. When Lord Listowel, who was on the Society's Committee, protested, it had to arrange another parliamentary question so that it could say the traffic was indeed still going on![32]

The next few years were a time of rising tension and rapid change. After Nasser nationalized the Suez Canal in 1956, Britain, France, and Israel invaded Egypt. American pressure and public outrage forced their withdrawal. Saudi Arabia broke off relations with Britain, and the Gulf rulers were deeply disturbed, but they looked to Britain as their protector. Two years later the Hashemite monarchy was overthrown in Iraq and there were a series of military coups in Syria. From Egypt, Nasser launched a vociferous program of revolutionary socialism aimed at ousting colonialism from the Arab world and replacing the "feudal" rulers.

In 1957, the British, in accordance with the Colonial Application clause asked the Gulf rulers to accept the 1956 Supplementary Slavery Convention. At first glance the authorities in Bahrain believed that it did not refer to domestic slavery but simply to "institutions and practices similar to slavery." Since most of these did not exist in the Gulf, the rulers would have had no trouble agreeing. None of them had agreed to the 1926 Convention. However, they were soon told that slavery was implied if not specifically mentioned. To sweeten the pill, it was emphasized that signatories were only bound to end it progressively.[33] Bahrain and Qatar accepted the treaty without difficulty. The Trucial rulers followed suit and told the political agent that slaves were now "at liberty to come and go at will." Evidently there had been a metamorphosis in their attitude since 1953. The shaykh of Kuwait agreed when told that other Muslim rulers had done so.[34]

Although all the Gulf shaykhs accepted the treaty, the Trucial rulers did not issue the necessary edicts and the British did not press the point at the time, arguing that there was no longer a slave trade, and any slaves who wished could apply to British officials for manumission. Slaves seemed "content with their lot" and were "by the letter of the law freemen."[35] Summing up the situation in 1961, the political agent explained that all the Trucial rulers had "some old slaves in their households" but they remained by choice. There might be some fifteen hundred of them. Masters could no longer appropriate the earnings of their slaves. The opening of jobs elsewhere in the Gulf was leading to an exodus of slaves and since very few people were now being enslaved, there was such a shortage of young slaves that the shaykh of Sharjah was considering employing Indian domestics.[36] There were still, however, rare cases of young girls being fraudulently married and then sold.

In 1961, sensational articles on the Trucial States and Arabia in the *Sunday Pictorial* and *The Times* led to renewed concern at the Foreign Office. An oil company employee, who had served in Oman, claimed to have seen a slave dug up for shipment to Arabia after being drugged and buried for a day. He described the bleached bones of a party of Iranian pilgrims dumped on shore by dhow owners and told to walk over the hill to Mecca. The young people had been taken away by slavers and the rest left to die. He claimed that children were kidnapped and shipped to Abu Dhabi en route for Riyad. He described manacled slaves herded onto planes in Buraimi and flown by "free booter" American pilots to Saudi Arabia.[37] Other articles followed about the traffic in Saudi Arabia.

British officials dismissed them as greatly exaggerated and the author as unreliable. They agreed that there were occasional cases of slaving, and slaves who asked for manumission often had been ill-treated. Horrifyingly, a few cases had come to light of Pakistani or Baluchi pilgrims landed on remote shores and left to fend for themselves by dhow owners who took their money. However, this was not necessarily linked to the slave trade.[38] The Foreign Office worried that these articles would attract the United Nations' attention and lead to questions in Parliament about British relations with the Gulf rulers.[39] By the beginning of 1962, they decided that the time had come to insist that the rulers issue the edicts outlawing slavery.[40] The shayhks insisted they had already banned it. But there was no record of any decrees.[41] There were further delays— the shaykh of Abu Dhabi, the only Trucial State producing oil at this time,[42] could not be approached because he was ill or in a bad humor, or it was Ramadan. The British wondered if they could modernize their image by ceasing to issue manumission certificates, but decided that a halfway measure of this kind would not help.[43] There had been twenty-six such certificates issued in 1961, eleven of them in Muscat, down from a high of one hundred and six in 1950.[44]

Then came the surprise news that Saudi Arabia had abolished slavery. It was now only legal in the British Arabian Protectorates and in Muscat and Oman, giving rise to comments at the United Nations and questions in Parliament.[45] Finally at the Trucial Council meeting in May 1963, the rulers of the northern six states agreed to sign a decree stating that slavery, like the slave trade, had long been forbidden in their territories.[46] The ruler of Abu Dhabi, who had not been at the meeting, was eventually pressured to follow suit. Thereafter, the only country in which slavery was legal was Oman.

THE ABOLITION OF SLAVERY IN MUSCAT AND OMAN

From 1957, the political situation in the Omani interior had gone from bad to worse. The leaders who had escaped to Saudi Arabia returned and led a revolt. British forces suppressed this revolt in 1959, and the sultan was finally installed in control of the whole country. Instead of instituting reforms, he lived in his palace in remote Salala, keeping contact with officials by radio-telephone. Increasingly out of touch with his subjects and despised in the Arab world as a British puppet, he depended on British ministers and advisors and a mercenary Baluchi army led by British officers. In return for military assistance, the British persuaded him to start a development plan in 1958. When the Anti-Slavery Society suggested that the suppression of slavery might be a condition of continued help, the Foreign Office replied that the slave trade had been suppressed and that giving the sultan military help did not entitle Britain to ask him to end an institution recognized by Muslim law.[47] The British believed he opposed manumission because he did not want to pay compensation. They defended their support of him on the grounds that Muscat was independent, there was no slave trading and any slave who wished was manumitted at the British request—although they knew this did not apply to the sultan's own slaves. In 1961, the British consul general reported that an average of some eighteen slaves a year had been freed in this way in the preceding decade, mostly because of ill-treatment.

The exact position is hard to determine. The British had no desire to clarify it. In 1956, *The Times* correspondent, James Morris, who had travelled across the country with the sultan, had been told by the British consul general that the sultan's servants and bodyguard had been manumitted, but the men had told him they could not leave. He asked the Foreign Office which was correct. The consul explained that they were "trusted servants" who were still called slaves. They did not leave because the sultan gave them all they wanted. The Foreign Office, called on to explain to Morris "when a slave was not a slave," and anxious to "steer the press off the subject" decided to give him just enough information to satisfy his curiosity.[48] When the political agent in the Trucial States claimed that domestic slaves in the Batinah area were all too commonly prevented by force from seeking manumission, the consul protested that he had little evidence of this.[49] Two anthropologists working in Suhar in the 1970s believed that slaves there had been freed between 1955 and 1960 and that many had gone as migrant labor to Kuwait.[50] In 1963, when an official asked why the sultan could not declare that slaves were free, he was told they were "unpaid family retainers who, being unpaid, represent wealth to their employers."[51]

This unsatisfactory situation continued for another seven years during which Britain was increasingly attacked at the United Nations for bolstering the autocratic sultan; and its satellites in the Gulf faced threats from Arab nationalists, as well as from Egypt, Saudi Arabia, Iraq, and Iran. The British felt it even more imperative to retain their alliance with the sultan. Reviewing their options in 1960 and again in 1963, they concluded that if he fell, the flow of oil from the Gulf might be cut off, and they would lose their air base on Masirah—a vital link on the route to Southeast Asia. There was no suitable alternative ruler, as his son, Qabus, was young and had seen little of his country. They decided that, though "far from ideal," they would continue to support him,[52] and they spent large sums building up his armed forces and financing development projects.[53]

The situation deteriorated as the sultan became more repressive and the opposition, spurred on by the discovery in 1964 of oil in exploitable quantities, became more vociferous at home and abroad. A revolt in Dhofar, in 1965, was contained but not quelled. Arab delegations to the United Nations condemned British "aggression" in Oman. After long wrangling and investigations, they accused the British in 1966 of "conducting a policy of mass extermination against the Omani people," and exploiting the country for their own benefit. The UN passed a resolution by an overwhelming majority, calling on Britain to withdraw.[54] It is notable that in these attacks at the United Nations, the British were not accused of countenancing slavery. This was a sensitive topic among Arabs, although it had theoretically at least lost its legal status everywhere. The attack was directed instead against colonialism. The Anti-Slavery Society drew attention to slavery in Oman, but its information was usually out of date and it got little support.[55]

Anticolonial feeling was rising in Britain, and in 1966 the Labor Party Conference voted for total withdrawal of all British forces east of Suez. In January 1968, after a financial crisis led to the devaluation of the pound, the Labor government announced that it would leave the Gulf and Oman by 1971. A coup against the sultan led by his son Qabus, endorsed by Britain, took place on 23 July 1970. Said bin Taimur abdicated and was flown to England.[56] Among the reforms which followed was the end of legal slavery in the same year.

THE ABOLITION OF SLAVERY IN SAUDI ARABIA

In 1951, the British tried to pass the burden of the antislavery campaign in Saudi Arabia to the United States, which was becoming increasingly involved in supporting the country with its valuable oil fields. They informed the State Department that they were no longer in a position to take a forceful stand over Saudi slavery and that the brunt of UN discussions on the subject would fall on the United States. They estimated there were fifty thousand slaves in the country and believed that numbers were increasing with oil wealth. They suggested that the American and British ambassadors in Jiddah might discuss the problem in view of the fact that there had been articles in Soviet publications attacking slavery in "reactionary Arab states," branded "puppets of the western imperialists."[57] Nothing seems to have resulted from this initiative.

Difficulties arose when the British tried, usually in vain, to retrieve slaves abducted from the Trucial Coast,[58] and when the Saudis tried to recover slaves who fled into the Gulf States. The ruler of Kuwait complained that he was faced with having either to buy off the owners of runaways or to refuse to return them, and he did not want to upset Ibn Saud. When the British protested, the Saudis denied complicity.[59] The Foreign Office also reported the gruesome information that twelve Baluchis belonging to

Ibn Saud, who had tried to escape, had been beheaded, three of them publicly in front of the palace in Riyad.[60]

During the 1950s, sensational articles appeared in the press. Some were surely exaggerated. For instance, a report reproduced in the *Sunday Dispatch* claimed that five thousand men, women, and children a month were abducted from French Africa, Uganda, Eritrea, and elsewhere, loaded onto trucks and shipped via Sudan to Mecca or Medina.[61] In 1953, however, the publication of the White Fathers, *Afrique Nouvelle,* reported a widespread traffic to Arabia from French West Africa, particularly Mauritania. It published the account of an African from Mali, who claimed he had been taken to Saudi Arabia by his African employer and sold, together with other servants, while on the pilgrimage. This was backed up with photographs and affidavits. Although there is no reason to doubt its accuracy, the American consul general in Dakar reported that the editor of the paper, Father Robert Rummelhardt, and his colleagues might have political, as well as humanitarian motives for their action. They were "patriotic Frenchmen" who bitterly resented "the Afro-Asia bloc's complaints about French policy in North Africa."[62]

However, the French ambassador in Jiddah reported that African merchants told him that Senegalese naturalized Saudis, posing as missionaries, offered to take Africans to Mecca. They trucked their clients across Sudan and then shipped them to Jiddah. There the authorities arrested them as illegal pilgrims, and handed them over to brokers. A young woman sold for two to three thousand riyals or two to four hundred francs. An old woman fetched some four hundred riyals and a man under forty about fifteen hundred riyals. The ambassador gave the names of the merchants implicated, and guessed that victims numbered several hundred a year, mostly from French West and Equatorial Africa. His inquiries ring true, but he also commented that a nation that traded in people was hardly equipped to attack France over human rights in Tunisia.[63]

The French consul in Ethiopia reported that there was still traffic through French Somaliland, and a Foreign Office "contact" in Djibuti said that some ninety African Muslims had been sold to Mecca in 1952. Twenty had escaped and made their way back to the Lake Chad area. He also believed that the Danakil were selling "Shankalla" to the Saudis.[64] In 1955, the French Assembly commissioned Pastor La Gravière to conduct an inquiry into slavery. He returned from Africa, convinced that there was still a slave trade.[65] The British representative in Jiddah agreed with him, and reported that prices had so increased that a pregnant young woman now fetched five hundred gold sovereigns or some twenty thousand riyals.[66] He thought most slaves came through Yemen and that Saudi officials supplemented their "uncertain" salaries by "turning a blind eye" to the traffic.[67]

In January 1961, the Egyptian newspaper *Al-Ahram* reported that Mali was attempting to get a chief extradited from Libya because, shortly before independence in 1960, he had taken many men, women, and children on the pilgrimage and sold them in Mecca. He then used the proceeds to set up a business in Libya.[68] Articles in the *Sunday Pictorial* 1961 and 1962 described a slave auction in Jiddah and the traffic from Sudan.[69]

By 1962, slavery had become a political issue in Saudi Arabia itself. Ibn Saud had forty-five sons, many of them dissolute and extravagant, but some eager for power and reform. Slavery was one of the platforms for Egyptian propaganda, and for complaint at the United Nations. It was also an issue that could be used by progressives at home. Thus when a freed slave made a public appeal for fifty thousand riyals to free his wife and children, a trade union leader took up his cause and was forced to flee to Egypt.[70] The same year, twenty Saudi princes involved in an abortive coup, also fled to Egypt, where they denounced slavery on the radio, fuelling Nasser's campaign against the Saudi royal family—a campaign that became more explicit as he increased his efforts to unite the Arab world under his aegis.[71]

A struggle for power ensued between the weak King Saud and his more able brother, Crown Prince Faysal. In June 1962, perhaps to diffuse criticism at home and abroad, a decree was issued forbidding the sale and purchase of slaves. In August, a younger son of Ibn Saud, Talal, an admirer of Nasser, and an advocate of constitutional government, announced that he was freeing his thirty-two slaves and fifty concubines. This gave the lie to Saudi claims at the UN that slavery had ended.

In September 1962, the Imam Ahmed of Yemen died. His successor, Muhammad Badr, was in sympathy with Nasser, but within days, a military coup replaced him with a president, who was supported by Egyptian soldiers. Civil war in Yemen followed. With this crisis on his doorstep, Faysal took over the Saudi government. He sent help to the new imam and mended his fences with the British, with whom diplomatic relations had been broken off after the Suez Crisis of 1956. The British sent military aid to him and to the royalists in Yemen. The United States called on Egypt to withdraw.

Faysal himself had owned slaves but had never bought any. The British had long ago reported that he did not like slavery. He had manumitted his own slaves after the Supplementary Slavery Convention was signed in 1956, although Saudi Arabia had not adhered to it. Now, doubtless to rally external and internal support, he announced a slate of reforms. At the first meeting of his new cabinet on 6 November 1962, he said:

> It is known that the Moslem Shari'a urges the manumission of slaves. It is also known that slavery in modern times lacks many of the stipulations imposed by Islam for the justification of slavery. The Saudi State has, ever since its inception, faced the problem of slavery and taken gradual steps towards its abolition. It started by prohibiting the importation of slaves and imposed penalties on slave importers. Lately it prohibited the sale or purchase of slaves. Now the government finds the time opportune for the total abolition of slavery and the manumission of slaves. It will compensate those who deserve compensation.[72]

This statement was considered to be a proclamation, and slavery was henceforth formally abolished. The Saudis did little to publicize their efforts, and material in the British archives is sketchy. In January 1963, committees were formed throughout the country to examine deeds of ownership and assess the compensation to be paid to owners, who entered claims before 21 July 1963. At this time there was no law forcing owners to free slaves but one was expected. The British estimated that there were between fifteen and thirty thousand slaves in 1962, less than half a percent of the total population of a little over three million. Most had been born in Arabia of African origin. Seventy percent belonged to the royal family and three other families.[73] Some 60 percent were women. Most were in domestic service and lived "in comparative luxury with moderate salaries as opposed to free but underpaid or unemployed workers."

The British believed that some twenty-five million riyals had been set aside for compensation and perhaps fifteen million had been spent. Radio Mecca announced in June that the equivalent of over ten million dollars had been paid to free some ten thousand slaves.[74] Some owners did not ask for compensation and it was believed that many slaves would remain with their masters. Faysal himself complained that all his household slaves wanted to stay with him. It was announced that a committee would be formed to rehabilitate former slaves, and on 11 September 1963 a decree was issued to provide them with work cards and identity papers.[75] By October 1963, the British considered that slave trading had "almost died out" and that few, if any, slaves were still imported.

This was refuted by those who believed that many more pilgrims entered the country than ever returned home. But the British ambassador explained the fallacy in this argument:

> It is difficult sometimes to disentangle the question of slavery from that of indigent Africans who smuggle their way to Saudi Arabia in order to go on the pilgrimage. There are many thousands of these in the Hejaz who having arrived either have no desire to return or have not the money to do so, and who remain. For example a large proportion of the native staff of this Embassy consists of such persons who have no passports or proper residence permits.

In 1963, the Saudis were trying to expel these foreign workers, and the ambassador did not believe that those who remained were enslaved.[76] The Mali embassy agreed with him. Mali was looking after the interests of over 90 percent of the slaves in Saudi Arabia, presumably because of sales of its nationals while on pilgrimage.

Charges that slavery and an active slave trade still existed in Saudi Arabia continued into the 1980s.[77] Their veracity cannot at this stage be verified but the need for labor was already being met by contract and other imported foreign labor.

THE SUPPRESSION OF SLAVERY IN THE
ADEN PROTECTORATES AND YEMEN

The position in the Aden Protectorate appears to have changed little in the 1950s. There was reportedly little slavery in the Western Protectorate but it was still "flourishing" in the Qu'ati and Kathiri states of the Hadhramaut, and the sultan of Mukalla had large numbers of slaves in 1956.[78] Manumission could still only be obtained in areas within reach of a British official. Occasionally cases of slave trading came to light. There were six such cases between 1957 and 1967, the latest in 1959.[79]

The next years were a time of turmoil. From being the veritable stepchild of empire, virtually ignored by, and unknown to the British public, Aden and its two Protectorates became the scene of intense conflict, leading to a humiliating British withdrawal.[80] Britain tried belatedly to weld the town of Aden, with its many Yemeni workers and its increasingly vociferous and politicized trade unions, into a federation with the administratively weak rulers of the interior. The rulers had few linkages with the town, and little liking for each other. In 1959, at British instigation, the sixteen rulers of the Western Protectorate and the colony of Aden formed the Federation of the Amirates of South Arabia (later the Federation of South Arabia).

Slavery had long been illegal in the colony, but in the Federation, only some of the rulers, now called sultans, had ended its legal status. The British claimed the others had not done so as there was no slavery.[81] The Anti-Slavery Society refuted this and regretted that abolition had not been a condition of British support for the rulers when the federation was formed. But the government claimed that it had not had the power to make such a demand.[82] In fact, it only legislated by agreement with the rulers and never attempted to impose laws.[83] Even the Supreme Council of the Federation could only urge states to take action. In response to criticism at the UN in 1962, and in the British Parliament, the council issued a "comprehensive denunciation of slavery,"[84] and the Federal Government began to draw up a law laying down punishments to serve as a model for the various states of the Federation.[85]

As late as 1967, some rulers had still not abolished the legal status of slavery. Criticism mounted when, in that year, the sultan of Lahej was reported to have brought a slave girl in his retinue to a London hotel. The Anti-Slavery Society claimed that Arab rulers often travelled with slaves and reiterated its plea for a UN slavery committee.[86] In Parliament an MP used the episode to attack the government's support of the "sultans and sheiks in South Arabia" for whose defense the British were paying.

In the Eastern Protectorate, the situation was just as unsatisfactory. There were four unfederated areas—the sultanates of Socotra and Mahra, and the Upper Yafa, and the Qu'ati and Kathiri States. In the last two, enslavement and possessing slaves were criminal offenses.[87] In 1966, the British admitted that "a technical form of slavery," whatever that was, possibly continued in "remote and unadministered parts of the Protectorate." They were guessing. Large areas of Mahra had still to be penetrated by representatives of the sultan and by British advisors, and there was no advisor in Socotra. As for Yafa, they stated that as far as they knew there was no slavery in the unadministered areas.[88] No cases of slave trading had come to light since 1959.

That the legal situation in South Arabia was unsatisfactory was clear, but even the Anti-Slavery Society believed that in practice slaves could leave their owners if they wished. Some held prominent positions. However, in the Society's eyes they were a "buffer" between the rulers and the people, facilitating the continuation of "feudal" practices such as hostage taking—an accusation refuted by the Colonial Office.

The fact that slavery continued in British South Arabia was the more embarrassing as the 1962 coup led to the outlawing of slavery in Yemen. Yemen had never given up its territorial claims to the Aden Protectorates, and the arrival of Egyptian troops was accompanied by intense political propaganda aimed at driving the British out of what it called "Occupied South Yemen." The British vacillated, failing to give adequate support to the rulers, and failing to win over the socialist parties in the colony, which became increasingly dominated, first by pro-Egyptian, and then by extreme communist elements.

The years from 1962 to 1967 were years of growing unrest during which slavery was not an important issue. The question was unresolved when, the British, defeated in their efforts to form a cohesive government that would ensure the security of their base at Aden—their major interest in the area—announced that independence would be granted in 1968. They searched in vain for a way to get out of South Arabia without leaving it in chaos, and finally left in disarray at the end of November 1967, handing it over to the extreme socialist National Liberation Front (NLF).

It was the extremist NLF that dealt slavery the coup de grace. As it took over the whole country, many of the rulers fled abroad. The remaining slaves were freed. Only local research will establish their fate, but many were said to have elected to remain with their former owners. Thus, ironically, given Britain's long campaign against the slave trade, it was their departure that precipitated its end in South Arabia.

By the 1970s, legal slavery in Arabia was a thing of the past, but, as will be seen, it was merely one of many different kinds of exploitation which remained alive and well. It was to their elimination that the humanitarian lobby, led as always by the Anti-slavery Society, now turned its full attention.

NOTES

1. Quoting memorandum by Selwyn Lloyd for the Cabinet, secret, C.P. (56) 98, 14 April 1956, CAB 129/80.

2. Draft directive to the commandant of the Trucial Oman Levies from the political resident in the Persian Gulf, FO 371/82175 EA 2181/82.

3. As Sir William Luce, a later political resident, used to say, Balfour-Paul, 110.

4. For the early problems of this force, see Lunt 1981.

5. Balfour-Paul, 110.

6. Persian Gulf: Annual Review for 1951, FOCP 18463.

7. Jacomb to Pelly, no. 5/32/51, 20 January 1951, enclosed in Pelly to Hay, no. 4 confidential (C2O/1/2/51), 5 February 1951, FO371/91360 E 2181/1.

8. Jacomb to Pelly, no. 5/166/51, 12 July 1951, enclosed in Pelly to FO, no. 101 (2182/26), 4 August 1951, FO 371/91360 EA 2181/3.

9. Minute by Jacomb, 28 July 1951, enclosed in Jacomb to Pelly, no. 5/166/51, 12 July 1951, enclosed in Pelly to Hay no. 101, 4 August 1951, FO 371/91360 EA 2181/3.

10. FO to Pelly, no. 149, 28 September 1951, and minutes on Pelly to FO no. 101, 4 August 1951, FO 371/91360 EA 2181/3.

11. Cranton to Hay, restricted, 18 December 1951, FO 371/91360 EA 2181/3.

12. Weir to political agent in Bahrain, 13 March 1952, enclosed in Hay to Eden, 17 April 1952, FO 371/98464 EA 2182/15.

13. Weir to Laver, no. 22/9/52, 14 April 1952, enclosed in Hay to Ross, 24 April 1952, and minutes, FO 371/98464 EA 2181/2.

14. Agency Kuwait to UN Department, restricted, 4 November 1957, FO 1016/589 2181/21/57. Earlier documents on Kuwait state that the British could not issue manumission certificates themselves. I am uncertain whether the procedure had changed by 1957. The result, however, seems to have been that slaves were freed without difficulty.

15. Hay to Ross, confidential, 1 June 1953, and minutes, FO 371/104447.

16. LeQuesne to Greenhill, confidential 2182/94/53, 19 October 1953, and minutes, FO 371/104447 EA 2182/16.

17. Hay to Eden, no. 50, restricted, 12 May 1952, and minutes, FO 371/98464 EA 2182/19/52; Ross to Hay, confidential, 20 December 1952, ibid., EA 2181/11.

18. Greenhill to Bird (Iraq Petroleum Co.), 24 July 1953, and Bird to Greenhill, confidential no. 8423, 29 September 1953, FO 371/104447 EA 2182/10.

19. Weir to Le Quesne, confidential, 13 May 1953 FO 1016/260 2182/33/53.

20. Hay to Eden, no. 18 restricted, 14 February 1953, FO 371/107151 EA 2182/19.

21. The Buraimi question is dealt with in many books. See inter alia Hawley 1970, Burrows 1990, Hay 1959, Heard-Bey 1982, Townsend 1977.

22. Weir to LeQuesne, no. 1370/10/53, 3 April 1953, and no. 1370/33/53, 14 May 1953, FO 371/104447 EA 2182/9; McGregor to Sharjah, telegram no. 39, 28 September 1953, ibid. EA 2182/15. See also documents in FO 1016/260.

23. LeQesne to Weir, confidential, 23 April 1953, FO 317/104447 EA 2182/16/53.

24. A relative of the ruler of Dubai, for instance, was believed to be involved in the shipment of a "boatload of female slaves" reported to have taken off from Beni Kaalb, heading for Saudi Arabia via Kuwait, Hay to FO, telegram no. 376, restricted, FO 371/104447, EA 2182/2.

25. Residency Bahrain to FO, confidential, 19 October 1953, FO 371/104447 EA 2182/96/53.

26. For the decision and the need to move fast, and a description of the occupation, see FO 1016/449.

27. Burrows 1990, 86–111, gives a personal account of the events in which he took part.

28. Note on the Persian Gulf by Selwyn Lloyd, secret C.P. (56) 122, 15 May 1956, CAB 129/81.

29. For these discussions and the role of the press, see above, chapter 19. Questions were asked and answered in Parliament on 18 April 1956. For press articles, see also letters to *Manchester Guardian* on 21 and 27 March 1956, and *The Times*, in FO 371/120691 EA 2185/2, EA 2185/2A.

30. Residency, Bahrain to FO, confidential telegram, 2 November 1955, FO 1016/450; Bahrain to FO, 6 March 1956, FO 371/120691 AE 2185/2. Four slave traders were arrested.

31. Minute by Riches, 30 April 1956 on parliamentary questions answered 7 May 1956, FO 371/120691 EA 2185/5.

32. The parliamentary questions were asked on 18 April and 9 July 1956; Listowel to Dodds Parker, 17 May and June 1956, and Dodds Parker to Listowel, 30 May and 13 June 1956, and minutes, and memoranda for the ASAPS, FO 371/120691 EA 2185/9.

33. Residency Bahrain to UN Department, confidential, 22 January 1957, FO 1016/589 2187/3/57; UN department to Residency, confidential, 27 February, ibid., 2187/5/59.

34. Gault to Selwyn Lloyd, no. 101 confidential, 19 July 1957, FO 1016/589; Tripp to Gault, no. 17, 19 July 1957, ibid.

35. Middleton to Selwyn Lloyd, no. 44 confidential, 23 May 1959, FO 371/140305 EA 2184/1.

36. Hawley to Davies, 28 June 1961, FO 1016/714 2181/61.

37. Articles by George Littledale, beginning on 28 June 1961. This reference to Iranian pilgrims may have been wrong since most of the persons duped were Pakistani. I am indebted to Sir Donald Hawley for this information.

38. Hawley to Wyatt, confidential no. 9, July 1961, FO 371/156716 no. B. 2181/7; Phillips to Wyatt, 11 July 1961, ibid., no. B.2181/8. Similar cases occurred in the Red Sea. The number of such incidents was unknown.

39. Wyatt to Hawley, confidential, 23 June 1961, FO 371/156716 B 2181/3.

40. Lamb to Man, Craig and Boustead, confidential, 8 January 1962, FO 371/162820 B2181/1.

41. The Gulf rulers did not issue many formal edicts or legislation at this time. I am indebted to Sir Donald Hawley for this information.

42. Oil production began in Abu Dhabi in 1962, and in Dubai only in 1969.

43. Summerscale to Brightly, no. 2188, 14 November 1962, FO 371/162820 B 2181/6.

44. The last three were issued in 1965. Since slavery was no longer legal, this was an anomaly, but as a Foreign Office official put it: "[S]o long as one person per year asks to be manumitted, and so long as the certificate has an effect, this ancient and honorable custom should continue." Its only effect was to give the recipient possible protection against re-enslavement. Wilcock to Summerscale, confidential, 18 February 1963, FO 371/168668 2181/1.

45. Given to Brown, confidential, 17 April 1963, FO 371/168668 B 2181/1; parliamentary question, 19 February 1963, ibid., B 2181/2.

46. This was signed by the rulers of Ajman, Dubai, Ras el-Khaimah, Umm el Qaiwain, Sharjah and Fujairah on 14 May 1963, FO 371/168961.

47. ASAPS to Selwyn Lloyd, 12 August 1957, Ormsby Gore to Fox-Pitt, 23 August 1957, FO 371/127019 EA 2184/6A.

48. Morris to Chauncey, 24 April 1956, Chauncey to Williams, no. 5325/3, 6 May 1956, Cole to Williams, confidential, no. 2185/6, Williams to Cole, no. 4094/36/56, 23 May 1956, and minutes, FO 371/120691. Morris simply wanted to get the facts right for his book, *Sultan in Oman*, 1956, personal communication from Jan Morris.

49. Hawley to Davies, 28 June 1961, FO 1016/714 2181/61; Phillips to Davies, 10 July 1961, ibid., 2183/4.

50. Barth 1983; Wikan 1982.

51. Rich to Given, confidential no. 2188, 1 June 1963, and enclosed memorandum: Slavery in the Southern Gulf: Present Situation, and minutes, FO 371/168668 B 2181/4.

52. Secret memorandum by Luce: Survey of the Political Situation in and Around the Persian Gulf, 6 April 1963, FO 371/168691. For development programs in Oman and the difficulties of the sultan's British advisors, see Townsend 1977, 64–76.

53. He was still in receipt of a subsidy awarded his predecessors in 1862 when Britain and France recognized Zanzibar's independence from Oman.

54. UK mission in New York to FO, telegrams no. 3159, 13 December 1966, nos. 3275 and 3276, 17 December 1966, and no. 496, 19 December 1966, FO 371/185370.

55. See for instance, *ASR*, VI, 12, no. 3, January 1966, p. 28.

56. Townsend, 74–77.

57. Abbey to State Department, no. 121, 2 October 1951, and enclosed British memorandum, USNA, 886a.064/10-251.

58. See, for instance, the correspondence over one victim in Pelham to Eden, no. 55 confidential, 23 April 1952, and enclosure, FO 371/96724 EA 2186/1, and Residency, Bahrain to Eden, no. 58 confidential, 30 May 1952, ibid., EA 2186/2.

59. See Ross to Hay, 27 August 1952, and draft Eden to Pelham, 17 October 1952, Pelham to Yusuf Yasin, 6 November 1952, and Yusuf Yasin, 26 November 1952, enclosed in Pelham to Eden, no. 127, 6 November 1952, FO 141/397 EA 2181/6.

60. Memorandum on the slave trade in Saudi Arabia 1952–1955 sent by the Foreign Office to the AS, copy in Listowel to Dodds Parker, 17 May 1956, FO 371/120691 EA 2185/9.

61. *Sunday Dispatch*, 7 December 1952, based on a communication to the UN by Jacques Alain, an explorer living in North Africa, FO 371/102611 J 2181/1.

62. Vaughan Ferguson to Department of State, no. 38, 26 August 1954, USNA, 886a.064/8–26J4.

63. Morillon to FMAE, no. 482/AL, 7 November 1953, enclosed in Listowel to Dodds Parker, 17 May 1956, FO 371/120691 EA 2185/9.

64. Memorandum on the slave trade in Saudi Arabia 1952–1955, sent by the Foreign Office to the AS, copy in Listowel to Dodds Parker, 17 May 1956, FO 371/120691 EA 2185/9.

65. *Le Monde*, 15 February 1956, FO 371/120691 EA 2185/8.

66. The high prices may have indicated a shortage of slaves.

67. Chancery to FO, confidential, 21 May 1956, FO 371/120691 EA 2185/10.

68. Segal 2001, 200–201. This information was based on a conversation that the editor had overheard between the Libyan foreign minister and a Mali delegate to a conference in Casablanca. Another version of this story came from the Anti-Slavery Society, which said that Mali had demanded the extradition from Saudi Arabia of a "tribal leader" reported to have taken a thousand followers on pilgrimage and sold them. The Saudi and Mali governments were said to be "hushing the matter up."

69. Sean O'Callahan article, 23 June 1961, FO 371/156716 B 2181/8.

70. Segal 2001, 201.

71. For the information that follows, I have relied heavily on Holden and Johns, 198–254.

72. Crowe to Home, no. 50 confidential, 12 September 1963, FO 371/168912 BS 2181/4; see also Holden and Johns 1981, 230.

73. The families listed were Saud, Faysal, Jiluwi, and Sudairi, Crowe to Home, no. 50 confidential, 12 September 1963, FO 371/168912 BS 2181/4. Holden and Johns put the number at thirty thousand. The figure of half a percent comes from Chancery to FO, 16 October 1963, ibid.

74. Holden and Johns 1981, 230, citing the *Daily Telegraph*, 3 June 1963.

75. Symons to Snellgrove, confidential, 11 September 1963, FO 371/168912 BS 2181/5; Crowe to Home, no. 50 confidential, 12 September 1963, ibid., BS 2181/4.

76. Crowe to Home, no. 50 confidential, 12 September 1963, FO 371/168912 BS 2181/4; Chancery to FO, 16 October 1963, ibid., BS 2181/6.

77. Segal, quoting inter alia John Laffin, *The Arabs as Master Slavers*, 1982, SBS Publishing: Engelwood, N.J.

78. Minute 7 March 1956, FO 371/120691 EA 2185/1.

79. McCarthy to Brenchley, 22 March 1967, and minute FCO 8/489.

80. This brief outline is based on Balfour-Paul 1991, 49–95.

81. The Audhali and the Lower Aulaqi sultanates and the Upper Aulaqi shaykhdom had done so.

82. Awad 1966, 156. For the UN inquiry and Awad's Report, see below, chapter 21.

83. Swan to Coles, confidential, 2 June 1965, FO 371/183694.

84. Slavery in South Arabia, confidential, and annex, 30 June 1965, FO 371/183694; Awad 1966, 157–58.

85. A year later, the draft law was still not satisfactory and was being reconsidered.

86. Draft reply to parliamentary question, 22 March 1967, FCO 8/489; articles in *The Sun*, 23 March 1967, and *The Observer*, 20 March 1967, and *Daily Telegraph*, 30 March 1967.

87. Awad 1966, 153–54.

88. Annex to IOC (66) 98, 30 June 1966, FO 371/189990, US 2183/13 (A). Compare this with the reply in Awad 1966, 154.

21

Slavery at the United Nations 1956–1966

THE POLITICAL BACKGROUND

By spelling out the various forms of exploitation under attack, the 1956 Supplementary Convention against slavery made it more difficult to get agreement on measures to enforce the treaty or even to monitor progress. It was to be nearly two decades before the humanitarian lobby, led by the Anti-Slavery Society, persuaded a reluctant United Nations to establish such mechanisms. Their efforts must be seen in the context of the changes resulting from the dismantling of the European colonial empires. The former colonies joined the United Nations and played an increasing role on the world stage, adding to the tensions generated by the continuing Cold War between the "Western bloc" led by the United States and the "Eastern bloc" led by the Soviet Union. Both sides courted the increasingly vociferous and ever growing number of "non-aligned" nations. Their revulsion against colonialism, already noted in connection with South Arabia and the Persian Gulf States, was inflamed by events in southern Africa, which were to have a direct bearing on the antislavery campaign.

South Africa's policy of racial oppression, known as apartheid, had been condemned at the United Nations in 1946, and, in 1962, a special committee was formed to consider it. Members were called upon to impose diplomatic and economic sanctions. There was strong feeling in Britain against apartheid, and South Africa left the Commonwealth over the issue in 1961, but the British government had taken no part in the UN committee and had abstained from many UN resolutions. It explained that the proposed sanctions would raise Britain's balance of payments deficit by an estimated £300 million a year. Moreover, enforcing them would require an expensive naval and air blockade, and have adverse effects on the British territories of Botswana (Bechuanaland), Lesotho (Basutoland), and Swaziland, then in process of establishing themselves as independent states.[1] In 1966, the United Nations voted to end South African rule in Southwest Africa (Namibia) but no action was taken to enforce the decision. In the Republic of South Africa itself, apartheid policies became more brutal by the year.

In 1965, Rhodesia issued its unilateral declaration of independence (UDI) after Britain refused to agree to a constitution that deprived the African majority of an effective role in government. African and Asian countries, led by Tanzania, urged the British to crush this white settler rebellion. For a variety of reasons, including opposition in Britain, logistical problems, and fears that Rhodesia might cut off the export of copper from Zambia, on which two million British jobs depended, the newly installed Labor government merely imposed sanctions.[2] These, as usual, were ineffective and the Rhodesian question festered on. African nationalists, supported by Tanzania and other independent states, launched a guerrilla war against the white governments in South Africa, Rhodesia, and the Portuguese colonies of Mozambique, Angola, and Guinea. Since some nationalist organizations received help from the Soviet bloc, the Western powers, afraid of the spread of communism, were reluctant to take radical action against South Africa.

By the mid-1960s, feelings in the Third World against the West were further inflamed by escalating United States participation in the war between South Vietnam and communist North Vietnam. Fuel was added by Israel's humiliating defeat of its Arab neighbors in the Six-day War in 1967. To add to the difficulty of getting any consensus against slavery, government after government in Africa succumbed to military coups. Nigeria was torn by civil war, while Western governments faced student rebellions and, in addition, the United States was torn by race riots instigated by the long oppressed black minority.

Humanitarian questions were frequently used as pawns in the unceasing propaganda war waged by the Eastern and Western blocs as each tried to win over public opinion and gain allies.

SLAVERY AT THE UNITED NATIONS 1956–1966

For a few years after the signing of the 1956 Supplementary Convention, the slavery question hung fire at the United Nations, but by 1959, a group of closely linked NGOs were agitating for either a UN commission of inquiry or the establishment of a committee of experts on slavery.[3] Women's organizations played an increasingly vociferous role in this campaign. Their support was welcomed by the Anti-Slavery Society, whose own membership had declined, leaving it in greater financial straits than usual.[4] Together, they got slavery placed on the agenda for the 1960 session of ECOSOC.[5] However, the British government delayed action by cosponsoring, with Denmark[6] and Uruguay, a resolution urging states to accede to the slavery conventions and inform the secretary-general of the steps taken to implement them. This was sufficiently innocuous to be carried easily. It was repeated in 1961, and again at the General Assembly in 1962, when 53 states sponsored it. But it netted few accessions.[7]

The campaign by nongovernmental organizations (NGOs) meanwhile gained momentum, aided by lurid articles on slavery in Arabia.[8] Lord Maugham roused public and parliamentary interest by announcing that he had bought a slave in Timbuktu for £37.10s.[9] The secretary of the Anti-Slavery Society, Commander Thomas Fox-Pitt,[10] assured surprised audiences that the traffic in children from Nigeria to other parts of West Africa had increased since independence. He also publicized the claim of an Egyptian woman in Cairo that her husband, a Saudi prince, had married some sixty-five women and sold them in Arabia for $5000 a head.[11] He played a trump card, however, when in an article in *New World* in January 1962, he appealed to the public to write to their members of Parliament demanding that Britain play a more active role against slavery at the United Nations.[12]

Public reactions showed that slavery could still evoke strong feeling. Some were more fanciful than useful. A group of Cambridge undergraduates, for instance, announced they were going to Timbuktu to buy a slave girl and bring her back to start life anew as their servant. College regulations, it appeared, allowed them to keep domestics.[13] More seriously, the Foreign Office was pestered with letters, petitions, deputations, and parliamentary questions.[14] Officials complained, with reason, that the public seemed unaware that Britain was not responsible for the policies of its former colonies.[15] Not all the interest was humanitarian either. As in France, there was an element of pique at the "hypocrisy" of African and Asian states, which attacked colonialism, but tolerated slavery.[16]

When the ILO investigated Ghana's charge that the Portuguese were violating the Forced Labor Convention in their colonies, the contrast between the ILO's response and the United Nations' inability to even inquire into violation of the antislavery conventions was not lost on Parliament.[17] The British government maintained that if it called for effective machinery against slavery, its former colonies might accuse it of interfering in their domestic affairs. The logical first step, it argued, was to continue to urge them to ratify the conventions.[18]

Fox-Pitt was "humiliated" to find that Nasser, pouring out propaganda from Cairo, had usurped Britain's traditional role of leader of the antislavery movement. After Saudi Arabia and Yemen abolished slavery in 1962, the Jordanian delegate to the UN pointed out that it was now legal only in Britain's Gulf satellites and Oman. On the latter, Fox-Pitt commented in disgust, "the Sultan, with the help of British planes, armored cars, officers and men—and at the expense of several British casualties—is fighting the Imam of Oman who has repudiated slavery in his area. The U.K. is lined up everywhere with slave owners."[19]

By the end of 1962, in spite of the resolutions, only 44 of the 104 members of the United Nations had acceded to the 1956 convention.[20] The next year, when twelve NGOs demanded a mechanism for implementing the treaties, the government fended them off with a new suggestion—the appointment of a UN Special Rapporteur to collect information on slavery.[21] This was less threatening than a committee, which might become permanent and even acquire powers of supervision. The British wanted "a forward policy" on human rights and they wanted these rights defined in the "Western" rather than the communist sense. However they did not want to extend all United Nations instruments to their remaining possessions, particularly those granting political rights. Hence, they opposed any UN body that might review government performance.[22]

THE SPECIAL RAPPORTEUR'S INQUIRY

ECOSOC agreed to the appointment of a rapporteur in July 1963, but his expenses could not be fitted into the budget until 1964. Dr. Mohammed Awad, an Egyptian geographer, formerly rector of Alexandria University and member of the UN Sub-Commission on the Prevention of Discrimination and the Protection of Minorities,[23] was chosen for the job. He had a long-standing interest in slavery, having attended meetings of the Anti-Slavery Society as a student at London University in the 1920s. He had served for many years as an expert on various projects of the Human Rights Division of the UN Secretariat and in UNESCO,[24] and was considered by his colleagues to be their "doyen" on slavery questions.[25] It was an interesting choice, too, since Egypt was spearheading the attack against the Arabian rulers accused of countenancing slavery.

Awad was given a broad mandate to receive information from governments, from the UN Specialized Agencies and, most important, from NGOs.[26] As in the past, governments had to be sent any information that concerned them, and their comments were published in the report. If they did not reply, the information could not be included. As a further safeguard, he could only approach NGOs in consultative status with the UN. This did not, of course, preclude them from sending in evidence they received from other organizations or from individuals, but all informants had to be willing to have their names published, and, as will be seen, producing evidence invited attack.

The Secretariat, in consultation with Awad, compiled a questionnaire, which was dispatched to all prospective informants in 1964.[27] Slavery was defined in accordance with the 1926 and 1956 conventions, and "related institutions" were debt-bondage, serfdom, forced marriage, and transactions leading to the exploitation of children. Governments were asked to describe their laws, the measures for enforcing them, and any other practices tantamount to slavery in their territories. Forced labor, trafficking in persons, consent to marriage, and minimum age of marriage were not included since they were already the subject of other treaties.[28]

The questionnaire was sent out again in 1965, when sixty-one states had not responded. Only seventy-eight finally answered.[29] Among the thirty-nine that did not reply were Saudi Arabia, Muscat, Mauritania, and Tanzania.[30] Most governments denied there was slavery of any kind in their territories. NGOs, however, contradicted some of these assertions. The International Council of Women, for instance, claimed that chattel slavery continued in remote non-Christian areas of Mindanao and Sulu. The government of the Philippines denied it. The Anti-Slavery Society reported that indigenous people in Brazil were enslaved by rubber pickers and tattooed to facilitate recapture if they escaped. The government said it had no evidence of this. The Society also maintained that poverty-stricken persons in Bolivia were selling or giving away their children. Some two hundred thousand of whom were employed as domestics in the cities. Bolivia replied that they had been "adopted" to work as domestic servants in private houses, an arrangement representing a kind of family life.

When the Anti-Slavery Society and the Friends World Committee claimed that the slave trade continued in Arabia, the Saudis threatened to call a debate on the prerogatives of NGOs. Such "wild accusations," they said, would turn the UN into an arena "for vindictive and acrimonious allegations." The Society, its consultative status threatened, sent in supplementary information praising Prince Faysal's courage in ending legal slavery. But it asked whether countries would be helped to find any of their nationals in Saudi harems who might want to return home. This raised the sensitive issue of concubines—slaves by definition—on whom the impact of Saudi abolition was unknown.

In some cases, the suppression of slavery was a political rather than a social and economic problem. Thus, the Anti-Slavery Society claimed that the president of Cameroon, although against slavery, needed the support of rulers in the north. He, therefore, allowed the *lamidos* of Ngaoundere and other areas to keep hundreds of slaves, including many women in their harems. Cameroon replied that these were wives and servants and that the missionaries, who provided the information, did not understand the workings of polygamy and tribal law. It admitted that the latter might "camouflage" some forms of exploitation, but did not reveal how the lamidos had acquired their "women and servants."[31]

The real problem was not chattel slavery, which now concerned few countries. It was "the slavery-like practices" spelled out in 1956, which prevented governments from acceding to the convention and led to less than candid replies to the questionnaire. Like the colonial rulers, the newly independent states had no desire to stir up a hornet's nest by attacking entrenched customs, which they did not consider forms of servitude. Many of these practices discriminated against women. Western women's organizations were vociferous in their denunciation of polygyny, of arranged marriages in which the bride had no right of refusal, of child marriage, widow inheritance, and payment of bride wealth.[32] They believed that these practices kept women in bondage, a view supported by some women's groups in the Third World.[33] However, in many countries they were the norm, hallowed by custom, and believed to be sanctioned by religion. Western attacks were resented as interference with their faith and their way of life.

The answers to the questionnaire showed that the borderline between chattel slavery and other forms of servitude and acceptable practice was open to interpretation. Thus, Chad agreed that the inheritance of widows was a form of slavery, while Uganda described it as a humanitarian custom, reflecting the fact that it provided a male protector for otherwise helpless women. The colonial rulers attacked it. Rhodesia had outlawed it, together with forced marriage. The Anglo-French government of the New Hebrides relied on missionary influence to end both practices. In their reply for South Arabia (the Aden Protectorate), the British acknowledged that marriage customs put such "social pressures" on girls that they "were not free agents," but did not suggest they had taken any action against them. The International Council of Women complained that Aborigines in Australia and women in the Trust Territory of New Guinea, although legally protected, were in practice forced into marriage.

Debt-bondage, including peonage, which had played such a part in the sabotaging of the Ad Hoc Committee of 1956 by Peru, and was to become a serious focus of attack in the decades to come, particularly in South Asia, was barely mentioned in the replies.[34] The Anti-Slavery Society reported that debt-bondage continued in Mysore. India admitted it had a problem, mostly among "tribal" peoples, whose poverty and ignorance made them an easy prey for moneylenders, but claimed that state governments were controlling usury and offering credit facilities. It also said that compensation was being paid for the release of bonded labor and that all children born after independence in 1947 were free.[35] Nepal and Pakistan did not mention the problem. Peru and Ecuador quoted their laws against peonage without comment.

As for the adoption of children in order to exploit them, a number of states said that their laws prevented this. Hong Kong and Singapore reported that mui tsai had died out. Given that they had introduced stringent laws and inspection arrangements, and that Communist China had cut off the major supply by ending sales of girls, this was probably true.[36] The British island of Dominica admitted to "a very limited practice" by which poor people with large families placed their children with persons who took care of them in return for domestic service. Since the parents could end this arrangement at any time, it denied that it was slavery. Spain reported rare cases of child exploitation. Sri Lanka (Ceylon) said nothing about it. Nigeria did not mention a trade in children, although the Anti-Slavery Society had publicly drawn attention to it. Haiti and Liberia, both of which had figured in the League Temporary Slavery Commission's discussions in this connection,[37] did not reply to the questionnaire. The cult slavery found in parts of West Africa by which children are dedicated to a temple to serve the priests for life was not mentioned in the report.[38]

Although trafficking in persons had been expressly omitted from the questionnaire, the British colony of Hong Kong replied that girls were being enticed into prostitution and that this was the only practice remotely akin to slavery. Egypt, Spain, and Laos also mentioned prostitution as a problem.

INTERNATIONAL POLITICS AND THE AWAD REPORT

Some states used their replies to make political points. The Russians claimed that the main factors upholding slavery and related institutions were "colonialism, apartheid and racism" and wanted "concrete," but unspecified, measures taken against them.

Mali denounced colonialism as "a new system of general slavery." Cuba stressed the need for "social revolution" to end "feudal regimes." Yemen replied that the revolution of 1962 had destroyed the "old reactionary despotism and established the equality of all citizens on the basis of democracy and justice."

The British struggled with an old difficulty—how to reply for the Gulf States without raising the question of how far they were really independent. They toyed with trying to "get away" with not replying for them, but, fearing this would be noticed, they attached a covering letter to the rulers' replies to make it clear they were not colonies.[39] As for South Arabia (Aden Protectorate), they worded their reply carefully to give the impression that slavery no longer existed,[40] but the Anti-Slavery Society reported that only a few states had abolished the legal status of slavery and that the ruling families still kept slaves. It conceded that they were well treated, free to leave, and often held positions of trust.[41] The Colonial Office eventually admitted to the Foreign Office that it did not know the precise position in any of the states, particularly Upper Yafa and the Eastern Protectorate, and could not predict whether they would enact legislation against slavery.[42]

AWAD'S RECOMMENDATIONS

Awad chided the UN agencies. The United Nations Educational, Scientific, and Cultural Organization (UNESCO) was not promoting educational programs voicing human rights ideals. The Food and Agriculture Organization (FAO) had not concentrated on land tenure problems, and the ILO was not investigating servitude among indigenous populations.[43] He also complained of the poor response from NGOs, except for the British Anti-Slavery Society to which he paid special tribute. The problem, of course, was that the agencies and many of the NGOs were wary of supplying information on so sensitive a subject for fear that governments might in the future deny them access for their main programs.[44]

Awad had asked for suggestions on measures to end slavery. Replies included raising the standard of living,[45] land tenure reform,[46] and technical, judicial, and other assistance from the specialized agencies,[47] NGOs,[48] and regional organizations like the Arab League.[49] Only Nigeria proposed a convention providing for international supervision and powers of enforcement. Spain suggested an inspectorate answerable to ECOSOC.[50] If most governments had no desire for mechanisms to implement the conventions, NGOs stressed the need for them.[51]

Awad himself advocated the highly controversial establishment of a slavery committee with an "appropriate" secretariat. Only such a committee, he argued, could deal with slavery in all its forms, promote and supervise the activities of specialized agencies and NGOs, cooperate with governments, and advise on measures to be taken. Moreover, it would be the "visible symbol" that the United Nations had a permanent interest in the question. He hinted that it might be empowered to send experts to countries needing help, and to investigate conditions on the spot like the Trusteeship Council, which oversaw territories under UN mandate.[52] He also advocated regional seminars to study the problems involved in suppression.[53] He even drafted a resolution for ECOSOC incorporating his suggestions—the main one being the establishment of a committee of seven independent experts to examine evidence from all sources and report on the steps needed to end slavery.[54]

RESULTS OF THE AWAD REPORT

Meanwhile, the British, still trying to avoid such a committee, had been toying with other ideas—among them the establishment of a High Commissioner for Human Rights, with the same status and powers as the High Commissioner for Refugees, who had his own staff and budget. This had been proposed by a number of NGOs anxious to strengthen United Nations machinery for the protection of human rights.[55] The Foreign Office thought that the commissioner could serve as a slavery "watchdog," among his other functions, but without the power to initiate investigations or take evidence from unofficial sources.[56]

The Anti-Slavery Society was willing to support a High Commissioner for Human Rights in addition to a committee, not instead of it.[57] It feared that he would relegate slavery to the end of a long list of other human rights violations. Moreover, its suppression was a "complicated and diverse subject" needing the "undivided attention" of experts. Some twenty other NGOS and a number of members of Parliament agreed with this.[58]

Under pressure to take the lead, the Foreign Office considered its options. A high commissioner would be able to exert discreet pressure behind the scenes. He might have more influence on governments than a committee, whose decisions would be scrutinized in ECOSOC where the Asian and African states would not "pillory" those who tolerated slavery. However, the Soviet and Afro-Asian blocs opposed the appointment and the project hung fire. The Foreign Office turned to the Anti-Slavery Society for advice.[59]

The Society had a new and dedicated secretary, Colonel Patrick Montgomery, who took over in 1963.[60] He had been interested in human rights from his youth, spurred by his father's tales of "blackbirding"—the buying of labor in the Solomon Islands to work on sugar estates in Queensland. On the eve of his retirement from a long career in the army, he had heard by chance of the Society's existence, and was sufficiently impressed by its humanitarian mission to offer his services for a nominal salary.[61] In 1965, the Society elected Sir Douglas Glover as chairman of the General Committee.[62] As a Conservative Member of Parliament, Glover was ideally placed to lobby politicians and put pressure on the government. Moreover, he was familiar with the working of the UN, having been the British parliamentary delegate to the General Assembly in 1962. He was both forceful and "tough," a power to be reckoned with.[63] He doubled the membership of the Society in his first three years, and, as will be seen, did much to enhance its influence in Parliament.[64] Together Glover and Montgomery were an indefatigable and effective team. The Society was also strengthened by the appointment to its Committee in 1964 of an advisor on diplomatic and United Nations affairs, John Alexander-Sinclair, who had served in both the British Foreign Office and the United Nations.[65]

They, and other NGOs, convinced the Foreign Office that the "psychological moment" had come to propose a committee, particularly, as the rapporteur—"an Arab to boot"—had "come down firmly in favor of it."[66] Officials realized there would be "hostile" questions in Parliament if they delayed any longer. To dissipate opposition from countries in which forms of servitude persisted, and from the communist bloc, which could be counted on to oppose attempts to make human rights treaties more effective,[67] they made it clear that the committee would be merely advisory, and that its recommendations would have no force unless they were accepted by ECOSOC. The British delegate, Sir Samuel Hoare, decided not to propose the committee himself as this would smack of neocolonialism and be the "the kiss of death." He thought it safer to support Awad's resolution, when it was discussed in the Social Committee of ECOSOC in July 1966.[68] Montgomery was jubilant:

> "We have scored a great victory...," he wrote, "... worked for by my predecessors relentlessly for 20 years. The F[oreign] O[ffice] have at last agreed (when driven into a corner) to support the recommendations of the Awad Report.... They have produced reason after reason—three different ones in the past five years, all specious, to justify their procrastination or plain objection to enable the Slavery Conventions to be implemented. At last we may see real progress . . . for the first time since 1939.[69]

Events were to prove him oversanguine.

THE DEFEAT OF THE PROPOSAL FOR A
UNITED NATIONS SLAVERY COMMITTEE

Predictably, the proposal was opposed by the Soviets, who claimed that additional mechanisms were not needed. Unexpectedly, it was opposed by the Americans, who objected to the cost. The coup de grace, however, came from W. E. Waldron-Ramsay, a West Indian lawyer, representing Tanzania. He claimed that the committee was designed by the colonial powers to expose practices they had not suppressed themselves, when they were in control. He played, with some sarcasm, on the fears of the "waverers." "They will go to your great country," he warned the Peruvian delegate, "and say that there is serfdom there: of course we all know that that is untrue, but they will say it." The real problems, he said, were apartheid and colonialism, not the "outdated forms" of slavery upon which Awad had focused. He deftly deflected opposition with such veiled threats as "My colleague of the United States would not like it said that his country supports apartheid."[70]

The delegate from Pakistan, whose speech had been written by Montgomery and Glover, tried in vain to counter his arguments.[71] Waldron-Ramsay carried the day when the representatives of Algeria, Gabon, and Iraq joined with him to sponsor a resolution to refer slavery, including the "slavery-like practices of apartheid and colonialism," to the Commission on Human Rights, with the request that it consider specific proposals for "effective and immediate measures" to end them.

The Foreign Office and the Anti-Slavery Society blamed each other for this "disaster." The British delegation thought the Society had frightened the Latin American and Afro-Asian delegates by emphasizing "slavery in all its forms,"[72] while the Society thought the British delegates could have avoided the mention of apartheid and colonialism if they had opened the debate by proposing a "strong resolution" in favor of a committee.[73]

Montgomery suspected that Waldron-Ramsay had been frightened by recent press reports that Kenya had released some thirty boys from what was described as either forced labor or slavery in Tanzania.[74] Whether or not this was the case, he was certainly expressing the frustrations of the Third World, led by Tanzania's president, Julius Nyerere, at Britain's policies particularly in southern Africa.[75] Once more, a humanitarian initiative had lost out to political considerations.

The new extension of the definition of slavery cost Britain the leadership of the international antislavery movement, which had been the source of so much national pride in the past. To add to the discomfort of the British delegates, Waldron-Ramsay dismissed their protest that referring slavery to the Commission on Human Rights, already overburdened with work, would be tantamount to "burying" it. Not at all, he assured them; the commission, which had recently been enlarged to include more representatives from the newly independent African and Asian states, would be only too eager to tackle the matter now that it included apartheid and colonialism. In fact, these might be the only forms of slavery it would consider![76] The whole episode had been a fiasco and an official commented gloomily:

> In the present state of international relations, even initiatives, which at one time were regarded as sensible and humane, like the slavery issue, are now simply twisted by knaves to make a trap for fools.[77]

NOTES

1. The history of Britain's South Africa policy at the United Nations at this time is beyond the scope of this work. A convenient summary is to be found in I.O.C. (68) 130, 1 October 1968, FCO 61/239.

2. Harold Wilson 1971, 109, 178–83.

3. The links are well demonstrated by the fact that one of their spokespeople, Mrs. Mary Nuttall, was on the committee of the Anti-Slavery Society as well as the Society of Friends and the Women's League of Peace and Freedom, *AS Annual Report* 1960, p. 3.

4. Its annual report for year ending 31 March 1960 showed an income and expenditure of under £3,000 and capital assets of less than £21,000. Support came, for instance, from the Associated Countrywomen of the World, the Association for Moral and Social Hygiene (formerly the Josephine Butler Society), the International Abolitionist Federation, the National Council of Women of Great Britain, and the Women's International League for Peace and Freedom, *AS Annual Report*, 31 March 1963.

5. The main NGOs concerned were the Friends World Committee for Consultation, which got the Human Rights Commission to put slavery on the agenda of the 1960 meeting of ECOSOC, the Women's International League for Peace and Freedom, which made a similar appeal, and the Anti-Slavery Society.

6. Danish interest appears to have been aroused by Mrs. Nuttall (see note 3 above) who persuaded a member of the Danish Parliament to ask a question on the subject, *AS Annual Report* 1960, p. 3. For the British and Danish resolutions see ECOSOC XXXII, 27 July 1961, when Uruguay also sponsored the resolution.

7. For a useful summary of UN activity and NGO lobbying at this time, and a list of ratifications with dates, see annex to brief for Minister of State meeting with the Society of Friends, 25 May 1965, FO 371/183694.

8. See above, chapter 20.

9. Robin Maugham published articles in *The People*, in 1960, followed by his book *The Slaves of Timbuctoo*, 1961. See Klein 1998, 237–38, 241, 247, for comment on his story.

10. Fox-Pitt was secretary of the Society from 1956–1963.

11. *Croydon Advertiser*, 27 June 1961.

12. "Slavery Today" in *New World*, the monthly organ of the United Nations Association.

13. "They're buying a slave girl," *News of the World*, 27 May 1962.

14. See letters and minutes in FO 371/166952, FO 371/166953, FO 371/166954. By July, some forty letters had been forwarded by MPs and five questions had been asked in Parliament. Letters were received from, for instance, the National Adult School Union, the Association for Moral and Social Hygiene, the Society of Friends, St. Joan's Alliance, Women's Liberation Federation, National Council of Women, and the Women's International League for Peace and Friendship.

15. Ibid.

16. See for instance the parliamentary question by Biggs-Davison, 11 July 1962, Hansard.

17. Parliamentary question 15 March 1962, reply and minutes, FO 371/166952. The final report of the Commission to examine Ghana's complaint that Portugal had not observed the provisions

of the Abolition of Forced Labor Convention of 1957 (no. 105) was released on 5 March 1962. For a further discussion of ILO methods, see chapter, 23 below.

18. Key to Attlee, confidential, 15 May 1962, and 5 June 1962, and to Salt, FO 371/166953 UNS 2183/37; FO to UK Mission New York, confidential, tel. no. 1980, 18 June 1962, ibid.

19. Fox-Pitt to Barbara Castle, 14 February 1963, MSS. Brit.Emp. s.19 D/25 file 1. For the British role in Muscat, see above, chapter 20.

20. *HRI*, 200–220, lists the states that signed, acceded to, or ratified these conventions, with the dates.

21. Confidential minute by UN (Economic and Social) Department of the Foreign Office 25 May 1965, FO 371/183694. The NGOs involved included the Anti-Slavery Society, the Associated Country Women of the World, Friends World Committee for Consultation, International Alliance of Women, International Council of Women, International Federation of Women Lawyers, St. Joan's International Alliance, World Christian Temperance Union, Women's International League for Peace and Freedom, World Young Women's Christian Association.

22. Taylor to Powell-Jones, 8 October 1964, and minutes, FO 371/178436 US 1733/3.

23. See below, chapter 22, for this subcommission.

24. AS statement at HRC 28, 1972, MSS. Brit.Emp.AS 1972–1981, folder UN 1972.

25. Personal communication from Peter Calvocoressi.

26. Resolution 960, ECOSOC XXXVI, 12 July 1963.

27. This questionnaire, together with the answers and Awad's recommendations, were published in Awad 1966.

28. The Convention for the Suppression of Traffic in Persons and the Exploitation of Prostitution of Others, 1949, consolidated earlier treaties. The Convention on Consent to Marriage, Minimum Age for Marriage and Registration of Marriages was signed in 1962. For further discussion of these conventions, see below, chapters 22 and 23. For the ILO Forced Labor Conventions see above, chapters 10 and 19.

29. This includes late replies, Awad 1966, 8. Disparities in the total number of UN members are inevitable as new members were constantly joining as they became independent.

30. Tanzania had ratified the 1956 convention in 1962. Awad, 8, lists states that did or did not reply.

31. For further developments in northern Cameroon, see below, chapter 22.

32. Some NGOs regarded bride wealth in Africa as tantamount to the sale of women—an accusation denied by the governments of the countries in which such payments were normal.

33. Ugandan women's organizations, for instance.

34. See below, chapter 24.

35. Awad, 74–77, 169–70.

36. For a description of the efforts made in Singapore, see Choo Chin Koh 1994.

37. See above, chapter 8.

38. For this type of slavery, see below, chapter 24.

39. Minutes on Turner [CRO] to Doyle, 26 October 1964, FO 371/178460 US 2183/4; Pridham to Phillips, confidential, 16 February 1965, ibid., US 2183/7 (64). The distinction was lost as Awad did not print the letter and the English versions of the replies were identical, giving the impression that they had been dictated.

40. Swan to Coles, confidential, 2 June 1965, and enclosure, and Cumming-Bruce to Coles, restricted, 2 July 1965, FO 371/183694, SSB/124/247/01; Jordan to Cumming-Bruce, 18 June 1965, ibid., US 2183/37. See above, chapter 20, for the real position.

41. CO minute "Slavery in South Arabia," 30 June 1965, FO 371/183694 2183/65.

42. Swan to Coles, confidential, 2 June 1965, FO 371/183694.

43. See Awad 1966, 8–9.

44. For further discussion of their problems, see below, chapter 22.

45. Reply from Spain, Awad, 303.

46. Replies from Cuba, and Senegal, Awad, 281, 27, 4-5.

47. Replies from Ecuador, Iran, Jamaica, the Netherlands, New Zealand, Nigeria, Peru, Senegal, United States, Awad, 281–303.

48. Replies from Cuba, Ecuador, Iran, Jamaica, New Hebrides, Romania, Peru, Spain, Sudan, Britain, United States.

49. Replies from Kuwait, Nepal; Awad, 273, 301.

50. Awad, 300–303.

51. Awad, 277–80, 293–95, 304–305.

52. Awad, 10–12, quoting House of Lords debate, 14 July 1960, on Slavery in Africa and Arabia, Hansard, vol. 225, no. 104.

53. A number of regional seminars were held on human rights but they could only be organized if a member state offered itself as host. Since it was unlikely that a country in which slavery existed would host such a seminar, Awad proposed that the seminars should be regional, Awad, p. 310; for British reactions see minutes on National Council of Women of Great Britain to Stewart, 29 June 1966, FO 371/189990 US 2183/20.

54. Awad, 311–12.

55. This was a revival of an earlier proposal. A brief history and a list of organizations sponsoring the proposal are in FO 371/178433.

56. Minute by Powell-Jones, restricted, 25 June 1965, and subsequent correspondence, FO 371/183694. The Foreign Office also considered suggesting the creation of a single UN committee to deal with the implementation of all human rights issues, Powell-Jones to Taylor, confidential, 24 February 1966, FO 371/189990 US 2183/1.

57. Memorandum from the Anti-Slavery Society, April 1966, FO 371/189990 US 2183/14.

58. See Standing Conference on the Economic and Social Work of the United Nations to Stewart, 13 December 1965, FO 371/183694.

59. Minutes headed "Slavery," confidential, May–June 1966, FO 371/189990 US2183/15, memorandum "Proposed amendments to draft resolution" on pp. 16–18 of E/4168 Add.3 and minute on ECOSOC Item 25 Slavery, 7 June 1966, FO 371/189990. The appointment of a high commissioner was being discussed in a special working group and its future was in doubt.

60. Montgomery was secretary from 1963–1980.

61. Personal communication from Montgomery.

62. Glover was appointed chairman of the General Committee in 1965 and resigned in 1973.

63. Personal communication from Dr. H. Charles Swaisland, who served on the Society's committee from 1965.

64. Montgomery to Lord Amulree, 6 February 1967, MSS. Brit.Emp. s.19 D10/20 file 3. For a discussion of his methods, see below, chapter 22.

65. He was later vice-chairman.

66. IOC (66) 98, 30 June 1966, FO 371/189990. For the role of the Anti-Slavery Society, see minute by Powell-Jones, "Slavery," 13 June 1966 and Glover to Pridham, 8 June 1966, and Powell-Jones to Glover, 20 June 1966, ibid. They were supported by the Friends Peace and International Relations Committee and the National Council of Women of Great Britain. Confidential Memorandum on Slavery, by Powell-Jones, 24 June 1966, and record of conversation with them, 27 June 1966, ibid., US 2183/18; National Council of Women of Great Britain to Stewart, 28 June 1966, and minutes, ibid., US 2183/20.

67. However, the Russians had called on the UN to take measures against slavery, Montgomery to Caradon, 21 February 1966, FO 371/189990 US 2183/66.

68. Personal communication from Montgomery, 1994, quoting the British delegate, Sir Samuel Hoare. The delegation had been given discretion to either introduce the resolution or support Awad's resolution with some changes.

69. Montgomery to Stewart Scott, 28 June 1966, MSS.Brit.Emp.s.19 D10/20 file 1. He attributed the Foreign Office's willingness to support the proposal, after some twenty years of opposition,

to the personal influence of Lord Caradon, Montgomery to Miller, 21 December 1966, ibid., file 3. I have found no evidence of this in the Foreign Office archives.

70. Montgomery described Waldron-Ramsay's tactics in a letter to Carter, 5 September 1966, MSS Brit.Emp. s.19 D10/20 file 3.

71. Ibid.

72. Reports of the UK Delegation on ECOSOC XLI, and minutes, August 1966, FO 371/190016.

73. Glover to Roberts, 31 August 1968, FCO 61/221. King notes for meeting between Roberts and the Anti-Slavery Society, 24 September 1968, ibid., US 13/17.

74. *The Anti-Slavery Society: Its Task Today*, p. 8, AS November 1966.

75. Nyerere had been the most vociferous of the Commonwealth leaders in urging Britain to use force in Rhodesia, Wilson 1971, 116, 181.

76. IOC (66) 124, FO 371/190016.

77. Gore-Booth minute, 23 August 1966, on Unwin to Stewart, no. 17, 8 August 1966, FO 371/190016.

The Final Struggle for a United Nations Slavery Committee 1966–1974

NEW INITIATIVES BY THE ANTI-SLAVERY SOCIETY

The defeat of the Awad proposal postponed the establishment of any machinery to implement the slavery conventions for nearly a decade. It reflected the concerns of the newly independent nations, which had seized the initiative in the social and economic organizations of the UN at a time when Britain's power and influence were on the wane.

In the light of this defeat, the Anti-Slavery Society reconsidered its tactics. In November 1966, Sir Douglas Glover and Colonel Patrick Montgomery were in New York, trying to promote an American antislavery society.[1] The United States had still not ratified the 1956 Slavery Convention owing to the conflict between the president and Congress over the signing of international instruments that might infringe the rights of states. In 1963, President Kennedy had tried in vain to get it accepted by Congress, together with the Forced Labor Convention. The State Department deplored this "diplomatic embarrassment" which made the failure of other powers to ratify the convention "more reputable" and provided ammunition for Soviet attacks.[2]

Glover and Montgomery spoke at the Johnson Foundation, a charitable organization based in Wisconsin. They gave talks and television interviews elsewhere in the Midwest. Although they had no success in founding an American sister society or in raising money, they believed they had aroused public awareness of the new forms of slavery, and hoped that public pressure would force America to ratify the Convention and play a more active antislavery role at the United Nations. They also made valuable contacts in Washington. In New York, they tried to persuade delegates to the UN that slavery should be considered separately from apartheid and colonialism, and that "appropriate machinery" should be set up to deal with it.[3]

Concluding that the new forms of servitude could not be ended while so many Arab, African, and Latin American states "considered them a good thing," they decided for the time being to concentrate on "slavery proper" and the remaining vestiges of the slave trade. Reliable evidence, however, was, as always, hard to find. Montgomery longed for a "cast-iron case," supported by eyewitnesses willing to face the camera. With little money for investigations, he relied on informants, who all too often refused to be named, leaving the Society to produce "smoke without fire."[4]

It was, in any case, hard to tell truth from fiction. Late in 1966, Montgomery admitted:

> We are dissatisfied with all our information really, though we believe that all we have published is true, in no case does it amount to enough to submit to a government with a request for action.[5]

Strange stories stretched the imagination, yet were not beyond the bounds of possibility. For instance, Glover was told that the *lamido* (sultan) of Rey Bouba in Cameroon had had one of his many slaves buried alive under his stool (throne) because a "witch doctor" had advised him that the "emanations would be good for his arthritis." Glover repeated this to one of the British delegates to the United Nations, who had himself called on the lamido, "laden with traditional gifts." He had seen no sign of the soil having been disturbed around the throne and was "inclined to pooh pooh" the story. Nevertheless, he was sufficiently worried to suggest that the British envoy in Yaounde should make enquiries about the "medicinal" use of slaves before embarking on further official visits to Rey Bouba.[6]

There were also difficulties with definition. A case in point arose when Halfdan Endresen, a member of the Norwegian Lutheran Mission, who had spent over thirty years in Cameroon, claimed that the lamidos in the north had thousands of slaves, and that many hundreds had been freed by the missionaries. The Anti-Slavery Society publicized his information. Awad included it in his 1966 report.[7] It was even broadcast in television films, one of which was made on the spot.[8] The government of Cameroon protested, quite truthfully, that slavery was illegal, but made no mention of whether it was enforcing the laws in the Muslim north.[9] However, in 1969 Endresen went out to investigate on behalf of the Anti-Slavery Society. He sent back the heartening news that fifty thousand people, previously regarded by the lamido as his personal property, were now free and that land reform and other measures were being taken to ensure "humane and realistic emancipation."[10] These were presumably the descendants of slaves captured in the nineteenth century or even as late as the 1920s. Whether they were really chattel slaves, or "agricultural serfs" owned by the lamido's officials, or simply oppressed subjects, depended upon definition. Endresen called three to four hundred women in his harem slaves, whereas Cameroon described them as "wives and servants." Their fate was not reported.

Montgomery used the term "slave" freely in his efforts to get public attention. He realized it was a "loaded" word, much "misused and misunderstood," which could arouse "hostility and suspicion."[11] Anxious not to alienate governments, he tried to approach them discreetly with his information and only resorted to publicity when this failed to stimulate action.

He also needed to protect his sources. A graphic example of the dangers faced by individuals who complained about slavery occurred in 1963. Two French schoolmasters, André Chalard and Jacob Oliel, teaching in Tindouf, on the Algerian-Mauritanian border, tried to recover one of their pupils, a little girl, who had been sold by her father's owner to a visiting Mauritanian noble. The Algerians expelled them as troublemakers. Back in Paris, Chalard, ignored by his own government and living a "hand-to-mouth existence," spent his free time raising support. In 1965, he founded a new society—*Action pour l'Abolition de l'Esclavage*. Its members and patrons included the writer André Maurois, Abbé Pierre, René Cassin, vice-president of the *Conseil d'État*, a longtime advocate of UN antislavery action, and former chairman of the Human Rights Commission,[12] as well as some well-known academics.[13] Perhaps for this reason the story had a happy ending. In 1967, the Algerian government informed Chalard that they had found the child, working as a goatherd in Mauritania to enable her master's children to attend school.[14]

The French society was a valuable ally for its British counterpart. It inspired articles in the press, lobbied the United Nations, corresponded with the presidents of Algeria and Mauritania and their ministers,[15] and extracted a promise from the Foreign Ministry that France would support the proposal for a slavery committee.[16] A French pastor, Emmanuel La Gravière, was an officer in both organizations.[17] At a joint meeting in London, early in 1968, the two societies announced that there could be ten million slaves spread over twenty countries. A French social anthropologist, Germaine Tillion, speaking from personal experience, said slavery continued in Algeria, Libya, Morocco, Mauritania, Senegal, Mali, and Niger. In some areas a woman could be freed for £150 and a man for half that sum, or ten camels. The Anti-Slavery Society's vice-chairman, Lord Wilberforce, accused the United Nations of "doing nothing more effective than talking" while this "disgrace to the twentieth century" continued.[18]

Another welcome addition to the NGO antislavery lobby was the Anti-Slavery Society of Norway, inspired by Endresen and inaugurated in the Central Church in Oslo in 1967. A Danish society was founded at the end of the year, and it was hoped a Swedish one would follow, and that they would pressure the Scandinavian delegates at the UN.[19]

The British society, still a miniscule operation facing an uphill struggle, welcomed these allies. It had changed its name in 1956 to the Anti-Slavery Society for the Protection of Human Rights to bring it more into line with the times, but this had done little to boost its membership. It still relied on subscriptions and donations and complained of competition from organizations using professional fund-raisers. Its income in 1965–1966 was a mere £2,113 and its capital only £23,113.[20] Although the number of members rose in that year from 572 to 649, the increase in subscriptions was offset by a jump in its rent from £234 to £865. The usual cost of sending a delegate to the

UN was around £250. A "strong delegation" to Geneva would cost upwards of £2,000—an almost prohibitive expenditure, which might bring no result. After the failure of the Awad resolution, Montgomery complained bitterly of the "complete disregard for humanitarian principles at Geneva."[21]

Whenever possible, the Society took advantage of the free publicity from press articles and broadcasts. The costs of pamphlets, meetings, and solicitations increased constantly, and did not always bring additional members.[22] The precious time of the overworked office staff of two was sometimes wasted answering well-meaning but misguided correspondents. One, for instance, expressed his "firm intention" to go to Africa to buy a slave—nothing would deter him. Would Algeria be a good location, he asked, and how would he find a market? Montgomery replied sadly that Maugham's purchase of a slave and his subsequent book "had had no effect whatsoever on slavery or public opinion" in Britain or elsewhere.[23] He urged the writer to join the Society, for £1 a year, or send a donation, but his appeal fell on deaf ears.[24]

The Society's offices were shabby. Its two employees willingly accepted low pay. They badly needed secretarial help. Members were asked to volunteer to work in the office, to urge their friends to join, to solicit donations, and even to donate a vacuum cleaner.[25] The *Anti-Slavery Reporter* was no longer published regularly.[26] Nevertheless, the Society's representatives attended three UN meetings in 1966–1967, addressed audiences in France, the United States, Switzerland, and Norway, published numerous letters and articles, appeared on television, spoke on the radio, and engineered questions in Parliament. Montgomery himself spoke at seventeen meetings to audiences totaling 1,100 people.

The Society's members were a motley collection of ordinary people and a few corporate groups. They were drawn from over twenty different countries, held differing political views, and practiced various religions, including Islam. Many were persuaded to join by their friends or were moved by articles in the press,[27] but there were still Wilberforces, Buxtons, and Cadburys carrying the torch passed to them by their forebears. As in the past, the joint presidents, vice-presidents, and committee members included an array of distinguished politicians,[28] academics,[29] churchmen,[30] and two African statesmen, Hastings Banda and Nnamdi Azikiwe. The atmosphere at committee meetings was "decidedly patrician," and most members were elderly.[31]

Owing to its august membership, its continuing ability to place articles in the press and arouse interest in Parliament, the Society's impact was still out of proportion to its size. The American delegate to the Commission on Human Rights in 1967 described it as the "eyes and the ears and the conscience of mankind," and marveled that an organization existing on less than $10,000 a year could "make so much noise."[32]

SLAVERY AND THE SUB-COMMISSION

The addition of apartheid and colonialism to the definition of slavery put the British "on the defensive," ending, for the time being, their "tradition of taking the initiative" at the

UN.[33] The Afro-Asian bloc, on the other hand, now had greater interest in pursuing the question. In 1967, the Commission on Human Rights (CHR), to whom ECOSOC had consigned the matter, referred it to the Sub-Commission on the Prevention of Discrimination and the Protection of Minorities (SPDPM). Henceforth, this was the UN body that dealt with slavery. Its composition and mandate are therefore important to our story.

In 1967, it had eighteen members, seventeen of them men.[34] They were appointed by the Commission on Human Rights from a list of nominees submitted by the secretary-general, but approved by their governments. They served for a limited period of years but could be reelected.[35] The world was divided into five geographic areas—Africa, Asia, Latin America, "Western Europe and others," and Eastern Europe. The Western bloc consisted of the democratic states. The Eastern Europeans formed a communist bloc. Before 1969, the number of members from each area was not fixed and the eight Western powers were the largest group. In that year, at the request of the African and Asian delegates to the Commission on Human Rights, the membership was increased to twenty-six to give fairer representation to the new members of the UN. Thereafter, the Afro-Asian members formed the largest bloc, with seven African and five Asian seats, against six for the Western powers, five for the Latin Americans, and three for Eastern Europe. There were always Russian, American, French, and British members.

Unlike ECOSOC and the Commission on Human Rights, which consisted of government representatives, the members of the Sub-Commission, like those on previous slavery committees, were theoretically independent experts. How independent they were depended on the government of the country to which they belonged. The more authoritarian it was, the less independence they had. In the British case, appointments did not necessarily follow a party line. Thus, although the British Labor government, which came to power in 1974, replaced Lady Elles when her time came up for renewal the following year, with a former Labor member of Parliament, Ben Whitaker, he remained on the Sub-Commission after a Conservative government took office in 1979.[36] The British members were encouraged to consult the Foreign Office over policy, but if they chose not to follow the government line, little could be done until they came up for reelection.[37]

Members were drawn from a variety of professions, but most were lawyers, sociologists, and other academics. Up to 1969, their relations, based on mutual respect, were good. "Cold War polemics" had been kept down and questions were debated on their merits in a way that was not possible in the UN bodies made up of government representatives. The British government paid tribute to the Sub-Commission's "cooperative spirit." The Anti-Slavery Society found it "a refreshing change" to lobby people not bound by government briefs and hence "relaxed and sympathetic." However, U.S. reports on its performance in 1967 complained that it had been "at its best" in academic discussion of general principles, and tried to avoid "substantive decisions."[38] After the Sub-Commission was enlarged, much of the early camaraderie was lost. More governments blatantly nominated civil servants, often diplomats, or chose delegates already representing them officially on other UN bodies. This, as the British complained, eroded both "the expert nature of the Sub-Commission and its independence from governmental influence."[39]

How expert members were on slavery or human rights depended on how their governments selected them. As each curriculum vitae was scrutinized by other governments, they usually had some plausible qualification in the field of human rights, but unlike the members of the League committees, they were unlikely to have any first-hand experience of slavery. In 1969, their election by the Commission on Human Rights was highly politicized. A list of candidates was circulated and governments informed one another of their choice, asked for support, and opposed the election of candidates they distrusted. Thus, the British and some other Western and Commonwealth delegations did not vote for Waldron-Ramsay, although they could not prevent his election. The Arabs lobbied successfully against the election of an Israeli, and the Turks prevented the election of a Greek Cypriot.[40] Personal qualities also played a part in rallying votes. British assessments of foreign candidates contain such comments as: "held to be a good judge . . . witty and gay at private parties . . . makes sardonic remarks about [his government's] policies . . . keen golfer . . . interest in cricket," "wife . . . socially pleasant," or "competent . . . civil servant . . . lacking in originality," but "well disposed towards Britain,"[41] or "unlikable" . . . with "classically Marxist" views.[42]

The Sub-Commission had a wide mandate. Its task was to recommend methods of preventing discrimination and other infringements of fundamental human rights, and to protect racial, religious, and linguistic minorities. In 1967, it discussed judicial administration, racial discrimination, genocide, and the treatment of minorities, as well as slavery. Since it only met for a few weeks a year, it often did not complete its exacting program. Consideration of an item could be accidentally delayed because the relevant documents had not been circulated or translated, or it could be deliberately postponed by placing it low on the agenda, or by filibustering so that time ran out before it could be debated.

Further delay was ensured because the Sub-Commission's reports, resolutions, and recommendations were drafted and redrafted as every word was carefully considered and debated. Its special reports were, in effect, laying the groundwork for conventions that might one day be negotiated. Then, once passed by majority vote, its recommendations had to be approved by the Commission on Human Rights and finally by ECOSOC. Both these bodies also discussed the resolutions, making changes of their own. Each of them might also run out of time and put off discussion to the next session or later. No more cumbersome system could have been devised to ensure that the wheels of the United Nations ground slowly at the best of times. In the worst cases, decisions could be put off for years.

The great weakness of the Sub-Commission was that, like the League committees, it had no executive authority. It could define problems, collect information from approved sources, study it, and make recommendations. The same problems might be raised year after year without hope of resolution. The only ultimate sanction was an appeal to public opinion. In this sphere, it had the advantage over the League committees in that it normally met in public.

However, to protect governments from embarrassing revelations, it heard accusations against them in private. As well as complaints from NGOs, the UN Secretariat received thousands of allegations of infringements of human rights from individuals. Until 1967, little was done with them. In that year, ECOSOC authorized the Commission on Human Rights and the Sub-Commission to examine "gross violations" of rights, such as apartheid. In 1970, it went a step further and authorized the "1503 procedure." This allowed accusations against a government to be considered if there was a consistent pattern of violations.[43] Accusations, euphemistically called "communications," had to be sent in writing to the secretary-general. They were then screened by a working group of the Sub-Commission, and then by the whole Sub-Commission. Those considered valid were forwarded to the Commission on Human Rights, which could appoint an ad hoc committee to investigate them, if the accused state agreed. The system was time consuming and usually achieved little because the Commission rarely took effective action.

It was also thoroughly unsatisfactory for the complainant, who only received a "receipt." The screening process was strict. Of 23,000 complaints considered in 1973, the year the system began, only eight were sent to the Commission. An NGO only knew whether its communication survived the process if it appeared months later on the agenda of the Commission on Human Rights. Moreover, once it had been discussed in the Commission it could never be raised again.[44] Unless a government replied, nothing more would be heard of it. The reason given for this blatant shielding of governments was that they would be more likely to cooperate if the proceedings were secret. However imperfect the procedure, it was welcomed by the Anti-Slavery Society because without it, none of the specific complaints would have even been seen by the Sub-Commission.[45]

Until 1973, NGOs were also not allowed actually to name governments when presenting their complaints to the UN, and the names were not mentioned in the reports. NGOs made a mockery of this by describing the countries at fault in phrases such as "a certain Asian country." This absurd procedure was dropped after Montgomery was challenged in the Commission on Human Rights to name an offending country, and he pointed out that NGOs had been warned only to name a state if they were praising it.[46]

THE APPOINTMENT OF ANOTHER
SPECIAL RAPPORTEUR ON SLAVERY

In 1967, the Sub-Commission recommended that the Commission on Human Rights authorize it to study measures to be taken against states that had failed to comply with the slavery conventions. Bold as this sounded, its actual proposals were cautious in the extreme. It suggested "international police action" to rescue people in danger of enslavement. But by this it meant simply that police forces should exchange information. It suggested the establishment of a panel of experts on slavery, but they were only to advise states that asked for help—an unlikely event. More promising was its request that one or more members of the Human Rights Division of the UN Secretariat be assigned to the "exclusive study" of slavery. Finally, it repeated the time-honored request that the secretary-general should urge states which had not done so, to accede to the conventions.[47] The U.S. member thought the resolution "not worth the paper it is written on."[48] Needless to say, the Commission accepted it.[49] The British delegates abstained. The government explained to Parliament that, although they supported the resolution against slavery, they could not endorse any action that included apartheid and colonialism in its definition.[50]

In May 1968, ECOSOC in turn agreed to the recommendations. It also called on members to protect persons escaping from slavery and asked the specialized agencies—the ILO, UNESCO, WHO, and FAO—to consider how they might help rehabilitate women and girls who had been freed. In a new departure, it included trafficking in persons for prostitution as a form of slavery. To the British dismay, it also made a point of calling on member states to combat apartheid and colonialism, affirming that the Master and Servant laws in South Africa, Southwest Africa, and Southern Rhodesia were "clear manifestations of slavery and the slave trade."[51] The British began to fear that it might take up a Tanzanian suggestion that the slavery conventions should be brought up to date to include apartheid and colonialism.[52] They wanted the Sub-Commission to put forward "serious and well argued proposals for implementation" which did not "confuse" slavery with apartheid and colonialism.

The Anti-Slavery Society reminded the Foreign Office that the Sub-Commission's meeting in September 1968 would be the last chance to achieve this before the additional Asian and African members took their seats in 1969. The British decided to lobby for the appointment of the British member, Peter Calvocoressi, as Special Rapporteur to study measures to implement the conventions.[53] He was "respected" by his colleagues and, although known for insisting on his independence, he kept in close touch with officials and with the Anti-Slavery Society.[54]

The plan misfired.[55] Calvocoressi tabled a draft resolution requesting the Commission on Human Rights to authorize the Sub-Commission to appoint the proposed Special Rapporteur from among its own members and argued that it should be considered separately from apartheid and colonialism. The Anti-Slavery Society and the Women's International League for Peace and Freedom made moving appeals for action. A number of members not only supported his resolution, but wanted it strengthened and agreed that apartheid and colonialism, although deplorable, were best tackled separately from slavery. It was even agreed that Calvocoressi would be the Rapporteur. "Everything," he wrote to Glover later, "went swimmingly up to the last minute." Then it was suggested that, as a "mere formality," a "matter of courtesy," the chairman "should have a private word with Awad." To the surprise, consternation, and embarrassment of all involved, Awad said he "would be delighted to do the job" himself. He was old and ailing and his term on the Sub-Commission was expiring, but "nobody could see how to get out of the mess." It was considered "too delicate a matter" to depute someone to tell him that he was too old.[56]

Awad's appointment was confirmed in June 1969. His mandate was to consider practical measures to eliminate slavery in all its forms including the possibility of using some of the techniques developed to help refugees and to counteract the narcotics traffic. He was to consult governments, but his main sources were to be the Specialized Agencies, intergovernmental regional organizations—such as the Organization of African Unity (OAU) and the Organization of American States (OAS), the Arab League—and NGOs. A single full-time member of the Secretariat was assigned to work on slavery.

PRESSURE RISES IN BRITAIN: THE ALL-PARTY PARLIAMENTARY GROUP ON SLAVERY

While Awad prepared his report, Glover found a new and effective method of putting pressure on the British government. In April 1969, he sent a *Sunday Times* article on Amerindians in Brazil to every member of Parliament (MP), inviting them to join the Anti-Slavery Society. At the same time he formed an All-Party Parliamentary Group on Slavery, launching it with a well-attended meeting presided over by the Speaker. This not only got press coverage but over thirty MPs joined the Society—boosting both its finances and its ability to organize parliamentary questions.[57] Most of the interest focused on the plight of indigenous peoples including "Amerindians" in South America, "Bushmen" in Africa, and "Negroid tribes" in the Southern Sudan, but Glover, true to the Society's dual mandate, also kept the spotlight on slavery. Later in the year, the group sent out letters asking for support to the heads of the legislative bodies of all members of the United Nations.

A deputation called on the minister of state at the Foreign Office, Goronwy Roberts,[58] and a debate urging the government to take stronger action at the United Nations was organized in the House of Commons. Roberts, afraid that the government would lose if it went to a vote, assured the House that Britain would henceforth take a stronger line.[59] A confident Montgomery informed Awad that he could be "more positive" in his recommendations, knowing that he had British support.[60] Once again, he was to be disappointed.

MORE AWAD REPORTS 1969–1971

When Awad presented an interim report in 1969 to the Sub-Commission only one morning was allotted to it.[61] Britain's fear that the new members would politicize the Sub-Commission was soon realized. Although Calvocoressi thought most of them were "good, some very good" and that governments had taken care to appoint "the right sort of people," time was wasted on polemics and on Waldron-Ramsay's "vacuous loquacity."[62] Awad himself frittered away precious minutes with a long, "largely irrelevant speech" and Montgomery feared that he had neither "the strength nor the will to produce a forthright report."[63]

As for the British government, it insisted that it could take no further action until Awad produced a final report.[64] To its chagrin, there was no hope of separating apartheid and colonialism from slavery. The problem over colonialism was partly removed, since the British had withdrawn from South Arabia in 1967 and had announced that they would leave the Gulf by 1971.[65] But the problems of Rhodesia and South Africa still loomed large. Lest they be forgotten, Waldron-Ramsay got the instructions to Awad amended to include the study of such specific manifestations of apartheid as forced and sweated African labor, the denial of trade union rights to Africans and the ill-treatment of Black prisoners.[66]

Awad presented an interim report in 1970 and the final one in 1971.[67] His consultations with the specialized agencies had yielded disappointing results. They had not wanted to be drawn into the problem[68] and some had little to offer. However, his discussions with them are of interest because they illustrate the difficulties that still dog action against slavery and other forms of servitude.

Awad reported that the basic reasons for the persistence of these practices were ignorance, poverty, and unemployment. UNESCO helped governments establish educational projects, including plans to increase literacy. He suggested that they could incorporate schemes to rally public opinion in the developing countries against slavery. However, UNESCO explained that it could only operate with the cooperation of governments and few of them gave priority to fostering any understanding of human rights.

The ILO had elaborate machinery for the implementation of the 250-odd conventions and recommendations which made up the International Labor Code setting labor standards.[69] Many of these agreements, such as the Forced Labor Conventions and the conventions and recommendations against debt-bondage, and against land tenure systems based on personal service, covered forms of servitude.[70] The organization had effective arrangements for persuading states to ratify its conventions and send in regular reports. If signatories failed to implement the conventions, it reviewed their difficulties with them. Its representatives were available to consult local officials and it also sent out experts to investigate complaints on the spot.[71] Awad suggested that its methods could be applied to the implementation of the slavery conventions. Moreover, since legal freedom was merely the first stage in the emancipation of slaves, the ILO could ease their transition to free labor by offering vocational training and other assistance. However, admirable as this machinery might be, it was useless against states that ignored or did not ratify the conventions, as the continuation of apartheid in South Africa made plain.

The FAO had been actively involved in helping governments eliminate serfdom and debt-bondage by land tenure reforms, and the provision of credit, and marketing institutions. Working together with the ILO, UNESCO, and the World Health Organization (WHO), it had been successful in improving the living standards of perhaps a fraction of the indigenous peoples in the Andes, but it too could only operate with government cooperation.[72]

Interpol had established machinery to facilitate police cooperation between more than a hundred countries and had a communications network encircling the globe.[73] It compiled statistics, kept individuals under surveillance, arranged arrests, and generally coordinated police work. It was ready enough to extend its operations to cover slavery in all its forms except apartheid. This was excluded because it was prohibited from intervening in cases with a racial, political, religious, or military character. It could only act within the framework of the laws of each country. For it to be involved, a state had to have declared slavery and the slave trade penal offenses carrying specific penalties. Even then, since it had no police force of its own, it had to rely on local police forces to enforce the laws, and for this they needed adequate numbers of well-trained personnel, and a cooperative public—conditions unlikely to exist where forms of servitude were entrenched.

Moreover, the laws had to be carefully drafted. Interpol's efforts to suppress trafficking in women for prostitution were hampered because the Convention for the Suppression of the Traffic in Persons and of the Exploitation of the Prostitution of Others signed in 1949 only allowed prosecution if it could be proved that victims were intentionally recruited for prostitution.[74] In many cases, they were tricked into the trade by promises of good jobs or marriage, or were given fraudulent contracts, making it impossible to prove that prostitution was the intention and not simply the result of recruitment. Hence, the recruiters went free. Similar problems could be expected in cases of enslavement in which victims were recruited voluntarily by the prospect of well-paid employment.

Awad believed that states were reluctant to admit that slavery existed in their territories because they had outlawed it and denied that it continued. Drug-producing states had likewise shown little interest in acting against the narcotics traffic until they had been encouraged to state their needs and apply to the United Nations for financial assistance. Awad suggested that if governments were offered a similar financial incentive to suppress slavery, they might welcome the help of United Nations organizations and even use the list of experts already established. He proposed that states should be asked to state their needs and the Sub-Commission should then prepare a five-year plan for technical cooperation.

The first step, however, was to get them to sign the existing slavery conventions, together with the conventions against trafficking in persons and against forced and child marriage.[75] He would have liked these consolidated into one convention. The Afro-Asian and communist members of the Sub-Commission supported this proposal, but the NGOs, led as usual by the Anti-Slavery Society, objected strongly. They feared it would be an excuse to defer further discussion on slavery until a new convention had been "drafted, adopted and ratified," a process which could take ten years.[76] Awad advocated regional meetings and seminars in which states with similar cultures and problems could cooperate. The Anti-Slavery Society objected that seminars were a waste of money. It was also rejected by the Sub-Commission in the belief that states where slavery continued would not participate. As the Society put it, countries with a "common cultural background" might share a common "traditional tolerance of slavery."[77]

The remainder of Awad's final report dealt with apartheid and colonialism. The details need not concern us here but it should be noted that he made it clear that these required different treatment from slavery. The Sub-Commission, however, insisted, in spite of the opposition of the British and French members, on retaining apartheid and colonialism in the definition of slavery. Finally, Awad reminded the Sub-Commission that in 1966 he had proposed a slavery committee, but he did not actually propose it again.

A UN WORKING GROUP ON SLAVERY FINALLY ESTABLISHED

The Sub-Commission passed a resolution incorporating most of Awad's suggestions but without any mechanism for implementing the conventions.[78] Acceptance of this uncontroversial resolution was deferred in 1972, because the Commission on Human Rights ran out of time. Outraged, twenty NGOs, led by the Anti-Slavery Society, demanded that ECOSOC instruct its subordinate bodies to get on with the job.[79] ECOSOC had been shocked by revelations of an illicit traffic in Africans brought to Europe, and then exploited and ill-treated. This modern version of the slave traffic had been operating for ten years without coming to international attention. As the Anti-Slavery Society said, there was nobody in the UN to look to for action, or even to collect information on slavery.[80] Pressured by the British delegate, ECOSOC reproved the Commission on Human Rights and ordered it to instruct the Sub-Commission to establish permanent machinery for the implementation of the slavery conventions.[81] This finally forced the issue, but it took two more years to bring results.

Two possible mechanisms were considered in 1972. One was the establishment of a committee of experts and the other the appointment of a slavery advisor. Ironically, the Anti-Slavery Society now came down strongly in favor of an advisor. Although it was not successful, its reasons are of interest because, as will be seen, they mirror those advanced in support of a similar proposal more than a quarter of a century later. The Society, Montgomery explained to Lady Elles, had "perhaps pigheadedly" gone on demanding a committee "until everyone at the UN was sick of the term." It had then suggested to Awad that there should be an International Slavery Board along the lines of the Permanent Central Narcotics Board, with its own secretariat and a budget. However, this had not even been discussed in the debate on his report, perhaps because it "looked too businesslike."[82] Late in 1972, the Society had decided that the best solution would be an advisor, with "loose" terms of reference, reporting annually to the Sub-Commission. To make the proposal more acceptable, his, or preferably her, title might be "Advisor on Social Development." He, or she, would have to be someone of "strong character," integrity, and courage, willing to use "a little of the stick as well as of the carrot" in dealing with governments. For continuity and to ensure expertise, the appointment should be full-time for at least five years. Such a person would need to travel, to have access to ministers, and freedom to receive, evaluate, and follow "all intelligence leads." He or she could thus respond quickly to reports of slavery, bring them discreetly to the notice of governments, present the facts and suggest remedies.[83]

Exactly what horse-trading went on behind the scenes in the Sub-Commission when the rival merits of an advisor versus a committee were discussed will not be known until the British and other official documents are opened. But the bare bones of the story can be pieced together from the UN reports, the Society's records, and other sources. In 1972, the Sudanese member of the Sub-Commission duly proposed the appointment of an advisor and the Ghanaian member proposed a working group of five experts to be chosen from the Sub-Commission's own members to meet for seven days just before its regular meeting. The Russian member opposed both proposals on the familiar ground that they were unnecessary and unlikely to be productive.[84] When it came to financial considerations, the advisor would have been cheaper than the committee. The decision was postponed to the following year.

In 1973, Lady Elles, now the British member, realized that the proposal for an advisor could not be carried, and rallied support for the establishment of the working group.[85] Finally, a resolution requesting its appointment was passed, and was agreed to by ECOSOC in May 1974. However, it was only to be allowed three days for its meetings. In spite of this authorization from on high, the Russian and Ecuadorian members of the Sub-Commission still opposed the proposal. The latter insisted that slavery no longer existed. However, this was successfully challenged and most speakers supported the establishment of the group. The Russian was finally persuaded to agree, provided slavery was only debated every other year.[86]

The group was to consist of five members, one from each of the geographical areas into which the UN had divided the world. It was to consider slavery and the slave trade in all their manifestations, including trafficking in persons and, of course, apartheid and colonialism. Its members were to be chosen by the chairman in consultation with the members from each area.

CONCLUSION: PAST EFFORTS AND FUTURE PROBLEMS

The Anti-Slavery Society's long battle for some international mechanism for implementing the slavery and related conventions had resulted in a Pyrrhic victory. It supported the establishment of the working group reluctantly—*faute de mieux.* The problems were obvious. The group would only meet for three days every other year at a fixed time. It could not react quickly even in a dire situation. Its members, changing constantly, could not become experts. It could not initiate investigations and was limited to the information provided by NGOs and other authorized sources. Worse still, but true to tradition, it had no executive powers and no authority to enforce the advice it was established to provide.

The Society had always looked back with nostalgia to the days of the Brussels Act, with its bureaus in Brussels and Zanzibar. However, the Act had outlawed only the African slave trade, and its office in Brussels merely published information supplied by governments. The one in Zanzibar collated information on slavers in the area. This facilitated action against them, but it depended on the cooperation of the powers to achieve results. The League of Nations had begun the process of extending the definition of slavery, but its committees had been toothless bodies. The first had called attention to the problems, and persuaded colonial governments to negotiate the first conventions against slavery and forced labor, as well as to begin to overhaul their laws, and, in some areas, to take tentative steps to help slaves gain their freedom. The second had insisted on the need for a permanent committee. The lone efforts of Maxwell had given the third one an impact, but mainly in the British Empire, and had focused some attention on problems, such as debt-bondage, hitherto ignored at the international level. The ill-fated ad hoc committee of 1949–1950 had, to its cost, brought peonage to the fore, but it had laid the foundations for the negotiation of the 1956 Convention, which had spelled out the various forms of servitude under attack.

By this time, chattel slavery and its associated slave trade had largely disappeared. What had come next was a whole new ball game. Colonial rulers vanished. Some states became richer as their resources were developed, and some, for various reasons, sank into greater poverty. These changes were under way by 1975, but as globalization intensified in the next quarter century, labor was mobilized in different ways, and began to flow, under various guises and, in ever increasing numbers, from poor areas into developing or richer ones. The arms and drug trades also intensified, together with the growth of organized crime. In the process, new forms of exploitation developed, some more cruel than many types of slavery.

To monitor this growing problem, the United Nations, by 1975, had established yet another small, powerless committee. Since it was impossible to separate economic and social problems from political ones, except at the level of academic discussion, it was highly politicized from the start, and, as Montgomery said, "over weighted" with members "from regions where Human Rights do not exist." He predicted it would be "worse than useless" because people would believe that some machinery for implementation had at last been established."[87] How far his gloom was justified will now be examined in a necessarily brief epilogue, based on published sources.

NOTES

1. AS *Annual Report,* 31 March 1967, pp. 5–6.

2. Sisco confidential memorandum for the Secretary of State, 26 May 1967, Soc. 14, State Department, USNA. The United States had signed the 1956 slavery convention but did not ratify it until 1967.

3. AS *Annual Report,* 31 March 1967.

4. Montgomery to Milett Wood, 23 February 1967, MSS. Brit.Emp. s.19 D10/20, file 5. For quotation and examples of information, see AS submission 1968 MSS. Brit.Emp. s.22 G884.

5. Montgomery to Daan van der Meulen, 19 December 1966, MSS. Brit.Emp. s.19 D10/20, file 5.

6. Warner to Pridham, restricted, 30 November 1966, FO 371/189990 US 2183/66.

7. For Awad's report, see above, chapter 21.

8. The film featuring Endresen, Glover, and Montgomery, was shown on the Frank McGee Program, NBC, 13 August 1967. A transcript is in FCO 61/22O.

9. Cameroon to the UN Secretariat, 31 January 1968. FCO 61/220.

10. AS *Annual Report,* 31 March 1970, 9–10.

11. Statement by the Anti-Slavery Society to the Commission on Human Rights, 7 March 1968, FCO 61/220.

12. Cassin won the Nobel Peace Prize in 1968.

13. These included the renowned Théodore Monod and the social anthropologist Germaine Tillion.

14. AS *Annual Report,* 31 March 1967, p. 4, and ASR series VI, vol. 12, no. 3 (pp. 16–18). To make amends, the Algerian government sent her to school in Algiers, with the sad result that she became too sophisticated to return to her family; interview with Jacques Oriel, Geneva, 2 August 1984.

15. For its activities and cuttings in *Liberté,* see MSS. Brit.Emp. s.22 G927.

16. FMAE to Chalard, 6 July 1966, FMAE NUO1 1033 folder, July 1961–December 1969.

17. Emmanuel La Gravière was one of the vice-presidents of the Anti-Slavery Society from the 1950s to the 1990s. He was a member of the French Assembly.

18. *Daily Telegraph,* 12 January 1968.

19. AS *Annual Reports,* 31 March 1967, p. 7, and 31 March 1968, pp. 10–11. The inauguration in Norway was attended by the Swedish professor, Bishop Bengt Sundkler, of the University of Uppsala.

20. This included a donation of £350 from Dr. Nnamdi Azikiwe, the President of Nigeria.

21. Montgomery to Carter, 9 September 1966, MSS. Brit. Emp. s.19 D10/20, file 3.

22. Even the cost of stationery and postage was a serious consideration.

23. Yule to Montgomery, 5 July 1966, Montgomery to Yule, 29 July 1966, MSS. Brit.Emp. s.19 D 10/20, file 1.

24. Montgomery to Yule, 29 July 1966, ibid. For Maugham's purchase, see above, chapter 21.

25. AS *Annual Reports* contain balance sheets, lists of members, appeals, and details of activities.

26. In the nineteen years from 1960–1979, it came out only in 1960, 1961, 1963, 1966, 1971, 1976, and 1979. Thereafter, it was published regularly.

27. Interview with Patrick Montgomery, 14 July 1981.

28. They included the Liberal, Rt. Hon. Joseph Grimond, the Labor Baroness Gaitskell, and the Conservative Lord Butler.

29. These included Dame Margery Perham, Thomas Hodgkin, and W. M. MacMillan.

30. These were the Bishops of St. Albans and Nottingham, the Rt. Rev. J. W. C. Wand, formerly Bishop of London, as well as the activist missionary, the Rev. Michael Scott, founder of the Africa Bureau and the Minority Rights Group.

31. Personal communication from Dr. H. Charles Swaisland. A former colonial servant, he was invited to join the committee in 1965 when he was 41, in order to introduce an element of youth.

32. AS *Annual Report*, 31 March 1967, p. 7.

33. Minute on the background to a parliamentary question by Archer, restricted, 2 July 1968, FCO 61/220.

34. This was up from fourteen a year earlier.

35. In 1969, members served for three years. In 1988, this was changed to four years.

36. Personal communication from Lady Elles, 28 August 1989. Whitaker was director of the Minority Rights Group.

37. Since, at the time of writing, the Foreign Office archives are closed from 1970, I do not know to what extent officials were consulted after that date.

38. US Mission, Geneva, to Department of State, 17 February 1967, A-1280 US Soc.14, US Archives.

39. Milton to Wilberforce, confidential, 24 March 1969, and IOC (69) 92, 26 August 1969, FCO 61/523. In 1969 at least seven of the successful candidates, including the French member, also

represented their governments on the Commission on Human Rights. These included also W. E. Waldron-Ramsey (Tanzania). Five others were serving civil servants.

40. Milton to Wilberforce, confidential, 24 March 1969, FCO 61/523.

41. See brief curricula vitae with comments in FCO 61/523.

42. IOC (69) 92, 26 August 1969, ibid.

43. It was called this because the resolution was no. 1503. For the text and comments, see Brownlie, 15–20.

44. AS *Annual Report* 1974, 4, Montgomery "Once is Enough." Personal communication from author of document deposited in UNCRP.

45. Montgomery, "Once is Enough," ibid.

46. Montgomery, "The Human Rights Contribution of NGOs," ibid.

47. E/CN.4/Sub.2/L.478/Add.6.

48. US Mission, Geneva, to Department of State, airgram, 15 October 1967, A-202, Soc.14 USNA.

49. ECOSOC resolution 14 (XXIV), 8 March 1968, E/CN.4/L.1036.

50. Parliamentary question, 1 April 1968; notes for supplementary questions by Pridham, 27 March 1968, FCO 61/220.

51. Resolutions 1330 and 1331 (XLIV), 17 June 1968, ECOSOC 44, item 13.

52. Tanzania had raised this question at ECSOC; minutes by Richards, 27 June 1968, and Coles, 3 July 1968, FCO 61/220.

53. Montgomery to foreign secretary, 9 August 1968, Glover to Roberts, 31 August 1968. Speaking notes by King, restricted, 25 September 1968, minutes by Coles, 27 September 1968, FCO 61/221.

54. Minutes by Wilberforce, 16 August 1968 and by King, 25 September 1968, FCO 61/221 US 13/17; Wilberforce to Ackland, restricted, 3 October 1968, CAB 134/210; UK Mission to secretary-general, 7 October 1968, FCO 61/221, circulated to Sub-Commission E/CN.4/Sub.2/290/Add.2.

55. For the various resolutions and the proceedings of this meeting, see E/CN.4/Sub.2/L507/Rev.1, E/CN.4Sub.2/SR.551, E/CN.4/Sub.2/SR.552.

56. Calvocoressi to Glover, 27 October 1968, MSS.Brit.Emp.s.22 G 889. Calvocoressi's official report on this meeting has been destroyed by Foreign Office "weeding" for no obvious reason.

57. For the correspondence with MPs and the activities of the Group, see MSS. Brit. Emp. N (Parliamentary 1972–1981).

58. Minute by King, 17 June 1969, and Record of Meeting between the Slavery and Primitive Peoples All-Party Parliamentary Group, 18 June 1969, FCO 61/534 UM 16/42.

59. Minute by King, 17 June 1969, FCO 61/534 UM 16/42; Debate 20 June 1969, Hansard.

60. Montgomery to Awad, 7 July 1969, MSS. Brit.Emp. s.22 G896.

61. E/CN.4/Sub.2/304.

62. Report by Calvocoressi, IOC (69) 133, 21 October 1969, FCO 61/523.

63. Montgomery's Report to the AS committee, September 1969, MSS. Brit.Emp. s.22 G896.

64. Speaking notes for meeting between minister of state and the All-Party Parliamentary Group, 11 September 1969, FCO 61/535 UM 16/42.

65. See above, chapter 20.

66. Resolution 4 (XXII), 10 September 1969. Apartheid and colonialism had been included in the amended resolution proposed by Calvocoressi in 1968, but had not been given such prominence. For the resolution and Waldron-Ramsey's amendment, see E/CN.4/Sub.2/L529/Rev 1, 9 September 1969. For British reactions, see documents in FCO 61/535.

67. E/CN.4/Sub.2/312, 1 July 1970 and E/CN.4/Sub.2/322, 16 July 1971.

68. Sawyer 1986, 225, citing a paper by Montgomery.

69. For details, see International Labor Conference, 53rd session, report 3, part 4.

70. As well as the Forced Labor Conventions, these included the Employment Policy Definition (no. 122) of 1965, the Social Policy (Basic Aims and Standards) Convention (no. 117) of 1962, the Freedom of Association and Protection of the Right to Organize Convention (no. 87) of 1948, the Right to Organize and Collective Bargaining Convention (no. 98) of 1949, the Convention for the Protection and Integration of Indigenous and Other Tribal and Semi-Tribal Populations (no. 107) of 1957.

71. For a brief and useful discussion of its methods, see Sawyer 1986, 226–28.

72. This was the Andean Indian Program launched by six governments in 1954 to improve the living standards of some ten million Indians of the Altiplano, living in "utter poverty" and "near serfdom." In 1973, it was only credited with having benefited 250,000 directly and the same number indirectly, ASR, 1973–1974, p. 3.

73. Interpol is an NGO recognized as a consultative body by ECOSOC.

74. For the text, see HRI, pp. 60–64. For further discussion of trafficking in persons, see below, chapter 24.

75. The Convention on Consent to Marriage, Minimum Age for Marriage and Registration of Marriages 1962, stipulated that marriage should only be entered into voluntarily and by persons

of full age and should be properly and publicly recorded. For text, see *HRI*, pp. 112–15, and subsequent recommendation, ibid., pp. 113–14.

76. Awad reports 1 July 1970, E/CN.4/Sub.2/312, paras. 132–5, and E/CN.4/Sub.2/322, 16 July 1971, para. 83; AS *Annual Report*, 1970–1971, p. 3; comments in Nuttall (Women's International League for Peace and Freedom) [WILPF] to Awad, December 1970, MSS. Brit.Emp. s.22 G898; Sawyer 1986, 223–24.

77. AS *Annual Report*, 1971–1972, p. 3.

78. Sub-Commission Report, E/CN.4/1070 and E/CN.4/Sub.2/323, 6 October 1971.

79. Statement to ECOSOC by NGOs, 17 May 1972, AS 1972–81, UN 1972.

80. AS submission to the Sub-Commission, 30 August 1972, AS 1972–81, UN 1972.

81. Sawyer 1986, 224.

82. Montgomery to Lady Elles, confidential, 15 August 1973, AS 1972–81, UN 1973.

83. Ibid.

84. For the two resolutions and the discussion, see E/CN.4/1101, E/CN.4/Sub.2/332, 28 September 1972.

85. Letter to the author from Lady Elles, 28 August 1989.

86. Sawyer 1986, 224.

87. Montgomery to Lady Elles, confidential, 15 August 1973, AS 1972–81, UN 1973.

Epilogue: The UN Working Group on Contemporary Forms of Slavery

THE UN WORKING GROUP ON SLAVERY STRUGGLES TO EXPAND ITS ROLE

The Working Group on Slavery met for the first time in Geneva in August 1975. Its five members, all lawyers, came from India, Britain, Yugoslavia, Sierra Leone, and Colombia. The Indian was elected chairman and rapporteur.[1] The British member, Benjamin Whitaker, had joined the Anti-Slavery Society in 1964 and was a staunch supporter of the cause.[2] Since all members spoke English, and since there were no interpreters, the atmosphere was informal. ECOSOC had not ruled on whether proceedings were to be public or private. The Group invited Montgomery, as the representative of the Anti-Slavery Society, first to attend their meetings, and then to participate in them, and finally they asked him if he would agree to be co-opted as a member for future sessions—an invitation he was all too ready to accept. "Clearly," he reported, "all members wanted to achieve positive results," although "some were keener than others."[3]

In the three days at its disposal, the Group held six meetings to determine its approach to work, to consider its terms of reference, and to draw up its report and recommendations to the Sub-Commission. The latter were deliberately drawn "as widely and loosely as possible," as a "*ballon d'essai*, festooned with ballast," which could be jettisoned "under attack." Members hoped by this means to get their most "essential" proposals accepted. These essentials were that the Group should be a permanent body, with longer sessions and broader terms of reference.[4] Its most controversial recommendations were that it should be allowed to seek and receive communications, visit countries where slavery existed, and invite governments, NGOs, and individuals to attend its meetings and "assist" in its work. Since trafficking and prostitution were a part of its mandate, it proposed that it should always have a female member—a request repeated twelve years later since few women were nominated and elected to UN bodies by their governments.[5] It called for the cooperation of the Specialized Agencies and

NGOs, and for states to ratify and implement the conventions against slavery and other forms of servitude. Finally, it asked that the UN publicize its work.

Needless to say, some of these recommendations struck fear into the hearts of certain members of the Sub-Commission. The Ecuadorian insisted that slavery no longer existed and should come off the agenda. The Egyptian opposed any widening of the terms of reference, as well as the inclusion of trafficking in persons. The Russian objected to the Group becoming a permanent body, to its receiving communications, to its paying visits, and to the inclusion of NGOs or individuals in its meetings. However, members from Ghana, Sudan, Sierra Leone, and Colombia, as well as those from Britain, the United States, France, and Italy, supported the recommendations. Eventually, the visits had to be dropped, but the Sub-Commission agreed that the Group's sessions should be extended to five working days and that individuals and NGOs could attend its meetings and take part in its work.[6] It was a heartening sign that only the Russian, Egyptian, and Ecuadorian members abstained from voting. Montgomery's expectations had been exceeded, although predictably nothing more was heard of the idea that he might be co-opted to serve on the Working Group.

These recommendations remained in suspense for three years. In 1976, the Commission on Human Rights was too busy to do more than take note of them. Thus neither the terms of reference nor the length of the session had changed when the Group met for its second session in that year. What had changed, however, was its composition. Only two of the original members remained.[7] Changes of personnel were to be a regular feature in the years to come.[8] For some years, Whitaker provided continuity, and Mr. Justice Abu Sayeed Chowdhury, from Bangladesh, served as chairman from 1978 until his death in 1987. Some long-term members of the Sub-Commission, such as Mrs. Halima Embarek Warzazi from Morocco, joined the Group intermittently.[9] These constant changes, together with a lack of vision on the part of some of its chairpersons, prevented the Group as a whole, as distinct from individual members, from developing either real expertise or a strong sense of purpose.

Since none of its recommendations had been acted upon, the Group repeated them in 1976. It also proposed special studies on the sale of children and the elimination of debt-bondage, and advocated the revival of the reporting and publication procedures required by the 1949 Convention on Trafficking in Persons and the Exploitation of the Prostitution of Others, which had fallen into disuse.[10] The only result of this meeting was that the Sub-Commission agreed that a permanent staff member from the Division of Human Rights should be appointed to deal with slavery. This would, at least, provide continuity and expertise in the Secretariat—the body that collected the information for each session from governments, NGOs, and Special Agencies, and undertook inquiries when requested. However, this concession came at a price. The Eastern European members agreed to it on condition that the Sub-Commission would only debate slavery in alternate years.[11] Thus, although the Group met annually, its recommendations were only to be considered biennially. Given the fact that any recommendations with financial implications had to be approved by the Sub-Commission, then the Commission on Human Rights and finally by ECOSOC, this was yet another delaying tactic.

When the Group met for its third session in 1977, once again neither its terms of reference nor the time allotted for meetings had changed, and the Secretariat had not appointed the promised expert. Its main recommendation at this session was that there should be two new studies—one on slavery to update the Awad report, and one on trafficking in persons and prostitution. In view of the many cases of forced labor and debt bondage brought before it, the Group also recommended that the ILO should be represented at all its meetings.[12]

The first public breach in the Group's unanimity now occurred. Whereas hitherto its reports had been unanimous, the Eastern European member now complained that the Group was exceeding its mandate. The Colombian member denied allegations of debt-bondage among the indigenous population of the Cauca River area of Colombia, which he had recently visited.[13] A flat denial of charges against a member's own government, or sometimes his or her geographical area was to become another a feature of the Working Group.

In 1977, when the Group had held three sessions and produced a crop of recommendations, none of which had been acted upon, the Anti-Slavery Society protested to the Commission on Human Rights at the built-in delays. A month later, the expert was finally appointed to the Secretariat. Montgomery considered this a "most important event." It was the first time since 1939 that there was someone at the international level responsible "for knowing about slavery let alone doing anything about it."[14] However, his jubilation was premature. For most of the next two decades, the Secretariat appointed only a part-time official in spite of annual complaints from the Group that this was inadequate.[15]

In 1978 the Group repeated, again in vain, its call for longer sessions and wider terms of reference. However, in response to its requests, two Special Rapporteurs were appointed—one to update the Awad report on slavery, and the other to report on the exploitation of child labor.[16] The Secretariat also sent out circulars and questionnaires asking states for reports on trafficking and the exploitation of women and children for prostitution. A further important point was won in 1979, when the Sub-Commission, moved by heartrending information on child labor, and an urgent appeal from the Group, led by Whitaker, agreed to consider its reports annually from 1980.[17]

By the early 1980s, the Working Group had achieved many of the "essentials" requested by its first members in 1975. It was now a permanent body, meeting annually for five days, and its recommendations were considered by the Sub-Commission each year. Meetings were in one of the smaller rooms in the imposing Palais des Nations in Geneva, a beautiful setting, overlooking the lake. Most importantly, the meetings were held in public with simultaneous translation in English, French, Spanish, and Russian. Sessions began with the election or reelection of the Chair/Rapporteur. Precious time was some-times wasted in laudatory speeches about his or her work or those of new members, and in superfluous ones on the purpose of the Group for the benefit of the often-nonexistent public. The Secretariat reviewed developments since the last meeting, the Specialized Agencies made their reports, and the NGOs presented their oral statements.

States accused of allowing forms of servitude were not only identified, but from 1981 they were sent copies of the charges against them, and invited to reply in writing and send representatives to meetings. Discussion as to what should be included in the Group's report followed, and decisions were made as to whether the allegations were serious and plausible enough to call them to the attention of the governments con-cerned. Usually such discussion was between members themselves, with some input from NGOs. Meetings were then adjourned while the report was prepared in private sessions, and doubtless further discussion took place at this stage. NGOs could com-ment on the draft, but the final report, which included the Group's recommendations, was presented at a public meeting, which NGOs attended but in which they could not participate. The Chair/Rapporteur then presented it to the Sub-Commission, which, until 1992, met immediately after the Group finished its session. From that year, the Group met well before the Sub-Commission in order to give that body time to exam-ine its reports. However, this did not ensure that the Sub-Commission would actually discuss them, in spite of the Group's frequent appeals that it should do so. Those rec-ommendations accepted by the Sub-Commission were then passed to the Commis-sion on Human Rights and ultimately to ECOSOC and even the UN General Assem-bly for approval. The secretary-general then invited states to keep the Group informed as to the measures they had taken to carry them out. The press was free to attend its public meetings and press releases were issued to publicize the Group's work.

For the NGOs, and the few members of the public who attended them, these early sessions were disheartening.[18] Whether the atmosphere was congenial or hostile de-pended largely on the attitude of the Chairman and members of the Group, and this de-pended on whether they took issue with the material presented. In the 1980s, it was rare for all five members to be in the room at once. Some dropped in for brief periods, cre-ating an atmosphere of restlessness; others never appeared. The submissions and reports were circulated to them, and there were often good reasons for absence.[19] However, the impression created was that the members regarded the public meetings not as unique opportunities for fruitful discussion between the Group, the NGOs, and the Specialized Agencies, but as charades to be endured. Serious discussion between them doubtless took place behind the scenes, but the extent of this must remain a mystery until official archives for this period are opened.[20] In 1987, the Group itself recommended that the UN take steps to ensure the presence of all its members at meetings. Moreover, frustrated at the lack of progress, it asked the Secretariat to report annually on the action that had been taken on its recommendations.[21] As the volume of work built up, it succeeded in getting its sessions extended to eight days. The fruitfulness of its discussions, however, depended largely on how much interest members showed, and on how well the meetings were chaired. If the chairperson lacked a clear goal and took the statements in haphazard order and not by subject, discussions tended not to get going.

The Group, pressed by NGOs and Special Rapporteurs, frequently recommended that its mandate be broadened to enable it to review the implementation of the conventions. A first step would have been to empower it to enter into direct dialogue with governments to seek information and discuss action.[22] Other proposals included holding meetings in areas where forms of servitude persisted; and sending experts out to exert pressure on governments and monitor results.[23] There was talk of appointing a Special Rapporteur on Slavery responsible to the Commission on Human Rights. Such a rapporteur would have the advantage of being able to visit problem countries, to respond quickly when abuses were reported, and be able to present annual reports to the Commission. Equally stillborn were proposals that there should be continuity of membership, that the Group should meet twice a year, and that it should be enlarged to include more experts with knowledge of the various forms of slavery, and that a new group should be appointed with wider powers.[24] Also ignored was the recommendation that there should be an emergency procedure to enable the Group to react swiftly in cases of gross violations of human rights.[25]

Since none of these suggestions were acted upon, the Group, like its predecessors, was doomed to remain a paper tiger, unable to realize its potential as the "focal point" for the collection and discussion of information on slavery at the UN. It repeatedly urged states to ratify the conventions, but could not even force them to explain why they had not done so. It could only ask the Secretariat to invite them to an informal exchange of views.[26] It could only "express the hope" that they would invite it to send out a delegation to enter into constructive dialogue.[27] It could only "study" ways of strengthening the machinery for implementing the conventions.[28] It could only urge other UN bodies and Special Rapporteurs to cooperate with it, send it information, and attend its meetings. It could only exhort the media and governments to inform and mobilize public opinion on the dangers of contemporary forms of slavery. By 1998, its reports were a repetitive litany of hopes, exhortations, and recommendations.

However, the Group was able to take some positive steps. Besides the Special Rapporteurs on Slavery and on Child exploitation, it also initiated the appointment of a Special Rapporteur on the Sale of Children, Child Prostitution, and Child Pornography.[29] Special Rapporteurs were appointed by the Commission on Human Rights, and sometimes by the Sub-Commission.

At the request of NGOs, the Group also initiated the establishment of the United Nations Voluntary Trust Fund on Contemporary Forms of Slavery in 1991 to help representatives of NGOs from different parts of the world to attend its sessions, and to assist victims of gross violations of human rights. The fund was administered by the secretary-general, assisted by a board of trustees, composed of members of NGOs from each of the five areas into which the UN divided the world.[30] It was financed by voluntary donations from governments, NGOs, and individuals. It enabled local NGOs to bring eyewitnesses and victims of exploitation to the sessions. This increased the number of firsthand accounts of the situation at the grassroots level—testimony which governments found it hard to ignore—and the local NGOs offered realistic solutions. However, few governments contributed funds and the Center for Human Rights failed to provide adequate secretarial assistance, even apparently forgetting in 1996 to send out invitations to NGOs whose attendance the trustees had agreed to support. It needed only $100,000 to run at a minimal level but, in spite of repeated appeals, it was in such financial straits in 1998 that the trustees could not meet, and the representatives of only two NGOs were brought to the Group. Both were from Nepal and one was a child who had been trafficked to India for prostitution.[31] By 2000, however, donations had risen and the fund was able to bring eighteen NGO representatives to Geneva and to fund seventeen field projects, some in Africa and Latin America.

In 1989, the Group began to organize its sessions around a theme. In that year, the focus was on the sale of children and their use in prostitution and pornography. In 1990, it was on child labor and debt-bondage, and in 1991 on the traffic in persons and the exploitation of the prostitution of others.[32] To do this effectively the topic had to be advertised well in advance and those governments, UN agencies, and NGOs particularly involved had to be invited to attend the session and to send in information in time to be read before the meeting. This required adequate secretarial support, which sadly was still not forthcoming.[33]

To encourage the implementation of the conventions, the Group, from the late 1980s, drew up Programs of Action. These specified the laws which governments needed to pass, and measures to be taken by specialized agencies and NGOs. They included changes in international development strategies, increases in foreign aid to combat poverty, and the encouragement of local community and self-help projects, as well as efforts to increase public awareness of the evils of contemporary forms of slavery. They stressed the need to rehabilitate the victims of exploitation, and to punish those responsible for their plight. The theme for 1994 was the implementation of the Program of Action on the Exploitation of Child Labor. This was followed by the Program of Action for the Prevention of Trafficking in Persons and the Exploitation of the Prostitution of Others. Subsequently this thematic approach became more diffuse, and there were no more Programs of Action. In 1995, the Group focused both on illegal adoptions and on domestic workers. In subsequent years, it focused on migrant labor, the commercial exploitation of children, pedophilia, on bonded labor, on trafficking in persons, and on the role of corruption in promoting contemporary forms of slavery.

The Programs of Action were incorporated into draft resolutions and sent to the Sub-Commission, which passed them on to the Commission on Human Rights. They were then returned to the Group for reformulation in the light of the comments made by these bodies, and by governments, Specialized Agencies, and NGOs.[34] The process was slow. For instance, the Program for the Elimination of the Exploitation of Child Labor, drawn up in 1990, was only adopted by the Commission on Human Rights in 1993. The Commission then invited states to report on the measures they had taken to implement the programs, and requested the Sub-Commission to submit a progress report every two years. Although these programs could only bear fruit if governments were willing and able to take the necessary action, they drew attention to the difficulty of eradicating modern forms of servitude. It became clear that structural changes in the world economy were needed, as well as administrative and legal reforms, and that efforts would have to be made to change public attitudes through education and the media.

By the early 1990s, significant changes had taken place on the world stage, which were reflected in the Working Group. Apartheid, vilified as gross discrimination against the Black majority in South Africa in the provision of jobs, education, and access to land, together with forced relocation and deprivation of political rights, drew to an end with the installation of majority rule. The decolonization of most of the European empires meant that colonialism was no longer a bone of contention between the Western powers and others. The new imperialists in fact included the Indonesians in East Timor, the Chinese in Tibet, and the Moroccans in the Western Sahara. Finally, the Cold War, which had paralyzed so many antislavery initiatives, came to an end.

These events helped to decrease friction within the Group, and between some members and the NGOs. Members became more concerned with trying to get their recommendations implemented than with scoring political points. Discussions between the Group and NGOs were more fruitful. From the mid-1990s, some governments entered into informal discussions with members of the Group, explaining why they had not ratified or implemented the various conventions.

By the late 1990s, in spite of the improved atmosphere, however, the Group had been, as one critic put it, floundering for several years "in a rather vague morass," largely because it was collecting information on a wider and wider range of subjects. Its value had been questioned in the Sub-Commission in 1983 on the grounds that it was expensive and inefficient, but the UN Assembly had decided to retain it. At that time, the Anti-Slavery Society defended it because it provided "admirable filtering and editing machinery," so that slavery questions arrived at the Sub-Commission, which had a "crowded" agenda, in "compact and digestible form." It had another value too. As the Society pointed out, it was the one body in which NGOs could raise almost any form of exploitation and be sure of a hearing.

However, by 1998, the Group was concerned because not all the contemporary forms of slavery, with which it dealt, were covered in international instruments, and because there was still no effective mechanism for responding to them. It therefore asked the member from the United States, David Weissbrodt, together with the direc-

tor of Anti-Slavery International, in consultation with other NGOs, to review all existing treaties and customary law covering "traditional and contemporary slavery-
related practices" as well as existing monitoring mechanisms.[35] The aim was to clarify
what were and were not slavery and slavery-like practices.[36]

They suggested three possible courses of action. One was to replace the Group
with a Special Rapporteur on Contemporary Forms of Slavery. Added to the advantages already noted, this would also be cheaper than reconstituting the Working
Group with a broader mandate and more efficient working methods. This option,
however, was rejected, at least for the time being, by a Working Group of the Commission on Human Rights.[37] A second option was that the Group, having announced
its primary theme for the following year, should invite the governments most concerned to submit reports and come to informal private discussions. Fourteen NGOs
supported this plan, and the Working Group included it in its recommendations. To
ensure continuity, the NGOs also proposed that there should only be two new members of the Group a year.[38] The Working Group merely acknowledged that there was
a need for continuity. It did not accept the NGOs suggestion that one member of the
Group should be authorized to visit a country, at its government's invitation, to investigate charges against it.

A third option was to appoint the Working Group as the monitoring body for the
slavery and trafficking conventions, with the same powers as the committees of experts
established under later UN conventions.[39] Signatory states were bound to furnish these
committees with regular full reports on the measures they had taken to implement the
conventions and the committees could ask for further information, and suggest other
measures. In 2001, the Group recommended the adoption of this option, and the Sub-
Commission endorsed it.[40] When the century ended, it remained to be seen whether this
recommendation would be acted upon, and whether, if the new protocols were added to
these conventions, the Working Group would actually be the monitoring body.

This would be a radical departure. Throughout the quarter century of its existence,
in spite if its endless appeals, nothing had been done to enhance its powers. It had been
designed to be toothless and virtually toothless it had remained. Nevertheless, it was
not quite the nonentity it had been in 1975. It had collected a great deal of information and had struggled to bring all aspects of contemporary forms of slavery to public attention. The Special Rapporteurs it had advocated had gathered useful evidence.
Its Programs of Action had identified at least some of the measures necessary to end
the various forms of slavery. A wide range of NGOs had found it a useful forum to
bring their concerns. It had increasingly netted them publicity. Its open hearing
process also enabled them to use it to call the attention of the ILO to abuses of
labor. UN Specialized Agencies and other bodies had also come, although their attendance still left much to be desired, and fell off in 2001, perhaps because it coincided

with an important ILO session on forced labor, or because it was no longer considered important, or because they had not found it cost-effective.

It was, of course, only a small group with no powers of implementation and it merely fed its information and recommendations to higher bodies, which only sometimes acted upon them. Other UN bodies and the ILO meanwhile negotiated a number of conventions touching on contemporary forms of slavery. The question now was whether the Working Group had reached the limit of what it could achieve in its existing form.

GOVERNMENTS AND THE WORKING GROUP
The success or failure of the Group's initiatives depended entirely on the cooperation of governments. They had been largely protected in the past by the fact that state sovereignty was sacrosanct. The only international pressure that could be applied was to impose economic sanctions or to withhold foreign aid, but these, and even diplomatic pressure involved political, economic, and strategic considerations, which usually outweighed humanitarian ones. Governments could, and often did, ignore the recommendations of the Working Group and its parent bodies, except in states where strong public opinion could be mobilized, usually by NGOs supported by a free and active press. However, by the last decades of the century, the expansion of communications was making it increasingly impossible to keep human rights violations from attracting media attention and rousing opposition. Governments were becoming more sensitive to criticism from an increasingly educated and informed international public opinion.

For many years, few governments bothered to reply to the Group's requests for information. In the five years ending in 1991, only 32 of the 105 states that had ratified the 1956 convention had replied. Those that had replied, and those which came to meetings to answer charges, usually merely recited their laws without discussing how they were enforced or how effective they were. Their responses were governed by such variables as their alignment in the Cold War, their commitment to antiapartheid policies, whether they were "developed" or "developing" nations, or great powers or minor ones. The Anti-Slavery Society reported that between 1989 and 1992 it had submitted reports on sixteen different countries, only three of which commented on them during the sessions, and entered into useful dialogue.[41] In the 1990s, although some governments regularly attended the Group's meetings and explained their policies, this was usually to refute charges that had been made against them.

Some governments resorted to countercharges rather than answering accusations or engaging in serious discussion of their problems. This was particularly true during the Cold War. For instance, in 1981, the Anti-Slavery Society flew in an Ethiopian witness who charged the communist government with forcibly recruiting thousands of people of both sexes and forcing them to work in appalling conditions on a state farm in Humera. The Ethiopian government representatives claimed that the witness was a Tigrean terrorist, who should not be allowed to speak, that the Society had paid for his testimony and was trying to destroy the Ethiopian revolution. The communist Eastern European member of the Group supported him. To keep the peace, the chairman agreed simply to refer to the allegations and the reply in the Group's report in an "impartial" way. The altercation failed to produce any discussion of the reasons why the Ethiopian government resorted to forced labor, nor of what might be done to avoid it in the future.[42]

The legacy of colonialism was often used as an excuse for inaction. India, for instance, charged with doing too little to erase debt-bondage, pointed out that British rule had impoverished rural India, and the government was struggling to remedy a situation it had inherited. It had passed the Bonded Labour System Abolition Act in 1976 freeing all bonded workers from debts, and was trying to rehabilitate them by attacking poverty and unemployment, but its resources were limited.[43] These were valid points. Many forms of servitude had their roots in colonial policies and in poverty—a fact reiterated over and over again and more and more forcefully during the 1990s. It was all very well, the argument ran, for NGOs to point out the failings of poorer nations, but it was useless to attack these symptoms of poverty without attacking its causes. The poverty of many developing states was compounded by their indebtedness. Only a concerted effort by the rich creditor states to bring about a new international economic order would end the unequal distribution of wealth and the forms of servitude it spawned.[44] The need for changes in the world economy was acknowledged by all members of the Working Group as well as by NGOs. However, the latter argued, neither poverty nor the legacy of colonialism should be used as a cover for failure to pass or enforce laws to end these abuses. Moreover, help could be sought from the UN Specialized Agencies.

As the Group became more established and its work better known, more governments, sensitive to its appeal to public opinion, sent observers to the meetings. Attendance fluctuated depending on the issues discussed, but whereas in 1981 only seven governments were represented, eleven years later, the number peaked at thirty, and they came from all areas of the world. The next year, however, it fell back to fourteen, but in 1995, it rose to twenty-seven. Attendance alone cannot be taken as evidence of interest in the Group or support for it. Some governments sent representatives simply to get their names in the report as having attended the session without staying for the meetings. However, it is significant that they even considered it worthwhile to appear to attend.

In some cases, however, the discussions became more fruitful. The government of India, for instance, attacked over and over again for doing too little to end debt-bondage, explained its policies and difficulties at length.[45] Governments also sometimes invited an NGO or a specialized agency to cooperate in a joint study. For example, in 1987 Argentina asked Defense of Children International to set up an international committee of experts to study sales of children.[46] In 1996, the government of Sweden hosted the World Congress Against Commercial Sexual Exploitation of Child Labor in collaboration with UNICEF, and ECPAT (End Child Prostitution in Asian Tourism) and the NGO Group for the Convention on the Rights of the Child. Brazil worked with the ILO and UNICEF to establish priority regions for the elimination of child labor. Peru started a national protection plan together with the ILO to prevent the exploitation of children. Pakistan asked the ILO to undertake studies of child labor and bonded labor.[47] Although the Working Group was not directly involved in these activities, the participants took pains to see that they were mentioned in its reports.

Governments, of course, had their own problems. Those of the poorer states, like the colonial powers before them, depended on the support of the elites and of business interests benefiting from the cheap labor. They were often ill served by corrupt officials and inefficient police. Their failure to respond to requests for information could sometimes be attributed to lack of resources in the face of the large number of such requests from the various UN bodies.[48] The governments of richer countries were often faced with difficult legal decisions, and, in cases of foreign workers, with the hostility of labor unions and the public.

THE GROWING INVOLVEMENT OF
UN BODIES AND SPECIALIZED AGENCIES

As time went on, more Specialized Agencies and other UN bodies were drawn into the attack on slavery. Whereas they had tried to remain aloof from it in the past, now, in response to direct invitations from the Group, they sent representatives to some meetings and furnished reports of their activities.[49] In 1980, only the ILO and the UN Center for Social Development and Humanitarian Affairs (CSDHA) attended the session, but the next year, UNCTAD (United Nations Conference on Trade and Development), the United Nations Educational Scientific and Cultural Organization (UNESCO), and the UN High Commission for Refugees (UNHCR) also came. In subsequent years, other agencies joined them and their involvement in antislavery activities increased.

The ILO played a key role with its surveys on the various forms of exploitation of labor. It held seminars on topics such as debt-bondage. It referred complaints to its Committee of Experts on the Application of Conventions and Recommendations. It negotiated conventions setting labor standards for signatories and offered technical assistance to governments. The Food and Agriculture Organization (FAO) studied the needs of groups such as rural children and persons in debt-bondage, and tried to ensure greater participation of the rural poor in administrative and political structures. It provided field experts to help governments reform land tenure systems, and reported on the passing of new laws against debt-bondage in Latin America and elsewhere. Its studies found that insufficient attention had been given to the impact of household duties, as well as agricultural labor, on education. It reported that girls worked harder than boys and did not attend school as often because their families depended on their labor.[50] In the days of apartheid, UNCTAD ran schemes to prepare African members of southern African independence movements to take over the administration when the White governments were overthrown, and helped neighboring countries to lessen their economic dependence on South Africa. The World Health Organization (WHO) was invited to come to meetings to discuss the health problems of servile groups, and of women and children, including the spread of AIDS. UNESCO was drawn in for its educational programs, including seminars on different forms of servitude. Its studies by experts provided valuable information. In 1988 for instance, they called attention to the increase in the migration of females from poor countries to rich ones, often resulting in their being forced into prostitution.[51] UNICEF ran a number of development programs to help children in exceptionally difficult circumstances, some in cooperation with NGOs. Thus in 1994, together with the Anti-Slavery Society and the World Association for Orphans and Abandoned Children (WAO-Afrique), it launched a regional campaign on child labor in West Africa. It was also active in setting standards for the legal adoption of children.

The UN Center for Social Development and Humanitarian Affairs (CSDHA) had a branch for the advancement of women, which considered prostitution, discrimination against women, and servile marriage. The UNHCR was mainly involved in the 1980s with helping refugees from South Africa, but it was expected also to assist individuals fleeing from servitude in their own countries, and it studied the abuse of child refugees. Interpol provided information on criminal organizations, on missing persons believed to be victims of trafficking, and it tracked prosecutions. In 1989, it raised the question of child pornography. The World Tourism Organization was invited by ECOSOC to take up the question of children in sex tourism and, by the late 1990s, it had organized a meeting to study ways of combating it.

However, none of these bodies, with their valuable information and important programs, attended the Group's sessions regularly in spite of its frequent appeals that they should do so.[52] This hampered the Group's efforts to be recognized as the focal point for the exchange of information and a forum for fruitful discussion.[53] Similarly a number of UN committees established to monitor particular forms of servitude covered by conventions, such as the Committee on the Rights of the Child, the Committee on the Elimination of Discrimination Against Women, and the Committee on Economic, Social and Political Rights, and even sometimes Special Rapporteurs, also failed to come in spite of repeated invitations. In some cases, lack of funding was the reason for failure to attend. The Working Group apparently did not ask ECOSOC for the necessary funds.[54]

THE VITAL ROLE OF NGOs

The NGOs were vital to the Working Group's existence. They supplied most of its information and offered solutions to the problems they exposed and even drafted many of its recommendations. Unlike the members of the Group who came and went, they had real expertise. As in the past, they were the mainspring of the antislavery campaign. In 1975, the Anti-Slavery Society was the only NGO to attend the session and it continued to provide much of its information, covering more forms of exploitation than other, more specialized organizations. By 1980, it had been joined by the Minority Rights Group, the International Federation of Women Lawyers, the International Union for Child Welfare, and the Internationalist Abolitionist Federation—a French society devoted to eradicating the exploitation of prostitution. Four years later, twelve NGOs sent representatives,[55] and others joined them as time went on. They fell into two categories—those with consultative status and those which supplied the group with information, with its consent. There was little danger of an NGO not being heard, as even those not accredited and not invited to supply information could get their points across under the umbrella of accredited organizations.

In the early days, although sometimes thanked for their efforts, NGOs were treated by some members of the Group as necessary evils, rather than sources of vital information. Their painstaking efforts to present in a nutshell[56] the sufferings of the victims of slavery often met with a petulant complaint from a member that his or her part of the world was always "picked on." In one farcical episode, the chairman, having treated the Anti-Slavery Society, which had supplied most of the submissions, with scant regard, suddenly realized that, but for the Society, his committee would have no information upon which to justify its existence. He was driven to ask the Society's secretary to draft the Group's report—an invitation that was accepted.[57]

Year after year, NGOs presented more and more examples of the same iniquitous practices, as well as new ones. Members listened to governments' claims that they were eliminating them, only to hear a year later from NGOs that nothing had changed. The only certainty was that if there were any results they would be long delayed. While the UN talked and governments made excuses, more people fell into debt-bondage, more women were forced into marriage, more children were sold and ill-treated, and more workers were exploited. Meanwhile governments, even impoverished ones, spent large sums on arms. Leaders salted away ill-gotten gains, and corrupt officials failed to enforce laws. Third World poverty was compounded by population growth, by the failure to construct a new and more equitable international economic order, and sometimes by structural adjustment demanded by the International Monetary Fund or the World Bank or by ill-conceived development projects.[58]

As time went on, NGOs became more appreciated by some members of the Group, and more feared by others. Specialized Agencies asked them to participate in their conferences, seminars, and researches. To give just one example, in 1984, UNICEF invited the Anti-Slavery Society to attend a conference in New York on the exploitation and abuse of children, and then commissioned and financed the Society's two research papers on these subjects.[59] NGOs were always in the vanguard of the antislavery movement, urging the UN to greater efforts. In 1985, the director of the Anti-Slavery Society,[60] Peter Davies, protested to the secretary-general that the UN Human Rights Center in Geneva "lacked dynamism." This was not surprising since it was composed of civil servants fearful of offending their own or other governments.

In 1986, the UN decided to save money by canceling the meeting of the Sub-Commission and all its Working Groups for the year. An outraged Davies raised thousands of dollars from NGOs and the Norwegian government for an unofficial meeting. This was attended by sixteen members of the Sub-Commission, including the four members of the previous year's Working Group, and all five of the members who were to serve in 1987. A number of other experts came, together with representatives of no less than fifty-two NGOs, forty-seven governments, the UN Center for Human Rights, the ILO, UNCR, UNICEF, and various other bodies. They presented their report and recommendations to the secretary-general. They protested that the Sub-Commission and its subordinate groups were "central to the defense" of oppressed people in all parts of the world. They deplored the increasing politicization of human rights questions, complaining that discussions at the UN were "an exercise in ideological or political confrontation" and problems were treated selectively on the "basis of geopolitical concerns." They called for cooperation between UN bodies and NGOs, for better coordination within the UN Human Rights programs, and for the participation in development plans of the people most affected. They made it clear that any further cancellation of sessions or cutbacks in human rights bodies would cause an "outcry."[61] The following year the Working Group's recommendations were aggressively aimed at the implementation of the conventions and at greater cooperation between the UN and NGOs.[62] Although this did not bring hoped-for results, at least no further sessions were cancelled.

A great problem for the NGOs was, as always, that their information was open to the challenge that it could not be verified. This was readily admitted by the Anti-Slavery Society, which remained a very small and impecunious operation. Although from 1978 it received grants from foundations for particular projects, it could only send out a few field researchers.[63] It often had to choose a case for study not because it was unique or the worst example, but simply because it could find someone to gather the necessary information. As a result, some forms of exploitation, such as bonded labor in the Indian subcontinent, were raised again and again, leading governments to complain that they were being "picked on."

Except in the rare cases when governments invited investigation, the Society's researches had to be carried out without attracting official attention. Since the Working Group itself could not send out representatives to verify its allegations, all too often its information and that of other NGOs was challenged as untrue or biased. In 1992, their difficulties were summed up in an ASI submission:

Non-governmental organizations have, in the main, extremely tight budgets, programmes and schedules. Submissions . . . are normally based on years of research. Contemporary forms of slavery are often hidden and subtle in methods of bondage; victims are extremely vulnerable, gullible and fearful; . . . the discrimination, which is the basis of much abuse and use, is deep-rooted in society and the issues extremely sensitive, politically, economically and socially. Not least is the problem of finding researchers who are able to work with sensitivity and intelligence, but also are willing to work in dangerous situations.[64]

In the early days, the Anti-Slavery Society lived in fear that, if its small size became generally known, states whose shortcomings it exposed might try to get its consultative status revoked.[65] This threat was made more than once, particularly by the Eastern European bloc. In 1977, the Society, together with the International League for Human Rights and Amnesty International, was accused of slandering socialist countries. The only reason a serious complaint was not lodged, when their consultative status was reviewed by ECOSOC the following January, was because a snowstorm prevented the plaintiff from appearing.[66] That the threat remained was clearly demonstrated when, in 1999, Christian Solidarity International's (CSI) consultative status was withdrawn at the request of Sudan.[67]

Another charge thrown up in the early years was that most NGOs were Western organizations and that their criticisms of poorer, less-developed countries smacked of cultural imperialism—an attempt to force Western standards on the rest of the world. In 1981, a member of the Working Group exhorted the Anti-Slavery Society to open branches around the world. There were already some non-Western NGOs, [68] but in the years that followed, more and more sprang up spontaneously in different areas to deal with specific problems, and they began to attend the Working Group. The Society welcomed them. It changed its name in 1990 to Anti-Slavery International (ASI) to "reflect" the "supportive role" it proposed to play towards these "vigorous indigenous agencies."[69] Among its main allies at that time were the Indian Bonded Labor Liberation Front and a similar group founded in Pakistan. The Society worked closely with them. In 1989, for instance, it held a joint seminar in India with the Bonded Labor Liberation Front.[70] The South Asian Coalition on Child Servitude grew out of a seminar on bonded child labor organized by the Society in the same year.[71] It also paid for them to send representatives to Geneva, and lobbied the UN to obtain financial help for them. Its efforts were rewarded in 1992, when the UN General Assembly established the Voluntary Trust Fund on Contemporary Forms of Slavery.[72]

By this time, there were NGOs promoting human rights in many countries.[73] For example, those combating the exploitation of children included one in Brazil working with street children, one in Haiti helping child domestic servants, one in Kenya trying to better the lot of children on coffee plantations, and another in Nepal concerned with children on tea estates. Others promoted the rights of children in Portugal, Pakistan, and Peru. NGOs also began building regional organizations such as Child Workers in Asia. NGOs in India, Pakistan, and Nepal launched a joint campaign against child labor in the carpet industry, supported by NGOs in Britain, Holland, Sweden, and Germany.[74] To encourage and publicize the work of these groups, the Society initiated a prize to be awarded annually to organizations or individuals who performed outstanding service in their own countries. The list of recipients reflects the diverse interests of non-Western NGOs.[75] In 1991, the prize went to the Indian Bonded Labor Liberation Front, in 1993 to the Thai-based End Child Prostitution in Asian Tourism (ECPAT), in 1996 to the Indigenous Organization of Atalaya, Peru (OIRA), an NGO working to help the Atalaya Indians escape from debt-bondage. In 1998, the first African won the award, Professor Cheikh Saad Bouh Kamara, a founder and chairman of the Mauritanian Human Rights Association. In 1999, it went to an Indian husband and wife team, Vivek and Vidyullata Pandit, the founders of Shramajeevi Sanghatana, a union to free and rehabilitate bonded laborers, and other rural poor. In 2000, the recipient was George Omona, Project Coordinator of Gulu Support the Children Organization, which had rehabilitated over a thousand children abducted by the Lord's Resistance Army rebels in Uganda. In 2001, the winner was the Association for Community Development, chosen for its outstanding work against trafficking in Bangladesh. In the intervening years, the award was given to outstanding individuals. The Brazilian priest, Father Rezende Figueira, won it in 1992 for his efforts to secure land tenure reform and to free bonded laborers in Amazonia. The winner in 1994 was a Haitian Episcopalian priest, Father Edwin Paraison. He worked with cane cutters from Haiti, who were lured to the Dominican Republic by promises of good jobs, only to find themselves forced to work long hours under guard on the sugar plantations, where they became ensnared in debt. The famous Chinese dissident Harry Wu won it in 1995, and, in 1997, the winner was a Brazilian woman, Dona Pureza Lopes Loiola, who campaigned to free hundreds of workers imprisoned on isolated, guarded estates. All too often, governments harassed local NGOs. Their members faced imprisonment and even death.[76]

Their arrival on the world scene boosted the antislavery campaign. They provided grassroots expertise, and advocated remedies compatible with local conditions. They also helped many individuals begin the long haul out of servitude, which often required psychological adjustment—an end to fatalism and subservience—as well as financial and other help. They could monitor the performance of their own governments more accurately and with greater insights into problems of implementation than foreign organizations and they could speak with greater effect of the plight of the exploited and abused. For the Western NGOs, their emergence helped end the impression that the antislavery movement was Western dominated and aimed at enforcing Western standards on the rest of the world for the benefit of Western workers.

As well as Third World NGOs, Western antislavery societies and groups existed in the United States, Australia, Norway, Denmark, Switzerland, and France. Many other NGOs also added contemporary forms of slavery to their agendas during the 1980s and 1990s. Others sprang up to get compensation for past iniquities such as the forced recruitment of "comfort women" to serve the Japanese troops, and the forced labor of prisoners of war during the Second World War. NGOs also began to band together to work against specific abuses. One of the most interesting changes in the second half of the century was the proliferation of NGOs, from under a thousand in 1956, to nearly five thousand five hundred in 1996. Not all were concerned with human rights, but they emerged as an important factor on the world scene, playing a part in molding public opinion, in shaping conventions, and changing government policies.[77] These NGOs, however, all had their own agendas and not all were reputable organizations. Some are mere fronts out to raise funds from gullible donors and willing to turn their attention to anything that the public or foundations might be persuaded to finance.

If NGOs were essential to the Working Group, they, in turn, valued the Group because its public meetings provided a forum for publicizing the various forms of servitude they were attacking.[78] Publicity, however, was often disappointing, in spite of press releases and conferences. The press, as the Anti-Slavery Society complained, had its own agenda and all too often its coverage of slavery issues was "simplistic, inaccurate, and lacking in balance."[79] Only the most sensational stories made the headlines. This encouraged some playing to the gallery.

Thus, in 1980, the show was stolen by Tim Bond, a representative of *Terre des Hommes* sponsored by the Minority Rights Group,[80] who produced receipts for two boys he had bought on the station platform in Bangkok for thirty-five dollars.[81] This distracted attention from his real message, which was that in northeastern Thailand people could barely survive from one rice harvest to the next. During the dry season, they were unemployed, and the sale of a child provided food for the rest of the family. He suggested remedies, such as irrigation schemes and the development of cottage industries, to alleviate their poverty.[82] His allegations, based on his eyewitness account, supported by documentary evidence, could hardly be denied, nor could they be blamed on colonialism, apartheid, or cold war politics. The Thai government immediately stated that it would crack down on child labor, admitting that an estimated five to six thousand children under twelve were working illegally in Bangkok, under agreements made with their parents. This was clearly a case in which UNDP, the ILO, and UNESCO could all offer help. Dramatically illustrated as it was, it attracted publicity, and, because Thailand was a small country, worried about its image, there was hope that change might result. As usual, however, it was many years before this hope was realized, if indeed it was realized during the twentieth century.

A significant change in the last two decades of the century was not only the proliferation of NGOs, but their increasing professionalism as executives moved from one to another, or came from other social service organizations. At the Anti-Slavery Society, the retired army or navy officers, colonial servants, who began as amateurs in the slavery field, gave way to more professionally oriented officers. Peter Davies had spent years in the British Council, and his successor had worked for various UN organizations. Two chairmen of the General Committee, Michael Harris and Reggie Norton, came from Oxfam, as did the first woman director, Lesley Roberts, appointed in 1990. Both she and her successor, Mike Dottridge, who came from Amnesty International, were younger than their predecessors.

When Roberts took over, there was no job description, and working methods were antiquated, at a time when the range of the Society's activities and demands for its support were increasing dramatically. The chairman and vice-chairman and some members of the General Committee were over seventy. The workload was beyond the capacity of the small staff. Research was time-consuming, and raising funds required "good research, careful presentation and personal visits," for which they had too little time.[83]

The Society hired consultants to help it to change its fuddy-duddy image, suggest new approaches to fund-raising, and streamline its working methods. A small executive committee was appointed to run the office. The General Committee, renamed the Council, became a consultative body of trustees to determine general policy. Its older members, including the chairman, retired. The Society itself, along with most charitable organizations, became a limited company to shield trustees and staff from personal liability if a lawsuit was launched against it for libel or some other offense—a growing danger in an increasingly litigious world. More staff members were hired. The office was moved from a rundown house in a shabby street to new, larger, and more suitable quarters. More of its work was computerized, its documents were catalogued, the format of the *Anti-Slavery Reporter* was changed, and most important, more grants were secured.[84]

At the end of the century, ASI remained the only NGO covering almost the full range of contemporary slavery, and it was in the vanguard of the attempts to expand the mandate of the Working Group or to replace it with a more powerful one. To bring this about, however, would require lobbying members of the Sub-Commission and the Commission on Human Rights over a period of several years—an expensive business. It might also arouse suspicions, since there were those who regarded the Working Group as a "backwater created for the Anti-Slavery Society" and who were jealous that it had "such a forum" to show its wares.[85]

NOTES

1. Report of the Working Group on Slavery on its First Session (henceforth WGCFS Report), E/CN.4/Sub.2/AC.2/3, 28 August 1975.

2. For many years, Whitaker played a prominent part in the Sub-Commission on Prevention of Discrimination and the Protection of Minorities (SPDPM). He had been a Labor MP, and was now director of the Minority Rights Group, a British NGO. He had joined Glover's All-Party Parliamentary Group, and had asked a number of slavery-related questions while in the House of Commons.

3. Report on first meeting of the Working Group AS 1972-81 UN 1975.

4. Ibid.

5. WGCFS Report 1987, E/CN4./Sub.2/1987/25.

6. One visit was eventually made to Mauritania, see below, chapter 24. The proposal that sessions should be ten working days was reduced to five to reduce the total cost of the per diem allowances drawn by members to $1,600.

7. These were the Colombian member and Whitaker, who was elected co-chairman/rapporteur with the new member from Kenya. The other two members now came from Thailand and Rumania.

8. Sometimes a member would drop out and then be reappointed later; sometimes he or she could not come to a session and a substitute was found.

9. Mrs. Warzazi served in a number of human rights organizations. She was a long-serving member of the Sub-Commission and was chairperson of the Working Group in 1996–1997, and 1999.

10. WGCFS Report 1976, E/CN.4/Sub.2/373.

11. AS *Annual Report*, 31 March 1980, in *ASR* 1980, VI, 12, 7 November 1980, p. 37. See also above, chapter 21.

12. WGCFS Report 1977, E/CN.4/Sub.2/389.

13. The allegations were made by Survival International, sponsored by the Anti-Slavery Society, E/CN.4/Sub.2/389, pp. 4, 6, 7.

14. AS *Annual Report*, 31 March 1981, p. 3.

15. This official was expected to ensure coordination with the Center for Human Rights and other organizations, to prepare documentation in advance of the meeting, and to "facilitate" the attendance of as many NGOs and intergovernmental organizations (IGOs) as possible.

16. Whitaker was chosen as rapporteur on slavery and Abdelwahab Boudhiba on child labor.

17. Report of the SPDPM, 20 September 1978, E/CN.4/Sub.2/417.and E/CN.4/1296; Report of SPDM, 5 October 1979, E/CN.4/1350. E/CN.4/Sub.2//435 para. 79. Initially, annual discussion of the report was conceded only for discussion of child labor, but it appears from 1980 to have been won for all the Group's fields of study.

18. I speak here from experience, having attended the 1980, 1981, 1984, 1988, 1993, and 1999 sessions.

19. Members might be ill, or attending another meeting scheduled at the same time. Finding replacements at the last minute and getting them approved by the outgoing chairman, according to rules, was often not possible. However, complaints were made about these absences by governments and others, SM notes, 8 February 1988.

20. I speak here of the British, French, and U.S. archives. I have not been able to find any United Nations archives.

21. WGCFS Report 1987, E/CN.4/Sub.2/1987/25.

22. WGCFS Report 1994, E/CN.4/Sub.2/1994/33.

23. Whittaker 1991, 37–39.

24. NGO Statement Concerning the Membership of the WGCFS and its Working Methods, 1992.

25. WGCS Report 1993, E/CN.4/Sub.2/1993/30.

26. A few governments accepted, see WGCS Reports, E/CN.4/Sub.2/1994/33; E/CN.4/Sub.2/ 1995/28.

27. WGCFS Report 1992, E/CN.4/Sub.2/1992/34.

28. WGCFS Report 1993, E/CN.4/Sub.2/1993/30.

29. The recommendation that there should also be a Special Rapporteur on Child Labor and Debt Bondage was not acted upon.

30. For instance, in 1995, the chairman was Swami Agnivesh, who also chaired the Indian Bonded Labor Liberation Front, and the other trustees were the Mauritanian activist, Cheikh Saad Kamara, Tatiana Maatveeva from the Russian Federation, and Jose de Souza Martins from Brazil. Its Western member resigned in protest at the lack of funding. In 1996, he was replaced by Lesley Roberts, the director of ASI, who was in turn later replaced by Theo Van Boven, who was wanted for his ability to persuade Western governments to allot funds.

31. WGCFS Report 1998, E/CN.4/Sub.2/ 1998/14. Whereas ILO programs received contributions from Ministries of Labor, this trust fund relied on contributions from Foreign Offices, which had more projects to support.

32. WGCFS Reports 1990, and E/CN.4/Sub.2/1991/41.

33. WGCFS Report 2001, E/CN.4/Sub.2/2001/30. According to the Group's reports, the secretary-general, after repeated requests, had at one time appointed the promised permanent full-time staff member to handle slavery questions, but this seems to have been short-lived.

34. See, for instance, Programs appended to Reports of WGCFS 1990, and 1991, E/CN.4/Sub.2/ 1990/44; E/CN.4/Sub.2/1991/41.

35. David Weissbrodt and Anti-Slavery International. "Review of the Implementation of and Followup to the Conventions on Slavery." E/CN.4/Sub.2/1999; C/CN.4/Sub.2/ 1999/CRP.1 (henceforth Weissbrodt and ASI).

36. Weissbrodt to Dottridge, 14 June 1998, ASI archives.

37. Report of the Inter-sessional open-ended Working Group on Enhancing the Mechanisms of the Commission on Human Rights, E/CN.4/2000/112, para.22. This working group decided to

keep the WGCFS, but advocated cutting down its sessions to five days and streamlining its working methods.

38. Statement by IMADR and thirteen other NGOs, 23 June 2000, Dottridge Notes, ASI Archives.

39. Weissbrodt and ASI. These were the Conventions for the Rights of the Child, for the Elimination of All Forms of Discrimination Against Women, and the 1966 covenants on civil and political rights, and on economic, social, and cultural rights. The covenants already required reports on the implementation of measures against slavery and forced labor. For the conventions, see Brownlie 1998, 182–202, 169–81; and for the covenants, ibid., pp. 114–24, 125–43.

40. WGCFS Report 2001, E/CN.4/Sub.2/2001/30; Sub-Commission on Human Rights Resolution 2001/14, E/CN.4/Sub.2/RES/2001/14.

41. ASI Submission to WGCFS 1992: "Evaluation of the activities of the WGCFS during the 14th, 15th, and 16th sessions."

42. The submission and the official Ethiopian response were published in *ASR* VII, 13, 1 December 1981, pp. 20–23. For the report of the Working Group, see E/CN.4/Sub.2/486. 21 August 1981.

43. SM notes 1981. A synopsis of the remarks of the Indian representative is in the WGCFS Report, E/CN.4/Sub.2/1983/27, Corr.1.

44. The need for a new international economic order as a fundamental necessity, if human rights were to be promoted, was the subject of a Special Rapporteur's report to the Sub-Commission in 1983, E/CN.4/Sub.2/1983/24 and Add.1–2.

45. See, for instance, WGCFS Reports 1988, E/CN.4/Sub.2/1988/32 and 1996, E/CN.4/Sub.2/1996/24.

46. Report of WGCFS, 22 August 1988, E/CN.4/Sub.2/1988/32.

47. WGCFS Report 2000, E/CN.4/Sub.2/2000/23.

48. WGCFS Report 1996, E/CN.4/Sub.2/1996/24.

49. This information took the form of notes from the secretary-general to the Working Group.

50. See, for instance, FAO report in note by secretary-general, 25 May 1988, E/CN.4/Sub.2/AC.2/1988/5.

51. Information sent by UNESCO on the International Meeting of Experts, Madrid 1987, in note by secretary-general, 25 May 1988, E/CN.4/Sub.2/AC.2/1988/5.

52. See, for instance, WGCFS Report 1987, E/CN.4/Sub.2/1987/25.

53. ASI Submission: "Evaluation of the activities of the WGCFS at its 14th, 15th, and 16th sessions, 1992."

54. The Working Group could have applied for such funds.

55. The International Abolitionist Federation, the Bureau International Catholique de l'enfance, Defense for Children Movement, International Association of Democratic Lawyers, International Commission of Jurists, International Federation of Women Lawyers, the Minority Rights Group, the International Federation of Women in Legal Careers, the International Federation of Women Lawyers, the International Movement for Fraternal Union among Races and Peoples, the Women's International League for Peace and Freedom, and the Pan Africanist Congress of Azania (a South African liberation movement).

56. NGOs had been warned in 1975 to keep their submissions brief. They therefore presented summaries to the Group, but sent fuller versions to the Secretariat where members could consult them.

57. SM notes 1984.

58. Chaudhury expressed his frustration at the whole system in a moving outburst in 1980, in which he blamed capitalism, colonialism, and the intransigence of governments for lack of action, SM notes, 12 August 1980.

59. AS *Annual Report*, 31 March 1985, p. 10.

60. The Society changed the title of the Secretary to Director in 1983.

61. "Recommendations and Conclusions" of the NGO Seminar on Human Rights in the UN Geneva, 8–10 September 1986 (available from ASI); AS *Annual Report*, 31 March 1987, p. 3, and 31 March 1994, p. 14.

62. WGCFS Report 1987, E/CN.4./Sub.2/1987/25.

63. Details of its finances were published in its *Annual Reports* or in the *Anti-Slavery Reporter*. In some years, these publications were produced in a single volume. The Society began to attract sizeable grants in 1978. Donors in this and later years included the Ford Foundation, the Gatsby Charitable Foundation, Gulbenkian Foundation, the World Council of Churches, the European Human Rights Foundation, UNICEF, Oxfam, Christian Aid, and sister societies in Norway, Denmark, and Switzerland.

64. ASI Submission to WGCFS 1992: "Evaluation of the Activities of the WGCFS at its 14th 15th, and 16th Sessions."

65. Private communication from Montgomery, 1981. The Society had 890 members in 1979, 1,124 in 1986–1987, 1,203 in 1989, 1,809 in 1990, 1,750 in 1995, *ASR*, VI, vol.12, no. 6, 1979, AS *Annual Reports*, 31 March 1987, 31 March 1989, 31 March 1990, AS General Committee Papers, 13 September 1995.

66. AS *Annual Report*, 31 March 1978, pp. 3–4.

67. A leader of the Sudanese rebels wanted to speak for CSI, to which he did not belong.

68. El Hor, for instance, was an NGO founded by freed slaves in Mauritania in 1974. The first of these NGOs to come to the Working Group were the Asian-African Peoples Solidarity Organization and the Pan Pacific and South East Asia Women's Association in 1982.

69. *AS Annual Report*, 31 March 1991, p. 5. In 1990, its full name was Anti-Slavery International for the Protection of Human Rights, but by 1994 it had been changed to Anti-Slavery International.

70. *AS Annual Report*, 1989–1990, p. 5.

71. *AS Annual Report*, 31 March 1994, p. 5.

72. This was five years after the Group recommended it in 1987, WGS Report 1987, E/CN.4/Sub.2/1987/25.

73. Welch 2001, 1.

74. Eliminating the Exploitation of Child Labour: International, National, and Local Action, NGO Group for the Convention on the Rights of the Child, Geneva, 1993.

75. The list of recipients and the reasons for the award are published annually in *ASR*. For more information on their work, see below, chapter 24.

76. Leaders of El Hor were arrested in Mauritania in 1980, ASI submission to WGCFS 1981: "Slavery in Mauritania in 1980." Members of the Pakistan's Bonded Labour Liberation Front were harassed. The chairman of SACCS was arrested, and a twelve-year-old bonded laborer turned campaigner was murdered in mysterious circumstances in Pakistan after receiving the Reebok prize in the United States in 1995. *ASR*, VIII, 1, 3, October 1995, ibid. The Episcopalian priest honored by the Anti-Slavery Society in 1994 was dismissed by the Bishop on his return to the Dominican Republic and his life was threatened. *ASR* VIII, 1, 1, February 1995.

77. Welch 2001; Korey 1998.

78. Private communication from Montgomery, 1981.

79. ASI submission to 1992. "Evaluation of the Activities of the WGCS at its 14th, 15th, and 16th sessions."

80. NGOs which did not have consultative status with a particular UN body could be sponsored by one that had it.

81. For the plight of Thai children, see below, chapter 24.

82. SM notes, 12 August 1980.

83. "Anti-Slavery International and its Future." October 1993, ASI archives.

84. There are many documents on this in ASI archives and copies in my possession since I was on the General Committee at this time.

85. Note by Mike Dottridge, 1 July 1996, ASI archives.

24

Contemporary Forms of Slavery

THE WORKING GROUP AND THE DEFINITION OF SLAVERY

As has been seen, the Working Group on Slavery discussed an ever-widening range of practices. This reflected the expansion of NGO activity and growing public awareness of the different forms of exploitation. In 1975, chattel slavery seemed to have virtually disappeared. Debt-bondage, however, was prevalent, especially in South Asia and South America. Child labor was a fact of life in much of the world, including parts of Europe. Servile forms of marriage kept millions of women in legal and social dependence on their husbands. Unknown numbers of women, children, and even men were being lured or forced into the sex industry and apartheid was still practiced in South Africa.

At its very first meeting, faced with evidence of all these practices, the Group declared that the definition of slavery in the two slavery conventions should be broadened. Some members suggested that it should be defined as "any form of dealing in human beings leading to the forced exploitation of their labor" or "all institutions and practices, which by restricting the freedom of the individual, are susceptible of causing severe hardship and severe deprivations of liberty." All agreed that the definition should be flexible enough to cover any new forms of servitude which might emerge. In 1980, Montgomery, after presenting horrendous accounts of the sufferings of prostitutes, suggested that the defining characteristic of modern slavery was not "ownership" but control, and that it should be defined as "the condition of a person completely under the control of an-other."[1] Dictionary definitions stressed both ownership and complete domination.

The following year, the Group commented in its report that since it was now the principal UN body monitoring not just the slavery conventions, but also that against trafficking in persons and the exploitation of the prostitution of others, it might change its name to "more accurately reflect its area of work."[2] In 1983, it recommended that it be called the "Working Group against Slavery, Apartheid, Gross Human Exploitations and Human Degradation."[3] When this came up in the Sub-Commission, a member suggested that the

"Working Group on Gross Human Exploitation" would be more appropriate. Another wanted it called the "Working Group on Apartheid and Slavery-like practices."[4]

However, no action was taken and as time went on many practices brought to the notice of the Group bore little relation to slavery as generally conceived or defined. They included the plight of "street children," who lived by their wits, sometimes alone, sometimes in gangs, begging, hawking, stealing, combing rubbish dumps, washing the windows of passing cars, even swallowing flames in hope of being thrown a coin or two. Many bedded down in the streets or in sewers. Although there were large numbers of them in the Third World, particularly Latin America, they were also found in the cities of Western Europe and the United States. They were runaways, orphans, or children abandoned by parents unable to provide for them. Their condition was deplorable, but they were neither owned nor controlled by anyone, with the exception of those who fell into the hands of drug pushers, pimps, or other criminals who forced them to work for them.

Even more remote from accepted definitions of slavery was the practice of female genital mutilation (also called cutting or circumcision). This took the form of operations of varying degrees of severity performed usually on young girls, even babies, in parts of Africa and the Middle East. It was hallowed by custom and considered necessary for hygienic reasons and to ensure premarital virginity. It was brought to the notice of the Working Group by the Minority Rights Group in response to appeals for help from African women anxious to end the practice.[5] The International Abolitionist Federation argued that it fitted the definition of slavery under the 1956 Convention because those concerned had lost control of their bodies. It was also often attacked as a form of male domination. However, the main support for the practice came from women, who believed that their daughters would not find husbands if they had not been circumcised. These women in no way considered themselves slaves. Members of the Working Group agreed that it did not "fall easily" within their terms of reference. They suggested that the Sub-Commission should take up the question as part of its efforts to end discrimination against women, and the Group eventually ceased to discuss it.[6]

Another practice in which victims had lost control over their bodies was the "honor" killing of Muslim women by their own relatives, because they had disgraced them by being caught in compromising situations. There were also reports that people were killed in order to sell their organs for transplants. The Group discussed this for many years, because it was suspected that Latin American children were kidnapped or sold so that their organs could be bought by recipients in the United States and other rich countries. The People's Republic of China openly sold the organs of prisoners who had been executed. However, reports of a clandestine traffic elsewhere were vague until 2001, when the Working Group was informed by India that mutilated bodies of children, whose parents had given them to an adoption agency, had been found.[7] Another case surfaced in Uzbekistan in which the victims had been lured into the hands of perpetrators with promises of jobs abroad.[8] Since the life expectancy of the recipient is extended if the organs are extracted from living donors, gruesome tales found their way into the press of victims having organs removed before death. The sale of human fetuses for use in the cosmetics and pharmaceutical industries was also called to the Group's attention,[9] but no government or NGO produced conclusive evidence that there was such a traffic. In 1997, the Group refused to consider cloning and "related" scientific excesses. However, it decided to hear evidence on religious and other "sects" who brainwashed their members, as well as on pedophilia and incest, but it had not discussed them in depth when the century ended.[10]

The ever-broadening scope of its mandate did not go unchallenged. Members of the Group often asserted that a particular practice was a violation of human rights and fell more logically into the province of the Sub-Commission. However, the Sub-Commission determined that slavery was "the exploitation of man by man" and as such was constantly taking new forms, and could not be a "static concept."[11] Hence, the Group continued to hear evidence difficult to incorporate into any existing definition of slavery, although NGOs, including ASI, warned against drawing the net so wide that the term slavery became meaningless.

One field, however, which was taken out of its hands, was the protection of indigenous peoples. The many submissions on this question, particularly from the Anti-Slavery Society, led the Sub-Commission to establish the Working Group on Indigenous Populations in 1981 (WGIP).[12] This group, which owed its existence to the precedent established by the Working Group on Slavery, proved a very effective body. Led for some fifteen years by a devoted and clear-sighted chairperson, it provided a forum for those indigenous peoples who not only suffered various forms of servitude, such as serfdom, debt-bondage, and forced labor on a large scale, but had also lost their rights to land, and faced discrimination and other infringements of human rights. Its achievements cannot be considered here, but it set the agenda for bettering their condition. It drafted a Universal Declaration on their rights, helped establish a Permanent Indigenous Forum under ECOSOC, and secured a well-funded trust fund to bring spokesmen to meetings, which attracted as many as a thousand people and where many governments exchanged views with their indigenous peoples.[13]

In 1987, the Working Group on Slavery again considered bringing its name into line with its work. Slavery was now a "catchall" term synonymous with extreme deprivation and exploitation. It was a useful tool to attract attention, but it was being used to describe practices ever more remote from chattel slavery—the form most commonly associated with slavery in the public mind. The solution arrived at was to change its name to the Working Group on Contemporary Forms of Slavery. This was considered "more descriptive of its actual interests, namely exploitation of sex [sic], debt bondage, sale of children, [and] apartheid."[14] This was the name by which it was to be known for the rest of the twentieth century.

It remains to consider how these forms of servitude were actually practiced at the grassroots level in the final decades of the century and what progress had been made towards their elimination by the year 2001.[15]

CHATTEL SLAVERY AND ITS "VESTIGES"

In July 1980, the Islamic Republic of Mauritania informed an astonished world that it had outlawed chattel slavery, although it had been outlawed by France in 1905, and was not recognized in the constitution promulgated at independence in 1960. A devastating drought in the 1970s and 1980s had wiped out much of the livestock, impoverishing many of the pastoralists—the Berber/Arab "White" Moors or Beydhan. These elites held the rights to the cultivatable land,[16] and wielded political power. Their slaves (Abid) were Black Africans, either born into slavery or recently acquired. They were chattels, dependent on their pastoral owners, whose animals they looked after or whose land they farmed. The Haratin were the descendants of freed slaves and of the indigenous population. They occupied a middle position. They could own land in theory, but not in practice. They were free to marry, to control their children, and to accumulate wealth. Some even owned slaves. Nonetheless, they had varying obligations to their former owners and could never equal them in social standing.[17] The Abid and Haratin greatly outnumbered the Beydhan, but were culturally aligned with them. They were collectively known as the Sudaan, or Black Moors, to distinguish them from the other Black Africans or Afro-Mauritanians in the country who had not been enslaved by the Beydhan, had maintained their own cultures, and wanted a share of political power.[18] The drought caused conflicts between the Sudaan, allied with the poorer Beydhan, and the richer Beydhan over land. In the countryside, some slaves refused to give part of their crop to masters, and Sudaan and poorer Beydhan flocked into the towns in search of work.

The country was further impoverished by an unsuccessful war in Western Sahara from which it withdrew in 1979, after a military coup. It was heavily dependent on foreign aid. In 1977, high taxes and masters' demands for part of their crop triggered a Haratin revolt, which was brutally suppressed. A military government seized power in 1978. Matters came to a head early in 1980, when El Hor, a clandestine organization founded by Haratin in 1974, staged protests after a girl was sold in a desert town. The government responded with a massive and brutal crackdown on El Hor militants on the one hand, and a declaration abolishing slavery on the other. It also promised a national commission to decide on the amount of compensation to be offered to owners.[19]

The Anti-Slavery Society sent an investigator to Mauritania, who reported that nothing had been done to carry out the declaration, which seemed to have been made to boost the country's international image and placate the Sudaan.[20] The Working Group referred the question to the Mauritanian government. UNCTAD and the ILO offered help. The question attracted considerable publicity. The BBC filmed a documentary in Mauritania with the assistance of the director of the Anti-Slavery Society,

Peter Davies. The government, at the Sub-Commission's suggestion, invited a mission to come out and investigate the position.[21] This mission, headed by the Belgian professor Marc Bossuyt, was accompanied by Davies at the insistance of the Mauritanian government. It spent eleven days touring the country in 1984, and interviewing a wide range of people, including members of El Hor.[22] As it turned out, this was to be the only such visit arranged by the Working Group. It has been characterized as the "high point" in the Group's efforts, but it achieved little and did not set a precedent.

Bossuyt reported that no laws had been passed detailing the rights of slaves or laying down penalties for their infringement, and owners had not been compensated. He recommended, among other things, that former slaves be paid wages, and be given access to land, credit, and education.[23] In 1984, a new Mauritanian government had seized power. It professed itself anxious to end slavery and requested economic assistance. However, help from Specialized Agencies and donor nations was disappointing. In the years that followed, the Western press tended to depict the struggle of slaves and Haratin to achieve equality with their masters as a simple struggle for freedom that had not been won when the century ended. Depicting it in this light attracted world attention. It also suited the Afro-Mauritanians, who, ironically, discriminated against the descendants of their own slaves,[24] but wanted the support of the Sudaan in their efforts to wrest some political power from the Beydhan.[25]

The Abid wanted access to land and education, as well as social equality with the Beydhan. By the late 1990s, many had been freed by owners who could no longer employ or feed them. Others had earned money as migrant workers and had bought land from the Beydhan and settled back into tribal life. Some had simply asserted their independence. Others had paid owners to manumit them.[26] Once freed, however, Abid could not rise socially beyond the status of Haratin, and, in general, they were still the poorest of a poor population.[27] Some Haratin had made money, and a few had risen to high office. Since land, jobs, and political power were still in the hands of the Beydhan, many Abid and Haratin chose to remain under their protection and domination, rather than risk losing their livelihood and suffer harassment. Activists attributed this acceptance of their lowly status to conservatism and to their Islamic faith, and believed that they, as much as the Beydhan, would have to be taught to change their attitudes if they were to attain real freedom. The problem was widespread on the desert fringes. As an informant explained to Maugham when he bought a slave in Timbuktu in 1958:

> In his head [the slave] knows that [by law] he is a free man. But in his heart he does not believe it. He knows he is . . . a slave. If he buys his freedom from his master, that is different. But otherwise, he believes that he belongs to his master, and so do his children.[28]

By the end of the century, however, many slaves had been freed, most of them males. However, masters had not been compensated and many still tried to assert their former rights, sometimes brutally, and particularly over women. They had always been reluctant to free slave women, since this meant giving up control of their progeny. Many owners, therefore, refused them permission to leave, to marry, to join absent husbands, or take custody of their children. Many children were still working for their mothers' owners. Some former masters claimed the possessions of slaves who died, beat up those who ran away, or charged them with theft, and generally harassed them. If a slave did win a case against his or her owner, the latter was not prosecuted.[29] Mauritania faced a particular dilemma when it came to prosecutions. It had promulgated a constitution, which protected human rights as conceived in the Western democracies. Some of these rights, however, conflicted with Muslim law, which took precedence over civil law. Hence, slavery was not recognized by the constitution but was recognized in Shari'a courts, which upheld masters' claims. Civil courts claimed they had no jurisdiction in slave cases.

In 1999, the chairman of the Mauritanian Human Rights Association (AMDH), Cheikh Saad Bouh Kamara, declared that slavery was still a "very deep social problem" and that the government had not implemented its law abolishing slavery.[30] This was hardly surprising for, like the colonial rulers of the past, it could neither afford to compensate the owners, nor risk losing their support; nor could it assume the cost of finding land or jobs for the freed. Western aid donors tolerated the situation for fear of destabilizing a country that provided a bulwark against Muslim fundamentalism. However, slavery in Mauritania was now being attacked by, among others, African Americans and members of the United States Congress. Ten human rights groups were also intensifying their efforts within the country to raise public awareness of slavery, which was no longer a "taboo subject" of discussion.[31] Nevertheless, it was still practiced, although on a reduced scale, and El Hor and a similar organization, SOS-Slaves, were mobilizing to attack it.

The disabilities of the slaves and freed slaves still existing in Mauritania were often described as "vestiges" of slavery. The term was used by governments, by the League and UN committees, scholars, and other observers, to describe practices based on slavery, but so attenuated that they were no longer considered oppressive. Once slavery had lost its legal status, once there was no longer a trade in slaves, once slaves could theoretically leave their owners, once they could keep their earnings, own property, marry, and control their own children, only "vestiges" of slavery remained. To activists, however, the situation in Mauritania was not one of "vestiges." It was the continuing manifestation of slavery itself.[32]

Elsewhere "vestiges" continued in varying forms, particularly along the southern fringe of the Sahara. In 2000, the Working Group was informed that all ethnic groups in Niger practiced slavery in some form. Public attitudes had not changed, and girls often changed hands.[33] Research on the Indonesian island of Sumba showed that in the last decades of the twentieth century there were still slave girls. They might accompany a bride to serve her in her new home, or be sold into a royal family, not to be married to a specific groom, but to bear children for the lineage.[34] More often, the vestiges took the form of discrimination in questions of marriage, inheritance, and the performance of rituals. Thus, among the Fulbe of Senegal, intermarriage between descendants of slave and free was unthinkable, the former could not lead prayers in the mosque, and they performed certain largely symbolic acts, such as cooking at feasts, for the descendants of their owners. When both groups migrated to Paris, the descendants of the slaves paved the way for the descendants of the free.[35] Among the highly stratified Soninke, migrants kept up their social distinctions to the point that if their French-born children attempted to intermarry, they ostracized, not just the couple, but their relatives in France and in Africa, even denying the latter access to mosques.[36] This discrimination was endorsed by the older generation of slave descent, perhaps because they saw the connections with former masters as an asset, or perhaps because deference was so ingrained that they accepted their status. At the end of the twentieth century, vestiges of slavery could still be found almost everywhere where chattel slavery had been practiced. In the United States, nearly a century and a half after emancipation and several decades after the launching of the Civil Rights movement, social, job, and housing discrimination against African Americans continued, although it had long been illegal.

Whereas in Mauritania, the problem was the continuation of existing relations of slavery. In Sudan in the mid-1980s, a resurgence of chattel slavery was reported.[37] In the past, the non-Muslim Dinka and Muslim Baggara (Rizeigat in South Darfur and Misseriya in West Kurdufan) raided one another in the age-old conflict between pastoral groups for control of water and pasture. Both took captives, as well as livestock, but periodically elders met, exchanged them, and settled their differences. Now, as a by-product of the war between the largely Muslim Arab North and the non-Muslim South, and of a devastating drought, such raids were stepped up. Baggara armed by the government, and sometimes supported by the army, raided Dinka and Nuer villages, killing the men, and carrying off the women and children. Some captives were ransomed by their relatives. The rest were kept or sold to owners in the north. Kidnapping, and sales of children by destitute parents, were also widespread. The new owners, as in the past, used their captives as concubines, domestics, and agricultural labor. Some were forced to convert to Islam, and even circumcised. Thus many decades after chattel slavery had been outlawed and had almost disappeared, it seemed to have resurfaced with all its cruelties. Abductions continued throughout the 1990s, in an increasingly complex war fuelled by the northern desire to gain control of the oil fields of the south, and complicated by the attempt of the government to impose Shari'a law.[38]

The whole question was the subject of intense publicity. Christian Solidarity International (CSI), a Zurich-based NGO with strong American connections, began ransoming victims in defiance of the conventional wisdom that this would lead to fraud, and would encourage slavery by providing a market for slaves, as well as provide the marauders with money to buy weapons for further raids. CSI claimed to have freed over forty-five thousand slaves between 1995 and 2001. The freed persons confirmed that they had been treated as chattels and subjected to forced labor and sexual abuse. The ensuing publicity brought donations from Western schoolchildren, religious groups, community organizations, members of the United States Congress, and NGOs, including the American Anti-Slavery Group (AASG), which contributed tens of thousands of dollars in 1999.[39] However, accusations soon appeared in the press claiming that at least some of these redemptions were an organized scam, and that much of the redemption money was shared between rural people masquerading as slaves, the "traders" who delivered them to the redeemers, and the administrators.[40]

After a UN Special Rapporteur confirmed that slaving and other infringements of human rights were taking place, and the General Assembly passed resolutions criticizing it, the government of Sudan acknowledged that there had been cases of what it called "abduction" and "forced labor." In 1999, it established the Committee for the Eradication of Abduction of Women and Children (CEAWC). Its mandate was to investigate abductions, bring the perpetrators to trial, and return the victims to their own people. It consisted of representatives of local communities and members of the Dinka Committee, a group established earlier to retrieve the abducted. Anxious to clear its image, the government invited the Anti-Slavery Society, which had issued a number of reports on slavery in Sudan, to visit the country in October 2000 to assess the situation. The information that follows comes from the Society's provisional report, dated March 2001. Information also comes from comments on the report by the Sudanese government, and the Society's reply to those comments.[41] ASI concluded that thousands of people had been abducted since the mid-1980s but that the CEAWC was now cooperating with the Dinka Committee to retrieve them. It had released hundreds of victims, and established centers, in collaboration with the British NGO, Save the Children, and with UNICEF, to rehabilitate them and help them to trace their relatives and return home. The Dinka Committee estimated that some fourteen thousand people had been abducted since 1986—far short of the two hundred thousand estimated by Christian Solidarity International.[42] The Dinka did not hesitate to call the victims slaves. The government of Sudan, on the other hand, denied that there was slavery, only "abductions," "enticement," and "forced labor." Similar problems of definition arose with the Baggara. Some victims had been ten years in captivity. Those taken as children were now young men and women. Some of the women had been forced to marry those who were holding them. Some of the children had been absorbed into Baggara families. Those who had acquired them claimed that these women and children were now family members. Clearly, before they were handed back, the victim's own wishes would have to be consulted.

It seemed that from 1999, the government had taken steps to identify and return the captives, but the pace was slow. Only 1,200 abducted persons had been documented by 2001. Moreover, there had been no prosecutions for abduction, enticement, or forced labor, let alone slavery. Worse still, the United Nations reported that 122 women and children had been abducted in a new raid in January 2001,[43] raising the question of how much control the government actually had over the raiders. At the end of the century, therefore, Baggara were still taking captives. But they were not the only raiders in Sudan. Southern pastoralists raided each other and had also seized small numbers of Baggara.[44] Moreover, the southern Sudanese People's Liberation Army was also accused of recruiting child soldiers and some of its members were said to be involved in slave redemption scams.[45]

DEBT-BONDAGE

Debt-bondage took many forms and was one of the most widespread forms of contemporary slavery. Year after year, for instance, the Working Group heard evidence of its practice in South Asia. India outlawed it in 1976, and Pakistan in 1992, but it was still entrenched at the beginning of the twenty-first century.[46] The debtors were usually illiterate, landless, rural poor. In India, they were often low caste or "tribal" people. A family eking out an existence on low pay might have to take out a loan simply to survive or to pay for a wedding, a funeral, medicines, fertilizer, or other necessities, and interest rates could run to 60 percent. In Muslim Pakistan, charging interest was illegal, but it could be disguised as an advance of pay. Once bonded, laborers lost all freedom of movement, and had to work for their creditors. The creditors were usually landlords—sometimes the very officials charged by the government with ending debt-bondage. However, as the informal industrial sector of the economy expanded in both countries in the last decades of the century, more and more creditors were the owners of factories, brick kilns, quarries, fisheries, and other businesses. Creditors could keep debtors in bondage indefinitely in two main ways. They could levy illegal fines, or charge for food, tools, fertilizer, and other essentials, while keeping wages too low for the debts ever to be repaid. Alternatively, they could maintain that all the labor performed by the debtor was collateral for the debt and could not be used to reduce it.

If the debtor could not perform all the tasks demanded of him, his wife and children might be forced to work and hence they, too, were bonded. Succeeding generations might never get out of debt, making bondage effectively hereditary. In one documented example in India, a man had borrowed thirty dollars for his wedding, and forty years later had not been able to repay it, although he had worked long hours, every day of the year. Parents also bonded their children in return for loans. In Pakistan in the late 1990s, whole families eked out a living in the brick kilns, working under guard, paid just enough to keep them working. Debtors who absconded were arrested by corrupt police, or their children were seized as hostages. Government inspectors were bribed to turn a blind eye. However, jobs were so scarce in some areas that laborers faced the choice of remaining in bondage or risk starvation. In 2001, Pakistan published a draft plan of action to abolish bonded labor, and free and rehabilitate the debtors, but it did not provide for the prosecution of those who kept them.[47]

In Nepal, where a number of bonded labor systems also existed,[48] many of the indigenous Tharu people had been drawn into bondage since the 1960s. By 2000, whole families of *Kamaya* lived and worked on the land and could be passed from one creditor to another—effectively sold.[49] In 2000, the king, as the result of Kamaya demonstrations and pressure from NGOs, issued an edict declaring all debt-bondage illegal. Monitoring committees were established to identify and rehabilitate victims. Since keeping them was now outlawed, landlords, forearmed, promptly evicted the Kamaya, displacing thousands of people. The government promised them land but it had not materialized by the end of the year. Half the freed were reported to be destitute in 2001 and the rest were once more Kamaya. They launched large-scale protests,[50] and foreign governments and UN agencies offered help. The former president of the United States, Jimmy Carter, together with fourteen NGOs, appealed to the Nepalese government to end the crisis. Nepal sought international funding, and began distributing land to the destitute in the far west, but the amount provided was not enough to provide for a family.[51] The crisis was unresolved as the century ended. The whole episode demonstrated once again that any plans to liberate unfree laborers must include plans to protect and rehabilitate them.

The governments of all South Asian countries were worried by the unfavorable publicity. NGOs orchestrated movements to withhold funding from development projects that employed bonded labor, and to boycott goods made by bonded laborers. One well-publicized effort was Rugmark, which had a system of inspection and verification enabling buyers to ensure that they only bought rugs made by free workers.[52] India and Pakistan regularly informed the Working Group of the steps they were taking to cancel debts and rehabilitate the laborers they liberated. Local NGOs also freed a number of people. Nevertheless, bondage continued in many areas. NGOs complained that the governments did not have the political will to enforce the laws. They believed that mobilizing the laborers would, in the end, prove the most effective way to free them, and NGOs were making them aware of their rights. By 2001, some bondsmen had tried to free themselves through self-help groups, or by appealing to the courts to order employers to pay them higher wages. However, they were faced with intimidation from which they could expect little protection in areas where the police were corrupt.[53]

Throughout the 1990s, the extent of bonded labor in other parts of the world was increasingly brought to light. In Brazil, it was the result of unemployment and extreme poverty in some areas and a great demand for labor for development in others. Contractors drove into the towns, promised the urban poor lucrative jobs, and gave them an advance of pay. On arrival, recruits found they were charged for their transport, food, housing, and tools, and that their wages were too low to repay their debts. Women were forced into prostitution. Men had to work fourteen-hour days, six days a week, for less than a dollar a day in forests, plantations, and mines. In the more re-mote areas of Amazonia, escape was almost impossible. Camps were patrolled by guards, and officials were bribed to return runaways. Medicines, sick leave, protective clothing, and even housing were virtually nonexistent. Moreover, whole families pro-ducing charcoal, or mining gold, were in danger from poisonous fumes.

These abuses were illegal, but, as elsewhere, the laws were not enforced. In 1995, in-vestors in the United States learned of conditions in the camps and threatened to with-draw funding. The government banned child labor in the charcoal industry in 1995. It set up a model camp, but all its workers were paid a pittance and were in debt. Else-where abuses continued. In 1998, the penalties for forced labor were increased but workers were afraid to lodge complaints. However, a special mobile inspection unit (flying squad) was created. This had freed nearly two thousand workers by 2001, but its funds were inadequate and only four employers had been prosecuted.[54]

Although more prevalent in poor countries, bonded labor was increasingly to be found in rich ones, particularly among migrants. Some women, many of them from the Philippines, found that the well-paid jobs they had been promised, particularly in the Gulf States, did not exist. They had to eke out a living as domestics, unable to pay off their debts to their recruiting agencies. In Western Europe, Canada, and the United States, mi-grant illegal aliens, many of them Chinese, were in debt to the gangs that imported them. They were forced to work for them under threat of retaliation against their relatives at home—a threat that was also used to extort further sums of money from them. Such abuses might only come to light if a victim tried to commit suicide or managed to escape.

In 2001, the UN estimated there were some twenty million people in bonded labor around the world, many of them indigenous peoples.[55] However, as the ILO report on Forced Labor made clear, estimating numbers was not easy, since not all forms of debt led to bondage.[56] Once identified and released, the only way to keep former bondsmen out of debt and prevent new persons falling into it was to provide those at risk with land or adequately paid jobs, as well as access to credit and compulsory free educa-tion.[57] All of these solutions required strong political will on the part of governments, as well as considerable expenditure and, in many cases, help was needed from the ILO and other UN agencies.

THE EXPLOITATION OF CHILDREN

The exploitation of child labor was the subject of special UN reports in the 1980s and 1990s.[58] Family labor or part-time work was acceptable for older children if they were not deprived of education, leisure, and normal childhood activities. If they were so deprived, they were considered exploited children or child slaves. Child laborers were in demand be-cause they were cheap and defenseless. The ILO conducted extensive investigations fo-cused on the minimum age of employment and on the safety of working conditions. The Anti-Slavery Society produced a series of publications on child labor from 1978,[59] and the Sub-Commission and Working Group heard evidence, which became more and more horrendous as the century drew to a close. The report of the first Special Rapporteur, published in 1982, concluded that in spite of the Declaration on the Rights of the Child proclaimed by the UN in 1959 and the ILO Convention on the Minimum Age for Employment of 1973,[60] more than 50 million children were working, many of them in conditions detrimental to their health. The problem was worldwide but was naturally greater in the poorer countries that in the richer ones. A few examples will illustrate the point.

In Thailand in the 1980s, poverty-stricken parents sold their children to recruiters either outright or in return for part of their wages. Others, as young as nine, were put on trains to Bangkok to find work for themselves. At the station "fisherwomen" offered to find them jobs in return for 50 percent of their wages. The children lived and worked in backstreet sweatshops. Their presence only became known to the authorities if a letter was smuggled out, if there was an accident, or if a desperate child escaped or committed suicide. In one factory in which two girls died, they had been given only one meal a day, and six children were crippled from being forced to sit for long hours at work. If any managed to escape, their parents were called on to refund part of their purchase price. This traffic in children was illegal, but the police were paid off by employers either with money or with the pick of the brothels.

On the Indian subcontinent, child labor was widespread. Some children worked with their families. Others were employed far from home in cottage industries, factories, quarries, circuses, and other occupations. In carpet factories, some were actually tied to looms. Many worked long hours, suffered physical abuse, and were denied contact with their parents. NGOs, including the Anti-Slavery Society, freed, sheltered, and educated small numbers of them. Criminal gangs in India used street children—the girls for prostitution and the boys for drug trafficking, theft, and begging.[61] In the 1990s, the ILO ran an active International Program for the Elimination of Child Labor (IPEC), and there was a widespread movement in richer countries to boycott goods made by children. Yet, in the late 1990s, children, some of them in bondage for the debts of their parents, were still extensively employed, despite frequent claims by the governments that they had taken action to protect children from exploitation.

In El Salvador, children as young as six were sent by their parents to scavenge in garbage dumps. Others worked fourteen hours a day wading in mosquito-ridden swamps searching for small mollusks in the mud, smoking cigars to keep off the insects, and taking amphetamines to keep awake.[62] In Tanzania in 2000, children worked in the Tanzanite mines delivering tools to miners working 300 meters below ground. They might work eighteen hours a day, suffering from intense heat, graphite dust, and poor nutrition for at most $1.20 a day.[63] In West Africa and in Haiti and elsewhere, hundreds of thousands of children, mostly girls, many under fourteen, were sent by poor parents to middle-class families in towns, ostensibly to go to school and learn urban ways. Many, however, were simply used as household drudges, isolated in homes, on call twenty-four hours a day, subject to physical abuse, and fed, like the mui tsai of the past, on leftovers.[64] Boys in West Africa were also sent to towns as unpaid "apprentices" condemned to a lifetime of low-paid employment.

There was also an export trade in child workers in West Africa. In 1994, a local NGO, WAO-Afrique, and ASI called for a regional and global solution and appealed to the Specialized Agencies to get involved. In April 2001, in a blaze of publicity, a boat carrying children from Benin, Mali, Guinea, Senegal, and Togo returned to Cotonou after Cameroon and Gabon refused to allow them to land.[65] These were the more fortunate. Unknown numbers, lured by the prospect of good jobs, had been exported over the years for domestic or plantation labor. Some were kept as virtual prisoners. After the revelation of conditions on cocoa plantations, the multinational chocolate companies, worried about their image, just as their predecessors had been over São Tomé more than 90 years earlier, and fearful of a boycott, agreed to a formal protocol to control conditions in the plantations.[66] The credit for this very important precedent must go to a society founded in the USA in 1999 by Kevin Bales as a sister society to ASI. Called Free the Slaves, it played a key role in winning Senate support and negotiating the protocol between the American and Ivory Coast governments and the chocolate industry. Signing the agreement was voluntary but once signed it became binding. The industry agreed to independent monitoring of conditions on the plantations to ensure that the "worst forms of child labor" would be eliminated by 2005, and to pay for the necessary research and for developing rehabilitation programs. Bales planned to extract similar agreements with other industries.[67]

Many children worked in life-threatening conditions: in fireworks factories in India or China, for example, and in the fume-ridden camps of Brazil. Small boys were sold, kidnapped, or lured from South Asia to ride in camel races in the Gulf States. In Bangladesh, the death of a seven-year-old jockey in April 2001 sparked protests by former child jockeys. The practice was outlawed in the United Arab Emirates after protests from ASI and other NGOs, but it continued.

Most dangerous of all, children were used in armed combat. In 1980, the Friends World Committee for Consultation reported that boys between twelve and seventeen had been forcibly recruited into the army or into rebel forces in Afghanistan, Angola, Cambodia, El Salvador, Ethiopia, Guatemala, Mozambique, Nicaragua, Peru, the Philippines, Sudan, Uganda, and Vietnam. This was just the beginning of the unfolding of the horrors of which children were both the victims and perpetrators. In Mozambique, Renamo forced some to kill their parents and then recruited them to fight. In Uganda in 1984–1985, orphans of genocide were recruited into General Museveni's army to fight the Acholi who had killed their parents. In the late 1990s, the Lord's Resistance Army, fighting a civil war in Uganda, kidnapped schoolchildren and forced them not just to fight for them, but also to kill recalcitrant comrades. Girls were abducted and forced into sexual slavery. A peak of bestiality was reached in Sierra Leone, when rebels recruited young boys and forced them to hack off the limbs of villagers, even babies, in a campaign aimed at terrorizing the population and gaining control of the government and of the diamond mines. The rehabilitation of children brutalized in this way posed particular difficulties. Settling down to a normal life was difficult enough but many were afraid to return home at the end of hostilities, because of the atrocities they had been forced to commit.[68] Over 2,500 child soldiers aged between eight and eighteen were demobilized by the Sudan People's Liberation Army and flown to the United States by UNICEF in February 2001, where they were distributed among host families. The United Nations estimated that some three hundred thousand children were still serving in thirty countries. For many of them, military service was their only means of livelihood. It also offered them much needed protection.[69] Numbers had escalated as small wars proliferated in the last decade of the twentieth century. In richer countries, criminal gangs recruited children. In 2001, for instance, boys were allegedly being used in the Western world as hit men in wars between drug gangs.[70]

The most pitiable of all exploited children were those of both sexes, but mainly girls, forced to work in brothels in both the developed and the developing world. In Brazil, in the 1990s, girls between ten and fourteen could earn so much money as prostitutes that their families lived on their takings.[71] NGOs working in Cambodia, Nigeria, and Mongolia reported cases of young prostitutes. Thousands of Nepalese girls were sold to brothels in India, and thousands of Indian girls were trafficked around the country. In India by 2001, adult women, fearful of contracting AIDS and more aware of their rights than in the past, were said to be demanding more pay and insisting that customers use condoms. As a result, younger and younger girls, especially virgins, were being forced into brothels. There were said to be some half a million young prostitutes in the country. Those who had been imported came from countries as far apart as China, Russia, and Latin America, and the majority were under eighteen.[72]

The children were kidnapped, or sold by parents in debt or too poor to feed them. Some parents, as in Thailand, were induced to part with their children by successful prostitutes, who returned home flaunting their riches. Many prostitutes, however, were kept in virtual slavery by force or through debt-bondage. Those who escaped, or were thrown out of brothels because of illness, were often shunned by the very parents who had sold them. Girls who were HIV positive or had AIDS were not wanted in their homelands. There were horrendous reports in the 1990s that Burmese victims expelled from Thailand were executed in Myanmar.

By this time, more forms of child sex abuse were coming to light, or the extent of existing ones was becoming better known. Girls and boys abducted, or lured away, from rich countries were forced to work as prostitutes in many parts of the world.

Similarly, those from poor areas, such as Latin America, were trafficked to the United States and other rich countries.

Thousands of children were drawn into the sex tourist industry. This was the provision of sex in poorer countries for tourists from richer ones. After the American withdrawal from Vietnam, the amusement centers to which the troops had been sent for rest and recreation were left without customers.[73] Tour operators began to advertise sex tours often as part of a package deal, and involving a range of deviant practices. Children were acquired from poverty-stricken parents, or unscrupulous traffickers.[74] Sex tourism was first raised at the Working Group in 1978. By 1989, it was rife in the Philippines, Sri Lanka, Thailand, and Taiwan, and by 1996, it was active in Brazil.[75] Sex tourism was fuelled by the growth of the worldwide tourist trade and, in some cases, it was run by organized crime. By the late 1990s, it was reported that men allegedly fearful of contracting AIDS, were demanding younger and younger children.[76]

The problem had to be attacked both in the rich countries from which the tourists came and the poor ones where the offenses were committed. But while the latter were reluctant to stem this source of much-needed foreign currency, the rich ones, like Britain, were reluctant to take action against crimes committed abroad, assuming extraterritorial rights required new laws, and there were difficulties about gathering evidence that would stand up in a British court of law. The first step taken by governments in the developed world was to make it illegal to advertise and sell tours offering child prostitutes.

However, during the 1990s, under pressure, the necessary extraterritorial powers were assumed by some of the richer powers, enabling them to prosecute not just their own nationals, but those of other countries, for crimes committed abroad. Thus, in 1995, the Belgians tried a British subject, the editor of *Spartakus Guide*, for advertising sex tourism involving children.[77] The Scandinavian states, and then Australia, led the way in the prosecution of their own nationals. Britain followed suit in 1997. Such prosecutions took time. France passed a law enabling such cases to be tried by jury in 1994, but only in 2000 was the first Frenchman sentenced to seven years in prison for having oral sex with an eleven-year-old girl in Thailand six years earlier. By the end of the century, however, many developed countries had changed their laws and were prosecuting tourists on their return.[78]

Interpol told the Group in 1989 that there was a growing international market for child pornography, defined as the "permanent visual depiction of the sexual molestation and exploitation of a child." Ominously, this traffic was encouraged by loosening moral standards in the developed world and by new technology. At that time, videocassettes were used,[79] but the development of the Internet, particularly chat rooms, offered ever-expanding opportunities for perpetrators. In 1990, on the recommendation of the Group, a Special Rapporteur was appointed to investigate sales of children, child prostitution, and pornography; and a working group was established by the

Commission on Human Rights to draft an optional protocol covering these abuses for the Convention on the Rights of the Child. Pornography was a growing industry and evidence was hard to come by. In June 2001, a British tourist was sentenced for hiring two seven-year-old girls to engage in sexual acts for pornographic photographs. He was only caught because his wife found the images on his computer.[80]

Children were also traded for adoption. In 1988, for instance, the Group heard from a Thai NGO that some ten thousand babies a year were kidnapped, or bought from prostitute mothers, and taken to Malaysia for adoption—a traffic more lucrative "than smuggling cigarettes."[81] Children were also sold in South America for adoption in Europe and North America. After the fall of its communist government, Romania was accused of allowing "wild adoptions." It maintained that it had taken steps to curb them by the mid-1990s. At this time, China was offering foundling girls for adoption in the United States and elsewhere at a cost to the adopters of some $20,000 each. In 1993, the Hague Convention on Protection of Children and Cooperation in Respect of Inter-Country Adoption, laid down rules to protect children from being adopted for exploitation. Genuine adoption conducted under these rules was considered to be in the interests of the child, and was not under attack.[82]

A problem for those attacking child labor was the lack of consensus over the age of majority. Some countries put it as low as twelve, others as high as eighteen or twenty-one. The ILO had adopted a piecemeal approach since its inception. It had negotiated conventions with varying minimum age limits depending on the occupation and the degree of danger. But the 1979 convention aimed at gradually ending all child labor, defined a child as anyone under fifteen.[83] There were serious problems with its application in poor countries where child labor was an important source of income for families. In India, for instance, it provided an estimated 23 percent of family income—vital for people on the edge of starvation. Although such labor was often illegal, governments were reluctant to take action for economic reasons. The carpet industry in Pakistan, for example, employed over a million children, and was an important source of foreign currency for the government.

Poor families often valued even unpaid labor. In Morocco, parents of girls working in backstreet rug factories were glad to have their daughters off the streets and given one meal a day, particularly as girls over the age of puberty were often not sent to school. Thus, what an NGO saw as exploitation, a poor family might regard as an asset. In 1998, ASI reported that NGOs in the Philippines were focusing not on the banning of child labor, but on improving the children's lives by, for instance, establishing meeting places for young domestics otherwise isolated in homes.

The challenge was to change the attitude of both parents and employers to child labor.[84] Poverty was the main problem. Destitute parents were lured into parting with their children by promises of a good job, or to secure a debt. Some abandoned them or sent them to towns, hoping they would find a way to survive. All too often, they became "street children," or fell into the hands of traffickers, pimps, or drug traders.

Although the first UN report on child labor was published in 1982[85] and the question was repeatedly brought to the attention of the Working Group and its parent bodies, the Convention on the Rights of the Child was only adopted in 1989. It laid down the basic rights of children, including the right to education and leisure, and set standards for their employment and care. States that were parties to the convention undertook to prevent the sale of children, and their use for prostitution, pornography, and hazardous occupations.[86] It begged the question of definition by stating that a child was anyone under eighteen *except in states where the legal majority was earlier*.

In the 1990s, serious attention began to be paid to the continuing exploitation of children. The Working Group on Contemporary Forms of Slavery drew up a plan of action to be sent to governments, UN bodies, and Specialized Agencies.[87] Special Rapporteurs were set up by the Commission on Human Rights to deal with various aspects of the exploitation of child labor. A real breakthrough came when the ILO decided to act. In the early 1990s, it established the International Program on the Elimination of Child Labor (IPEC). IPEC established programs to eliminate child labor, and withdraw children from the work force, within a definite time period in countries whose governments were ready to cooperate. A much-publicized Global March Against Child Labor, cofounded by ASI, began in the Philippines in January 1998—the year of the fiftieth anniversary of the Universal Declaration of Human Rights. It spanned five continents and 107 countries covering 50,000 miles. It ended with marchers from around the world arriving in Geneva for the opening of the ILO conference. It called on governments to protect the rights of children.[88] The ILO estimated that there were some 250,000 working children in the world between between the ages of five and twelve; nearly half of these worked every day of the year. Seventy percent of them worked in hazardous conditions. In June 1999, the ILO adopted the Worst Forms of Child Labor Convention (No.182)—eighty years after its first convention on child labor[89] and nearly a quarter of a century after the matter was first raised at the Working Group.

This convention defined a child as anyone under eighteen. Signatories were bound to end the sale of children, and were not to allow them to be kept in debt-bondage or serfdom, to be recruited as soldiers, to be used as prostitutes or for pornography, or other criminal activities such as drug dealing. They were not to be employed in occupations detrimental to their health or morals. However, some of the force was lost by the recommendations on enforcement and monitoring which were appended to the convention (Recommendation 190). These allowed children over the minimum age for employment, but under eighteen to be employed in hazardous occupations for vocational training, as long as safety standards were met. Although treated as a separate issue, this enabled Britain, the United States, and other states to continue to recruit younger persons into their armed forces, as long as they did not put them in the front line. The convention was widely ratified, but at the end of the century, it remained to be seen how effective it would be.

ADULT TRAFFICKING AND FORCED PROSTITUTION

No subject caused greater controversy than adult prostitution. Everyone agreed that the kidnapping or fraudulent recruiting of adults for forced prostitution was a violation of basic human rights. However, there was a clear division between those who believed that all prostitution was a form of slavery and should be a criminal offense, and those who maintained that consensual prostitution should be tolerated because it was a matter of free choice, an inevitable fact of life, and impossible to stamp out. Finally, there were those prostitutes, who regarded themselves as sex workers—professionals—entitled to the same protection and benefits as other workers. Some of them told horrendous tales of how they had to take up prostitution to feed their families because it was the only career open to them. Others simply found it a lucrative career, which enabled them to enrich themselves and help their families. They saw it as their right to have a free choice of occupation. Those who objected to any legalized prostitution argued that it encouraged an exploitative global sex industry, including sex tourism and mail-order brides, and fostered discrimination by targeting particular ethnic groups.

The 1949 Convention for the Suppression of the Traffic in Persons and the Exploitation of the Prostitution of Others made it an offense to procure or entice another person into prostitution, even with their consent. This prevented a number of powers, including Britain and the Netherlands, from signing it because they would have had to criminalize consensual prostitution. The convention was also considered out of date by the last decades of the century because it only forbade trafficking for prostitution, and people were trafficked for other reasons such as labor, or forced marriage; and because it did not offer sufficient protection to the vulnerable.

By the mid-1990s, it was becoming increasingly clear that both forced and consensual prostitution were increasing. New sources, mostly of women and girls, but also of males including young boys, were being exploited. Western Europe and North America saw a great influx of women from the former Soviet Union and Eastern Europe. Where figures existed, they were daunting, if unreliable. An estimated forty to fifty thousand women and children were reported to be trafficked to the United States each year.[90] Most were economic migrants lured with the promise of good jobs, but many were kidnapped by gangs linked to the drug trade and organized crime, which also ran brothels. Some suffered extraordinarily brutal treatment and many became drug or alcohol addicts or were HIV positive. In 1997, the Working Group asked the International Movement Against all Forms of Discrimination and Racism (IMADR), a Tokyo-based NGO, to analyze the international regime against trafficking and the exploitation of prostitution. Its working paper was chilling. In the half century since 1949, trafficking had become "more pernicious and pervasive." Criminal networks were more organized and powerful. Officials, community members, and even some families looked to prostitution to generate income. Laws were passed but not implemented.

The NGOs and governments were hopelessly divided over whether to criminalize, or to legalize and control, consensual prostitution. What was now a global sex industry (GSI) had expanded exponentially, aided by increasing poverty in some areas and facilitated by the development of air travel. The Internet was being used to promote prostitution, sex tours, the trafficking of mail-order brides, pornography, live sex shows, and rape videos. Apart from its moral and criminal aspects, prostitution was also a health hazard as it contributed to the spread of HIV/AIDS and other sexually transmitted diseases. A coherent global strategy was needed to combat it. IMADR suggested inter alia that there should be mandatory national plans of action and mandatory reports from governments, as well as mechanisms for individuals to make complaints, and to enable victims to bring civil suits against the perpetrators. It also urged the appointment of either a Special Rapporteur or a Working Group to gather facts and build up a consensus as to what might be done.[91]

In 1999 IMADR organized a consultation between UN agencies and NGO and Inter-Governmental Organizations (IGOs) on the need for a "human rights framework" to attack the global sex industry. It was assisted by the New York based Coalition Against the Trafficking in Women (CATW), and by the Bangkok-based Global Alliance Against Trafficking in Women (GAATW) and by ASI. The conference met in Geneva immediately before the Working Group. The aim was to reach consensus between those who opposed all prostitution, led by CATW, and those prepared to accept consensual prostitution, led by GAATW, and to suggest measures to be taken. A compromise was reached on common objectives. However, in its report for 2001, the Working Group failed to follow this up and took the extreme view endorsed by CATW, and recommended that prostitution should never be legalized, because it was a violation of human rights, incompatible with human dignity, and it fostered sex trafficking and sex tourism. The Group also attacked the term "sex worker" because it implied that prostitution was acceptable.[92]

More importantly, there was no agreement among governments as to whether or not to legalize consensual prostitution. Some states had done so. They even controlled brothels and taxed prostitutes. In others states, prostitution was a crime, whether it was consensual or not. A point at issue in the latter case was that, if there were prosecutions, it was usually the prostitutes who were prosecuted and not their customers. Sweden announced in 2001 that it was changing this by making the "purchase of sexual services" a criminal offense. In most countries fear of arrest on the one hand, and of brutal reprisals from pimps and gangs on the other, prevented victims of forced prostitution from giving evidence to the authorities. Whether prostitution was legal or not, all agreed that prostitutes should be offered rehabilitation and other chances of employment rather than being treated as criminals. In 2001, a number of countries told the Working Group that they were taking steps to ensure the protection of victims of trafficking. In the United States and the Netherlands, for instance, they could be granted residence permits on humanitarian grounds. These grounds, however, were not specified.[93]

In the early 1990s, representatives of surviving "comfort women," mainly Koreans and Filipinas forced into brothels to serve Japanese soldiers during World War II, used the Working Group to press claims for compensation from Japan. The Japanese government maintained that under the peace treaties all such debts had been settled. The Group discussed it for years trying to get an amicable agreement and finally, in 2001, stated that it had fulfilled its mandate and would no longer consider it. That the women and other prisoners of the Japanese were entitled to compensation was generally acknowledged. In 1995, a Special Rapporteur on systematic rape, sexual slavery, and slavery-like practices in war, reported that in the Balkan wars of the 1990s, women were raped as part of the campaigns of ethnic cleansing. Special Rapporteurs identified cases from other areas, such as Peruvian soldiers fighting the Shining Path, the rape of Chinese women in Indonesia in 1998, and the rape of women by Indonesian troops in East Timor, Irian Jaya, and Aceh.[94] However, rape was only a form of slavery if, as in the case of the "comfort women," it was sustained over time, and became sexual slavery, as happened, for instance, in the late 1990s in Uganda, where the Lord's Resistance Army kidnapped schoolgirls and forced them into "marriage" or simply made them serve its soldiers. Similar outrages took place in the rebel-held areas of Sierra Leone.[95]

SERVILE MARRIAGE, EARLY AND FORCED MARRIAGE

In the early 1990s, the Anti-Slavery Society turned its attention to what it called servile marriage. In many parts of the world, women did not have the same marital rights as men. In Africa,[96] in South Asia, and in many Muslim societies,[97] such discrimination was the norm. Women's rights varied considerably from country to country. In some, they could be divorced at will and had no rights to the custody of their children. Marriages were polygynous. Women could not own property. Wife beating was legal, and women had to defer to their husbands or other male relations, who were the recognized heads of families. In Afghanistan under the rule of the Taliban, they were denied education and jobs, and could not venture out without being completely covered and accompanied by a close male relative. Elsewhere, in the Islamic world women were educated, could hold high office, own property, and follow less stringent rules for clothing. In some African societies, they had no rights to land or property or child custody and were doomed to a life of frequent childbearing and hard agricultural work. In others, girls were educated and many women worked outside the home, although they might not be able to keep their own wages.[98]

Many governments tried to end or modify this discrimination by educating girls and giving women more rights. In some societies in Africa and South Asia, women formed self-help units and obtained credit to start small businesses. However, discrimination against women was hard to change since it involved entrenched attitudes and religious beliefs. Even when laws were changed, the women themselves often did not want to flout custom or risk ostracism. They accepted discrimination as the norm and resented the efforts of militant Western feminists to "free" them. The international covenants on political, social, economic, cultural, and civil rights and the 1979 Convention on the Elimination of All Forms of Discrimination Against Women were designed to give women the same rights as men.[99] A number of the states that signed the latter made reservations that rendered it pointless.

NGOs focused not on general discrimination against women in marriage but on two practices which could more nearly be considered forms of slavery—early marriage and forced marriage—which were both covered in the 1956 slavery convention. The former, in which a girl was betrothed by her family at a very young age and had no right of refusal when she reached marriageable age, was considered a form of forced marriage. A difficulty, however, was that each country set its own age of consent. It ranged from twelve to eighteen. In some countries, even younger girls were married. Moreover, a bride's age could not be established where birth certificates were not issued and marriages were not recorded. Another form of forced marriage was the inheritance of widows, who in some African societies automatically become the wives of their husband's brother or other close relation. As has been seen, this was a means of providing a widow with a male protector. However, it could also condemn her to an unhappy marriage, to neglect, or even by the end of the twentieth century expose her to AIDS.

The colonial powers, as has been seen, had no desire to interfere with marriage customs. At the end of the century, local NGOs, working to ameliorate the lot of women, relied on education to change public attitudes rather than trying to rescue girls who might then find themselves free but ostracized. The Working Group decided only in 2001 that it would concentrate on forced and early marriage and the sale of wives at its session in 2003. By this time attention had been focused on the question by immigrants who tried to force their Western-educated children into arranged marriages. The British, for instance, were freeing some one hundred sixty British girls a year, who had been taken by their parents for holidays in their homelands—usually Pakistan, India, Bangladesh, and Yemen—and forced into marriage. How many cases remained undetected because the girls could not escape is unknown. Those who returned to England risked being shunned by their parents, and those who had been forced into pregnancy had to leave their children behind.[100]

In China, after the relaxation of communist control, girls were kidnapped and forced into marriage. Government efforts to end this traffic, which also included girls from overseas, were often thwarted by corrupt police and officials. It was cheaper to acquire a bride through force than to pay the customary price to a girl's family—a problem made worse by the one-child policy, which led to a shortage of girls. Thousands of girls were freed by the authorities, but unknown numbers remained in forced marriage. Often they were kept locked up until they produced a child, after which they were less likely to want to leave.[101]

CULT OR RITUAL SLAVERY

Cult slavery, in which a person, usually a young girl, was dedicated to a god or goddess, took a number of forms. Under the Devadasi system in parts of India, the girl was sacrificed by her family to ensure their own future, usually because of grinding poverty. She was then considered to be married to the local god, and became a saint bound to work in the temple. Any female children born to her became Devadasi and were thus in hereditary bondage.[102] In some cases, the temple became a virtual brothel. In others, girls were sold to pimps. However, some women were said to find that life as a Devadasi gave them more freedom and opportunities than those of ordinary married women.[103] In 1995, the Anti-Slavery Society believed that some ten thousand children were dedicated annually, but it admitted that evidence was hard to obtain. The government of India outlawed the practice in the late 1970s. It passed laws against it and claimed to have taken steps to rehabilitate victims.[104]

In southeastern Ghana, among the Ewe, virgin girls were dedicated to a shrine by their families to atone for offenses committed by relatives. A nine-year-old, for instance, was sent to the shrine because her grandmother had stolen a pair of earrings. Known as *Trokosi*, the girls were employed by the guardian of the shrine as agricultural and domestic labor. Some were released and allowed to marry, but others faced lifelong servitude. Many were forced to sleep with the priest, and their children were born in bondage. The Anti-Slavery Society showed the Working Group a film on Trokosi in 1995. Ghana only outlawed the practice in 1998, and two years later, no priest had been prosecuted. A local NGO, International Needs Ghana, however, released and rehabilitated many Trokosi.[105] Since the custom was deeply rooted in religion, its eradication required a change in community outlook, and the cooperation of the priests, as well as legislation. Elsewhere there were less harsh forms of cult slavery. The Osu in southern Nigeria, for instance, were similarly dedicated to a deity, and were forced to live apart and marry only other Osu. They suffered extreme discrimination but no physical harm, as people were afraid of them.

FORCED LABOR AND SWEATSHOPS

Many instances of forced labor were regularly reported to the Working Group. It was usually imposed by governments. Sometimes it was a weapon of war. A long-term offender was the government of Myanmar (Burma), which, as part of its long battle against insurgent ethnic minorities, conscripted Shan, Karenni, Karen, and Mon women and children to work, often in hazardous conditions. Some were sent ahead of the army into minefields. Many were moved into camps or new towns and then conscripted as porters or construction workers for the army, or for labor on roads, railways, and other forms of infrastructure, sometimes in areas where foreign companies were exploring for oil and gas.[106] Others were made to work on plantations, shrimp farms, and tourist projects. These abuses increased in the early 1990s. In 2000, the ILO took the rare step of calling on Myanmar's trading partners to impose sanctions. By the summer of 2001, however, the call had not been answered.[107]

In Communist China, forced labor was also used to crush dissent, and to provide cheap labor for domestic construction, for agriculture, or for the production of goods for export. Political and religious dissenters were sentenced to labor camps—*laogai*—or "reform through labor." Many of them described the grueling work in camps, factories, and mines.[108] Conditions were reported to be worsening in the 1990s as these inefficient businesses lost money.[109] Haitian cane cutters in the 1980s were sold to the Dominican Republic as contract labor. By 1999 after protests by the ILO that the Forced Labor Convention was being infringed, they were no longer sold but were tricked into signing contracts, which the army then enforced.[110]

Forced labor was also found in the private sector in sweatshops and on farms. In sweatshops, labor laws were not enforced. Working conditions were abysmal. Working hours were long. Overtime was demanded but not paid. Sweatshops producing for the U.S. market, for instance, were uncovered in Vietnam, Indonesia, Central America, and elsewhere. In some cases, workers did not complain because sweated labor was better than unemployment. Whether these voluntary laborers should be classed as slaves or forced labor is debatable since they could leave and they earned money—although a pittance. However, some were kept by force, and were certainly unfree labor. In 1999, for instance, garment factories on the American island of Saipan were employing some forty thousand young Asian women, who had been promised good jobs but were imprisoned in compounds, threatened with violence, and forced to work twelve hours a day, seven days a week producing goods for well-known U.S. firms.[111] Such factories were attacked through the 1990s by trade unions, religious groups, and left-wing organizations. By the late 1990s, the protesters were joined by students and antiglobalization activists. Threatened with boycotts, producers, worried about their image and their markets, began to demand that their suppliers improve the conditions of labor and terms of employment. But sweatshops had a way of popping up wherever labor laws were not enforced. Their existence raised the question of whether global trade placed corporate profits above human rights and welfare.

Migrant labor was particularly vulnerable to forced labor in the private sector. Abuses took many forms and were to be found virtually all over the world. In Britain and elsewhere in Western Europe, the United States, and Canada, for instance, domestic servants entering on restricted visas and unable to change employers were sometimes ill-treated. Their passports were taken away. Their pay was withheld and some suffered physical abuse. Kept isolated in homes, often unable to speak the local language, they were totally at the mercy of their employers. If they escaped, they did not go to the authorities for fear of deportation, and as they often had families dependent on their earnings, they were driven to prostitution. The problem of their restricted visas had been raised in the 1970s in connection with diplomats working in the United States for the United Nations.

The problem escalated as more servants were imported. In the 1990s, after a campaign mounted by NGOs, Canada and Britain took steps to allow them to change employers and to ensure that both they and their employers understood the terms of their contracts. Canada went further and introduced model contracts and spot checks.

Migrant women going to the Gulf States were often tricked into thinking they would have good jobs as doctors, nurses, or engineers, only to find themselves forced into domestic service, where some faced similar abuses at the hands of their employers. Filipinas and others going to Japan, Hong Kong, or elsewhere to seek work were often forced into prostitution and otherwise abused. After some tragic cases, particularly in the Gulf States, the government of the Philippines, which relied on the billions of dollars of foreign currency remitted by migrants, insisted that it had taken steps to protect its nationals.

In 1990, an International Convention on the Protection of the Rights of All Migrant Workers and their Families was signed,[112] and in 1997 the Commission on Human Rights established a Working Group of Experts to consider the difficulties of migrants who were often denied the protection and benefits of other workers, were forced to live away from their families, and were often the victims of racism and violence. Under the convention, they were to have the same civil rights as other workers and be eligible for social security. Millions have indeed exercised these rights, but with increasing numbers of illegal aliens, desperate economic refugees seeking a better livelihood in the richer areas of the world—opportunities to exploit them proliferated. Unable to go to the authorities for fear of deportation, often with families dependent on them, migrants were willing or forced to work in sweatshops for a pittance. In the United States, such businesses have been uncovered in California and elsewhere, and are particularly a feature of the garment and footwear industries.[113] In Italy some thirty thousand men, women, and children were found working in sweatshops outside Florence. In the United States, the National Workers Exploitation Task Force, set up to combat modern slavery, stated that ten people had been convicted for holding people in slavery in 1999. One concerned Mexican women and girls forced to work in a brothel. In another case, Guatemalan and Mexican farmworkers were subjected to forced labor in Florida. The problem was not limited to immigrants. In Florida in 2001, a homeless man escaped from a farm on which, together with other workers, he had been kept by force, paid a pittance, and worked from dawn to dusk.[114]

Although governments and the public had all been alerted, the desperation of economic refugees, and public resentment against them, made it likely that only the tip of the iceberg had been discovered and that these abuses would continue into the twenty-first century.

NOTES

1. SM notes, 15 August 1980.

2. WGS Report 1976, E/CN.4/Sub.2/373.

3. WGS report 1983 E/CN.4/Sub.2/1983/27/Corr.1.

4. Sub-Commission Report, E/CN.4/Sub.2/1983/43, p. 40.

5. For the background to this, see Minority Rights Group 1980. The Anti-Slavery Society also became involved in combating the practice, financing pilot schemes to help women in Africa achieve self-sufficiency, *ASR*, VI, 12, 7 November 1980, pp. 39–41.

6. WGCFS Report, E/CN.4/Sub.2/1983/27; Sub-Commission Report, E/CN.4/Sub.2./1983/43, Annex II p. 1, and 1984/3. Sub-Commission Special Rapporteurs considered the question as part of the problems of traditional practices affecting the health of women and girls, and under the rubric of violence against women.

7. WGCFS Report 2001, E/CN.4/Sub.2/2001/30.

8. For the Uzbek case, see *Sunday Times*, 9 July 2001. For an article on the voluntary sale of organs by poor donors in India, Turkey, and Iraq, see *Sunday Telegraph*, 24 June 2001. A BBC documentary showed Moldavians being encouraged to sell their organs to Istanbul for Israeli recipients.

9. WGCFS Report 1987, E/CN.4/Sub.2/1987/25.

10. WGCFS Report 1997, E/CN.4/Sub.2/1997/13.

11. Whitaker 1991, *Slavery*, p. 4.

12. The peoples in this category included Aborigines in Australia, Native Americans, hunter-gatherer groups (commonly called Sarwa, San, or "Bushmen") in Southern Africa, Nagas in India, Amerindian groups in Latin America, the Hmong of Thailand, as well as the indigenous peoples of Papua, New Guinea, East Timor, and the Western Sahara. Their protection had been part of the mandate of the Anti-Slavery Society since its amalgamation with the Aborigines Protection Society in 1909 (see above, chapter 5). It was a particular interest of Jeremy Swift, who was chairman of the General Committee of the Society from 1974 to 1987.

13. I am indebted to David Weissbrodt for this view of the reasons for the success of the WGIP.

14. WGS Report 1987, E/CN.4/Sub.2/1987/25.

15. For a brief summary of the discussion that follows and references to information on the Internet, see Miers 2000.

16. Land was held communally by tribes, whose elders decided on its allocation.

17. McDougall 1988; Ruf 2000. The actual terms of service between slaves and owners varied, allowing some slaves greater independence than others.

18. These were Fulbe, Wolof Bambara, and Soninke.

19. The Declaration and the Ordinance were published as annexes to Bossuyt's report, E/CN.4/Sub.2/1984/23, 2 July 1984.

20. AS Submission to WGCFS: "Slavery in Mauritania," August 1981; *ASR*, VII, vol. 13, no. 1, December 1981. For the full report, see Mercer 1981.

21. *ASR*, VII, 13, no. 2, 1985.

22. Bossuyt Report E/CN4/Sub.2/1984/23, 2 July 1984.

23. Bossuyt, "Final Report on the Mission to Mauritania," 17 July 1987, E/CN.4/Sub.2/1987/27. Measures had already been promulgated to introduce private ownership of land.

24. Kamara 2000.

25. Ruf 2000; Saleck 2000; Messaoud 2000.

26. *ASR*, VII, 13, no. 3; Ruf 2000.

27. Bales 1999, 80–200. Bales visited Mauritania surreptitiously in 1997.

28. Maugham 1961, 164.

29. For examples of these abuses, see Messaoud 2000.

30. *ASR*, VII, 5, 1, January 1999; see also Messaoud 2000.

31. *ASR*, VII, 5, 4, October 1999.

32. For an activist viewpoint on Mauritania, see Messaoud 2000. He was a founding member of both El Hor and SOS-Slaves. For a scholar's more nuanced views, see Ruf 2000.

33. WGCFS Report 2000, E/CN.4/Sub.2/2000/23.

34. Hoskins, forthcoming.

35. Clark 1998.

36. Sy 2000.

37. ASI submission to WGCFS 1998: "Slavery in Sudan."

38. For a discussion of the complexities, ethnic, religious, and linguistic and their relationship to the war and to slaving, and for further references, see Bola 2000.

39. For the activities of CSI, see reports of CSI visits to Sudan in 1995, 1998, and 1999; Paul Harris, *Daily Telegraph*, 8 February 2000; article by John Eibner of CSI, in *International Herald Tribune*, 29 June 2001. For a personal account of ransoming slaves, see Bombay 1998; and Boyd 1998. AASG has no affiliation with ASI.

40. For a description of how the scam is conducted, see "The Great Slave Scam," *Irish Times*, 23 February 2002. I am indebted to Kevin Bales for sending me this article. These accusations are hotly denied by the groups involved in funding these redemptions. The redoubtable English Baroness Cox was one of the original redeemers, but gave it up and broke her ties with CSI.

41. "Is there Slavery in Sudan? Provisional observations of a visit to Sudan by Anti-Slavery International representatives (18 to 28 October 2000)." Exchange of faxes between CEAWC (dated 30 August 2001) and ASI (12 October 2001).

42. For a discussion of such estimates see below, chapter 25.

43. *ASR*, January 2001. For more on slavery in Sudan, see Mahmud and Baldo, 1987; Report of the United Nations Special Rapporteur, Situation of Human Rights in Sudan, UN no. E/CN.4/1994/58; *HRW Reports* 1995, and 1996; *HRW World Report 1999*; Verney 1997; Hargey 1998. For the government committee, see ASR VIII, October 1999, 5; ASR submission to WGCFS 1999: "Effective Measures to free Sudanese Held Captive and Forced to Work."

44. For instance, the Dinka and Nuer, both southern pastoralists, made an agreement to stop mutual abductions, and CEAWC had returned 118 Baggara to their families in the north; see Sudanese government fax to ASI, 30 August 2001.

45. See below for the use of child soldiers.

46. The information that follows is based on the submissions of ASI and other NGOs to the Working Group, on the *ASR,* and on Bales 1999. The information on Brazil is based on the same sources and on Sutton 1994.

47. WGCFS Report 2001, E.CN.4/Sub.2/2001/30.

48. See for instance, Sattaur 1993, and Chalise et al. 2001.

49. For the plight of the *Kamaya,* see ASI submission to the WGCFS Report 1994, E/CN.4/ 1994/ 33; Chalise et al. 2001. For the development of the system, see Robertson and Mishra 1997.

50. *ASR* VIII, January 2001.

51. *ASR* VIII, April 2001 and July 2001; ILO, *Stopping Forced Labour* 2001.

52. The campaign was supported by the more reputable factory owners in order to stifle competition from the employers who employed such labor.

53. WGCFS Report 2000, E/CN./Sub.2/2000/23; WGCFS 2001. E/CN.4/Sub.2/2001/30; *ASR,* see inter alia VIII, April 1999, April and October 2000, July 2001; Bales 1999, 223–31.

54. *ASR,* January 2001. WGCFS Report 2000, E/CN./Sub.2/2000/23.

55. See inter alia *Enslaved Peoples in the 1990s*, ASI and IWGIA, Copenhagen 1997.

56. ILO, *Stopping Forced Labour,* p. 35.

57. Ibid., pp. 32–43.

58. Bouhdiba 1982; reports by Vitit Mutarbhorn, submitted to UN General Assembly in 1995, A/49/478, and by O. Calcetas-Santos, on the Sale of Children, Child Prostitution, and Child Pornography, February 1997, E/CN.4/1997/95.

59. The Society published fifteen booklets between 1978 and 1997, on child labor in Morocco, India, Spain, Thailand, Italy, Jamaica, South Africa, Britain, Portugal, and Nepal. Some were on particular industries such as the carpet industry in the Indian subcontinent and Morocco, and one was on child domestic workers.

60. The Declaration and the Convention (ILO no. 138) are published as annexes in Bouhdiba 1982.

61. WGCFS E/CN.4/Sub.2/2001/30.

62. IPEC Country Profile: El Salvador, 2000. ILO.

63. IPEC Country Profile: United Republic of Tanzania 2000. ILO.

64. WGCS Report 1995, E/CN.4/Sub.2/1995/28; 1998, E/CN.4/Sub.2/1998/14.

65. WGCFS Report 2001, E/CN.4/Sub.2/2001/30; *ASR* VIII, July 2001. This was widely covered in the press.

66. In 2001, a documentary film, "TrueVision," made for Channel 4 in Britain and HBO in the United States, exposed conditions on cocoa plantations. It was based on the groundbreaking book, Bales 1999.

67. I am indebted to Kevin Bales for providing me with this information and for the agreement between ASI and Free the Slaves. The latter is an independent but closely affiliated society with an interlocking directorship. For more information on Bales and his work, see Bales 2002, and <www.freetheslaves.net>.

68. For illustrated examples, see *The Times*, 15 May 2001, *Sunday Times Magazine*, 19 August 2000.

69. *ASR* VIII, April 2001.

70. *Sunday Times*, 29 July 2001.

71. WGCS Reports 1996 and 1997, E/CN.4/Sub.2/1996/24; E/CN 4/Sub.2/1997/13.

72. WGCFS Report 2001, E/CN.4/Sub.2/2001/30.

73. Altink 1995, 18.

74. WGCS Report 1978, E/CN.4/Sub.2/410, for more on this, see below.

75. Report of WGCS 1996, E/CN.4/Sub.2/ 1996/26.

76. Report of WGCS 1996, E/CN.4/Sub.2/ 1997/13.

77. Report of WGCS 1995, E/CN.4/Sub.2/ 1995/28.

78. The British Sex Offenders Act was passed in 1997.

79. Report of WGCS, 28 August 1989, E/CN.4/Sub.2/1989/39.

80. *The Times*, 19 June 2001.

81. ASI submission to WGCFS, 1988.

82. In the Chinese case, the homes of the adopters were visited and their qualifications verified. The operation appeared to be a means of getting rid of unwanted girls. They were said to be

foundlings abandoned for various reasons, including the difficulties faced by parents who produced a second child, infringing the one child per family policy.

83. ILO Convention 138.

84. WGCFS Report 1998, E/Cn.4/ Sub.2/1998/14.

85. Bouhdiba 1982.

86. Brownlie, 182–202.

87. WGCFS 1990, E/CN.4/Sub.2/1990/44.

88. See *ASR,* March 1998, and AS *Annual Report,* 1997/8.

89. A 1919 convention set the minimum age of employment at fourteen. It was followed by a number of other conventions on the subject.

90. WGCFS Report 2001, E/CN.4/Sub.2/2001/30; *State Department Report, 1999.*

91. WGCFS Report 1998, E/CN.4/Sub.2/1998/14.

92. WGCFS Report 2001, E/CN.4/Sub.2/2001/30.

93. WGCFS Report 2001, E/CN.4/Sub.2/2001/30. For a definition of trafficking and the Protocol against transnational trafficking, see below, chapter 25.

94. Linda Chavez, Preliminary Report of the Special Rapporteur on the Situation of Systematic Rape, Sexual Slavery and Slavery-like Practices during Periods of Armed Conflict, 16 July 1996, E/CN.4/Sub.2/ 1996/26; Reports of the Special Rapporteur on Violence against Women, R.Coomaraswamy, 12 February 1997, E/Cn.4/1997/47, 26 January 1998, E/CN.4/1998/54, 21 January 1999, E/CN.4/1999/68 Adds.1, 3, 4.

95. WGCS report 1998, E/CN.4/Sub.2/ 1998/14. U.S. forces were also accused of starting the Southeast Asian sex industry during the Vietnam War.

96. Many books have been written on women in Africa but see inter alia the studies in Stichter and Parpart, eds. 1988, Hay and Wright, eds. 1982; Guyer 1987.

97. See inter alia Bodman and Tohidi, eds. 1998.

98. I had personal experience of an African schoolteacher who could not marry as her husband would then be entitled to her wages, which her father claimed as he had paid her school fees and wanted to use her money to pay those of her siblings. She did not dare to refuse in case he cursed her.

99. For the 1979 convention, see Brownlie 1998, 169–81.

100. *ASR* VIII, October 2000. For personal accounts, see *The Times,* 12 May 2001; Muhsen 1991.

101. Jaschok and Miers 1994, 264–65.

102. Bales 1999, 199–201.

103. Altink 1995, 24.

104. Report of WGCS, 1995, E/CN.4/Sub.2/1995/28.

105. *ASR* VIII, January 2000.

106. Martin Smith 1994; Delang, ed. 2000, and inter alia WGCFS report, 1995, E.CN.4/1995/28.

107. *International Herald Tribune*, 3 May 2001.

108. See inter alia Wu 1992, Wu and Wakeman 1994.

109. *International Herald Tribune*, 15 June 2001.

110. Plant 1987; Report of WGCS, 28 August 1990, E/CN.4/Sub.2/1990/44; *ASR* VIII, October 1999.

111. Miers 2000 (b), 736.

112. Brownlie 1998, 203–40.

113. For the plight of illegal aliens in the United States, see Lewis 1980.

114. Article by T. C. Tobin, *St. Petersburg Times*, 16 August 2001.

Conclusion:
The Antislavery Campaign
in the Twentieth Century

THE LEAGUE OF NATIONS AND SLAVERY

At the outset of the twentieth century, chattel slavery was still widespread. Although it had been outlawed in Europe and the Americas, it was practiced by native peoples in many parts of the world, including those living under European, American, and Ottoman rule. The first aim of the colonial masters was to suppress the raids and the trade, which kept it alive. By 1914, this had been largely achieved. The colonial powers met their labor needs with wage, contract, and forced labor. These could degenerate into slavery but they were quite different in theory and often in practice. A contract worker's service ended with his contract. Forced labor was for a limited time. Other devices, such as land alienation and taxes, were used to force free people into the labor market. Chattel slavery had lost its legal status in most colonies in the first decade of the century but little had been done by 1920 to make its demise a reality. The colonial powers, with some exceptions, merely made it legally possible for slaves to free themselves. They hoped that most would stay with their owners until the institution withered away with the imposition of peace, and with changing economic and political conditions. Many slaves did leave, but probably the greater number stayed where they were, but over time renegotiated their terms of service. In Ethiopia, Arabia, and parts of India and Burma, and the remoter areas of Africa, however, both slavery and the slave trade and, in some places, even slave raiding, continued on a reduced scale.

The international antislavery campaign before 1890 had focused on preventing the export of slaves, particularly from Africa, the main supplier. The British network of treaties had been laboriously constructed in the nineteenth century for this purpose. The Brussels Act of 1890, however, bound all the maritime and colonial powers not only to end the export trade from Africa, but also to end slave raiding and trading on the continent. This was slowly achieved because the colonial powers wanted to keep labor at home, and under their control, and because they needed to keep the peace in

the interests of good government and economic development. By 1919, they had succeeded to the point that they abrogated the Brussels Act, claiming that it was no longer
needed. The Covenant of the League of Nations introduced a new element by binding
members to secure "fair and humane" conditions of labor. Since these conditions were
not defined, this merely paid lip service to the antislavery cause. A single article in one
of the three treaties of St. Germain-en-Laye, which replaced the Brussels Act, bound
signatories to "secure the complete suppression of slavery in all its forms" as well as the
slave trade by land and sea. The phrase "in all its forms" opened the way to a new conception of slavery. Hitherto, the international attack had been limited to the much
publicized and well-understood form of chattel slavery. Moreover, the creation of the
International Labor Organization (ILO) in 1920 brought into being a new effective
weapon for the protection of all forms of labor.

The slavery question, however, would probably have remained dormant had there
not been a resurgence of slave raiding and trading in Ethiopia and a revival of the export traffic across the Red Sea. When this news reached the Anti-Slavery Society, its
secretary, John Harris, had the perspicacity to realize that the League of Nations was a
new weapon, which could be brought to bear in the fight not just against slavery, but
also against other forms of exploitation. His efforts were to lead to the establishment
of the three League of Nations Slavery Committees.

The first and most imaginative, and in the long run, the most influential, of these
was the Temporary Slavery Commission (TSC). This included qualified experts—
former colonial administrators, some of them recognized as men of stature, who had
had experience of slavery. They realized that the real task ahead was the protection of
colonial peoples from exploitation by their rulers, as well as from a range of indigenous practices, which included various forms of servitude. They, therefore, widened
the attack on slavery to include some of the devices used by the colonial powers to exploit labor—forced labor, the mistreatment of migrant and contract labor, as well as
practices "restrictive of the liberty of the person," notably forced marriage, "quasi-
adoption," serfdom, and debt-bondage. These were now projected onto the international stage as abuses to be eliminated. Labeling them forms of slavery called attention
to them, and kept them within the mandate of the TSC.

The commission was instrumental in forcing governments to negotiate the Slavery
Convention of 1926. This was the first international instrument against slavery, and although it did not name the various other forms of servitude, subsumed under "slavery in all its forms," they were clearly identified in the TSC report. The convention was
still in force at the end of the twentieth century. By including forced labor as a form of
slavery and recommending action to limit it, the TSC also played a part in stimulating
the negotiation of the Forced Labor Convention of 1930 by the International Labor
Organization.

The next League antislavery committee—the Committee of Experts on Slavery of 1932—contributed little in the way of new ideas, but it showed up, even more forcibly than its predecessor, the fact that governments were failing to provide full and impartial information. It also demonstrated, to a greater degree than its predecessor, how a committee of experts on slavery could be used to further national interests. Its main achievement was to fulfill the expectation of its British sponsors by paving the way for the first official permanent international antislavery body—the Advisory Committee of Experts on Slavery (ACE).

This committee was soon dominated by its British member, George Maxwell. He came to it fresh, with expertise learned in Malaya giving him a grasp of debt-bondage and child welfare, neither of which had been considered in any depth by the TSC. His contribution was pragmatic rather than idealistic. He set out to defuse conflict by whittling down the definition of slavery. The fact that the TSC had decided that its defining characteristic was ownership, and that it had been so defined in the Slavery Convention, enabled him to rule out many of the practices that it had condemned as forms of slavery. If he had had his way the committee would have collected all available information and then handed over its responsibilities to more powerful bodies, particularly the ILO. Slavery "in all its forms" would thus have been divided into its component parts, and the term only applied to chattel slavery. However, the outbreak of the Second World War ended the committee's active life. Whether Maxwell would have succeeded in passing on most forms of servitude to other bodies remains a matter of conjecture. The committee's reports, however, caused the British and the French to refine their slavery laws, and, to some extent, their policies.

The weakness of these committees was that they were mainly composed of members of the European colonial powers and the ILO. Furthermore, their information was limited to published sources, petitions, personal experience, government reports, and evidence from carefully vetted NGOs. The government reports were rarified documents, voicing what administrators were willing to divulge, or in the case of the British ones, containing what Maxwell could extract from them. Many governments, including Saudi Arabia, did not send reports. The slave voice, such as it was, was relayed through nongovernmental organizations (NGOs), particularly the Anti-Slavery Society and the Bureau de la Défense des Indigènes. The reports of all three committees were published after evaluation by governments to ensure that they contained, on the one hand, as little damaging information as possible, and on the other, as much praise as for their activities as possible. The reports were used to explain inaction as well as to paint colonial aggression as antislavery activities.

For all their failings, however, these League committees focused attention on slavery for the best part of two decades. By 1938, the Slavery Convention had been ratified, or acceded to, by forty-four states. Colonial governments had at least voiced the ideal of complete eradication, and some had reviewed and strengthened their anti-slavery laws, and made some changes in their policy.

The 1920s, 1930s, and early 1940s saw the virtual eradication of slave raiding, a great decline in the slave trade, and an end to the legal status of chattel slavery everywhere, except in parts of Arabia. Slavery was eroded at the grassroots level mainly by political, economic, and social change. However, the reforms stimulated by the spotlight on slavery at the League, and by the 1926 Slavery Convention, had resulted in some colonies passing new laws, or restating old ones, which helped many slaves to leave their owners or renegotiate their terms of service. Moreover, the fact that slavery was under attack was not lost on Saudi Arabia and Yemen, both of which took the first tentative steps to pay at least lip service to ending slave imports.

The League committees also played a part in raising public awareness of the many other forms of exploitation used by the colonial powers and other governments, particularly forced labor, forced crop cultivation, and abuses of contract labor. They also began the attack on such practices as debt-bondage, child labor, forced marriage, cult slavery, fraudulent adoption, and serfdom. Although all these were still widely practiced at the outbreak of the Second World War, the colonial powers had, at least, voiced the ideal of complete eradication.

In terms of their composition and powers, the League committees provided a model for the future. They were minor bodies, run on a shoestring, meeting for only a few days. They had little prestige, and no power to launch investigations. The ACE, in particular, was hamstrung by stringent rules of procedure that precluded taking evidence that was not published or provided by governments. The Secretariat assiduously collected published material and received petitions from private organizations, mostly British, but real investigation was impossible. Nongovernmental organizations could not come in person to give testimony or discuss the questions at issue.[1] No evidence came directly from slaves. Moreover, meetings were private, so publicity was limited to the published reports. These were all published by permission of the Council, but they were vetted by governments, and the committees took care to word them as tactfully as possible.

In sum, the League slavery committees were one step in the move to bring social and economic questions onto the international stage. They were born from the doctrine of trusteeship and were part of the effort to set minimum international standards for the treatment of slaves and other exploited groups. They were fairly successful as far as slavery was concerned, because this was no longer the widespread and important institution it had been in the past. It was well in decline in most areas by the time the committees began their work. They were less successful in tackling debt-bondage (including peonage), forced labor, child labor, and other exploitative practices, which were widely practiced methods of procuring and controlling cheap labor. However, the fact that these had even been proclaimed to be forms of slavery meant that they were part of the legacy the League passed to the United Nations.

The lack of any official powers of investigation and supervision, and the complete lack of any enforcement mechanism, meant that these committees could do little more than call attention to problems and trust to public opinion to force governments to take action.

THE UNITED NATIONS AND SLAVERY TO 1975

The United Nations was a much more effective body than the League, which it succeeded in 1946. It operated in a new world setting. The European colonial powers, which had been so powerful at the League, one by one lost their colonies and with that, much of their influence. The United States and the Soviet Union held center stage and their rivalry and mutual hostility prevented concerted action for many years. The UN suffered, like the League, from the fact that national sovereignty was still inviolate. The gradual appearance of new members as the result of decolonization was to change the setting within which the antislavery campaign was conducted. It was no longer possible to bring matters to a head by agitation in Europe. Each government had to be approached separately, and more and more the objects of attack were those practiced in the so-called Third or Developing World.

The changes came gradually. Thus, Greenidge, as secretary of the Anti-Slavery Society, was able to get slavery put on the agenda of the United Nations, and to get the appointment of the Ad Hoc Committee in 1949. In a new and permanent departure, its members were chosen from the five geographical areas into which the UN divided the world.[2] A further new departure, which was short-lived, was that Greenidge was appointed a member. The committee was only advisory and temporary. It met in private, but its members sought and secured unprecedented press coverage. Although it ended in disagreement and Peru cut short its proceedings, it succeeded, through the efforts of Greenidge, in laying the groundwork for the negotiation of the Supplementary Convention of 1956. This convention reverted to the concept of slavery in all its forms as laid out by the TSC. It also defined them for the first time, to the consternation of some of the new states that emerged in the next two decades. Like its predecessors, the convention contained no mechanism for enforcement. Moreover the Royal Navy's long cherished, but now barely used, rights to search foreign shipping were finally ended as part of the bargaining process over certain articles of the convention.

The Anti-Slavery Society continued its battle to get a permanent slavery committee established, but until the early 1970s, it ran into widespread opposition from both the colonial powers and many of their successor states. The latter finally agreed to it only after apartheid and colonialism were added to the already broad definition of slavery. The British only agreed to it after legal slavery had ended in their Arabian satellites and Oman. Finally, in 1975 the Working Group on Slavery was appointed as a subsidiary body to the Sub-Commission on the Prevention of Discrimination and the Protection of Minorities. Its five members, one from each region of the world, were elected by the Sub-Commission. It had some advantages over its predecessors. It met in public and the UN issued press releases to publicize its work. Unlike the League committees, it took evidence from NGOs, which, in fact, produced the bulk of its information. Its meetings were also attended by Specialized Agencies, other UN bodies, and government representatives. But, of course, it had no effective powers of investigation or monitoring.

THE ACHIEVEMENTS AND FAILINGS OF THE UN WORKING GROUP

When, in 1983, the Working Group was attacked at the UN as expensive and inefficient, the Anti-Slavery Society defended it as an "admirable filtering and editing" machine which brought questions to the busy Sub-Commission in "compact and digestible form." In 1987, the Society appreciated the fact that a wide range of abuses, such as female genital mutilation, could be raised at its sessions and solutions discussed. In 1998, Mary Robinson, Commissioner for Human Rights, praised it for the "flexibility that had enabled it to take account of all developments in the field." To her, its value lay in its willingness to consider an ever-growing range of practices under the rubric of contemporary forms of slavery. Other observers, however, saw this as a weakness and believed the Group was losing focus. The fact that it covered so much ground meant that by 2001 it had collected an enormous amount of material, and provided a forum to which numerous NGOs could bring their concerns. It also solicited publicity, issuing press releases and asking for media coverage. In this respect, its achievement, together with that of the growing number of NGOs, was impressive.

In 1975, most people believed that slavery implied only chattel slavery, and that this had already been eradicated. It was a thing of the past and not the present. Now other forms of servitude had been called forcefully to public attention, and were equated with slavery. By 2001, as the result of the information brought to the Group by the NGOs and of the propaganda efforts of the latter, the situation had changed dramatically. By the late 1990s, most people had heard of at least some of the contemporary forms of slavery. Almost daily, press articles covered one or another form. Sensational accounts appeared on chattel slavery in Mauritania and Sudan, on forced marriage, on debt-bondage, on the exploitation of child labor, on forced labor, and so on. The efforts of the Group and NGOs to arouse public indignation were reinforced by such dramatic ploys as the Global March against Child Labor of 1998 as well as by the many congresses, conferences, and seminars held around the world on various forms of servitude. In all the turmoil of exposure, the Working Group remained a forum for serious discussion of contemporary social and economic problems. Thanks to the Voluntary Fund and NGO efforts, victims were able to come to Geneva to testify to their personal experiences. The appointment by the Commission on Human Rights and the Sub-Commission of Special Rapporteurs, some of them on the recommendation of the Group, yielded considerable information, much of it from on-the-spot investigations. The Group's Programs of Action provided valuable guidance on the steps required to end certain abuses.

The failings of the Working Group, however, were all too clear. Its inability, or lack of will, to initiate enquiries, and its lack of monitoring and supervisory mechanisms threatened to render it irrelevant as just another toothless UN committee. This failing was compounded by the fact that unlike the League committees, its personnel changed continually. Recommendations to enlarge it by appointing permanent members with real expertise at the grassroots level were ignored. The constant changes meant that the new "experts" often knew little about the subjects being discussed and were unaware of the recommendations made in previous years. In theory, they should have read them in the Group's reports to the Sub-Commission, but in practice, they often appeared not to have done so. Constant changes in membership meant that there was no opportunity for the emergence of dominant figures with clear aims such as Lugard, Maxwell, and Greenidge. These changes were not simply due to the periodic changes in the personnel of the Sub-Commission as their terms of service expired. They were also due to the fact that this was not a popular committee on which to serve and members often failed to stand for reelection. One can only speculate that this was at least partly due to frustration at hearing a catalogue of the same abuses year after year and watching so many of the Group's recommendations ignored or shelved.

Another failing was that the Group's reports were couched in diplomatic language designed to avoid giving offense to governments and sometimes to hide the source of its information. They were also stuffed with repeated appeals to Special Agencies to cooperate and to attend sessions, to governments to enforce their laws and act on the Group's recommendation, and with admonitions to the media to educate the public. They were full of lines beginning the Working Group "considers," "further considers," "requests once more," until finally they delivered a weak recommendation, which was all too often ignored or watered down, and often failed to name the specific countries in which abuses took place.

These failings were not the fault of the Group, but of the members of the UN, who established it to satisfy NGO demands for action against slavery, but ensured that it had neither the powers nor the personnel to make it really effective. Nonetheless, its efforts compare unfavorably with those of the Working Group on Indigenous Populations and the Working Group on Minorities, both of which had had the advantage of continuity of leadership. The question at the end of the century was whether the WGCFS had reached the limit of its useful life. If so, should it be replaced by a more powerful and prestigious body? This could be a committee of independent experts along the lines of those which monitor the two UN conventions on political and civil rights, and social, economic, and cultural rights. Alternatively, should it be replaced by a special rapporteur for slavery questions, who would be able to make on-the-spot visits, establish working relationships with governments, and report directly to the Human Rights Commission? Finally, should it simply be scrapped and its duties taken over by other bodies such as the ILO, UNESCO, WHO, and so on, along the lines suggested by Maxwell more than seventy years earlier?

THE NEED FOR RIGOROUS DEFINITIONS IN CONVENTIONS

The Working Group's constantly expanding definition of slavery in the last quarter of the twentieth century raised a very practical problem. Whereas calling a particular abuse "slavery" ensured that it would get public attention, the conventions negotiated by the United Nations, including the ILO, required careful definitions if signatories were to prosecute offenders. For example, the Convention on the Rights of the Child set labor standards, which distinguished acceptable child labor from child slavery. A child was not a slave if he or she had time for education and recreation, if he or she worked in a healthy environment, and was paid a market wage, and was above the minimum age for work outside the family. Similarly, the two ILO Forced Labor conventions of 1930 (no. 29) and 1957 (no. 105) stipulated that forced labor was acceptable if it was for a short term, was performed near home for public purposes, and was in the interests of those conscripted. Moreover, the worker had to be paid at the market rate, work only for specified hours, and be provided with adequate food, housing, and health care. Using forced labor for military purposes, for economic development, for disciplining labor, or for suppressing political dissent were punishable offenses. Rigorous standards were also set by the ILO in its attempt to protect migrant workers, foreign contract workers, illegal aliens, and other vulnerable groups. Without such definitions, prosecutions might fail.[3]

Obviously the definition of slavery in the 1926 Convention as "the status or condition of a person over whom any or all of the powers attaching to the rights of ownership are exercised" in the 1930 Convention did not fit what was designated slavery in the late twentieth century. The 1956 convention defined some "practices similar to slavery," but did not cover all those considered by the Working Group, such as pedophilia, incest, and the forced sale of organs. A more useful definition was adopted in a Protocol to supplement the Convention against Transnational Organized Crime.[4] This defined trafficking in persons as:

> The recruitment, transportation, transfer, harboring or receipt of persons, by means of the threat or use of force or other forms of coercion, of abduction, of fraud, of deception, of the abuse of power or of a position of vulnerability or of the giving or receiving of payments or benefits to achieve the consent of a person having control over another person, for the purpose of exploitation. Exploitation shall include, at a minimum, the exploitation of the prostitution of others or other forms of sexual exploitation, forced labor, or services, slavery or practices similar to slavery, servitude, or the removal of organs.

This, together with other provisions of the protocol, made clear the circumstances under which the various practices it detailed were exploitative, and when they were acceptable.[5] However, the protocol only applied to transnational crime. Slavery remained undefined. In 1999, the Rome Statute of the International Criminal Court listed it as one of the offenses to be tried by the International Criminal Court, along with Genocide and other crimes. But it was still defined as "the exercise of any or all of the powers attaching to the right of ownership over a person," though with the addition of "the exercise of such power in the course of trafficking in persons, particularly women and children."[6]

New treaties and new national legislation were needed with clear definitions of slavery, forced labor, and other exploitative practices. They would make it plain that slavery as conceived at the end of the century was a whole conglomeration of abuses embracing many forms of exploitation. This was not new and was certainly recognized when the phrase "slavery in all its forms" was inserted into the League Covenant, but by the year 2000, the Working Group was using the term to cover such a wide range of practices as to be virtually meaningless. Only a new clear definition in international law could untangle the morass, set clear standards, and allow governments to prosecute offenders, and victims to seek redress through the courts.

At the end of the twentieth century, another legal problem that came to the fore was the lack of a time limit for bringing cases to court for human rights abuses, including slavery and forced labor. This problem emerged in the Working Group when the former prisoners of war of the Japanese and the so-called "comfort women" called on Japan for apologies and compensation. Not only had these abuses taken place over fifty years earlier, but many victims had died. The question at issue was not just whether these victims and their heirs were entitled to reparations, but how far back into history exploited groups and their descendants could go in making their demands. Also, how was compensation to be assessed? If the victims had died, to whom would it be paid? Such problems arose at the Durban World Conference against Racism, Racial Discrimination, Xenophobia, and Related Intolerance in September 2001, when African Americans and African groups demanded reparations for the slave trade and for colonialism. Some governments, even when willing to admit that their predecessors had inflicted grievous wrongs, were afraid to offer so much as an apology for fear of becoming the focus of class actions. Another question was how far old abuses should be allowed to eclipse the immediate grievances of living victims, such as the Dalits (Untouchables) of India, who had hoped to get greater attention in Durban. These problems were unresolved at the beginning of the twenty-first century.

RESULTS OF THE ANTISLAVERY CAMPAIGN IN THE TWENTIETH CENTURY

By the end of the twentieth century, chattel slavery, and its attendant raiding and trading, was no longer the widespread oppressive institution it had been. Outlawed everywhere, its vestiges continued in various forms, some doubtless more exploitative than was generally known or acknowledged, but governments everywhere had proclaimed it illegal, even if, as in Sudan, it appeared to have resurfaced. Some of what were called contemporary forms of slavery had also been condemned and in some cases had been ended or were under serious attack. Others, however, were still widespread and the impact of the campaign was hard to assess. For instance, most governments had passed laws against debt-bondage, and had even taken steps to free some of its victims. In Brazil and the Indian subcontinent, NGOs were actively helping debtors to achieve freedom. It was also widely recognized that they would need access to credit and land or jobs if they were not to fall back into debt. Nevertheless, debt-bondage continued to be a scourge. It was even emerging in new areas, such as Britain, where aliens, particularly illegal ones, were in debt to the agencies or the criminal gangs who had imported them. The gangs used them as they wished, demanded payoffs from their families in their home countries, and threatened to harm the families if the victims resisted. Since the victims were afraid to give evidence, the laws to protect them were unenforceable and their numbers were unknown.

Child labor in its worst forms had been universally condemned, but it was too much to hope that children would not continue to be recruited into guerrilla and other armies, or forced into prostitution, used for pornography, subjected to forced labor, or made to perform grueling, even dangerous, labor in factories, quarries, farms, and plantations. Again, these abuses could only be eradicated with political will, incorruptible inspectors, sufficient resources, and public cooperation. Similarly, sweatshops were apt to spring up as fast as they were shut down in the eternal search for cheap labor on one side and the desperate need for jobs on the other. The rise in organized crime threatened to undermine efforts to end forced prostitution. Girls were still abducted or tricked into forced prostitution by unscrupulous and often sadistic operators. Servile marriage was not even condemned in some societies, and forced and underage marriage also continued.

Nonetheless, treaties had been negotiated. Standards had been set. Some groups had been mobilized to claim their rights. Efforts had been made to alert the public to the whole range of abuses. Boycotts of goods produced by sweated and child labor had been organized. Many branches of the UN had discussed the issues. Large numbers of NGOs were active. But there remained no mechanism to enforce the conventions. Governments did not have to adopt and ratify them, let alone enforce them. They might be exposed, vilified, even forced to pay lip service to the eradication of admitted abuses, but national sovereignty was only beginning to be breached, now that a range of abuses, including slavery and trafficking, could be prosecuted in the International Criminal Court. But in the last resort, the Court had to rely on national governments to hand over the perpetrators, or on the international community to force them to do so.[7]

The antislavery campaign seemed to be foundering as contemporary forms of slavery flourished in the face of increasing poverty, of disparities in the wealth of nations, of the great increase in the number of the world's children, as well as the proliferation of small wars and rebellions, and the sheer scale of the practices under attack. The problem was compounded by the growth of the underground or "second economy," and the expansion of organized crime. The latter was significantly aided by the proliferation of tax havens and banking secrecy. These provided opportunities to launder money obtained through forced prostitution, sex tourism, pornography, and other forms of exploitation. The Internet made communications for the perpetrators easier and faster. Urbanization and migration put more people at risk as they moved out of the poorer areas to seek opportunities elsewhere.

The result of these changes was that by the year 2001, unprecedented numbers of people were in various forms of servitude. Exact numbers could not be ascertained. Just as Harris exaggerated the number of slaves in Ethiopia back in the 1930s, so NGOs tended to inflate figures to make an impact. Thus estimates of, say, twenty million bonded laborers in the world, were often mere guesses. But once such figures are reported to the Working Group or another UN body, and appear in their reports, they take on the appearance of fact. However, a very careful and conservative estimate by Kevin Bales puts the number of slaves at twenty-seven million. To arrive at this estimate, he defines actual slavery as:

> The loss of free will, where a person is forced through violence or the threat of violence to give up the ability to sell freely his/her labor power. In this definition, slavery has three key dimensions: control by another person, the appropriation of labor power and the use or threat of violence.[8]

This definition rules out some of the iniquitous forms of servitude already described. If these are included, the numbers are clearly very much higher.

In sum, it may be stated that while chattel slavery was almost a thing of the past at the end of the century, unprecedented numbers of people were in some form of "contemporary slavery" and it was both widespread and perhaps increasing. Moreover, new forms were constantly springing up. There seemed no end to people's ability to exploit one another. All was not black, however. Much was now known about many forms of servitude and the need for a new approach, and new mechanisms had been recognized. There was hope that the slow and halting steps towards a more equitable world order would eventually provide adequate treaties and laws to protect, and if necessary rehabilitate, the weak and vulnerable.

NOTES

1. The only exception was the evidence on Ethiopia presented to the CES in 1932.

2. Only four were eventually appointed; see chapter 19.

3. Unocal, a United States multinational company, was accused of using forced labor supplied by the government of Myanmar. A successful prosecution depended not only on a clear definition of forced labor, but also on whether the government had assumed the legal rights to try crimes committed in another country, and whether this could be done if the government of the other country was involved.

4. Protocol to Prevent, Suppress and Punish Trafficking in Persons, Especially Women and Children, Supplementing the United Nations Convention Against Transnational Organized Crime, G.A. res. 55/25, annex II, 55 U.N. GAOR Supp. (No. 49) at 60, U.N. Doc. A/45/49, Vol. 1, 2001.

5. For instance, the removal of children's organs for medical reasons, with the consent of their parents, is acceptable.

6. Rome Statute of the International Criminal Court, 1999, article 7c <http://www.un.org/law/icc/statute/99-corr/1.html>.

7. The Rome Statute of the International Criminal Court came into operation in 2002, but among the powers that refused to agree to it were the United States, Russia, and China.

8. Bales and Robbins 2001. This article reviews definitions of slavery in international instruments.

Bibliography

NATIONAL AND INTERNATIONAL ARCHIVES

Afrique Occidental Française, Dakar, Senegal. (AOF)

Botswana National Archives, Gaborone. (BNA)

British Cabinet Papers, Public Record Office, Kew, U.K. (CAB)

British Colonial Office, Public Record Office, Kew, U.K. (CO)

British Colonial Office, confidential prints. (COCP)

British Foreign Office, Public Record Office, Kew, U.K. (FO, FCO)

British Foreign Office, confidential prints. (FOCP)

India Office, British Library, London, U.K. (IO)

Ministère des Affaires Étrangeres, Paris, France. (FMAE) Some reference numbers have been changed since the research was done for this work.

Archives Nationales, Section Outre-Mer, Aix-en-Provence, France. (ANSO)

Archives of the Department of State, College Park, Maryland, U.S. (USAN)

League of Nations Archives, Geneva, Switzerland. (LON)

National Archives of Nigeria, Ibadan. (NANI)

National Archives of Swaziland, Lobamba. (NAS)

COLLECTIONS OF PRIVATE PAPERS

Archives of the British Anti-Slavery Society, Rhodes House, Oxford and ASI, London. These files are catalogued to 1972 and are prefixed by AS and the reference number. Uncatalogued files,

1972–1981, are shown in references as AS 1972–1981, followed by the year and the number or name on the folder. Most files from 1972 to date are in ASI library, London.

The papers of Anthony Arkell, School of Oriental and African Studies, 2nd Batch, London.

The papers of René Claparède, League of Nations Archives, Geneva, Switzerland.

The papers of Lt. Col. A. Curle (in the possession of Mrs. Christian Curtis).

The papers of Frank de Halpert, Rhodes House, Oxford University, and the Hampshire Record Office, Winchester, U.K.

The papers of Frederick, Lord Lugard, Rhodes House, Oxford University, Oxford. These papers were given to me by Dame Margery Perham. I deposited them in Rhodes House, where they have now been catalogued, together with later deposits of Lugard papers that had been retained by Dame Margery. My references are to the date and recipient or sender.

United Nations Career Records Project (UNRCP), Bodleian Library, Oxford.

The papers of Daniel Sandford (extracts in the possession of Eleanor Casbon).

INTERVIEWS

Peter Davies, Chipstead, Surrey, 25 August 1988.

Kiponda wa Mavuo, Madina, Marafa, Kenya, 3 November 1974.

Janet Lim, Brisbane, Australia, 1–2 September 1989.

Patrick Montgomery, Buxted, Kent, 14–15 July 1981.

Jacob Oliel, Geneva, 2 August 1984.

OFFICIAL PUBLICATIONS

Child Labor Surveys: Results of Methodological Experiments in Four Countries 1992–93. ILO, Geneva.

Documents Relatifs à la Repression de la Traite des Esclaves, 1893–1913. Brussels Anti-Slave Trade Bureau, Ministère des Affaires Étrangères, Brussels, Belgium. (BMFA)

British and Foreign State Papers, HMSO, London. (*BFSP*)

Parliamentary Papers (British). (*PP*)

Instructions for the Guidance of H. M. Naval Officers engaged in the Suppression of the Slave Trade. This is in the Foreign Office Library and has been updated a number of times.

Lugard, F. D. 1906, *Confidential Instructions to Political Officers in Northern Nigeria on Subjects Chiefly Political and Administrative,* Waterlow and Sons, London.

IPEC Country Profile: El Salvador, 2000. ILO, Geneva.

IPEC Country Profile: United Republic of Tanzania, 2000. ILO, Geneva.

Eliminating the Worst Forms of Child Labor, IPEC pamphlets, 2001. ILO, Geneva.

Stopping Forced Labor: Global Report under the Follow-up to the ILO.

Declaration on Fundamental Principles and Rights at Work, 2001. ILO, Geneva.

Reports on Slavery from Member States 1923–1939. League of Nations, Geneva.

Reports of the Temporary Slavery Commission, 1924–1925. League of Nations, Geneva. (TSC)

Reports of the Committee of Experts on Slavery, 1932. League of Nations, Geneva. (CES)

Reports of the Advisory Committee of Experts on Slavery 1935–1938. League of Nations, Geneva. (ACE)

Proceedings of the League of Nations Assembly, Geneva.

Proceedings of the League of Nations Council, Geneva.

League of Nations Journal, Geneva.

Reports of the Working Group on Contemporary Forms of Slavery, United Nations, Geneva.

Reports of the Sub-Commission on Prevention of Discrimination and Protection of Minorities, United Nations, Geneva.

Reports of the Commission on Human Rights, United Nations, Geneva.

Human Rights: A Compilation of International Instruments, United Nations, New York 1978. (*HRI*)

U. S. Department of Labor Reports (periodic reports on labor questions such as Chinese "gulags").

U. S. Department of State Reports (periodic reports on Human Rights Issues, including trafficking, in various countries).

BOOKS, ARTICLES, AND PAPERS

Abdullah, Muhammad Morsey. 1978. *The United Arab Emirates: A Modern History*. Croom Helm: London.

Abir, M. 1968. *Ethiopia in the Era of the Princes: The Challenge of Islam and the Re-unification of the Christian Empire 1769–1855*. Longmans, Green and Co.: London.

Ahmad, Abdussamad H. 1999. "Trading in Slaves in Bela-Shangul and Gumuz, Ethiopia: Border Enclaves in History, 1897–1938." *JAH* 40, 1 (1999): 433–46.

Al-Amer, Muhammad. 1978. *The Hijaz under Ottoman Rule 1869–1914: Ottoman Vali, the Sharif of Mecca, and the Growth of British Influence*. Riyadh University Publications: Riyadh.

Ali, Abbas Ibrahim Muhammad. 1972. *The British, the Slave Trade and Slavery in the Sudan, 1820–1881*. Khartoum University Press: Khartoum.

Allen, Richard B. 1999. *Slaves, Freedmen, and Indentured Laborers in Colonial Mauritius.* Cambridge University Press: Cambridge.

Alpers, E., Gwyn Campbell, and Michael Salman, eds. Forthcoming. *Slavery and Resistance in Africa and Asia.* Vol.1: *Resistance to Slavery and Servitude in Asia and the Indian Ocean.* Vol. 2: *Bonds of Resistance.*

Altink, Sietske. 1995. *Stolen Lives: Trading Women into Sex and Slavery.* Scarlet Press: Chipping Norton, United Kingdom.

Anene, J. C. 1966. *Southern Nigeria in Transition 1885–1906.* Cambridge University Press: Cambridge.

Anstey, Roger. 1975. *The Atlantic Slave Trade and British Abolition 1760–1810.* Humanities Press: Atlantic Highlands, N.J.

———. 1979. "Slavery and the Protestant Ethic." In Michael Craton, ed., 157–72.

———. 1980. "The Pattern of British Abolitionism in the Eighteenth and Nineteenth Centuries." In C. Bolt and S. Drescher, eds., 19–41.

———. 1981(a). "Parliamentary Reform, Methodism and Anti-Slavery Politics, 1829–1833." *S & A* 2, 3: 211–26.

———. 1981(b). "Religion and British Slave Emancipation." In Eltis and Walvin, 37–61.

Archer, Leonie J., ed. 1988. *Slavery and Other Forms of Unfree Labour.* Routledge: London.

Ashworth, John. 1987. "The Relationship between Capitalism and Humanitarianism." *AHR Forum* 92, 4 (October). Also in Bender, ed., 1992, 180–99.

———. 1992. "Capitalism, Class and Antislavery." In Bender, ed., 263–89.

Asiegbu, Johnson U. J. 1969. *Slavery and the Politics of Liberation 1787–1861: A Study of Liberated African Emigration and British Anti-Slavery Policy.* Longmans: London.

Austen, Ralph A. 1977. "Slavery among the Coastal Middlemen: The Douala of Cameroon." In Miers and Kopytoff, 305–33.

Awad, Mohammed. 1966. *Report on Slavery.* United Nations: New York.

Baker, Randall. 1979. *King Hussein and the Kingdom of Hejaz.* Cambridge University Press: Cambridge.

Bales, Kevin. 1999. *Disposable People: New Slavery in the Global Economy.* University of California Press: Berkeley.

———. 2002. "The Social Psychology of Modern Slavery." *Scientific American* (April 2002): 1–8.

Bales, Kevin, and Peter T. Robbins. 2001. "No One Shall Be Held in Slavery or Servitude: A Critical Analysis of International Slavery Agreements and Concepts of Slavery." *Human Rights Review* 2, 2 (January–March): 18–45.

Balfour-Paul, Glen. 1991. *The End of Empire in the Middle East: Britain's Relinquishment of Power in Her Last Three Arab Dependencies.* Cambridge University Press: Cambridge.

Banaji, D. R. 1933. *Slavery in British India.* D. B. Taraporevala and Sons: Bombay, India.

Barber, James. 1968. *Imperial Frontier: A Study of Relations between the British and the Pastoral Tribes of North East Uganda.* East African Publishing House: Nairobi.

Barker, Anthony J. 1996. *Slavery and Antislavery in Mauritius, 1810–33.* MacMillan Press: Basingstoke.

Barth, Frederik. 1983. *Sohar: Culture and Society in an Omani Town.* Johns Hopkins University Press: Baltimore.

Bender, Thomas, ed. 1992. *The Antislavery Debate.* University of California Press: Berkeley.

Benedict, Burton. 1980. "Slavery and Indenture in Mauritius and Seychelles." In Watson, ed., 135–68.

Bethell, Leslie. 1970. *The Abolition of the Brazilian Slave Trade: Britain, Brazil and the Slave Trade Question 1807–1869.* Cambridge University Press: Cambridge.

Birmingham, David, and Phyllis Martin, eds. 1983. *History of Central Africa,* vol. 2. Longmans: London.

Blackburn, Robin. 1988 (a). *The Overthrow of Colonial Slavery, 1776–1848.* Verso: London.

———. 1988 (b). "Defining Slavery—Its Special Features and Social Role." In Archer, ed., 262–79.

Boahen, A. A. 1964. *Britain, the Sahara and the Western Sudan.* Clarendon Press: Oxford.

Bodman, Herbert L., and Nayereh Tohidi, eds. 1998. *Women in Muslim Societies: Diversity with Unity.* Lynne Rienner: Boulder, Colo.

Bola, Ahmed Bachir Abdalla. 2000. "Soudan: les séquelles de la honte." *Journal des Africanistes* 70, 1–2: 197–216.

Bolland, O. Nigel. 1986. "Labour Control and Resistance in Belize in the Century after 1838." *S & A* 7, 2: 175–87.

Bolt, Christine, and S. Drescher, eds. 1980. *Antislavery, Religion and Reform: Essays in Memory of Roger Anstey.* Dawson: Folkestone.

Bombay, Carl R. 1998. *Let My People Go!* Multnomah Publishers: Sisters, Oregon.

Botte, Roger, ed. 2000 (a). L'ombre portèe de l'esclavage: Avatars Contemporains de l'oppression sociale." *Journal des Africanistes* 70, 1–2.

Botte, Roger. 2000 (b). "De l'esclavage et du daltonisme dans les sciences socials." *Journal des Africanistes* 70, 1–2: 7–43.

Bouche, Denise. 1968. *Les Villages de Liberté en Afrique Noire Française 1887–1910.* Mouton and Co.: Paris.

Bouche, Denise. 1991. *Histoire de la Colonisation Française,* vol. 2, Flux et Refluxe (1815–1962). Fayard: France.

Bouhdiba, Abdelwahad. 1982. *Exploitation of Child Labor.* United Nations: New York. E/CN.4/Sub.2/479/Rev.1.

Boyd, Andrew. 1998. *Baroness Cox: A Voice for the Voiceless.* Lion Publishing: Oxford.

Bradley, Ian. 1985. "Wilberforce the Saint." In Hayward, ed., 69–85.

Brown, Carolyn A. 1996. "Testing the Boundaries of Marginality: Twentieth-Century Slavery and Emancipation Struggles in Nkanu, Northern Igboland, 1920–29." *JAH* 37: 51–80.

Brownlie, Ian. 1998. *Basic Documents on Human Rights,* 3rd edition. Clarendon Press: Oxford.

Brunschvig, R. 1960. "Abd." *Encyclopaedia of Islam,* new ed., I, pp. 24–40. E. J. Brill: Leiden.

Buell, R. L. 1928. *The Native Problem in Africa,* 2 vols. Macmillan: New York.

Burroughs, Peter. 1976. "The Mauritius Rebellion of 1832 and the Abolition of British Colonial Slavery." *JICH* 4: 243–65.

Burrows, Bernard. 1990. *Footnotes in the Sand: The Gulf in Transition 1963–1958.* Michael Russell: Salisbury.

Busch, B. C. 1971. *Britain, India and the Arabs, 1914–1921.* University of California Press: Berkeley.

Campbell, Gwyn, ed. Forthcoming. *Slave Systems in Asia and the Indian Ocean: Their Structure and Change in the Nineteenth Century,* 2 vols. Vol.1, *Slavery and Other Forms of Unfree Labor in Asia and the Indian Ocean.* Vol. 2, *Abolition and Its Aftermath in the Western Indian Ocean.* Frank Cass: London.

Caplan, Gerald L. 1970. *The Elites of Barotseland 1878–1969: A Political History of Zambia's Western Province.* C. Hurst and Co.: London.

Caplan, Lionel. 1980. "Power and Status in South Asian Slavery." In Watson, ed., 169–94.

Carter, Marina. 1993. "The Transition from Slave to Indentured Labour in Mauritius." *S & A* 14, 1: 114–30.

Casbon, Eleanor. 1993. *The Incurable Optimists: Chris and Dan Sandford of Ethiopia.* United Writers Publications Ltd.: Penzance, Cornwall.

Cassanelli, Lee V. 1988. "The Ending of Slavery in Italian Somalia: Liberty and the Control of Labor 1890–1935." In Miers and Roberts, eds., 308–31.

Cecil, Robert, Viscount Cecil of Chelwood. 1941. *A Great Experiment.* Jonathan Cape: London.

Chalise, Mahendra, et al. 2001. "A Step Towards Elimination of Slavery, Unfree Labor and Revolt in Nepal." Paper presented at the International Conference on Slavery, Unfree Labour and Revolt in Asia and the Indian Ocean Region, Avignon, 4–6 October.

Chatterjee, Indrani. 1999. *Gender, Slavery and Law in Colonial India.* Oxford University Press: Oxford.

———. Forthcoming. "Abolition by Denial: Slavery in South Asia after 1843." In Campbell, ed., vol. 2.

Chattopadhyay, A. K. 1977. *Slavery in the Bengal Presidency 1772–1843.* Golden Eagle: London.

Clarence-Smith, W. Gervase. 1979. *Slaves, Peasants and Capitalists in Southern Angola, 1840–1926.* Cambridge University Press: Cambridge.

———. 1985. *The Third Portuguese Empire 1825–1975: A Study in Economic Imperialism.* Manchester University Press: Manchester.

———. 1993 (a). "Cocoa Plantations and Coerced Labor in the Gulf of Guinea, 1870–1914." In Klein, ed., 150–70.

———. 1993 (b) "Labor Conditions in the Plantations of São Tomé and Principe, 1875–1914." In Twaddle, ed., 149–67.

Claridge, W. W. 1964 (first published 1915). *A History of the Gold Coast and Ashanti*, 2nd ed. Frank Cass: London.

Clark, Andrew F. 1994. "Slavery and Its Demise in the Upper Senegal Valley, West Africa, 1890–1920." *S & A* 15, 1: 51–71.

———. 1995. "Freedom Villages in the Upper Senegal Valley, 1887–1910: A Reassessment." *S & A* 16, 3: 311–30.

———. 1998. "The Ties That Bind: Servility and Dependency among the Fulbe of Bundu." In Miers and Klein, eds., 91–108.

———. 1999. *From Frontier to Backwater: Economy and Society in the Upper Senegal Valley (West Africa) 1850–1920.* University Press of America: Lanham, Md.

Clayton, A., and D. C. Savage. 1974. *Government and Labour in Kenya 1891–1963.* Frank Cass: London.

Conquest, Robert. 1978. *Kolyma: The Artic Death Camps.* Macmillan: London.

———. 1990. *The Great Terror: A Reassessment.* Oxford University Press: New York.

Conrad, Robert. 1972. *The Destruction of Brazilian Slavery 1850–1888.* University of California Press: Berkeley.

Cookey, S. J. S. 1968. *Britain and the Congo Question 1885–1913.* Longmans, Green and Co. Ltd.: London.

Cooper, Barbara M. 1997. *Marriage in Maradi: Gender and Culture in a Hausa Society in Niger, 1900–1989.* Heinemann and James Currey: Portsmouth, N.H.

Cooper, F. 1977. *Plantation Slavery on the East Coast of Africa.* Yale University Press: New Haven, Conn.

———. 1980. *Slaves to Squatters: Plantation Labor and Agriculture in Zanzibar and Coastal Kenya, 1890–1925.* Yale University Press: New Haven, Conn.

Coquery-Vidrovitch, C. 1972. *Le Congo au Temps des Grandes Companies Concessionaires, 1898–1930.* Mouton: Paris.

Cordell, Denis. 1988. "The Delicate Balance of Force and Flight: The End of Slavery in Eastern Ubangi-Shari." In Miers and Roberts eds., 150–71.

Corwin, Arthur. 1967. *Spain and the Abolition of Slavery in Cuba 1817–1886.* Institute of Latin American Studies, University of Texas Press: Austin.

Coupland, R. 1933 (1964). *The British Antislavery Movement.* Frank Cass: London (references are to the 1964 edition).

Crais, Clifton. 1990. "Slavery and Freedom Along a Frontier: The Eastern Cape, South Africa 1770–1838." *S & A* 11, 2: 190–215.

Craton, Michael. 1974. *Sinews of Empire: A Short History of British Slavery.* Temple Smith: London.

———, ed. 1979. "Historical Reflections: Roots and Branches." *Current Directions in Slave Studies* 6, 1.

———. 1985. "Emancipation from Below? The Role of the British West Indian Slaves in the Emancipation Movement, 1816–34." In Hayward, ed., 110–31.

———. 1988. "Continuity Not Change: The Incidence of Unrest among Ex-Slaves in the British West Indies, 1838–1876." *S & A* 9, 2: 144–70.

———. 1992. "The Transition from Slavery to Free Labour in the Caribbean 1790–1890: A Survey with Particular Reference to Recent Scholarship." *S & A* 13, 2: 37–67.

Crowder, Michael. 1988. *The Flogging of Phineas McIntosh: A Tale of Colonial Folly and Injustice, Bechuanaland 1933.* Yale University Press: New Haven, Conn.

Cumpston, I. M. 1953. *Indians Overseas in British Territories, 1834–1954.* Oxford University Press: London.

Curtin, Philip D. 1964. *The Image of Africa: British Ideas and Action, 1780–1850.* University of Wisconsin Press: Madison.

———. 1969. *The Atlantic Slave Trade: A Census.* University of Wisconsin Press: Madison.

Daget, Serge. 1980. "A Model of the French Abolitionist Movement and Its Variations." In Bolt and Drescher, eds., 64–79.

———. 1981. "France, Suppression of the Illegal Slave Trade, and England, 1817–1850." In Eltis and Walvin, eds., 193–217.

Darity, W. 1988. "The Williams Abolition Thesis before Williams." S & A 9, 1: 29–41.

Darley, Henry. 1972. First published 1926. *Slaves and Ivory: A Record of Adventure and Exploration in the Unknown Sudan, and Among the Abyssinian Slave Raiders.* Reprint by Metro Books Inc.: Northbrook, Ill.

Dasgupta, Keya. Forthcoming. "Plantation Labour in the Bramapura Valley: Regional Enclaves in a Colonial Set-Up, 1881–1921." In Campbell, ed., vol. 2, chapter 9.

Davenport, J. R. H. 1977. *South Africa: A Modern History.* University of Toronto Press: Toronto.

Davis, D. B. 1966. *The Problem of Slavery in Western Culture.* Cornell University Press: Ithaca, N.Y.

———. 1975. *The Problem of Slavery in the Age of Revolution 1770–1823.* Cornell University Press: Ithaca, N.Y. Chapters 1, 5, 8, are reproduced in Bender, ed. 1992.

———. 1980. "Slavery and Progress." In C. Bolt and S. Drescher, eds., 351–66.

———. 1984. *Slavery and Human Progress.* Oxford University Press: New York.

———. 1992. "The Perils of Doing History by Historical Abstraction: A Reply to Thomas L. Haskell's *AHR Forum* Reply." In Bender 1992, 290–309.

De Jonghe, E., ed. 1949. *Les Formes D'Asservissment dans les Sociètés Indigènes du Congo Belge.* Georges Van Campenhout: Brussels.

Delang, C. O., ed. 2000. *Suffering in Silence: The Human Right Nightmare of the Karen People of Burma,* Karen Human Rights Group, Universal Publishers: Parkland, Fla.

De Monfried, see Monfried.

Deschamps, Hubert. 1971. "French Colonial Policy in Tropical Africa between the Two World Wars." In Gifford and Louis, eds., 543–69.

Deutsch, Jan-Georg. 1998 and 1999. "The Freeing of the Slaves in German East Africa: the Statistical Record 1890–1914." In Miers and Klein, eds., 109–32.

———. 2001. "Slavery under German Colonial Rule in East Africa c.1860–1914." Habilitationsschrift, Humboldt: University at Berlin.

Ditchfield, G. M. 1980. "Repeal, Abolition, and Reform: A Study in the Interaction of Reforming Movements in the Parliament of 1790–1796." In Bolt and Drescher, eds., 101–18.

Donham, D., and Wendy James, eds. 1986. *The Southern Marches of Imperial Ethiopia: Essays in History and Social Anthropology.* Cambridge University Press: Cambridge.

Drescher, Seymour. 1977. *Econocide: British Slavery in the Era of Abolition.* University of Pittsburgh Press: Pittsburgh.

———. 1980. "Two Variants of Anti-slavery: Religious Organization and Social Mobilization in Britain and France, 1780–1870." In Bolt and Drescher, eds., 43–63.

———. 1986. "The Decline Thesis of British Slavery since Econocide." *S & A* 7, 1: 3–24.

———. 1987. *Capitalism and Antislavery: British Mobilization in Comparative Perspective.* Oxford University Press: Oxford.

———. 1988. "The Slaving Capital of the World: Liverpool and National Opinion in the Age of Abolition." *S & A* 9, 2: 128–43.

———. 1989. "Manumission in a Society without Slave Law: Eighteenth Century England." In McGlynn, ed., 85–101.

———. 2002. *The Mighty Experiment: Free Labor versus Slavery in British Emancipation.* Oxford University Press: Oxford.

Duffy, J. 1967. *A Question of Slavery.* Harvard University Press: Cambridge, Mass.

Dumett, Raymond E. 1981. "Pressure Groups, Bureaucracy, and the Decision-making Process: The Case of Slavery Abolition and Colonial Expansion in the Gold Coast, 1874." *JICH* 9, 2: 193–215.

Dumett, Raymond E., and Marion Johnson. 1988. "Britain and the Suppression of Slavery in the Gold Coast Colony, Ashanti, and the Northern Territories." In Miers and Roberts, eds., 71–116.

Duncan Rice, C. 1980. "Literary Sources and the Revolution in British Attitudes to Slavery." In Bolt and Drescher, eds., 319–34.

Echenberg, M. 1991. *Colonial Conscripts: The Tirailleurs Senegalais in French West Africa, 1857–1960.* Heinemann and James Currey: Portsmouth, N.H.

Eckert, Andreas. 1998 and 1999. "Slavery in Colonial Cameroon, 1880s–1930s." In Miers and Klein, eds., 133–48.

Eldredge, Elizabeth, and Fred Morton, eds. 1994. *Slavery in South Africa: Captive Labor on the Dutch Frontier.* Westview Press: Boulder, Colo.

El Hamel, Chouki. 2001. "Race, Slavery and Islam in the Maghrebi Mediterranean Thinking: The Question of the *Haratin* in Morocco." Paper presented at the African Studies Association Annual Meeting, Houston, Texas, 15–18 November.

Elphick, Richard, and Hermann Giliomee, eds., 2nd ed., 1988. *The Shaping of South African Society, 1652–1840.* Wesleyan University Press: Middletown, Conn.

Eltis, David. 1981. "The Impact of Abolition on the Atlantic Slave Trade." In Eltis and Walvin, eds., 155–75.

———. 1982. "Abolitionist Perceptions of Society After Slavery." In Walvin, ed., 201–202.

———. 1987. *Economic Growth and the Ending of the Transatlantic Slave Trade.* Oxford University Press: Oxford.

———. 1993. "Labour and Coercion in the English Atlantic World from the Seventeenth to the Early Twentieth Century." *S & A* 14, 1 (April) Special Issue, Michael Twaddle, ed., 207–22.

Eltis, David, and James Walvin, eds. 1981. *The Abolition of the Atlantic Slave Trade.* University of Wisconsin Press: Madison.

Engerman, Stanley L. 1981. "Some Implications of the Abolition of the Slave Trade." In Eltis and Walvin, eds., 3–17.

———. 1982. "Economic Adjustments to Emancipation in the United States and British West Indies." *Journal of Interdisciplinary Studies* 13, 2: 195–205.

———. 1985. "Economic Change and Contract Labour in the British Caribbean: The End of Slavery and the Adjustment to Emancipation." In Richardson, ed., 225–44.

Engerman, Stanley L., and David Eltis. 1980. "Economic Aspects of the Abolition Debate." In Bolt and Drescher, eds., 272–93.

Ennew, Judith. 1981. *Debt Bondage: A Survey.* ASI Report no. 4, London.

Eno, Omar. Forthcoming. "Abolition and Its Impact on the Benadir Coast." In Campbell, ed., vol. 1.

Ensor, R. C. K. 1966. *England 1870–1914.* Clarendon Press: Oxford.

Evans-Pritchard, E. E. 1949. *The Sanusi of Cyrenaica.* Clarendon Press: Oxford.

Ewald, Janet. 1990. *Soldiers, Traders, and Slaves: State Formation and Economic Transformation in the Greater Nile Valley, 1700–1885.* University of Wisconsin Press: Madison.

Falola, Toyin, and Paul Lovejoy, eds. 1994. *Pawnship in Africa: Debt Bondage in Historical Perspective.* Westview Press: Boulder, Colo.

Finley, M. I. 1980. *Ancient Slavery and Modern Ideology.* Chatto and Windus: London.

Fogel, Robert William. 1991. *Without Consent or Contract: The Rise and Fall of American Slavery.* W. W. Norton: New York. First published 1989.

Foner, Eric. 1983. *Nothing but Freedom: Emancipation and Its Legacy.* Louisiana State University: Baton Rouge.

———. 1994. *Slavery and Freedom in Nineteenth-Century America: An Inaugural Lecture Delivered before the University of Oxford on 17 May 1994.* Clarendon Press: Oxford.

Forster, S., W. J. Mommsen, and Ronald Robinson, eds. 1988. *Bismarck, Europe and Africa: The Berlin West Africa Conference 1884–1885 and the Onset of Partition.* The German Historical Institute, London. Oxford University Press: Oxford.

Fraginals, M. M., F. M. Pons, and S. Engerman, eds. 1985. *Between Slavery and Free Labor: The Spanish Speaking Caribbean in the Nineteenth Century.* Johns Hopkins University Press: Baltimore.

Fromkin, David. 1989. *A Peace to End All Peace: The Fall of the Ottoman Empire and the Creation of the Modern Middle East.* Avon Books: New York.

Gann, L. H. 1988. "The Berlin Conference and the Humanitarian Conscience." In Forster, Mommsen, and Robinson, eds., 321–31.

Garretson, P. 1986. "Vicious Cycles: Ivory, Slaves and Arms on the New Maji Frontier, Southern Marches." In Donham and James, eds., 196–218.

Gavin, R. J. 1962. "The Bartle Frere Mission to Zanzibar, 1873." *The Historical Journal* 5: 122–48.

———. 1975. *Aden under British Rule 1939–1967.* Barnes and Noble: New York.

Getz, Trevor. Forthcoming. *Slavery and Reform in West Africa: Towards Emancipation in Nineteenth-Century Senegal and the Gold Coast.* Ohio University Press: Athens.

Gide, André. 1962, trans. First published 1927. *Travels in the Congo.* University of California Press: Berkeley.

Gifford, P., and Wm. Roger Louis, eds. 1971. *France and Britain in Africa: Imperial Rivalry and Colonial Rule.* Yale University Press: New Haven, Conn.

Ginneken, Anique van. 1996. "Forced Labour as Seen from Geneva: The Situation in the League of Nations Mandates." Seen in mss.

Goldberg, Jacob. 1986. *The Foreign Policy of Saudi Arabia: The Formative Years, 1902–18.* Harvard University Press: Cambridge, Mass.

Grace, J. 1975. *Domestic Slavery in West Africa: With Particular Reference to the Sierra Leone Protectorate, 1896–1927.* Frederick Muller Ltd.: London.

Grandclément, Daniel. 1990. *L'incroyable Henry de Monfried.* Bernard Grasset: Paris.

Gray, Richard. 1961. *A History of the Southern Sudan 1839–1889.* Oxford University Press: London.

Green, William A. 1976. *British Slave Emancipation: The Sugar Colonies and the Great Experiment 1830–65.* Clarendon Press: Oxford.

———. 1985. "Was British Emancipation a Success?" In Richardson, ed., 183–202.

Green-Pederson, Svend E. 1981. "Slave Demography in the Danish West Indies and the Abolition of the Danish Slave Trade." In Walvin and Eltis, eds., 231–57.

Grey of Falloden, Viscount, 1925. *Twenty-Five Years, 1892–1916,* 2 vols. Hodder and Stoughton: London.

Griffith, W. B. 1987. *Ordinances of the Settlements on the Gold Coast and of the Gold Coast Colony in Force April 1887.* Stevens and Son: London.

Guyer, Jane I. 1987. *Women and the State in Africa: Marriage Law, Inheritance and Resettlement.* Boston University African Studies Center, Boston University, Working Paper no. 129, Boston.

Hailey, Lord. 1945. *An African Survey: A Study of Problems Arising in Africa South of the Sahara,* 2nd edition. Oxford University Press: London.

Halbersleben, Karen I. 1993. *Women's Participation in the British Antislavery Movement 1824–1865.* E. Mellen Press: Lewiston, N.Y.

Hamilton, David. 1967. "Imperialism Ancient and Modern: A Study of English Attitudes to the Claims to Sovereignty to the Northern Somali Coastline." *Journal of Ethiopian Studies* 5, July: 9–35.

Hanna, A. J. 1956. *The Beginnings of Nyasaland and North Eastern Rhodesia 1859–95.* Clarendon Press: Oxford.

Hargey, Taj. 1981. "The Suppression of Slavery in the Sudan 1898–1939." D. Phil. diss., Oxford University: Oxford.

———. 1998. "Festina Lente: Slavery Policy and Practice in the Anglo-Egyptian Sudan." In Miers and Klein, eds., 250–72.

Harris, Alice, and John Harris. autobiographical notes, ASI Library, London.

Harris, John. 1912. *Dawn in Darkest Africa.* E. P. Dutton and Co.: London.

Harris, Joseph E. 1971. *The African Presence in Asia: Consequences of the East African Slave Trade.* Northwestern University Press: Evanston, Ill.

Harrison, Brian. 1980. "A Genealogy of Reform in Modern Britain." In Bolt and Drescher, eds., 119–48.

Haskell, Thomas L. 1985 (a). "Capitalism and the Origins of Human Sensibility, Part 1." *AHR* 90, 2 (April), reprinted in Bender, ed. 1992, 107–35.

———. 1985 (b). "Capitalism and the Origins of Human Sensibility, Part 2." *AHR* 90, 3 (June). Reprinted in Bender, ed. 1992, 136–60.

———. 1987. "Convention and Hegemonic Interest in the Debate over Antislavery: A Reply to Davis and Ashworth." *AHR Forum* 92, 4 (October). Reprinted in Bender, Thomas, ed., 200–59.

Hawley, Donald. 1970. *Trucial States.* Allen and Unwin: London.

Hay, Rupert. 1959. *The Persian Gulf States.* Mid-East Institute, Washington, D.C.

Hay, Margaret Jean, and Maracia Wright, eds. 1982. *African Women and the Law: Historical Perspectives.* Boston University Papers on Africa, No. 7, Boston.

Hay, Margaret Jean, and Sharon Stitcher, eds. 1984. *African Women South of the Sahara.* Longmans: London.

Hayward, Jack, ed. 1985. *Out of Slavery: Abolition and After 1833–1983.* Frank Cass: London.

Heard-Bey, Frauke. 1982. *From Trucial States to United Arab Emirates: A Society in Transition.* Longmans: Harlow Essex.

Herlehy, Thomas J., and F. Morton. 1988. "A Coastal Ex-Slave Community in the Regional and Colonial Economy of Kenya: The WaMisheni of Rabai, 1880–1963." In Miers and Roberts, 254–81.

Hertslet, E. 1840–1924. *Commercial Treaties,* London, 30 vols.

Hertslet, L. and E. 1909, reprinted 1967. *The Map of Africa by Treaty,* 3rd ed., 3 vols. Frank Cass: London.

Heywood, Linda M. 1988. "Slavery and Forced Labor in the Changing Political Economy of Central Angola, 1850–1949." In Miers and Roberts, eds., 415–36.

Hickey, Dennis. 1984. "Ethiopia and Great Britain, Political Conflict in the Southern Borderlands 1916–1936." Ph. D. diss., Northwestern University.

Higman, B. W. 1976. *Slave Population and Economy in Jamaica 1807–1834.* Cambridge University Press: Cambridge.

———. 1984. *Slave Populations of the British Caribbean 1807–1834.* Johns Hopkins University Press: Baltimore.

Hitchcock, R. K. 1978. *Kalahari Cattle Posts: A Regional Study of Hunter-Gatherers, Pastoralists, and Agriculturists in the Western Sandveld Region, Central District, Botswana,* 2 vols. Ministry of Local Government and Lands: Gaborone.

Hjejle, B. 1966. "Slavery and Agricultural Bondage in South India in the Nineteenth Century." *The Scandinavian Economic History Review* 14, 2: 71–126.

Hochschild, Adam. 1999. *King Leopold's Ghost: A Story of Greed, Terror and Heroism in Colonial Africa.* Houghton and Mifflin: Boston.

Hodges, Tony, and Malyn Newitt. 1988. *São Tomé and Principe: From Plantation Colony to Microstate.* Westview Press: Boulder, Colo.

Hogendorn, J. S., and Paul E. Lovejoy. 1988. "The Reform of Slavery in Early Colonial Nigeria." In Miers and Roberts, eds., 391–414.

Holden, David, and Richard Johns. 1981. *The House of Saud: The Rise and Rule of the Most Powerful Dynasty in the Arab World.* Pan Books: London.

Hollis, Patricia. 1974. *Pressure from Without in Early Victorian England.* Edward Arnold: London.

———. 1980. "Anti-Slavery and British Working-Class Radicalism in the Years of Reform." In Bolt and Drescher, eds., 294–315.

Holmboe, K. 1936. *Desert Encounter: An Adventurous Journey through Italian Africa.* George Harrap: London. First published in Danish in 1931.

Hoskins, Janet. Forthcoming. "Slaves, Brides and Other 'Gifts': Resistance, Marriage and Rank in Eastern Indonesia." In Alpers, Campbell, and Salman, eds., vol. 2.

Howarth, David. 1965, 1980. *The Desert King: The Life of Ibn Saud.* Quartet Books: London.

Hutson, Alaine. 2002. "Enslavement and Manumission of Africans and Yemenis in Saudi Arabia, 1926–1938." *Critique* 11, 1: 49–70.

Iadarola, A. 1975. "Ethiopia's Admission to the League of Nations: An Assessment of Motives." *IJAHS* 8: 601–22.

Igbafe, P. A. 1975. "Slavery and Emancipation in Benin 1897–1945." *JAH* 15, 3: 409–29.

———. 1979. *Benin under British Administration: The Impact of Colonial Rule on an African Kingdom 1897–1938.* Humanities Press: Atlantic Highlands, N.J.

Ingrams, Doreen. 1970. *A Time in Arabia.* John Murray: London.

Ingrams, W. H. 1936. *A Report on the Social, Economic and Political Condition of the Hadhramaut.* Colonial no. 123, HSO London.

———. 1966. *Arabia and the Isles,* 3rd ed. John Murray: London.

Isaacman, Allen, and Barbara Isaacman. 1983. *Mozambique: From Colonialism to Revolution, 1900–1982.* Westview Press: Boulder, Colo.; and Gower: Hampshire, England.

James, Wendy. 1988. "Perceptions from an African Slaving Frontier." In Archer, ed., 130–41.

Jaschok, Maria. 1988. *Concubines and Bondservants: The Social History of a Chinese Custom.* Zed Books: London.

———. 1994. "Chinese 'Slave' Girls in Yunan-Fu: Saving (Chinese) Womanhood and (Western) Souls, 1930–1991." In Jaschok and Miers, eds., 171–97.

Jaschok, Maria, and Suzanne Miers, eds. 1994. *Women and Chinese Patriarchy: Submission, Servitude and Escape.* Zed Books Ltd. and Hong Kong University Press: London.

Jewsiewicki, B. 1986. "Rural Society and the Belgian Colonial Economy." In Birmingham and Martin, eds., 95–125.

Jewsiewicki, B., and Mumbanza Mwa Bawele. 1981. "The Social Context of Slavery in Equatorial Africa in the Nineteenth and Twentieth Centuries." In Lovejoy, ed.

Johansen, Hans Christian. 1981. "The Reality behind the Demographic Arguments to Abolish the Danish Slave Trade." In Eltis and Walvin, eds., 221–30.

Johnson, Douglas. 1988. "Sudanese Military Slavery from the Eighteenth to the Twentieth Century." In Archer, ed., 142–56.

Jonghe, Ed. de, ed., see de Jonghe.

Jumare, Ibrahim M. 1994. "The Late Treatment of Slavery in Sokoto: Background and Consequences of the 1936 Proclamation." *IJAHS* 27, 2: 303–22.

Jumeer, Musleem 2000. "Slave Systems in Mauritius: Structure and Change (Eighteenth to Twentieth Centuries)." Paper presented at the International Workshop on Slave Systems in Asia and the Indian Ocean, Avignon, 18–20 May.

Kamara, Ousmane. 2000. "Les divisions statutaire des descendants d'esclaves au Fuuta Tooro mauritanien." *Journal des Africanistes* 70, 1-2: 265–89.

Kea, Ray A. 1995. "Plantations and Labor in the South-East Gold Coast from the Late Eighteenth to the Mid-Nineteenth Century." In Law, ed.

Kelly, J. B. 1964. *Eastern Arabian Frontiers.* Faber and Faber: London.

Klein, Martin A. 1988. "Slave Resistance and Slave Emancipation in Coastal Guinea." In Miers and Roberts, eds., 203–19.

———, ed. 1993. *Breaking the Chains: Slavery, Bondage, and Emancipation in Modern Africa and Asia.* University of Wisconsin Press: Madison.

———. 1993 (a). "Slavery and Emancipation in French West Africa." In Klein, ed., 171–96.

———. 1993 (b). "Introduction: Modern European Expansion and Traditional Servitude in Africa and Asia." In Klein, ed., 3–36.

———. 1998. *Slavery and Colonial Rule in French West Africa.* Cambridge University Press: Cambridge.

Kloosterboer, W. 1960. *Involuntary Labour since the Abolition of Slavery: A Survey of Compulsory Labour throughout the World.* E. J. Brill: Leiden.

Knight, Franklin W. 1970. *Slave Society in Cuba during the Nineteenth Century.* University of Wisconsin Press: Madison.

Koh, Choo Chin. 1994. "Implementing Government Policy for the Protection of Women and Girls in Singapore, 1948–66: Recollections of a Social Worker." In Jaschok and Miers, eds., 122–40.

Kopytoff, Igor, and Suzanne Miers. 1977. "African 'Slavery' as an Institution of Marginality." In Miers and Kopytoff, eds., 3–81.

Korey, William. 1998. *NGOs and the Universal Declaration of Human Rights: A Curious Grapevine.* St. Martin's Press: New York.

Kumar, Dharma. 1993. "Colonialism, Bondage, and Caste in British India." in Klein, ed., 112–30.

Law, Robin, ed. 1995. *From Slave Trade to "Legitimate Commerce": The Commercial Transition in Nineteenth-Century West Africa*. Cambridge University Press: Cambridge.

Lee-Wright, Peter. 1990. *Child Slaves*. Earthscan Publications: London.

Levine, Nancy E. 1980. "Opposition and Interdependence: Demographic and Economic Perspectives on Nyinba Slavery." In Watson, ed., 195–222.

Lewis, Bernard. 1990. *Race and Slavery in the Middle East: An Historical Inquiry*. Oxford University Press: Oxford.

Lewis, Sasha G. 1980. *Slave Trade Today: American Exploitation of Illegal Aliens*. Beacon Press: Boston.

Likaka, Osumaka. 1997. *Rural Society and Cotton in Colonial Zaire*. University of Wisconsin Press: Madison.

Lim, Janet. 1958. *Sold for Silver: An Autobiography by Janet Lim*. William Collins and Sons: London. Reprinted 1985, Oxford University Press: Singapore.

Livingstone, David. 1857. *Missionary Travels and Researches in South Africa*. John Murray: London.

Lloyd, Christopher. 1968. *The Navy and the Slave Trade: The Suppression of the African Slave Trade in the Nineteenth Century*. Frank Cass: London.

Louis, Wm. Roger. 1967. *Great Britain and Germany's Lost Colonies 1914–1919*. Clarendon Press: Oxford.

Louis, Wm. Roger, and Jean Stengers. 1968. *E. D. Morel's History of the Congo Reform Movement*. Clarendon Press: Oxford.

Lovejoy, Paul E. 1981. "Slavery in the Context of Ideology." In Lovejoy, ed., 11–38.

———, ed. 1981. *The Ideology of Slavery in Africa*. Sage Publications: Beverley Hills.

———. 1983. *Transformations in Slavery: A History of Slavery in Africa*. Cambridge University Press: London.

Lovejoy, Paul E., and Jan S. Hogendorn. 1993. *Slow Death for Slavery: The Course of Abolition in Northern Nigeria, 1897–1936*. Cambridge University Press: Cambridge.

Lugard, F. D. 1893. *The Rise of Our East African Empire: Early Efforts in Nyasaland and Uganda*, 2 vols. William Blackwood and Sons: London.

———. 1964. First published 1922. *The Dual Mandate in British Tropical Africa*. Archon Books: Hamden, Conn.

Lunt, James. 1981. *Imperial Sunset: Frontier Soldiering in the Twentieth Century*. Macdonald Futura: London.

Mackenzie, K. 1952. "Great Britain and the Abolition of the Slave Trade by Other Powers (1812–22)." B. Litt. thesis, Oxford University.

Mahmud, U. A., and S. Baldo. 1987. *The Diein Massacre: Slavery in the Sudan.* Sudan Relief and Rehabilitation Association: London.

Manchuelle, François. 1987. "Forced Labor in French West Africa, 1881–1946." Paper presented at the African Studies Association Meeting, Denver, 22 November.

———. 1989. "The Patriarchal Ideal of Soninke Labor Migrants in West Africa from Slave Owners to Employers of Free Labor Migrants." *CJAS* 23: 106–25.

———. 1997. *Willing Migrants: Soninke Labor Diasporas, 1848–1960.* Ohio University Press: Athens; James Currey: London.

Marcus, Harold G. 1975. *The Life and Times of Menelik II: Ethiopia 1844–1913.* Clarendon Press: Oxford.

———. 1995. First published 1987. *Haile Sellassie I: The Formative Years, 1892–1936.* Red Sea Press: Lawrenceville, N.J.

Marks, Shula, and P. Richardson, eds. 1984. *International Labour Migration: Historical Perspectives.* Maurice Temple Smith: London.

Maugham, Robin. 1961. *The Slaves of Timbuktu.* Harper and Brothers: New York.

Mbodji, Mohamed. 1993. "The Abolition of Slavery in Senegal, 1820–1890: Crisis or the Rise of a New Entrepreneurial Class." In Klein, ed., 197–211.

McCalman, Iain. 1986. "Anti-Slavery and Ultra-Radicalism in Early Nineteenth-Century England: The Case of Robert Wedderburn." *S & A* 7, 2: 99–117.

McDougall, E. Ann. 1988. "A Topsy-Turvy World: Slaves and Freed Slaves in the Mauritanian Adrar, 1910–1950." In Miers and Roberts, eds., 362–88.

McGlynn, Frank, ed. 1989. *Perspectives on Manumission.* Special issue of *S & A* 10, 3 (December).

McSheffrey, G. 1983. "Slavery, Indentured Servitude, Legitimate Trade and the Impact of Abolition in the Gold Coast, 1874–1901: A Reappraisal." *JAH* 24, 3 (1983): 349–68.

Meillassoux, Claude. 1975. *L'esclavage en Afrique Précoloniale: Dix-sept études présentées par Claude Meillassoux.* François Maspero: Paris.

———. 1991. Translation, first published in French 1986. *The Anthropology of Slavery: The Womb of Iron and Gold.* University of Chicago Press: Chicago.

Meltzer, M. 1993. *Slavery: A World History.* Da Capo Press: New York.

Mercer, John. 1981. *Slavery in Mauritania Today.* ASI: London.

Messaoud, Boubacar. 2000. "L'esclavage en Mauritanie: De l'idèology du silence à la mise en question." *Journal des Africanistes* 70, 1-2: 291–337.

Metcalfe, G. E. 1964. *Great Britain and Documents of Ghana History 1807–1957.* University of Ghana Press: Legon.

Midgley, Clare. 1992. *Women against Slavery: The British Campaigns, 1780–1870.* Routledge: London.

Miège, J. L. 1961. *Le Maroc et L'Europe (1830–1894),* 4 vols. Presses Universitaires de France: Paris.

Miers, Suzanne. 1975. *Britain and the Ending of the Slave Trade.* Longmans: London.

———. 1988. "Humanitarianism at Berlin: Myth or Reality." In Forster, Mommsen, and Robinson, eds., 333–45.

———. 1989. "Diplomacy versus Humanitarianism: Britain and Consular Manumission in Hijaz, 1921–1936." In McGlynn, ed., 102–28.

———. 1994. "Mui Tsai through the Eyes of the Victim: Janet Lim's Story of Bondage and Escape." In Jaschok and Miers, eds.

———. 1997. "Britain and the Suppression of Slavery in Ethiopia." *S & A* 18, 3 (December): 257–88.

———. 1998. "Slave Raiding, Cattle Rustling and Ivory Poaching in the Ethiopian Borderlands. How Plausible Was Darley?" Paper presented at the African Studies Association Annual Meeting, Chicago, 29 October–1 November.

———. 2000 (a). "Slavery to Freedom in Sub-Saharan Africa: Expectations and Reality." In Temperley, ed., 238–64.

———. 2000 (b). "Contemporary Forms of Slavery." *CJAHS* 34: 714–47.

———. Forthcoming(a). "Slavery and the Slave Trade in Saudi Arabia and the Persian Gulf States 1920s-1960s." In Campbell, ed., vol. 2.

———. Forthcoming(b). "Slave Resistance and Rebellion in the Aden Protectorate in the 1930s and 1940s." In Alpers, Campbell, and Salmon, eds., vol. 1.

Miers, Suzanne, and Michael Crowder. 1988. "The Politics of Slavery in Bechuanaland: Power Struggles and the Plight of the Basarwa in Bamangwato Reserve, 1926–1940." In Miers and Roberts, eds., 172–200.

Miers, Suzanne, and Martin A. Klein, eds. 1999. *Slavery and Colonial Rule in Africa.* Frank Cass: London. First published as an occasional volume in *S &A* 19, 2 (August 1998).

Miers, Suzanne, and Igor Kopytoff, eds. 1977. *Slavery in Africa: Historical and Anthropological Perspective.* University of Wisconsin Press: Madison.

Miers, Suzanne, and Richard Roberts, eds. 1988. *The End of Slavery in Africa.* University of Wisconsin Press: Madison.

Miners, Norman. 1987. *Hong Kong under Imperial Rule, 1912–1941.* Oxford University Press: Hong Kong.

Minority Rights Group, Report no. 47, 1980. *Female Circumcision, Excision and Infibulation, the Facts and Proposals for Change.* MRG: London.

Monfried, Henry de. 1934. *Secrets of the Red Sea* (translated from French). Faber and Faber: London.

Montana, Ismael Musa. 2001. "Islamic Law, the Religious Establishment and the Abolition of Slavery in the Regency of Tunis." Paper presented at the Annual Meeting, African Studies Association, Houston, Texas, 15–18 November.

Montgomery, J.R. Patrick. "Once Is Enough." UN Career Records Project (UNRCP), Bodleian Library, Oxford.

———. "The Human Rights Contribution of NGOs." UNRCP, Bodleian Library, Oxford.

Morrell, E. D. 1906. *Red Rubber: The Story of the Rubber Slave Trade Flourishing in the Congo in the Year of Grace 1906.* Allen and Unwin: London.

Morris, James. 1957. *Sultan in Oman: Venture into the Middle East.* Pantheon Books: New York.

Morton, R.F. 1994. "Captive Labor in the Western Transvaal after the Sand River Convention." In Eldredge and Morton, eds., 167–85.

Muhsen, Zana, with Andrew Crofts. 1991. *Sold: One Woman's Account of Modern Slavery.* Futura: London.

Mundle, Sudipto. 1986. "Debt Bondage in Colonial Palamau: A Re-examination of the Servitude Hypothesis." Paper presented at the Ninth International Economic History Congress, Berne.

Murray, David. 1980. *Odious Commerce: Britain, Spain and the Abolition of the Cuban Slave Trade.* Cambridge University Press: London.

Nelson, Samuel H. 1994. *Colonialism in the Congo Basin 1880–1940.* Ohio University Center for International Studies, Athens.

Newbury, C. W. 1965. *British Policy towards West Africa: Select Documents 1786–1874.* Clarendon Press: Oxford.

———. 1971. *British Documents towards West Africa: Select Documents 1875–1914: With Statistical Appendices 1800–1914.* Clarendon Press: Oxford.

———. 2000. "Patrons, Clients and Empire: The Subordination of Indigenous Hierarchies in Asia and Africa." *Journal of World History* 11, 2: 227–63.

Newbury, Gertrude E., and C. W. Newbury. 1976. "Labor Charters and Labor Markets: The ILO and Africa in the Interwar Period." *Journal of African Studies* 3, 3 (1976): 311–27.

Newitt, Malyn. 1981. *Portugal in Africa: The Last Hundred Years.* Longmans: Harwell, Essex.

Nicholls, C. S. 1971. *The Swahili Coast, Policy, Diplomacy and Trade on the East African Littoral, 1798–1856.* Allen and Unwin: London.

Norregard, Georg. 1966. *Danish Settlements in West Africa 1658–1850.* Boston University Press: Boston.

Northedge, F. S. 1986. *The League of Nations: Its Life and Times 1920–1946.* Leicester University Press: Leicester.

Northrup, David. 1988 (a). "The Ending of Slavery in the Eastern Belgian Congo." In Miers and Roberts, eds., 462–82.

————. 1988 (b). *Beyond the Bend in the River: African Labor in Eastern Zaire, 1865–1940.* Ohio University Center for International Studies: Athens.

————. 1995. *Indentured Labor in the Age of Imperialism 1834–1922.* Cambridge University Press: Cambridge.

Nwulia, Moses D. 1981. *The History of Slavery in Mauritius and the Seychelles, 1810–1875.* Fairleigh Dickenson University Press: Rutherford, N.J.

Ochsenwald, W. 1980. *Religion, Society and the State in Arabia: The Hijaz under Ottoman Control, 1840–1908.* Ohio State University: Columbus.

Ohadike, D. 1988. "The Decline of Slavery among the Igbo People." In Miers and Roberts, eds., 437–61.

O'Hear, Ann. 1997. *Power Relations in Nigeria: Ilorin Slaves and Their Successors.* University of Rochester Press: Rochester, N.Y.

Okia, Opolot. 2000. "The Northey Crisis: A Symptomatic Reading." Paper presented at the annual meeting of the African Studies Association, Nashville, Tennessee, 16–18 November.

Oliver, Roland. 1965 (2nd ed.). *The Missionary Factor in East Africa.* Longmans: London.

O'Shea, Raymond. 1947. *The Sand Kings of Oman.* Methuen and Co.: London.

Packwood, C. O. 1975. *Chained on the Rock: Slavery in Bermuda.* Eliseo Torres and Sons: New York.

Parsons, Neil. 1988. Prologue in Parsons and Crowder, eds., xi–xxiv.

Parsons, Neil, and Michael Crowder, eds. 1988. *Monarch of All I Survey: Bechuanaland Diaries 1929–37 by Sir Charles Rey.* Botswana Society, Gaborone, and L. Barber Press: New York.

Paterson, Orlando. 1991. *Freedom in the Making of Western Culture.* Basic Books: New York.

Patterson, Orlando. 1982. *Slavery and Social Death: A Comparative Study.* Harvard University Press: Cambridge, Mass.

Peires, J. B. 1988. "The British and the Cape 1814–1834." In Elphick and Giliomee, eds., 472–518.

Perham, Margery. 1969. *The Government of Ethiopia*, 2nd ed., Northwestern University Press: Evanston, Ill.

———. 1956. *Lugard: The Years of Adventure 1858–1898.* Collins: London.

———. 1960. *Lugard: The Years of Authority 1898–1945.* Collins: London.

Philby, H. St. John. 1957. *Forty Years in the Wilderness.* Robert Hale Ltd.: London.

Plant, Roger. 1987. *Sugar and Modern Slavery.* Zed Books: London.

Prakash, Gyan. 1993. "Terms of Servitude: The Colonial Discourse on Slavery and Bondage in India." In Klein, ed., 131–49.

Prouty, Chris, and Eugene Rosenfeld. 1981. *Historical Dictionary of Ethiopia.* Scarecrow Press: Metuchen, N.J.

Ramm, Agatha. 1944. "Great Britain and the Planting of Italian Power in the Red Sea 1868–85." *English Historical Review* 59: 211–36.

Rashid, Ismail. 1998 (1999). "Do Daddy nor lef me Make dem Carry me: Slave Resistance and Emancipation in Sierra Leone, 1894–1928." In Miers and Klein, eds., 208–31.

Rawley, James A. 1993. "London's Defence of the Slave Trade 1787–1807." *S &A* 14, 2: 48–69.

Renault, François. 1971. *Lavigerie, l'esclavage Africain et L'Europe,* vol. 1: *Afrique Centrale,* vol. 2: *Campagne antiesclavagiste.* De Bocard: Paris.

———. 1975. *L'abolition de l'esclavage au Sénégal: L'attitude de l'administration française, 1848–1905.* Société Française de l'histoire d'Outre-Mer: Paris.

———. 1976. *Libération d'esclaves et nouvelle servitude: Les rachats de captifs Africains pour le compte des colonies francaises après L'abolition de L'esclavage.* Les Nouvelles Éditions Africaines: Abidjan.

Richardson, D., ed. 1985. *Abolition and Its Aftermath: The Historical Context, 1790–1916.* Frank Cass: London.

Roberts, Karen. 1992. "Slavery and Freedom in the Ten Years War, Cuba, 1868–1878." *S & A* 13, 3: 181–200.

Roberts, Richard L. 1987. *Warriors, Merchants and Slaves: The State and the Economy in the Middle Niger Valley, 1700–1914.* Stanford University Press: Stanford, Calif.

———. 1988. "The End of Slavery in the French Soudan, 1905–1914." In Miers and Roberts, eds., 282–303.

Roberts, Richard L., and Martin A. Klein. 1980. "The Banamba Slave Exodus of 1905 and the Decline of Slavery in the Western Sudan." *JAH* 21: 375–94.

Robertson, Adam, and Shisham Mishra. 1997. "Nepal: The Struggle against the Kamaiya System of Bonded Labor." In *Enslaved Peoples in the 1990s,* ASI and International Work Group for Indigenous Affairs (IWGIA), Copenhagen, Document no. 83, 83–106.

Robertson, Clare C., and Martin A. Klein, eds. 1983. *Women and Slavery in Africa.* University of Wisconsin Press: Madison.

Rodney, Walter. 1981. *A History of the Guyanese Working People, 1881–1905.* Johns Hopkins University Press: Baltimore.

Romero, P. W. 1986. "Where Have All the Slaves Gone? Emancipation and Post–Emancipation in Lamu, Kenya." *JAH* 27, 3: 497–512.

———. 1997. *Lamu: History, Society, and Family in an East African Port City.* Marcus Wiener: Princeton, N.J.

Ross, E. A. 1925. *Report on Employment of Native Labor in Portuguese Africa.* Abbott Press: New York.

Ross, Robert. 1993. "Emancipation and the Economy of the Cape Colony." *S & A* 14, 1: 131–48.

Rubin, V., and A. Tuden, eds. 1977. *Comparative Perspectives on Slavery in New World Plantation Societies.* Annals of the New York Academy of Sciences, CCXCCI (1977): 343–67.

Ruf, Urs Peter. 2000. "Du neuf dans le vieux: La situation des haratin et abid en Mauritanie rurale." *Journal des Africanistes* 70, 1–2: 239–54.

Saleck, El Arby Ould. 2000. *Journal des Africanistes* 70, 1–2: 255–63.

Samarin, William J. 1989. *The Black Man's Burden: African Colonial Labor on the Congo and Ubangui Rivers, 1880–1900.* Westview Press: Boulder, Colo.

Sattaur, Omar. 1993. *Child Labour in Nepal.* ASI: London.

Sawyer, Roger. 1984. *Casement: The Flawed Hero.* Routledge and Kegan Paul: London.

———. 1986. *Slavery in the Twentieth Century.* Routledge and Kegan Paul: London.

———. 1988. *Children Enslaved.* Routledge: London.

Sbacchi, Alberto. 1997. *Legacy of Bitterness: Ethiopia and Fascist Italy, 1935–41.* The Red Sea Press: Lawrenceville, N.J.

Schuler, Monica. 1980. *"Alas, Alas, Kongo": A Social History of Indentured African Immigration into Jamaica, 1841–1865.* Johns Hopkins University: Baltimore.

Scott, Rebecca. 1985 (a). *Slave Emancipation in Cuba: The Transition to Free Labor, 1860–1899.* Princeton University Press: Princeton, N.J.

———. 1985 (b). "Explaining Abolition: Contradiction, Adaptation, and Challenge in Cuban Society, 1860–1886." In Fraginals, Pons, and Engerman, eds.

Segal, Ronald. 2001. *Islam's Black Slaves: The Other Black Diaspora.* Farrar, Straus, and Giroux: New York.

Sever, Adrian. 1993. *Nepal under the Ranas.* Oxford and IBH Publishing Co.: New Delhi.

Sheridan, Richard B. 1993. "From Chattel to Wage Slavery in Jamaica, 1740–1860." *S & A* 14, 1: 13–40.

Sheriff, Abdul. 1987. *Slaves, Spices and Ivory in Zanzibar: Integration of an East African Commercial Empire into the World Economy, 1770–1873.* James Currey: London.

Shirreff, David. 1995. *Barefeet and Bandoliers: Wingate, Sandford, the Patriots, and the Part They Played in the Liberation of Ethiopia.* Radcliffe Press: London.

Sikainga, Ahmad Alawad. 1991. *The Western Bahr Al-Ghazal under British Rule: 1898–1956.* Ohio University Press: Athens.

———. 1996. *Slaves into Workers: Emancipation and Labor in Colonial Sudan.* University of Texas Press: Austin.

Simon, Kathleen. 1929. *Slavery.* Hodder and Stoughton: London.

Sinn, Elizabeth. 1994. "Chinese Patriarchy and the Protection of Women in Nineteenth-Century Hong Kong." In Jaschok and Miers, 141–70.

Smith, M. G. 1960. *Government in Zazzau, 1800–1950.* International African Institute, Oxford University Press: Oxford.

Smith, Martin. 1994. *Ethnic Groups in Burma: Development, Democracy and Human Rights.* ASI: London.

Smith, Mary. 1954. *Baba of Karo, 1877–1951.* Faber and Faber: London.

Solzhenistsyn, Aleksandr. 1963, translation. *One Day in the Life of Ivan Denisovich.* Praeger: New York.

———. 1974. *The Gulag Archipelago 1918–56: An Experiment in Literary Investigation,* vol.1, 1973. Harper and Row: New York; vol. 2, 1975, vol. 3, 1978, Collins: London.

Spaulding, Jay. 1988. "The Business of Slavery in the Central Anglo-Egyptian Sudan 1910–1930." *African Economic History* 17: 23–44.

Spiers, Fiona. 1985. "William Wilberforce: 150 Years On." In Hayward, ed., 47–68.

Stark, Freya. 2001. First published 1936. *The Southern Gates of Arabia: A Journey in the Hadhramaut.* Random House: New York.

Stichter, Sharon B., and Jane L. Parpart, eds. 1988. *Patriarchy and Class: African Women in the Home and Workforce.* Westview Press: Boulder, Colo.

Sundiata, Ibrahim K. 1980. *Black Scandal: The United States and the Liberian Labor Crisis, 1929–1936.* Philadelphia Institute for the Study of Human Issues: Philadelphia.

———. 1996. *From Slaving to Neoslavery: The Bight of Biafra and Fernando Po in the Era of Abolition, 1827–1930.* University of Wisconsin Press: Madison.

Suret-Canale, Jean. 1966. "La fin de la chefferie en Guinea." *JAH* 7, 3 (1966): 459–93.

Sutton, Alison. 1994. *Slavery in Brazil: A Link in the Chain of Modernization, the Case of Amazonia.* ASI: London.

Swaisland, H. C. 1967. "The Aborigines Protection Society and British Southern and West Africa." D. Phil. diss., Oxford University.

Sy, Yaya. 2000. "L'esclavage chez les Sonninkés: Du village à Paris." *Journal des Africanistes* 70, 1–2: 43–69.

Tamuno, T. N. 1972. *The Evolution of the Nigerian State: The Southern Phase 1898–1914.* Longmans: London.

Temperley, Howard. 1972. *British Antislavery 1833–1870.* Longmans: London.

———. 1974. "Antislavery." In Hollis, ed., 27–51.

———. 1977. "Capitalism, Slavery and Ideology." *Past and Present*, 94–118.

———. 1980. "Anti-Slavery as a Form of Cultural Imperialism." In Bolt and Drescher, eds., 335–50.

———. 1981. "The Ideology of Antislavery." In Eltis and Walvin, eds., 21–35.

———. 1985. "Abolition and the National Interest." In Hayward, ed., 86–109.

———. 1991. *White Dreams, Black Africa: The Antislavery Expedition to the River Niger 1841–1842.* Yale University Press: New Haven, Conn.

———. 1994. Review of Bender, ed., 1992 in *S & A* 15, 1 (April 1994): 121–23.

———, ed. 2000. *After Slavery: Emancipation and Its Discontents. S & A* Special Issue 21, 2 (August).

Thesiger, Wilfred. 1984. First published 1959. *Arabian Sands.* Harmondsworth, Penguin Books: London.

Thompson, E. P. 1966. First published 1963. *The Making of the English Working Class.* Vintage Books: New York.

Tibebu, Teshale. 1995. *The Making of Modern Ethiopia 1896–1974.* Red Sea Press: Lawrenceville, N.J.

Tinker, Hugh. 1993, 2nd edition. First published 1974. *A New System of Slavery: The Export of Indian Labour Overseas 1830–1920.* Hansib: London.

Tlou, Thomas. 1977. "Servility and Political Control: Botlhanka among the Batawana of Northwestern Botswana, ca. 1750–1906." In Miers and Kopytoff, eds., 367–90.

Toledano, Ehud. 1982. *The Ottoman Slave Trade and Its Suppression, 1840–1890*. Princeton University Press: Princeton, N.J.

———. 1993. "Ottoman Concepts of Slavery in the Period of Reform, 1830s–1880s." In Klein, ed., 37–63.

———. 1998. *Slavery and Abolition in the Ottoman Middle East*. University of Washington Press: Seattle.

Townsend, John. 1977. *Oman: The Making of the Modern State*. Croom Helm: London.

Treat, Ida. 1934. *Pearls, Arms and Hashish: Pages from the Life of a Red Sea Navigator, Henry de Monfried*. Coward-McCann: New York.

Triulzi, A. 1981. *Salt, Gold and Legitimacy: Prelude to the History of a No-Man's Land, Bela Shangul, Wallaga, Ethiopia, c. 1800–1898*. Instituto Universitario Orientale Seminario di Studi Africani: Naples.

Turley, David. 1991. *The Culture of English Antislavery, 1780–1860*. Routledge: London.

Twaddle, Michael. 1988. "Slaves and Peasants in Buganda." In Archer, ed., 118–29.

———, ed. 1993. *The Wages of Slavery: From Chattel Slavery to Wage Labour in Africa, the Caribbean and England*. Frank Cass: London; also *S &A* Special Issue 14, 1 (April).

Ullendorf, Edward. 1977. *My Life and Ethiopia's Progress, 1892–1937: The Autobiography of Emperor Haile Sellassie I*, translated and annotated. Oxford University Press: Oxford.

Uzoigwe, G. N. 1974. *Britain and the Conquest of Africa: The Age of Salisbury*. University of Michigan Press: Ann Arbor.

Vail, Leroy, and Landeg White. 1980. *Capitalism and Colonialism in Mozambique: A Study of Quelimane District*. Heinemann: London.

Van Ginneken, see Ginneken.

Vaughan, James H., and Anthony H. M. Kirk-Greene, eds. 1995. *The Diary of Hamman Yaji: Chronicle of a West African Muslim Ruler*. Indiana University Press: Bloomington.

Verney, Peter. 1997. *Slavery in Sudan*. Sudan Update and ASI: London.

Walker, Julian. 1999. *Tyro on the Trucial Coast*. The Memoir Club: Durham.

Walvin, James. 1977. "The Impact of Slavery in British Radical Politics, 1787–1838." In Rubin and Tuden, eds.

———. 1980. "The Rise of Popular Sentiment for Abolition 1787–1832." In Bolt and Drescher, eds., 149–62.

———. 1981. "The Public Campaign in England against Slavery, 1787–1834." In Eltis and Walvin, eds., 63–79.

———. 1982. "The Propaganda of Anti-Slavery." In Walvin, ed., 49–68.

———, ed. 1982. *Slavery and British Society*. Macmillan: London.

———. 1985. "Freeing the Slaves: How Important Was Wilberforce?" In Hayward, ed.

Ward, W. E. F. 1969. *The Royal Navy and the Slavers: The Suppression of the Atlantic Slave Trade.* Allen and Unwin: London.

Warren, James Francis. 1994. "Chinese Prostitution in Singapore: Recruitment and Brothel Organization." In Jaschok and Miers, eds., 77–107.

Watson, James L. 1980. "Slavery as an Institution: Open and Closed Systems." In Watson, ed., 1–5.

———, ed. 1980. *Asian and African Systems of Slavery.* Basil Blackwell: Oxford.

Watson, R. L. 1990. *The Slave Question: Liberty and Property in South Africa.* Wesleyan University Press: Hanover, N.H.

Welch, Claude E., ed. 2001. *NGOs and Human Rights: Promise and Performance.* University of Pennsylvania Press: Philadelphia.

White, Luise. 1988. "Domestic Labor in a Colonial City: Prostitution in Nairobi, 1900–1952." In Stitchter and Parpart, eds., 139–60.

———. 1990. *The Comforts of Home: Prostitution in Colonial Nairobi.* University of Chicago Press: Chicago.

Whitaker, Benjamin. 1982. *Slavery.* UN/CN.4Sub.2/1982/20/Rev.1.

Whitney, Robert. 1992. "The Political Economy of Abolition: The Hispano-Cuban Elite and Cuban Slavery, 1868–1873." *S & A* 13, 2 (1992): 20–36.

Whittaker, Alan, ed. 1991. *Children in Bondage: Slaves of the Subcontinent.* No. 10, ASI Child Labour Series: London.

Wikan, Unni. 1991 First published 1982. *Behind the Veil in Arabia: Women in Oman.* University of Chicago Press: Chicago.

Williams, Eric. 1944. *Capitalism and Slavery.* Russell and Russell: Chapel Hill, N.C.

Willis, Justin, and Suzanne Miers. 1997. "Becoming a Child of the House: Incorporation, Authority and Resistance in Giryama Society." *JAH* 38: 479–95.

Wilmsen, Edwin N. 1989. *Land Filled with Flies: A Political Economy of the Kalahari.* University of Chicago Press: Chicago.

Wilson, M., and L. Thompson, eds. 1983. *History of South Africa to 1870.* Oxford University Press: Oxford; and Westview Press: Boulder, Colo.

Wilson, Harold. 1971. *The Labour Government, 1964–1970: A Personal Memoir.* Weidenfield and Nicholson: London.

Wolfson, Freda. 1950. "British Relations with the Gold Coast, 1843–1888." Ph.D. diss., London University.

Worden, Nigel. 1985. *Slavery in Dutch South Africa.* Cambridge University Press: Cambridge.

——. 1986. "Slavery and Post-Emancipation Reconstruction in the Western Cape." Paper presented at the University of Cape Town, Centre for African Studies, July.

——. Forthcoming. "The Slave System of the Cape Colony and Its Aftermath." In Campbell, ed., vol. 2.

Wright, Marcia. 1993. *Strategies of Slaves and Women: Life Stories from East/Central Africa.* Lilian Barber Press: New York.

Wrigley, C. C. 1971. "Historicism in Africa: Slavery and State Formation." *African Affairs* 70, 279: 113–24.

Wu, Harry, and Carolyn Wakeman. 1994. *Bitter Winds: A Memoir of My Years in China's Gulag.* John Wiley and Sons: New York.

Wu, Hongda Harry. 1992. Trans. *Laogai: The Chinese Gulag.* Westview Press: Boulder, Colo.

Wylde, A. B. 1888. *'83 to '87 in Sudan.* Remington and Co.: London.

Zewde, Bahru. 1976. "Relations between Ethiopia and Sudan on the Western Ethiopian Frontier 1898-1935." Ph.D. diss., University of London.

Index

Abdallah, emir of Transjordan, 87
Abdul al Aziz ibn Saud, King of Saudi Arabia,
88, 179, 343; anti-German stance of, 306;
conquest of Hijaz by, 95–96; consular
manumission and, 179–82, 254–60; and
Italy, 257; League of Nations and, 254;
slave trade and, 181, 184, 179–80, 258–60,
307, 309; slavery and, 179, 181, 258–59,
310; slaves of, 180–81, 255; territorial
claims of, 256–57, 311, 340, 342–43. *See
also* Buraimi Oasis; Saudi Arabia; Treaty
of Jiddah
Abolition Act of 1807 (British), 3–4
Abolition of Forced Labor Convention 1957,
331–32, 373
Aborigines Protection Society (APS), 20, 53,
62–63. *See also* Anti-Slavery Society
Aboye, Walda Giyorgis, 67
Abu Dhabi, 260, 264, 306, 311–12. *See also*
Persian Gulf States; Saudi Arabia; Trucial
States
Abyssinia. *See* Ethiopia
Abyssinia Association, 247, 301
ACE: Aden Protectorate and, 268, 271; British
discontent with, 231, 290–91; debt-
bondage and, 228–29, 287–88; definition
of slavery and, 219–21; demise of, 289–92;

effects of, 292, 447; and Ethiopia, 228,
230, 246; formation of, 216–18; frequency
of meetings of, 216, 218–19, 278; and
India and Burma, 229, 282–83; Maxwell,
Sir George, and, 231–32, 278–79, 289–90,
292; members of, 217–18; mui tsai and,
225, 284, 286; Persian Gulf and, 265;
reports of governments, 221–24, 224–29,
278–80, 282; rules of procedure, 216,
218–19, 231–32, 294; and serfdom,
288–89; shortcomings of, 294; slave trade
and, 226–29, 271, 278–80; slavery and,
279–83; Yemen and, 261. *See also*
Ethiopia; Gohr, Albrecht; Lugard,
Frederick; Maxwell, Sir George
Action pour l'Abolition de l'Esclavage, 375
Ad Hoc Committee on Slavery: attack
against, 325; British and, 320–21;
difficulties of, 323–25; methods of,
324–25; results of, 325–26, 449. *See also*
Greenidge, Charles
Aden Protectorate: abolition of slavery in,
352; ACE and, 268, 271; British
withdrawal from, 352; freed slaves in,
304–05; concubines in, 268; marriage
customs in, 363; royal slaves, 268, 305;
slave trade in, 268–69, 270–71, 304–06;

About the Author

Suzanne Miers (née Doyle) was born in the Belgian Congo, of American parents, and brought up in Brussels and London. Her first husband was Brigadier Richard Miers (British army) by whom she had two children. He died in 1962 and she is now married to Professor Roland Oliver. They spend half the year in England and half in Florida. She is emerita professor of African history at Ohio University. She has also taught at the Universities of Wisconsin, London, and Malaya (Singapore). She is the author of *Britain and the Ending of the Slave Trade* (1975) and numerous articles. She coedited *Slavery in Africa: Historical and Anthropological Perspectives* (1977) with Igor Kopytoff; *The End of Slavery in Africa* (1988) with Richard Roberts; *Women and Chinese Patriarchy: Submission Servitude and Escape* (1994) with Maria Jaschok; and *Slavery and Colonial Rule in Africa* (1998) with Martin A. Klein.